Dor

T5-AGP-807

THE ACADIENSIS READER: VOLUME TWO

mgen
(Don)

Atlantic Canada
After Confederation

THE ACADIENSIS READER: VOLUME TWO
SECOND EDITION

COMPILED AND EDITED BY
P.A. BUCKNER
AND
DAVID FRANK

ACADIENSIS PRESS
FREDERICTON
1988

ACADIENSIS PRESS 1988

Canadian Cataloguing in Publication Data

Main entry under title:
Atlantic Canada after Confederation

Essays originally published in the journal Acadiensis.
Includes bibliographical references.
ISBN 0-919107-18-4 (bound)
ISBN 0-919107-16-8 (pbk.)

1. Maritime Provinces — History — 1867-.* 2. Newfoundland — History. I.
Buckner, Phillip A. (Phillip Alfred), 1942-. II. Frank, David Alexander. III.
Title: Acadiensis (Fredericton, N.B.). IV. Title: The Acadiensis reader,
volume two.

FC2011.A862 1988   971.5'03   C88-098562-3
F1033.A862 1988

H.W. WILSON PRINTING

FC
2005
.A8127
1988
v.2

CONTENTS

PREFACE

During the 1960s and 1970s a revolution began to take place in Canadian historiography. The traditional focus on "national" themes was abandoned by a growing number of historians who turned to a wide range of more limited topics. Regionalism was one of those topics and was eagerly embraced by scholars in the hinterlands of Canada who felt that the older emphasis on nation-building relegated their regions to a secondary and largely reactive position in Canada history.[1] These developments were viewed with approval -- and even encouraged -- by such leading figures in the Canadian historical profession as Ramsay Cook and Maurice Careless. In 1967 Cook had suggested that "Perhaps instead of constantly deploring our lack of identity we should attempt to understand and explain the regional, ethnic and class identities that we do have. It might just be that it is in these limited identities that 'Canadianism' is found". In a widely quoted article published in 1969 Careless popularized the term "limited identities", which became the most important new concept employed by Canadian historians in the 1970s.[2]

It was against this background that *Acadiensis* was launched in 1971.[3] The pressure to found *Acadiensis* came from many directions but a key role was played by the late Ken Windsor who insisted on the need for a journal which would -- in his words -- "recover the past" of the Atlantic Region. The timing was fortuitous. University history departments in the region were still in the process of expansion and a substantial number of graduate students were in the process of completing theses on regional topics. George Rawlyk, whose graduate seminar at Queen's University produced many of these students, predicted in 1969 that a new "Golden Age of Maritime Historiography" was about to begin.[4] During the 1970s his prophecy seemed on the verge of fulfillment. Particularly through the pages of *Acadiensis*, a new generation of scholars began to reshape the contours of our regional and national historiography.[5] There was also a refreshing amount of interdisciplinary con-

---

1 For a brilliant critique of the traditional historiography, see E.R. Forbes, "In Search of a Post-Confederation Maritime Historiography, 1900-1967", *Acadiensis*, VIII, 1 (Autumn 1978), pp. 3-21.

2 Ramsay Cook, "Canadian Centennial Cerebrations", *International Journal*, XXXI (Autumn 1967), p. 663; J.M.S. Careless, " 'Limited Identities' in Canada", *Canadian Historical Review*, L (March 1969), pp. 1-10.

3 For comments on the origins of the journal and its antecedents, see P.A. Buckner, "Acadiensis II", *Acadiensis*, I, 1 (Autumn 1971), pp. 3-9, and "Acadiensis: The First Decade", *Acadiensis*, X, 2 (Spring 1981), pp. 3-4.

4 George Rawlyk, "A New Golden Age of Maritime Historiography?", *Queen's Quarterly*, 76 (Spring 1969), pp. 55-65.

5 See W.G. Godfrey, " 'A New Golden Age': Recent Historical Writing on the Maritimes", *Queen's Quarterly*, 91 (Summer 1984), pp. 35-82.

tact in the journal, which was most notable in the contributions of historical geographers. In 1977 an historian from outside Canada, commissioned to prepare a survey of "Canadian History in the 1970s", declared: "I am conscious in reading *Acadiensis* that work on Maritime history is cumulative in a sense in which work published in the *Canadian Historical Review* is not and perhaps cannot be because the range of topics covered is so wide".[6]

Ironically just as the new Golden Age seemed to have arrived, some historians began to predict its demise. In 1977 Ramsay Cook, while praising the results of the new historiography, cautiously warned regional historians not to ignore "the 'national' experience".[7] In 1978 Lovell Clark delivered an attack on those Canadian historians who "add to the focus of disunity by jumping on the bandwagon of regionalism", and in 1980 Donald Swainson emphasized that Canadian historians had "allowed the pendulum to swing too far" in the direction of regionalism.[8] Maurice Careless -- once described by Ramsay Cook as "the patron saint of the new approaches to our history" -- announced that the search for "limited identities" had gone too far: "limited identities threaten to take over, and settle the matter of a Canadian national identity, by ending it outright, leaving perhaps a loose league of survivor states essentially existing on American outdoor relief".[9] Even those who remained sympathetic to the more general historiographical revolution that had taken place wondered whether the "increasing emphasis on 'region' as the crucial variable which explains sundry problems of Canadian development" was not "misplaced".[10]

The flight from regional studies was due to several factors. As Ramsay Cook pointed out, the historians "at least partly reflected the direction in which the society itself was moving".[11] The growing fear of Quebec separatism in the late 1960s and early 1970s had inspired the desire to find an explanatory concept which all Canadians -- including Québécois -- could accept. Limited identities seemed to provide that concept. But after the Quebec referendum separatism no longer seemed a threat and Canadian historians -- in tune with the national mood -- began to re-emphasize their commitment to the search for

---

6   H.J. Hanham, "Canadian History in the 1970s", *Canadian Historical Review,* LVIII (March 1977), p. 10.

7   Ramsay Cook, "The Golden Age of Canadian Historical Writing", *Historical Reflections,* 14 (Summer 1977), p. 148.

8   Lovell Clark, "Regionalism? or Irrationalism?", *Journal of Canadian Studies,* 13/2 (Summer 1978), p. 119; D. Swainson, "Regionalism and the Social Scientists", *Acadiensis,* X, 1 (Autumn 1980), p. 144.

9   Cook, "The Golden Age", p. 139; J.M.S. Careless, "Limited Identities -- ten years later", *Manitoba History,* I (1980), p. 3.

10 Greg Kealey, "Labour and Working-Class History in Canada: Prospects in the 1980s", *Labour/Le Travailleur,* 8 (Spring, 1981), p. 74. Compare Bryan Palmer's 1972 assessment in "Most Uncommon Common Men: Craft and Culture in Historical Perspective", *Labour/Le Travailleur,* 1 (1976), p. 21.

11 Cook, "The Golden Age", p. 139.

a "national" identity. Too few were prepared to heed David Alexander's pleas for a stronger Canadianism which might learn something of value from the regional experience and incorporate some of the virtues of the other identities in which Canadians have participated.[12] There was also a feeling -- particularly among the older generation of historians -- that the profession and the discipline had been fragmented by the variety of new approaches which had developed in the 1970s. Some historians legitimately criticized the imprecision with which the terms "region" and "regionalism" were -- and are -- used.[13] There was nothing "peculiarly Canadian" about these developments. American historiography, which so greatly influences Canadian, followed a similar pattern in the 1980s.[14]

One might have some sympathy with these attitudes if an historiographical revolution really had taken place in Canada. Yet, as Chad Gaffield has written, the new approaches of the 1970s have become "institutionalized" in new journals in the "periphery" while "mainstream" historical attention focuses on traditional topics.[15] While work in new fields such as social history, women's history and working-class history is frequently welcomed, few historians have been prepared to accept the need to re-think some of the traditional categories and periodization of Canadian history.[16] Even a cursory examination of the recent literature reveals the limited impact of the new scholarship. Most books on "national" subjects pay lip-service to the need to convey the variety of the regional experience in Canada but too frequently contain only token materials or passing reference to the Atlantic Region. And most textbooks in Canadian history retain their traditional Central Canadian and to a lesser degree Western Canadian focus.[17] Until our national historiography really does incorporate the insights contained in journals like *Acadiensis* the flight from regional concerns in the 1980s seems, at best, premature.

It is to make these insights more widely accessible that we have decided to issue two volumes of essays drawn from *Acadiensis*. Since our primary concern was to choose articles which were most likely to be of use in undergraduate survey courses, a large number of scholars were asked to par-

---

12 David Alexander, *Atlantic Canada and Confederation: Essays in Canadian Political Economy* (Toronto 1983).

13 See Ramsay Cook, "Regionalism Unmasked", *Acadiensis*, XIII, 1 (Autumn 1983), pp. 137-42.

14 For example, see Carl N. Degler, "Remaking American History", *The Journal of American History*, 67 (1980), pp. 7-25 and Thomas Bender, "The New History -- Then and Now", *Reviews in American History*, 12 (December 1984), pp. 612-22.

15 See his review of *Hopeful Travellers* in the *Urban History Review*, XI (February 1983), p. 81.

16 For efforts to do so, see Michael S. Cross and Gregory S. Kealey, eds., *Readings in Canadian Social History*, 5 vols. (1983-1984), and Marie Lavigne, Jennifer Stoddart, Micheline Dumont et Michèle Jean, *L'histoire des femmes au Québec depuis quatre siècles* (Montréal 1982).

17 See Bill Godfrey, "Canadian History Textbooks and the Maritimes", *Acadiensis*, X, 1 (Autumn 1980), pp. 131-5.

ticipate in the process of selection. The end product is not comprehensive and many fine articles had to be omitted. In order to publish the volumes as inexpensively as possible, the articles also had to be reprinted precisely as they originally appeared in the journal and they are presented without comment by the editors. Nonetheless, we hope that these volumes will introduce students, both within and without the Atlantic Region, to some of the important literature that has appeared in *Acadiensis* and whet their appetite for more. If they do serve that function, they will help not only to fulfill Ken Windsor's dream of recovering the past of this region but also to re-integrate this history into the mainstream.

DAVID ALEXANDER

Reprinted from Vol. V, No. 2
(Spring 1976)

Newfoundland's Traditional Economy and Development to 1934

The price of being a country is willingness to bear a cross. For Germany it is the cross of beastliness; for Russia it is stolidity; the United States must rise above material wealth; and Canada is required to find a national identity. The burden which Newfoundland has carried is to justify that it should have any people. From the Western Adventurers of the seventeenth century to Canadian economists in the twentieth, there has been a continuing debate as to how many, if any, people should live in Newfoundland. The consensus has normally been that there should be fewer Newfoundlanders — a conclusion reached in the seventeenth century when there were only some 2,000 inhabitants, and one which is drawn today when there are over 500,000.

Newfoundland's economic history has centred around valuation of its natural resource endowment in relation to the size of its population. The particular object of debate has been (and still is) the size and well-being of the traditional or rural economy, and the likelihood that it could expand extensively at acceptable standards of life, or that other sectors can be developed to absorb labour exports from the traditional sector. The economic characteristics of a traditional economy can be stated simply enough. Labour and natural resources, or 'land', are the most important factors of production, and capital plays a very minor role. If it is assumed that land is a constant, then the average output of labour is a simple function of the ratio of labour to land. Thus, if the population expands and the ratio increases, then average per capita output falls; that is, standards of living fall. If it is further assumed that the economy is closed to emigration, then the prospects are those of deteriorating standards to a very low level of physical security and comfort. To make matters still more depressing, a once-and-for-all technical improvement in the traditional economy (say the introduction of the cod trap) which shifts average per capita output upwards, is of little long-term benefit, for the gains in living standards will be eaten away by the likelihood of strengthened population growth: one ends up with a larger economy, but not necessarily a more prosperous one. The only routes to a long-run improvement in living standards are a widening resource base and technical change (including organizational changes such as the growth of domestic and international market activity).[1] These assumptions imply a movement away from the traditional economy with capital growth (both reproducible and human) defining the growth of total and per capita income.

The stark features of this simple model obviously fail to capture accurately the complexities of Newfoundland's economic history. Yet it does identify some realities of its economic problems and, what is just as important, perceptions of the problems. When Newfoundland's traditional economy reached an apparent limit to extensive expansion in the second half of the nineteenth century, a struggle was waged to expand the resource base and modernize both the structure of production and the composition of output. This campaign ended in collapse and that collapse led directly to union with Canada. In 1949 the effort to 'develop' was resumed under new constitutional dress. But the historical record sketched in this essay suggests that Confederation did not introduce any especially new perceptions of Newfoundland's economic problems and potential, and some might argue that it simply reinforced a depressing tendency to neglect the province's most obvious natural resource — the sea.

At the time of its discovery Newfoundland's fishery was an international open access resource, exploited by fleets from France, Portugal and Spain. At this time (unlike today) the volume of factors of production available to exploit the resource, the primitive techniques, and the size of the markets, meant the resource base was in no danger of over-exploitation in the sense of significant reductions in maximum sustainable yield. For the continental countries, the adoption of a 'green cure' meant the issue of settling Newfoundland did not arise, since the Island was mainly a convenient watering and repair station. But this was not the case with the West of England fishery, which developed in the second half of the sixteenth century.[2] Whether in response to relatively high costs of salt or to local tradition, the West Country fisherman pursued a light salted, sun dried fishery at Newfoundland. Land resources were consequently important to the Westcountrymen, as wood was needed for flakes and stages, and shore facilities for drying. The consequences of this technology were two-fold: first, an undignified annual rush by the West of England fishing boats to Newfoundland to claim *seasonal* property rights over the best fishing 'rooms'; and secondly, opposition to establishment of 'plantations' or any other settlement of the Island, whether by Englishmen or foreigners, which would prejudice seasonal claims to ownership over essential land inputs.

---

1   See C. H. Fei and Gustav Ranis, "Economic Development in Historical Perspective", *American Economic Review*, LIX (1969), pp. 386 - 400.

2   On this point see K. Matthews, "A History of the West of England-Newfoundland Fishery" (Unpublished D.Phil. thesis, Oxford University, 1968).

The short fishing season and poor winter employment opportunities in Newfoundland as well as the grim agricultural potential, favoured a migratory fishery; but very slowly in the course of the seventeenth and eighteenth centuries the difference in the rates of return between a migratory and a settled fishery shifted in favour of the latter. Rising European shipping costs and the development of regular and lower cost supplies of food and other imports from the North American colonies, were critical factors in this shift. Nonetheless the growth of a resident population was painfully slow. In 1650 it was around 2,000 and by 1750, with sharp fluctuations, reached only 6,000. The turning point came in the second half of the eighteenth century. The French fishery declined after the Seven Years' War and the New England fishery following the Revolution, and neither fully recovered until the end of the Napoleonic Wars. By the end of the century the West Country merchants had translated an international migratory fishery at Newfoundland into a colonial industry in Newfoundland. Between 1750 and 1804 Newfoundland's population grew at an annual rate of 2.3% reaching over 20,000 and in the next twelve years more than doubled to 50,000, implying a growth rate of over 8% per annum.[3]

The transition from a British fishery at Newfoundland to a Newfoundland fishery was significant in two ways. It meant the foundation of a new country in the world, for while it is customary (at least in Newfoundland) to claim a history of many hundreds of years, it is more realistic to view Newfoundland as one of the nineteenth-century countries of European settlement. Secondly, while there was always a possibility (however remote up to the nineteenth century) that an expanding migratory fishery would deplete an open access resource, there was now a better possibility that a settled traditional economy would expand to the point of impoverishing a country.

The inshore salt cod industry dominated Newfoundland's economic history in the nineteenth century and continued to be the single most important source of employment and market income well into the twentieth. Table 1 is the basis for suggesting that in terms of the gross value of (export) production, prices and physical output, there were three long cycles running between 1815 and 1934: the first covering 1815/19 to 1850/54; the second between 1855/60 to 1895/99; and a third between 1900/04 to 1930/34. Mean volumes, prices and export values tended to be higher in each period, but as Table 2 indicates fluctuations around the means were extreme, especially with respect to prices and export values. It is clear that prices were more volatile than physical production, and that on a quinquennial basis gross export values were less stable than either output or prices. The industry was obviously an unstable one upon which to found a country's external earnings

---

3   Calculated from figures in S. Ryan, "Collections of C.O. 194 Statistics" (unpublished manuscript, Newfoundland Studies Centre, Memorial University, 1970).

and such a large fraction of its national income, and it is hardly surprising that with responsible government politicians launched an effort to widen the country's production base.

TABLE 1
QUINQUENNIAL AVERAGES AND VARIATIONS IN SALT COD EXPORT VOLUMES, PRICES AND GROSS VALUES 1815/19 - 1930/34

PERIOD	VOLUMES (000 Quintals)			PRICES ($ per Quintal)			GROSS EXPORT VALUE (000 Dollars)		
	$\overline{X}$	S	V	$\overline{X}$	S	V	$\overline{X}$	X	V
1815-19	1,018	50	5%	3.90	1.07	27 %	2,968	1,429	48%
1820-24	883	30	3	2.46	0.23	9	2,175	224	10
1825-29	923	37	4	2.08	0.11	5	1,942	174	9
1830-34	763	110	14	2.42	0.32	13	1,840	326	18
1835-39	788	65	8	2.78	0.04	1	2,193	201	9
1840-44	944	59	6	2.79	0.13	5	2,637	216	8
1845-49	963	115	12	2.66	0.16	6	2,547	226	9
1850-54	955	108	11	2.61	0.38	15	2,454	161	7
1855-59	1,205	128	11	3.33	0.34	10	4,008	605	15
1860-64	1,172	140	12	2.65	0.50	14	4,218	266	6
1865-69	969	81	8	3.86	0.45	12	3,731	450	12
1870-74	1,273	175	14	3.93	0.02	0.5	5,026	896	18
1875-79	1,134	132	12	3.88	0.31	8	4,354	432	10
1880-84	1,460	70	5	3.82	0.13	3	5,582	615	11
1885-89	1,192	112	9	3.66	0.52	14	4,316	374	9
1890-94	1,101	70	6	3.60	0.04	1	3,957	461	12
1895-99	1,224	81	7	2.89	0.16	5	3,549	559	16
1900-04	1,302	78	6	4.19	0.03	0.6	5,562	289	5
1905-09	1,574	112	7	N/A	N/A	N/A	N/A	N/A	N/A
1910-14	1,346	122	9	5.66	0.51	9	7,583	599	8
1915-19	1,517	250	16	9.35	2.80	30	15,650	6,030	41
1920-24	1,499	183	12	8.67	2.29	26	13,265	4,974	37
1925-29	1,398	162	12	8.37	0.76	9	11,587	584	5
1930-34	1,179	52	4	5,90	1.87	32	7,010	2,464	35

NOTES: $\overline{X}$ — Arithmetic Mean
       S — Standard Deviation
       V — Coefficient of Variability (V = S/X . 100)

SOURCE: Calculated from Government of Newfoundland, *Historical Statistics of Newfoundland* (St. John's, 1970), vol. I, Table K-7.

TABLE 2
MEAN VALUES OF QUINQUENNIAL COEFFICIENTS OF VARIATION FOR THE SALT COD INDUSTRY

PERIOD	VOLUMES %	PRICES %	GROSS VALUES %
1815/19 - 1930/34	8.88	11.09	15.57
1855/59 - 1895/99	9.33	7.50	12.11
1900/04 - 1930/34	9.43	17.77	21.83

Although high volumes, prices and export values characterized the cod fishery in the first years of the century, output volumes grew by only 0.08% per annum from the mid-1820s to mid-1850s, and in four out of six quinquennia were below the trend for 1805/08-1915/20. During the same period prices rose by only 0.13% per annum and in five quinquennia were below trend for 1821/25-1900/04. Accordingly, the value of cod exports grew by only 0.9% per annum and in all six quinquennia was below trend for 1805/09-1900/14.[4] Over the same period population grew at slightly over 2.5% per annum, and the apparent depression of the first half of the century would appear worse if the initial benchmark for measurements was the values of 1809/15 — a quinquennia when many people were encouraged to migrate to Newfoundland. But it does not follow necessarily that for the economy as a whole the productivity of labour and living standards were falling. It is possible that a decline in per capita export values was compensated by a general decline in unit costs of imports, for while a U.S. wholesale price index for farm products rose from 59 in 1826/30 to 84 in 1851/55 (with a dip to 55 in 1841/45), a United Kingdom merchandise export price index fell from 169 in 1826/30 to 104 in 1851/52[5]. Moreover, within Newfoundland the rapid growth of the seal fishery softened the depression in the cod fishery, and it is also a reasonable hypothesis that over the period some fraction of total domestic expenditure was shifted from imports to domestic production. In addition to the non-market output which a rural community could generate through increasing familiarity with its environment, the very rapid growth of St. John's (reaching some 20% of the population by 1857) suggests development of import substituting commodity and service production.

Between the grant of responsible government in 1855 and the mid-1880s, Newfoundland's basic industry flourished, although there were always bad years, frequently coupled with indifferent ones. But prices grew by 1.17% per annum in 1850/54-1880/84 and were above the trend referred to earlier in every quinquennia. Volumes grew by 1.25% per annum and were above trend in four out of six quinquennia. Accordingly, over the same interval, export values grew by 2.14% per annum and were above the trend in each quinquennia. Over the period 1857-1884 population growth decelerated to an annual rate slightly over 1.7%. Furthermore, while according to the censuses the labour force (occupied population) was growing at just over 2% per annum, the male fishing labour force grew by only 1.7%. Thus, the industry's

---

4   Calculated from Government of Newfoundland, *Historical Statistics of Newfoundland and Labrador* (St. John's, 1970), vol. I, Table K-7.

5   Calculated from Department of Commerce, *Historical Statistics of the United States* (Washington, 1962), Series E1-12; and B. R. Mitchell, *Abstract of British Historical Statistics* (Cambridge, 1962), ch. XI, Table 15. It is a reasonable assumption that wholesale prices for Canadian farm products which Newfoundland bought moved in directions similar to the American.

share in total employment fell from 90% in 1857 to 82% in 1884, and the implication (under the assumption of constant factor proportions) is a modest growth in total productivity. The trend in living standards, however, is unclear. The U.S. wholesale price index for farm products rose sharply from 83 in 1856/60 to 117 and 130 in the two quinquennia of the 1860s, then fell to 86 in 1880/84. The U.K. merchandise export price index moved in the same direction, rising from 110 in 1856/60 to a plateau of about 126 in the three quinquennia between 1861-75 and then falling off to 93 in 1881/85. But whatever the implications of the terms of trade for living standards, behind the growth rates for the fishing economy an alarming situation was emerging. The absolute level of employment in the fishing industry grew from some 38,500 men in 1857 to around 60,400 in 1884, and fishing rooms in use expanded from some 6,000 to around 10,500[6]. This meant that the average volume of production per fisherman was falling from around 30 quintals in the 1850s and 60s to a low of some 23 quintals in the late 1880s, after which there was a modest recovery.[7] We know little about trends in man-hours among fishermen and the growth of employed capital, and it is therefore difficult to be certain about changes in labour and total factor productivity. But contemporaries were convinced that the traditional fishing economy had reached a limit to extensive growth.

The size of national income produced by this traditional economy is impossible to estimate precisely. In 1884 the value of all exports was $6.6M and almost all of this was accounted for by fish products — notably salt codfish and oil, while the remainder consisted of mineral and other primary product shipments.[8] Primary employment (the export sector) accounted for 87% of the labour force, the secondary sector some 10% and the service sector some 3%.[9] If we assume that the value of output in the secondary and tertiary sectors was a proportional fraction of their labour forces to the *realized* output of the primary sector, then the realized national income would be around $7.5M.[10] There was a great deal of production in rural Newfoundland, however, that did not move through markets. In the late 1930s it was estimated that income in kind amounted to some 55% of the value of fish exports.[11]If the

6   *Tenth Census of Newfoundland and Labrador,* 1935, Part 1, vol. II, p. 87.

7   Calculated from *loc. cit.*

8   P. Copes, "Role of the Fishing Industry in the Economic Development of Newfoundland" (unpublished manuscript, Newfoundland Studies Centre, 1970), Table 3.

9   Calculated from *Tenth Census of Newfoundland, op. cit.*

10   By 'realized' output is meant that fraction which enters into markets. For estimates of 'National Cash Income' in this period see Steven D. Antler, "Colonialism as a Factor in the Economic Stagnation of Nineteenth Century Newfoundland: Some Preliminary Notes" (unpublished manuscript, Newfoundland Studies Centre, 1973), Table 3.

11   R. A. MacKay, ed., *Newfoundland: Economic, Diplomatic and Strategic Studies* (Toronto, 1946), Anonymous, Appendix B.

same proportion of non-market income was produced in 1884, then this would add some $4.1M to the realized national income, for a total national income of some $11.6M and a per capita income of around $60. Probably this is a low estimate. If realized income accounted for, say, only around half of a *fishing family's* total income, then the output of factors in the secondary and tertiary sectors should be at least doubled (otherwise there would have been migration from the urban to rural sector), yielding a realized national income of $8.4M and a total national income of around $12.5M. Even this figure may underestimate the national income, for despite the strains of the Depression period, impressionistic evidence suggests the economy was less oriented to markets in the nineteenth century than during the 1930s. At the later date a smaller fraction of the labour force was geographically and occupationally situated to generate income in kind and consumption patterns were by then more oriented through taste and availability of cash towards marketed foodstuffs and manufactures. Thus as an 'outside' estimate, if we impute an income in kind at least equal in value to that of primary exports, then the estimate of national income rises to around $15M with income per capita of $75.[12]

Even if this high estimate is accepted, then it is clear that Newfoundland's traditional economy was by no means an affluent component of the North Atlantic world. Comparisons are fraught with dangers, but as a rough indicator, it can be noted that Canada's per capita national income in 1880 (without adjustment for income in kind) was around $135.[13] It is probably true that with a more sophisticated and market oriented economy, the burden of capital depreciation and taxation on personal incomes was higher in Canada than in Newfoundland at this time; nonetheless the gap in average material well-being must have been substantial.

Newfoundland's traditional economy underwent a crisis in the late 1880s and 1890s. Export prices for salt codfish sank from $3.82 a quintal in 1880/84 to $2.89 in 1895/99 — a collapse of around 32%. Production volumes also fell from about 1.5M quintals in 1880/84 to some 1.2M in 1895/99 — a 20% decline. Accordingly, industry gross earnings sagged from $5.6M to $3.6M — a decline of 36%.[14] But the impact on the real level of national income and per capita consumption was probably less severe than these figures suggest. Table 3 represents a rough indicator of Newfoundland's terms of trade up to the end of World War I for the fishing sector. It suggests that the terms of trade actually moved in Newfoundland's favour in the two quinquennia

12 More accurately, this is an estimate of total domestic income as no allowance has been made for depreciation and the balance of net property income from abroad.

13 Calculated from M. C. Urquhart and K. A. H. Buckley, *Historical Statistics of Canada* (Toronto, 1965), Series E2.4-244.

14 Calculated from *Historical Statistics of Newfoundland*, Table K-7.

1884-94 relative to the 1870s and first half of the 1880s, although there was a sharp deterioration during 1895-99. But the point remains that employment levels reached in 1884 could not be maintained, quite apart from the additional burden of absorbing into the traditional economy increments from natural increase. The male labour force engaged in catching and curing fish fell back from an historic peak of 60,000 in 1884 to just under 37,000 in 1891. Employment inched up again during the prosperous first decade of this century and reached almost 44,000 in 1911; but then it began a slow decline to some 35,000 in 1935.[15]

The sharp decline in employment in the traditional economy after 1884 and its relative stability during the first half of this century, was achieved in part through the absorption of labour into other sectors; but a major contribution also came through slower rates of growth of population and labour force. Whereas in 1874-84 population grew at a rate of 2.1% per annum, it was close to stationary in 1885-91 at 0.3% and remained below 1% per annum until World War II.[16] Deceleration of population growth was not principally a function of changes in fertility or mortality. The crude birth rate was around 30 per thousand in 1884, 33 in 1891 and 35 in 1901. The crude death rate which was 14 per thousand in 1884 rose to 22 in 1891 and fell back to 15 in 1901.[17] Throughout the 1920s and 1930s the crude birth rate was above 20 per thousand — in the high twenties during the relatively prosperous 1920s and the low twenties during the Depression — while the crude death rate fluctuated around 12 per thousand.[18] It follows that population and labour force growth could only have been held down by substantial net emigration. Trends in net migration can be estimated by noting population levels at census periods and imputing what it should have been with no migration at the estimated Rate of Natural Increase. By this method, net immigration at an annual average of less than 1000 prevailed between 1869-84. But from 1884 to 1935 a large flow of emigrants began. Between 1884-1901 it probably ranged between 1,500 to 2,500 per year, and from 1901 to 1945 between 1,000 to 1,500 per year.[19]

15 Calculated from *Tenth Census of Newfoundland, op. cit.*

16 *Historical Statistics of Newfoundland,* Table A-1.

17 Calculated from *Census of Newfoundland,* 1901, Table J, p. XVII. The sharp increase in the death rate in 1891 may represent an unusual year or a weakness in the census.

18 Dominion Bureau of Statistics [hereafter DBS], *Province of Newfoundland Statistical Background* (Ottawa, 1949), Tables 21 and 22.

19 Sources for these estimates are the *Census of Newfoundland,* 1901, 1911 and 1935; and DBS, *Statistical Background,* Table 23. Michael Staveley, "Migration and Mobility in Newfoundland and Labrador: A Study in Population Geography" (Unpublished Ph.D. thesis, University of Alberta, 1973), p. 71, also concludes that a flood of emigration began around 1884.

TABLE 3

TERMS OF TRADE FOR THE TRADITIONAL ECONOMY

Period	(1) Index of Salt Cod Prices 1913-100	(2) UK Merchandise Export Index 1913-100	(3) Terms of Trade with UK Exports/Imports	(4) Canadian Export Price Index 1913-100	(5) Terms of Trade with Canada Exports/Imports	(6) USA Merchandise Export Index 1913-100	(7) Terms of Trade with USA Exports/Imports	(8) UK	(9) Canada	(10) USA	(11) All Country Weighted Index of Terms of Trade
								— Country Share in Newfoundland Imports %			
1870-74[1]	69	130	53	78	88	N/A	N/A	40	30	30	67
1875-79[1]	68	110	62	83	82	N/A	N/A	40	30	30	70
1880-84	67	99	68	84	80	102	66	40	30	30	71
1885-89	65	87	75	81	80	88	74	39	36	35	77
1890-94	63	87	72	84	75	81	78	35	41	24	75
1895-99	51	80	64	78	65	71	72	33	35	32	67
1900-04	74	81	91	86	86	83	89	29	38	33	88
1905-09	N/A	91	N/A	96	N/A	91	N/A	25	37	38	N/A
1910-14	100	96	104	100	100	98	102	26	35	39	102
1915-19[2]	165	N/A	N/A	180	92	168	98	11	42	47	96
1920-24[3]	153	236	65	178	86	117	131	24	44	33	97
1925-29	148	164	90	158	94	138	107	23	44	33	97
1930-34	104	130	80	106	98	97	107	20	44	36	98
1935-39	82	135	61	117	70	113	73	26	40	34	69
1940-44[4]	172	N/A	N/A	142	121	250	69	7	60	33	100
1945-49[5]	281	300	94	222	127	252	112	5	60	35	120

[1]Calculated with 1881-85 distribution of trade between the three trading partners, and with the USA the 1880-84 terms of trade.
[2]Calculated with 1910-14 terms of trade with the UK.
[3]Calculated with 1923-24 only as weights.
[4]Calculated with 1935-39 UK terms of trade.
[5]Calculated with 1945-48 only as weights.

SOURCES:
Historical Statistics of Newfoundland, Table K-7; D.B.S., *Province of Newfoundland Statistical Background,* Table 98; *Historical Statistics of Canada,* Series J84-95 and J108-117; *Historical Statistics of the United States,* Series U21-44; *British Historical Statistics,* ch. 11, Table 15.

It is clear that the 1880s is an important benchmark in Newfoundland's economic history. The traditional economy reached a limit to its extensive growth and further development was perceived as a function of the emergence of modern resource industries, with emigration acting as a mechanism to balance a labour force growing faster than employment opportunities. Since the acquisition of responsible government in 1855, the ever pressing task which confronted ministries was to raise market incomes in the traditional sector and to substitute domestic job creation for the humiliating, costly and enervating mechanism of emigration. Indeed, during the decades when the traditional economy was approaching its maximum extensive growth, government had begun to search for a development strategy which would reduce the rate of inshore fishery expansion and initiate its relative decline. The most famous statement of this goal was the report of the Whiteway Committee which declared that "no material increase of means is to be looked for from our fisheries, and . . . we must direct our attention to the growing requirements of the country."[20] The strategy the committee proposed contained the essential features of the national development policy pursued by all nineteenth-century territories of European settlement.[21] Through railway technology the country would be shaken free from dependence upon coastal resources, and a moving frontier of inland settlement would open export sectors in agriculture and minerals — resources whose existence in Newfoundland was confirmed by geological survey. There was also a hint in the committee's report that St. John's would provide a market for country products, and presumably with the growth of the latter, would emerge as a centre of domestic manufacturing. At one stroke, a blow was dealt to the one product export economy and the income leakages resulting from high foreign trade dependence. In general, Newfoundland's economic problem was seen not as an actual or approaching over-abundance of labour relative to resources, but of labour relative to resources currently being exploited.

In the latter part of the nineteenth century this strategy was pursued with a legislative ferocity which took second place to no developing country. In 1873 a Homestead Law was passed to encourage "Agriculture and the more speedy settlement of the Wilderness" and the Companies Corporation Act provided the legal framework for establishing limited liability companies in manufacturing, mining and commerce. In 1875 a system of bounties was introduced to speed up land clearance and cultivation. Two years later there was an "Act for the Encouragement of Manufacturing" providing subsidies on imports of flax, cotton and wool used in fishing gear and textiles. An act of

---

20 "Report of the Select Committee to Consider and Report upon the Construction of a Railway", *Journal of the House of Assembly,* 1880, p. 126.

21 For a discussion of this point see A. J. Youngson, "The Opening up of New Territories", *Cambridge Economic History* (Cambridge, 1966), vol. VI, Part I, ch. 3.

1880 offered large blocks of land to licensees who would settle farming families. In the same year the Receiver General was authorized to issue debentures for construction of a railway from St. John's to Notre Dame Bay, and in the next year the first railway contract was brought down for a line to Halls Bay with branches to Conception Bay. The 1880 session also introduced one of many bounty schemes to encourage ship building for the Bank fishery, and legislation was passed in 1882 providing assistance to New York promotors to establishing the Newfoundland Dock Company — the railway and drydock being the two great infastructure investments of the late nineteenth century.[22]

The 1882 session included a flight of fancy, in legislation for the "Great American and European Short Line Railway". It provided the promotors with incentives to build a southern line from St. John's to the Southwest Coast, there to link up by steamer with railways to be built or running rights to be acquired, through Eastern Canada and the United States — a scheme perhaps no more ridiculous in its historical context than the Canadian dream of an Imperial transportation link between Europe and the Orient. In any case, it was an early manifestation of Newfoundland's continuing fascination with its supposed locational advantages in the North Atlantic. In 1884 an act closely modeled on Canadian legislation provided for the survey of Newfoundland into townships, sections and quartersections, with a further development of homesteading, mining and forestry law. This was followed two years later by an "Act for the Promotion of Agriculture" which established agricultural districts under the direction of a superintendent and staff to direct settlement, road building and other public works as well as the promotion of scientific agriculture. In 1889 these measures were supplemented by the establishment of a Board of Agriculture to supervise local agricultural societies, and found a model farm to introduce improved stock, seeds and farm equipment.[23] In 1896 the trans-insular railway was completed, but the decade saw the projection of fresh schemes including a line from the Canadian border to the Labrador coast.

Throughout the late nineteenth century the St. John's newspapers followed the progress of secondary manufacturing, giving close attention to technical accomplishments, the level of employment and the likelihood of staunching imports. Gaden's Ginger Ale Factory was applauded for beating out imported mineral waters. The carriage factory of Messrs. W. R. Oke and Sons was hailed for developing a wooden tricycle for the French Consul which could be marketed at a quarter the cost of steel models. Archibald's Tobacco

---

22 For the statutes embodying these provisions see *Statutes of Newfoundland,* 36 Vict., c.7, c.8; 38 Vict., c.18; 40 Vict., c.10; 43 Vict., c.3, c.4; 44 Vict., c.2; 43 Vict., c.5; and 45 Vict., c.3.

23 See *ibid.,* 45 Vict., c.4; 47 Vict., c.2; 49 Vict., c.3; and 52 Vict., c.8.

Works, employing some 120 people, produced a Newfoundland plug tobacco. Stained glass, with designs in a national idiom, was made by the Newfoundland Glass Embossing Company. Newfoundland fruit was bottled in a new factory on Mundy Pond Road and samples were sent to the Queen with the hope of acquiring a royal appointment. Boots and shoes were turned out in a plant at Riverhead in St. John's employing close to 150 people, and since its work could "compare more than favourable with work turned out in any part of the world" it was anticipated that imports would be reduced.[24] The seriousness with which manufacturing development was viewed was symbolized by a government decision in 1891 to fund an Industrial Exhibition at St. John's "for the encouragement of the national and mechanical products of this colony."[25]

Like Canada's National Policy, Newfoundland's first development strategy envisioned a moving frontier of agricultural settlement (facilitated by investments in inland transportation) linked to an initially protected and subsidized industrial sector. The results were disappointing. Improved acreage doubled from 36,000 acres in 1874 to 86,000 in 1901, but on a per capita basis this meant a growth from only 0.28 acres to 0.32.[26] Similarly, there was modest growth in the livestock population — from 90,000 cows and cattle to 148,000, and from 180,000 sheep to 350,000 — but the country had hardly made a dent in its domestic import bill and certainly had not emerged as one of the world's frontiers of agricultural investment.[27]   In the industrial sector the value of factory output per capita grew from only $10 in 1884 to $12 in 1901 and $14 in 1911.[28] It is, accordingly, a reasonable conclusion that agriculture and secondary manufacturing developments brought no important shifts in the composition of output. Nonetheless, the structure of employment in the country was significantly different in 1911 compared with 1884, as shown in Table 4. Between these dates almost 30% of the labour force — a growing labour force — was shifted out of fishing and into other occupations. Over half of this 30% represented small gains to defined primary, secondary and service occupations, while the other 13% was accounted for by the census aggregate 'Others'. This category likely included workers in a variety of personal service occupations, although the sharp increase in the category between 1884 and 1891 suggests another analysis which supports its allocation

24 I am grateful to Mrs. B. Robertson of the Newfoundland Historical Association for drawing my attention to these references. See *The Daily Colonist*, 30, 9 July 1887; 1 April, 13 September 1886; 8 October 1888; 4 June 1889.

25 54 Vict., c.10.

26 Calculated from *Census of Newfoundland*, 1911, vol. I, Table XXI.

27 *Ibid.*, Table XXII.

28 *Ibid.*, Table XXIII. Some large firms, however, did not report, such as Reid-Newfoundland, Angel Engineering and A. Harvey.

TABLE 4

DISTRIBUTION OF THE LABOUR FORCE: 1857 - 1935

	1858	1869	1874	1884	1891	1901	1911	1921	1935
Labour Force	43,251	47,024	53,309	73,796	56,984	67,368	82,426	80,327	88,710
Primary:	94%	90%	89%	87%	70%	69%	63%	59%	55%
-Agriculture	4	4	2	2	3	4	4	4	5
-Fishing	89	84	86	82	64	61	53	51	⎤ 48
-Lumbering	1	1	1	2	1	2	3	3	⎦
-Mining	—	1	—	0.5	2	2	2	1	2
Secondary:	5	9	10	10	22	23	27	28	24
-Mechanics	5	4	4	5	5	5	7	6	7
-Factory Workers	—	—	—	—	2	1	2	2	
-Others	—	5	6	5	15	17	18	20	17
Service:	1.9	1.6	1.5	3.8	7.9	8	11	12	22
-Professional	0.3	0.4	0.4	0.4	2	2	2	2.6	3.6
-Merchants	1.6	1.3	1.1	1.2	1.4	1.5	1.6	1.3	⎤ 8.7
-Clerical	—	—	—	2.2	3.4	3.5	5.6	6.2	⎦
-Government	—	—	—	—	—	—	—	—	7.3

NOTE: A 'modern' occupational classification was introduced in the 1935 census which renders comparisons with previous years difficult. The category 'others' for 1935 includes employees in electric power, construction, transportation and unspecified areas. Prior to 1935 employees in personal service were enumerated under 'others' insofar as they were recorded at all. The error would hence inflate secondary employment and deflate service employment in earlier years relative to 1935.

SOURCE: *Tenth Census of Newfoundland and Labrador, 1935*, Part I, vol. II.

to secondary employment. Between 1884 and 1891 railway construction and a number of urban service projects got underway, and the upswing in the category 'Others' probably reflects the emergence of a large labour force in transportation, communications, public utilities and construction. If this is so, then a large share of employment diversification in this period was secured by a flow of public, and largely foreign private funds, into capital projects. Indeed it was two of the largest of these investments — the Bell Island iron mine and the Harmsworth newsprint plant at Grand Falls — which accounted for the decline in fish products as a percentage of exports (despite rising values from 1900) from over 90% in the 1880s to less than 70% by the opening of the War.

It is very probable that gross domestic product grew substantially in real terms between the mid-1880s and 1911. But the gains to gross national product and to personal incomes would be less dramatic; for both the railway, the new resource industries, and the expanding urban services must have increased the gross investment ratio and introduced for the first time into the Newfoundland economy substantial payments abroad for technology, capital and entrepreneurship.

The assumptions guiding Newfoundland's first development strategy were akin to those shaping the nineteenth-century territories of settlement. The weight of development was to be assumed by Newfoundlanders — native born and immigrants — accumulating capital and absorbing modern technology through the formation and expansion of small agricultural and industrial enterprises. Their efforts would be complemented by footloose entrepreneurs who, with government backing, would tackle large and complex capital investments. These assumptions began to give way by the beginning of the twentieth century. It is true that interest in native Newfoundland enterprise remained strong in the St. John's newspapers. For example, in 1912 excitement built up over the prospect of a rubber goods factory employing "all local capital", but it was abandoned when it was found that "the smallest plant which could be established . . . would produce enough stock in about four to five weeks to accommodate the demand."[29] It was also suggested at various times that factory hands should boycott merchants who carried imported lines when local products were available.[30] But the bulk of development legislation from the turn of the century was devoted not to the stimulation of local enterprise, but to a search for foreign, direct investment firms to develop modern resource industries through a package of advanced management and technology.

The reasons for this shift are clear. The original development strategy had failed. The high cost of land clearance and fertilization of an acidic soil made

29 *The Daily News,* 16 January 1912.
30 *The Evening Telegram,* 9 July 1908.

the land marginal to Newfoundlanders and the European migrants who flooded into the prairie lands of Australia and South and North America. With manufacturing, the size of the domestic market doomed firms to sub-optimal scale, and the absence of an industrial tradition in the country among capitalists and workers made it unlikely that Newfoundland firms would overcome the difficulties of entering foreign markets to achieve optimum scale. The remaining avenue to development was primary manufacturing industries, where possession of a scarce natural resource provided cost advantages for entry into international markets. Unlike the fishing industry, however, the minimum size of the firm in modern resource-based manufacturing was large and Newfoundland, with its tiny national income, had neither the savings, the entrepreneurs, nor the skilled workers to launch and control such developments.

The resulting wedding between Newfoundland and the international corporation can be traced back to the nineteenth-century contracts for railways, the drydock and the Bell Island mines. But the volume of such contracts accelerated with the successful Anglo-Newfoundland Development Company agreement in 1905 for a paper mill at Grand Falls. In the following year the Marconi Company was given a monopoly over telegraphy in return for a commitment to improve the Island's communications. In 1910 the "Coal Development Act" provided the Newfoundland Exploration Syndicate with tariff guarantees on coal imports if the company established a commercial mine. A similar inducement was given in 1910 to the Newfoundland Oil Fields Limited of London. In 1911 the British-Canadian Explosives Company, also of London, was offered protection to establish a manufacturing plant of sufficient capacity at least to supply local demand. In the same year an agreement was reached with the International Carbonizing Company to manufacture peat fuel, and two Maine promoters were offered various inducements to build five cold storage plants for fish products. In the next year the American-Newfoundland Pulp and Paper Company of Grand Rapids, Michigan, entered into an agreement for a pulp and paper mill at Deer Lake. In 1913 the Orr Newfoundland Company was empowered to construct five reduction plants to manufacture glue and fertilizer from dogfish, while the Canadian North Atlantic Corporation revived an old vision of a railway from Quebec City to the Labrador coast.[31]

The war years slowed down but did not staunch the flood of industrial promotions. In 1915 the Newfoundland-American Packing Company received concessions for cold storage facilities to pack fresh water fish, fruits and berries, and the Newfoundland Products Corporation was launched to manufacture fertilizers on the Humber. In the first year of peace the St. George's

31 See *Statutes of Newfoundland,* 5 Ed. VII, c.9, c.8; 10 Ed. VII, c.23, c.24; 1 Geo. V, c.11, c.20, c.22; 2 Geo. V, c.7; 3 Geo V, c.8, c.14.

Coal Fields Company revived the prospect of domestic coal supplies. In 1920 the St. Lawrence Timber, Pulp and Steamship Company offered prospects for the development of pulp mills on Bonne Bay, while the Terra Nova Sulphite Company was planning a similar facility at Alexander Bay. In 1921 the D'Arcy Exploration Company was granted leases for oil exploration, while the Pulp and Paper Corporation of America proposed mills in Labrador — probably only to acquire rights to export pulpwood and pitprops. In 1923 an agreement with the Newfoundland Power and Paper Corporation resulted in the mill at Corner Brook — one concrete success. In 1924 the Newfoundland Milling Company was founded to mill cereals with a guarantee of a twenty year monopoly and tariff protection. In 1929 the Newfoundland Mines and Smelters Limited was granted concessions over a large part of the Avalon to mine and process lead, copper, zinc and other ores. In 1930 one of the most imaginative — and enduring — schemes was launched by the Great Lakes-Atlantic Newfoundland Company for a transhipment port at Mortier Bay. In the last years, as the edifice of responsible government slipped away, the Terra Nova Oils Company was granted privileges to distil for export.[32]

Each of the agreements had common threads. Any provision for Newfoundland equity participation, either public or private, was absent. The Newfoundland Government provided concessions in the form of Crown Land grants, drawbacks on duties on new construction materials, machinery and raw materials, tax holidays, and where applicable, the promise of protective tariffs. In return for these privileges, the companies promised to employ Newfoundland labour wherever possible and to invest certain minimum amounts over specified time periods — a guarantee which was commonly extended for further grace periods by amending legislation. But for all the hopes and effort embodied in these agreements, few resulted in any investment and still fewer in any permanent additions to the country's productive capacity.

In contrast to the late nineteenth century, legislation involving Newfoundland entrepreneurship was remarkably scarce and, with two exceptions, unoriginal. In 1908 the Model Farm Act provided for an agricultural experimental station to undertake original and applied research. In 1917 the Newfoundland Knitting Mills and the Riverside Woolen Mills, both apparently Newfoundland firms, were given relief from import duties on machinery and raw materials and a limited subsidy for fifteen years. In 1928 a Harbour Grace merchant was given a three year monopoly to establish a shark oil industry — a trade perhaps better fitted to some of the foreign concessionaires. A more promising direction was offered in the Tourist Commission Act of 1927 which

32 *Ibid.,* 6 Geo. V, c.3, c.4; 9 & 10 Geo. V, c.25; 11 Geo. V, c.6, c.2; 12 Geo. V, c.8, c.9; 14 Geo. V, c.1; 15 Geo. V, c.1; 20 Geo. V, c.12; 21 Geo. V, c.6; 22 Geo. V, c.5; 23 & 24 Geo. V, c.5.

established a public corporation drawing revenues from a tax on hotels, steamships and similar enterprises, to promote a tourist traffic and a "wider knowledge of the colony's natural resources". Undoubtedly the most important legislation in these years seeking to upgrade the efficiency and returns to Newfoundland enterprise was the two acts which made up the Coaker Regulations.[33] The acts established national quality controls in the production of salt fish and an organized approach in the markets for all Newfoundland output. Regrettably, the regulations foundered on divisions within the trade and were repealed in the following year.[34] It was not until the economic collapse of the 1930s when prospects of attracting foreign capital for resource development dried up, that attention to fishery legislation revived. In the interval Newfoundland's position as the world's largest exporter of salt cod weakened in the face of a growing competitiveness in Scandinavia and the development of national fishing fleets in traditional importing countries.[35]

"No colony of the British Empire", it was stated in 1910, "has made such progress in recent years as has Newfoundland." It was "one of the most progressive states in the Western hemisphere" and "no people in the world maintain a more comfortable and contented existence than the Newfoundland fishermen . . . ."[36] Twenty years later, on the eve of Newfoundland's economic and political collapse, Joseph Smallwood wrote at length of the country as a budding industrial Michigan set down in a North Atlantic Arcadia.[37] But the structural transformation so often planned, predicted and seen, had not in fact arrived. Between 1911 and 1935 Newfoundland's population grew from 243,000 to 290,000, an annual rate of 0.8% as compared with about 1.7% in Canada. As a consequence of emigration, the labour force grew more slowly than population at an annual rate of 0.3%, whereas in Canada it grew faster than population at slightly over 1.8%.[38] In other words, the demographic trends were not those of a country which had surmounted a development hump into modern economic growth.

33 *Ibid.,* 8 Ed. VII, c.7; 8 Geo. V, c.1, c.2; 18 Geo. V, c.1; 11 Geo. V, c.25, c.27.

34 See Ian McDonald, "Coaker the Reformer" (unpublished manuscript, Newfoundland Studies Centre, 1975).

35 See G. M. Gerhardsen and L. P. D. Gertenbach, *Salt Cod and Related Species* (Rome, Food and Agricultural Organization, 1949).

36 Anon., "The Golden Age of Newfoundland's Advancement" (n.p., 1910), pp. 1, 8. Internal evidence suggests this to be a Harmsworth promotional pamphlet.

37 J. R. Smallwood, *The New Newfoundland* (New York, 1931).

38 The Canadian rate is calculated for employed population 1911-31. The dependency ratio was not, however, remarkably different. Both countries had heavy child dependency ratios of 35% in Newfoundland in 1935 and 31% in Canada for 1931. That the Newfoundland ratio was not more unfavourable may be attributable to the apparently higher infant mortality rate (see DBS, *Statistical Background,* Table 24) and differing marriage and fertility patterns. Whatever the explanation, the occupied labour force was 34% of the population in 1911 and only 30% in 1935.

The foreign trade statistics appeared, superficially, to indicate considerable growth and diversification. Exports and re-exports grew from \$11.7M in 1906/10 to a peak of \$40.0M in 1929/30, or from about \$50 per capita to around \$135, while fishery products fell from some 80% to 40% of total exports.[39] Indeed, per capita exports from Newfoundland were higher than in Canada, which stood at \$40 in 1911 and \$115 in 1929. But given the small volume of domestic production for home consumption, Newfoundland needed very high levels of exports per capita to emulate the North American pattern of consumption which, as Smallwood noted, was increasingly emulated and desired.[40] Moreover, the gains to levels of consumption from rising per capita exports could not have been very great since, as Table 3 suggests, the export price indices of countries from which Newfoundland drew most of her imports rose by 40% to 60% between the immediate pre-war years and the second half of the 1920s. Secondly, duties as a percentage of imports rose from around 20% to 28% over the period,[41] and expenditures for servicing foreign debt rose from 20% of revenue in 1919-20 to 35% in 1929-30.[42] Thirdly, the per capita value of exports in pre-war Newfoundland reflected much more realistically returns for consumption to factors of production in Newfoundland than was the case by the late 1920s. The new resource industries in mining and forest products, which accounted for over 55% of the value of exports in 1929-30, required substantial payments out of the gross value of sales for capital depreciation, payments to foreign suppliers of intermediate inputs and non-resident management and ownership. For the same reason, the apparent diversification of the economy is misleading. Newfoundland had progressed from a domestically owned one product export economy to a substantially foreign owned three product export economy, for in 1929-30 some 98% of exports were accounted for by fish, forest, and mineral products.

Diversification of output for the export economy had no dramatic impact on the distribution of the labour force. In Table 4 the apparently strong growth in service employment and the decline in secondary shares between 1911 and 1935 is largely a statistical illusion arising either from a failure to enumerate personal service before 1935, or its allocation to 'Others' in earlier periods. The Table suggests a continuation of long-run trends rather than sharp discontinuities. Relative to the labour force, primary employment was declining, service employment was increasing, but secondary employment was stabilizing at around 20-25% of labour force. This was the share reached in the 1890s when the modern transportation, communications and construc-

39   DBS, *Statistical Background,* Table 97.

40   *New Newfoundland,* p. 211.

41   DBS, *Statistical Background,* Table 97.

42   Dominons Office, Newfoundland Royal Commission, *Report* (London, 1933, Cmnd. 4480), pp. 57, 63.

tion labour force began to emerge. Fishing and lumbering in 1935 continued to employ almost half the labour force, while factory and shop employment, despite the paper mills and electrical power stations, still employed only about 7%, while all occupations in the service sector showed small relative gains. The modern resource industries attracted to Newfoundland since the turn of the century had had a much greater impact on the composition of domestic product than on the structure of the labour force. The *trends* in labour's sectoral allocation were the same as those affecting other countries in the western world,[43] but the strength of demand for labour in Newfoundland's non-primary sectors and the growth of labour productivity in the primary sector had generated a much slower pace of transition than elsewhere. Thus, while the employment trends were toward the 'modern' allocation, at each date the secondary sector and, to a lesser degree, the service sector were more weakly developed.

Table 5 compares the sectoral allocation of employment with distribution of earning in 1935 and gives the resulting sectoral average per capita earnings. The Table is misleading as to the share in earning of the fishing industry in 'normal' times, as the price collapse of fish products was more severe than in other export industries. Still, even if the export value of fish products for 1928/29 (some $16M) is allocated entirely to labour income in Newfoundland and no adjustment is made for depressed earnings in other sectors — obviously a gross bias in favour of the fishing industry in normal times — the sector would have received only about 45% of earnings, and per capita earnings would have stood at around $350. It is more likely that in good years some 35-40% of earnings went to this sector which, according to the 1935 census, directly and indirectly employed and supported some 40% of the population. It is true that fishermen had to outfit themselves from earnings, but it is also the case that non-market income was more available to the rural than the urban labour force. The best guess is that in normal times standards of living for the mass of workers in the fishing sector did not differ sharply from those for the mass of workers in other sectors of the economy. If this is so, then the reason for the small absolute decline of the fishing labour force in the first half of the twentieth century is not simply a function of employment potential in other sectors. The critical fact is that the economy as a whole could not provide sufficient employment for the growing population and potential labour force, necessitating emigration from *both* urban and rural sectors. With stronger growth in secondary and tertiary sectors the level of emigration would have fallen, but it would have required a massive boom in demand for secondary and service output and a correspondingly sharp rise in per capita earnings in those sectors to have attracted large amounts of labour out of the primary sector.

---

43   See Simon Kuznets, *Modern Economic Growth* (New Haven, 1966), ch. 3.

TABLE 5

OCCUPATIONS AND EARNINGS IN NEWFOUNDLAND 1935

	% Total Employment	% Total Earnings	Per Capita Earnings
All Industries	(88,710)	($24,952,700)	($280)
Forestry, Fishing, Trapping	48 %	24 %	$ 140
Services:	15	19	350
-Professional (Male)	1.3	5.4	830
-Public Administration (Male)	2.3	6	750
-Personal Service (Female)	6.5	2	60
Unspecified	8	4	140
Trade	7	16	640
Manufacturing	7	14	610
Transportation and Communication	5	10	500
Agriculture	5	4	155
Construction	3	4	350
Mining	2	4	500
Electric Power	0 (0.3)	1	1,100
Finance	0 (0.2)	1	1,350

NOTE: All calculations are rounded in the major breakdowns to the nearest 1%.

SOURCE: Calculated from *Tenth Census of Newfoundland and Labrador*, 1935.

The Newfoundland government struggled with the prospect of bankruptcy during the early years of the Depression, and finally surrendered independence and Dominion status early in 1934. The Commission appointed from Britain a year earlier to review the causes of impending collapse, attributed it largely to the irresponsibility of politicians in the management of public funds.[44] But from its own evidence it is difficult to make the case that there was a riot of spending. Revenues grew steadily from $8.4M in 1920/21 to $11.6M in 1929/30, but current expenditures actually declined from $8.9M to $7.2M and in every year between were under $7M.[45] It is true that the budget was in surplus only in 1924/25, whereas it was in surplus in every year after 1922 in Canada; but the great development expenditures of the Canadian government were over by the 1920s, whereas in the twenty-eight years between 1885 and 1913 the Canadian budget had been in deficit in all but six of those years.[46] In 1933 the per capita public debt in Newfoundland stood at around $344 compared

44 1933 Commission, *op. cit.*, p. 43.

45 *Ibid.*, pp. 57, 63.

46 Calculated from *Historical Statistics of Canada*, Series 621-24 and 626-44.

with $540 for all levels of government in Canada,[47] which given relative income levels implied a heavier burden in Newfoundland.[48] Analysis of the Newfoundland public debt in 1933 shows that 35% was attributable to development of the railway; 60% was accounted for by the railway and other development expenditures on fisheries, agriculture, schools, roads, urban development and similar accounts; that over 70% was chargeable to these and the war debt, and finally that the lion's share of borrowings made to cover budget deficits was in order to keep the railway operating.[49]

Whatever the peccadillos of its politicians, Newfoundland's collapse was not the result of corruption or even unwise, as distinct from unfruitful, spending of public funds. With the grant of responsible government, Newfoundland had set out to replicate the economic performance of its continental neighbours. The levels and patterns of North American consumption were the goal, and it is not surprising that development strategies to achieve it were imported as well. From hindsight, some of the reasons for failure are apparent. The matter of scale was crucial, for it was only by the output of massive volumes of several primary products and the simultaneous enlargement of domestic markets, that servicing of development expenditures could be covered, a measure of isolation from the swings of international prices secured, and dependence upon external capital markets reduced. Newfoundland was unfortunate. The economy was too narrowly based to benefit from war demand in 1914-18 and at best only a small commodity trade surplus was achieved. Moreover, unlike Canada, Newfoundland had to finance much of her war effort by borrowing in London and New York. The economy emerged from the war without a sharply diversified structure or increased capacity, with a casualty ridden labour force, and an increased external debt.

In the 1920s weak primary product prices offered no relief, and unlike Canada the country could not escape from the treadmill of external borrowing to service existing debt and to seek the elusive breakthrough into modern economic growth and structure. Hence the country was extremely vulnerable in the face of the international economic crisis which was steadily building throughout the 1920s. Newfoundland's export earnings dropped by 22% in 1930/31 - 1934/35 over their level in 1925/26 - 1929/30 — a rather modest decline compared with the almost 50% collapse in Canada's foreign earnings in 1931-35 over 1925-29.[50] But the smaller percentage decline had a much

47 Calculated from 1933 Commission, *op. cit.*, p. 253; *Historical Statistics of Newfoundland*, Table A-1, and *Historical Statistics of Canada*, Series 696-710.

48 In Canada in 1933 debt charges of all governments as a per cent of revenues amounted to 40% as compared with 63% for Newfoundland in 1932/33. Calculated from *Historical Statistics of Canada*, Series 662-82, 683-710, and 1933 Commission, *op. cit.*, pp. 57, 63.

49 Calculated from 1933 Commission, *op. cit.*, p. 253.

50 Calculated from DBS, *Statistical Background*, Table 97, and *Historical Statistics of Canada*, Series F242-245.

greater impact on Newfoundland since a larger share of national income was derived from foreign trade, the fishing industry (which was the most important in terms of payment to resident factors) was most severely hit, and government revenues, out of which payments on development capital had to be met, were almost entirely derived from customs.

Emulation of the style of life and the development strategies by which the new continental countries had achieved it, resulted in ruin for Smallwood's 'New Newfoundland'. For the impatient public servants of the 1933 Royal Commission, it was a case of a "people misled into the acceptance of false standards" and a "country sunk in waste and extravagance."[51] A blunter conclusion was reached in the 1940s by MacKay and Saunders: "the Newfoundland economy cannot, in normal times, provide the revenue required to supply the Island with the public services demanded by a Western people".[52] In short, Newfoundland was not a fit place for white men, or at least very many of them.

E. H. Carr has suggested that history rarely repeats itself because man is conscious of the past.[53] But in Newfoundland the past has not been well understood and the range of choice has been severely restricted. After the 1934 collapse succeeding decades have brought a repetition of earlier development cycles. During Commission Government in the 1930s and 1940s, attention reverted to improving the efficiency and expanding the capacity of indigenous enterprise; in the 1950s and 1960s as a province of Canada, there was a further round on 'infastructure' investment and strenuous efforts to woo international capital and corporations. In the 1970s the province confronts the highest per capita debt and burden of taxation and the lowest credit rating in Canada. Almost half of provincial revenues are transfers from the federal government, and consumer expenditure and private investment is heavily supported by direct and indirect federal expenditures and transfers. The level of unemployment hovers around 20% of a labour force with a low participation rate, and many of the provinces hard-won industrial projects, such as the electric reduction plant, the linerboard mill and the oil refinery, are either heavily subsidized or operating at a loss. The Labrador mineral and hydro-electric projects have not generated major returns to the province and their prospect for further expansion is now dim. On the Island and coastal Labrador a large rural population remains, reluctant to move to the Mainland, and dependent upon the tattered remnants of a once great fishing industry wrecked by unfavourable trends in the international economy and hopelessly ineffec-

51 1933 Commission, *op. cit.,* p. 43.

52 MacKay, *Newfoundland,* p. 190.

53 *What is History?* (New York, 1972 ed.), pp. 84-89.

tive national trade and fisheries policies.[54] As Newfoundlanders once hoped that paper and mining companies would finally bring prosperity, they now await the discoveries of international oil companies on the Labrador coast.

If there are lessons from the past, however, they suggest that the province's natural potential lies on the sea, not the land, and that international resource corporations will not effect the economic transformation so long awaited. It might be wiser for Newfoundland to define and accept more modest goals and expectations, or perhaps more accurately, different ones. The development which a country achieves is not simply a quantitative measure of real output, but a qualitative valuation of the levels and patterns of consumption secured with that output, and its mental independence from valuations made by other influential countries. A tropical island will be poor no matter how much fish, fruit, sunshine and leisure its economy can provide if its people want, or are persuaded to want, cars and apartment towers. It is possible Newfoundland could develop a more prosperous economy and more self-confident society if its people adjusted to a pattern of consumption somewhat different from that of the Mainland, and its labour and capital were more effectively linked to its obvious natural endowment.

---

54   This issue is to be detailed in a forthcoming monograph by the author on the post 1945 Newfoundland fishing industry.

PATRICIA A. THORNTON Reprinted from Vol. XV, No. 1
(Autumn 1985)

The Problem of Out-Migration from Atlantic Canada, 1871-1921: A New Look

THE PERIOD FROM THE 1860s TO THE 1920s was a crucial one for Atlantic Canada. During this period both the Maritimes and Newfoundland failed to develop successfully. The Maritimes, despite optimistic beginnings, were ultimately unable to complete their industrial transformation. Newfoundland was unable to diversify out of its single-resource base, which in turn never modernized sufficiently to compete with "newer" fishing nations. Meanwhile a net figure of close to half a million people left the Maritimes and an unknown but considerable number left Newfoundland. Pondering such data in 1927, R.H. Coats of the Dominion Bureau of Statistics stated that "generally speaking the trend in population, especially in a 'new' country, is regarded as an index of its prosperity....The study of population tendencies in the Maritimes...may therefore be regarded as illustrating and reflecting the course of their economic development".[1] In this respect Coats was simply expressing the conventional wisdom of economists concerning migration theory and projecting it, as others have done before and since, onto the region to "explain" demographic trends over the preceding half-century.

Just what role did out-migration play in the relative economic fortunes of the region? Economic historians offer diverse and somewhat conflicting interpretations. In the Maritimes, the most commonly held view is that out-migration was (and indeed still is) a *consequence* of the failure of the region to industrialize successfully,[2] whereas in Newfoundland overpopulation (and hence a lack of sufficient out-migration) is seen as a *cause* of worsening economic conditions.[3]

The author wishes to acknowledge the help and thank Dr. David Frost for the hours of work he put in programming the procedures used in this study and generating the SYMAP data base.

1 DBS, *The Maritime Provinces since Confederation: A Statistical Study of their Social and Economic Condition during the Past Sixty Years* (Ottawa, 1927), p. 3.

2 See for example, Canada, Dominion Bureau of Statistics [DBS], *The Maritime Provinces since Confederation* (Ottawa, 1927); New Brunswick, Office of the Economic Adviser, *Migration, New Brunswick, 1871-1967: A Statistical and Economic Analysis* (Fredericton, 1967); O.J. Firestone, *Canada's Economic Development 1867-1950* (London, 1958); S.A. Saunders, *Economic History of the Maritime Provinces* (Fredericton, 1984 [1939]); Alan Brookes, "Out-Migration from the Maritime Provinces, 1860-1900: Some Preliminary Considerations", *Acadiensis*, V, 2 (Spring 1976), pp. 26-56; and Alan Brookes, "The Golden Age and the Exodus: The Case of Canning, Kings County", *Acadiensis*, XI, 1 (Autumn 1981), pp. 57-82; David Alexander, "Economic Growth in the Atlantic Region, 1880-1940", *Acadiensis*, VIII, 1 (Autumn 1978), pp. 47-76; Kari Levitt, *Population Movements in the Atlantic Provinces* (Halifax, 1960).

3 One of the earliest discussions of overpopulation can be seen in "Report of the Select Committee

Thus, in one part of the Atlantic Region (the Maritimes) out-migration is considered a consequence of failure, while in another part of the region (Newfoundland) it is felt that out-migration would have been beneficial but in insufficient numbers it was a cause of economic failure. At best this is confusing both theoretically and empirically.

The empirical literature leads us to believe that migration can be both a cause and a consequence of economic conditions. The theoretical literature, although somewhat ambiguous on this topic, generally assumes that migration is a consequence of economic forces.[4] Similarly, both the empirical and the theoretical literature are ambiguous on the effects of out-migration. It has been argued that migration can be both a "good" and a "bad" phenomenon.[5] In fact, despite a not inconsiderable literature on out-migration from the region, the consequences of out-migration on the region have never been examined in any systematic way.[6] Indeed regional historians appear not to have been conscious of

to Consider and Report on the Construction of the Railways", Newfoundland, *Journals of the House of Assembly, 1880*, p. 126; the most recent discussion of this topic can be found in Parzival Copes, *The Resettlement of Fishing Communities in Newfoundland*, (Ottawa, 1972). For the best overview of the topic see David Alexander, "Newfoundland's Traditional Economy and Development to 1934", in J. Hiller and P. Neary, eds., *Newfoundland in the Nineteenth and Twentieth Centuries*, (Toronto, 1980), pp. 17-39.

4   Economic theories of migration all presume that migration is the dependent variable responding to inter-regional changes in economic opportunity. See for example J. Isaac, *Economics of Migration* (London, 1947) and more recently work by L.A. Sjaastad, 'The Costs and Returns of Human Migrations", *Journal of Political Economy*, 70 [supplement] (1962), pp. 80-93.

5   See Isaac, *Economics of Migration*, and other neo-classical economists who believe that migration usually results in regional equalization. On the other hand advocates of the core-periphery school usually assume that migration tends to increase rather than decrease regional disparities: see John Friedmann, *Regional Development Policy: A Case Study of Venezuela* (Cambridge, 1966) and Gunnar Myrdal, *Economic Theory and Under-developed Regions* (London, 1957). They all nevertheless believe that migration comes about because of the existence of regional disparities and the tendency for labour to move from areas of low wages and productivity to areas of higher wages and productivity.

6   Most of the work has focused on the spatial patterns of out-migration, particularly the places of origin and destination and the apparent causes of large-scale out-migration. Much of this has been dependent upon sources which identify migrants from the United States end. In addition to the work by Brookes already mentioned and his Ph.D. thesis, "The Exodus: Migration from the Maritime Provinces to Boston during the second half of the Nineteenth century", University of New Brunswick, 1979, see also the companion volumes by M.L. Hansen and J.B. Brebner, *The Mingling of the Canadian and American Peoples, 1604-1938* (New Haven, 1940) and L.E. Truesdell, *The Canadian-Born in the United States, 1850-1950* (New Haven, 1943). Of the remaining work which has focused on the Atlantic Region end of the process there has been a considerable literature concerned about the impact of the continued drain of out-migration on the viability of the region: see the three volumes brought out by the Dominion Bureau of Statstics: *The Maritime Provinces since Confederation* (1927), *The Maritime Provinces in their Relation to the National Economy of Canada: A Statistical Study of their Social and Economic Condition since Confederation* (Ottawa, 1934), and *The Maritime Provinces in their Relation to the National Economy of Canada: A Statistical Study of of their Social and Economic Condition since Confederation* (Ottawa, 1948). More recently two works by economists have followed in the same vein: Levitt, *Population Movements in the Atlantic Provinces* (1966) and D.J. McDonald,

the theoretical issue at stake and seem to have absorbed by osmosis the *a priori* theoretical assumption that migration is necessarily a consequence of economic conditions. This assumption, however, is both ambiguous and inadequately substantiated.

There are, therefore, two problems. Within the regional literature we need to clarify our arguments and specifically address the question of the consequences of migration for the region. Within the theoretical literature, we need to overcome the too narrow assumptions and lack of a temporal perspective. To do this we need to look at the region's experience consciously in terms of the theoretical issue: is out-migration necessarily a consequence of economic failure or can it also be a cause? In this paper the principal focus is on the regional experience of out-migration. Theory is examined to provide a framework for studying the consequences of out-migration on Atlantic Canada. In turn the regional case helps to establish the inadequacy of the available theory, which will need to be reassessed and restated in order to accommodate the empirical findings.

An examination of decadal intercensal rates of population growth in Atlantic Canada (see Table One) and out-migration in the Maritimes (see Table Two) compared with Quebec, Ontario and Canada as a whole from 1851 to 1931 is instructive in that it is open to conflicting interpretations. Looking back retrospectively from the present, several studies have shown that Atlantic Canada grew much more slowly than Quebec, Ontario and Canada as a whole since 1880,[7] and that in total more than 600,000 people left the Maritimes, which resulted in a net loss to the region of more than 460,000 people, or some 50 per cent of the population still present in 1931 at the end of the period.[8] These authors have interpreted this demographic history as symptomatic of economic stagnation and underdevelopment. However a closer examination could support an alternative interpretation.

Table One shows two distinct phases of population growth. Between 1851 and 1881, growth rates in the region were high and on a par with levels elsewhere in Canada. Only after 1881 and then for the entire period until 1931 were growth

Population, Migration and Economic Development in the Atlantic Provinces (Fredericton, 1968). All these studies however start from the assumption that out-migration in the 19th century was a consequence of economic stagnation, although Levitt and McDonald in particular do discuss the consequences of continued and persistent out-migration on the economic development of the region in the 20th century.

7   *Ibid.*, pp. 3-21; Levitt, *Population Movements*; McDonald, *Population, Migration and Economic Development*.

8   Several independent estimates have been made of the extent of out-migration from the Maritimes between 1881 and 1931, although as yet none exist for Newfoundland prior to 1907. In 1927, 1934 and 1948 the Dominion Bureau of Statistics, concerned about increasing regional disparity, estimated *gross* out-migration from the Maritimes over the period at approximately 600,000 and *net* out-migration at 470,000: DBS, *The Maritime Provinces*, p. 20. Similarly Nathan Keyfitz estimated *net* out-migration at 463,000: "The Growth of the Canadian Population", *Population Studies*, Vol. IV, No. 1 (1950-51), pp. 52-3); while Yolande Lavoie estimated *gross* out-migration at 618,000: Y. Lavoie, *L'Emigration des Canadiens aux Etats Unis avant 1930* (Montreal, 1972), p. 39.

Table One

Percentage Population Change by Decade, 1851-1961

	1851-61	61-71	71-81	81-91	91-01	01-11	11-21	21-31	31-41	41-51	51-61
Newfoundland*	15.0	18.0	21.0	3.0	9.0	9.0	8.0	7.0	10.0	19.0	27.0
Prince Edward Island	29.0	16.3	15.8	0.2	-5.3	-9.2	-5.5	-0.7	8.0	3.6	6.3
Nova Scotia	19.5	17.2	13.6	2.2	2.0	7.1	6.4	-2.1	12.7	11.2	14.7
New Brunswick	30.1	13.3	12.5	0.0	3.1	6.3	10.2	5.2	12.0	12.7	15.9
Maritimes	24.5	15.6	13.5	1.2	1.5	4.9	6.6	0.9	12.0	11.2	14.6
Ontario	46.6	16.1	18.9	9.7	3.2	15.8	16.1	17.0	10.4	21.4	35.6
Quebec	24.9	7.2	14.1	9.5	10.8	21.6	17.7	21.8	15.9	21.7	29.7
Canada	32.6	14.2	17.2	11.8	11.1	34.2	21.9	18.1	10.9	21.8	30.2

Sources: Newfoundland, *Census*, 1857, 1869, 1874, 1884, 1891, 1901, 1911, 1921, 1935; *Census of Canada*, 1951, 1961; Michael Staveley, "Aspects of Migration in Newfoundland and Labrador", Ph.D. thesis, University of Alberta, 1973, p. 70.

*Note that before 1891 the four intercensal periods for Newfoundland are 1857-69, 1869-74, 1874-84 and 1884-91.

Table Two

Net Migration Estimates, 1851-1931:
Maritime Provinces, Quebec, Ontario, Canada

	1851-61	1861-71	1871-81	1881-91	1891-1901	1901-11	1911-21	1921-31
in thousands								
Maritimes	+ 23	− 13	−25	−101	− 89	− 75	− 76	−122
Quebec				−132	−121	− 29	− 99	− 10
Ontario				− 84	−144	+ 74	+ 46	+129
Canada	+171	−191	−85	−205	−181	+715	+113	+103
as % of base population								
Maritimes	+ 4.3	− 2.0	− 3.3	− 11.6	− 10.1	− 8.4	− 8.1	− 12.2
Quebec				− 9.7	− 8.1	− 1.8	− 4.9	− 0.4
Ontario				− 4.3	− 6.8	+ 3.4	+ 1.8	+ 4.4
Canada	+ 7.0	− 5.9	− 2.3	− 4.7	− 3.7	+ 13.3	+ 1.6	+ 1.2

Note: All rates are calculated on the total population at the beginning of the decade.
Source: 1881-1931: Keyfitz, "The Growth of Canadian Population", *Population Studies*, Vol. IV, No. 1 (1950-51), pp. 52-53; 1851-1881: D.J. McDonald, *Population, Migration and Economic Development in the Atlantic Provinces* (Fredericton, 1968), pp. 9-13.

rates extremely low in the Maritimes. Although considerably higher in New-foundland, they were nevertheless lower than elsewhere in Canada. By contrast, despite somewhat retarded growth in the 1880s and 1890s in Ontario, there were no abrupt changes in demographic growth and this sluggish period lasted only 20 years there compared with 50 in Atlantic Canada. Table Two confirms that the turning point in the demographic growth of the Maritimes compared to the rest of Canada occurred in the 1880s, when out-migration was for the first time higher than the level experienced in the rest of Canada. However, these data also show that net out-migration had commenced more than two decades earlier and that the major difference between the Maritimes and the rest of Canada really surfaced around the turn of the century. After 1900 chronic out-migration con-tinued in the Maritimes while Ontario and to a lesser extent Quebec showed a recovery, with in-migration exceeding out-migration in some cases by significant proportions.

Economic historians have largely agreed that the economic recession of the 1880s and 1890s was no worse in the Maritimes than elsewhere in Canada and that the major reason for concern about the fate of the Maritimes came after the turn of the century when the great economic boom which swept the rest of Can-ada produced only slight reverberations in the Maritimes.[9] H.T. Johnson goes still further to challenge conventional wisdom by suggesting that the 1870s, far from being a decade of stagnation, witnessed pronounced increases in the rate of economic development, productivity and urbanization: indeed between 1871 and 1891 levels of urbanization appeared inexplicably high in the Maritimes.[10] Yet it was at precisely this time that massive and sustained out-migration occurred and population growth faltered. How then can demographers and economic his-torians alike, studying the region, continue to assume that such out-migration was a consequence of economic stagnation and not possibly a significant cause of subsequent economic stagnation? It may be suggested, then, that massive and sustained net losses of about 15 per cent of the region's population per decade may have seriously jeopardized the potential of the region to complete its indus-trial transformation. Certainly by the 1920s there could be no doubt about the economic stagnation and backwardness of the region — as the large number of official enquiries into this matter bear witness.[11]

But what about Newfoundland? Except for David Alexander's work[12] there have been no attempts to "bridge the Cabot Strait" to compare demographic and economic trends in the Maritimes and Newfoundland, and cast them in a

9 Alexander, "Economic Growth in the Atlantic Region", p. 48.

10 H.T. Johnson, "Urbanisation and Economic Growth in Canada, 1851-1971", Research Report 7321, Department of Economics, University of Western Ontario, 1973, p. 11.

11 Many of them, as we have seen, looked specifically at this question of the relationship between out-migration and economic development. See for example, the three reports published by the Dominion Bureau of Statistics in 1927, 1934 and 1948, Levitt, *Population Movements*, New Brunswick, Office of the Economic Adviser, *Migration, New Brunswick, 1871-1961*, and McDonald, *Population, Migration and Economic Development*.

12 Alexander, "Economic Growth in the Atlantic Region".

similar framework. For this reason it is perhaps not surprising that out-migration in Newfoundland should have been interpreted in such a different fashion from the Maritimes. Population numbers and growth have been seen as Newfoundland's prime economic problem: too many people in relation to too few resources.[13] Why then, as Table One would suggest, was out-migration insufficient to reduce growth rates to the level achieved in the Maritimes? In the absence of estimates of out-migration from Newfoundland, the plethora of economic studies would nevertheless lead us to question seriously whether the higher levels of population growth in Newfoundland relative to the Maritimes between 1881 and 1931, presumably reflecting lower levels of out-migration, necessarily indicate a more satisfactory economic performance. Instead it seems more likely that continued population growth may indicate nothing more than greater barriers to out-migration. In this context they can be expected only to have contributed to further impoverishment.

The regional literature thus points to an interesting question that has to be asked: Was out-migration a significant contributing factor to economic stagnation in the Maritimes, and just what was its extent and effect on Newfoundland? Just how many people left, from where and when? In the Maritimes did they leave in sufficiently large numbers *before* the marginal productivity of labour and economic opportunites had deteriorated? Did they not leave in sufficiently large numbers in Newfoundland until *after* productivity and economic opportunity had deteriorated? The regional literature also shows us clearly that the crucial period to study to answer this question at least for the Maritimes lies between 1870 and 1900. The theoretical literature shows us how we might address this question.

Economic theories of migration presume that migration is the dependent variable responding to inter-regional changes in economic opportunity. Assuming that there are no obstacles to migration and that migration costs are negligible, economists believe that people will move from low-income to high-income areas in response to differences in the marginal productivity of labour and available opportunities. Under such circumstances there are two schools of thought about the impact of migration on regional income and employment disparities. Neoclassical theorists believe, assuming labour to be homogeneous, that such migration will result in regional equalization of income.[14] Centre/periphery theorists, on the other hand, maintain that such migration will serve only to increase wage and productivity differences because migrants are demographically and economically selective and because money and investment concentrates where economies of scale, agglomeration, market potential and productivity are greatest.[15]

13 Alexander, "Newfoundland's Traditional Economy and Development to 1934"; "Report of the Select Committee on the Construction of the Railway", *Journals of the Newfoundland House of Assembly, 1880*, p. 126.

14 Isaac, *Economics of Migration*.

15 Friedmann, *Regional Development Policy*, and Myrdal, *Economic Theory and Underdevelopment*.

Migration theory, such as that developed by the International Labour Office and by Everett Lee, has removed some of the oversimplifications and further clarified such theory. They recognize that there are barriers to migration imposed by such factors as costs, inertia, distance, migration laws or inadequate information channels. More importantly, they recognize that there are basically two sets of economic forces operating: "push" and "pull" forces.[16] Where "push" factors at origin are strongest (such as rural poverty, low wages and incomes, few or declining opportunities, absence of amenities, poor education facilities and the like) then migration is less demographically and economically selective. Under these circumstances out-migration may be beneficial to the region, relieving it of surplus labour. However, where "pull" forces are strongest (such as the lure of cheap farm land, virgin forests, attractive opportunities for employment, promotion or good salaries, along with readily available amenities such as schools and hospitals) then migration is usually highly selective of the young, dynamic, better-educated and more highly skilled. Under these circumstances out-migration may deprive the region of the very people on whom self-sustained growth depends. The impact of migration on economic development, therefore, depends to a large extent on the conditions at origin and destination. In addition, the extent and timing of migration are determined as much by the quality of the links between areas,[17] the strength of the "pull" forces,[18] and the general level of prosperity (booms stimulating greater migration than busts).[19] Also important is the level of relative deprivation, that is the difference between such factors as unemployment and economic opportunity levels of two places

16 E.S. Lee, "A Theory of Migration", *Demography*, 3 (1966), pp. 47-57. The best review of migration theory by a staff member of the International Labour Office is W.R. Böhning, "Elements of a Theory of International Economic Migration to Industrial Nation States", in M. Kritz et al., eds., *Global Trends in Migration*, (New York, 1981), pp. 28-43. But see also the numerous studies and papers put out by that office either as independent studies or through the two journals they publish, *The International Labour Review* and *Industry and Labour*.

17 It is this notion of the quality of links between areas which underlies the now well-substantiated "laws" of migration: that most migration occurs over short distances; that over long distances migration tends to form distinctive streams and counterstreams where, in both cases, the quality of links would presumably be better; and the volume of migration increases over time and especially with economic development as the quality of links improve.

18 See for example Peach's study of West Indian Immigration to Britain before the restrictions were imposed in 1962, which showed that the volume of migration was most clearly associated with the need for unskilled labour in Britain rather than conditions in the West Indies, with fluctuations in numbers best correlated with fluctuations in employment opportunities in Great Britain, with a certain lag for the transatlantic flow of information: G.C.K. Peach, *West Indian Migration to Britain* (Oxford, 1968). Empirical studies at the regional level confirm these findings. See for example D. Friedlander and R. Rossiter, "A Study of Internal Migration in England and Wales", *Population Studies*, 19 (1966), pp. 239-79 and 20 (1966) pp. 45-60; and P.J. Schwind, *Migration and Regional Development in the United States, 1950-1960*, Research Paper No. 133, Department of Geography, University of Chicago, 1971.

19 See especially Hart's work on inter-regional migration within Britain in which he demonstrates that gross migration flows were mainly between more prosperous regions: R.A. Hart, "A Model of Inter-regional Migration in England and Wales", *Regional Studies*, 4 (1970), pp. 279-96.

rather than absolute levels,[20] the relative awareness of alternative opportunities, and the perceived value ascribed to them.[21]

Because conventional economic wisdom assumes that migration is primarily a consequence rather than a cause of economic growth, relatively little attention has been paid to the impact of migration on economic development, or on why regions might not always respond in the same way. In this respect Bernard Okun and Richard W. Richardson's study of the United States is particularly helpful.[22] They have stressed the necessity of looking at the relationship between place of origin and place of destination to explain variations in the quantity of net migration and the "quality" of migrants. This, they suggested, would help in understanding the differential impact of migration on regional economic growth. They categorized regions according to an income level — high or low — and the direction of economic change — growing or stagnating — thereby identifying four types of regions: *low stagnant regions; high growing regions; low growing regions; high stagnant regions.*

Low stagnant regions (perhaps such as Newfoundland) specializing in primary, normally labour-intensive production, where the marginal productivity of labour is low and the opportunity costs nil, are likely to be places of origin only for migrants. Net migration of unskilled families in both short and long runs is likely to be beneficial because it raises per capita incomes and encourages capitalization. Equally straightforward, *high growing regions* (such as New England in the second half of the 19th century and Ontario between 1900 and the 1920s) will predominate as a destination for migrants, and in the long run will experience beneficial cumulative economic growth from continued net immigration.

Much more complex are the cases of the two other types of regions. *Low growing regions* (such as some parts of the Maritimes in the 1870s and 1880s) will be net exporters of population in industrial countries. While they might experience short-term benefits from out-migration (except where they are sparsely settled) in the long run and especially in the context of a shift from primary to manufacturing sectors such regions are likley to experience severe shortages of labour which will deter the rate of economic growth. This will be especially true

---

20 See especially Oliver's classic study, in which he found that levels of *relative* employment, expressed in terms of the difference between the regional and national unemployment rate, were more important than absolute levels of unemployment in determining migration. Nevertheless, it should be added that Oliver found only contradictory support for his model: "There is a large measure of disparity in response to changes in unemployment condition in the various regions": F.R. Oliver, "Inter-regional Migration and Unemployment, 1951-1961", *Journal of the Royal Statistical Society*, 127A (1964), pp. 42-75.

21 This has been developed by behaviouralists into the notion of "place-utility": see J. Wolpert's seminal paper on this topic "Behavioural Aspects of the Decision to Migrate", *Papers and Proceedings, Regional Science Association*, 15 (1965), pp. 159-69.

22 B. Okun and R.W. Richardson, "Regional Income Inequality and Internal Population Migration", in J. Friedmann and W. Alonso, eds., *Regional Development and Planning* (Cambridge, 1964), pp. 303-18.

where industrialization is also associated with a secular decline in the birth rate as occurred in the late 19th century. *High stagnant regions* associated with the presence of industries which enjoyed their peak at an earlier stage (such as the "wood, wind and sail" economy of the Maritimes) and have subsequently failed to attract sufficient new and rapidly growing industry are also likely to be net exporters of migrants. The channels of information are available, access to them is well-developed and high incomes allow people to move more readily, while since they are skilled and educated there is considerable demand for their labour. On the other hand such regions will not tend to receive many immigrants because their economy is stagnating, though migrants may come from *low stagnant regions* because of the relatively better opportunities for education, welfare, and domestic service resulting from higher incomes and levels of urbanization. At the same time net out-migration is likely to be detrimental in both the short and the long run. The drain of population combined with the "quality exchange" of migrants — poor, uneducated immigrants replacing skilled, educated and wealthier out-migrants — works severely against the region's ability to develop economically and attract growth industries and will in turn ultimately bring down per capita incomes. (Okun and Richardson believe that out-migration "will contribute to, but is not initially responsible for the impairment of the region's economy").[23]

If the Maritimes is typical of such "low growing" or "high stagnant" industrial regions then we might expect out-migration to be high, highly selective of the young active population and also of skilled craftsmen from industrial and urban areas as well as rural areas. If such migration also preceded to some extent economic stagnation, its extent and selectivity could be expected to have seriously jeopardized the capacity of the region to industrialize fully. On the other hand, if Newfoundland is characteristic of economically backward "low stagnant" primary producing regions, "push" factors would predominate, making for relatively less demographic and economic selectivity among migrants. Furthermore, if out-migration from Newfoundland was on a relatively small scale, and not from the most over-populated but the most "open" regions, it might be expected to do little to relieve population pressure. At the same time the proximity of the Maritimes, its openness to information, and the availability of transportation channels to New England could also have heightened the feeling of relative deprivation among Maritimers. On the other hand, in Newfoundland, which was relatively more isolated, feelings of relative deprivation would not be as great, despite the more dire economic conditions.

A serious examination of the relationship between migration and economic development in Atlantic Canada must not only be based upon sound theoretical premises but must also involve a systematic quantitative assessment, at the sub-provincial level, for Newfoundland as well as the Maritimes, of how many people left, from where, and, most importantly, when. What follows, therefore, is an attempt to estimate net migration levels and rates by age and sex at the

23 *Ibid.*, p. 315.

county level for all four Atlantic Provinces and place them within the theoretical framework outlined above. Such an analysis of the extent, timing and geographic and demographic characteristics of the migration process with its implications for regional economic growth is designed to provide a statistical and theoretical basis for future micro-scale studies. For only at this scale will it be possible to demonstrate conclusively the nature of the impact of out-migration on the economic development of the region.

Since no data exist on migration *per se* except those gleaned indirectly from the United States census,[24] we can calculate only the extent of net migration: that is, the population increase between censuses less natural increase (or decrease). In the absence of vital statistics of births and deaths prior to 1921,[25] we are forced to find some other way to calculate natural increase. Fortunately, from 1871 to 1901 in the Maritimes and from 1874 to 1884 and 1891 to 1921 in

24 While immigrants are, at least officially, recorded, no record is kept of out-migrants. One method used extensively by researchers on this topic has been to use the records of recipient countries — in this case the United States. Perhaps the most widely used U.S. source has been the Census (both published and unpublished manuscript) which contains information on Canadian-born residents. See for example Hansen and Brebner *The Mingling of the Canadian and American Peoples*, Truesdell, *The Canadian Born*, and Brookes "Out-Migration from the Maritime Provinces". These sources, it is widely agreed, grossly understate actual levels of immigration of Canadians: see Keyfitz, "The Growth of the Canadian Population", p. 48.

25 Universal and standardized mandatory vital registration commenced in Canada only in 1921 — with Quebec joining in 1926. Nevertheless several provinces did collect vital statistics of varying quality prior to this period. Nova Scotia collected and published vital statistics for a brief period between 1864 and 1875, when the statistics were highly unreliable, and then not again until 1908-1909: see the "Annual Report of Births, Marriages and Deaths", in appendices to the *Journal of the House of Assembly, Nova Scotia, 1864-1875* and *Journal of the Legislative Council, Nova Scotia, 1878.* In New Brunswick "Annual Reports of Registration of Births, Deaths and Marriages" exist for 1888-1894 published as appendices to the *Journals of the Legislative Assembly of the Province of New Brunswick.* These appear to under-record births by about one-third. Reliable registration commenced in 1917-1918 under the Chief Medical Officer and can be found in the "Annual Report of the Chief Medical Officer with Vital Statistics", published annually by the Department of Health, New Brunswick. In Prince Edward Island some registration exists for the years 1906-1907 to 1928, published as the "Annual Report of the Registrar General of Births, Marriages and Deaths" in the appendices of the *Journal of the Legislative Assembly, Prince Edward Island.* No reports have been found for 1911-1912, 1920, 1922 and 1923. The number of registered births was always so low, however, that a large proportion of births evidently escaped registration. Newfoundland began to publish its own vital statistics from 1896, which can be found in the "Annual Report of Births, Marriages and Deaths", Department of Health, Newfoundland. Of course Newfoundland vital statistics were not published by the Dominion Bureau of Statistics until after Confederation in 1949. It should be remembered, however, that even after the commencement of universal standard registration in Canada in 1921 the total number of births registered from 1921 to 1945 have been considered sufficiently deficient to warrant a correction for under-registration. Government estimates of completeness of registration were 94 per cent for 1931 and 97 per cent for 1941. It is generally agreed that registration was unlikely to be much more than the minimum 90 per cent required by DBS when the national vital statistics system commenced in 1921. For a detailed discussion of vital registration in Canada especially prior to 1921 see R.R. Kuczynski, *Birth Registration and Birth Statistics in Canada* (Washington, 1930).

Newfoundland, censuses record population by age and sex at the county level and at regular intervals, thus making cohort analysis possible. Basically intercensal cohort analysis calculates net migration as the difference in the numbers of people in each age group from one census year to the next, less those who died in the interim. Given the age structure of a population in a census year and a comparable age structure for the same population ten years later, survival factors are used to project forward from the first census the number expected to survive until the next census and backwards from the terminal population to adjust for those who could be expected to have died during the period. The difference between the expected and the actual populations gives two estimates of net migration for each age group, which when averaged give a final approximation.[26] These can then be summed to give the total net migration and converted into rates by dividing them by the average of the base populations for the two census years.

The problems associated with this technique have been extensively discussed elsewhere,[27] and it is necessary only to itemize those points which affect the interpretation of the results. 1) Five-year age groups after 1881 in the Maritimes and 1891 in Newfoundland allow the most detailed breakdown of migration by age. For the intercensal period 1871-1881 only ten-year age groups can be used in Nova Scotia and New Brunswick. This does not affect the comparability of overall estimates of net migration, although it does affect estimates of age-specific net migration rates. In Prince Edward Island and Newfoundland, however, incomplete age breakdowns and age group breakdowns which are larger than ten years mean that these figures have to be adjusted to make their total estimates comparable over time and space.[28] 2) For reasons of reliability only those born before the first census, or who were younger than 60 by the first census are used to calculate net migration. Nevertheless the total base popula-

26 In the first case all the expected deaths are assumed to occur within the area prior to out-migration. In the latter case they are assumed to occur only to the population remaining after migration. Thus the forward method gives higher estimates of deaths than the number taking place and hence understates the net outflow, while the reverse projection has the opposite effect. Hence the consistently lower estimates of net out-migration given by the forward projection relative to the reverse projection. By taking the average of these two estimates we assume that there was an even flow of migrants during the decade and that half of the deaths among migrating cohorts occurs after migration. In the older cohorts, where the difference between the two estimates is greatest, this assumption is less likely to be true, as the proportion of deaths occurring at the beginning of the decade is likely to be greatest and this may account for the tendency for the oldest cohorts to show positive net migration, while all other cohorts were experiencing net losses.

27 See P.A. Thornton, "The Extent and Consequence of Out-Migration from Atlantic Canada, 1871-1921", paper presented to the Annual Meeting of the Association of American Geographers, Washington, April 1984.

28 The 1871-1881 estimates for Prince Edward Island had to be adjusted by a factor of 1.016, and for Newfoundland by as much as 1.113. These adjustment factors were based upon the difference in the 1880s estimates of net migration using the 1870s cohort breakdown rather than the complete quinary age cohorts.

tions are used to calcuate the rates as if net migration among the very young and the very old was negligible. By and large, therefore, these figures represent conservative estimates. 3) Swedish life tables have been used to calculate survival factors.[29] Canadian and Massachusetts life tables were discarded on the grounds of unreliability and temporal incompleteness.[30] The English and United States ones were discarded on the grounds that they do not reflect the economic and social conditions prevailing in Atlantic Canada at the time as accurately as the equally reliable Swedish data do.[31] In particular, in the late 19th century both Sweden and Atlantic Canada had approximately similar levels of urbanization, were similarly affected by heavy out-migration and were relatively less industrialized than the adjacent United Kingdom and United States respectively. All these factors are important in determining survival chances.[32] Moreover the migration estimates based upon Swedish life tables render both consistent results and estimates which are intermediate between those derived using English and New World life tables.

Two caveats are in order. Local mortality differences were very pronounced in the late 19th century, especially between rural and urban areas.[33] By applying

29 The Swedish mid-decade survival factors were calculated from life tables published by N. Keyfitz and W. Flieger, *World Population: An Analysis of Vital Data* (Chicago, 1968) for 1873-7 (p. 485), 1883-7 (p. 488), 1893-7 (p. 490). Three other potential sets of life tables exist and have been used in other studies to calculate net migration in Canada.

30 Canadian life tables do exist: Canada, DBS, Social Analysis Branch, *Canadian Abridged Life Tables 1871, 1881, 1921, 1931* (Ottawa, 1939) based upon Canadian census estimates of age-specific mortality rates and were used by me in an earlier report on this study: P.A. Thornton, "The Extent and Consequences of Out-Migration from Atlantic Canada, 1870-1920", in L.R. Fischer and E.W. Sager, eds., *Merchant Shipping and Economic Development in Atlantic Canada* (St John's, 1982), pp. 187-218. These life tables are widely agreed to be grossly inaccurate: see Keyfitz, "The Growth of the Canadian Population", p. 57 and D.M. McDougall, "Immigration into Canada, 1851-1920", *Canadian Journal of Economics and Political Science*, 27 (1961), pp. 162-75. The early Dominion Bureau of Statistics studies of out-migration from the Maritimes all used Massachusetts and later United States life tables. See P.R. Uhlenberg, "A Study of Cohort Life Tables: Cohorts of Native born Massachusetts Women, 1830-1920", in *The Demographic History of Massachusetts* (New York, 1976), p. 419 and United States, Bureau of the Census, *United States Life Tables, 1890, 1901, 1910, and 1901-1910* (New York, 1976), pp. 102-33. A comparison of results based upon these three and the Swedish life tables for the time confirm that both the Canadian and Massachusetts data are unreliable.

31 Keyfitz, "The Growth of the Canadian Population" and McDougall, "Immigration into Canada" both used English life tables modified in various ways to better fit Canadian conditions. The English and United States data though reliable do not reflect the economic and social conditions prevailing in the Maritimes at the time as well as the Swedish data do.

32 For example, between 1871 and 1891 both the Maritimes and Sweden exhibited similar levels of urbanization, which increased from approximately 12 per cent in the Maritimes and 13 per cent in Sweden in 1871 to 18.8 per cent in both places in 1891. At the same time Massachusetts and England were between 60 and 80 per cent urban, the United States as a whole 25 to 40 per cent.

33 See R. Woods, "The Structure of Mortality in mid-nineteenth century England and Wales", *Journal of Historical Geography*, Vol. 8, No. 4 (1982), pp. 373-94. For example Woods found variations in life expectancy at birth among the 631 registration districts of England and Wales in 1861 ranging from a low in Liverpool of 26 years for males and 27 years for females to a high of

"national" survival factors at the county level, differences in mortality will appear as differences in net migration. Generally speaking, therefore, in urban and to a lesser extent in industrial counties, mortality is likely to be underestimated and net out-migration overestimated. Nevertheless the margin of error is not sufficiently large to negate the estimates of the extent and degree of local variations in net migration in the Atlantic Region. A more serious problem stems from the way in which net migration techniques disguise actual flows of migrants and especially hide internal rural-urban migration. Hence migrants who perhaps moved from rural Queens County, Nova Scotia to Halifax, to fill positions vacated by Haligonians who moved to the "Boston States", would in effect appear to have migrated directly from Queens to New England, disguising both the extent of out-migration from Halifax County and the "quality exchange" of migrants. These problems aside, however, intercensal cohort analysis does provide us with reasonably accurate estimates of net migration at the county level broken down by age and sex.[34]

A provincial summary of the extent of net out-migration from the Atlantic Region is contained in Table Three.[35] By the 1870s the region was already losing through migration more people than it was gaining: the net loss amounted to 46,000 people or a little more than four per cent of the total population of the region. By the 1880s, however, out-migration had reached epidemic proportions: the net loss represented some 112,000 people or 12.5 per cent of the population of the Maritimes alone. This exodus slackened off only slightly in the 1890s, when the net loss was 101,000 people from the Maritimes and 123,000 people from the whole of the Atlantic Region, representing some 11 per cent of the population.[36] Unfortunately, in the absence of age-sex breakdowns at the county level after 1901 we do not know what happened in the Maritimes after the turn of the century. We do have data for Newfoundland until 1921, but not for the crucial decade of the 1880s when out-migration was supposed to have been very high.[37] It would seem that out-migration waned somewhat in the 1900s but rose

55 years for males and 57 years for females in Oakhampton, Devon.

34 The variation in estimates of net migration resulting from the use of the wide range of survival estimates is amazingly small both absolutely and from one county to the next and renders the results reliable within a maximum range of + / − 10 per cent, except in Newfoundland and Prince Edward Island in the 1870s.

35 These results have been revised from the earlier estimates printed in Thornton, "The Extent and Consequences of Out-Migration". The present results are based upon mid-decade estimates of mortality using Swedish life tables while the originals used beginning-of-decade Canadian estimates.

36 These estimates are between 10 and 15 per cent above Keyfitz and DBS estimates and the same below Lavoie's if beginning-of-decade estimates are used in all cases. See Keyfitz, "The Growth of the Canadian Population", pp. 52-3, DBS, *The Maritime Provinces* (1927), p. 20, and Lavoie, *L'Emigration de Canadiens*, p. 39.

37 See Michael Staveley, "Aspects of Migration in Newfoundland and Labrador", Ph.D. thesis, University of Alberta, 1973, and P.A. Thornton, "Dynamic Equilibrium: Population Ecology and Settlement in the Strait of Belle Isle", Ph.D. thesis, University of Aberdeen, 1980, Chapter 8.

Table Three

Intercensal Net Migration Levels:
Maritime Provinces 1870s to 1890s, Newfoundland 1870s to 1910s

	1870s*		1880s		1890s	
	Migration (000s)	Net-Migration Rate per 1000	Migration (000s)	Net-Migration Rate per 1000	Migration (000s)	Net-Migration Rate per 1000
Prince Edward Island	-3.3**	-32.5	-15.8	-144.5	-18.5	-169.4
New Brunswick	-16.9	-55.5	-46.9	-146.8	-36.4	-113.2
Nova Scotia	-19.1	-45.8	-48.9	-109.8	-46.0	-103.3
Maritime Provinces	-39.3		-111.6		-100.8	

Newfoundland

	1870s*	1880s	1890s	1900s	1910s
Net-Migration (000s)	-6.9**	n.a.	-21.9	-16.7	-32.1
Net-Migration Rate per 1000	-38.5	n.a.	-105.7	-80.4	-154.9

** data adjusted
* Newfoundland data represent the intercensal period 1874–1884

to its highest levels in the 1910s. It is frustrating that we do not know more of what happened in the 1920s, when out-migration was once again a topic of national concern.[38]

In the 1870s out-migration was greatest from New Brunswick and least from Prince Edward Island, with Nova Scotia, the most urbanized and industrialized province, nevertheless not exempt from the exodus. By the 1880s Prince Edward Island was experiencing levels of out-migration as high as New Brunswick, with Nova Scotia managing to retain a significantly larger proportion of its population. By the 1890s out-migration from Prince Edward Island had reached an all-time high of 17 per cent of the total population at mid-decade, significantly above that for the remaining provinces who otherwise showed little variation (10.5 per cent). Out-migration from Newfoundland appears to have been on a par with the lowest levels achieved by any Maritime Province.

One of the major advantages of the cohort method of estimating net out-migration is that it reveals the age and sex characteristics of the net migrating population. The diagnostic features of the demography of out-migration are evident from Table Four. Females appear to have had a greater propensity to leave the region than men, although this may in part be a spurious by-product of the fact that males predominated among immigrants.[39] Migration was heavily concentrated among the young active age groups who lost between 20 and 50 per cent of their numbers in any decade, or three to four times the rate from the population at large. Out-migration was considerably less age-selective in Newfoundland than the Maritimes, and there is some tendency for age-selectivity to decrease over time.

What does this mean? The female-led nature of migration tends to support the contention that migration in the Atlantic Region was primarily to cities, and cities moreover that were not perceived as being geographically or culturally distant, since it is held that it was primarily over short distances and to the cities that women predominated among migrants.[40] Although this runs contrary to evidence derived from local studies, such as Alan Brookes' study of Canning, Nova Scotia, it should be mentioned that studies based upon nominative sources often do disguise female involvement since they depend upon household data and family names. Indeed Brookes' study also documents the significant participa-

---

38 In his report on the Newfoundland census of 1921, the Newfoundland Colonial Secretary deplored the loss by emigration of the younger people and showed how this had resulted in a declining birth rate in rural districts, with districts showing a constant diminution of population since 1884: *Census of Newfoundland, 1921*, Introduction.

39 It is not surprising, therefore, that the greatest differential between male and female levels of net migration were found in the 1870s when immigration was still significant. In the 1870s out-migration was only 3.6 times in-migration, while in the 1880s it was 11.6 times and in the 1890s 6.5 times. See DBS, *The Maritime Provinces* (1927), p. 20.

40 Ravenstein was the first to demonstrate that rural-urban migration in the 19th century was predominantly female-led: see D. Grigg, "E. G. Ravenstein on the Laws of Migration", *Journal of Historical Geography*, 3 (1977), pp. 41-54. On the other hand overseas immigrants were predominantly male.

Table Four

Age and Sex Characteristics of Net Out-Migration
(Net Migration Rates [NMR] per 1,000 population)

	Column 1 Male Net-Migration Rate	Column 2 Female Net-Migration Rate	Column 3 NMR Largest Male Cohort	Column 4 Ratio: Col. 3 : Col. 1	Column 5 NMR Largest Female Cohort	Column 6 Ratio: Col. 5 : Col 2
1870s						
Nova Scotia	39.6	52.1	184(16-20/26-30)	4.65	225(21-30/31-40)	4.32
New Brunswick	53.8	57.4	217(16-20/26-30)	4.03	253(21-30/31-40)	4.41
Prince Edward Island*	23.2	42.0	258(16-20/26-30)	11.13	329(16-20/26-30)	7.83
Newfoundland*	34.1	43.2	76(20-29/30-39)	2.24	129(20-29/30-39)	2.99
1880s						
Nova Scotia	100.1	119.6	374(20-24/30-34)	3.74	397(20-24/30-34)	3.32
New Brunswick	142.4	149.9	435(15-19/25-29)	3.05	421(20-24/30-34)	2.81
Prince Edward Island	141.3	148.3	490(20-24/30-34)	3.47	473(20-24/30-34)	3.19
Newfoundland	n.a.	n.a.	n.a.	n.a.	n.a.	n.a.
1890s						
Nova Scotia	91.4	115.3	372(20-24/30-34)	4.07	397(20-24/30-34)	3.44
New Brunswick	107.3	119.3	380(15-19/25-29)	3.54	359(20-24/30-34)	3.01
Prince Edward Island	169.3	169.6	578(20-24/30-34)	3.41	525(20-24/30-34)	3.10
Newfoundland	94.2	117.6	248(20-24/30-34)	2.63	324(20-24/30-34)	2.76
1900s						
Newfoundland	89.4	71.1	232(20-24/30-34)	2.61	328(20-24/30-34)	4.61
1910s						
Newfoundland	142.6	167.7	354(20-24/30-34)	2.48	479(15-19/25-29)	2.85

* adjusted rates

tion of women in the industrial economy of Nova Scotia and a growing tendency for women to seek employment in the factories of Canada and the United States.[41] Moreover it is now widely agreed that the Industrial Revolution was built on the backs of the cheap labour of women.[42] If the degree of age-selectiveness indicates the importance of "pull" forces at destination relative to "push" forces at home, then these data would corroborate that "pull" forces in New England were more significant than "push" forces at home throughout the period. Moreover, "pull" forces were more significant in Nova Scotia than New Brunswick and surprisingly crucial for Prince Edward Island emigrants in the 1870s and 1880s.[43] "Push" forces at home were apparently more significant among Newfoundland emigrants, although it should be noted that the more inclusive age categories for Newfoundland in the 1870s would significantly deflate the index of age-selectivity for that decade.

These provincial statistics, however, disguise considerable variation among counties in both the level and age-selectivity of migrants. Figures One to Five show for each decade the levels of out-migration by county. In the 1870s out-migration was already widespread — only eight out of the 53 counties experiencing net in-migration. These can be described as either sparsely settled counties in New Brunswick and Newfoundland which were still experiencing some initial settlement, or the cities of Halifax and St. John's. As we might expect, the immigration to the frontier was predominantly male-led and relatively less age-selective, while cityward immigration was heavily female-led and highly concentrated among the young single age-groups. Saint John, New Brunswick, on the other hand, experienced the highest out-migration of any county — losing close to 29 per cent of its total population, 40 to 50 per cent of its young active population. The major fire which struck Saint John in 1877 may help explain the extent of out-migration from Saint John, but the age and sex selectivenes of that migration suggests that the out-migration was real and not simply a temporary displacement of people from the city to surrounding areas. This is supported by the fact that although out-migration was much less from the surrounding rural part of the county the countryside did not appear to have received the large numbers of displaced urbanites. Moreover, out-migration from the surrounding counties was among the highest in New Brunswick. Overall out-migration was considerably more severe from New Brunswick than elsewhere, and was most heavily concentrated in the counties closest to and best connected with the United States. In Newfoundland, both the older-settled Conception Bay counties, known for over-population,[44] and the more open communities along the

41 Brookes, "The Golden Age and The Exodus", pp. 67-9.

42 See for example S.M. Trofimenkoff, "One Hundred and Two Muffled Voices: Canada's Industrial Women in the 1880s", *Atlantis*, Vol. 3, No. 1 (Fall 1977), pp. 66-82.

43 It could be that these "pull" forces for Prince Edward Island out-migrants were more social or cultural than economic relative to Nova Scotia: see Brookes, "Out-Migration from the Maritime Provinces", p. 37.

44 See P.A. Thornton, "The Demographic and Mercantile Bases of Initial Permanent Settlement in

FIGURE 1

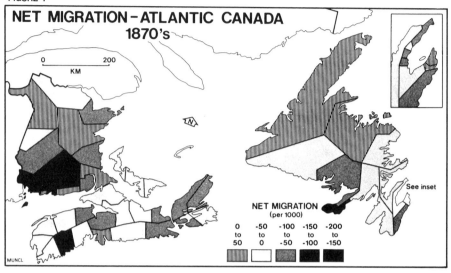

FIGURE 2

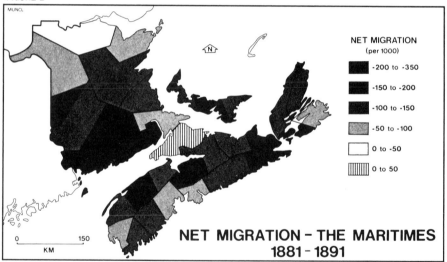

South Coast, experienced rates of out-migration on a par with the Maritimes, and considerably above the rest of the Island.

By the 1880s all of the Maritimes but the industrial Cumberland County was experiencing net out-migration of epidemic proportions, although it was still lower in the most remote counties as well as on the Atlantic seaboard (shipping

the Strait of Belle Isle", in J. Mannion, ed., *The Peopling of Newfoundland: Essays in Historical Geography* (St. John's, 1977), pp. 152-83.

FIGURE 3

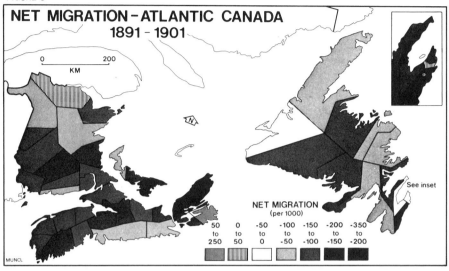

NET MIGRATION – ATLANTIC CANADA
1891 – 1901

NET MIGRATION
(per 1000)

| 50 to 250 | 0 to 50 | -50 to 0 | -100 to -50 | -150 to -100 | -200 to -150 | -350 to -200 |

FIGURE 4

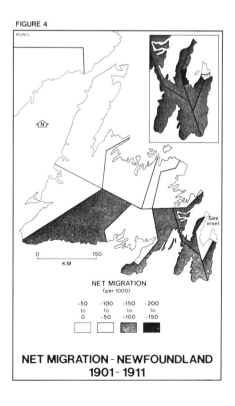

NET MIGRATION
(per 1000)

| -50 to 0 | -100 to -50 | -150 to -100 | -200 to -150 |

NET MIGRATION – NEWFOUNDLAND
1901 – 1911

FIGURE 5

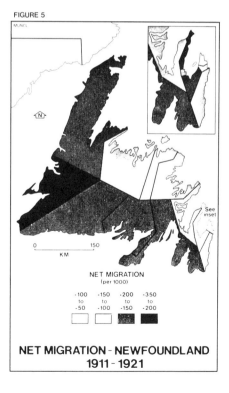

NET MIGRATION
(per 1000)

| -100 to -50 | -150 to -100 | -200 to -150 | -350 to -200 |

NET MIGRATION – NEWFOUNDLAND
1911 – 1921

counties) and in the industrial counties of Nova Scotia. The highest levels of net out-migration — where more than 20 per cent of the total population and close to 60 per cent of the young active age groups left — were experienced in four counties in the St. John River Valley area. Nevertheless levels of between 15 and 20 per cent were widespread throughout the region. Even counties containing cities such as Charlottetown, P.E.I. and Saint John, N.B. along with counties in which the shipping industry was important, such as Hants and Northumberland, were not exempt from high rates of out-migration.

Heavy out-migration persisted through the 1890s, although the centres of greatest net out-migration had shifted somewhat. Only industrializing Cape Breton County showed immigration and that was on a large scale and dominated by young men. Many probably came from the adjacent rural counties of Victoria, Inverness, Richmond and Antigonish, all of which experienced very high levels of out-migration. A large number also came from Newfoundland (see Table Five). Prince Edward Island experienced massive out-migration and even counties which had previously managed to retain relatively more of their population were now no longer able to, although more remote frontiers and city counties still remained relatively less affected. Out-migration from Newfound-

Table Five

Newfoundland Immigrants Resident in the Maritimes, 1901

County	Number of Immigrant Newfoundlanders 1851-1901	Newfoundlanders as Percentage of Immigrants
Cape Breton, N.S.	6246	54
Victoria, N.S.	735	33
Halifax, N.S.	7014	27
Lunenburg, N.S.	264	24
Guysborough, N.S.	386	17
Pictou, N.S.	1725	16
Cumberland, N.S.	1570	14
Shelburne and Queens, N.S.	468	10
Albert, N.B.	324	15

Note: only places in which Newfoundlanders made up more than 10 per cent of immigrants are included. Data for Shelburne and Queens were aggregated in census reports for 1891 and are aggregated here for consistency.
Source: *Census of Canada, 1901.*

land was smaller than might be expected from the literature,[45] although it was most concentrated in the older-settled overpopulated regions of Conception Bay and the Southern Shore. By the 1910s, when emigration was at its highest in Newfoundland, the West Coast joined these longstanding areas of out-migration, but the traditional inshore fishing areas of the East and North-East coast still showed lower levels of out-migration.

In general, then, out-migration peaked earlier in New Brunswick and Prince Edward Island than in Nova Scotia, but only in Saint John, New Brunswick did out-migration peak in the 1870s. Moreover it would seem that it was in the urban, shipping, fishing and industrial counties that migration peaked later, suggesting that these more "industrialized" or "modernized" counties were relatively speaking better able to hold onto their populations or at least replace them for a longer time. In Newfoundland both the overpopulated Conception Bay and the "open" South and later West coasts, with strong mercantile connections with the mainland, were consistently more prone to out-migration than the more inward-looking traditional inshore fishing communities of the East and North-East coasts.

The individual county age-sex profiles of net migrants fall into five distinct categories, although the large majority — 70 per cent of all pyramids in the Maritimes over three decades — fall into the classic profile category, the first profile shown in Figure Six, represented by Kings County, New Brunswick, 1881-1891. Its essential characteristics are the pronounced "V" shape, showing out-migration strongly concentrated among the young active age groups. These areas often lost as much as 40 to 60 per cent of their population in any decade, and young children and families are poorly represented. Females show a slightly greater propensity to migrate than men. This profile is typical of "short-distance" migration which is generally a response to "pull" forces. Two other factors displayed by this profile also seem typical: the disproportionately low rate of out-migration among people 45-49 at the opening of the decade and 55-59 by the close of it, and the tendency for migration to show a net gain among males 50-60. These may reflect inadequacies of either age-reporting or survival estimates or both.

The second profile, Harbour Grace, Newfoundland, 1891-1901, represents, by contrast, the classic Newfoundland profile in which out-migration predominates. This differs significantly from the one above in that there is a much less pronounced "V" shape, showing less age-selectivity and a high proportion of children and families represented. This profile is more characteristic of a population among whom out-migration is largely a response to "push" forces at home.

The remaining profiles represent only a relatively few cases. The third profile, Saint John, N.B., 1881-91, is both a good and a bad example of a city profile. It is typical in that all cities experienced in-migration among young females, especially among the 10-14/20-24 range, even, as is especially apparent in this

45 See footnotes 37 and 38.

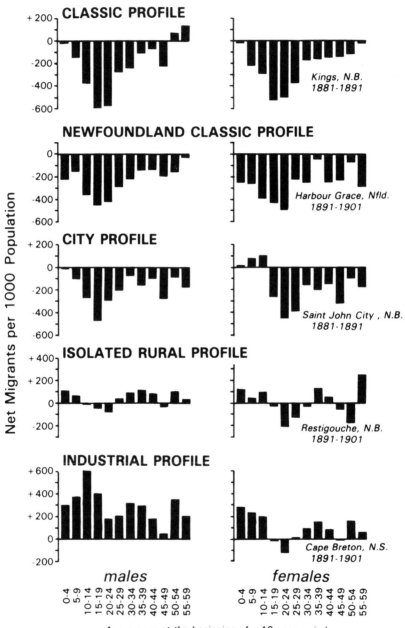

FIGURE 6
AGE-SEX PROFILES OF MIGRANTS

Age groups at the beginning of a 10 year period

MUNCL

FIGURE 7
REGIONAL AGE-SEX PROFILES OF MIGRANTS
NEWFOUNDLAND, 1874-1884

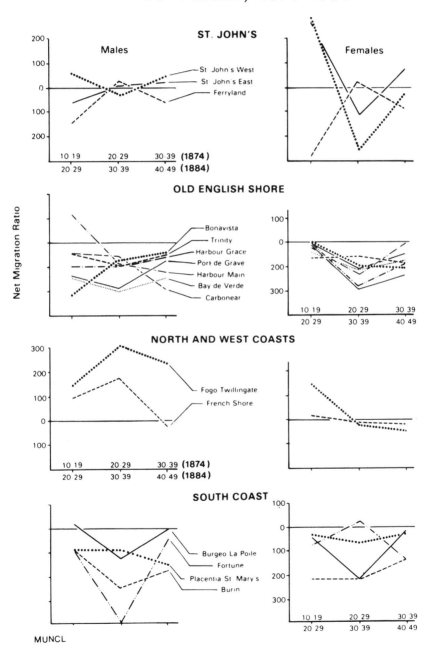

MUNCL

case, when the overall tendency was wholesale out-migration. This net gain of young girls, who were perhaps attracted by the greater opportunity in the city for entering service, was usually counterbalanced by a net outflow of women in the 15-24/25-29 age group, who were probably returning home to marry. This reciprocal relationship is best exemplified by the net-migration age-sex profile of Ferryland relative to St. John's (Figure Seven). What is atypical of the Saint John, N.B. profile is the extent of net out-migration — as much as 40-50 per cent of all males between the ages of 15-19 at the beginning of the decade and 25-29 by the end — and the excess of male migrants over female migrants.

The next profile, of Restigouche, N.B., 1891-1901, is typical of a small number of rural counties in New Brunswick and Newfoundland — namely Victoria, Westmorland, Northumberland and Gloucester in New Brunswick and Fogo, Twillingate, St. Barbe and St. Georges in Newfoundland — which experienced periods of in-migration as well as out-migration. There are a variety of reasons why such rural areas should experience in-migration, but for the most part these were responses to specific local conditions rather than more general ones. In all cases, however, they created new opportunities for rural settlement. In this case in-migration exceeds out-migration, although both were clearly operating. Such pyramids are characterized by a "ragged" shape, with little age-selectivity among migrants, and male migrants outnumbering females.

Finally, the last profile, Cape Breton, Nova Scotia, 1891-1901, is unique in this study. It is a pyramid, characteristic of a vibrant industrializing county. Similar features are found only in Cumberland County a decade earlier, where they are much less pronounced. In both net immigration predominates, although it rarely lasts more than a decade, and is male-led. Cape Breton also shows somewhat greater age-selectivity among migrants than either Restigouche or Cumberland County, where the number of young males actually shows a net loss.

Figure Seven shows the age composition of migrants by district for Newfoundland from 1874 to 1884 and is instructive for two reasons. First, it shows that age-sex profiles of migrants can be used to distinguish regional patterns of migration: St. John's and its drawing area (Ferryland); the overpopulated English Shore with Bonavista and Trinity Bay, somewhat different from Conception Bay; the expanding "frontiers" on the North and West Coasts; and the "open" well-connected South Coast. Secondly, it further corroborates the relationship between age-selectivity and the relative strength of "push" versus "pull" forces. The overpopulated English shore — where "push" forces can be expected to have been strongest — showed less age selectivity than the North and West "frontiers" and the "open" South Coast, where migrants could be expected to have been responding to "pull" forces.

The empirical evidence on the extent, timing and geographic and demographic characteristics of out-migration presented here strongly supports the thesis that out-migration may have been a significant contributing factor in the economic decline of the region, and may have worked in different ways in Newfoundland and the Maritimes to this same end. In the Maritimes out-migration occurred on a massive scale throughout the late 19th century. A steady net loss was already well underway by the 1870s, and was to reach epidemic proportions in the 1880s and 1890s. This was at a time when, as Alexander and others have shown, the economy of the region was well developed and still growing, and (at least for the 1880s) growing faster than Ontario in terms of real output and gross value of production in manufacturing.[46] It would seem, therefore, that endemic out-migration from the Maritimes, such as that which occurred in the 1880s, largely anticipated the economic downturn in the region's economy, which did not really set in until the decade of the 1890s. Migration was moreover highly selective of the young productive age groups and probably, therefore, of the more educated and highly skilled. It was greatest from those counties closest to and most connected to New England, where the pull of the "Boston States" was most likely to have been strongest. Moreover, in the 1870s out-migration occurred disproportionately from urban parts of counties. This is especially true for Prince Edward Island and Nova Scotia where only 13 and 23 per cent of the population respectively was urban but 22 and 42 per cent of net out-migration was from urban areas. Nevertheless, with the exception of Saint John, New Brunswick, shipping and industrial counties as well as those containing cities appear to have been better able to hold onto population somewhat longer than other counties, though in the end even they were affected severely by out-migration.

A significant qualitative exchange of migrants also seems to have been occurring in the Maritimes, both through rural-urban redistribution within the region, and through immigration of presumably less-skilled workers from Newfoundland replacing more highly skilled out-migrants. Between 1880 and 1900, 150 to 200 per cent of the region's net out-migration came from rural areas. The excess 50 to 100 per cent of regional out-migration measured at the county level, therefore, represented a rural to urban redistribution of the region's own population. This step-by-step migration up the rural-urban hierarchy must have had a detrimental effect on economic growth, inevitably involving a qualitative exchange of migrants: young, unskilled, rural workers moving to the city to replace skilled, urban out-migrants, and in turn themselves acquiring skills only to become the next wave of skilled out-migrants. This process is empirically documented by local studies such as those of Alan Brookes and T.W. Acheson, who moreover suggest that migration was also occupationally selective of craftsmen and traders, rather than farmers, lumbermen and unskilled labourers, although these latter did make up a large proportion of out-migrants, especially in later decades.[47] At the same time a large number of presumably less skilled New-

---

46 See Alexander, "Economic Growth in the Atlantic Region", pp. 58, 60. In the 1880s the decadal increase in gross value of production in mining and manufacturing were both above the Canadian levels. By the 1890s, however, the rates were significantly below those for Canada as a whole. But this was only after 20 years of sustained out-migration.

47 In Brookes' sample of 1524 Nova Scotians (of whom 450 were adult males) entering the United

foundlanders immigrated to the Maritimes during the last half of the 19th century, concentrating especially in the urban counties, such as Halifax, and certain industrial counties, such as Cape Breton (See Table Five). The end result was a constant drain of the Atlantic Region's young active population which certainly reduced the size of the region's labour force: the proportion of the total population who were of working age slipped from about one per cent less than the Canadian average in 1881 to close to five per cent less than Ontario by 1901. Thus, out-migration was a significant and incremental drain on the region's productive population compared to Central Canada.[48]

In Newfoundland by contrast, out-migration occurred on a slightly smaller scale, may not have peaked until this century, and was less age-selective. Although it did occur from the most "overpopulated" districts in Conception Bay, the quality of the links with the Maritimes and New England also seemed to have played a role in determining the level of out-migration. Out-migration was also high from the "open" and well-connected districts with traditional mercantile links with the Maritimes and New England. It was much less pronounced in the most distant, traditional, inward-looking inshore fishing communities, where population density was ultimately greatest, but where fishermen may have been trapped by merchant indebtedness resulting from the operation of a closed truck system. Moreover, population pressure on the traditional inshore fishery of Newfoundland was particularly acute in the 1880s.[49] This would seem to coincide with and even anticipate the period of massive out-migration from Newfoundland.

Finally the existence of traditionally strong links between the Maritimes and

States in 1872, 102 were farmers, 109 were mariners, 127 servants, 72 carpenters, 64 labourers and 33 were merchants: Brookes, "Out Migration from the Maritime Provinces", p. 37. See also T.W. Acheson, "A Study of the Historical Demography of a Loyalist County", *Histoire sociale/ Social History*, 1 (April, 1968), pp. 63-4. Similar evidence is found in E. Kerr, *Imprint of the Maritimes: Highlights in the Lives of 100 Interesting Americans Whose Roots are in Canada's Atlantic Provinces* (Boston, 1959).

48 The distribution of the population of labour force age is as follows:

Per Cent of Population of Labour Force Age

	1871[1]	1881[2]	1891[2]	1901[2]
Maritimes	52.0	54.5	54.9	55.4
Newfoundland	n.d	n.d	53.9	54.8
Ontario	50.7	55.8	58.4	60.3
Canada	n.d	55.6	57.2	58.3

Source: *Census of Canada*, 1871, 1881, 1891, 1901;
Census of Newfoundland, 1891, 1901.
[1] labour force age is 20-69.
[2] 1881 onwards labour force age is 15-64.

49 This was especially true following the introduction and widespread adoption of the cod-trap which restricted the number of berths (sites) that could be used and hence access to the fish resource: see Alexander "Newfoundland's Traditional Economy", and E.W. Sager, "The Traditional Outport Economy", paper presented to the Canadian Historical Association, Halifax, June 1981.

New England in the late 19th century, meant that information on opportunities was both readily available, and the demand for skilled labour high, at precisely the time when the region itself most needed increased investment in its labour force and was least in a position to release surplus labour.[50] Newfoundland, by contrast, remained initially relatively isolated from New England and as its population had fewer skills to offer for the market, the demand for their labour was less at a time when the out-migration of excess population might well have encouraged greater capitalization in the fishing industry.

Existing theory, in taking a static view of migration, has largely ignored the crucial question of whether migration can be both a *cause* as well as a *consequence* of the economic well-being of a region. This is all the more surprising in light of the empirical evidence put forward by economists such as Brinley Thomas. He argues that migration flows between Britain and West Europe to the New World in the 19th and early 20th centuries were the *cause* of the economic swings on those two continents and also explain their inverse relationship. Each of the three upsurges in emigration from Europe — 1863-72, 1870-90, and 1898-1907 — was accompanied by a boom in British capital exports, thus precipitating a downswing in domestic investment in the British economy and an upswing in the Canadian and American economies.[51] It should not come as a surprise that out-migration from one *region* (such as the Maritimes) should be highest when economic growth in the nation or continent (Canada and United States) was also most rapid, and lowest when economic growth slowed down. Since trends in economic activity in the region paraliel (even if at a lower level) those in the nation as a whole, large-scale out-migration is likley to occur when the region is most in need of increased rather than decreased investment in its labour force, and when surplus skilled labour is probably in shortest supply.

It is ironic that economic historians have consistently looked to Central Canada, Confederation and the National Policy to explain the demise of the Maritimes and to the internal social structure of Newfoundland and its colonial connections to explain that nation's impoverishment. In both cases the root of the problem may have lain in the pull of the neighbouring "Boston States", which acted as a drain on the "bone and sinew" of the Maritimes population and as an insufficient pull on the fishing population of Newfoundland.

Only when migration is seen as part of a system — rather than a specific or even repeated set of events — does it become possible to overcome the static, cause-effect view of migration which pervades existing migration theory. Migra-

---

50 McDonald argues this point passionately. He bases his argument on two criteria: (1) The timing of migration is usually at a point when economic growth is at its greatest and not at its lowest, and economic trends in the region usually parallel those of the nation as a whole; (2) The selectivity of migration means that instead of losing surplus manpower the region loses the very people on whom self-sustained growth depends. "In essence the Maritimes are being divested of a dynamic element which is a precondition to self-sustained growth": McDonald, *Population, Migration and Economic Development*, pp. 22, 41.

51 B. Thomas, *Migration and Urban Development: A Reappraisal of British and American Long Cycles* (London, 1972).

tion usually exists within some larger context of economic and social change which determines the nature of the inter-relationship between area of origin, area of destination, and the characteristics of migrants. This wider context both fuels the process of migration and is in turn affected by it. In 19th century Atlantic Canada the structural context was the industrialization of North America with its concomitant integration of regional economies into one national or even continental economy, involving in turn the concentration and centralization of investment. Such a theoretical framework requires that we see migration as both a consequence and a cause of the economic well-being of the region.[52]

The evidence presented here should be seen as suggestive rather than proof of the role of out-migration in regional underdevelopment in Atlantic Canada. In that sense it is offered as an hypothesis which needs to be tested in micro-scale studies. The major weakness of this approach stems from what is termed statistically "the ecological fallacy", which arises out of the problems which almost inevitably occur when conclusions about individuals are drawn on the basis of aggregate statistics. Nevertheless, the current confusion in the regional literature, the dubious theoretical assumptions on which migration studies are based in this respect, the failure to address the issue of the consequences of out-migration in any serious way, and the absence of studies providing a data base at the sub-provincial level anywhere in the region or for Newfoundland at all, all make such a broad survey an essential first step. Local studies are needed: of individual migrants in terms of their opportunity structures and their decisions to migrate, of economic sectors, such as an examination of potential shortages of skilled or non-skilled labour in certain Maritime industries, and of the effects of out-migration on the development of economies of agglomeration. Only then will it become possible to fully assess the role of out-migration in regional underdevelopment.

52 A.L. Mabogunge pioneered the systems approach to migration. Most specifically he highlighted the importance of the flow of information operating within institutional control systems and the role of feedback amplifying or counteracting the original stimulus and thereby reinforcing or dampening continued migration: A.L. Mabogunge, "A Systems Approach to a Theory of Rural-Urban Migration", *Geographical Analysis*, 2 (1970), pp. 1-18. The most useful and recent systems framework for the study of migration is that provided by R.E. White and R.I. Woods, *The Geographical Impact of Migration* (London, 1980).

Appendix One

Total Net Migration in the Maritimes by County
1871-1901

County	1871-1881	1881-1891	1891-1901
NOVA SCOTIA	−19088.5	−48900.4	−46012.1
Inverness	−1768.0	−3027.1	−3938.2
Victoria	−800.4	−1445.3	−2748.0
Cape Breton	−1178.6	−1880.9	+7941.2
Richmond	−1233.8	−2643.6	−2464.5
Guysborough	−1784.1	−3001.3	−1489.7
Halifax City	+1114.5	−2123.2	
Halifax Rural	−1125.1	−3699.0	
(Halifax Co.)	(−10.4)	(−6148.0)	−6953.0
Lunenburg	−581.2	−2675.2	−3589.7
Queens	−1500.7	−1082.4	
Shelburne	−68.2	−2118.1	
(Queens+Shelburne)	(−1568.9)	(−3200.5)	−3930.6
Yarmouth	−1004.4	−2099.3	−2560.9
Digby	−787.2	−2839.9	−2373.9
Annapolis	−401.5	−3204.4	−2176.3
Kings	−1565.7	−3360.2	−2832.8
Hants	−1847.1	−3905.8	−4141.9
Colchester	−882.1	−2980.1	−4745.9
Pictou	−1585.8	−4477.6	−3779.3
Antigonish	−1044.5	−3218.9	−3130.7
Cumberland	−1072.2	+1253.1	−3957.6
NEW BRUNSWICK	−16886.2	−46926.6	−36362.5
Albert	−697.8	−3068.6	−1658.6
Saint John City	−5072.6	−3694.5	
Saint John Rural	+93.0	−4327.8	
(Saint John Co.)	(−4982.6)	(−8022.2)	−2820.6
Charlotte	−3211.8	−4701.4	−3926.0
Kings	−2677.4	−4992.5	−3369.7
Queens	−1845.5	−3078.7	
Sunbury	−1023.2	−1338.5	
(Queens+Sunbury)	(−2891.7)	(−4449.1)	−2759.4
York	−1659.0	−3541.3	−3281.9
Carleton	−542.7	−3496.7	−3284.5
Victoria	+228.4	−1454.8	−1593.0
Westmorland	+1129.7	−3494.5	−5528.1

Kent	−1139.2	−3425.4	−4207.5
Northumberland	+45.3	−3728.2	−1826.3
Gloucester	−1973.4	−2188.4	−2664.4
Restigouche	−37.8	−364.2	+192.1
PRINCE EDWARD ISLAND[1]	−3312.7	−15775.4	−18464.9
Prince	−630.5	−4400.3	−3062.3
Queens	−2046.5	−819.4	−7152.6
Kings	−732.6	−3138.5	−8247.1
NEWFOUNDLAND[2]	−6863.0		
St. John's East	+933.6		
St. John's West	+632.5		
Harbour Main	−446.4		
Port de Grave	−765.1		
Harbour Grace	−862.7		
Carbonear	−198.0		
Bay de Verde	−725.7		
Trinity Bay	−852.2		
Bonavista Bay	−364.3		
Fogo+Twillingate	+311.0		
St. Barbe/St. George	+320.1		
Burgeo/LaPoile	−276.4		
Fortune	−426.4		
Burin	−960.0		
Placentia/St. Marys	−455.0		
Ferryland	−663.5		

---

1 Adjusted by a factor of 1.016.

2 Adjusted by a factor of 1.113. The intercensal period for Newfoundland is 1874-1884.

Appendix Two

Total Net Migration in Newfoundland by County
1891 - 1921
(000s)

County	1891-1901	1901-1911	1911-1921
St. John's East	−2465.7	−201.1	−1963.1
St. John's West	+170.8	−1031.9	−1011.1
Harbour Main	−1126.4	−1302.4	−1810.2
Port de Grave	−1479.0	−1255.6	−1151.8
Harbour Grace	−3015.4	−2367.0	−2215.4
Carbonear	−1323.5	−564.3	−921.3
Bay de Verde	−1492.4	−1213.8	−1466.5
Trinity Bay	−2510.0	−2727.0	−2681.7
Bonavista Bay	−1151.1	−1598.4	−2740.2
Fogo	−557.9	−689.0	−918.3
Twillingate	−1943.5	−1013.6	−1985.7
St. Barbe	−586.0	−136.6	−1192.8
St. Georges	−78.1	−166.4	−1816.1
Burgeo/Lapoile	−936.2	−810.2	−1139.1
Fortune	−850.0	−760.1	−1257.1
Burin	−1032.3	−1095.1	−1479.8
Placentia/St. Marys	−726.6	−2026.9	−2611.0
Ferryland	−868.9	−769.6	−627.0
NEWFOUNDLAND	−21920.6	−16686.1	−32132.8

GEORGE F. G. STANLEY Reprinted from Vol. II, No. 1
(Autumn 1972)

The
Caraquet
Riots
of 1875

In April 1871, four years after the confederation of the British North American provinces, an education bill was introduced into the legislature of the province of New Brunswick. This measure was, apparently, the work of the attorney-general, the Honourable George Edwin King, a graduate of the Methodist college at Sackville, who represented Saint John county in the legislature. The object of King's bill was to establish a non-sectarian school system supported by public funds. The Roman Catholic minority, very much alive to the question of separate schools after their inclusion in the Manitoba Act in 1870 at the insistence of Louis Riel, pressed upon the provincial government the need for the establishment of a separate school system in New Brunswick. Some twenty-two petitions were sent to Fredericton, and Timothy Anglin's *Morning Free-man* in Saint John and Norbert Lussier's *Moniteur Acadien* in Shediac repeatedly demanded equal school rights for the Catholic citizens of the province. The press and public generally, however, supported the principle of non-sectarian schools, and on 5 May the Bill passed the Protestant-dominated Assembly, twenty-five votes to ten, with six abstentions. After a narrow squeak through the Legislative Council, where an amendment proposing that public funds should be made available to all schools was defeated on an even division, the bill became law in May 1871.

Not only was the Common Schools Act offensive in principle to the Roman Catholic minority, the detailed regulations adopted under authority of the Act were even more objectionable. Such, for instance, as Regulation 20, forbidding the display in the school room of symbols or emblems of any national or other society, or of any political or religious organization. Applied literally, this meant that no member of a religious order could be employed as a teacher. There was no specific mention of French as a language of instruction in the Act, although a reference in Regulation 16 to the selection of text books in French would imply that the Act was directed primarily against denominational schools rather than against French language schools.

The constitutional validity of the Common Schools Act was challenged both in parliament and in the courts. Petitions were sent to the prime minister, Sir John A. Macdonald, begging him to disallow the Act. Sir John, aware that his French Canadian supporters in Quebec had accepted Confederation on the understanding that education would be a purely provincial matter, declined to intervene. Timothy Anglin, Auguste Renaud and John Costigan, the federal members for Gloucester, Kent and Victoria, argued the case in Ottawa, but all they could obtain in the way of concessions were pious expressions of regret that the new legislation should have proven displeasing to so large a segment of the New Brunswick population and suggestions that legal opinion should be obtained regarding the validity of the impugned legislation. The provincial authorities did not like the idea of turning the matter over to the judges. Nevertheless, the question did come before the courts as a result of the initiative of Auguste Renaud. Not that the provincial ministers need have worried very much. In January 1873 the New Brunswick Supreme Court unanimously agreed that the Act was *intra vires*, although some of the judges were disposed to criticize certain regulations adopted under the Act, particularly Regulation 20.[1] A year later the Judicial Committee of the Privy Council confirmed the verdict of the provincial court.

Two months before the judgement of the Judicial Committee had been handed down, George King, who had become premier in 1872, called an election. "Vote for the Queen against the Pope" was the premier's battle cry.[2] It was a good one, for religious prejudice was widespread enough to give him a good majority. When the electioneering was over and the votes counted, it was found that thirty-four candidates favouring the Common Schools Act had been returned and only five supporters of separate schools.[3] The latter all came from counties with Acadian majorities, Gloucester, Kent and Madawaska.

Meanwhile the Catholic minority kept up its pressure. Finally the Board of Education began to show signs of yielding, not on the principle of a single non-sectarian school system, but in the direction of concessions on points of detail. In 1872, Regulation 20 was modified to permit the wearing of religious symbols by the teachers and in 1873 this concession was extended to include religious garb. Behind the scenes the Bishops of Saint John and Halifax were endeavouring to achieve further concessions; Sweeney was working on King in Fredericton, and Connolly upon Macdonald in Ottawa. Connolly, for instance, urged Sir John to do something about removing that "brainless and raving bigot" Lemuel Allan Wilmot from his appointment as Lieutenant-Gov-

1 Canada, *Sessional Papers*, 1873, No. 44, p. 77.

2 R. Rumilly, *Histoire des Acadiens* (Montréal, 1935), p. 763.

3 They were Théotime Blanchard, Kennedy F. Burns, Urbain Johnson, Henry O'Leary and Lévite Theriault.

ernor. "Without that," the Bishop wrote to the Canadian Prime Minister, "I look upon the cause as hopeless."[4] It was easy enough for Macdonald to oblige Connolly. Wilmot was near the end of his term, and just before the Conservative Government went down to defeat in 1873, as a result of the Pacific Scandal, Macdonald named his old Maritime colleague, Sir Leonard Tilley, as Lieutenant-Governor. The Methodist Wilmot was thus removed from the political scene; but it is questionable whether the appointment of the Anglican Tilley provided the distressed Roman Catholics in New Brunswick with much comfort or encouragement.

Despite the slight relaxation of the education regulations, the Catholic minority still found itself liable for the "odious" — to use Connolly's word — school taxes. The courts upheld the non-sectarian school system as valid and there was no way of getting out of paying the school taxes as long as the provincial authorities were determined to apply the law to the letter and to use the legal machinery to the fullest extent. Neither religious principles nor private conscience deterred the tax collector. If the money was not forthcoming, then stock, farm goods, or other items of private property were seized by the bailiffs and put up for public auction. The cows belonging to the curé of Cocagne, the stove belonging to the curé of St. Charles, and the books belonging to another curé, were seized and sold. In other instances, priests were arrested and placed in prison. In Saint John the horses and carriage, given to Bishop Sweeney by the city people on his return from the Vatican Council, were seized and sold for seven dollars less than the amount of school taxes due on the Roman Catholic School properties in the city, for which the Bishop was held personally responsible.[5]

Actions such as these, legal though they may have been, began to raise questions in some minds as to whether the law ought to be carried this far. During 1874 some members of the local legislature wondered whether the wiser course of action might not be to soft-pedal the punitive aspects of the new school policy. James Nowlan went so far as to move the repeal of the School Act of 1871. The answer was a firm 'no'. Nowlan's motion was able to muster only thirteen votes against twenty-five.[6] There would be no weakening, no compromise, no appeasement, if the premier and attorney-general, George E. King, had anything to say about it. Not at least until after two men had been killed in Caraquet.

4 Connolly to Macdonald, 30 September 1873, quoted in Peter M. Toner, "The New Brunswick Separate Schools Issue, 1864-1876" (unpublished M.A. thesis, University of New Brunswick, 1967), p. 92.

5 For those arrests and confiscations see *Le Moniteur Acadien*, 28 mai, 15 octobre, 22 octobre, 10 décembre 1874.

6 *Journal of the House of Assembly of the Province of New Brunswick*, 1874, pp. 202-3. See also Katherine F. C. MacNaughton, *The Development of the Theory and Practice of Education in New Brunswick 1784-1900* (Fredericton, 1947), p. 210.

II

The troubles which led to the outbreak of violence at Caraquet in January 1875, began with a parish meeting held under the chairmanship of Théotime Blanchard, the local member for Gloucester in the Legislative Assembly. The purpose of the meeting was to nominate the various parish officers for the year. The nominations were made and, as required by law, were reported to the Gloucester County Sessions for confirmation? Unfortunately, by far the greater number of ratepayers who attended and voted at the meeting were men who had not paid their school taxes and who, like the chairman himself, had no intention of doing so.

Fully aware of the weak ground on which Blanchard and the others had acted, a small group of English-speaking ratepayers residing in the parish of Caraquet called a second meeting on 4 January. This meeting was presided over by the Honourable Robert Young, a former member of the legislature who had been defeated by Blanchard in the provincial election of 1874, but who at this time held an appointment in the Legislative Council. Young's supporters then proceeded to draft a document, bearing nineteen signatures, pointing out the flaw in the proceedings of the earlier meeting, asking that the previous nominations be rejected and requesting the approval by the Gloucester Sessions of the new parish officers named in the document. The Sessions admitted the validity of the argument in Young's petition and, disregarding the facts that the second meeting had been given no publicity and could by no stretch of the imagination be regarded as representative of the people of the parish, approved the new nominations. When it is recalled that the census of 1871 showed 3111 inhabitants in Caraquet, of whom only 79 were Protestants, it is hard to escape the conclusion that the Sessions were moved more by the letter than by the spirit of the law. But this is scarcely surprising. To the English-speaking Protestant, the law was a religion; to the French-speaking Roman Catholic, religion was the law.

With the authority of the Sessions behind them, two of the new parish officers, James Blackhall[8] and Philip Rive, the latter the representative of the Jersey fishing interests, called a public meeting of the parish on 14 January 1875 for the purpose of imposing a District School Tax. Spirits were running high and the people of the parish turned out in good numbers to oppose the imposition of the tax. When the chairman attempted to speak, several men rushed forward and hustled him out of the building. Fabien Lebouthillier grabbed the papers from Blackhall's hands. In the midst of shouting and arm waving the meeting broke up[9]

7 Maud Hody, "The Development of Bilingual Schools in New Brunswick" (unpublished D. Education thesis, University of Toronto, 1964), p. 59. See also New Brunswick, *Synoptic Reports of Debates of the the House of Assembly*, 11 March 1875, p. 38.

8 Blackhall held the appointments of magistrate, coroner, collector of customs, postmaster, and, as he stated in his evidence at the trial, "five or six other public offices".

9 This account is taken from reports appearing in the Saint John *Morning Freeman* and the Shediac *Moniteur Acadien*, during January and February 1875, and from two typescript accounts in the

Believing that the English Protestants might make another attempt to hold a secret meeting, a group of French-speaking inhabitants, about thirty in number, went to the school the next day. The weather was bitterly cold and when they found the door of the schoolhouse locked against them, they went to Blackhall's office where they demanded and were refused the key. At this point they moved to Charles Robin's store where they obtained a gallon of rum. It is doubtful that this was the only alcohol they had to drink, for contemporary evidence suggests that the crowd was boisterous and belligerent. Having heated their heads as well as warmed their feet, they returned to Blackhall's office, some of them bellowing the *Marseillaise.* In the general melee some papers were torn from the wall, a stove was pushed over, and some windows were broken. Under duress Blackhall finally signed a pledge promising to have nothing more to do with school meetings. Rive, who lacked Blackhall's strength of character, had already done so earlier. At this point, the crowd moved off to the premises occupied by the Honourable Robert Young. Young was not at home, and his wife, terrified by the noise and the sight of the crowd, some of whom were carrying clubs and guns, locked herself indoors with her children. Young's clerk, Colson Hubbard, gave the leaders, who included Joseph Chiasson and Philéas Mailloux and his three brothers, Joseph, Bernard and Louis, all of them big, strong, hot-tempered men, a few provisions and they moved away. Their object, at this point, seems to have been to intimidate those members of their own community who had showed a disposition to go along with the authorities in supporting the School Act by paying their school taxes, and who were known locally as the "Bourbons." After threatening Hubert Blanchard, they went to Martin Haché's to force him to sign a document promising to withdraw all support of the School Act, then to Stanislas Legere's for the same purpose, and to Alexander's store, where they extorted $4.00 from the manager, Thomas Ahier. When, by argument or intimidation, they had persuaded most of the "Bourbons" to change sides, they returned to their homes. There was nothing more to be done, only to wait until Robert Young should return, when they would endeavour to convince him that it was to his best interest to throw in his lot with the majority of the people of Caraquet.

There is no doubt that the demonstrators acted illegally on 15 January at Robin's store and elsewhere, but there was small justification, at this time, for the *New Brunswick Reporter* of Fredericton to look upon the events of the day as a fanatical, dangerous, anti-Protestant riot prompted by "the incendiary and revolutionary" incitements of the Catholic *Freeman* of Saint John[.10] Neither

Archives of the Université de Moncton, Adélard Savoie, "L'émeute de Caraquet" (a term paper prepared at the Université de Saint Joseph), and J. Médard Léger, "Notes sur les Troubles Scolaires de Caraquet 1875".

10 *The New Brunswick Reporter and Fredericton Advertiser*, 20 January 1875. The *News* of Saint John declared that "the ruffians" of Caraquet would have to be dealt with "in a manner that will teach them New Brunswick is not quite ripe for the Commune, nor for a reign of terror of the Riel, Lépine or any other pattern". The frequent references to the Riel troubles suggest that the events in Manitoba made a deeper impression on the Maritimes than western Canadian historians have realized.

was there much justification for the rather flippant attitude of the *Freeman* which reported on 28 January that "for shipwrecks without storms and riots without violence, Caraquet has no equal in the Dominion just now."" The situation was one which demanded tactful handling. A false step, by either side, might well precipitate serious trouble in Caraquet.

Meanwhile, frantic and terrified, Mrs. Young had sent a telegram to her husband in Fredericton telling him to come home at once because his family was in danger. Robert Young, however, was not at Fredericton. Following a meeting of the provincial cabinet he had set out on his return journey by way of Saint John and Sackville. He was in the vicinity of the latter town when the telegram reached him late on Friday the 15th. He hurried on to Shediac that night, and hired a carriage to take him to Chatham on the Miramichi. At Chatham, on Sunday, the 17th, Young received another communication which suggested that his own life was in danger and that the Caraquet mob was planning to burn his store and destroy all his business records.[12] For this, or for some other reason which remains obscure, Young did not hurry home. Instead, he remained at Chatham, probably in consultation with his political colleague, the Honourable William Kelly. It was not until Friday, 22 January, that Young arrived at Caraquet, one week exactly after Chiasson, Mailloux and their companions had frightened the wits out of Mrs. Young. At this time Young found the parish in a state of tranquillity. There were no mobs, no damage, no obvious signs of the riotous situation about which some of the newspapers, like the *News, Telegraph* and *Reporter*, were writing in such alarming terms. But there was a feeling of tension in the air.

III

On Sunday, 24 January, the Abbé Joseph Pelletier read two statements from the pulpit of the parish church in Caraquet. The first was an expression of his disapproval of the excesses of the 14th and 15th. The second was a letter which he said he had just received prior to the service. This letter ordered him, in emphatic terms, to stop the "band of pirates" responsible for the earlier troubles, under pain of having his presbytery burned to the ground should he fail to do so.

---

11 *The Morning Freeman*, 28 January 1875. The *Freeman* of the 19th had poked fun at the alarmist reports in the *Telegraph, Globe* and *News*: "If we may believe some of the newspapers and their Caraquet correspondents, civil war is actually raging in Gloucester county, where a dozen loyal citizens have actually been obstructed in their attempt to rob all their neighbours in due form of law, and, horrible to add — if we may believe these correspondents — a stove has been knocked down and a gallon of whiskey — at least one gallon — has been drunk."

12 The message Young received at Chatham was reported in the *Freeman* (28 January 1875) as follows: "They say they are done with us Protestants except you. They threaten to take your life the moment you arrive. From what happened yesterday we are afraid you are not safe. If they gather and get liquor, which they are bound to have when they meet, they do not know where to stop. They say after they put you through they are going to all the merchants to make them burn all mortgages and accounts up to date."

So seriously was this threat regarded, that the Sisters of Notre Dame took the precaution of packing their effects so that they would be ready to remove them to safety in the event of fire.[13] The author of this letter remains a mystery. It hardly seems likely that a man like Young, familiar with the people of the parish and holding a responsible position in the government of the province, would have been guilty of such a stupid provocation; all that we know is that Colson Hubbard, Young's clerk, was seen to give a letter to the sexton, who in turn gave it to Pelletier on the morning of the 24th.[14] Beyond that we cannot go.

The immediate result of the threat to the Abbé Pelletier was a storm of indignation among the members of the priest's congregation. A number of those who attended Mass that day resolved to take the matter up with the Honourable Robert Young the following morning. About 10:00 a.m. on the 25th a group of some 100 men set out to see Young. There is nothing to suggest that they were intent upon violence, if only because of Pelletier's Sunday exhortations that they should conduct themselves in a peaceable way. But Young obviously expected a violent confrontation. He had barricaded the doors and windows of his premises, and had assembled a few "well-armed" friends to help him defend his improvised fortification.[15] When the Acadians demanded to see him, he refused to open the door or to talk with any of them. His curt refusal only aggravated their already raw tempers. Who was this man who was treating them in such a cavalier manner? None other than the man whom they had elected to office only a few years before, and with whom they had done business for many years. Why should he act this way? It was his duty as a member of the provincial government to listen to their grievances. Despite their irritations they did not take to sticks and stones, but returned to talk the matter over at André Albert's house and plan their course of future action.

Young had already made his plans. On the information of Hubbard and Ahier, warrants for the arrest of the rioters had been put in the hands of the High Sheriff of Gloucester on 23 January. Now was the time to serve them. Young sent word to Sheriff Robert B. Vail at Bathurst to come to Caraquet with a force of constables to arrest the troublemakers. Vail set out from Bathurst late on Monday, arriving at Caraquet about 3:00 a.m. on Tuesday, 26 January. He brought with him four constables, Stephen Cable, Alfred Gammon, Joseph Gammon and Robert Ramsay. En route he picked up William Eady and David Eady at New Bandon. At Caraquet they were joined by John Sewell and Richard Sewell from Pokemouche. Vail went at once to Young's, telling his

13 Extrait du "Journal des Révérendes Soeurs de Notre Dame," cited by Savoie, *op. cit.* The pages of the Savoie transcript are not numbered; however, this reference appears on page 12.

14 Savoie, *op. cit.*, p. 13.

15 *The Telegraph* (26 January 1875) stated: "Some of the men approached and knocked on one of the doors, but did not attempt to break in." See also *Le Moniteur Acadien*, 28 janvier 1875. Mrs. Young gave similar evidence at the trial.

men to report to him there after they had had something to eat. During the course of the morning Vail's constables made several arrests, the prisoners being taken to Young's premises where they were detained until arrangements could be made to remove them to the gaol at Bathurst.[16]

Meanwhile, influenced by Young's alarmist view of the situation, Vail had applied to the Hon. William Kelly, Board of Works Commissioner, at Chatham, for additional men.[17] The High Sheriff of Gloucester had, of course, no jurisdiction outside his own county, and to enrol men in the neighbouring county of Northumberland was as remarkable as it was irregular. He ought, instead, to have approached the local Justices of the Peace, Théotime Blanchard and P. J. Ryan of Caraquet, both of whom were available. In the absence of positive documentary evidence, one may assume from some of the remarks at the trial of the rioters that, while he had been at Chatham, Young had already broached the question of sending reinforcements to Caraquet to back up the small force of constables available to the High Sheriff. The very fact that no fewer than 20 men from Chatham and Newcastle were rapidly assembled and despatched to Caraquet on sleighs on the afternoon of the 26th, suggests that Vail's request came as no surprise to Kelly. The Miramichi party, after a difficult journey over almost impassable roads via Tracadie, arrived at Young's in Caraquet about 7:00 a.m. on the 27th; it included Sam Wilcox, Peter Manderson, Robert Manderson, James Loggie, George Loggie, Dudley Wells, Philip Perlay, Hugh Marquis, John Cassidy, Donald McGruer, Allan Rand, Isaac Clark, Charles Call, William Reid, James Chapman, John Gifford, Henry Burbridge, Henry Bannister, William Carter and William Fenton. Technically these men were not constables. Vail did not swear them in as such. He looked upon them as "volunteers" and instructed them to "assist in the arrest of those persons that were to be arrested."[18]

From his operational headquarters at Robert Young's, Sheriff Vail ordered that more arrests should be made on the morning of the 27th. Several men were brought in, one of whom offered strong resistance to his arrest; "pretty rough" was how constable Gammon described the experience.[19]   Learning

16 The proceedings of the trial of the Acadian rioters were reported in detail in the newspapers of the day, particularly in *Le Moniteur Acadien* for November 1875. There is also a manuscript of the legal proceedings in the Robidoux Papers in the Archives of the Université de Moncton. This manuscript appears to be a verbatim record of the trial. It is in poor condition but quite legible, and may be checked against the newspaper accounts. Material in this paragraph is taken from the evidence of Alfred James Gammon, one of Vail's constables.

17 *Synoptic Reports*, 9 April 1875, p. 104.

18 Evidence of George W. Loggie. Bannister gave evidence to the same effect. A frequent error in the accounts of these events which have appeared in French is the confusion of the so-called "volunteers" from the Miramichi with the Militia. Savoie, Léger, Rumilly, Turgeon and others use the words "milice" and "soldats" when referring to the constables and the "volunteers." The Militia, however, did not appear on the scene until after the troubles were at an end.

19 Evidence of Alfred James Gammon. The man who resisted was Gervais Chiasson.

from an informer that a number of those who had taken part in the events of the 14th and 15th had gathered at André Albert's house, Vail ordered his deputy, Stephen Cable, to take a party of men to Albert's and seize the offenders. Cable's party set out, with the necessary warrants, about 3:00 p.m. It numbered about 20 men, including both constables and "volunteers."[20] Blackhall went with them as interpreter because few of Cable's men were familiar with the language spoken by the great bulk of the inhabitants of Caraquet.

The arrests made on the 26th and the morning of the 27th had aroused alarm and consternation among the Acadian population. They had heard reports of violence, broken windows and even shooting. But what disturbed them most was the presence of "Orangemen" from the Miramichi among those whom they were disposed to refer to as "Young's Army." Rumours were circulating from one end of the community to the other that Young was going to arrest everybody he could find. For the moment the Acadians did not know what to do. Perhaps the best thing would be to get together and work out some kind of a plan. With this object in view they made their way to André Albert's house at the other end of the town.[21]   Some of them sat down to play cards, while the others talked. When they were thus engaged, Télésphore Brideau rushed in to tell them that "Young's Army" was on its way to Seraphin Albert's house to make arrests there. He told them that the constables and "volunteers" were armed and that there was no point in trying to offer any resistance.[22]   Brideau then hurried away, followed by several others, like Jules Chiasson and Isaac Albert, who preferred to run away and live to demonstrate another day. The others, apparently, did nothing but talk until they were aroused to action by the noisy arrival of Cable's men. Bernard Albert shouted the warning: "We are all dead. There is Young's Army coming, armed with guns and bayonets — let us hide ourselves."[23]   With no thought of anything but their own safety, the Acadians hurriedly climbed into the attic of André Albert's house. Perhaps there they would escape detection and thereby escape arrest.

While Cable arranged his men outside the house to watch the doors and windows, Blackhall went to the back door and knocked. He and some of the deputy sheriff's party entered and exchanged greetings with Albert. Speaking in French, Blackhall asked if Charles Parisé, one of those for whom Cable had a warrant, was in the house. At the subsequent hearing Albert stated that he had misunderstood Blackhall's question, believing him to be enquiring about the whereabouts of Xavier Parisé; he therefore replied honestly that he did

---

20 The party included Cable, Chapman, Alfred Gammon, Joseph Gammon, Ramsay, Wilcox, Cassidy, two Loggies, Manderson, Rand, Marquis, Call, Wells, David Eady, Richard Sewell, Burbridge, Bannister, Richie, Gifford and Blackhall.

21 There is no evidence to support the statement which appeared in *The New Brunswick Reporter* (3 February 1875) that Albert's house was "fortified and loop-holed."

22 Evidence of Jean Louis Frigault.

23 Evidence of Bernard Albert.

not know. While Blackhall and Albert were talking, the room filled with armed men. One of them, catching sight of a movement by one of the two women in the house towards a pot of water on the stove, and assuming that she intended to hurl the boiling water at the constables, held his gun to her face. She and her companion were then shoved into another room in the house.[24]   Meanwhile a noise overhead attracted the attention of constable Robert Ramsay. He raised his rifle and fired through the opening in the ceiling leading to the attic, with the object, he maintained, of frightening the men obviously hiding above. At this point, Sewell and Burbridge rushed to the opening, but when they attempted to get into the attic they were pushed back by some of the Acadians. Several other constables and "volunteers" then thrust their bayonets upwards in an effort to pry loose some of the planks in the ceiling. While they were thus engaged, a shot was fired from the attic. The trapped Acadians had had several rifles with them and these they had taken upstairs when they had fled for safety. This shot apparently struck the stove on the ground floor but did no damage.[25]   In all probability this, like Ramsay's shot, was fired as a deterrent rather than with murderous intent.

At this stage, the events and sequence of events become as obscure to the historian as they must have appeared to the actual participants through the gunsmoke and dust in André Albert's attic. Any historical reconstruction based upon the evidence at the subsequent trial can be no more than a reasonable, credible guess at accuracy. It does seem clear, however, that about this time Sewell and Loggie managed to climb into the attic, while John Gifford was endeavouring to hoist himself through another opening in the ceiling. Gifford succeeded in getting his head and shoulders above the level of the attic floor, and while in this position may well have fired a shot from his revolver.[26]   Then another shot was fired; this time it came from the gun of Louis Mailloux. Gifford was hit in the head and fell to the floor below.[27]   The shooting which followed was as wild as it was senseless. Loggie stated later that he fired three times in the direction of the Acadians. Sewell emptied his revolver at them. Burbridge, who was now in the attic, pressed the trigger of his weapon only to have it misfire. James Chapman, on the floor below, without seeming to realize that he might injure one of his own comrades in the attic above, fired several times through the ceiling. It was in this confusion that Louis Mailloux was hit — both Loggie and Sewell saw him fall to the floor.[28]   That others were

24 The two women were Madame André Albert and Clothide Chiasson.

25 Evidence of Henry Burbridge. According to David Eady's evidence Sewell shouted: "the sons of bitches are up there."

26 Gifford was armed with a Smith and Wesson 22 calibre revolver. When the revolver was recovered later it was found that one shot had been fired from it. See evidence of George Loggie.

27 Evidence of George Loggie and David Eady.

28 Sewell subsequently boasted that he had shot Mailloux. When he was questioned about this boast by the Defence during the trial the question was not allowed by the judge.

not hit at the same time is more a tribute to their good fortune than to the judgement of Cable's men. Unquestionably the gunsmoke which concealed the Acadians from view explains the absence of further casualties.

In the confusion one or two Acadians in the attic managed to escape. Agapit Albert jumped to the floor below, much to the surprise of James Chapman, and then "ran like the devil" to safety.[29] Another Acadian, Stanislas Albert, who attempted to do likewise, was hit with a rifle butt and left lying in the snow. In the attic, Sewell, out of ammunition, grabbed Peter Manderson's gun, but the Acadians were anxious to give themselves up. According to their own evidence, they had tried to do so earlier but no one had listened to them,[30] a thing understandable enough in the darkness, confusion, shouting and noise of the moment. The prisoners were then marched off to Young's store. Two of them, Joseph Duguay and Bernard Albert, had wounds in the face. Later in the day, when the constables returned to examine the scene of the shooting, they found Mailloux. He was still breathing but died shortly afterwards. Gifford had been killed instantly.

The next day, the 28th, the prisoners seized at Caraquet were removed to Bathurst and lodged in gaol. During the journey most of them suffered extensively from the bitter cold; some of them even had their feet and hands frozen.[31] Post-mortems were held on Gifford and Mailloux and on 2 February Mailloux was buried. There were no demonstrations. The shootings had taken the heart out of the population and there was little need for the Abbé Pelletier's appeal to his parishioners to abandon all thought of resistance and useless shedding of blood.[32]

The events of "bloody Wednesday" had not only frightened the Abbé Pelletier, they had frightened the civil authorities at Bathurst even more. No one had ever anticipated that two men might die by gunfire while arrests were being made. Perhaps there might be further shootings. Accordingly an appeal was made to the military authorities for assistance. Senator John Ferguson and two other Justices of the Peace immediately got in touch with the Hon. William Kelly at Chatham, urging him to lose no time in arranging for the despatch of an organized military force to Gloucester to assist in "suppressing

---

29 Evidence of James Chapman.

30 Evidence of Bernard Albert. Joseph Chiasson had cried: "Stop! Stop!" when the shooting began; and Bernard Albert cried: "I'll go with you." The only answer they received was "God Damn Frenchmen, I'll kill you."

31 The *Morning Freeman* (30 January 1875) published a telegram from Bathurst: "Thirteen of the men arrested at Caraquet have just arrived here with the Sheriff. They appear inoffensive and have anything but a bloodthirsty appearance."

32 The *New Brunswick Reporter* (3 February 1875) quoted Pelletier as saying: "It is better one hundred times to submit to no matter what trouble, rather than to expose the life of one man." The complete letter Pelletier wrote to his parishioners may be found in *Le Moniteur Acadien*, 25 février 1875.

a riot" at Caraquet. At Kelly's request, Lt. Col. C. McCulley, the brigade major of the 3rd brigade at Chatham, called out the Militia. On the 28th, at 3:00 p.m., a detachment comprising 2 officers and 41 other ranks of the Newcastle Field Battery, under the command of Major R. C. Call, set out for Bathurst with two nine-pounder cannon. They were followed, several hours later, by a second detachment, this time an infantry force made up of 4 officers and 46 other ranks of the 73rd Battalion (later known as The North Shore Regiment).[33] Both detachments found the going difficult, "having to shovel through immense snow banks, and long pieces of the road that were drifted full of snow as high as the fences"; however, they arrived safely in Bathurst the following day, the 29th January.[34] The gunners were asked by the Justices of the Peace to remain in Bathurst to guard the gaol and the prisoners. The infanteers were sent on to Caraquet, where they acted as guards and provided escorts for those prisoners who were arrested after the affair at Albert's. It does not appear from the records that the militiamen made any arrests; this was solely the responsibility of the civil power represented by the High Sheriff and his men.

On the evening of 3 February the situation was deemed sufficiently quiet for the infantry detachment to be withdrawn and returned to Chatham. The artillery, however, remained on guard duty at Bathurst for a period of six weeks. When they were finally withdrawn in March, Senator Ferguson and a number of his fellow citizens addressed a letter to the commanding officer, complimenting him on the "readiness with which you responded to the call of the authorities, and the manner in which you have performed duties, in many respects most difficult . . . ."[35] There was no such letter from the Acadians at Caraquet; nevertheless they could not help but contrast the strict discipline and good conduct of the Militia soldiery, with the lack of discipline and irresponsibility displayed by the Miramichi "volunteers," whose presence in Caraquet had proven more of an embarrassment than assistance to the civil authorities.

IV

The inquests into the shootings of Mailloux and Gifford were conducted by G. C. Blackhall, acting in the capacity of coroner. The coroner's jury, in the absence of the necessary evidence, found that Mailloux had been killed by a "ledden" bullet fired by some person unknown. In the case of Gifford, a verdict was found against the rioters, and nine persons were named as participants in the death of the "volunteer" from Miramichi; namely, Joseph Chiasson, Prudent Albert, Luc Albert, Bernard Albert, Stanislas Albert, Agapait Albert, Joseph Duguay, Moïse Parisé and Jean Louis Paulin. Following the inquest,

33 Today known as the 2nd Battalion, The Royal New Brunswick Regiment (North Shore).

34 McCully to the Deputy Adjutant General, 6 February 1875, in Canada, *Sessional Papers*, 1876, No. 7, pp. 50, 54-55.

35 Ferguson and 37 Justices of the Peace and others to Major Call, Lieutenant Mitchell, non-commissioned officers and men of the Newcastle Field Battery of Artillery, *ibid.*

the men named appeared before the stipendiary magistrate, D. G. McLaughlin, on 1 February. John Young, a brother of Robert Young, acted as court interpreter. After a short hearing the accused were charged with murder and ordered to be held in custody pending the sitting of the court in September. The other prisoners, who had been arrested on the 24th and 25th January and who were charged with rioting, were released on bail. The editor of the *Moniteur*, who throughout January had generally followed a moderate line, wrote bitterly on 11 February: "This is an example of the justice the Acadians receive from their persecutors! Where is equality? Where is the impartiality of the law?"

At once friends of the prisoners began to make plans for the defence of those charged with murder. Pierre Landry, a young Acadian lawyer, later federal member of Parliament for Westmorland, first Acadian to become Chief Justice and a knight bachelor, volunteered his services. Onésiphore Turgeon, a Quebec-born French Canadian living at Bathurst, had other ideas. He wanted the Hon. J. A. Chapleau, one of Canada's outstanding lawyers who had gained considerable popularity in French Canadian circles as a result of his defence of Riel's lieutenant, Ambroise Lépine, in 1873. Turgeon had, in fact, already approached Chapleau and obtained the consent of the New Brunswick Bar for Chapleau to plead the prisoners' cause. Two other friends of the prisoners, the Abbé Pelletier and Kennedy Burns, one of the members of the legislature for Gloucester, had their reservations about Chapleau. Would it be a good idea, they argued, to bring into the province an outstanding lawyer and politician from Quebec to defend the prisoners? Might not this lead to an English back-lash? Accordingly arrangements were made by Burns to obtain the services of a well-known lawyer from Saint John, S. R. Thompson, and provide him with Pierre Landry as his assistant. At the same time an appeal was made to Pascal Poirier, an Acadian then employed by the federal government in Ottawa, to do what he could to raise money to assist in the defence of the Caraquet prisoners. According to Turgeon, it was Poirier's efforts as a fund-raiser that "saved the situation."[36]

The proceedings opened at Bathurst on 7 September 1875. The presiding judge was John Campbell Allen. The Crown was represented by George E. King, the provincial premier and attorney-general, and D. S. Kerr; the Defence by S. R. Thompson and P. Landry. On the 9th, the Grand Jury found acts of accusation against the nine prisoners cited for the murder of John Gifford. The following day acts of accusation were found against eight of the prisoners for riot on 15 January, and against ten for riot on the 25th of January.

The trial of the rioters on six separate charges began on 17 September. The Defence raised several points of law, suggesting that the High Sheriff of the

36 Onésiphore Turgeon, *Un Tribut à la race acadienne, mémoires 1871-1927* (Montréal, 1928), pp. 27-8.

county was incompetent to summon the Grand Jury, since he was himself an interested party; Thompson also questioned the eligibility of several jurors owing to their blood relationship with various constables who had arrested the alleged rioters. Other points were also raised, and it was not until the 24th that the petty jury was finally selected. It included among its twelve members, nine Roman Catholics, of whom seven were French-speaking. The Crown took the view that there had been a state of continuous riot from 15 to 25 January. In reply the Defence argued that the significance of the events had been grossly exaggerated and that the evidence before the court proved no more than trespass on 15 January, certainly no criminal intent. After two weeks of hearing the evidence of witnesses and the arguments of counsel, the petty jury found nine of the accused guilty of illegal assembly on 15 January. The others, notably Eloi and Gustave Lanteigne, were acquitted. In view of the number of points of law which had been raised, Judge Allen reserved judgement and ordered the release on bail of the convicted prisoners with the order that they should appear in court to hear sentence at the next sitting of the assizes.

The court then proceeded to the second and more important trial, that of the nine men charged with the murder of Gifford. The proceedings on this occasion were marked by strong feeling and strong words. At one point a Crown attorney accused one of the Defence lawyers of lying, and was obliged to pay a fine of fifty dollars for his outburst. A hint that this trial was going to be no cut and dried affair came during the selection of the jury. A panel of 150 men had been summoned for jury duty, and the Crown made liberal use of its right to challenge those whom it suspected of sympathies with the accused. Despite Thompson's protest, the Attorney-General ordered all Catholics to stand aside. According to the Defence lawyers, this action was taken at the instigation of the Hon. Robert Young. Whatever the truth of this charge, the fact was that the petty jury was made up wholly of Protestants.[37]   The editor of *Le Moniteur Acadien* wrote sarcastically: "How good it is to live under English rule, so vaunted for its equality of justice, such as understood and interpreted by the Attorney-General of New Brunswick and his rabble (sans culottes)."[38]

The first of the accused to stand trial was Joseph Chiasson. He pleaded "not guilty." For several weeks the jury listened patiently to a number of witnesses, several of whom contradicted each other on the essential issues of who fired first and how many shots were fired. Interestingly enough it was a Crown witness, the constable Robert Ramsay, who admitted that he fired the first shot, and that he did so with the intention of intimidating the Acadians who had hidden in Albert's attic. And yet there were witnesses who solemnly declared that they had not heard or seen Ramsay's shot!

37 The *New Brunswick Reporter* (15 December 1875) wrote: "The jury composed of Protestants and, we understand, all intelligent men, did not shrink from doing their whole duty."

38 *Le Moniteur Acadien*, 11 novembre 1875.

The Defence endeavoured to draw attention to the conduct of the constables and volunteers prior to reaching Albert's house, to justify the fears and alarms of the accused; but Judge Allen would tolerate no evidence of any actions prior to their entry to Albert's; neither would he allow the Defence to introduce evidence which had been given at the Coroner's inquest, even though he was prepared to permit the Crown to use this evidence to throw doubt on the credibility of witnesses for the Defence. Basically the Crown case was that the men at Albert's house had assembled there for the purpose of resisting legal arrest by the Sheriff's constables. The case for the Defence was that the men at Albert's were there for legal purposes — to play cards — and that there was no intention of resisting arrest. When they fled to the attic, they did so because they were afraid of "Young's Army." Because the Miramichi men were not properly sworn constables they were not entitled to the rights of arrest and the Acadians were, therefore, acting in self defence. Finally the Judge put several questions to the jury: (a) did the accused know that Cable's men were constables? (b) did the accused assemble at Albert's for the purpose of resisting arrest? (c) did the accused take refuge in the attic through fear and with no intention of resisting arrest? (d) did the accused resist the attempt of the constables to get into the attic? and (e) was Gifford shot by one of the accused carrying out a common intention of resisting the law? After five hours' deliberation the jury brought in a verdict of guilty against Joseph Chiasson.

Judge Allen was not prepared to pass judgement on Chiasson. He felt that there were too many points at issue which he believed should be referred to the Supreme Court. He therefore used his good offices to obtain the consent of the Defence attorney to an agreement that "in consideration of the other prisoners indicted with Chiasson withdrawing their pleas of 'not guilty' and pleading 'guilty of manslaughter' all of the objections taken by the prisoner's counsel in this case should be reserved, and should inure to the benefit of the prisoners, in case this conviction should be quashed" by the higher court.[39] Thompson agreed to these conditions. Meanwhile the nine men went back to their cells to wait until the meeting of the Supreme Court in June 1876.

Additional funds were raised by the Acadian defence committee to finance the appeal. Nazaire Dupuis, the founder of Dupuis Frères, and a descendant of an Acadian exile from St. Jacques l'Achegan, conducted the fund-raising in Montreal, as did J-C. Taché in Ottawa. Two large meetings were held in the Salle Gésu in Montreal, one presided over by Louis Jetté, a French Canadian Nationalist who had defeated Sir George Cartier in the election of 1873, and the other by Charles Devlin, one of the great orators of his day. Pascal Poirier lent his aid as a speaker.

39 This is taken from a printed court report, *The Queen vs. Joseph Chasson*, issued by Judge C. Allen at Fredericton, 1 February 1876. This document is in the Archives de l'Université de Moncton.

The Supreme Court reviewed both the riot and murder cases in June 1876. The justices sitting on the bench included John Campbell Allen, the judge who had tried the Acadian rioters at Bathurst,[40] together with Charles Fisher, Charles Duff, John Wesley Weldon and Andrew Rainsford Wetmore; Allen served as Chief Justice. In the case of the rioters, the majority of the court, Allen, Fisher and Duff, affirmed the conviction. Weldon and Wetmore dissented. In the murder and manslaughter cases, the court, while upholding Allen in several instances, concluded that he had been in error on other points of law and procedure, and that the convictions should be quashed. The prisoners were therefore released. As far as the rioters were concerned, it was considered that in view of the lapse of time since their offence — a matter of eighteen months — there was no point in imposing any punishment upon them. The Acadian population in Caraquet was overjoyed, and George King, the premier, was content to let the whole tragic incident remain buried in oblivion.

V

One might well have anticipated that the outbreak of physical violence in the village of Caraquet would have been followed by verbal violence in the chambers of the Legislature. The surprising thing is that the provincial members were remarkably reticent about raising the issue in the House of Assembly in 1875. It would appear that, without any formal agreement, they decided that a discussion of Caraquet would only serve to exacerbate racial and religious feelings in the province. Once only did emotions show signs of overriding good sense, when Théotime Blanchard introduced a measure to legalize the proceedings of the original parish meeting at Caraquet. The Hon. J. J. Fraser, Provincial Secretary and member for York, heatedly accused Blanchard not only of condoning breaches of the law but encouraging them by refusing to pay his school taxes. How far Fraser's indignation was real and how far it was assumed for effect, does not emerge from the pages of the *Synoptic Reports.*[41]
It was probably real enough, for the members of the Assembly studiously watched their language after Blanchard's bill was defeated. Only occasionally do we find them making references to the events at Caraquet. One such instance was when, in opposition to a bill to incorporate the Loyal Orange Lodge in New Brunswick, Kennedy Burns of Gloucester suggested that the Orangemen of Chatham were not "free from blame" for the "unfortunate affair" at Caraquet.[42] Another occasion was when a bill was introduced to establish a police force and a lock-up at Caraquet;[43] and again when the Legislature was

---

40 The Chief Justice of New Brunswick, E. J. Ritchie, was appointed to the newly established Supreme Court of Canada in 1875 and Judge J. C. Allen was appointed to fill his vacancy. Thus it was that Allen found himself in the unusual position of hearing an appeal from his own court.

41 *Synoptic Debates,* 1875, 12 March 1875, p. 38.

42 *Ibid.,* 3 March 1875, p. 20.

43 *Ibid.,* 8 April 1875, p. 97.

called upon to approve payment of the federal bill for the aid rendered to the civil power by the Militia. Burns suggested that the Militia gunners had been sent on a fool's errand when they hauled their two nine-pounder cannon through the snow to Bathurst; Blanchard remarked sarcastically that there had been no need "for the calling of the Prussian Army to Caraquet by the Bismarcks and Kaisers of Gloucester."[44]

In Ottawa, John Costigan returned to the charge with his annual effort to secure an amendment to the British North America Act which would guarantee publicly supported separate schools for New Brunswick, but he urged those who might take part in the debate to refrain from making any references in their speeches to the unfortunate events at Caraquet.[45]   As in previous years the debate on the Costigan motion in 1875 cut across racial and party lines. Quebec Conservatives who had been foremost in the defence of Louis Riel, such as L. F. R. Masson, gave full support to Costigan; so too did some of the Liberals like Charles Devlin of Montreal. The Hon. Joseph Cauchon, newly appointed to Mackenzie's Cabinet, supported his chief, by arguing that, unfortunate as the absence from the B.N.A. Act of the guarantees demanded by Costigan might be, it would be even more unfortunate to try now to alter the compact which the provinces had entered upon at the time of Confederation. Costigan's motion had no chance of success without Government support and it suffered defeat, the third since 1872.

If the troubles in Caraquet were not directly debated either in Fredericton or in Ottawa, that does not mean that they were without interest to the people of the province. On the contrary. The impact they made was deep enough in 1875, and lasting. Neither French nor English, Catholic or Protestant wanted to see any repetition of what had occurred on the North Shore. That is why they all welcomed the news that a group of Roman Catholic members of the Legislature, encouraged if not actively assisted by Bishop Sweeney, had resumed talks with the provincial cabinet. Early in August a formal agreement was arrived at. This agreement, known generally as "The Compromise" or the *Modus Vivendi* of 1875, provided that all Roman Catholic children could be grouped together in the same school or schools; that official recognition would be granted to certificates issued by the Superior of any teaching order in lieu of attendance at the Normal School, provided any such teacher took the examination required for a licence; that text books would be carefully selected to eliminate those containing anything likely to offend Roman Catholic susceptibilities; and buildings belonging to the Roman Catholic Church could be rented for school purposes without any restriction being placed on their use after school hours. The Roman Catholic minority did not gain the right to state-supported schools, but they did gain the right to send their children to the school of their choice, to expose their children to the catechism, and to

44 *Ibid.*, 9 April 1875, pp. 103-4.
45 Canada, House of Commons, *Debates*, 1875, p. 561.

have them taught by members of Catholic religious orders.[46] The Compromise fell short of what the Roman Catholics would have considered as equality, but it was accepted as the best possible arrangement which could be obtained at the time. In his circular letter of 3 January 1876, addressed to the clergy of the Diocese of Chatham, Bishop James Rogers wrote:

> . . . in the present temper of the Government and of the majority of the population of our Province, we have no alternative but to cease the active opposition which however conscientious and justifiable, is found to be not only unavailing but has given occasion to men, esteemed otherwise just and kindly disposed, to outrage and oppress their fellow citizens . . . In order then not to give even innocent occasion to greater evils, we must simply tolerate what we cannot prevent.
>
> Thus, while still protesting against the objectionable feature of the School Law in question, we consent, through necessity, to work under it, hoping that the good judgement and a delicate sense of right on the part of our fellow citizens administering the law will do much practically to neutralize its radical defect and utilize whatever acknowledged advantages it may otherwise possess.[47]

Half a loaf was better than none at all.

With the acceptance of the Compromise of 1875, opposition to the School Act of 1871 subsided. For five years that Act had been a source of bitter controversy, a barrier to goodwill, and in the end, a prod to violence. Too often, in Canadian history, compromise has come only after force, and justice after bloodshed. Are we incapable of learning any lesson from history?

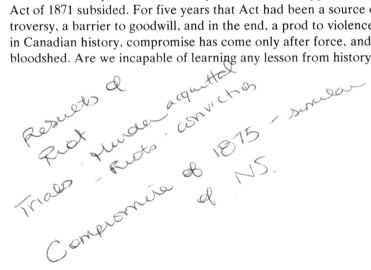

---

46 Hody, *op. cit.*, Appendix E. See also Rumilly, *op. cit.*, pp. 769-770.

47 Hody, Appendix F. The pages including the several appendices in Dr. Hody's thesis are not numbered. They are to be found at the end of the thesis.

COLIN D. HOWELL

Reprinted from Vol. VIII, No. 2
(Spring 1979)

W. S. Fielding and the Repeal Elections of 1886 and 1887 in Nova Scotia

On 15 June 1886, after a number of unsuccessful attempts to redress Nova Scotia grievances through existing political channels, the Liberal Government of Premier William S. Fielding contested the provincial elections of 1886 on the issue of secession from Confederation, winning 29 of the province's 38 seats. In the federal elections held less than a year later, John A. Macdonald's Conservative party reversed this apparent repeal victory, winning 14 of 21 seats. Almost immediately the repeal campaign collapsed. Unfortunately, the important relationship of the secession question to the electoral *volte-face* of 1886 and 1887 in Nova Scotia has not yet received comprehensive analysis. Lacking the information provided by the Fielding papers, most historians have hitherto dealt with repeal only in passing, treating it either as a minor incident in federal-provincial relations,[1] or as one of those occasional outbursts of regional discontent that help make up Nova Scotia's protest tradition.[2] Not only has this resulted in a tendency to divorce the secession agitation from the socio-economic and political conditions out of which it emerged, but also it has left us with an incomplete understanding of Fielding's objectives and behaviour during the elections of 1886 and 1887.[3]

In July 1886, Fielding's contemporary, James W. Carmichael, described repeal in the narrowest way possible: it was simply "a lever to obtain better terms".[4] But repeal was more than just a device to wring financial concessions out of the Federal Government. It was related to the decline of Nova Scotia's traditional sea-based and export-oriented economy in the post-Confederation period. Nova Scotian separatism developed logically out of a regional ideology that attempted both to explain and to remedy the area's declining economic

1 J. Murray Beck, *The Government of Nova Scotia* (Toronto, 1957), pp. 159, 330; and *The History of Maritime Union. A Study in Frustration* (Fredericton, 1969); Donald Creighton, *John A. Macdonald: The Old Chieftain* (Toronto, 1955), p. 453; and Peter B. Waite, *Canada 1874-1896. Arduous Destiny* (Toronto, 1971), pp. 184-8.

2 Colin D. Howell, "Nova Scotia's Protest Tradition and the Search for a Meaningful Federalism", in David Jay Bercuson, ed., *Canada and the Burden of Unity* (Toronto, 1977), pp. 169-91; G.A. Rawlyk, "Nova Scotia Regional Protest, 1867-1967", *Queen's Quarterly*, LXXV (Spring 1968), pp. 105-23.

3 See Phyllis Blakeley, "The Repeal Election of 1886 in Nova Scotia", Nova Scotia Historical Society *Collections*, 26 (1945), pp. 131-53; Bruce Fergusson, *Hon. W.S. Fielding. The Mantle of Howe* (Windsor, N.S., 1970), vol. I, ch. 4; and Colin Howell, "Repeal, Reciprocity, and Commercial Union in Nova Scotian Politics, 1886-1887" (MA thesis, Dalhousie University, 1967).

4 Carmichael to Edward Blake, 6 July 1886, J.W. Carmichael Papers, vol. 394, no. 411, Public Archives of Nova Scotia [hereafter PANS].

mixture of different elements

fortunes. This regional ideology, although never a coherent body of thought, was an amalgam of the following elements: a belief in a pre-Confederation Golden Age; a conviction that Confederation itself was responsible for the region's decline; a feeling that the financial terms of Confederation needed revision; a belief that prevailing national policies were detrimental to the region; a feeling that closer commercial ties with the United States were desirable; and a conviction that the Maritimes could prosper as independent states if left to their own devices. In coming to terms with political secessionism, therefore, it is important to keep in mind its relationship both to economic decline and fiscal disability, and to this broader and more comprehensive regional ideology.

The re-emergence of repeal as a political movement in 1886 reflected, among other things, a deep concern about the disintegration of a traditional maritime economy based upon the wooden sailing ship, the international carrying trade, and the export of staple products. As steam-powered shipping and the iron hull gradually supplanted the sailing ship in the international shipping trades, fewer and fewer vessels were being constructed in the once active building centers in the province. In 1864, the high point in Nova Scotia's shipbuilding activity before Confederation, ship construction amounted to 73,038 tons. Shipbuilding remained an important component of the regional economy after 1867, but in the mid-1870s the industry entered into a decline from which it would not recover. In 1886 and 1887, the years in which repeal was a public issue, ship tonnage constructed in Nova Scotia had declined to 21,193 and 14,266 tons respectively.[5]

Nova Scotia's economic difficulties also encouraged a significant out-migration from the province and a consequent decline in the rate of population growth after 1880. Although the population of Nova Scotia increased by 15% between 1861 and 1871 and grew another 12% between 1871 and 1881, between 1881 and 1891 the rate of growth slowed to a mere 2%.[6] At the same time, with the National Policy of 1879, the post-Confederation expansion of coal production, the revolution in transportation that accompanied the railroad boom, and the related enterprises that developed in response to these changes, there was a significant movement of population from the countryside to the towns, and from rural counties to areas of industrial growth. The most rapidly industrializing county was Cumberland which experienced a 26.2% increase in population

---

5   S.A. Saunders, *The Economic History of the Maritime Provinces. A Study Prepared for the Royal Commission on Dominion-Provincial Relations* (Ottawa, 1939), pp. 110-11. See also K. Matthews and G. Panting, eds., *Ships and Shipbuilding in the North Atlantic* (St. John's, 1977); and L. Fischer and E. Sager, eds., *The Enterprising Canadians: Entrepreneurs and Economic Development in Eastern Canada, 1820-1914* (St. John's, 1978); C.R. Fay and H.A. Innis, "The Economic Development of Canada, 1867-1921: The Maritime Provinces", *Cambridge History of the British Empire* (Cambridge, 1930), VI, pp. 659-67.

6   Alan A. Brookes, "Out-Migration from the Maritime Provinces, 1860-1900: Some Preliminary Conclusions", *Acadiensis*, V (Spring 1976), pp. 30-1.

between 1881 and 1891. Lunenburg, Halifax, Yarmouth, Colchester, Cape Breton, Queen's, Shelburne, and Digby also registered gains of between 0.9 and 5.1%, but in every case except Queen's the county's growth rate was substantially below that of the preceding decade. Moreover, all the other counties in the province suffered significant population declines from a high of -10.8% in Antigonish, -6.0% in Annapolis and -5.6% in Hants to a low of -0.3% in Victoria.[7]

The economic development of Nova Scotia during the 1880s proceeded unevenly. While the introduction of Macdonald's National Policy and the expansion of the coal industry spurred development in some parts of the province, especially in Cumberland and Cape Breton counties, a general economic downturn in Canada and the United States after 1882 led to shrinking markets for those parts of the province dependent upon the export of agricultural and fish products. In the five years between 1885 and 1889, the average annual value of fish exported from Nova Scotia was 9.9% less than that of the preceding five year period.[8] This decline was largely the result of the termination of the fisheries clauses of the Treaty of Washington in July 1885, and the consequent restoration of the more restrictive provisions of the Convention of 1818. In August 1885 the United States Consul General at Halifax reported that these new regulations diminished dry fish and lobster exports from Halifax to the United States by over 75% and thereby encouraged "a general business depression in the Provinces".[9] A temporary decline in fish sales to the West Indies between 1885 and 1889 further compounded Nova Scotia's difficulties.[10]

If the economic disabilities of declining areas provided the general context for the development of Nova Scotian separatism, it was the political subordination of the Maritimes within Confederation that prompted Fielding to make repeal an issue in 1886. To Fielding, the source of the province's difficulties was the inflexible financial settlement of 1867. Under the initial terms of Union, Nova Scotia had been granted an annual subsidy amounting to 80¢ per head of population, a further grant of $60,000 per annum in support of the legislature, and a debt allowance of $8,000,000. In 1869 the Howe-Macdonald better terms agreement increased the provincial debt allowance to $9,186,000 and revised the annual subsidy upwards by $82,698 for a ten-year period beginning 1 July 1867. During the 1870s the revised arrangement provided the province with more than enough revenue to undertake extensive road and bridge construction and to

---

7   Computed from population statistics published in *Census of Canada,* 1881, 1891.

8   Eric Sager, "The Shipping Fleet of Halifax, 1820-1903" (paper presented to the Atlantic Canada Studies Conference, Fredericton, 1978), p. 18.

9   Consul General Phelan to Secretary of State Porter, 15 August 1885, United States Consulate (Halifax), Dispatches, vol. 14, n.p., Dalhousie University Library (microfilm).

10 Waite, *Arduous Destiny,* p. 185.

initiate railroad development.[11] But when the additional subsidy lapsed in 1877 and the Government of Nova Scotia faced serious financial difficulties, Ottawa offered no further assistance. Prime Minister Alexander Mackenzie and his Finance Minister Richard Cartwright, and later John A. Macdonald as well, categorically refused an extension of the better terms annuity.[12]

One source of Nova Scotia's financial distress in these years was the absence of an effective system of municipal government which would have reduced the province's responsibility for financing essentially local services. In 1879 the Conservative Government of Simon Holmes took the first step to remedy this deficiency with the passage of the County Incorporation Act. This legislation made the incorporation of counties compulsory, and empowered municipal councils to make assessments in support of various local services.[13] The primary object of the County Incorporation Act was to encourage counties to tax themselves directly in order to maintain roads and bridges, and thereby to relieve the pressure on the provincial treasury, but it was decidedly unpopular in most parts of the province.[14] The Holmes Government's policy of retrenchment and its unsuccessful attempt to secure a subsidy increase from Ottawa further upset an already discontented electorate.[15] In the provincial election of 1882 the Conservatives went down to defeat; the Liberals won twenty-four of thirty-eight seats in the province.

The Liberal Government that assumed power in 1882 faced serious difficulties of its own. While in opposition the Liberals had been a seriously divided party. Apart from their united opposition to the County Incorporation Act, Liberal MLAs had demonstrated a significant resistance to party discipline. The election victory of 1882 did little to improve matters. Although the party had operated earlier under the nominal leadership of Alfred Gayton of Yarmouth, a Liberal party convention in 1882 passed over Gayton and offered the Premiership to Fielding. When Fielding declined the offer in order to continue as editor of the Halifax *Morning Chronicle*, William T. Pipes, a New Glasgow lawyer and the youngest man in the legislature, assumed the post. But Pipes lacked both the political presence and experience to unite the party. Facing serious opposition from Gayton and Otto S. Weeks of Guysborough, Pipes resigned in 1884 and Fielding became Premier.[16]

11 James A. Maxwell, "Financial History of Nova Scotia, 1848-1899" (PhD dissertation, Harvard University, 1926), p. 110.

12 James A. Maxwell, *Federal Subsidies to the Provincial Governments in Canada* (Cambridge, 1937), pp. 68-70.

13 C. Bruce Fergusson, *Local Government in Nova Scotia* (Halifax, 1961), p. 10.

14 J. Murray Beck, *The Evolution of Municipal Government in Nova Scotia 1749-1973* (Halifax, 1973), pp. 25-8.

15 James A. Fraser suggested that although the Holmes government pressed faithfully for better terms, when it went for re-election it failed to make the province aware of the reason for its financial distress. *Morning Chronicle* (Halifax), 26 February 1886.

16 Fergusson, *The Mantle of Howe*, pp. 22-55.

As Premier, Fielding seized upon the revenue crisis as the issue that would bring his divided party together. Better terms was an issue that enjoyed almost universal support. In 1884, for example, the Conservatives joined with the government in an address to the federal cabinet explaining that "an additional revenue has become an absolute necessity to this Province. . .as our people will not submit to direct taxation for local purposes".[17] In January, 1885 a delegation travelled to Ottawa to further argue the Province's claim to an increased subsidy. But when the Provincial Legislature opened in February, the province had not yet received a reply to its request for better terms. In the meantime some members of the House, led by James Fraser of Guysborough, were beginning to demand repeal. If better terms were not offered, Fielding confided to Blake, "men who have hesitated to commit themselves to a repeal cry will no longer hesitate".[18]

One should not assume, however, that Fielding had rejected repeal out of hand. Like many Liberals who initially refused to support secession, Fielding accepted the repealers' explanation for the region's decline. Fielding believed that the province had been dragooned into Confederation on terms that limited its future possibilities. Nowhere was this more evident than in politics, where a small province like Nova Scotia was denied sufficient power and means to command respect. "So long as the Province is financially embarrassed, as at present", he wrote to Edward Blake, "the whole affair must tend downward and the best men who get into the political arena will be glad to get out of it again".[19] But in the summer of 1885 Fielding was not yet ready to call for independence. "I may say", he explained to Blake, "that while I have not forgotten and cannot forget the wrong of '67 and am not satisfied that Nova Scotia can be as happy in the Union as she was before, I should shrink from. . .a repeal agitation if such could fairly be avoided".[20] On the other hand, if the Federal Government continued to treat the province with apparent contempt, it would demonstrate the unworkability of Confederation, and independence would be the only option.

In July 1885 Fielding wrote a final time to Ottawa, reiterating "the absolute necessity of large grants from the Federal Treasury for the support of services assigned to the Local Government",[21] and urging Macdonald to reply to the memorial of 1884. It was six months before the province received a rejection of its claim. Macdonald denied the provincial petition, explaining lamely that

---

17 Nova Scotia, *Journals,* 1886, Appendix 12, p. 5.
18 Fielding to Blake, 6 July 1885, Fielding Papers, vol. 490, no. 635, PANS. Unless otherwise noted all subsequent references to the Fielding Papers are to volume 490 which contains the Fielding Letter Books from 1883-1888.
19 Fielding to Blake, 8 January 1886, Fielding Papers, no. 160, PANS.
20 Fielding to Blake, 6 May 1886, *ibid.*
21 Nova Scotia, *Journals,* 1886, Appendix 12, p. 6.

Nova Scotia had "withdrawn from the credit of the debt account large amounts which they had expended in Railway extension and other Public works".[22] The *Morning Chronicle,* whose editorial policy still displayed Fielding's influence, considered this a turning point in the province's relationship with Ottawa. "That announcement calls for a most important change of some sort in Nova Scotia politics. . . . Only two alternatives are open to us — direct taxation or repeal".[23] Fielding was equally irate. In a letter to Edward Blake he wrote:

> I am an Anti Confederate. I cannot forget the manner in which Nova Scotia was forced into the union. . . . At all events I do not conceal from anybody the fact that I regard Confederation as a *wrong* and a substantial *injury* to Nova Scotia and I would gladly join in any legitimate movement which would give promise of obtaining repeal.[24]

Earlier, Fielding had been reluctant to move repeal resolutions in the House, because there seemed to be little prospect of success. Faced with the rejection of the provincial claim for increased subsidies and the prospect of having to impose direct taxation, however, Fielding became convinced that repeal would be "a ground on which we can unite nearly all our own party".[25] On 5 May 1886 he rose in the legislature, outlined the declining fortunes and limited future of the province within Confederation, and proceeded to introduce resolutions calling for repeal of the British North America Act and the establishment of an independent Maritime Union.[26]

Fielding's strategy in the ensuing campaign was to unite advocates of independence, proponents of better terms, and supporters of reciprocity into a broad political coalition. To the extent that Fielding could encourage the repeal, reciprocity and better terms questions to dissolve into one another, he would provide the electorate with a romanticized explanation of its fiscal and economic disability, and direct provincial discontent away from his government. During the summer election campaign of 1886, however, the marriage of convenience between secessionists and advocates of better terms came unstuck. It was not just that secessionists and unionists had different things in mind when they talked repeal, but that many unionists doubted the propriety of raising the issue in the first place. The most vigorous opposition to repeal in Liberal party circles arose in the northern and eastern parts of the province which were most successfully industrializing under the National Policy. S.M. MacKenzie, Liberal editor of the New Glasgow *Eastern Chronicle,* announced that despite "great excuse

22 *Ibid.,* Appendix 6, p. 13.
23 *Morning Chronicle,* 26 February 1886.
24 Fielding to Blake, 8 January 1886, Fielding Papers, no. 151, PANS.
25 Fielding to J.V. Ellis, 6 March 1886, Fielding Papers, no. 218, PANS.
26 Nova Scotia, *Debates,* 5 May 1886, pp. 394-5.

for the extreme measures adopted by Mr. Fielding and his followers, we cannot follow him to the full extent of his resolutions".[27] In Amherst, William Pipes criticized Fielding for dragging out the "putrid carcass of repeal".[28] Similarly, in Cape Breton County Liberal candidates George H. Murray and Ronald Gillis announced an independent stance on the repeal question.[29] Opposed to repeal because it threatened continued expansion of the coal industry, Murray and Gillis acknowledged the National Policy's importance to Cape Breton's economic well-being.[30] Not to have done so would have meant their certain defeat, for opposition to repeal on Cape Breton Island was overwhelming. At a public meeting at the Sydney court house on May 15, a resolution passed without opposition calling for separation of Cape Breton from Nova Scotia if repeal succeeded.[31]

Even in Guysborough County, itself a hotbed of repeal, the separatist issue caused difficulty. D. C. Fraser, a staunch unionist and opponent of repeal, threatened to run as an independent Liberal if the party nomination went to repealers Otto Weeks and James A. Fraser. Fearing that a split vote would endanger a safe Liberal riding, Fielding tried to bring the maverick Fraser into line. He wrote:

> I am told that you do not fully agree with us on the repeal question, but I am sure there can be no substantial difference between us on the question. It can hardly be possible that you do not desire repeal. The most you could say I judge is that we are not likely to get it. That is not a reason why we should fail to declare our wishes.

In the end it was Fielding's offer of a seat on the Legislative Council that resulted in Fraser's acquiescence.[32]

In Halifax County and along the eastern and southern shore, a traditionally Liberal part of the province, Liberal candidates made repeal a high-profile issue. Given the party's admirable record in the Assembly, the improvements in steamship service along this coastline, and the southerly orientation of Fielding's railway policy,[33] prospects for a Liberal victory were good. At the

---

27 *Eastern Chronicle* (New Glasgow), 13 May 1886.

28 *Colonial Standard* (Pictou), 18 May 1886. Fielding resented this outburst. In December 1886, he described repeal to Pipes as "a lively. . .corpse" which was "everyday bearing good fruit and will continue to bear such". Fielding to Pipes, 31 December 1886, Fielding Papers, nos. 18-9, PANS.

29 *Morning Herald* (Halifax), 9 June 1886.

30 Roselle Green, "The Public Life of Honorable George H. Murray" (MA thesis, Dalhousie University, 1962), pp. 7-10.

31 *Morning Chronicle,* 17 May 1886.

32 Fielding to D.C. Fraser, 17 May 1886, Fielding Papers, nos. 285-8, PANS.

33 Howell, "Repeal, Reciprocity, and Commercial Union in Nova Scotia Politics", pp. 19, 24, 29.

same time there was a close relationship here between the repeal and reciprocity issues. Some Liberals no doubt supported repeal in the hope that it might prompt the reopening of reciprocity negotiations with Washington. But this does not diminish the importance of the repeal question. The key to understanding the secession agitation is to recognize the way in which better terms, reciprocity, Maritime Union, and repeal blended together to appeal broadly to those concerned about the passing of the older commercial order.

In Halifax, the Liberal *Morning Chronicle* provided the most consistent expression of this regional ideology. The *Morning Chronicle's* campaign focused on the declining prosperity of the province after the "betrayal" of 1867. Confederation meant the loss of financial autonomy, excessive taxation in support of public works projects in the "barren west", little support for important provincial services in the east, and the closing of Nova Scotia's natural markets to the south. Added to this was the impact of the "diabolical tariff". Instead of opening markets in Ontario and Quebec for Nova Scotian products, the *Chronicle* argued, the National Policy turned the Maritimes into a "slaughter market" for Central Canadian suppliers.[34] The remedy was repeal:

> If Nova Scotians were now free from the Union with a fair share of the public debt of the Dominion cast upon her, the taxes which are now collected within this province would furnish a revenue sufficient to provide more liberally for every public service in the province than they are at present provided for, and leave in addition an annual surplus of half a million dollars in the treasury of the province . . . . We thrived before we endured the exactions of Canucks, we shall thrive when we are once again free from those exactions.[35]

On the other hand, a second Liberal newspaper in Halifax refused to support the repeal agitation. The *Acadian Recorder* stressed the legislative record of the Fielding government and made a strong case in favor of reciprocity. The editor, James Wilberforce Longley, was also the Liberal candidate for Annapolis County, and later Attorney-General in the Fielding government. Although Longley had "the gravest misgivings both as to the wisdom and propriety of the repeal agitation",[36] he had little faith in the future of Confederation. During the initial debate on the repeal resolution on May 8, Longley had declared Confederation a "failure, a total failure".[37] Not convinced that Confederation

---

34 *Morning Chronicle*, 10, 12, 15 June 1886.

35 *Ibid.*, 18 May 1886.

36 J.W. Longley to Edward Blake, 25 February 1887, Blake Papers, Provincial Archives of Ontario.

37 Nova Scotia, *Debates*, 8 May 1887.

itself explained Nova Scotia's disabilities, Longley blamed the "unnatural attempt to force inter-Provincial trade among Provinces which have no trade with each other",[38] and called for Commercial Union rather than repeal. "Secure unrestricted trade relations between this country and the United States", the *Recorder* suggested, "and the Repeal agitation in Nova Scotia will fade away".[39]

Because repeal, reciprocity and better terms were not always kept separate during the campaign, it is not possible in every case to distinguish those candidates who desired repeal from those who simply wanted better terms or reciprocity. But if one takes the candidates at their word, it is possible to discern three shades of opinion within the Liberal party. There was a repeal faction, which argued consistently in favor of repeal during the campaign; a group of moderate repealers, who expressed support for repeal but chose not to make it the central issue of the campaign; and a group of Liberal unionists who stated clearly their opposition to independence. The repeal group, Weeks and Fraser of Guysborough, Fielding, William Roche and William Power of Halifax, Albert Gayton and William Law of Yarmouth, Jeffrey McColl of Pictou, William F. McCoy of Shelburne, John S. McNeil of Digby, and Leander Rand of Cornwallis, King's County, represented those parts of the province whose products sought markets in the United States or the United Kingdom. This was also the case for many of the moderate repealers, a group made up of Henry M. Robicheau of Digby, George Clarke and Frederick A. Laurence from Colchester, Allan Haley of Hants County, Thomas W. Johnson of Shelburne, Joseph Henry Cook of Queen's County, Charles Church and George A. Ross from Lunenburg, Angus MacGillivray and Colin F. McIsaac of Antigonish. The unionist group, which included Thomas R. Black and C. J. MacFarlane of Cumberland County, Murray and Gillis from Cape Breton, John MacKinnon and Daniel McNeill from Inverness and Longley from Annapolis, represented areas of industrial growth or agricultural counties whose produce was consumed locally.[40]

The June 15 election added significantly to the strength of Fielding's government in the House. The 29 seats won by the Liberals represented an increase of five over the election of 1882, and four over the number of Liberals in the House at dissolution. The Liberals gained two seats in Colchester and Inverness counties, and one seat in Yarmouth, Antigonish, Halifax, Hants and Pictou. At the same time they lost two seats in Cape Breton county and one each in Richmond and Annapolis. In Cumberland, Thomas Black won a seat

38 *Acadian Recorder* (Halifax), 27 May 1886.

39 *Ibid.,* 14 May 1886.

40 In some cases there was insufficient evidence to indicate a candidate's attitude towards repeal. Included in this unknown category are Archibald Frame (Hants), Joseph Matheson (Richmond), and John A. Fraser (Victoria).

that had gone to the Conservatives in 1882, but this did not represent an increase in Liberal party strength since Black had been elected to the legislature in a by-election in 1884.[41]

As Table 1 reveals, the results of the election show a basic cleavage within the province. In the western counties and along the southern and eastern shore where prosperity was dependent upon access to international export markets and where repeal was a prominent issue, the Liberals won all the seats but two, an increase of six seats over 1882. More significantly, all eleven repealers and ten moderates in the province were elected, many of the former with commanding majorities. In Yarmouth County, repealers William Law and Alfred Gayton took 3388 of 4167 or 81.3% of the votes cast and in the process unseated the incumbent Thomas Corning. In Halifax, Liberal repealers Fielding, Michael Power and William Roche ran up majorities of 1061, 950, and 841 votes respectively, and in so doing defeated the incumbent Conservative W. D. Harrington who had led the poll in Halifax in 1882. In Pictou, repealer and annexationist Jeffrey McColl broke the Conservative hegemony in the county, running second to Tory leader Adam Bell. In Guysborough, James Fraser and Otto Weeks won by a significant majority polling 63% of the vote. The remaining repealers William McCoy, Daniel McNeil and Leander Rand each won their constituencies with comfortable majorities.

Conservative party strength was concentrated in the industrializing northeast. Cape Breton County, whose expanding coal output depended upon the maintenance of a 60¢ per ton duty on imported coal, elected two Conservatives, as did Pictou, while Cumberland and Richmond elected one each. In Victoria County Dr. J.L. Bethune ran as an independent Conservative and won with a majority of 316 votes. While Liberal candidates won election to two seats in Inverness, and one each in Pictou and Cumberland, they were often as hostile to repeal as their Conservative opponents. Daniel McNeil, a Liberal candidate in Inverness County, for example, pledged to resign if Fielding persisted in demanding secession after the election of 1886.[42]

The split between export-oriented counties and those experiencing significant industrial growth is also revealed in the occupational pursuits of the various candidates. In areas where repeal and reciprocity were attractive issues, export merchants were particularly prominent. Moderate repealers Joseph Henry Cook of Queen's County, Charles Church and George Ross of Lunenburg, and Thomas Robertson of Shelburne were all merchants with an export orientation, while Allan Haley of Hants operated as secretary of the Shipowners Marine Insurance Company. The repeal group included William Law, owner of

41 *Canadian Parliamentary Guide,* 1883, pp. 276-7; Nova Scotia, *Journals,* 1887, Appendix 12, pp. 1-21.
42 *Morning Herald,* 17 January 1887.

Table 1: *Electoral Behaviour and Affiliation of Successful Candidates, 15 June 1886*

County	Candidate	Affiliation	Election Majority 1882	Election Majority 1886	Majority as % of Votes Cast 1882	Majority as % of Votes Cast 1886
Annapolis	J. W. Longley	(L)	unionist	+79	+21	1.5	0.0
	Frank Andrews	(C)	unionist	—	+5	—	0.0
Antigonish	Angus MacGillivray	(L)	moderate	550	+434	19.6	10.8
	Colin F. McIsaac	(L)	moderate	—	+369	—	9.1
Cape Breton	Colin Chisholm	(C)	unionist	−401	+380	−7.2	7.3
	William McKay	(C)	unionist	—	+309	—	6.0
Colchester	George Clarke	(L)	moderate	—	+271	—	3.6
	Frederick A. Laurence	(L)	moderate	—	+156	—	2.1
Cumberland	Thomas Black	(L)	unionist	—	+144	—	1.7
	Richard Black	(C)	unionist	—	+125	—	1.5
Digby	Henry Robicheau	(L)	moderate	+296	+586	8.3	22.4
	John S. McNeil	(L)	repealer	+234	+464	6.6	17.7
Guysborough	James A. Fraser	(L)	repealer	+296	+471	10.9	15.3
	Otto Weeks	(L)	repealer	+355	+366	13.1	11.9
Halifax	William S. Fielding	(L)	repealer	+21	+1061	0.1	5.2
	William Roche	(L)	repealer	—	+950	—	4.6
	Michael Power	(L)	repealer	+48	+841	0.3	4.1
Hants	Allan Haley	(L)	moderate	+25	+44	0.5	0.7
	Archibald Frame	(L)	unknown	−32	+14	−0.6	0.2
Inverness	John McKinnon	(L)	unionist	−97	+491	−2.1	8.3
	Daniel McNeill	(L)	unionist	—	+401	—	6.7
King's	Leander Rand	(L)	repealer	—	+100	—	1.6
	William Bill	(C)	unionist	−78	+25	−1.4	0.4
Lunenburg	Charles Church	(L)	moderate	+344	+449	6.6	9.0
	George Ross	(L)	moderate	+291	+323	5.5	6.5
Pictou	Adam Bell	(C)	unionist	+62	+279	0.4	1.8
	Jeffrey McColl	(L)	repealer	−62	+41	−0.4	0.3
	C.H. Munroe	(C)	unionist	+78	+13	0.5	0.1
Queen's	Jason Mack	(L)	unknown	+139	+165	5.5	6.0
	Joseph Cook	(L)	moderate	+134	+140	5.4	5.1
Richmond	Joseph Matheson	(L)	unknown	−53	+161	−2.9	7.0
	David Hearn	(C)	unionist	—	+79	—	3.4
Shelburne	Thomas Johnson	(L)	moderate	+255	+328	8.1	10.5
	William F. McCoy	(L)	repealer	+246	+203	7.9	6.5
Victoria	John L. Bethune	(IC)	unionist	—	+316	—	10.8
	John A. Fraser	(L)	unknown	—	+47	—	1.6
Yarmouth	William Law	(L)	repealer	—	+966	—	23.2
	Albert Gayton	(L)	repealer	+461	+864	14.2	20.7

Source: *Canadian Parliamentary Guide, 1883*, pp. 276-7; *Journals and Proceedings of the House of Assembly of the Province of Nova Scotia, 1887*, Appendix 12, pp. 1-21.

a successful Yarmouth shipping business, William Roche, a Halifax coal merchant and steamship agent, Leander Rand, a King's County farmer engaged in the export of potatoes and other vegetables to the United States, and merchants Albert Gayton of Yarmouth and William Power of Halifax. In the more industrialized counties, on the other hand, Liberal and Conservative candidates were drawn primarily from the professional classes. David Hearn, George Murray, Charles Munro, John Bethune, Daniel McNeill, Alexander Campbell, Angus McLennan, Colin Chisholm, and William McKay, were all either doctors or lawyers.[43]

In a somewhat different way the business dealings of repealer Jeffrey McColl provide a clue to the curious election results in Pictou, where two unionists and a repealer won election to the legislature. In 1886 McColl was president of the Pictou Bank, which, during the early 1880s, had assisted in the industrialization of Pictou County by carrying a number of industrial accounts. At the time of Fielding's repeal resolutions in May 1886, however, the bank was on the verge of bankruptcy as a result of the failure in 1884 of its largest customer.[44] It would thus be incorrect to attribute McColl's repeal advocacy and election to the passing of an older commercial order based upon international commerce. More likely McColl's success in Pictou reflected the county's concern about the weakness of its infant industry in a period of extended business depression.

Despite the success of repealers and moderates at the polls, McColl included, it would be a mistake to regard the 1886 election as merely a repeal victory. Local issues and the record of the Fielding government were also important in the campaign. In February, Fielding had announced to the legislature that his government had "faithfully and justly managed the public affairs of the province. Unless something occurs . . . to mar that record, we can go to the country and claim and receive the confidence of those who placed us in the position we occupy".[45] During the campaign Liberal newspapers stressed the legislative accomplishments of the government. Included were amendments to the County Incorporation Act, an electoral bill extending the franchise by some 1,500 voters in Halifax alone, improvements to academic and agricultural education, increased support for road and bridge construction, and a railway policy directed at railway consolidation and the completion of the 18 mile "missing link" between Digby and Annapolis on the Halifax-Yarmouth railway line. Moreover, because the railway policy of the Fielding government had a

43 Biographical and occupational data was compiled from C.B. Fergusson, *A Directory of the Members of the Legislative Assembly of Nova Scotia, 1758-1958* (Halifax, 1958); *The Canadian Parliamentary Guide*, 1883, 1889; and the Vertical MSS files of the Public Archives of Nova Scotia.

44 James Frost, "Principles of Interest. The Bank of Nova Scotia and the Industrialization of the Maritimes 1880-1910" (MA thesis, Queen's University, 1978), pp. 63-5.

45 Nova Scotia, *Debates*, 26 February 1886, p. 15.

southwestward orientation, and because Fielding left railway development in the north and northeast to the Federal government, differences between the southern and northern parts of the province, evident in the case of repeal, were further magnified.[46]

Notwithstanding the divisions in the Liberal party over the secession question, some observers were concerned that Fielding's victory would make a vigorous repeal agitation in 1887 more likely. "Possibly in some counties our opponents were not serious in this", wrote the Tory John F. Stairs. "Success will, I am afraid, make their party a united one . . . . Many of them are talking as strongly now as the most rabid Irishman against Ireland's union with England".[47] Rather than uniting the party, however, the Liberal sweep increased the anxiety of Liberal unionists about Fielding's future course of action and threatened to divide the party even further. Fearing that Fielding and Alfred G. Jones of Halifax were planning to make repeal the issue of the upcoming federal campaign, the New Glasgow shipbuilder, industrialist, and erstwhile anti-Confederate J. W. Carmichael warned Edward Blake that "the overwhelming victory fairly dazed the Gov't. and our friends in Halifax. They are miscalculating the real value of the repeal movement".[48] In Carmichael's opinion the end of repeal should be better terms rather than secession. Carmichael had little faith that Nova Scotians wanted independence, since many of the same people who voted for repeal in 1867 voted in support of the National Policy in 1882. The province, Carmichael believed, had long since made its choice to remain in Confederation. If Fielding pushed secession, "with Halifax and certain Western Counties determinedly Repeal, Cumberland, Colchester and the whole of Cape Breton determinedly opposed", he would succeed only in "wrecking the party, but assuredly not in obtaining Repeal".[49]

The problem, of course, was one of interpreting the results of the June election. Did they represent a victory for repeal, or simply a mandate for negotiating better terms? In Pictou, the Conservative *Colonial Standard* noted that the Liberals were divided on the secession question. "Two, at least, of their supporters from Cape Breton, one from Hants, one from Cumberland, and one from Digby", it observed, "are against repeal".[50] Charles Hibbert Tupper agreed:

> That the election resulted in a victory for Mr. Fielding is true. It was, however, the result of a party fight, a party united solely by party ties, but

46 See *Acadian Recorder,* 14 May 1886; *Eastern Chronicle,* 27 May 1886; *The Advance* (Liverpool), 2 June 1886.
47 Stairs to Macdonald, 17 June 1886, Macdonald Papers, vol. 117, Public Archives of Canada.
48 Carmichael to Blake, 6 July 1886, Carmichael Papers, vol. 394, no. 411, PANS.
49 Carmichael to Blake, 6 July 1886, *ibid.,* vol. 394, no. 412.
50 *Colonial Standard,* 17 June 1886.

divided on this question of repeal. Many of Mr. Fielding's supporters refused to commit themselves upon this question, while another pronounced himself as strongly opposed to a repeal of the union of 1867.[51]

Jeffrey McColl, the successful repeal candidate in Pictou County, appreciated the potential hazards in proceeding towards independence with a divided party. In an open letter to his constituents in the fall of 1886 McColl pointed out that the Liberals had not won simply because of repeal, but because of a host of "side issues". Although McColl reiterated his personal support for repeal, he did not want it imposed if a sizeable minority in the province wished to remain within Confederation. The only real method of determining the extent of secessionist sentiment was to hold a referendum on the issue. If two-thirds of those voting wished to secede, then and only then should the government proceed towards independence.[52]

But Fielding ignored this counsel of caution and between the elections of 1886 and 1887 vigorously promoted an independent Maritime Union apart from Canada. Although Maritime Union had been included in Fielding's repeal resolutions in the legislature, it had not been an important issue in the campaign. It made obvious sense to determine whether Nova Scotia wanted repeal before proceeding towards Maritime Union. At the same time Fielding recognized that the Mother Country would be unlikely to grant independence to Nova Scotia alone: "I believe that if the Maritime Provinces would take united action to that end, we could get out of the Union. But I hardly expect that any one province will be allowed to go".[53] Arguing that the election of 1886 revealed a desire to co-operate with "New Brunswick and Prince Edward Island in a movement for separation from Canada and the formation of a Union of the Maritime Provinces",[54] Fielding travelled to Charlottetown in July to confer with L.H. Davies and other influential figures in Prince Edward Island political circles. In addition, he corresponded with New Brunswick Premier A.G. Blair, Liberal Association President George McLeod of Saint John, and a number of New Brunswick assemblymen including John V. Ellis and C.W. Weldon of Saint John, and M.C. Atkinson of Bristol.[55] In a letter to James A. Fraser in August 1886, Fielding outlined the attitude of the other provinces, and his strategy for promoting Maritime Union:

51 C.H. Tupper to Editor, London *Standard*, 22 November 1886, C.H. Tupper Papers, PANS (microfilm).

52 Jeffrey McColl, "To the Electors of the County of Pictou, 1886", Vertical MSS File, PANS.

53 Fielding to J.V. Ellis, 6 March 1887, Fielding Papers, no. 218, PANS.

54 Fielding to James H. Crockett, E.H. Allen, and H.S. Bridges, 16 June 1886, Fielding Papers, PANS.

55 Fielding to Hon. A.G. Blair, 19 June 1886, Fielding Papers, PANS.

I know that if official action was taken now in the direction of Maritime Union we could get no aid from the Governments of New Brunswick and Prince Edward Island. The island Government is *Tory,* the New Brunswick Government is *timid.* If we make application to the Tory Government of England for release of Nova Scotia we shall as the case now stands almost certainly receive a flat refusal. I prefer to work up the movement among the public men and among the people too in New Brunswick and Prince Edward Island and will go again and am contemplating a trip to New Brunswick in the same way. If we can get some public indication of sympathy from those Provinces we can secure the active cooperation of some parties in our own province who up to this time have fought shy of repeal.[56]

From the other provinces Fielding asked for neutrality. "The repeal issue", he explained to Oliver Mowat, "goes beyond the question of better terms. . . [to] a separation which will be better for all concerned".[57] It was Fielding's hope that Ontario would not contemplate the prevention of secession by force of arms.

Given the opposition to repeal within Nova Scotia and the reluctance of the other Maritime governments to take up this issue, the Federal election of 1887 in Nova Scotia assumed a decisive importance, if independence were to be had. "If we could elect 21 men to stay away from Ottawa", Fielding wrote to Fraser, "it would be the most effective move".[58] Unfortunately for Fielding the only four repeal candidates contesting the elections of 1887 were J.A. Kirk of Guysborough, J.D. Eisenhauer of Lunenburg, H.H. Fuller of Halifax, and John Lovitt of Yarmouth. Fielding did what he could to improve matters. "I wish you or somebody else would come out squarely on the repeal issue", Fielding wrote to George Murray. "I am persuaded that if favorably presented that issue would prove a winning one in any part of C.B.".[59] In the long run, however, he was fighting a losing battle. In addition to Murray, the unionist ranks included William Pipes in Cumberland, J.D. McLeod in Pictou, Adam Bell and Samuel McDonnell in Inverness, W.B. Vail in Digby, Michael Slattery in Cape Breton, Edward Flynn in Richmond, and William F. McCurdy in Victoria. Other candidates like W.H. Ray from Annapolis, Jason Mack from Queen's, Thomas Robertson from Shelburne, William Curry from Hants, F.W. Borden from King's, Angus McGillivray from Antigonish, Silas McLellan from Colchester, and Alfred Jones from Halifax stopped short of repudiating repeal but gave it little support.[60]

56 Fielding to James A. Fraser, 25 August 1886, Fielding Papers, nos. 505-7, PANS.

57 Fielding to Oliver Mowat, 7 July 1886, Fielding Papers, PANS.

58 Fielding to James A. Fraser, 8 July 1886, Fielding Papers, nos. 422-3, PANS; and Fielding to J.A. Smith, 12 August 1886, Fielding Papers, no. 476, PANS.

59 Fielding to George H. Murray, 4 December 1886, Fielding Papers, nos. 728-9, PANS.

60 The *Morning Herald* noted on 15 February 1886 that "in Cape Breton there are no less than five

One reason for the limited support for secession in 1887 was the obvious incompatibility of repeal and the national platform of the Liberal party. It seemed inconsistent for Liberal candidates to demand secession in one breath and to support Edward Blake and the national party in the next. Liberal candidates now emphasized reciprocity rather than repeal. "If there is any one thing that the people of the province are more in earnest about than another following the defeat of the present administration", Alfred Jones remarked, "it is to have free commercial intercourse with the people of the United States, who are our natural customers".[61] Even the Halifax *Morning Chronicle* took a more moderate position on repeal than it had in 1886. "It is only by repeal, or by a change of government at Ottawa", the *Chronicle* announced on 10 February, "that reciprocity may be obtained".[62] Other Liberal newspapers, among them the *Acadian Recorder,* the Liverpool *Advance,* and the *Eastern Chronicle,* supported reciprocity and avoided repeal. The one exception was the Yarmouth *Herald* which still considered repeal essential: "One remedy alone remains. The electorate must demand a change of Government, a return to economy and lower taxation, and at the earliest moment a complete severance of the bonds of Union".[63]

Another explanation for repeal's limited popularity in 1887 was the obvious opposition to Nova Scotian separatism in the Mother Country. This became a particularly important question with the publication of an apparently unfavorable comment about repeal in a letter from William Ewart Gladstone to Charles Hibbert Tupper. In response to Tupper's assurance that Nova Scotian Liberals were divided on the repeal question, Gladstone expressed his pleasure with "the very conclusive evidence which you have given. . . as to the solidarity of the. . . [Union], which has done so much for British North America and for the solidarity and harmony of the Empire".[64] Coming from an influential supporter of Irish Home Rule, Gladstone's remarks suggested that there would be vigorous Imperial opposition to any attempt to dismantle Confederation. Later Gladstone argued that his remarks were taken out of context, but his corrective, coming as it did only one week before the 1887 federal election, did not compensate for the damage already done to the repeal campaign.[65]

unionists in the field. In the peninsula proper Messrs. Pipes, Curry, McLelan, and Vail have not expressed themselves in favor of repeal, while Messrs. McGillivray, McLeod, Ray, Borden, Mack, etc., are known to be using the repeal cry only in secluded districts as a political kite". In King's County, Frederick Borden's campaign manager, W.E. Roscoe, was a repealer, but there is little evidence of repeal in Borden's speeches. Carmen Miller, "The Public Life of Sir Frederick Borden" (MA thesis, Dalhousie University, 1964), pp. 33-5.

61 Speech of Alfred Jones at Halifax, 18 January 1887, quoted in *Morning Chronicle,* 20 January 1887.

62 *Ibid.,* 10 February 1887.

63 *The Herald* (Yarmouth), 16 February 1887.

64 Gladstone to C.H. Tupper, 31 December 1886, Charles H. Tupper Papers, PANS (microfilm).

65 Gladstone to William Annand, 15 February 1887, Fielding Papers, PANS.

Throughout the campaign the Conservatives ridiculed the vacillating attitude of the Liberals toward repeal. If repeal were really an issue, the Halifax *Morning Herald* asked, why were most Liberals supporting Blake? "Whatever his other weaknesses. . . [Blake] is not yet a secessionist".[66] The Antigonish *Casket* preached from a similar text, pointing out that if the Liberals "are earnest Repealers they are not supporters of Blake; if they are supporters of Blake, they are not earnest Repealers".[67] Furthermore, if the Liberals themselves were divided on the issue of repeal, was a successful separation of Nova Scotia from Canada likely? "To get . . . [repeal] our people must be unanimous", said Conservative candidate John F. Stairs. "We are not only not unanimous, but the party that have taken up the cry is itself divided upon this question".[68]

The difficulties confronting the Liberal party were reflected in the election results of 1887. The Liberals captured but 7 of the 21 seats in the province, a figure unchanged from the previous federal election of 1882. Predictably, Liberal strength was concentrated along the province's eastern and southern shores, while the Conservatives controlled the industrializing northern districts and towns along the railroad line and through the Annapolis Valley. The Conservatives swept Cape Breton Island with the exception of Richmond, took both seats in Pictou, and won in Annapolis, Antigonish, Colchester, Cumberland, Digby and Hants. The largest Conservative majorities were run up in Colchester, Cumberland, and Pictou. A.W. McLelan, Finance Minister in Macdonald's government, defeated Silas McLellan by 627 votes in Colchester; in Cumberland Sir Charles Tupper led William Pipes by 668 votes; and in Pictou Charles Hibbert Tupper and John MacDougall defeated J.D. McLeod and Adam Bell by 6747 to 5662 votes. For the Liberals, three repealers, Lovitt in Yarmouth, Kirk in Guysborough and Eisenhauer in Lunenburg, won comfortable victories, with majorities of 683, 352 and 122 votes respectively. In addition, Liberal candidates won in Shelburne, Halifax, and King's counties, where repeal had not been a prominent issue and in Richmond where the candidate was a unionist.

The results of the election of 1887 constituted a vote of confidence in Confederation and a repudiation of repeal. For Fielding, who had been predicting 16 to 19 Liberal seats, the results were particularly disappointing.[69] With only three repealers winning election, he realized that repeal was all but dead. When the provincial legislature opened in March, Fielding found repeal a source of embarrassment. While most Liberals seemed inclined to accept J.W. Longley's

---

66 *Morning Herald,* 12 February 1887.

67 *The Casket* (Antigonish), 10 February 1887.

68 Speech of John F. Stairs at Dartmouth Reform Club Hall, 1 February 1887, quoted in *Morning Herald,* 3 February 1887.

69 Fielding to Blake, 5 October 1886, Fielding Papers, nos. 582-7, PANS.

advice to forget repeal and return to "honest government",[70] there was a diehard repeal faction in the provincial House, including James Fraser, Otto Weeks, William McCoy, William Roche and Jeffrey McColl. Fielding was boxed. To repudiate secession would anger the sincere repealers within the party; to support it would alienate the unionists. The Premier, the Halifax *Morning Herald* pointed out, was damned if he supported repeal, and damned if he rejected it.[71]

On 21 April 1887 Fielding rose in the House to recount his version of repeal's collapse and to urge its suspension. He observed that "in several counties in June last the repeal issue, though put to some extent before the people was not made the paramount issue. . . . The government was sustained. . .on the general record of their four years management of the affairs of the country". There were a few counties in 1886 where repeal was significant, but in 1887 even fewer candidates than before were ready to call for separation. "The policy was not followed throughout the whole province", Fielding continued, "and you cannot carry on a repeal movement without insisting on such a policy".[72] Fielding then introduced a resolution which suspended the repeal agitation indefinitely. After considerable debate the resolution passed the House on April 27. The Halifax *Morning Herald* had the last word: "At midnight on the 27th of April, A.D. 1887, the legislature of Nova Scotia consigned the repeal jackass to the silent tomb. . . . Succeeded he will doubtless be by some other donkey with a different name, mayhap 'Commerical Union'."[73]

With the suspension of the repeal campaign, Fielding and the Liberals followed the more orthodox policy of encouraging reciprocity with the United States, expanding the coal industry through the attraction of capital investment from outside the region, and involving the province in a broad movement for provincial rights. For those regions most closely tied to the old commercial economy, reciprocity or Commercial Union seemed an acceptable alternative to repeal. At the same time, the expansion of the coal industry promised to foster industrial development and to augment provincial revenues through increased royalty payments. And finally, the question of better terms could be pursued in the context of provincial rights rather than repeal. In October 1887, Fielding, Longley and Angus McGillivray represented the province at the Inter-provincial Conference at Quebec, to discuss such matters as disallowance, Senate reform, provincial boundaries, the protection of public works, and provincial finances. Although the recommendations of the Quebec Conference in the area of financial terms were subsequently ignored by the Federal Govern-

---

70 J.W. Longley to Edward Blake, 25 February 1887, Blake Papers, Provincial Archives of Ontario.

71 *Morning Herald,* 3 March 1887.

72 Nova Scotia, *Debates,* 21 April 1887, pp. 252-3.

73 *Morning Herald,* 29 April 1887.

ment, the significance of the Conference should not be overlooked. It facilitated the transformation of a separatist movement into a more orthodox movement for provincial rights.[74]

In retrospect, Fielding's campaign for repeal seems to have been related to the erosion of a traditional economy based upon the international carrying trade. The depression of the 1870s and 1880s prompted those most affected by the passing of the older order to suggest a series of remedies, including better terms, Maritime Union, reciprocity, and repeal. In each case the objective was the same: restoration of a mythical pre-Confederation "Golden Age". Secession was simply the most dramatic expression of this desire to turn the clock back. But repeal alone was no real solution. Lacking a rational explanation for Nova Scotia's disabilities and devoid of a positive program for future economic development, the repealers were offering little more than the faint hope that what was now past might somehow be recovered. At the same time, as J. W. Carmichael suggested and the election of 1887 confirmed, many Nova Scotians were coming to accommodate themselves to the new industrial order. Under the umbrella of the protective tariff new manufacturing opportunities were opening in the textile industry, in coal and steel, in rope and cordage manufacture, in the confectionary industry, and in sugar refining.[75] For those who saw the National Policy as an appropriate and progressive development strategy for the region, repeal seemed reactionary and destructive by comparison. Only later would they realize that the industrial capitalist hope, symbolized in the "National Policy" of John A. Macdonald, would create as many problems as it solved.

74 For a fuller treatment of the alteration of Liberal party tactics after the suspension of repeal, see Howell, "Repeal, Reciprocity, and Commercial Union in Nova Scotian Politics", ch. IV.

75 T.W. Acheson, "The National Policy and the Industrialization of the Maritimes, 1880-1910", *Acadiensis*, I (Spring 1972), pp. 3-28.

JOHN G. REID

Reprinted from Vol. XII, No. 2
(Sprng 1983)

The Education of Women at Mount Allison, 1854-1914

"IT WOULD BE SUPERFLUOUS to advocate what must now be considered a settled principle: that the introduction of the abstruser sciences into a course of study for females, is of the highest utility". This confident assertion of the desirability of a rigorous academic education for female students was contained in the *Mount Allison Academic Gazette* of December 1855, in an editorial almost certainly written by Mary Electa Adams, chief preceptress of the ladies' academy that had opened at Mount Allison in the previous year. Attacking "the ordinary modes of female education" as tending to produce "that impatience of thought, that tendency to the desultory and the superficial, which are proverbial failings of young ladies", the editorial promised that Mount Allison would offer a systematic programme of study aimed at producing women of intellectual vigour.[1] Logical as that goal might be, its successful accomplishment was no simple matter in a society where women were commonly expected to live their lives according to closely circumscribed roles as daughters, wives, and mothers.

Just how much knowledge of "the abstruser sciences" was it proper for a woman to have in order to enrich the life of her family? The *Academic Gazette* admitted to no doubts on this score. "The ornamental branches", it declared, "without being depreciated or displaced, will always be pursued in subserviency to the solid studies"; even in the home, the influence exerted by Mount Allison women, so the argument went, would be all the greater for being characterized by intellectual strength.[2] This was a debatable point in British North America in the 1850s, however, and the debate became more complex during the later decades of the century as Canadian women began in increasing numbers to undertake professional careers. The development of the ladies' academy (renamed "ladies' college" in 1886) was profoundly influenced by that debate. By 1914 the ladies' college had come to be more dominated by the accomplishments of the drawing-room than would have been approved by Mary Electa Adams. Yet the strong academic bent with which the institution began had not been lost. It had resulted not only in the creation of professional schools of music, fine arts, and home economics, but also in important innovations at the adjoining Mount Allison University: the first woman to receive a bachelor's degree at any institution in the British Empire was a Mount Allison graduate of 1875, who received the degree of Bachelor of Science and English Literature, and she was followed seven years later by the first woman to receive a Bachelor of

1 *Mount Allison Academic Gazette* (December 1855), pp. 5-6.
2 *Ibid.*, p. 6.

Arts degree in Canada. Although the academic emphasis at the ladies' college was in serious jeopardy by 1914, and although profound ambiguities remained as to the ultimate goals of women's education, Mount Allison over the previous 60 years had been responsible for a significant widening of the educational opportunities open to women in Canada's Maritime Provinces.

The opening of educational opportunities to the young of the three Maritime Provinces had been a paramount objective at Mount Allison since the first Wesleyan Academy for boys in Sackville, New Brunswick, had opened in 1843. Charles Frederick Allison, the Sackville merchant whose financial contributions had made the foundation of the institution possible, had insisted that the school be built in Sackville, rather than in a larger urban centre such as Saint John, in order that it should be easily accessible to students from throughout the Maritime region.[3] Sackville, situated just a few miles from the border between New Brunswick and Nova Scotia and within easy reach of the crossing-points from Prince Edward Island, was obviously an ideal choice to fulfill this requirement. Allison also envisaged the academy as an open institution in other respects. Although it should be, he wrote in 1839, under the control of the Wesleyan Methodist denomination, he did not seek to restrict attendance to Methodists, and other denominations were represented among the students from the beginning. Furthermore, as the newly-appointed principal of the academy, Humphrey Pickard, made clear in his speech at the official opening of the institution in June 1843, the intention was "to extend the benefits of the Institution as widely as possible" in a social sense. Although this did not mean that Mount Allison's clientele, any more than that of other academic educational institutions of the period, would be fully representative of the social classes of the region, Pickard declared that government grants from the provinces of New Brunswick and Nova Scotia would be used to keep tuition fees as low as possible.[4] The age range of the students was also wide, as New Brunswick school inspector James Brown remarked when he visited Sackville in October 1844. Of the 84 students in attendance, Brown reported, "six are under 10 years

---

3   C.F. Allison to W. Temple, 4 June 1839, Wesleyan Methodist Missionary Society Archives [WMMSA], Box 101, file 11b, School of Oriental and African Studies, University of London; letter of Enoch Wood to *The Wesleyan* (Halifax), 19 May 1882.

4   "An Inaugural Address, Delivered at the Opening of the Wesleyan Academy, Mount Allison, Sackville, New Brunswick, by the Principal, the Rev. H. Pickard, A.M.", *British North American Wesleyan-Methodist Magazine* (August 1843), p. 289. At £25 per annum for the primary department (including both residential and tuition fees) and up to £30 for the higher departments, the fees were approximately equivalent to the total year's wages, over and above board and lodging, of the average New Brunswick agricultural labourer of the time; though it was also possible to attend a single term for £8/15/-, or (as in the case of the Bathurst carpenter James Dawson during the mid-1840s) to pay fees in the form of work. Wesleyan Academy, *Catalogues*, 1843-7; Richard Shepherd to C.F. Allison, 5 October 1843, C.F. Allison Papers, 7946/3, Mount Allison University Archives [MAA]; Graeme Wynn, *Timber Colony: A Historical Geography of Early Nineteenth Century New Brunswick* (Toronto, 1981), pp. 80-2.

of age, eleven are over 10 and under 12, thirteen over 12 and under 14, twenty-four over 14 and under 16, fifteen over 16 and under 18, seven over 18 and under 20, and eight 20 years old and upwards".[5] As such an age range dictated, the curriculum was varied: it ranged from a primary course, consisting of basic instruction in areas such as English grammar and arithmetic, to a "collegiate" course introduced in 1846. The collegiate course could, if the student wished, lead to the examinations for the external degree of Bachelor of Arts at King's College, in the provincial capital of Fredericton, although most instruction at the academy continued to be conducted at the non-degree level. Between the primary and the collegiate courses was an "intermediate" course designed to be completed in two years (as opposed to the four years of the collegiate course) and was composed chiefly of non-classical subjects.[6]

The Wesleyan Academy, therefore, strove to make its educational services widely available to the boys and young men of the Maritime Provinces. Yet the institution — despite Inspector Brown's statement in 1844 that it was "perhaps, the very best Educational Establishment in the Province" —[7] could hardly claim to be serving its constituency without restriction as long as attendance was confined to male students. In the summer of 1847 a joint meeting of the Methodist districts of New Brunswick and Nova Scotia passed a resolution in favour of "the necessity and desirableness of establishing an Institution under the controal [sic] of our Church similar to that we have in the case of the Sackville Academy for the religious education of females". The resolution did not specify that the proposed academy for girls and young women would be located in Sackville, but it did appoint Humphrey Pickard in his capacity as principal to investigate the feasibility of the plan. In the following year, the New Brunswick district heard and accepted a proposal by "the Wesleyans and their friends, in Sackville and its Neighbourhood" to provide a sum of £2,000 — half of which was to be given by Charles Allison — and a lot of land for the new institution.[8]

The way towards the opening of the academy for female students was not smooth. "Whether it will be judged prudent," wrote Pickard to a correspondent in December 1848, "to proceed next spring with the Building for the Academy for Females is now, owing to the business state of the Country, somewhat doubtful".[9] It was not until late 1851 that fund-raising efforts were resumed; in

5 Report of James Brown, 26 November 1844, *New Brunswick Assembly Journal*, 1845, Appendix, p.ciii.

6 Wesleyan Academy, *Catalogue*, 1846, 1852. The eventual structure of the curriculum became clear in 1851, when the intermediate course was formed out of the elements of previous "classical" and "literary and scientific" courses.

7 Report of James Brown, 26 November 1844, *New Brunswick Assembly Journal*, 1845, Appendix, p.civ.

8 Minutes of New Brunswick District, United Church of Canada, 3 July 1847, pp. 425-6, 18 May 1848, p. 463, United Church of Canada, Maritime Conference Archives.

9 Pickard to Robert Alder, 29 December 1848, WMMSA, Box 32, file 229. On the depression of

September 1852, Pickard announced that the plans would proceed, and by early 1853 work had begun on a building to be constructed under the personal supervision of Allison.[10] Even with the completion of what the *Mount Allison Academic Gazette* described as a "commodious and beautiful edifice" — a three-storey wooden building located near the existing male academy — further delays were threatened when the scheduled opening date in August 1854 coincided with a major outbreak of cholera in Saint John. Despite the postponement of the formal opening ceremony, the new institution began its first term on 17 August 1854 with "an unexpectedly large company" of between 80 and 90 students. A week later, the building had reached its planned capacity of 70 boarders, and 29 day-scholars were also enrolled. In the first term, enrolment would reach 118, surpassing by six that of the male academy. It was, as Pickard remarked, "an auspicious beginning of the new epoch".[11]

That this was indeed a new epoch at Mount Allison could hardly be questioned. The presence of such a large number of female students and a staff of seven women teachers altered permanently the hitherto male-dominated environment of the institution. This was a cause of some concern. In June 1854 readers of the *Academic Gazette* were assured that "the Family and Class organizations [of the female branch] will be entirely distinct from those of the other Academy, and the Students of the different branches will not be allowed to associate or even meet, either in public or in private, except in presence of some of the officers of the Institution".[12] The daily walks allowed to the students were carefully planned so as to avoid chance meetings, and even at church separate seating was provided for male and female students. The very need for such regulations showed the magnitude of the change that had taken place. The opening of the female branch also brought about other changes in the academy's clientele. An early student recalled that "many of the village girls attended the seminary as day pupils myself among the number although quite young in years".[13] Analysis of the composition of the student body in the first three years of the female academy confirms her recollection, for there was a heavy concentration of pupils from the local area. In the second year, more than one-third of the students came from Sackville, and almost half were from the county of

1848-51, see W.S. MacNutt, *The Atlantic Provinces: The Emergence of Colonial Society, 1712-1857* (Toronto, 1965), pp. 234-7; MacNutt, *New Brunswick: A History, 1784-1867* (Toronto, 1963), pp. 315-25.

10 *The Wesleyan*, 14 February 1852; *The Provincial Wesleyan* (Halifax), 9 September 1852, 24 March 1853; see also Raymond Clare Archibald, *Historical Notes on the Education of Women at Mount Allison, 1854-1954* (Sackville, N.B., 1954), p. 1.

11 *Mount Allison Academic Gazette* (December 1853), p. 7; *ibid.*, (December 1854), pp. 2-4; *The Provincial Wesleyan*, 10 August 1854. See also Geoffrey Bilson, "The Cholera Epidemic in Saint John, N.B., 1854", *Acadiensis*, IV, 1 (Autumn 1974), pp. 85-99.

12 *Mount Allison Academic Gazette* (June 1854), p. 7.

13 Mrs. C. Christie to R.C. Archibald, 22 April 1904, Archibald Papers, 5501/13/9, p. 40, MAA.

Westmorland in which Sackville was located. As a result, when the total student body from both branches is examined, the proportions of local students were higher than at any time previous to the opening of the female branch, except for the opening year of 1843. Nor, in the case of the female academy, was this a passing trend. In 1856-57, fully 35 per cent of the female students came from Sackville; the proportion among the male students was only 16 per cent, and the combined proportion was 24.4 per cent.[14]

The student population of the female academy was also notable for the relatively low proportion of those who came from urban areas, and this had the effect of strengthening a trend already apparent in the male academy. From the beginning the academy had professed to serve the overall population of the Maritime region, and on this basis had been awarded legislative grants. That population was overwhelmingly rural; and yet substantial proportions of the students had come from major cities of the region and especially from Saint John. In 1852, 23.4 per cent came from Saint John, with a further 9.4 per cent each from Halifax and Charlottetown.[15] This, however, was the peak year of urban attendance, and in the male academy in 1856-57 these cities supplied only 19.1 per cent of the students. The year 1852 had been exceptional as a year when the major population centres of the region were experiencing a rapid recovery from the economic depression of 1848-51, but the figures also reflected the growth of alternative educational opportunities in urban areas, and notably the operation of Methodist academic day schools in Halifax and Saint John. The female academy, on the other hand, never had such a high percentage of students from the major cities, and thus its opening accentuated the shift away from urban recruitment. In 1856-57, the proportion of urban students was 18.4 per cent, and the combined proportion for the male and female branches was 18.8 per cent.[16] The composition of the student body was coming more nearly to resemble that of the population it professed to serve, though with a confirmed bias towards those who originated from Sackville or nearby.

The opening of the female branch clearly had a significant effect upon Mount Allison. Did it also affect in an important way the education of women in the region? Certainly, the institution could not claim total originality. Boarding schools for girls were by no means rare either in Great Britain or in the United States. Even college education had been opened to women at Oberlin College in Ohio by 1837 and at other institutions soon afterwards.[17] In British North

14 *Mount Allison Academic Gazette*, 1854-57. Comparative data for the male academy before 1854 are available in the *Catalogues* of Wesleyan Academy, 1843-53.

15 Wesleyan Academy, *Catalogue*, 1853.

16 See *Mount Allison Academic Gazette*, 1854-57; also Judith Fingard, "Attitudes Towards the Education of the Poor in Colonial Halifax", *Acadiensis*, II, 2 (Spring 1973), p. 23; *New Brunswick Assembly Journal*, 1855, pp. 106, 337.

17 Frederick Rudolph, *The American College and University: A History* (New York, 1968), pp.

America, initiatives in Methodist women's education had been located chiefly in Canada West, the co-educational Upper Canada Academy opened at Cobourg in 1836 being a major example. In the Maritimes, also in 1836, the Baptist denomination had taken the lead by opening its Fredericton seminary to both male and female students. That the Baptists and Methodists should have led in women's education was not surprising, since both denominations had strong traditions of earnest evangelical zeal that suggested the value of a disciplined education as an antidote to idleness or frivolity in either women or men. Yet the Cobourg and Fredericton experiments were short-lived. The "female department" of the Upper Canada Academy was discontinued in 1842 with the institution's acquisition of college status, smaller schools in Cobourg henceforth taking up the work of women's education, while the Fredericton seminary also allowed its female department to lapse in 1843 in the face of competition from private schools in the city.[18] Private girls' schools in the Maritimes had existed since the late 18th century, and their number grew rapidly during the earlier decades of the 19th. In 1839, for example, a school in Halifax was advertised by "the Misses Tropolet", who offered instruction "in English Reading, Writing and Arithmetic, Ancient and Modern History, Geography, Plain Needle Work, and Fancy Work, Music and Drawing, and the Use of Globes". Eleven years later, a girls' school was opened much closer to Mount Allison, when Mrs. C.E. Ratchford advertised a "Female Seminary" in Amherst.[19] The scale of the female branch of the Sackville academy, however,

311-2. The admission of women to college education at Oberlin and other midwestern coeducational institutions, however, did not imply an equal concern for the intellectual development of male and female students. See Jill K. Conway, "Perspectives on the History of Women's Education in the United States", *History of Education Quarterly*, 14 (1974), pp. 6-7, and Sheila M. Rothman, *Woman's Proper Place: A History of Changing Ideals and Practices, 1870 to the Present* (New York, 1978), p. 27.

18 George Edward Levy, *The Baptists of the Maritime Provinces, 1753-1946* (Saint John, N.B., 1946), pp. 119-22; Edward Manning Saunders, *History of the Baptists of the Maritime Provinces* (Halifax, 1902), p. 234; Allison A. Trites, "The New Brunswick Baptist Seminary, 1833-1895", in Barry M. Moody, ed., *Repent and Believe: The Baptist Experience in Maritime Canada* (Hantsport, N.S., 1980), pp. 106-9. The female department of the Fredericton seminary would be reopened in 1857. Also in the late 1850s, the private girls' schools which would be the forerunners of the Acadia Seminary — the chief rival of the Mount Allison ladies' academy in the later years of the 19th century — were established in Wolfville. See *Memorials of Acadia College and Horton Academy for the Half-Century 1828-1878* (Montreal, 1881), pp. 107-8; and James Doyle Davison, *Alice of Grand Pré: Alice T. Shaw and her Grand Pré Seminary: Female Education in Nova Scotia and New Brunswick* (Wolfville, N.S., 1981), *passim*. On the Cobourg academy and its successors, see Marion Royce, "Methodism and the Education of Women in Nineteenth Century Ontario", *Atlantis*, 3, No. 2 (Spring 1978), pp. 130-43, and C.B. Sissons, *A History of Victoria University* (Toronto, 1952), pp. 23, 30-1, 47, 76. For discussion of the contribution of evangelical Christianity to women's education and to the feminist movement, see Olive Banks, *Faces of Feminism: A Study of Feminism as a Social Movement* (New York, 1981), pp. 13-27, 39-46.

19 *The Wesleyan*, 12 August 1839, 12 January 1850. Early girls' schools in the Maritimes are discussed in Davison, *Alice of Grand Pré*, pp. 33-42.

and the absence of any comparable denominational institution, made it at the time of its founding the major school for girls in the region. In June 1854 the *Mount Allison Academic Gazette* proclaimed that the female academy was "designed to be in every respect, in proportion to its extent, equal to any public Institution devoted to the advancement of Female Education on this continent".[20]

The nature of the education offered to female students at Mount Allison was profoundly influenced by the first chief preceptress. This office was the highest in the school held by a woman and carried essentially the duties of a principal, although subject to the nominal authority of Humphrey Pickard as principal of the two branches of the academy. Mary Electa Adams was a native of Lower Canada who had grown up in Upper Canada and had studied there and in the United States. She had finished her education at the Cobourg Ladies' Seminary, one of the successor institutions of the Upper Canada Academy. Subsequently, Adams had been Lady Principal of the Picton Academy, again in Canada West, and had spent four years teaching at the Albion Seminary in Michigan. Still only 30 years old when she arrived in Sackville in 1854, she nonetheless brought considerable experience to her position. Although she stayed only three years before family deaths forced her return to Canada, her influence was soon apparent not only in the devotion which she evidently evoked in her pupils, but also in the nature of the academy and particularly in the curriculum offered to female students.[21]

When the trustees of the academy had petitioned the New Brunswick legislature in early 1854 for an operating grant for the female academy — an annual allocation of £300 was voted beginning in 1855 — the proposed curriculum had stressed training in the social graces rather than a rigorous academic programme "In addition to the Elementary Branches of Education", the assembly had been informed, "that of the French and other polite Languages, Music, Drawing, Painting, and other ornamental Branches, will be taught".[22] By June 1854, although parents were assured in the *Academic Gazette* that "the cultivation of refined taste and lady-like manners" would receive due attention, academic content was accorded a new prominence: "The Course of Study in Literature and Science, the principles of Classification, and the general routine of

20 *Mount Allison Academic Gazette* (June 1854), p. 7. The phrasing of this declaration, comparing the Sackville institution with others throughout North America, suggests the intention of attracting students who might otherwise have gone from the Maritimes to the United States to further their education. Certainly, a number of Maritime students attended Mount Holyoke Seminary, in Massachusetts, during the 1850s. See Davison, *Alice of Grand Pré*, pp. 26-31; and, on Mount Holyoke and other seminaries in the United States, Phyllis Stock, *Better Than Rubies: A History of Women's Education* (New York, 1978), pp. 185-6.

21 Elsie Pomeroy, "Mary Electa Adams: A Pioneer Educator", *Ontario History*, 41 (1949), pp. 107-10.

22 *New Brunswick Assembly Journal*, 1854, pp. 93, 223; *ibid.*, 1854-5, pp. 108, 189-90, 261.

the intellectual training will correspond, as nearly as may be, with the plan which is . . . published for the other Branch, and which has been so successfully tried. There will be here as in the other Branch, three departments — the Primary, the Intermediate, and the Collegiate — each with its own appropriate portion of the course of study suitably modified".[23]

The nature of the suitable modifications was revealed when the detailed curriculum was published in the following year. The Primary Department curriculum was similar to that of the equivalent in the male branch, though with the addition of "occasional Oral Instructions in Physiology, Domestic Economy, and Natural History". The intermediate course also resembled its counterpart, though with the omission of Latin and certain subjects such as book-keeping and surveying, and their replacement by classes in map-drawing and mythology. The collegiate course for female students was divided into three years, rather than the four years prescribed in the male branch: the difference lay chiefly in the omission of Greek language and literature, and of two out of six Latin authors; also omitted were political economy and mineralogy. Vocal music, along with English composition, was continued throughout the collegiate course, while instrumental music and fine arts were available to all students at added cost.[24] Thus, the education offered to female students at the academy was characterized by a lesser concentration on classical subjects and the omission of subjects pertaining to careers and social roles considered inappropriate for women. Yet it was equally clear that the courses of study were not exclusively designed to cultivate good taste and the accomplishments of the drawing-room. As the *Academic Gazette* editorial pointed out in December 1855 in the course of its attack on "the ordinary modes of female education", literary and scientific subjects were strongly represented. Mary Electa Adams had ensured that the school began with a curriculum that neglected neither the academic nor the "ornamental" emphasis, but gave pre-eminence to the academic. The practical development of those two emphases, and the balance between them, would depend in the future not only upon her successors but also upon the social and economic development of the region from which the students were primarily drawn.

For some 15 years after the departure of Mary Electa Adams in 1857, the fortunes of the female branch of the Wesleyan Academy were dominated by struggles for survival that were not uncommon among new educational institutions of the era. The optimism generated by the school's successful beginning grew quickly to new heights during the later 1850s, with the arrival of John Allison, a 36-year-old Methodist minister and a cousin of Charles Frederick Allison, who became principal of the newly-renamed "ladies' academy". His wife Martha Louisa Allison became preceptress. Both held A.B. and A.M.

23 *Mount Allison Academic Gazette* (June 1854), p. 7.
24 *Ibid.*, (December 1855), p. 7.

degrees from institutions in New York State (John Allison from Syracuse University, Martha Allison from Genesee College), and Martha Allison became the first woman to hold a professorial position at Mount Allison, with the title of Professor of Natural Sciences, Ancient and Modern Languages, within the ladies' academy.[25] Enrolment continued to grow and when the number rose to 189 students during the 1859-60 year the facilities of the school became, as John Allison commented, "uncomfortably crowded"; the result was the addition of a new wing to the academy building by the end of 1860.[26] Just as quickly, however, prosperity faded. The new addition to the building had been constructed on borrowed money, and a short-lived expansion of the teaching staff put further strain upon the institution's finances. By 1864, the debt had risen to more than $16,000 and the Allisons resigned amid rumours of mismanagement. The ill health of Martha Allison had compounded the situation, and there had also been persistent personal rivalry between John Allison and Humphrey Pickard, principal of the male academy. These problems had affected public confidence in the school, and at a time when development of the public school systems of the provinces was opening alternative educational opportunities for girls. By 1864, enrolment at the ladies' academy had fallen to some 20 resident students and 30 local day students.[27] The result of the crisis was the reappointment of Pickard as principal, with the day-to-day management of the ladies' academy being entrusted to J.R. Inch (hitherto a teacher in the male academy) as vice-principal. Inch became principal in his own right on Pickard's retirement in 1869, and under his direction the prosperity of the institution, and its student enrolment, was gradually rebuilt. By 1871-72, annual attendance had reached 82, of whom 54 were boarders, and there was further modest expansion during the remaining years of the decade. Though enrolment levels were still short of those of the earliest years, survival had been ensured.[28]

25. Leonard Allison Morrison, *The History of the Alison or Allison Family In Europe and America* (Boston, 1893), p. 197; Ladies' Academy, *Catalogue*, 1859.

26 Ladies Academy, *Catalogues*, 1859, 1860; *The Provincial Wesleyan*, 4 April 1860; Minutes of Board of Trustees, 1858-1899, pp. 26-7, MAA; John Allison to Leonard Tilley, 26 December 1860, RG4, RS24/861/re/1, Provincial Archives of New Brunswick [PANB].

27 *New Brunswick Assembly Journal*, 1865, Appendix No. 5, p. 52; Thomas Wood to Mr. and Mrs. Trueman, 8 February 1861, Wood Papers, MC218/8/23, PANB; John Allison to John A. Clark, 11 October 1862, John A. Clark Papers, 7412, MAA; Minutes of Board of Trustees, 1858-1899, pp. 40-5, MAA; *The Mount Allison Academic Gazette* (June 1863), p. 8; David Allison to W.G. Watson, 4 March 1921, David Allison Papers, 0126/1, MAA; Archibald, *Historical Notes*, p. 4. For discussion of developments in public school education, and of the 1864 Nova Scotia Free School Act, see William B. Hamilton, "Society and Schools in Nova Scotia", in J. Donald Wilson, Robert M. Stamp, and Louis-Philippe Audet, eds., *Canadian Education: A History* (Scarborough, Ont., 1970), pp. 99-102; also Hamilton, "Society and Schools in New Brunswick and Prince Edward Island", *ibid.*, pp. 115-7.

28 For enrolment figures, see *Nova Scotia Assembly Journals*, 1871, Appendix 21, p. 40; 1872, Appendix 13, p. u; 1873, Appendix 14, p. 42; 1874, Appendix 15, p. 46; 1875, Appendix 14, p. 52; 1876, Appendix 7, p. 56; 1877, Appendix 5, p. S. See also Archibald, *Historical Notes*, p. 4.

Inevitably, the travails induced by the financial crisis of the early 1860s had their effects upon the teaching process at the ladies' academy, and to some extent restricted the services that the institution was able to offer to its students. John and Martha Allison, shortly after their arrival in 1857, had instituted a revised curriculum, in which the number of courses offered was reduced to two: a "preparatory course", based on elements of the old primary and intermediate course, and a "graduating course for ladies". The graduating course was a three-year programme based upon the old collegiate course but incorporating some changes: students could now study Greek as well as Latin if they wished, but it was also possible to complete the course without any study of classical languages, by substituting French for Latin and German for Greek. Graduates must also have "some knowledge of Music or Drawing". Those who completed the full three years were promised "a beautiful and appropriate diploma". While this new curriculum represented a move away from the structured academic content favoured by Mary Electa Adams, it retained considerable academic demands. From the early 1860s onwards, the graduating diploma carried the title of "Mistress of Liberal Arts".[29] The decline in enrolment, however, severely limited the number of students wishing to take the course. During the three-year period from 1859 to 1861, there were at least 30 graduates; but it took until 1874 for the next 30 to be recorded.[30]

Another initiative of the Allisons that had limited results was an attempt in 1860 to link the ladies' academy directly to the training of teachers for the New Brunswick parish school system, which was expanding under the terms of the 1858 Parish School Act. In late 1860, John Allison informed Leonard Tilley, the provincial secretary, that "we are now educating a few [students] at reduced rates who expect to become teachers". Allison's suggestion that a special government grant be made in recognition of this service was not accepted. Similarly, an earlier attempt to obtain provincial sanction for an arrangement by which academy students could obtain parish school teaching licenses by examination at the provincial training school without actually having to attend classes there had been given the non-committal response, "each case will be dealt with according to its own merits".[31] Academy students could apply for examination

29 Ladies Academy, *Catalogues*, 1857-8, 1859. The Mistress of Liberal Arts Diploma was the highest Mount Allison qualification open to a woman until the opening of college-level degrees to women in 1872. Thereafter, the M.L.A. continued to be awarded, normally to students who chose not to pursue their studies at the more demanding B.A. level.

30 Ladies' College, *Catalogue*, 1909-10. This catalogue was the first to publish a list of graduates dating from the beginning of the graduating course. The list may be incomplete for the earliest years.

31 John Allison to Leonard Tilley, 26 December 1860, RG4, RS24/861/re/1, PANB; Board of Education Minutes, 12 April 1860, RG11, RS113/RED/BE/1/2, PANB. On the instruction offered at the training school in Saint John, which had been open to female students from 1849 onwards, see Katherine F.C. MacNaughton, *The Development of the Theory and Practice of Education in New Brunswick, 1784-1900* (Fredericton, 1947), pp. 139-43.

Table I: Occupations of Graduates of Mount Allison
Ladies' Academy/College 1857-1904

	Teacher (Ladies' Academy/ College)	Private teacher of music or elocution	Teacher/ educator (other)	M.D.	Mission-ary	Nurse	Musi-cian	Gover-ness	Further study	No known formal occupa-tion	Total
1857-60	6		2							17	25
1861-70	2			1	1					37	41
1871-80	1									33	34
1881-90	4	2	1	3	5	1				54	70
1891-1900	1	2	5		1		1			83	93
1901-04	3	8	3		1	3		1	4	26	49

Source: [Raymond C. Archibald], "Our Graduates, 1854-1904", *Allisonia*, II (1904-05), pp. 139-54.

Note: Based upon a survey carried out by R.C. Archibald, teacher of music and mathematics in the ladies' college, in 1903-4, this table includes occupations known to have been followed by graduates at any time during their post-graduation career. The data gathered by Archibald were as complete as he could obtain, chiefly by mail enquiries, but it is possible that there were some (particularly among the earliest graduates) who had undertaken occupations that were not recorded in the survey.

without attendance, as Mary and Alice Gallagher of Sackville successfully did in July 1860, but it would remain a privilege rather than a right; and the large majority of those ladies' academy students who took up teaching after graduation would continue for the time being to do so at the academy itself.[32]

Interest in the "ornamental branches" was at a high level during the late 1850s, with many students studying music and art despite the substantial fees charged for those subjects over and above the regular academic tuition fees. Of the 153 students listed in the 1859 catalogue, 120 were studying instrumental music and 105 vocal music; of all the subjects taught these totals were exceeded only by composition (140) and penmanship (130). Even arithmetic (97), reading (86) and English grammar (78) were well behind. The fine arts enrolments were divided into ten separate classes, but were substantial also, with the highest enrolments — in drawing and in "coloured crayon" — reaching 36, and five others ranging between 21 and 27.[33] Despite the popularity of the "ornamental branches", they were often plagued by financial constraints. The succession of music professors was continuous from 1855 onwards, although few stayed for long. Theodore Martens, for example, who arrived from the Leipzig Conservatory as professor of music in 1869, was the sixth individual to hold the position and himself stayed only three years.[34] Yet if Martens became another music professor who was unwilling for long to put up with limited facilities and low pay, his counterpart in fine arts — the landscape artist John Warren Gray — was even less fortunate. Gray became in 1869 the first professor to be appointed in the field of art. Trained in England and later to have a distinguished career as a practising artist in Montreal, he was nonetheless invited to leave Mount Allison in 1873 on the recommendation of Inch "that he considered it undesirable to continue the services of Mr. Gray as Teacher of Painting, his salary being greater than the profits yielded to the Institution financially".[35] It would be 20 years before Mount Allison again had a professor of art, and in the meantime teaching was carried on by an assistant teacher. Under Inch's careful financial management the "ornamental branches" were expected to pay their own way.

32 Board of Education Minutes, 13 July 1860, RG11, RS113/RED/BE/1/2, PANB; see also Table I. On the increasing entry of women into the teaching profession, see Alison Prentice, "The Feminization of Teaching in British North America and Canada, 1845-1875", in Susan Mann Trofimenkoff and Prentice, eds., *The Neglected Majority: Essays in Canadian Women's History* (Toronto, 1977), pp. 49-65.

33 Ladies' Academy, *Catalogue*, 1859, p. 12. The basic charge for elementary tuition and board at the ladies' academy in 1859 was £9/3/4 per term, or £27/10/- per academic year. Additional fees for music and fine arts ranged up to £2/13/4 per term for instrumental music, and £2 per term for oil painting.

34 See [R.C. Archibald], "An Historical Note: Music at Mt. Allison", *The Argosy* (May 1895), p. 8; also Mount Allison *Catalogue*, 1869-70.

35 Minutes of Board of Trustees, 1858-1899, p. 120, MAA; see also Virgil Hammock, "Art at Mount Allison", *Arts Atlantic*, I, 3 (Summer/Fall 1978), p. 17; and Obituary of John Warren

At the same time as subjects taught for "ornamental" purposes were experiencing these constraints, the academic education of women at Mount Allison was making significant advances, and the balance between the two traditions was once again being altered. In 1862 the degree-granting Mount Allison Wesleyan College had opened on a site adjoining the two academies. Enrolment at the college was small at first and by 1870-71 it stood at only 17 in Arts and seven in Theology.[36] Up to that time, only male students had been admitted to the degree programmes of the college, but on 26 May 1872 a radical change was proposed by Inch to the college board, with the support of the theological professor Charles Stewart. The minutes of the meeting recorded the occasion tersely: "Moved by Prof. Inch seconded by Dr. Stewart that: Ladies having regularly matriculated and completed the course of study prescribed by this board shall be entitled to receive the degrees in the arts and faculties upon the same terms and conditions as are now or may hereafter be imposed upon male students of the college".[37] If there was any opposition to this crucial change, it was not apparent. David Allison, the president of the college, was known to hold rather different views from those of Inch on the matter of women's social role. Several years later, when they shared the platform at the ladies' academy closing exercises of 1880, Inch declared that "years of experience had taught him that young ladies can compete with the sterner sex in either intellectual acuteness or the power of acquisition". Allison's view was that "any woman's best and highest sphere [was in] . . . aiding some good, honest, faithful man in discharging the duties of life". Yet even Allison acknowledged that "any Education that differentiates between the sexes is wrong", and although he believed that relatively few women would ever desire to go to college he did not create barriers for those who did.[38]

It is likely that the decision to admit women was hastened by the financial crisis that arose at Mount Allison in early 1872, when the New Brunswick provincial subsidy was cut off in the wake of the 1871 Common Schools Act. One historian of higher education in the United States has remarked that by increasing enrolment in the late 19th century "coeducation helped to save many one-time men's colleges of the small denominational type from being put out of business".[39] While there was no immediate influx of women students to Mount Allison, the college was certainly widening its constituency by permitting their attendance. Indeed, the decision was often cited in appeals for endowment

Gray, clipping from Saint John *Globe*, 2 March 1921, Archibald Papers, 5501/13/13, p. 100, MAA.

36 See Table II.

37 Minutes of College Board, 1863-1941, pp. 44-5, MAA.

38 *The Chignecto Post and Borderer* (Sackville), 3 June 1880.

39 Rudolph, *The American College and University*, p. 323; see also Rosalind Rosenberg. *Beyond Separate Spheres: Intellectual Roots of Modern Feminism* (New Haven, 1982), pp. 30-1.

funds. Inch declared publicly on 28 May 1872 that in "this liberal policy" Mount Allison now "led all Seminaries in these Provinces"; while the editor of the Saint John *Globe* shortly afterwards praised it as an action "in keeping with the spirit of the times" and called upon wealthy individuals to contribute to the endowment fund "on patriotic grounds".[40] Nevertheless, although the admission of women students undoubtedly had its practical advantages, the origins of the decision taken in 1872 went back much further than the immediate crisis of that year.

The roots of the change lay in two previous decisions. The first was the determination of Mary Electa Adams in 1854 that the new female branch of the Wesleyan Academy should impose rigorous intellectual standards upon its pupils and should emphasize systematic study. This decision established the foundations for the collegiate programme which provided the indisputable evidence that female students were as capable as males. The second was the decision shortly after the opening of the Mount Allison College to allow senior ladies' academy students to attend college classes as part of their own collegiate course. Exactly how and when this was arranged was never recorded, and was not publicized, no doubt to avoid the denunciation of those who believed that male and female students had no business in the same classroom together. Nonetheless, the results obviously impressed the anonymous correspondent who described the Mount Allison examinations of November 1871 in the *Provincial Wesleyan*, and wrote of "one fact [which], in view of the various 'new departures' in modern education, deserves to be noted in respect to the lady students. It is their marked success in the college classes with which they have been associated. This success they have striven to make the rule and they have done it. No comment is needed".[41] Similarly, a *Provincial Wesleyan* editorial pointed out in June 1872 that "we have seen ladies in those college classes years ago maintaining their ground in the most spirited scholastic contests", and the Saint John *Globe* recalled that the custom went back to the very beginning of the college's existence.[42]

The *Provincial Wesleyan* drew the conclusion that the change made in 1872 was "not a new decision", and claimed that if the women students of past years had not taken degrees "it was not owing to any restrictions in the rules of the college".[43] This assertion, designed to allay any lingering opposition to coeducation, was not as ingenuous as it seemed. It was quite true that there was nothing either in the college charter or in the catalogue to say that women could not matriculate and graduate; but neither was there anything to say that they could, and the very action of the college board in 1872 showed that a deliberate

40 *The Provincial Wesleyan*, 5, 12 June 1872.
41 *Ibid.*, 22 November 1871.
42 *Ibid.*, 5, 12 June 1872.
43 *Ibid.*, 5 June 1872.

Figure 1: *Top:* Mount Allison College graduating class, 1875, including Grace Annie Lockhart; *Bottom:* Students and staff in the Mount Allison ladies' academy park, c. 1885 (Mount Allison University Archives).

measure was required in order to remedy the omission. From 1872 onward, the catalogue provided explicitly that students were "admitted irrespective of sex".[44] Mount Allison's action may also have been influenced to some extent by external factors. Less than a year previously, in the summer of 1871, the board of trustees of Wesleyan University in Connecticut had similarly resolved that there was "nothing in the charter to prevent ladies from being admitted to the privileges of the University". In view of the close ties existing between that Methodist institution and Mount Allison it was certain that this precedent would not go unnoticed. There were also concurrent discussions of coeducation at Cornell University — which decided favourably in 1872 — and other United States institutions.[45]

Admission of women to Mount Allison College as regular students, therefore, was a genuine and far-reaching change, although it had antecedents both in the previous arrangements at Mount Allison, and in American precedents which had been known and discussed in the Maritimes. Elsewhere in Canada, and throughout the British Empire, women's struggle to gain access to higher education was more protracted.[46] Thus it was a Mount Allison student, Grace Annie Lockhart, who in 1875 attained the distinction of being the first woman to be awarded a bachelor's degree at any institution in the British Empire. A native of Saint John, Lockhart enrolled in the ladies' academy in 1871 at the age of 16. Most of her courses were in fact taken while she remained a ladies' academy student, and it was only in her final year, after obtaining her M.L.A. diploma in 1874, that she was officially registered as a student of the college. Her graduation on 25 May 1875 with the degree of Bachelor of Science and English Literature — no woman had as yet enrolled in the full Bachelor of Arts programme — passed with little comment. The Halifax *Herald* noted that "this was the first occasion on which the College had conferred a degree on a member of the female sex", while the newly-inaugurated Mount Allison student magazine, the *Argosy*, was only a little bolder in asserting that "Miss Grace A. Lockhart is, we

44 Mount Allison *Catalogue*, 1872.

45 Carl F. Price, *Wesleyan's First Century: With an Account of the Centennial Celebration* (Middletown, Conn., 1932), p. 172; Rudolph, *The American College and University*, pp. 316-23.

46 Girton College, Cambridge, for example, was incorporated in 1874, but its students could not qualify for degrees, despite the strong arguments advanced by the Mistress of the college, Emily Davies. Even London University, well known for its liberal admission policies, had refused to allow women to matriculate, as Davies and her colleague Elizabeth Garrett had found out when they had attempted to gain admission in 1862. In Canada, McGill University came close to admitting women in 1870, but a favourable resolution of the institution's board of governors in that year was not implemented. See Mary Cathcart Borer, *Willingly to School: A History of Women's Education* (London, 1976), pp. 273-6, 288-90; M.C. Bradbrook, *'That Infidel Place': A Short History of Girton College, 1869-1969* (London, 1969), chs. i, ii; Stanley Brice Frost, *McGill University: For the Advancement of Learning, Vol. I, 1801-1895* (Montreal, 1980), pp. 251-6; Margaret Gillett, *We Walked Very Warily: A History of Women at McGill* (Montreal, 1981), pp. 51-8; Stock, *Better Than Rubies*, pp. 179-83.

believe, the first lady in these provinces to receive a college degree".[47] Lockhart herself made little mention of her academic achievement in later years, and it is doubtful whether either she or J.R. Inch was aware at the time that her graduation had been so great an innovation throughout the British Empire. For all that, Inch was proud of the achievement that the ladies' academy had made possible. "While other institutions were halting and hesitating and putting the door ajar", he recalled in 1880, Mount Allison "boldly opened its doors to all irrespective of sex".[48]

The opening of degree programmes to women, and the conferral of the first degree upon a candidate who had carried out most of her studies in the ladies' academy, was an undeniable tribute to the academic standing of that institution. Yet it was a tribute that had unpredictable implications for the future, especially in view of the age range of the students. The ladies' academy had begun as an institution for girls of all ages, and during the earlier years a substantial proportion of the students had been under 15 years of age.[49] After the enrolment crisis of the mid-1860s, however, and increasingly as the public schools continued their expansion, the ladies' academy tended to cater to older pupils. Between 1870 and 1872, the average age reached as high as 19, though by the mid-1870s it dropped to 17. The age-group under 15 had not been abandoned entirely, but a large majority of the students were aged 15 or more.[50] Now that the degree courses of the college were open to women students, there was an obvious possibility that the ladies' academy would soon be left with a dangerously narrow clientele of students, or that it would become in effect a finishing school, offering instruction in the "ornamental" tradition to students who did not aspire to a full college education. When J.R. Inch resigned as principal in 1878 to become president of the college, the finances and the enrolment of the ladies' academy were healthy. Yet the institution had serious questions to face as to its educational mission. Furthermore, it would face competition not only from public schools but also from such direct competitors as the Wesleyan Academy in Charlottetown, and the Acadia Seminary in Wolfville.[51]

---

47 *Morning Herald* (Halifax), 26 May 1875; *The Eurhetorian Argosy* (June 1875), p. 60.

48 *The Chignecto Post and Borderer*, 3 June 1880. On the later career of Grace Annie Lockhart, see "G.A. Lockhart", Biographical Files, MAA.

49 In December 1858, for example, John Allison reported to the government of Nova Scotia that of the 157 pupils in his care, 5 were aged between 8 and 10 years, 20 were between 10 and 12, 45 were between 12 and 15, 50 were between 15 and 18, and 37 over 18: Returns of Mount Allison Wesleyan Academies, December 1858, MG17, Vol. 17, No. 90, Public Archives of Nova Scotia.

50 *Nova Scotia Assembly Journals*, 1871, Appendix 21, p. 40; 1872, Appendix 13, p. u; 1873, Appendix 14, p. 42; 1874, Appendix 15, p. 46; 1875, Appendix 14, p. 52; 1876, Appendix 7, p. 56; 1877, Appendix 5, p. S.

51 On the Acadia Seminary, see *Memorials of Acadia College*, pp. 107-08; enrolment figures for the Wesleyan Academy in Charlottetown are found in *First Annual Report of the Educational Society of the Methodist Church of Canada* (Toronto, 1875), p. 10.

The 1880s proved to be an expansionist decade for the ladies' academy, and for reasons that were linked in part to social and economic changes in the Maritime Provinces. By now, the days of shipbuilding, and of the large merchant fleets which had operated from Maritime ports in the middle decades of the century, were numbered. From 1879, however, with the adoption of the National Policy by the federal government, Maritime industries enjoyed the protection of a large tariff barrier against foreign imports, and benefited too from the favourable freight rate structure of the Intercolonial Railway. The prosperity thus attained by such centres as Moncton and Amherst was not evenly distributed throughout the region, and time would reveal that the industrialization of the 1880s and 1890s was not as securely based as it seemed at first. Yet there were enough prosperous Methodist merchants and industrialists to see Mount Allison through a brief but acute financial crisis in 1881, associated with the termination of grants to denominational institutions by the province of Nova Scotia. Thereafter a growing demand for higher education, along with the ability of more families than ever before to afford to educate their children, launched the college on a period of expansion that was symbolized by the adoption of the title "university" in 1886.[52] The ladies' academy also shared in this growth: in 1886 the title of the institution was changed to "ladies' college", to complement the university's change of name, and throughout the decade enrolment grew: the student attendance of 174 in 1890-91 was more than double that of ten years before.[53]

One result of growth, however, was to sharpen the already-existing tensions within the ladies' college over the primary purpose of the education it offered, and to bring out once again the conflict between academic and "ornamental" traditions. "The attendance during the past year of 140 students", declared the ladies' college catalogue for 1887-88, "a number not equalled in the previous history of the Institution, — many of whom came exclusively for Music and the Fine Arts — is evidence of the unrivalled excellence of these departments". Commented a correspondent of the *Wesleyan* in 1889, "it doesn't seem to make any difference what other seminaries or colleges arise, lady students continue to flock to Mt. Allison".[54] Not all were convinced that this kind of expansion was

52 On the effects of the National Policy on Maritime industry, see T.W. Acheson, "The National Policy and the Industrialization of the Maritimes, 1880-1910", *Acadiensis*, I, 2 (Spring 1972), pp. 3-12. See also Acheson, "The Maritimes and 'Empire Canada'", in David Jay Bercuson, ed., *Canada and the Burden of Unity* (Toronto, 1977), pp. 87-114; Ernest R. Forbes, "Misguided Symmetry: The Destruction of Regional Transportation Policy for the Maritimes," *ibid.*, pp. 60-86; and S.A. Saunders, *The Economic History of the Maritime Provinces: A Study Prepared for the Royal Commission on Dominion-Provincial Relations* (Ottawa, 1939), pp. 1-22. The effects of the expansionist period on the Mount Allison College, as distinct from the ladies' academy, are sketched in John G. Reid, "Mount Allison College: The Reluctant University", *Acadiensis*, X, 1 (Autumn 1980), pp. 43-6.

53 See Table II.

54 Ladies' College, *Catalogue*, 1887-88; *The Wesleyan*, 24 January 1889.

Table II: Enrolment at Mount Allison Institutions,
Selected Years, 1870-1911

	1870-71	1880-81	1890-91	1900-01	1910-11
College/University[1]	17	25	62	73	155
Theology	7	10	17	18	43
Post-Graduate	-	2	2	3	2
Ladies' Academy/College	78	76	174	168	303
Male Academy and Commercial College	78	66	73	103	154
Special Students and Others	10	2	13	12	21
Total	190	181	341	377	678

Source: Mount Allison, *Catalogues* and *Calendars*, 1870-1911.

1 This category comprises only those enrolled in the regular undergraduate degree courses. 'Special Students', who would be enrolled to take only a few university-level courses, are not included; nor are theological students, unless also registered in Arts.

desirable. Thomas Hart, for example, Methodist minister in Berwick, Nova Scotia, wrote to B.C. Borden , also a minister, and principal of the ladies' college since 1885, to express concern that the daughter of a family on his circuit had "in some way formed the opinion that some of the Lady Students care more for a little finish than for a good Education".[55] Such a perception certainly contradicted the stated intentions of the institution, for each year the catalogue carried the statement that "the ornamental branches . . . [are] regarded only as the accessories and embellishments of learning — not its substitute . . .".[56] A related perception was that the institution was catering more and more to the rich. The suspicion that the traditional clientele was being replaced by students from wealthier familes was given public voice during the summer of 1884 by a correspondent of the *Wesleyan* using the pseudonym "A Lover of Mount Allison". While praising Mount Allison's achievements, the letter complained that the dresses worn by the ladies' academy students at the recent closing exercises had been too elaborate. "Apart from the love of display engendered", it continued, "we object on account of the heavy expense to parents. If allowed to continue it must end in excluding from the academy all but the daughters of the richest".[57] The same concern was raised in a different context two years later by E.E. Rice of Bear River, Nova Scotia, in a letter to Borden. He was debating , he wrote, whether to send his daughter back for another year at Mount Allison, as he had heard that she would have a new room-mate, and feared that she might have a similar experience to that of his son at Acadia, who had been led astray by the bad company he had fallen in with there. "I expected Sackville was stricter in carrying out dissiplin [sic] but have great fears in regard to it as there is to many rich folks children goes and they must have their way as at home or leave and the School cannot spare them".[58]

Rice was apparently satisfied by Borden's reply, for his daughter was once again registered in the year 1886-87; but he had raised an important question. If the ladies' college were to be, or even to seem to be, an institution that was inaccessible to the ordinary Methodist people of the region, or one where their children would be alienated from them, great damage would be done to the standing of Mount Allison in its constituency. Yet as Rice implied, there could be no question of discouraging wealthy families from enrolling their daughters, without destroying the competitive position of Mount Allison in regard to other institutions in the region. Despite repeated admonitions in the ladies' college catalogue that "it is especially desired that the dress of students shall be simple

---

55 Thomas D. Hart to B.C. Borden, 14 January 1887, Borden Papers, 7508, 1886-1910, p. 15, MAA.

56 Ladies' College, *Catalogue*, 1886-87.

57 *The Wesleyan*, 13 June 1884. An editorial note added that comments in the same vein had been made to the editor by others.

58 E.E. Rice to B.C. Borden, 28 July 1886, Borden Papers, 7508, 1886-1910, p. 19, MAA.

and inexpensive", the matter of dress continued to arouse controversy.[59] In June 1895, the local *Chignecto Post* reported comments made by a farmer attending a recent ladies' college reception that the extravagant dresses worn by the students were enough to exclude those from families of limited means. The *Post* commented, with due caution, that "it is just possible that those who govern Mount Allison might in this respect hold the reins a little tighter", and drew an immediate rejoinder from "a resident of Sackville", who denied that dress at Mount Allison was luxurious by comparison with standards elsewhere. A father "in moderate circumstances", the writer suggested, need have no hesitation on that ground in sending his daughter to Mount Allison, where scholarship and Christian morality were the prime concerns. Yet this letter also emphasized the social advantages of a Mount Allison education: "If we speak of the matter of style, let us not forget that the beautiful and suitable in dress have an educative effect and it is one of the acknowledged advantages of a ladies' school, that there girls from quiet country homes may gain a knowledge of what is customary in dress and deportment in the great world outside".[60]

It remained true that many of the students of the ladies' college continued to come from rural homes. Analysis of the home backgrounds of those students who originated in the Maritime Provinces in census years between 1870 and 1911 — when Maritimers comprised more than 90 per cent of the overall student body — shows that although the proportion of those coming from small communities (unincorporated areas, or incorporated places with a population of 1,000 or less) declined significantly during the period, there were still 32.8 per cent of such students in the 1910-11 year. With 37.8 per cent coming from Sackville in that year, and 5.0 per cent from other small towns with a population within the 1001-2500 range, the ladies' college continued to cater for a largely rural and small-town clientele.[61] How far the institution was maintaining its aspiration of openness to those "in moderate circumstances" is more difficult to gauge, owing to the lack of available data for most of the period. For the six consecutive academic years beginning in 1903, however, a college register has survived which includes the fathers' names of all students listed. By use of provincial directories, occupations can be identified and an indication obtained of the social background of the students. Of the 414 students whose background was identified, 109 were the daughters of retail or wholesale merchants, the majority

59 Ladies' College, *Catalogue*, 1886-87.

60 *Chignecto Post*, 27 June, 11 July 1895. The writer of the letter was identified by R.C. Archibald, a teacher of mathematics at the ladies college at this time, as Nellie Greenwood Andrews, the first woman graduate of Victoria University and now the wife of a Mount Allison college professor; see Archibald Papers, 5501/13/2, p. 7, MAA.

61 Mount Allison, *Catalogues* and *Calendars*, 1870-1911; Canada, *Census of Canada, 1931*, Vol. 2, Table 8, pp. 8-14. For background analysis of population movements affecting the Maritimes during this period, see Alan A. Brookes, "Out-Migration from the Maritime Provinces, 1860-1900: Some Preliminary Considerations," *Acadiensis*, V, 2 (Spring 1976), pp. 26-55.

of whom were rural or small-town (population 2500 or less) general or provision merchants: 58 fell into that sub-category.[62] Another 70 were farmers' daughters, while the next-largest group included the 63 who were daughters of industrial and commercial proprietors and managers. Forty of the students were daughters of clergymen, while other substantial minorities included daughters of non-manual workers such as railway clerks and office employees (30) and of manual workers such as fishermen, miners, carpenters, and railway running crew (37). The professions, including doctors, lawyers, teachers, and others, were represented by the fathers of 28 students, while government officials, sea captains, and commercial travellers comprised lesser numbers. The clientele of the ladies' college thus was not restricted to any one group within regional society, although there was a bias towards the daughters of retail and wholesale merchants and, to a lesser extent, of farmers and of those participating as proprietors and managers in the industrial and commercial economy of the region.

To some extent, therefore, the ladies' college could be defended convincingly against the allegation that it was becoming a finishing school for the children of wealthy families. Yet the perception of it as such was not easy to combat. As numbers had risen between 1880 and 1911, so too had the proportion of students from towns and cities with populations in excess of 2,500: from 14 in 1880-81 (18.7 per cent of the Maritime students) to 64 in 1910-11 (24.4 per cent). Urban students were not necessarily wealthy students, but of those social groups represented in the years 1903-09, 21 of the 28 students whose fathers' occupations were classed as "professional" were from towns and cities with populations of more than 2,500, as were 39 of the 63 industrial and commercial proprietors and managers.[63] An anonymous correspondent of the *Wesleyan* described his visit to a ladies' college reception in 1894 by observing with approval that "it was evident at a glance that the Sackville Institutions must have the patronage of the first families of the provinces"; his comment would be mirrored by that of the disgruntled farmer who felt a year later that this was not a matter for congratulation.[64] Principal Borden, in his report at the college graduation exer-

---

62 See Table III. The sub-category of rural or small-town general or provisions merchants is obtained by cross-referencing places of origin with Canada, *Census of Canada, 1931*, Vol. 2, Table 8, pp. 8-14. Some general cautions are in order regarding the use of Table III. Substantial numbers of students could not be included for reasons discussed in the notes to the table, and the results are subject to error for this reason. Also, the classification of occupations is subject to the precision or imprecision of the directory entry for each father of a student. The category of "farmer", for example, could include a variety of circumstances ranging from large landowner to smallholder; also, the category of "industrial and commercial proprietors and managers" cannot always be sharply distinguished in directory entries from that of "retail and wholesale merchants". For these reasons, the data in Table III should be regarded as comprising an indication of social background rather than a precise portrayal.

63 See Table III; also Mount Allison *Calendars* and *Catalogues*, 1880-1911; and Canada, *Census of Canada, 1931*, Vol. 2, Table 8, pp. 8-14.

64 *The Wesleyan*, 8 February 1894; *Chignecto Post*, 27 June 1895.

Table III: Occupations of the Fathers of Maritime Provinces
Female Students at Mount Allison Ladies' College and University, 1903-1909

	University students	Ladies' College[1] students	Total	University graduates, 1904-12	Ladies' College[2] graduates, 1904-10
Professional	6	28	34	6	6
Clergy	15	40	55	11	11
Government officials	2	15	17	2	4
Industrial & commercial proprietors & managers	6	63	69	3	17
General merchants & provision merchants (retail & wholesale)	3	74	77	2	6
Other retail & wholesale merchants	6	35	41	5	5
Commercial travellers/salesmen	2	10	12	-	5
Sea captains	-	12	12	-	3
Farmers	12	70	82	10	11
Non-manual workers	1	30	31	-	4
Manual workers	-	37	37	-	4
Total	53	414	467	39	76
Not included: non-Maritime	9	76	85	6	11
father deceased	8	52	60	5	8
cannot identify[3]	4	56	60	4	13
no data[3]	15	249	264	11	9

Source: Ladies' College Register, 1903-09, MAA; *McAlpine's Nova Scotia, Magdalen Islands, and St. Pierre Directory, With a Business Directory of Newfoundland, 1902* (Halifax, n.d.); *McAlpine's Nova Scotia Directory, 1907-08* (Halifax, n.d.); *McAlpine's New Brunswick Directory for 1903* (Saint John, n.d.); *McAlpine's Prince Edward Island Directory, 1900* (Saint John, 1899).

1 Included in this category are those ladies' college students who did not attend the university as undergraduates; those ladies' college students who were also undergraduates are classified as university students.

2 Not included in this category are the eight students who graduated from both university and ladies' college.

3 Those in the "cannot identify" category are the students included in the college register whose fathers could not be traced in directories; those listed as "no data" are those who were not included in the register even though their names appeared in the annual student lists in the college catalogue. It is likely that those in this latter category were students whose connection with the college was tenuous, such as students attending for weekly music lessons only, but this cannot be verified conclusively from existing data.

cises of May 1895, recalled that, over a period of years, the ladies' college had surrendered the lower grades of education almost entirely to the public schools: "while we are prepared to take pupils in all grades", he went on, "this college is especially strong (I will not say as a 'finishing school' as I do not like the expression) but as a school where advanced pupils in literary courses, as well as in music and the fine arts, may enjoy exceptional advantages".[65] That he should have felt the need to go out of his way publicly to express his disapproval of the term "finishing school" indicated that the term was being used more often than he liked.

Along with the unwelcome perception that the ladies' college had responded to social change by serving a wealthier clientele and giving more attention to the "ornamental" aspects of education, the academic quality of the institution was also under threat, for serious doubts could be raised as to whether it was meeting the real needs of women in the late 19th century. The "Ladies' College Notes" in the *Argosy* in May 1894 declared that "politically, intellectually, socially, the position of women today is a commanding one", and that "'Home is Woman's Sphere' is a wrong principle if it must shut her out from all other avenues of usefulness".[66] The small numbers of women who in fact broke through the barriers of the more prestigious male-dominated professions would later show the writer's comments to have been over-optimistic. Yet the ladies' college, at the close of the 1880s, could look back on a decade when a number of M.L.A. and music graduates had found career opportunities. Of the 70 graduates of the period 1881-90, seven had become teachers: four at the ladies' college itself, two as private teachers of music, and one as musical director at a seminary in Massachusetts. Three had become medical doctors, after further study in the United States; one of the three, Jane Heartz, subsequently moved to Halifax to take over the practice of Maria Angwin, a ladies' college graduate of 1869 who had been the first such graduate to take a medical degree.[67] A further five graduates had become missionaries, and one had become a nurse. Thus, although there was still a substantial majority of those who did not enter the work force, the ladies' college in the 1880s was providing training for a significant number who wished to enter professions.[68] The question was, however, whether the ladies' college could continue to function in this way during the 1890s, as women of

65 *Daily Times* (Moncton), 28 May 1895.

66 *The Argosy* (May 1894), pp. 9-10.

67 See Table I; also the details in [Raymond C. Archibald], "Our Graduates, 1854-1904", *Allisonia*, II (1904-05), pp. 139-54. According to Archibald, Maria Angwin had been the first woman doctor to practise in Halifax.

68 For discussion of the effects of industrialization in altering the career patterns of women, and of the entry of women into certain specific professions, see Linda Kealey, "Introduction", in Kealey, ed., *A Not Unreasonable Claim: Women and Reform in Canada, 1880s-1920s* (Toronto, 1979), pp. 1-14; Wendy Mitchinson, "Canadian Women and Church Missionary Societies in the Nineteenth Century", *Atlantis*, 2, Part 2 (Spring 1977), pp. 57-75; Prentice,

ability were increasingly attracted to the degree programmes of universities.

At Mount Allison, the attendance of women at the university increased markedly during the 1890s. Following the graduation of Grace Annie Lockhart in 1875, seven years had gone by before Harriet Starr Stewart became the next woman graduate, the second woman graduate in Canada and the first to receive the degree of Bachelor of Arts. Only three others emulated her accomplishment during the 1880s, and in 1884 J.R. Inch publicly expressed regret "that more young ladies had not availed themselves of the opportunities offered".[69] The 1890s, however, saw a different pattern, for during the period from 1891 to 1900 there were 31 women graduates, the majority of whom took up some form of employment after graduation. Although 15 of these were listed in a 1903 survey as having no formal employment, 11 had become teachers, one a missionary, one a doctor, one a stenographer, and one a governess. Three had entered journalism, although by 1903 only one was active in that field. In other words, more than half of the women graduates had attained at least for the time being a position of independence in society based upon the education they had received at Mount Allison.[70] Furthermore, the proportion of women enrolled in degree programmes at Mount Allison was still well in advance of the average at Canadian universities, and was growing apace. In the 1900-01 year, the university women at Mount Allison numbered 11 out of a total enrolment of 73: 16.4 per cent, compared with a national proportion of 11 per cent. By 1910-11, there were 41 university women at Mount Allison, well over one-quarter of the total enrolment of 155.[71] Like the students of the ladies' college, the university women came from families of varied background, though there were especially large contingents whose fathers were clergymen or farmers, and almost none from the homes of lower-paid manual or non-manual employees. While most of the students of the ladies' college would not receive (nor, presumably, seek)

"The Feminization of Teaching", pp. 49-65; Wayne Roberts, "'Rocking the Cradle for the World': The New Woman and Maternal Feminism, Toronto, 1877-1914", in Kealey, *A Not Unreasonable Claim*, esp. pp. 31-40; Veronica Strong-Boag, "Canada's Women Doctors: Feminism Constrained", in Kealey, *A Not Unreasonable Claim*, pp. 109-29.

69 *Chignecto Post*, 5 June 1884.

70 [Raymond C. Archibald], "A list of the names of those persons on whom degrees have been conferred by the University of Mount Allison College", 1 May 1903, Archibald Papers, 5501/14, MAA; *The Argosy*, March 1899, April, November 1901, January, February, March, May 1902. See also Roberta Frankfort, *Collegiate Women: Domesticity and Career in Turn-of-the Century America* (New York, 1977), pp. 56, 60, 112, for data regarding career patterns of women graduates at certain institutions in the United States. Significant comparison with Mount Allison is hindered, however, not only by the differences in traditions of women's education between Canada and the U.S., but also by the small size of Mount Allison at this time and the consequently low number of graduates.

71 University of Mount Allison College, *Calendars*, 1901, 1911; see also Ramsay Cook and Wendy Mitchinson, eds. *The Proper Sphere: Women's Place in Canadian Society* (Toronto, 1976), p. 120.

diplomas at the end of their studies, most of the university women could expect to graduate: of the 89 who attended the university between 1903 and 1909, 65 obtained degrees by 1912.[72] Unlike their colleagues at certain other Canadian universities — notably McGill and the University of Toronto — the university women were not faced with stern battles over the merits of coeducation.[73] At Mount Allison, that issue had been settled decisively in 1872. Every year, by the early 20th century, the university calendar remarked proudly that women received their education at Mount Allison on a basis of "perfect equality with men". Perfection, in reality, was too high a claim, for no women had yet enrolled in engineering, nor in the regular programmes in theology. Yet in the arts and science programmes, women undoubtedly comprised a substantial and growing proportion of the student population.[74]

Given the increased presence of women at the university, what was the future for the ladies' college, if not to serve only as an outpost of the "ornamental" tradition? The academic character of the ladies' college was powerfully defended during the late 19th century not only by Borden as principal, but also by the vice-principal, Mary Mellish Archibald. How far they could hope to be successful was always a matter for doubt, but their efforts nonetheless created new opportunities in several fields for the women students of the region. When Borden had been appointed principal in 1885, he had been selected from among seven male nominees. The notion of a woman principal had not yet been seriously considered, although Mary Electa Adams and Louisa Allison had both exercised considerable influence despite being nominally subject to higher (male) authority. During the principalships of Inch and his immediate successor David Kennedy, the position of chief preceptress had been held by a series of younger teachers for periods of only a year or two, and none had attained the stature of either Adams or Allison. In 1885, however, the situation changed. Among the teachers at the ladies' academy during Inch's regime, Mary Mellish had taught mathematics and natural science between 1869 and 1873, and had been chief preceptress during the last two of those years. In 1873 she had left to be married, but returned in 1885 after the death of her husband, to become once again chief preceptress. Just a year older than Borden, Mary Mellish Archibald had both the experience and the determination to put her imprint upon the ladies' college, and her successful partnership with Borden lasted until her early death of pneumonia in 1901.[75] She was succeeded by Emma Baker, an experienced administrator of women's colleges in Ontario and Pennsylvania, who had

72 See Table III.

73 See Gillett, *We Walked Very Warily*, ch. iv; and Roberts, "New Woman and Maternal Feminism", p. 32.

74 University of Mount Allison College, *Calendar*, 1910-11. The *Calendar* was correct in a technical sense, however, in that there was no formal barrier to the enrolment of women in any degree programme. A few women did study as "special students" in theology, in preparation for missionary work.

75 See Ladies' Academy, *Catalogues*, 1869-73; Archibald, *Historical Notes*, pp. 9-10. Mary Mellish Archibald's title was changed from "chief preceptress" to "vice-principal" in 1897.

attained the distinction in 1903 of receiving the first Ph.D. degree in philosophy granted by the University of Toronto, and one of the first two doctoral degrees in any discipline granted by that university to women. Baker's graduation brought to two the number of ladies' college faculty members who held the Ph.D. degree, at a time when the university, by comparison, had none.[76] That a candidate as strong as Baker should become vice-principal showed clearly that after Mary Mellish Archibald there could be no question of a return to the previous custom of relying upon an inexperienced teacher as the chief female administrative officer of the ladies' college.

The strategy adopted by Borden and Archibald in their efforts to preserve the academic quality of the ladies' college was a simple one, involving the frank recognition that many students of the institution attended not in order to study the literary and scientific disciplines that were also taught at the university, but to study music and fine arts. This did not imply, however, that these must necessarily be taught as purely ornamental subjects. On the contrary, if the high intellectual standards of the literary departments (the primary, matriculation, and M.L.A. courses) could be matched by the highest of artistic standards in the other departments, then the entire institution would be strengthened. Accordingly the late 1880s and the 1890s saw a series of measures directed at the development of systematic and demanding courses of study in what had hitherto been regarded as the "ornamental branches". In the fall of 1887, a new four-year diploma course was introduced which provided for the first time a coherent and graduated programme of art study, with the final two years devoted largely to oil painting.[77] Five years later negotiations began for the acquisition by the ladies' college of the extensive teaching collection which had been built up in Saint John by the Owens Art Gallery, and in particular by its curator John Hammond. When the Owens collection was transferred to Mount Allison in 1893 (and accommodated two years later in a new gallery building) Hammond became the first professor of fine arts since the departure of John Warren Gray some 20 years before. Hammond became a full member of the Royal Canadian Academy in the same year, and it was by virtue of acquiring the services of an artist of his quality, even more than by securing the Owens collection, that Mount Allison established itself as an important regional and national centre of the fine arts.[78]

Parallel developments were also taking place in the field of music with the construction of a new conservatory, opened in 1891. Initiated in a proposal made by Archibald in 1888 to the alumnae society of the ladies' college, which

76 *Allisonia* (November 1903), pp. 3-4, May 1905, p. 183. The other holder of the Ph.D. degree on the ladies' college faculty was R.C. Archibald, son of Mary Mellish Archibald, who taught mathematics and music.

77 Ladies' College, *Catalogue*, 1886-87.

78 See J. Russell Harper, *Painting in Canada: A History* (2nd ed.; Toronto, 1977), pp. 198, 226-8.

undertook to raise half of the cost of construction, the new building was intended "to make it unnecessary for persons wishing to obtain a thorough and complete musical education, or to prepare themselves to teach music, to go outside of the Maritime Provinces".[79] The curriculum was strengthened not only by the addition to the existing diploma course in piano of equivalent courses in violin, pipe organ, and vocal culture, but also by the requirement that all students should study musical history and theory.[80] As the 1890s went on, increasing stress was placed upon theoretical work. Writing in the *Argosy* in 1897, music professor John J. Wootton argued strongly that the prejudice that music was of no intellectual value was held by all too many individuals who "musically considered, cannot tell a harp from a handsaw".[81] For Wootton, music was a demanding discipline and an important professional occupation, and this view was reflected in the diploma courses of the conservatory, which led either to a "teacher's diploma" or an "artist's diploma". "The performer who does not understand these sciences", admonished the college catalogue with reference to the study of harmony and theory, "is much like a person reciting a poem in a foreign language, while not understanding a word of what he is speaking".[82] While some students continued to attend the Mount Allison ladies' college to study music and fine arts as "ornamental" subjects, the reforms of the late 1880s and early 1890s ensured that every student had the opportunity to study these subjects in a more systematic way.

Also implied by these reforms, and particularly by the introduction of the teacher's diploma in music, was the recognition that the ladies' college must also cater directly for women who wished to be trained for a professional career. Another development in that direction was the introduction in the 1889-90 year of "courses in shorthand and typing . . . designed to meet the needs of those who wish to fit themselves for employment in business offices".[83] Although overshadowed by the more extensive commercial training offered to both male and female students by the male academy, this programme continued in the ladies' college until 1905. Meanwhile, domestic science had been introduced as a field of study in 1904. The inauguration of a programme of "domestic chemistry" had been proposed in 1891 by W.W. Andrews, the professor of science at the university.[84] The notion was enthusiastically supported by the alumnae society,

79 Ladies' College, *Catalogue*, 1890-91. See also Minutes of Alumnae Society, 27 May 1888, MAA.

80 Ladies' College, *Catalogue*, 1890-91.

81 *The Argosy* (April 1897), pp. 3-5.

82 Ladies' College, *Catalogue*, 1890-91. Some 17 years earlier, the anonymous author of a series of "Confidences" of "A Girl of the Period", published in the *Canadian Monthly*, had complained of her feelings of being "utterly helpless and dependent"; as a pianist, she went on, "I am a *brilliant success*, and yet a humbug as regards the science of music". Quoted in Cook and Mitchinson, *The Proper Sphere*, p. 65.

83 Ladies' College, *Catalogue*, 1888-89.

84 *The Wesleyan*, 7 May 1891; see also Gillett, *We Walked Very Warily*, p. 347.

on a resolution proposed by Mary Mellish Archibald, but financial constraints prevented its implementation until 1904, when Andrews's related proposal for a school of engineering at the university was also put into effect.[85] By that time, Mount Allison was following other institutions in introducing instruction in household science, and financial assistance obtained from Lillian Massey-Treble, a wealthy member of the National Council of Women of Canada — ensured that the Mount Allison school would have close links with the Toronto school of household science that already bore her name.[86] The Massey-Treble school at Mount Allison opened in the spring of 1904 with the expectation, expressed by the local *Tribune* that "girls will go out from this school fully equipped to grapple with domestic difficulties and as veritable household angels, to comfort and bless". More prosaic, but just as welcome, was the verdict of the New Brunswick department of education: J.R. Inch, who had been provincial superintendent of education since resigning as president of the university in 1891, informed Borden that the ladies' college diploma would henceforth be accepted as a sufficient qualification in domestic science for teachers in the public schools.[87] That the schoolteacher was indeed a more typical product of the Massey-Treble school than the "household angel" is suggested by consideration of the later careers of the early graduates. Despite incomplete data — information for this period must be gleaned from the alumnae columns of the ladies' college magazine, *Allisonia* — 14 of the 25 household science graduates of the years from 1904 to 1910 are known to have taken employment after graduation: six taught in the schools of New Brunswick and six at schools in other provinces or in the United States, while one returned to teach at the ladies' college and one became a dietician in New Jersey.[88]

Through new curriculum developments, therefore, the ladies' college had been equipped to serve new demands and to offer new career opportunities considered appropriate for women students. Yet by the beginning of the second decade of the 20th century, a new principal of the ladies' college, G.M. Campbell, appointed in 1911, seemed ready to accept a more limited role for the ladies' college. "'Women for Homes'", declared Campbell at the year-end ceremonies

85 Minutes of Alumnae Society, 1 June 1891, MAA.

86 *Allisonia* (January 1904), pp. 34-6; see also Roberts, "New Woman and Maternal Feminism", p. 22.

87 *The Tribune* (Sackville), 19 May 1904; p. 50, Inch to Borden, 10 May 1904, Archibald Papers, 5501/13/9, p. 50, MAA.

88 *Allisonia*, Vols. 3-10 (1905-13); for graduation lists, see Ladies' College, *Catalogue*, 1910-11. The career patterns of graduates of other diploma programmes are more difficult to assess. Graduates in oratory, literature, and art were fewer in numbers (19, 13, and 9 respectively) and most were not mentioned in the *Allisonia* columns. Of the 68 music graduates of the academic years from 1904 to 1910, 35 are known to have taught, but in the majority of cases it is unclear whether this was an occupation from which they derived a livelihood, or whether they only took a few pupils on a limited and perhaps temporary basis.

of 1912, "is the consistent and the peculiar motto of Mount Allison . . .".[89] Campbell's assertion represented an apparent departure from the principles of his predecessors in office, but it conveyed a certain realism nonetheless. First of all, the large majority of those who enrolled at the ladies' college were not availing themselves of the diploma programmes offered: of the 847 women who attended the institution between 1903 and 1909, only 117 (or 13.8 per cent) would obtain a diploma by 1910.[90] Even those who did pursue a full course to graduation did not necessarily have the intention of subsequently taking employment; certainly the majority of those graduating between 1901 and 1904 are not known to have done so. Of those who did take employment, moreover, the great majority did so in fields, such as teaching and nursing, which had come to be part of the accepted "woman's sphere", appropriate for the maternal or nurturing qualities of women. Thus, in this sense the initiatives launched by the ladies' college had had limited results.[91] Furthermore, there were signs that the new departments so carefully developed at the ladies' college during the late 19th and early 20th centuries might soon be absorbed by the university. The introduction of a bachelor of music degree programme in 1912 was one indication of this possibility.[92] Just as the opening of university degree courses to women in 1872 had been a tribute to the academic standing of the ladies' college, but had also raised serious questions as to the institution's future clientele, so the further encroachment of the university upon ladies' college programmes might again raise such doubts. If the ladies' college were, as Campbell's comment implied, to be an institution avowedly offering instruction in the "ornamental" tradition, this goal might well seem dangerously limited if the economic health of the Maritime Provinces were ever to decline to the point where enrolment was affected. Already by the eve of the First World War the signs of such a decline were beginning to appear.[93]

By 1914, therefore, the Mount Allison ladies' college faced a future that was less assured than could be apparent from the institution's customary large enrolments. Over its 60-year history, however, the institution had contributed significantly to the development of educational opportunities for women. The insistence of Mary Electa Adams in 1854 that academic disciplines should take priority over "the ornamental branches" in the curriculum of the ladies'

---

89 *The Tribune*, 30 May 1912.

90 See Table III.

91 See Table I. See also Conway, "Perspectives on the History of Women's Education", pp. 8-9; Kealey, "Introduction", pp. 7-8; Roberts, "New Woman and Maternal Feminism", pp. 29-31; Rosenberg, *Beyond Separate Spheres*, pp. 48-50.

92 University of Mount Allison College, *Calendar*, 1912.

93 See Acheson, "The Maritimes and 'Empire Canada'", p. 95; also Ernest R. Forbes, *The Maritime Rights Movement, 1919-1927: A Study in Canadian Regionalism* (Montreal, 1979), pp. 17-22.

academy was fully in accordance with the principles already established at the male academy. Yet, since limiting definitions of the appropriate social role of women were so deeply entrenched in society at large, that early decision involved Mount Allison in debate over the purposes of women's education that ultimately had significance far beyond the confines of the institution. A direct result of the academic emphasis at the ladies' college was the opening of university degree programmes to women in 1872, a decision unprecedented in Canada. With the beginning of co-education at the university level, however, came new difficulties for the ladies' college, intensified by the social and economic changes which created an increased demand for a "finishing school" education for the daughters of well-to-do families, while at the same time opening up careers in certain professions to women who would now require systematic instruction as a preparation for taking employment. Survival for the ladies' college required that an attempt be made to meet both of these demands, and the curriculum innovations in such fields as music, fine arts, and household science represented efforts to accomplish this task. These new developments, together with the increasing enrolment of women in the degree programmes of the university, prompted J.R. Inch to declare in 1904 that Mount Allison provided "courses to meet the demands of the most exacting advocate of the educational needs of women".[94] Women's needs would be redefined by succeeding generations, and even by 1914 there were signs that Mount Allison's role in women's education would require redefinition also. Yet strenuous efforts had been made over a 60-year period to resolve the dilemmas that came from the tension between the academic and the "ornamental" traditions in women's education and from the deeper uncertainties as to the role in society of the educated woman. All ambiguities had not been resolved, but the result of the attempt had been significant change in the nature of the education available to women in the Maritime Provinces and in Canada as a whole.

94 *Allisonia* (November 1904), p. 59.

DAVID ALEXANDER

Reprinted from Vol. VIII, No. 1
(Autumn 1978)

Economic Growth in the Atlantic Region, 1880 to 1940

It has been customary for historians to treat the Maritimes and Newfoundland as two regions rather than one. This reflects, very probably, nothing more credible than an academic inertia about widening horizons. While there were profound differences in the level of economic activity and in the rate of growth of the two economies before World War II, Caves and Holton rightly pointed out nearly two decades ago that they shared a common economic niche.[1]

This essay has several purposes. The first is to encourage historians of the Atlantic region to make more efforts to bridge the Cabot Strait. This effort would add fresh perspectives on the troubles and successes of both the Maritimes and Newfoundland. It would also conform to modern political, economic and planning reality. A second purpose is to provide a systematic quantitative assessment of the growth of the Newfoundland economy from 1880 to 1940 in relation to the Maritimes. While work has been done on the Maritimes, little exists for Newfoundland for this period. This effort is only a beginning, but it does offer a new approach to the Island's economic record before Confederation. The final objective is controversial. In the Maritimes, even among some cautious academics, there is an 'underground hypothesis' that the provinces sacrificed their economic potential by entering the union with Canada in the 1860s and 1870s. By contrast, the sometimes unhappy history of Newfoundland is commonly attributed to its stubborn rejection of the 'Canadian wolf' until 1949. Given the economic and social similarities, it is unlikely that these two contradictory hypotheses can both be true. Therefore, does the comparative economic performance suggest that the date of entry into Confederation was a critical variable in the progress of either the Maritimes or Newfoundland?

The union of the British North American colonies provoked both fear and optimism in the Maritimes — fear that the provinces would be reduced to colonies of Upper Canada, and optimism that they would develop into the workshop of the new Dominion. That such opposite predictions existed is perhaps a sign of the critical turning point upon which the Maritimes was poised in the 1860s; that it became a dependency rather than a workshop, however, is not in itself proof that the doubters were prescient. The brief

1 R. E. Caves and R. H. Holton, *The Canadian Economy* (Cambridge, Mass., 1961), p. 145.

trade recession following Confederation, and the deeper recession of the 1880s and 1890s, were taken by opponents of the union as confirmation of their fears. But both were general to Canada and proved nothing. The great boom which swept Canada at the turn of the century, while only generating a mild flutter in the Maritime economy, could be taken as a more serious sign. But Maritime consciousness of economic stagnation and relative decline within the Dominion of Canada only assumed the stature of certainty and reality in the 1920s.[2] Since the Maritimes still commanded some weight in the country and the presence of sharp regional inequalities was something that still surprised and concerned Canadians as a whole, the interwar period was rich in official enquiries of royal stature. These enquiries were usually highly specific — fiscal problems and industry problems — which was a suggestion that the difficulties were not thought to be irrevocable. They began with Sir Andrew Duncan's enquiry into the coal industry in 1925, followed shortly by the more far-reaching enquiry into fiscal arrangements.[3] Two years later distress in the fishing industry and the 'trawler question' generated a study by Hon. Justice MacLean.[4] Duncan returned in 1932 with another study of the coal industry,[5] and finally in 1934 the Province of Nova Scotia assembled a distinguished commission to undertake a wide-ranging enquiry into that province's economic troubles.[6] A year later Sir Thomas White reviewed the earlier work of Duncan on Maritime claims.[7]

After 1935, however, the specific problems of the Maritime region were absorbed into the general problem of metropolitan Canada and 'the regions'. The great *Royal Commission on Dominion-Provincial Relations* began this tradition,[8] although unlike its successor in the 1950s, the Gordon Commission,[9] it at least published a background study on the Maritimes rather than simply a study of regionalism. It was left to Nova Scotia to undertake a major piece of postwar planning, under R. MacGregor Dawson.[10] But apart from

2   See E. R. Forbes, "The Origins of the Maritime Rights Movement", *Acadiensis*, V (Autumn, 1975), pp. 55 - 61.

3   *Royal Commission Respecting the Coal Mines of Nova Scotia* (1926) and *Royal Commission on Maritime Claims* (1926).

4   *Royal Commission Investigating the Fisheries of the Maritime Provinces and the Magdalen Islands* (1928).

5   *Royal Commission Respecting the Coal Mines of Nova Scotia* (1932).

6   *Nova Scotia Royal Commission Provincial Economic Enquiry* (1934).

7   *Royal Commission on Financial Arrangements between the Dominion and the Maritime Provinces* (1935).

8   S. A. Saunders, *The Economic History of the Maritime Provinces* (Ottawa, 1939).

9   R. D. Howland, *Some Regional Aspects of Canada's Economic Development* (Ottawa, 1957).

10 *Royal Commission on Provincial Development and Rehabilitation* (1944).

another, almost inevitable study of postwar slump in the coal industry,[11] the nation eschewed further enquiries into the Maritimes of the formal magnificence of the interwar royal commissions. Since the problems had not disappeared, this might seem curious. It reflected, in part, the institutionalization of analysis within expanded provincial and federal civil services, where much more enquiry was undertaken in a continuous way rather than by the grand royal commission.[12] Moreover, the urgency of enquiry was muted by the growth of prosperity in the region, even if much of it was accounted for by unearned income. One also suspects that some of the urgency that was felt in the interwar years about the decline of the Maritimes was lost simply because the region had become an insignificant fraction of the nation, and its economic plight was accepted as lacking a solution.

Having ceased to be an important area of national concern,[13] the burden of research fell upon the region itself. Perhaps this is as it should be, but in the 1950s the universities, while numerous, were mainly weak and it is only in recent years that any volume of work has emerged, frequently sponsored by government and private organizations.[14] Historical analysis of the decline of the Maritimes is still not voluminous. The established interpretation began in the interwar period with Saunders, a product of the staples school of geographic determinism, who accepted Maritime decline as a function of the obsolescence of 'wind, wood and sail'.[15] This was a narrow interpretation of the structure and dynamism of the nineteenth-century Maritime economy, and it has never been satisfactorily explained why the equally 'woody and windy' Scandinavians managed to pass, at great profit, into the vulgar world of oil-fired turbines.

This same geographic determinism accepted the inevitability of manufacturing and financial activity migrating to Upper Canada, and at the end of the Second War this resigned pessimism was given a scientific basis. B. S. Keirstead argued that the increasing size of firms at the turn of the century favoured growth in Ontario and Western Quebec, with its large population, excellent communications, and agglomerations of labour skills, capital and inter-industry linkages. The decline of the Maritimes, located on the fringe

---

11   *Royal Commission on Coal* (1946).

12   As, for example, in the recent study by the Economic Council of Canada, *Living Together: A Study of Regional Disparities* (Ottawa, 1977).

13   For example, it is unlikely the Department of Regional Economic Expansion would have been established in the absence of political and economic troubles in the Province of Quebec.

14   Dalhousie's Institute of Public Affairs was an early contributor to regional studies, and the establishment of APEC and later the Atlantic Development Board have contributed enormously to the production of regional studies.

15   Saunders, *Economic History, op cit.*

of the tariff protected Canadian market, was inevitable, as was the relocation of its financial institutions.[16] Historians have recently suggested that the process was not as neutral as Keirstead's arguments imply. E. R. Forbes points to the loss of regional control over the rate structure of the Inter-colonial Railway in 1918 as the cancellation of a critical tool of regional development which had served the Maritimes well during the previous forty years.[17] T. W. Acheson has shown that Maritime entrepreneurs were remarkably successful in the early decades of Confederation in shifting the economy from a North Atlantic to a continental focus, although ultimately the absence of a strong regional metropolis left the region's industries vulnerable to takeover, and weak in pressing regional interests in national policy.[18] The most direct attack on the widely-held Keirstead explanation of Maritime underdevelopment, however, was Roy George's demonstration that there were no cost disadvantages to manufacturing in Nova Scotia for the Atlantic and Central Canadian market in the 1960s which could explain the concentration of manufacturing in Ontario and Quebec.[19] Stagnation in the region, in other words, was not inevitable and it is not beyond correction.

The accepted interpretation of Newfoundland's economic development is radically different from that of the Maritimes, for no one has argued that Newfoundland became relatively poorer or less developed, and few have been so bold as to suggest that it had any assured prospects. The first thorough enquiry into the country's economic state and prospects came with the Amulree Commission in 1933, which recommended the country be closed down.[20] At the end of World War II, the volume of studies by MacKay was generally gloomy about the country's past and future,[21] and a more powerful unpublished work by Mayo saw little prospect for Newfoundland either as a Province of Canada or as an independent country.[22] For a long time such pessimism was submerged by the ebullience of the Province's first premier,

16 B. S. Kierstead, *The Theory of Economic Change* (Toronto, 1948), pp. 269 - 81.

17 E. R. Forbes, "Misguided Symmetry: The Destruction of Regional Transportation Policy for the Maritimes", David Jay Bercuson, ed., *Canada and the Burden of Unity* (Toronto, 1977), pp. 60 - 86.

18 T. W. Acheson, "The National Policy and the Industrialization of the Maritimes, 1880 - 1910", *Acadiensis,* I (Spring, 1971), pp. 3 - 28; and "The Maritimes and 'Empire Canada' ", Bercuson, *Burden of Unity,* pp. 87 - 114.

19 Roy George, *A Leader and a Laggard* (Toronto, 1970), pp. 102 - 5.

20 *Newfoundland Royal Commission* (1933).

21 R. A. MacKay, ed., *Newfoundland: Economic, Diplomatic and Strategic Studies* (Toronto, 1948).

22 H. B. Mayo, "Newfoundland and Canada: The Case for Union Examined" (unpublished D.Phil. thesis, Oxford University, 1948).

activity in the new resource frontier in Labrador, and the general prosperity
which swept the Western World in the 1950s and 1960s. But underneath the
new optimism was the serious problem of a huge, decaying fishing industry
and its dependent rural population. When this issue re-emerged in the mid-
1960s a bitter and still unresolved debate ensued between those who recommended a planned reduction of the Island's population,[23] and those who
fought for a revitalized rural fishing economy.[24] While the relatively late
development of the province's university has meant that historical work on
Newfoundland's economic development is only in its infancy, what exists
has not confirmed the argument that the Province was or is hopelessly un-
productive.[25] Indeed, the economist Gordon Goundrey has noted that the
proportion of Gross Provincial Product arising in the goods producing sectors
in Newfoundland exceeds that for Canada as a whole.[26]

Although identification of the turning point is still uncertain, it is agreed
that by 1940 the Maritimes' economy had declined in size relative to Canada.
But what was its position compared with Newfoundland? Population and
labour force growth is a crude and sometimes misleading index of economic
expansion, but a useful beginning to analysis. From the mid-nineteenth to the
mid-twentieth century population growth was highest in the territories of
overseas settlement, such as Australia, the United States and Canada, all of
which recorded rates of growth of over 19% per decade.[27] Between 1871 and
1941 the Canadian rate of growth was 1.64% per annum. In the Maritimes it
was only 0.55% compared with 1.0% in Newfoundland between 1869 and 1935.
The Maritimes' share of the national population fell by 50%, compared with

23 P. Copes, *The Resettlement of Fishing Communities in Newfoundland* (Ottawa, Canadian
   Council on Rural Development, 1972).

24 This has largely been the creation of Memorial University's Institute for Social and Economic
   Research. Among many publications are Cato Wadel, *Marginal Adaptations and Moderniza-
   tion in Newfoundland* (St. John's, 1969); Ottar Brox, *Newfoundland Fishermen in the Age of
   Industry* (St.John's, 1972); Nelvin Farstad, *Fisheries Development in Newfoundland* (Oslo and
   Bergen, 1972); and David Alexander, "The Political Economy of Fishing in Newfoundland",
   Journal of Canadian Studies (February, 1976), pp. 32 - 40.

25 See Peter Neary, *The Political Economy of Newfoundland* (Toronto, 1973), and David
   Alexander, "Development and Dependence in Newfoundland", *Acadiensis*, IV (Autumn,
   1974), pp. 3 - 31; "Newfoundland's Traditional Economy and Development to 1934",
   Acadiensis, V (Spring, 1976), pp. 56 - 78; "The Decline of the Saltfish Trade and Newfoundland's Integration into the North American Economy", Canadian Historical Association, *Historical Papers*, 1976, pp. 229 - 48; and *The Decay of Trade* (St. John's, 1977).

26 "The Newfoundland Economy: A Modest Proposal", *Canadian Forum* (March, 1974), p. 18.

27 Simon Kuznets, *Modern Economic Growth* (New Haven, 1966), Table 2:5.

25% in Ontario and 9% in Quebec.[28] In the United States, where a comparable westward shift took place, there was not an equivalent imbalance of regional population growth. Between 1860 and 1950, the North East share of population declined by 22% and the South by only 12%.[29] The labour force in the Maritimes also fell during this period, from 18% of the Canadian in 1891 to 9% in 1941. Between 1891 and 1911 the Maritime labour force grew by only 0.3% compared with a rate five times greater in Ontario and Quebec, and in 1911 - 41 the absolute and relative performance was no better. In international perspective the Maritimes was also a poor performer; between 1913 and 1938 small countries like Denmark, the Netherlands, Norway and Sweden increased the size of their labour force by 27 to 49% compared with less than 14% in the Maritimes, which ranked with larger, troubled countries like Belgium (4%), Italy (9%) and France (-11%).[30] In Newfoundland, however, the labour force actually grew faster between 1891 and 1911 (1.9% per annum) than in Ontario and Quebec, and in 1911 - 1941 at a rate close to that of Ontario.[31]

Although Newfoundland's population and labour force grew substantially faster than in the Maritimes, this is not unequivocal evidence of a more satisfactory economic performance. The utilisation of the labour force on the Island is almost impossible to measure, and there were also more formidable barriers to emigration. The faster growth might indicate nothing more than an increasingly impoverished population, both absolutely and relatively. If this were so, it should be revealed in the structural stagnation of the labour force.

In 1901, as Table I reveals, the distribution of labour force in the Maritimes was much more concentrated in agriculture and fisheries than was the case in Quebec and Ontario, with relative under-representation concentrated more in the industry than the services sector. Between 1901 and 1941 the reallocation of labour from primary industries proceeded rapidly in Ontario but at about the same rate in the Maritimes and Quebec. Quebec had the most 'modern' distribution in 1901, but this mantle had passed to Ontario by

28 Calculations from M. C. Urquhart and K. A. H. Buckley, *Historical Statistics of Canada*, Series A2 - 14; and Government of Newfoundland, *Historical Statistics of Newfoundland*, Table A1. For migration patterns in the Maritimes, see Alan A. Brookes, "Out-Migration from the Maritime Provinces, 1860 - 1900: Some Preliminary Considerations", *Acadiensis*, V (Spring, 1976), pp. 26 - 55.

29 Calculated from Peter B. Kenen, "A Statistical Survey of Basic Trends", Seymour E. Harris, ed., *American Economic History* (New York, 1961), Table 2, p. 68.

30 See Angus Maddison, *Economic Growth in the West* (London and New York, 1964), Table D-2, p. 213.

31 All calculations from the 1891 and 1941 *Census of Canada,* and the 1935 and 1945 *Census of Newfoundland and Labrador.*

1941. The most dramatic labour force shifts, however, occurred in Newfoundland. While labour force allocation to the industrial sector in 1901 was not massively below that of the two large Maritime Provinces, service sector employment was strikingly under-represented. Between 1901 and 1945 there was a major shift of labour out of primary activities, a growth in industry employment equivalent to that on the Mainland, and a massive gain in service employment. This latter phenomenon reflected the expansion of the transport

TABLE 1: LABOUR FORCE DISTRIBUTION

	Primary			Industry			Services		
	1901 %	1941 %	Change %	1901 %	1941 %	Change %	1901 %	1941 %	Change %
Canada	42	27	-15	31	32	1	27	41	14
Maritimes	47	31	-16	28	31	3	25	38	13
N.S.	44	25	-19	30	35	5	26	40	14
N.B.	47	31	-16	29	31	2	24	38	14
P.E.I.	67	59	- 8	15	12	-3	18	29	11
Nfld.	65	33	-32	26	30	4	9	37	28
Ont.	41	19	-22	32	37	5	27	44	17
Que.	39	22	-17	34	37	3	27	41	14

Note: 'Industry' includes logging, mining, manufacturing, construction and unspecified labourers. 'Services' includes all professional and personal service employment, trade, finance, clerical, public service, transport and communications. 'Primary' therefore includes only agriculture, fishing and trapping. The terminal date for Newfoundland is 1945. For 1901 in Newfoundland, 10% of those enumerated as 'otherwise employed' are assumed to be in transport and communications (the 1935 share) and are allocated to services. All calculations omit those without stated occupations.

Source: *Census of Canada,* 1941; *Tenth Census of Newfoundland and Labrador,* 1935; and Dominion Bureau of Statistics, *Province of Newfoundland: Statistical Background* (Ottawa, 1949), Table 81.

TABLE 2: LABOUR FORCE LOCATION QUOTIENTS

	MARITIMES		NEWFOUNDLAND	
	1911	1941	1911	1945
Agriculture	0:97	1:30	[16:40	13:90]
Fishing	10:17	2:26		
Logging	1:50	2:14	2:17	2:89
Mining	2:66	2:58	1:32	1:07
Manufacturing	0:66	0:52	0:50	0:33
Construction	0:80	0:93	—	1:03
Transport	1:03	1:13	—	0:99
Trade and Finance	0:78	0:86	0:20	0:80
Professional	0:96	1:19	1:03	1:36
Clerical	0:75	0:62	1:40	0:54

Note: The location quotient is:

$$LQ = \frac{S_i/S}{R_i/R}$$

where, S_i = number in industry 'i'
     in the region
  S = number in industry 'i'
     in the 'nation'
  R_i = number in regional
     labour force
  R = number in 'national'
     labour force.

The 'nation' includes Newfoundland, the Maritimes, Quebec and Ontario.

Source: *Census of Canada*, 1941; *Census of Newfoundland and Labrador*, 1935 and 1945.

and communications system on the Island, as well as the rapid development (from a rather backward starting point) of modern educational, health and public service facilities.

A three sector analysis of labour force distribution is, of course, a blunt instrument of analysis. Table 2 calculates labour force location quotients for a more detailed breakdown, wherein a value in excess of 1:00 indicates a specialization greater than would be expected given the region's share of the total labour force.[32] In this case the regions are the Maritimes and Newfoundland while the 'nation' includes these and Central Canada.[33] In 1911 the Maritimes had a roughly balanced share of employment in agriculture, transportation and professional services. Not surprisingly, it had a disproportionately large share of fishing employment and a less dramatically large share of logging and mining employment. On the other hand, it was under-represented in manufacturing employment and in construction, which may be taken as an index of fixed capital investment, and trade and financial activity, which may be an index of entrepreneurial activity. Between 1911 and 1941 the disproportionate concentration in fishing was modified, but otherwise the heavy specialization in primary activities solidified, and the manufacturing ratio deteriorated. The disproportionate share of professional employment reflects the large educational and health establishment relative to the labour force which remained in the region, and perhaps the tendency for the region's middle class to concentrate in socially prestigious professions when entrepreneurial opportunities were poor. In Newfoundland, the fragility of the 1911 census invites caution in intertemporal comparison, although the data does suggest an equivalent structural development to the Maritimes. By the 1940s both sub-regions of the 'nation' were well established as producers and transporters of primary products, and dependent upon the central sub-region for finished goods and entrepreneurial and associated labour force activity.

Since population and labour force data are inconclusive indices of relative economic growth, it is essential to compare output data. The difficulty here is that no compatible set of output statistics exists. For the Maritimes, the most satisfactory are Alan Green's Gross Value Added (GVA) series for 1890, 1910, 1929 and 1956. No comparable series exists for Newfoundland, and the prospects for creating one are doubtful. The only recent estimate of output is a limited three sector Gross Value of Production (GVP) series pre-

---

32   For a discussion of the location quotient, see W. Isard, *Methods of Regional Analysis* (Cambridge, Mass., 1960), pp. 123 - 6.

33   The West has been excluded because its growth from the turn of the century distorts trends in the older settled regions, which must be the reference point for analysis of Atlantic development.

TABLE 3: GROSS VALUE OF PRODUCTION: NEWFOUNDLAND

($000 1935 - 39)

	Agri.	Forest.	Mining	Fish	Manuf.	Total	Per Capita
1884	1,245	214	761	9,456	2,520	14,196	72
1891	1,693	447	935	9,220	2,175	14,470	72
1901	3,383	755	1,513	12,242	3,311	21,204	96
1911	5,368	1,396	1,931	13,119	3,982	25,796	106
1921	6,116	3,386	446	7,846	4,320	22,114	84
1929	6,318	14,581	3,003	12,867	6,711	43,480	156
1939	7,980	14,928	8,903	6,869	9,596	48,276	160

NOTE: Agricultural output 1891 - 1921 derived from Department of Overseas Trade, *Industries and Resources of Newfoundland for 1925*
(HMSO, 1926), p. 14. These estimates include the value of the animal
stock, which in 1921 was about 40% of the value of field crops and
animal products. Census returns indicate the ratio of animals to
field crop production was relatively constant, and hence the Department of Trade estimates for 1891 - 1921 have been deflated accordingly. Output in 1884 is estimated by the value of output in 1891
weighted by the relative physical productivity of field crops in the
two years. For 1929 the estimate is the 1935 field crop output plus
the 1921 animal products ratio. For 1939 as given in Newfoundland
Industrial Development Board, *Industrial Survey*, vol. 1, p. 92.

—All other sector estimates derived from the Newfoundland Customs
Returns, *Journals of the House of Assembly*, and *Census of Newfoundland and Labrador*, 1884, 1891, 1901, 1911, 1921 and 1935: and
for 1939 as estimated in Industrial Development Board, *Industrial
Survey*, vol. 1, p. 92. The forestry sector includes only lumbering
and pulp and paper. The manufacturing sector is net of pulp and
paper. The fishing sector includes an estimate for domestic consumption.

—All estimates deflated by the General Wholesale Price Index for
Canada in M. C. Urquhart & K. A. H. Buckley, *Historical Statistics
of Canada*, Series J34, and for mining J35.

pared by the Royal Commission on the Economic State and Prospects of Newfoundland and Labrador, for various years between 1891 and 1948.[34] Therefore, in order to compare Newfoundland and Maritimes development it is necessary to create a new set of indices. Tables 3 to 5 provide a GVP series in five goods producing sectors for Newfoundland, the Maritimes and Canada, using published Dominion Bureau of Statistics estimates for the Mainland, and a wider variety of sources for the Island.[35] Tables 6 and 7 attempt to compare real output growth rates and sectoral contributions to real output growth for the three economies.

There are a number of limitations surrounding the use of these data. It proved impossible to create long term estimates of output in construction, electric power, transportation and the service industries. The assumption, nonetheless, is that this more limited series will serve as a proxy of the comparative rate of growth of the three economies, and that there is no serious distortion of the progress of one against the others.[36] Secondly, since the estimates are of GVP rather than GVA, the absolute values must be used with caution as indicators of comparative productivity and well-being.[37] Thirdly, the series have been deflated by the General Wholesale Price Index to estimate the value of real output growth. While the use of sectoral deflators would more accurately estimate real GVP in Canada and the Maritimes, whether this would also be true for Newfoundland is less certain. It is true that the Island's growing dependence on Canada and the competitive nature of much of its output, suggests that Canadian sectoral deflators would be appropriate. But on crude data, a crude deflator seemed less risky than a finer one. Finally, the early 1880s was chosen as the initial date because of data limitations before that decade. The terminal year of 1939 was adopted because the War had powerful stimulative effects on both Newfoundland and the Maritimes which inflates the historic growth performance prior to Newfoundland's entry into Confederation. For any of the economies it may be argued that some other date would be more appropriate than the one chosen. This objection is insurmountable unless one has annual estimates of output, or some other index of trade cycle behaviour. In their absence, and

---

34 Alan G. Green, *Regional Aspects of Canada's Economic Growth* (Toronto, 1971), Appendix B; Newfoundland, *Report of the Royal Commission on the Economic State and Prospect of Newfoundland and Labrador* (St. John's, 1967), Table 3. GVP is the value of shipments, while GVA is this less the value of inputs.

35 Where possible, all Newfoundland estimates were double checked against other sources.

36 In the case of the service sector, the labour force analysis gives some support for these assumptions.

37 In the case of the Maritimes and Newfoundland, however, the broad similarities of industrial mix and the state of technology in most sectors should not lead to serious distortions.

TABLE 4: GROSS VALUE OF PRODUCTION: MARITIMES

($000 1935 - 39)

	Agric.	Forest.	Mining	Fish	Manuf.	Total	Per Capita
1880	41,956	13,297	3,115	14,918	42,626	115,912	133
1890	40,222	16,194	6,112	15,465	71,978	149,971	170
1900	58,763	17,199	14,424	20,253	56,414	167,053	187
1910	71,447	26,619	18,683	19,627	85,915	222,291	237
1920	81,283	22,317	18,235	9,183	105,642	236,660	237
1929	87,726	21,160	26,301	14,976	108,354	258,517	259
1939	77,241	30,164	31,198	14,935	124,120	277,658	252

NOTE: Agricultural output 1900-1939 from *Canada Year Book*, 1914, Table 9; 1924, pp. 203 - 4; 1934 - 35, pp. 254 - 5; 1941, pp. 152 - 3. For 1880 and 1890, O. J. Firestone, *Canada's Economic Development* (London, 1958), Table 69, p. 193, estimate of Canadian agricultural gross value of production. For Maritimes' share, Maritimes share of occupied farms in Canada weighted by the relative productivity in 1900 as estimated from *Canada Year Book*, 1914, Table 9.

—Forestry sector includes lumber and pulp and paper, from Canada, *The Maritime Provinces Since Confederation* (Ottawa, 1927), pp. 60 - 61; and Canada, *The Maritime Provinces in their Relation to the National Economy of Canada* (Ottawa, 1948), pp. 68 - 9, and 73.

—Mining from *Maritime Provinces in Relation, op. cit.,* Table 30, pp. 85 - 8.

—Fisheries is marketed value from *Maritime Provinces in Relation,* Table 13, p. 58.

—Manufacturing is net of lumber and pulp and paper as calculated from *Maritime Provinces in Relation, op. cit.,* Table 36, pp. 98 - 100.

—All estimates deflated by the General Wholesale Price Index for Canada in M. C. Urquhart & K. A. H. Buckley, *Historical Statistics of Canada,* Series J34, and for mining J35.

given the close relationship among the three economies, the decision was made to measure at common dates. The value of any decennial comparison is doubtful; but the approach should not seriously compromise conclusions drawn from growth rate calculations of over sixty years, or even for sub-periods of thirty years.

What were the sectoral and aggregate growth patterns in these three economies? It is logical to begin with agricultural production, where Newfoundland has always faced a comparative weakness. In 1880 agricultural output represented 44% of goods production (excluding construction) in Canada, 36% in the Maritimes and only 9% in Newfoundland.[38] By 1939 the relative contribution of agriculture to output had declined by 48% in Canada but only 22% in the Maritimes. In Newfoundland, however, the government launched a major initiative at the turn of the century to stimulate food production and, despite the climate and soil conditions, output expanded under the watchful eyes of a myriad of local agricultural societies and a newly established Department of Agriculture from 9% of goods production in 1884 to 21% in 1910. In subsequent decades the relative share fell as other sectors of the economy expanded rapidly, but in 1939 agricultural output still accounted for a respectable 17% of goods production.

From the 1880s into the interwar period, the number of people employed in the farm sector of the Maritimes declined, from 140,000 in 1880 to 96,000 in 1941, or from 18% of the population to 8%. In Newfoundland the full-time agriculturalist was a rarity, but the absolute number of full-time farmers rose from 1500 in 1891 to 4200 by 1935. While this represented only 1.5% of the population, the bulk of the country's 35,000 fishermen were also subsistence farmers. In Canada, employment in agriculture rose from 662,000 in 1881 (15% of population) to over one million by 1921, after which it stabilized to 1941, representing 9% of the population. Thus, over the period the relative commitment of population to agriculture was about the same in the Maritimes as in Canada, but the numbers shrank in the former while they rose in the latter into the interwar period.

The number of occupied farms in the Maritimes rose from 78,000 to 113,000 in 1891, after which the number declined steadily. In Canada, because of Western settlement, farm numbers increased until 1931, but not in the Central Provinces for neither Quebec nor Ontario had significantly more farms at the end of the interwar period than they had after Confederation. Yet, while the trends were the same in the Maritimes and in Central Canada, the decline in occupied farms in the Maritimes between 1891 and 1941 was 45% compared with only 17% in Ontario and 12% in Quebec. Nor

---

38 Henceforth, the qualification "excluding construction" will not be made.

TABLE 5: GROSS VALUE OF PRODUCTION: CANADA

($000 1935 - 39)

	Agri.	Forest.	Mining	Fish	Manuf.	Total	Per Capita
1880	369,080	45,960	14,125	20,195	385,345	385,345	192
1890	456,035	76,900	26,290	26,400	623,205	1,208,830	250
1900	647,435	88,225	97,805	34,550	682,700	1,550,715	289
1910	924,840	101,565	123,150	28,170	1,383,760	2,561,485	355
1920	739,175	218,300	103,230	24,235	1,605,790	2,690,730	306
1929	1,309,055	313,780	220,385	38,365	2,802,960	4,684,545	467
1939	1,182,770	311,400	441,210	40,480	3,198,485	5,174,345	459

NOTE: For the forestry sector, sawmilling, pulp and paper production estimated as 60% of 'Wood Products' in Firestone, *Canada's Economic Development*, Table 78, p. 213. For 1900 and 1910 *Canada Year Book*, 1924, pp. 293 - 4 and 296. For 1920 - 39, Canada, *The Maritime Provinces in their Relation to the National Economy of Canada*, Tables 20 and 24, pp. 69, 74.

—Agricultural output 1880 - 1920 as in Firestone, *op.cit.*, Table 69, p. 193. For 1929 and 1939 farm output as in *Canada Year Book*, 1934 - 35, pp. 254 - 5; and 1941, pp. 152 - 3.

—Mining for 1880 - 90 as in *Canada Year Book*, 1941, pp. xiv - xvi plus coal. For 1900 - 39 all metallic and non-metallic production (excluding cement) as in M. C. Urquhart & K. A. H. Buckley, *Historical Statistics of Canada*, Series N1-26 and N89-119 and N170.

—Manufacturing is net of lumber and pulp and paper, as derived from *Maritime Provinces in their Relation, op.cit.*, Table 36, p. 100.

—Fisheries as in *Maritime Provinces in their Relation, op.cit.*, Table 13, p. 58.

—All estimates deflated by the General Wholesale Price Index for Canada in *Historical Statistics*, Series J34, and for mining J35.

was this relatively greater loss of farms in the Maritimes compensated by growth in average farm size. Improved acreage per farm was 36 acres in 1871 compared with 48 acres in Quebec and 51 acres in Ontario. By 1941 there was no significant change in the acreage of the average Maritime farm, but the Quebec farm was by then two-thirds larger and the Ontario farm was twice as large.[39] Compared with Western Europe, the average Maritime farm was not especially small, for in England in the 1930s improved acreage per farm was 51 acres, in Denmark 39, Germany and France 21, and in Sweden 18 acres.[40] But European farmers in this period were not very prosperous, and compared with the Maritime farmer they had access to large urban markets and better opportunities for exploiting possibilities of 'high farming'.

Newfoundland farm output grew by over six times, although from an insignificant base of $1.2 million in 1884 to only $8.0 million in 1939. The fastest rate of growth was secured in the 1884 - 1911 period at 5.6% per annum, and this accounted for some 35% of the real growth in output for the economy. Very clearly, there were important dividends gained from the agricultural programme introduced during these years, as well as from the opening of the west coast of the Island and improved transport links to the urban markets. In the 1911 - 1939 period, however, the growth rate fell back to 1.4% per annum, which reflected both the strong relative growth of other sectors of the economy and the real limits to output imposed by natural conditions and the small urban market.

The Maritime output of $42 million in 1880 and $77 million in 1939 was obviously huge compared with Newfoundland; but the growth performance of the sector was relatively weak. In 1880 - 1910 output grew at 1.8% per annum and in 1910-1939 at only 0.3%, compared with 3.1% and 0.9% for Canada. In the period when the West was opened, it is understandable that Canadian growth should be higher than in a long-established region like the Maritimes. And while a growth rate of only 0.3% in 1911 - 1939 might appear dismal, it was no worse than the performance of Quebec and Ontario combined.[41] Moreover, through rural depopulation in the 1920s, Maritime farm efficiency drew very close to that of Quebec/Ontario. In 1910 real output per acre in the Maritimes was about $21 compared with $28 in Quebec/Ontario; by 1939 this had narrowed to $24 compared with $26.[42] The difference in the two

39 Calculated from, Canada, *The Maritime Provinces in their Relation to the National Economy of Canada* (Ottawa, 1948), Table 3, pp. 44 - 5.

40 W. S. and E. S. Woytinsky, *World Population and Resources* (New York, 1953), Table 209, pp. 44 - 5.

41 The comparable Quebec/Ontario rate calculated from deflated values in *Canada Year Book*, 1914, Table 9; 1924, pp. 203 - 4; 1934 - 35, pp. 254 - 5; and 1941, pp. 152 - 3.

42 Cash farm sales in the Maritimes were substantially lower than in Quebec/Ontario, but this reflects relative marketization and not the well-being of the population.

TABLE 6: REAL OUTPUT GROWTH RATES
(% per annum)

	Agri.	Forest.	Mining	Fish	Manuf.	Total	Per Capita
NFLD.							
1884-1911	5.6	7.2	3.5	1.2	1.7	2.2	1.4
1911-1939	1.4	8.9	5.7	-2.3	3.2	2.3	1.5
1884-1939	3.4	8.0	4.5	-0.6	2.4	2.2	1.4
MARITIMES							
1880-1910	1.8	2.3	6.1	0.9	2.3	2.2	1.9
1910-1939	0.3	0.4	1.8	-0.9	1.3	0.8	0.2
1880-1939	1.0	1.4	4.0	0.0	1.8	1.5	1.1
CANADA							
1880-1910	3.1	2.7	7.4	1.1	4.3	3.8	2.0
1910-1939	0.8	3.9	4.4	1.2	2.9	2.4	0.9
1880-1939	2.0	3.3	6.0	1.2	3.7	3.2	1.5

NOTE: Calculated from Tables 3 to 5. All calculated rates are compound rates per annum and not fitted trends.

TABLE 7: SECTORAL CONTRIBUTIONS TO REAL OUTPUT GROWTH
%

	Agri.	Forest.	Mining	Fish	Manuf.
NFLD.					
1884-1911	35.5	10.2	10.1	31.6	12.6
1911-1939	11.6	60.2	31.0	-27.8	25.0
1911-1939 (exld fish)	9.1	47.1	24.3	—	19.5
MARITIMES					
1880-1910	27.7	12.5	14.6	4.4	40.7
1910-1939	10.5	6.4	22.6	-8.5	69.0
1910-1939 (exld fish)	9.6	5.9	20.8	—	63.6
CANADA					
1880-1910	32.2	3.2	6.3	0.5	57.8
1910-1939	9.9	8.0	12.2	0.5	69.5

NOTE: Calculated from Tables 3 to 5.

farming regions came from the larger average farm size up the St. Lawrence, for in 1939 output per farm was $1,726 in Quebec/Ontario and $1,465 in the Maritimes. But if a comparison is made with Ontario alone, the disparities widen. For example, the value of output per head of population in 1939 was $68 in the Maritimes, $62 in Quebec and $100 in Ontario. Nonetheless, Maritime farming was not a notably deficient sector of the economy, since it grew at a rate comparable to Quebec/Ontario (although not Ontario alone, with its urban market advantages) and the contribution of the sector to the growth of total output was comparable to that for the Canadian economy. If one is searching for explanations of Maritime economic problems in the period, enquiry into the farm sector will not yield large dividends. In Newfoundland's case, there were greater opportunities for gains in output and productivity given the very low initial base. Clearly, some of these gains were being harvested, since output expanded throughout the period at a higher rate than in either the Maritimes or Canada.

Rather than the agricultural sector, difficulties in the forest industry are more obviously important in explaining sluggish growth in the Maritimes. Towards the end of the century the Maritime lumber industry entered a long period of depression as a result of demand shifts and supply competition. While pulp mills were established in the region in the 1890s, it was not until the late 1920s that newsprint mills were built. In 1911 pulp production represented only 7% of lumber output, rising to 55% by 1926. In the 1930s expanding pulp and paper output overtook the badly depressed lumber sector.

The lumber industry in the Maritimes contracted sharply in the interwar period under the impact of less competitive wood supplies and trade protectionism, and the recovery which emerged in the second half of the 1930s was weaker than in Canada as a whole. In the 1920s the real capital/labour ratio was comparable to the national level,[43] but the output/labour ratio was 20% to 30% lower.[44] In the 1930s the position of both ratios moved sharply against the Maritimes relative to Canada. The efficiency of capital employment (as measured by the output/capital ratio) was also substantially lower in the Maritimes in the 1920s, although it improved in the 1930s. The pulp and paper industry compensated for some of the problems in the lumber sector, but here too output growth was slower than in Canada, as the mills were generally smaller and less efficient.[45] These troubles were reflected in the comparative

---

43   In 1926 it was $3,618 in the Maritimes and $3,833 for Canada. Calculated from *Maritime Provinces in Relation*, Table 20, pp. 68 - 9.

44   In 1926 it was $2,337 in the Maritimes and $2,958 for Canada, *loc. cit.*

45   The Maritime capital/labour ratio in pulp and paper in the 1920s was about 20% lower, as was output per worker. In the 1930s, however, with the spread of newsprint mills the Maritime ratios converged with the Canadian.

growth rates. Over the period 1880 - 1939 real output expanded at 1.4% compared with 3.3% for Canada. In the sub-period 1880 - 1910 the relative performance was more satisfactory (2.3% and 2.7%) and it was really in the 1910 - 1939 period that the Maritimes' industry stood virtually still compared with Canada (0.4% and 3.9%). Accordingly, while the forest sector accounted for some 6% of total output growth in the Maritimes, it contributed some 8% to the faster growing Canadian economy.

Newfoundland had not possessed the kind of forest resources which had allowed the Maritimes to develop a large lumbering industry at an early stage in its history. In 1873 the country imported over $76,000 of lumber and other forest products against exports of only $7,100.[46] Expansion was rapid in subsequent years, however, and by 1901 (before the establishment of pulp and paper) the lumbering labour force had grown from 450 to 1,400, and by 1911 Newfoundland earned a surplus on non-pulp and paper trade of $63,500.[47] Depressed markets for lumber in the interwar period, however, meant that the mills were forced back into dependence upon domestic consumption. Most of these mills were small, two-man and part-time operations; while there were a handful of large mills each employing several hundred, the 534 licensed mills in 1929 only produced some $400,000 of lumber, compared with $15.5 million in the 650 Maritime mills.[48] In 1938 lumber output was still only $450,000 and at the end of the interwar period net imports of lumber were about 20% of the value of domestic output.[49]

The transformation of Newfoundland's forest industry came with the establishment of pulp and paper capacity. The big newsprint mill opened at Grand Falls in 1910 produced $1.2 million of products compared with $1.5 million in the twelve Maritime pulp mills; and with the addition of the Corner Brook mill in 1925 Newfoundland's output equalled that of the Maritimes. In 1938 the two Newfoundland mills employed only 70% of the employees, but paid-out in wages and salaries 90% of the compensation paid in Maritime mills. The average Newfoundland wage was 27% higher than in the Maritimes and 21% higher than in Canada,[50] and this high wage characteristic has persisted to the present.[51] It was for no idle reason that a good job in Newfoundland

46 Customs Returns, *Journal of the House of Assembly*, 1873.

47 *Ibid.*, 1912.

48 Department of Overseas Trade, *Economic Conditions in Newfoundland* (London, HMSO, 1931), p. 28; and *Maritime Provinces in their Relation*, Table 20, pp. 68 - 9.

49 Newfoundland Industrial Development Board, *Industrial Survey* (St. John's, 1949), vol. II, pp. 34 - 5.

50 Calculated from *Industrial Survey*, vol. II, p. 37; and *Maritime Provinces in their Relation*, Table 24, pp. 74 - 5.

51 Economic Council, *Living Together*, p. 43.

was known as a 'Grand Falls job'.

The expansion of output for the domestic lumber market, the large packaging industry for the fishery, and the spectacular growth of pulp and newsprint in the twentieth century, were reflected in the industry growth rate for Newfoundland. Beginning from a low base, the sector grew at a rate of 7.6% per annum to 1901 (prior to the first newsprint mill) and by 8.9% in the 1911 - 1939 period. The sector accounted for nearly half of non-fisheries goods production growth in the period, and nearly a third of the value of measured goods production by 1939. Even though the industry was foreign owned and purchased substantial inputs from outside Newfoundland, in 1935 wages paid in logging and paper manufacturing probably accounted for up to 25% of earnings in the economy.[52] In 1880 forest products accounted for only 1.5% of goods production in Newfoundland compared to 5.5% in Canada and 11% in the Maritimes. In subsequent decades, the relative importance of the sector in the Maritimes was unchanged, while it rose modestly to 6.0% in Canada, and rose enormously in Newfoundland to 5.4% in 1910 and 31.0% in 1939. The sector offered a major net addition to output in Newfoundland, whereas in the Maritimes pulp and paper mainly offset the decline of the lumber industry.

The mining industry, because of its instability and harsh working conditions, has had a greater social and economic impact on the Atlantic region than is reflected in its contribution to output. In 1880 mining contributed 5% of goods production in Newfoundland, 3% in the Maritimes and 2% in Canada; by 1939 these shares had risen to 18%, 11% and 9% respectively. Nova Scotia dominated mining in the Maritimes with gold, gypsum and coal. It was the latter, of course, which gave Nova Scotia its prominence, and coal production was never less than 80% of total mineral output. In the 1880s and 1890s Maritime mineral output was close to 25% of the Canadian total, but with expansion in Northern Quebec and Ontario, Alberta and British Columbia, this share fell to 15% in 1900 - 1910 and to 7% by 1941. It is less well known that Newfoundland was an important mineral producer by the last quarter of the nineteenth century. The Notre Dame Bay copper mines, opened in 1864 and operated until 1917, made the country the fourteenth largest copper producer in the world.[53] This was followed by the opening of the Bell Island iron mines in 1895, which quickly came to account for some two-thirds of mineral exports. This had fallen to around 40% by the end of the 1930s, reflecting both uncer-

---

52   An estimate derived from wages paid in 1938, as given in *Industrial Survey*, vol. II, pp. 32 - 6, and total earnings for 1935 as given in *Tenth Census of Newfoundland and Labrador, 1935*, vol. II, part 1, sec. II, p. 85.

53   Michael J. Prince, *Provincial Mineral Policies: Newfoundland 1949 - 75* (Kingston, Centre for Resource Studies, 1977), p. 4.

tain markets for iron ore, and the opening of the base metal mines at Buchans in 1928 and the fluorspar mine at St. Lawrence in 1933.

In the 1880 - 1910 period, world output of the major metallic, non-metallic and mineral fuels was growing at 4.5% per annum.[54] Expansion in Canada (7.5%) and the Maritimes (6.1%) was substantially in excess of world growth, but it was lower in Newfoundland (3.5%). In 1910 - 1939, however, while world output expansion fell to 2.3%, the Canadian rate remained substantially higher (4.4%). In the Maritimes, the coal industry confronted growing competition from the United States as well as the postwar shift to alternative fuels, and this, combined with the absence of major new mining developments, yielded a comparatively slow rate of growth (1.8%). In Newfoundland, on the other hand, the new ventures opened in the interwar years, combined with the high productivity of the Wabana iron fields, generated a growth rate (5.7%) substantially above both world and Canadian levels.

Mineral output per head was normally substantially higher in the Maritimes than in Canada until the interwar period. It was then that the relatively poor growth performance began to tell, and by 1941 output was about $26 per person in the Maritimes compared with about $40 for Canada. Until the 1930s Newfoundland's output per head was substantially lower than in either Canada or the Maritimes, but with output of some $22 per head in 1941 the country was pointed towards its postwar stature as the major mining centre of the Atlantic region. In Canada the growth of mining output contributed some 12% to total growth of goods production, but in the Atlantic region it was much more important at 20% and 24% in the Maritimes and Newfoundland. While Newfoundland's growth rate substantially exceeded that of the Maritimes and Canada in 1911 - 1939, the expansion of the industry did not generate the same local benefits as noted with the forest products sector. While the sector accounted for 18% of goods production in Newfoundland in 1939, it accounted for less than 5% of total earnings in 1935.[55]

The major structural difference between Newfoundland and the Maritimes is revealed in the relative dependence of the two economies on the fishing industry. In 1884 some 67% of goods production in Newfoundland was accounted for by fish products, compared with only 13% in the Maritimes and 2% in Canada. If fishing and agriculture are combined, the difference in relative dependence on primary activities is narrowed (75% and 50%) but remains striking, and emphasizes the vulnerability of Newfoundland's dependence upon a one product export economy. By 1910 the fishery contribution to output had fallen to 51% in Newfoundland and 9% in the Maritimes,

54 Woytinsky, *World Population*, Table 322, p. 571.
55 Calculated from *Tenth Census of Newfoundland*, vol. II, p. 85.

and by 1939 (reflecting the interwar depression in the industry) only 14% and 5% respectively. By that time the Maritimes was relatively more dependent upon fisheries and agriculture than Newfoundland (33% compared with 31%), although that also reflected the comparative poverty of arable food production on the Island.

Large and old industries, like the Atlantic fishery, are often characterized by relatively low rates of growth, and this was certainly the case with the fishing sector. In Newfoundland in 1884 - 1911 fisheries output grew by only 1.2% and in the Maritimes at less than 1.0% per annum. It was in 1910 - 1939, however, that the industry was overwhelmed by troubles. In Newfoundland real output growth contracted at a rate of -2.3% and in the Maritimes at almost -1.0% per annum. The industry was extraordinarily dependent upon international trade, and returns to production factors were especially sensitive to the host of interwar disturbances, including the postwar inflation, rising protectionism, the Depression, and the collapse of the multilateral payments system in the 1930s. Compounding these external problems was a highly conservative and defeatist approach to potential changes in product, catching and marketing on the part of industry and government.[56] The less bad performance of the Maritimes reflected its greater product diversification and its access to the United States market, for Newfoundland was much more dependent upon saltfish and the highly competitive and disturbed European markets. Given the unusual importance of the industry to the Newfoundland labour force, and hence to the revenues of the government, its virtual collapse in the interwar period seriously compromised the gains which were won from expansion of other sectors of the economy. Thus, while in the Maritimes fisheries contraction was -8.5% of total output growth, in Newfoundland it was -27.8% over the 1911 - 1939 period.

Economic policy in Newfoundland consistently focussed upon developing and expanding resource sectors. In the Maritimes there were much greater expectations for manufacturing. The contribution of manufacturing (excluding lumber and pulp and paper throughout this discussion) to the three economies in 1880 ranged from a low of 18% of goods production in Newfoundland to 37% in the Maritimes and 46% in Canada. By 1939 this had risen only to 20% in Newfoundland, but it was now 45% in the Maritimes and 62% in Canada. Relative to Canada, therefore, the contribution of manufacturing to total output had declined over the period in both Newfoundland and the Maritimes.

In 1880 current dollars, manufacturing gross value was $40 per capita in the Maritimes, $60 in Canada and only $10 in Newfoundland. By 1890 the Maritimes relative position improved from 63% of the Canadian level to

---

56   This is discussed in Alexander, *Decay of Trade*, ch. 1.

68%, with a per capita production of $67. Much of this output consisted of unsophisticated raw material processing and small shop output (as it did everywhere at this time); nonetheless, the Maritimes and Canada ranked favourably with other countries in the world. While such comparisons are fraught with difficulties, the order of achievement is suggested by an 1888 output per head (in $U.S.) of $117 in the United Kingdom, $65 in France and Germany, $50 in Sweden and the Netherlands, and as little as $25 in Italy and Spain.[57] Although there are special difficulties with the Newfoundland data which lead to underestimation of finished goods production, clearly it was not a significant manufacturer by any standard.[58]

By 1937 the Maritimes relative position had changed dramatically. Per capita output in that year was $140, compared with $80 in Newfoundland and $330 in Canada. Between 1890 and 1937, therefore, the Maritimes' position relative to Canada had fallen from 68% to 42%, and it had even deteriorated against Newfoundland. In the United Kingdom in 1935 output per head was $290, in Germany $285 and in Italy about $115.[59] If basic iron and steel manufacturing is removed from the Maritime data, then its output per head falls to $95, which is not substantially in advance of the Newfoundland level. Between 1880 - 1910 real manufacturing output grew at 2.3% per annum in the Maritimes compared with 4.3% in Canada.[60] In the 1880s the Maritime growth rate was probably higher than Canada's (around 5.4% compared with 4.9%), but it fell below the Canadian performance in the 1890s and sub-stantially so in 1900 - 1910 (4.3% and 7.3%). Manufacturing's contribution to total output growth was only 41% in the Maritimes compared with 58% in Canada. In the 1910 - 1939 period, Maritimes real output grew at a much lower rate than before the War, and at only half the Canadian rate (1.3% and 2.9%). The 1920s was an especially bad period for the Maritimes, with a growth of only 0.3% compared with 6.1% in Canada. Still, in the badly de-pressed interwar economy of the Maritimes, this slow growing manufacturing sector still accounted for 69% of total output growth, which was almost the same as in Canada.

It is well established that Maritimes' manufacturing stagnated after the War. While its position relative to Canada was not one of equality at the

57 Calculated from Woytinsky, *World Population,* p. 1003.

58 The lower level of market activity in Newfoundland biases the results against the Island for all sectors. For the development of the manufacturing sector, see John Joy, "The Growth and Development of Trades and Manufacturing in St. John's, 1870 - 1914" (unpublished M.A. thesis, Memorial University of Newfoundland, 1977).

59 Woytinsky, *World Population,* Table 423, p. 997.

60 For both the Maritimes and Canada the actual rate might be somewhat higher because of a change in reporting which reduced the enumeration of output in 1910 relative to 1880.

beginning of Confederation, the Maritimes was relatively strong both nationally and internationally. Except in the 1880s, however, non-forest products manufacturing grew much more slowly than in Canada and the world, leaving the region more backward by the end of the interwar period than it had been in the last quarter of the nineteenth century. Newfoundland had no significant manufacturing capacity in the 1880s, and despite tariff barriers that came to exceed Canadian levels, it did not have a large per capita output by 1939. Nonetheless, in the 1910 - 1939 period, the country achieved a rate of growth of non-forest products manufacturing equal to that of Canada, and by 1947 domestic production of manufactures accounted for 25% of domestic consumption.[61] With the removal of the tariff barriers in 1949 much of this capacity was wiped out; but in a few product lines local firms were able to meet the competition and even export to the Mainland. Thus, even in Newfoundland it was possible for efficient secondary manufacturing to locate and produce for the national market.

This review of growth in five key sectors of the Atlantic economy now allows for a general answer to the first question posed at the beginning of this paper: how did Newfoundland's economic growth compare with the Maritimes in the decades prior to its union with Canada? A succinct answer is possible. In both 1880 and 1911 goods production in Newfoundland was about 12% of the Maritimes level, but by 1939 it had increased to about 20%. Relative to Canada, the Maritimes accounted for 14% of goods production in 1880, only 9% in 1911 and 5% by 1939. The Maritimes economy, therefore, shrank relative to both Newfoundland and Canada.

Behind these trends in relative size lies the growth rates for goods production in the three economies. In the 1880 - 1910 period Newfoundland and the Maritimes grew at the same rate (2.2%), which was 50% less than the growth rate in Canada (3.8%). Angus Maddison has estimated the growth of Gross Domestic Product (GDP) in twelve European and North American economies over 1870 - 1913 to average 2.7% per annum, ranging between 1.4% for Italy and 4.3% for the U.S.A.[62] If our estimates of goods production parallel that of GDP,[63] then the results suggest a pace of development in the Atlantic region more akin to that of the large and developed economies of Western Europe than the North American territories of settlement.

In the 1910 - 1939 period growth everywhere in the world was slower than in the preceding decades. For example, total output in Denmark, Sweden and

61 *Industrial Survey,* vol. 1, p. 90.

62 Maddison, *Economic Growth,* p. 28.

63 Maddison's GDP estimate for Canada is 3.8%, which is identical to our estimate for goods production growth.

the Netherlands expanded by some 2.2% per annum and in Norway at a somewhat faster rate of 2.8%.[64] In Canada and Newfoundland, goods production expanded by 2.4% per annum,[65] a rate three times greater than that achieved in the Maritimes. Although the Canadian rate was equalled by Newfoundland, on a per capita basis Newfoundland was consistently the least productive of the three economies. In 1884 with $72 per capita of goods production, it stood at only 54% of the Maritimes and 40% of Canada. By 1910 its position relative to the Maritimes had fallen to 45% and relative to Canada to 34%. But the industrial developments of the 1910 - 1939 period reversed this trend, and in 1939 Newfoundland's per capita output relative to the Maritimes had improved sharply to 64%. Still, with goods production in 1939 of only $160 compared with $460 in Canada, it is obvious that the Island was extremely vulnerable to the kind of trade and financial crisis which overwhelmed it in the 1930s. In terms of growth performance, it is also apparent that Newfoundland was developing from its low initial base at a more satisfactory pace than the Maritimes secured from its stronger initial position. Both communities were growing at a per capita rate on the level of Maddison's twelve countries in 1870 - 1913. But between 1910 - 1939 per capita growth in Newfoundland was higher than in Canada (1.5% and 0.9%), while in the Maritimes there was little real per capita growth in the goods producing sector (0.2%).

The sectoral contributions to aggregate growth in the Newfoundland economy were characterized by a major shift after the turn of the century. In 1884 - 1911 a third of the growth of output was gained in the agricultural sector, another third in fisheries, and the remainder was spread relatively evenly across forestry, mining and manufacturing. Agricultural contributions to growth were only slightly less important to the Maritimes and Canada, but the major sectoral contribution for both came from manufacturing. In the Maritimes, however, manufacturing provided only 40% of the contribution to total output that it did in Canada, with forestry, mining and fishing contributing much larger shares.

In the 1911 - 1939 period, negative growth in the fisheries was a major drag on output growth in Newfoundland, as it was in the Maritimes. Almost half of positive contributions to Newfoundland output were accounted for by the lumber and paper industry, and another quarter by mining. The relative contribution of manufacturing fell in this period, and the gains from the agricultural sector were modest. In the Maritimes and Canada, both agriculture and forestry were minor contributors to output growth, as was mining for Canada. Manufacturing in Canada, however, contributed over two-thirds of

64   *Ibid.* Table A-2.

65   Maddison's estimate of total production growth in Canada for 1910 - 38 is 2.0%.

the growth in the period, whereas it added 20% less in the Maritimes. On a net value of production basis, of course, the contribution of the manufacturing sector would be substantially less; but the data do pinpoint the relative weakening of finished goods production in the Maritimes relative to Canada. Thus, the rapid rate of growth in Newfoundland had its origins in the expansion of two new resource sectors. Had these sectors not developed when they did, the economic troubles of the country would have been still more terrible. In the Maritimes the resource sectors had undergone earlier and more substantial development, and the region could not look to these areas for fresh impetus to growth. Manufacturing growth was essential to the development of the Maritimes if it was to maintain its stature within Canada and relative to Newfoundland. This was not accomplished, and while the sector contributed almost 60% of output growth in the 1910 - 1939 period, it was a contribution to a real growth in total output that was absolutely and relatively very small.

A postwar estimate of Newfoundland's per capital national income for the years 1936 - 1939 showed it to be only 62% of the weighted average of the Maritime provinces.[66] This was probably a substantial *relative* improvement over what it had been some sixty years earlier. In 1880 Newfoundland was structurally backward in terms of its labour force and output distributions. Much of the responsibility for this lay in the natural obstacles to food production, for if the same per capita production had been achieved in Newfoundland (output in other sectors remaining the same), per capita goods production would have been 86% of the Maritimes' level rather than 54%. Given the low productivity levels in the fishery, it is reasonable to believe that output in other sectors would not fall under such an assumption. Indeed, given an adequate agricultural base, there is little doubt that population would have been larger, monetization of the economy more pervasive, and incomes substantially higher in all sectors. The effort that was made to raise agricultural output was important, but there was nothing Newfoundland could do about the weather and the soil. The task before the country was to overcome this natural disadvantage by maximum efficiency in other sectors. In the 1884 - 1911 period, although the impact of modernization and diversification efforts had little quantitative impact,[67] by Canadian, Maritime and Western European standards the growth of goods production was at a reasonable rate. Population growth, however, absorbed a large share of this with the consequence that output per capita in 1911 was lower relative to the

---

66   Calculated from MacKay, *Newfoundland,* Appendix B. The gross value of production series which has been used in this essay shows a ratio of 63%.

67   See David Alexander, "Traditional Economy", *op cit*

Maritimes and Canada than it had been in 1880. For Newfoundland, the 1884 - 1911 period was one of *extensive* growth within the traditional economic framework, notwithstanding the industrial developments which dominated the final years of the period. Unless one posits major changes in the general level of education and the quality of entrepreneurship, it is difficult to see how in this period Newfoundland could have developed at a more satisfactory rate than it did.

The Maritimes was a more sophisticated and prosperous economy in 1880 than Newfoundland, with a per capita output which was closer to the Canadian average than Newfoundland's was to the Maritimes. The major economic advantages which the region enjoyed were the early commercial potential of its agricultural and forestry resources, and its location closer to the markets and stimulus of the fast-growing eastern seaboard of the United States. While goods production did not grow any faster in the Maritimes than in Newfoundland, the ease of emigration lowered population growth, and in 1911 per capita goods production relative to Canada was only three percentage points lower than it had been in 1880. With its already highly developed primary sectors, the Maritimes had to rely more upon expansion in finished goods or export sales of services, such as shipping, to maintain or improve its position. But the shipping industry collapsed and manufacturing output expanded at little better than half the Canadian rate.

While the roots of the changes lay in the earlier period, a major break with continuity was visible in both Newfoundland and the Maritimes in the 1910 - 1939 period. Newfoundland began rapidly to assume its modern character as a major resource production centre, with an aggregate growth of output which matched that of Canada. Heavy emigration in the 1920s generated a per capita growth in goods production which was substantially higher than in Canada. The country's major failure, however, lay in the fisheries sector. Spectacular rates of growth could not be expected in the difficult trading climate of the 1920s and 1930s, but a long term growth between 1910 - 1939 of at least 1.5% per annum was possible for an efficient and imaginative fishing country.[68] If such a growth rate had been achieved (making no adjustments for population growth or linkage impacts on other sectors), total per capita output in 1939 would have been $237 rather than $160, representing 52% of the Canadian level rather than 35%. Yet, whatever opportunities were

68 Between 1920 and 1937, Newfoundland's share of output in the North Atlantic fishery fell by twelve percentage points, and in the markets the country steadily lost ground against its major competitors. Whatever the trading difficulties (and they were not uniquely faced by this country) they were compounded by a backward technology in primary fishing, poor product quality, and inefficient and fragmented marketing. See Alexander, *Decay of Trade*, chs. 2 and 3.

missed in Newfoundland in this period, its overall performance was exceedingly good compared with the Maritimes, where on both a total and a per capita basis goods production fell drastically relative to both Canada and Newfoundland. No sector of the economy which was measured grew at as much as half the rate of the equivalent Canadian sector, or even close to the rates in Newfoundland. The obvious question is whether this performance was in some way inevitable?

The Maritimes' agricultural sector was not markedly inferior to Ontario and somewhat better than Quebec by some measures. The slightly higher growth of output for Canada was largely attributable to the residue of Western expansion. Unlike the situation in Newfoundland and much of Canada, the forestry sector was already a mature industry. Newsprint manufacturing was relatively slow in coming to the Maritimes, and while higher growth was a possibility in the sector, the rate of growth recorded in Newfoundland was not. The mining growth rate was the highest in the Maritime economy, due partly to coal subsidies, but unlike Newfoundland, Quebec, Northern Ontario and the West, there were no mining frontiers to be opened in the Maritimes. Fisheries production was as badly handled in the Maritimes as it was in Newfoundland, but it was also relatively less important to the total or per capita growth rate. Thus, while margins for gains exist in any sector in any economy, it is clear that if the Maritimes was to maintain its relative well-being and stature within the country, it had to be secured in the finished goods sector.

If in the 1880 - 1910 period manufacturing output had grown at the national rate, then the real value of output in 1910 would have been $130 million rather than $85 million. If one also allows Maritime population to grow at the national rate, then total output per head in 1910 would have been $384 rather than $274. Making no allowances for inter-industry effects, total output per head would have been 77% of the national level rather than 67%. If one projects the same assumptions through the 1910 - 1939 period, the effect is to raise per capita goods production to 84% of the Canadian level as compared with the 55% which existed. The least important objection to this extrapolation is that expansion in manufacturing output would mean less output in other sectors, leaving the Maritimes with a different distribution of output but not with any major gains in total and per capita output. The Maritime economy in this period, however, was not burdened with factor supply constraints (assuming that national financial institutions were indeed national) and the likely effect of manufacturing growth at the national rate would be a regional output and income growth path which converged towards national equality. But having posited that as a reasonable prediction, was it possible for the Maritimes to achieve the Canadian rate of growth in manufacturing?

The truthful answer is that we do not know, and perhaps in the historical sense, it is unknowable. Keirstead, as we noted, argued that over most manufacturing sectors there were growing diseconomies to location in the Maritimes for the national market. Roy George has presented arguments that the cost disadvantages are insignificant today, which does not prove that they always were. Apart from the 1880s the rate of growth of manufacturing output in the Maritimes was substantially lower in both 1880 - 1910 and 1910 - 1939, with the interwar years being those when most of the trouble was concentrated. Acheson's work indicates a far from hopeless prospect for Maritime manufacturers up to the First War, and in many industries there was real strength. Forbes' analysis of the transportation issue strongly suggests that the absorption of the Intercolonial Railway into a national system, and the resulting loss of regional control over freight rates, killed-off any hopes of maintaining or strengthening manufacturing in the interwar period. The possibility that economic decline was a reflection of local entrepreneurial lassitude has been undercut by David Frank's study of the stunning ineptitude of the distinguished external management of one major Maritime industrial complex.[69] Until much more work is done, the best conclusion is that manufacturing in the Maritimes for the national market did involve locational costs, but that it was rendered virtually impossible by national transportation policy and the absence of national incentives to overcome the disadvantages. If one accepts that a basic objective of any country is to equalize opportunities across the land, and to implement policies which ultimately turn regional diseconomies into positive advantages, then the legitimate grievance of the Maritimes is that there was no place for it in twentieth-century Canada.

The evidence is unmistakable that, despite remaining outside the Canadian economic and political union, population and output grew faster in Newfoundland than it did in the Maritimes. Does it therefore follow — and this was our second question — that Newfoundland gained from standing apart, and that development in the Maritimes was retarded by its earlier absorption? Indices of economic growth do not provide a conclusive answer. It is possible to argue, for example, that Newfoundland's growth rate would have been even higher as a Province of Canada, as a consequence of a better supply of infastructure and a more attractive and stable climate for Canadian and foreign investment. The historical experience of the Maritimes, however, does not encourage such predictions. It is impossible to know how the Maritimes would have responded to a less open economic and political environment. The romantic hypothesis is to predict a burst of creativity, as a function of the concentration of skills and energies occasioned by real and patriotic constraints on the migration of labour and capital. The pessimist would predict stagnation at higher aggregate, but lower per capita, income.

Despite the impressive growth performance of Newfoundland during its

---

69   David Frank, "The Cape Breton Coal Industry and the Rise and Fall of the British Empire Steel Corporation", *Acadiensis*, VII (Autumn, 1977), pp. 3 - 34.

years of political independence, its history does not support the romantic interpretation. It is true that aggregate output grew faster in Newfoundland, and that there was some catching-up in terms of output and income per capita. But little of that is obviously attributable to the genius of the Newfoundland people operating within the constraints and incentives of their own nation state. Newfoundland's stronger growth performance mainly reflected the opening of an unexploited natural resource frontier by foreign corporations. It was principally the impact of rapid development of large newsprint mills and mines that lifted the Newfoundland economy onto a more respectable level relative to the Maritimes. This development was quite independent of whether Newfoundland was a Province of Canada or a quasi-sovereign Dominion. Indeed, the major domestically controlled sector of the economy, the fishery, was the sector which was the poorest performer and which contributed most to the financial and political collapse of 1933.

In the absence of a more creative development of domestically controlled sectors of the economy, Newfoundland in fact paid a price for its political independence. An earlier entry into Confederation would not have quickened the pace of development in foreign enclave sectors. It would not have guaranteed Newfoundlanders a higher rate of return from those resource sectors. It would not have conferred any important social welfare benefits, for these were mainly a product of the postwar years. Certainly, if the Maritimes are to be taken as a model, it would not have done anything to spark a more dynamic domestic sector. But it can be said that an earlier entry into Confederation would have relieved the country of its intolerable, externally held public debt which, in the crisis of the Depression, brought the country to its knees. Almost all of this debt had been acquired to support the railway system and to pay for the War effort. With the decline of exports during the early years of the Depression, payments of interest and principal could not be met, and the debt could not be rolled-over. Hence, the country collapsed in 1933, lost its Dominion status, suffered the ignominy of suspended democratic institutions, and as a result of these things, has harboured a sense of exploitation and vulnerability ever since.

The only demonstrably clear lesson from Newfoundland's experience is that very small countries are financially precarious. They survive only if international trade and payments systems are liberal; if they profit from international conflicts; if they avoid, relative to their size, colossal investment blunders; and if, like Iceland, they rely upon internally generated sources of growth and development. Union with a larger country provides an element of stability, and this is a benefit not to be taken lightly. It does not, however, necessarily bring improved opportunities for regional growth and development, as Maritimers well know. In terms of expectations, Maritimers might well be right to complain that Confederation generated disappointing long term results. But the Newfoundland example of externally generated growth and domestic entrepreneurial stagnation, perhaps suggests that the political question is fundamentally uninteresting. If the Dominion of Newfoundland is accepted as the historical analogy, then at least it can be said that Confederation allowed the Maritimes to maintain a shabby dignity.

T. W. ACHESON

Reprinted from Vol. I, No. 2
(Spring 1972)

The National Policy and the Industrialization of the Maritimes, 1880-1910

The Maritime provinces of Canada in 1870 probably came the closest of any region to representing the classic ideal of the staple economy. Traditionally shaped by the Atlantic community, the region's industrial sector had been structured to the production and export of timber, lumber products, fish and ships. The last was of crucial significance. In terms of the balance of trade, it accounted for more than one-third of New Brunswick's exports at Confederation. In human terms, the manufacture of ships provided a number of towns with large groups of highly skilled, highly paid craftsmen who were able to contribute significantly to the quality of community life. Against this background, the constricting British market for lumber and ships after 1873 created a serious economic crisis for the area. This was not in itself unusual. Throughout the nineteenth century the region's resource-based economy had suffered a series of periodic recessions as the result of changing imperial policies and world markets. Yet, in one respect, this crisis differed from all earlier; while the lumber markets gradually returned in the late 1870's, the ship market did not. Nova Scotians continued to build their small vessels for the coasting trade, but the large ship building industry failed to revive.

In the face of this uncertain future the National Policy was embraced by much of the Maritime business community as a new mercantilism which would re-establish that stability which the region had enjoyed under the old British order. In the first years of its operation the Maritimes experienced a dramatic growth in manufacturing potential, a growth often obscured by the stagnation of both the staple industries and population growth. In fact, the decade following 1879 was characterized by a significant transfer of capital and human resources from the traditional staples into a new manufacturing base which was emerging in response to federal tariff policies. This development was so significant that between 1881 and 1891 the industrial growth rate of Nova Scotia outstripped all other provinces in eastern Canada. The comparative growth

---

1 Nova Scotia's industrial output increased 66 percent between 1880 and 1890; that of Ontario and Quebec by 51 percent each. Canada, *Census* (1901), III, pp. 272, 283. Bertram estimates that the per capita value of Nova Scotia's industrial output rose from 57.8 percent to 68.9 percent of the national average during the period. Gordon Bertram, "Historical Statistics on Growth and Structure of Manufacturing in Canada 1870-1957", Canadian Political Science Association Conference on Statistics 1962 and 1963, *Report,* p. 122.

of the period is perhaps best illustrated in St. John. The relative increase in industrial capital, average wages, and output in this community significantly surpassed that of Hamilton, the Canadian city whose growth was perhaps most directly attributable to the protective tariff.[2]

Within the Atlantic region the growth of the 1880's was most unequally distributed. It centred not so much on areas or sub-regions as upon widely scattered communities.[3] These included the traditional Atlantic ports of St. John, Halifax, and Yarmouth; lumbering and ship building towns, notably St. Stephen and New Glasgow; and newer railroad centres, such as Moncton and Amherst. The factors which produced this curious distribution of growth centres were human and historical rather than geographic. The one characteristic shared by them all was the existence in each of a group of entrepreneurs possessing the enterprise and the capital resources necessary to initiate the new industries. Strongly community-oriented, these entrepreneurs attempted, during the course of the 1880's, to create viable manufacturing enterprises in their local areas under the aegis of the protective tariff. Lacking the resources to survive the prolonged economic recessions of the period, and without a strong regional metropolis, they acquiesced in the 1890's to the industrial leadership of the Montreal business community. Only at the century's end, with the expansion of the consolidation movement, did a group of Halifax financiers join their Montreal counterparts in asserting an industrial metropolitanism over the communities of the eastern Maritimes. This paper is a study in that transition.

I

The Maritime business community in the 1870's was dominated by three groups: wholesale shippers, lumber and ship manufacturers, and the small scale manufacturers of a variety of commodities for purely local consumption. As a group they were deeply divided on the question of whether the economic salvation of their various communities was to be found in the maintenance of an Atlantic mercantile system, or in a programme of continentalist-oriented industrial diversification. A wedding of the two alternatives appeared to be the ideal situation. While they had warily examined the proposed tariff of 1879, most leading businessmen accepted its philosophy and seriously attempted to adapt it to their community needs.[4]

2 Canada, *Census* (1901), III, pp. 326-9. The increase between 1880 and 1890 was as follows:

	St. John	Hamilton
Population	−3%	34%
Industrial Capital	125%	69%
Industrial Workers	118%	48%
Average Annual Wage	12%	2%
Value of Output	98%	71%

3 See Table I.

4 For a sampling of business opinion on the National Policy see K. P. Burn's reply to Peter Mitchell in the tariff debate of 1883, Canada, House of Commons, *Debates,* 1883, pp. 551-2; the opinion of Josiah Wood, *ibid.,* pp. 446-8; and the view of John F. Stairs, *ibid.,* 1885, pp. 641-9.

TABLE I

Industrial Development in Principal Maritime Centres 1880-1890

	Population	Industrial Capital	Employees	Average Annual Wages	Output	Industry by Output (1891)
Halifax (1880)	39,886	$2,975,000	3,551	$303	$6,128,000	Sugar**
Dartmouth (1890)	43,132	6,346,000	4,654	280	8,235,000	Rope*
						Cotton
						Confectionary
						Paint
						Lamps
St. John (1880)	41,353	2,143,000	2,690	278	4,123,000	Lumber**
(1890)	39,179	4,838,000	5,888	311	8,131,000	Machinery***
						Smelting
						Rope**
						Cottons
						Brass*
						Nails*
						Elect. Light**
New Glasgow (1880)	2,595	160,000	360	255	313,000	Primary Steel*
(1890)	3,777	1,050,000	1,117	355	1,512,000	Rolling Mills**
						Glass
St. Stephen (1880)	4,002	136,000	447	314	573,000	Cottons
Milltown (1890)	4,826	1,702,000	1,197	320	1,494,000	Confectionary
						Fish Canning
						Soap
						Lumber
Moncton (1880)	5,032	530,000	603	418	1,719,000	Sugar
(1890)	8,765	1,134,000	948	333	1,973,000	Cottons
						Woolens
						Rolling Stock
Fredericton- (1880)	7,218ᵃ	1,090,000ᵃ	911ᵃ	221ᵃ	1,031,000ᵃ	Cottons
Marysville (1890)	8,394	2,133,000	1,526	300	1,578,000	Lumber
						Foundry Product
Yarmouth (1880)	3,485	290,000	211	328	284,000	Cotton Yarn*
(1890)	6,089	783,000	930	312	1,234,000	Fish Canning
						Woolens
Amherst (1880)	2,274	81,000	288	281	283,000	Foundry Product
(1890)	3,781	457,000	683	293	724,000	Shoes
						Doors

a Estimates. Marysville was not an incorporated town in 1880, and totals for that date must be
  estimated from York County figures.

* Leading Canadian Producer; ** second; *** third.

Source: Canada. *Census* (1891), III, Table I; *Ibid.,* (1901), III, Tables XX, XXI.

For a variety of reasons the tariff held the promise of prosperity for the region's traditional commercial activities and, as well, offered the possibilities for the development of new manufacturing industry. For most Nova Scotian business leaders the West Indies market was vital to the successful functioning of the province's commercial economy. It was a major element in the region's carrying trade and also provided the principal market for the Nova Scotia fishing industry. These, in turn, were the foundations of the provincial ship-building industry. The successful prosecution of the West Indies trade, however, depended entirely upon the ability of the Nova Scotia merchants to dispose of the islands' sugar crop. The world depression in the 1870's had resulted in a dramatic decline in the price of refined sugar as French, German, British and American refineries dumped their surplus production on a glutted world market. By 1877 more than nine-tenths of Canadian sugar was obtained from these sources,[5] a fact which threatened the Nova Scotia carrying trade with disaster. A significant tariff on foreign sugar, it was felt, would encourage the development of a Canadian refining industry which would acquire all of its raw sugar from the British West Indies. Through this means, most Nova Scotian wholesalers and shippers saw in the new policy an opportunity both to resuscitate the coastal shipping industry of the province and to restore their primacy in the West Indies.

Of the newer industries which the National Policy offered, the future for the Maritimes seemed to lie in textiles and iron and steel products. The optimism concerning the possibilities of the former appears to have emerged out of a hope of emulating the New England experience. This expectation was fostered by the willingness of British and American cotton mill machinery manufacturers to supply on easy terms the necessary duty-free equipment, and by the feeling of local businessmen that the market provided by the tariff and the low quality labour requirements of such an enterprise would guarantee that a profitable business could be erected and maintained by the efforts of a single community. Behind such reasoning lay the general assumption that, despite major transportation problems, the Maritimes, and notably Nova Scotia, would ultimately become the industrial centre of Canada. The assumption was not unfounded. The region contained the only commercially viable coal and iron deposits in the Dominion, and had the potential, under the tariff, of controlling most of the Montreal fuel sources. Under these circumstances the development of textiles and the expansion of most iron and steel industries in the Atlantic area was perhaps not a surprising project.

Despite a cautious enthusiasm for the possibilities offered by the new federal economic dispensation, there was considerable concern about the organizational and financial problems in creating a new industrial structure. The Maritimes was a region of small family firms with limited capital capabilities. Other

5 Quoted by J. F. Stairs in the tariff debate of 1886, Canada, House of Commons, *Debates*, 1886, p. 775.

than chartered banks, it lacked entirely the financial structure to support any large corporate industrial entity. Like the people of Massachusetts, Maritimers were traditionally given to placing their savings in government savings banks at a guaranteed 4 percent interest than in investments on the open market.[6] Regional insurance, mortgage and loan, and private savings corporations were virtually unknown. The result was to throw the whole financial responsibility for undertaking most manufactories upon the resources of individual entrepreneurs.

Since most enterprises were envisioned as being of general benefit to the community at large, and since few businessmen possessed the necessary capital resources to single-handedly finance such an undertaking, most early industrial development occurred as the result of co-operative efforts by groups of community entrepreneurs. These in turn were drawn from a traditional business elite of wholesalers and lumbermen. In Halifax as early as May, 1879, a committee was formed from among the leading West Indies shippers "to solicit capital, select a site and get a manufacturing expert" for the organization of a sugar refinery.[7] Under its leadership $500,000 was raised, in individual subscriptions of $10-20,000, from among members of the Halifax business community. This procedure was repeated during the formation of the Halifax Cotton Company in 1881; more than $300,000 was subscribed in less than two weeks, most of it by thirty-two individuals.[8]

The leadership in the development of these enterprises was taken by young members of traditional mercantile families. The moving spirit in both cases was Thomas Kenny. A graduate of the Jesuit Colleges at Stonyhurst (England) and St. Gervais (Belgium), Kenny had inherited from his father, the Hon. Sir Edward Kenny, M.L.C., one of the largest wholesale shipping firms in the region. In the early 1870's the younger Kenny had invested heavily in shipyards scattered throughout five counties of Nova Scotia, and had even expanded into England with the establishment of a London branch for his firm. Following the opening of the refinery in 1881, he devoted an increasingly large portion of his time to the management of that firm.[9] Kenny was supported in his efforts by a number of leading merchants including the Hon. Robert Boak, Scottish-born president of the Legislative Council, and John F. Stairs, Manager of the Dartmouth Rope Works. Stairs, who had attended Dalhousie University, was a member of the executive council of Nova Scotia, the son of a legislative councillor, and a grandson of the founder of the shipping firm of William Stairs, Son and Morrow Limited.[10]

6 *Monetary Times*, 4 June, 6 September 1886. Forty-five of the fifty savings banks in the Dominion were located in the Maritimes.

7 *Monetary Times*, 16 May 1879.

8 *Monetary Times*, 20 May 1881.

9 George M. Rose, ed., *Cyclopedia of Canadian Biography* (Toronto, 1886-8), II, pp. 729-31 (henceforth cited as *CCB*).

10 *Encyclopedia of Canadian Biography* (Montreal, 1904-7), I, p. 86; *CCB*, II, p. 155; W. J. Stairs, *History of Stairs Morrow* (Halifax, 1906), pp. 5-6.

In contrast to Halifax, St. John had always been much more a manufacturing community and rivalled Ottawa as the principal lumber manufacturing centre in the Dominion. Development in the New Brunswick city occurred as new growth on an existing industrial structure and centred on cotton cloth and iron and steel products. The New Brunswick Cotton Mill had been erected in 1861 by an Ulster-born St. John shipper, William Parks, and his son, John H. Parks. The latter, who had been trained as a civil engineer under the tutelage of the chief engineer of the European and North American Railroad, assumed the sole proprietorship of the mill in 1870.[11] In 1881 he led the movement among the city's dry goods wholesalers to establish a second cotton mill which was incorporated as the St. John Cotton Company.

The principal St. John iron business was the firm of James Harris. Trained as a blacksmith, the Annapolis-born Harris had established a small machine shop in the city in 1828, and had expanded into the foundry business some twenty-three years later. In 1883, in consequence of the new tariff, he determined to develop a completely integrated secondary iron industry including a rolling mill and railway car plant. To provide the resources for the expansion, the firm was reorganized as a joint stock company with a $300,000 capital most of which was raised by St. John businessmen. The New Brunswick Foundry, Rolling Mills and Car Works, with a plant covering some five acres of land, emerged as the largest industrial employer in the Maritimes.[12] The success of the Harris firm induced a group of wholesale hardware manufacturers under the leadership of the Hon. Isaac Burpee, a former member of the Mackenzie Government, to re-establish the Coldbrook Rolling Mills near the city.

Yet, despite the development of sugar and cotton industries and the expansion of iron and rope manufactories, the participation of the St. John and Halifax business communities in the industrial impulse which characterized the early 1880's can only be described as marginal. Each group played the role of participant within its locality but neither provided any positive leadership to its hinterland area. Even in terms of industrial expansion, the performance of many small town manufacturers was more impressive than that of their city counterparts.

At the little railway centre of Moncton, nearly $1,000,000 was raised under the leadership of John and Christopher Harris, John Humphrey, and Josiah Woods, to permit the construction of a sugar refinery, a cotton mill, a gas light and power plant, and several smaller iron and textile enterprises. The Harris brothers, sons of an Annapolis ship builder of Loyalist extraction, had established a shipbuilding and shipping firm at Moncton in 1856.[13] Under the aegis of their firm they organized the new enterprises with the assistance of their

11 *Canadian Biographical Dictionary* (Montreal, 1880-1), II, pp. 684-5 (henceforth cited as *CBD*); Parks Family Papers, F, no. 1, New Brunswick Museum.

12 *CBD*, II, pp. 684-5; *Monetary Times*, 27 April 1883, 22 June 1888.

13 *CCB*, II, pp. 186-7, 86.

brother-in-law John Humphrey, scion of Yorkshire Methodist settlers of the Tantramar, longtime M.L.A. for Westmorland, and proprietor of the Moncton flour and woolen mills. They were financially assisted in their efforts by Josiah Wood (later Senator) of nearby Sackville. The son of a Loyalist wholesaler, Wood first completed his degrees (B.A., M.A.) at Mount Allison, was later admitted to the New Brunswick bar, and finally entered his father's shipping and private banking business.[14]   The leadership of the Moncton group was so effective that the owner of the *Monetary Times*, in a journey through the region in 1882, singled out the community for praise:

> Moncton has industrialized . . . business people only in moderate circumstances but have united their energies . . . persons who have always invested their surplus funds in mortgages are now cheerfully subscribing capital for the Moncton Cotton Co. Unfortunately for industrial progress, there are too many persons [in this region] who are quite content with receiving 5 or 6% for their money so long as they know it is safe, rather than risk it in manufactures, even supposing it yielded double the profit.[15]

At St. Stephen the septuagenarian lumber barons and bankers, James Murchie and Freeman Todd, joined the Annapolis-born ship builder, Zechariah Chipman, who was father-in-law to the Minister of Finance, Sir Leonard Tilley, in promoting an immense cotton concern, the St. Croix, second largest in the Dominion at the time. The son of a local farmer, Murchie, whose holdings included more than 200,000 acres of timber lands — half of it in Quebec —, also developed a number of smaller local manufactories.[16]   At the same time two young brothers, Gilbert and James Ganong, grandsons of a Loyalist farmer from the St. John Valley, began the expansion of their small confectionery firm,[17]   and shortly initiated construction of a soap enterprise in the town.

At Yarmouth a group of ship builders and West Indies merchants led by the Hon. Loran Baker, M.L.C., a shipper and private banker, and John Lovitt, a shipbuilder and member of the Howland Syndicate, succeeded in promoting the Yarmouth Woolen Mill, the Yarmouth Cotton Manufacturing, the Yarmouth Duck Yarn Company, two major foundries, and a furniture enterprise.[18] The development was entirely an internal community effort — virtually all the leading business figures were third generation Nova Scotians of pre-Loyalist

14 *CCB*, II, pp. 354-5; *CBD*, II, p. 693; Henry J. Morgan, ed., *Canadian Men and Women of the Time* (Toronto, 1898), p. 1000.

15 *Monetary Times*, 16 December 1882.

16 *CCB*, II, pp. 221-2; *CBD*, II, pp. 674-5; Harold Davis, *An International Community on the St. Croix (1604-1930)* (Orono, 1950), chapter 18; *Monetary Times*, 1 August 1890.

17 Canada, *Sessional Papers*, 1885, no. 37, pp. 174-97.

18 *Monetary Times*, 11 December 1885; *Canadian Journal of Commerce*, 3 June 1881; *CBD*, II, pp. 409-10, 510; *Canadian Men and Women of the Time* (1898), p. 44.

American origins. A similar development was discernible in the founding of the Windsor Cotton Company.[19]

A somewhat different pattern emerged at New Glasgow, the centre of the Nova Scotia coal industry. Attempts at the manufacture of primary iron and steel had been made with indifferent results ever since Confederation.[20]   In 1872, a New Glasgow blacksmith, Graham Fraser, founded the Hope Iron Works with an initial capital of $160,000.[21]   As the tariff on iron and steel products increased in the 1880's so did the vertical expansion of the firm. In 1889, when it was amalgamated with Fraser's other enterprise, the Nova Scotia Forge Company, more than two-thirds of the $280,000 capital stock of the resulting Nova Scotia Steel and Coal Company was held by the citizens of New Glasgow.[22] Fraser remained as president and managing director of the corporation until 1904,[23]   during which time it produced most of the primary steel in the Dominion,[24]   and remained one of the largest industrial corporations in the country.[25]

Fraser was seconded in his industrial efforts by James Carmichael of New Glasgow and John F. Stairs of Halifax. Carmichael, son of a prominent New Glasgow merchant and a descendant of the Scottish founders of Pictou, had established one of the largest ship building and shipping firms in the province.[26] Stairs' investment in the New Glasgow iron and steel enterprise represented one of the few examples of inter-community industrial activity in this period.

The most unusual pattern of manufacturing development in the region was that initiated at Fredericton by Alexander Gibson. Gibson's distinctiveness lay in his ability to impose the tradition and structure of an earlier semi-industrial society onto a changing pattern of development. A St. Stephen native and the son of Ulster immigrants, he had begun his career as a sawyer, and later operated a small lumber firm at Lepreau. In 1865 he bought from the Anti-Confederationist government of A. J. Smith extensive timber reserves on the headwaters of the Nashwaak River,[27]   and at the mouth of that river, near Fredericton, built his own mill-town of Marysville. Freed from stumpage fees by his fortunate purchase, the "lumber king of New Brunswick" was producing as

19 *Canadian Journal of Commerce*, 10 June 1881.

20 W. J. A. Donald, *The Canadian Iron and Steel Industry* (Boston, 1915), chapter 3.

21 *Monetary Times*, 28 April 1882.

22 *The Canadian Manufacturer and Industrial World*, 3 May 1889 (henceforth cited as *Canadian Manufacturer*).

23 Henry J. Morgan, ed., *Canadian Men and Women of the Time* (Toronto, 1912), p. 419; C. W. Parker, ed., *Who's Who and Why* (Vancouver, 1916), VI & VII, p. 259 (hereafter cited as *WWW*).

24 *Canadian Manufacturer*, 1 April 1892.

25 *Ibid.*, 7 March 1890.

26 *CBD*, II, pp. 534-5.

27 A. G. Bailey, "The Basis and Persistence of Opposition to Confederation in New Brunswick," *Canadian Historical Review*, XXIII (1942), p. 394.

much as 100,000,000 feet of lumber annually by the 1880's — about one third of the provincial output. His lumber exports at times comprised half the export commerce of the port of St. John.[28]

One of the wealthiest industrial entrepreneurs in the Dominion, Gibson determined in 1883 to undertake the erection of a major cotton enterprise entirely under his own auspices.[29] He erected one of the largest brick-yards in the Dominion and personally supervised the construction of the plant which was opened in 1885.[30] In that same year he employed nearly 2,000 people in his sundry enterprises.[31] By 1888 his sales of cotton cloth totalled nearly $500,000.[32] That same year the Gibson empire, comprising the cotton mill, timber lands, saw mills, lath mills, the town of Marysville, and the Northern and Western Railroad, was formed into a joint stock company, its $3,000,000 capital controlled by Gibson, his brother, sons and son-in-law.

Several common characteristics distinguished the men who initiated the industrial expansion of the 1880's. They were, on the whole, men of substance gained in traditional trades and staples. They sought a substantial, more secure future for themselves within the framework of the traditional community through the instrumentality of the new industrial mercantilism. Averaging fifty-four years of age, they were old men to be embarking upon new careers.[33] Coupled with this factor of age was their ignorance of both the technical skills and the complexities of the financial and marketing structures involved in the new enterprises.

The problem of technical skill was overcome largely by the importation of management and skilled labour, mainly from England and Scotland.[34] The problem of finance was more serious. The resources of the community entrepreneurs were limited; the costs of the proposed industry were almost always far greater than had been anticipated. Moreover, most businessmen had only the vaguest idea of the quantity of capital required to operate a large manufacturing corporation. Promoters generally followed the normal mercantile practice and raised only sufficient capital to construct and equip the physical plant, preferring to finance operating costs through bank loans — a costly and inefficient process. The Halifax Sugar Refinery perhaps best illustrated these

28 *Monetary Times*, 9 January 1885.

29 *Ibid.*, 11 May 1883.

30 *Our Dominion. Historical and Other Sketches of the Mercantile Interests of Fredericton, Marysville, Woodstock, Moncton, Yarmouth, etc.* (Toronto, 1889), pp. 48-54.

31 Canada, *Sessional Papers*, 1885, no. 37, pp. 174-97.

32 Canada, Royal Commission on the Relations of Labour and Capital (1889), *Evidence*, II, p. 448.

33 American industrial leaders of the same period averaged 45 years. See W. F. Gregory and I. D. New, "The American Industrial Elite in the 1870's: Their Social Origins", in William Miller, ed., *Men in Business* (Cambridge, 1952), p. 197.

34 Canada, Royal Commission of the Relations of Labour and Capital, *Evidence*, II, pp. 256, 458 and III, pp. 78, 238, 249; *Canadian Manufacturer*, 24 August 1883; *Monetary Times*, 17 June 1887.

problems. When first proposed in 1879 it was to have been capitalized at $300,000. Before its completion in 1881 it was re-capitalized twice to a value of $500,000.[35] Even this figure left no operating capital, and the refinery management was forced to secure these funds by loans from the Merchants Bank of Halifax. At the end of its first year of operation the bank debt of the corporation totalled $460,000,[36] which immediately became a fixed charge on the revenues of the infant industry. Fearing bankruptcy, the stockholders increased their subscriptions and kept the business functioning until 1885 when they attempted a solution to the problem by issuing debenture stock to a value of $350,000 of which the bank was to receive $200,000 in stock and $50,000 cash in settlement of debts still owed to it.[37]

While many industries received their initial financing entirely from local capitalists, some projects proved to be such ambitious undertakings that aid had to be sought from other sources. The St. Croix Cotton Company at St. Stephen, for example, was forced to borrow $300,000 from Rhode Island interests to complete their huge plant.[38] Some industries came to rely so heavily on small community banks for perpetual loans for operating expenses that any general economic crisis toppled both the industries and the banks simultaneously. The financing of James Domville's enterprises, including the Coldbrook Rolling Mills, was a contributing factor in the temporary suspension of the Maritime Bank of St. John in 1880,[39] while such industrial loans ultimately brought down the Bank of Yarmouth in 1905.[40]

II

The problem of industrial finance was intricately tied to a whole crisis of confidence in the new order which began to develop as the first enthusiastic flush of industrial expansion paled in the face of the general business downturn which wracked the Canadian economy in the mid-1880's. At the heart of this problem was a gradual deterioration of the British lumber market, and the continued shift from sea borne to railroad commerce. Under the influence of an increasingly prohibitive tariff and an extended railroad building programme a two cycle inter-regional trading pattern was gradually emerging. The westward cycle, by rail into the St. Lawrence basin, left the region with a heavy trade imbalance as the central Canadians rapidly replaced British and American produce in the Maritime market with their own flour and manufactured materials.[41] In return, the region shipped to Montreal quantities of primary

---

35 *Monetary Times*, 18 March 1881.
36 *Ibid.,* 17 February 1882.
37 *Ibid.,* 19 March 1886.
38 *Canadian Journal of Commerce*, 26 October 1883.
39 *Monetary Times*, 18 October 1880.
40 *Ibid.,* 10 May 1905.
41 *Ibid.,* 8 January 1886.

and primary manufactured products of both local and imported origins. The secretaries of the Montreal and St. John boards of trade estimated the extent of this inter-regional commerce at about $15,711,000 in 1885, more than 70 percent of which represented central Canadian exports to the Maritimes.[42] By contrast the external trade cycle moved in traditional fashion by ship from the principal Maritime ports to Great Britain and the West Indies. Heavily balanced in favour of the Maritimes, it consumed most of the output of the region's resource industries. The two cycles were crucially interdependent; the Maritime business community used the credits earned in the external cycle to meet the gaping deficits incurred in the central Canadian trade. The system worked as long as the equilibrium between the two could be maintained. Unfortunately, as the decade progressed, this balance was seriously threatened by a declining English lumber market.[43]

In the face of this increasingly serious trade imbalance, the Maritime business community became more and more critical of what they regarded as the subversion of the National Policy by central Canadian interests. Their argument was based upon two propositions. If Canadian transportation policy was dedicated to creating an all-Canadian commercial system, then this system should extend not from the Pacific to Montreal, but from the Pacific to the Atlantic. How, in all justice, could the Montreal interests insist on the construction, at a staggering cost, of an all-Canadian route west of that city and then demand the right to export through Portland or Boston rather than using the Maritime route? This argument was implicit in almost every resolution of the Halifax and St. John boards of trade from 1880 onward.[44]

The second proposition maintained that, as vehicles of nationhood, the railways must be considered as a means of promoting national economic integration rather than as commercial institutions. The timing of this doctrine is significant. Before 1885 most Maritime manufacturers were competitive both with Canadian and foreign producers. Nails, confectionery, woolens, leather, glass, steel and machinery manufactured in the Maritimes normally had large markets in both central Canada and the West.[45] The recession of 1885 reached a trough in 1886.[46] Diminishing demand coupled with over-production, particularly in the cotton cloth and sugar industries, resulted in falling prices, and made it increasingly difficult for many Maritime manufacturers to retain their

42 *Monetary Times*, 30 January 1885. Principal Maritime imports from Central Canada included flour, shoes, clothing, textiles, alcoholic beverages and hardware; exports to Quebec and Ontario centered on sugar, coal, cotton cloth, iron and fish.

43 Exports of New Brunswick lumber declined from 404,000,000 board feet in 1883 to 250,000,000 feet in 1887. *Monetary Times*, 9 January 1885, 2 and 7 January 1887, 21 January 1898.

44 See particularly, *Proceedings of the Ninth Annual Meeting* of the Dominion Board of Trade (1879), pp. 65-73; *Monetary Times*, 27 January 1882; Minute Book of the St. John Board of Trade (1879-87), 14 October 1887, New Brunswick Museum.

45 Canada, *Sessional Papers*, 1885, no. 34, pp. 86-125.

46 Bertram, p. 131.

central Canadian markets. The *bête noir* was seen as the relatively high freight rates charged by the Intercolonial Railway. The issue came to a head late in 1885 with the closing of the Moncton and the two Halifax sugar refineries. The response of the Halifax manufacturers was immediate and decisive. Writing to the Minister of Railways, John F. Stairs enunciated the Maritime interpretation of the National Policy:

> Four refineries have been set in operation in the Lower Provinces by the policy of the Government. This was right; but trade having changed so that it is now impossible for them to work prosperously it is the duty of the Government to accomodate its policy to the change. The reduction in freight rates asked for is necessary to this . . . . If in answer to this you plead that you must manage so that no loss occur running the I.C.R., we will reply, we do not, and will not accept this as a valid plea from the Government . . . and to it we say that the people of Nova Scotia, nor should those of Ontario and Quebec, for they are as much interested, even admit it is essential to make both ends meet in the finance of the railroad, when it can only be done at the expense of inter-provincial trade, and the manufacturers of Nova Scotia . . . . How can the National Policy succeed in Canada where such great distances exist between the provinces unless the Government who control the National Railway meet the requirements of trade . . .[47]

At stake, as Stairs later pointed out in a confidential memorandum to Macdonald, was the whole West Indies trade of Nova Scotia.[48] Equally as important and also at stake was the entire industrial structure which had been created in the region under the aegis of the National Policy.

The Maritimes by 1885 provided a striking illustration of the success of that policy. With less than one-fifth of the population of the Dominion, the region contained eight of the twenty-three Canadian cotton mills — including seven of the nineteen erected after 1879[49] — three of five sugar refineries, two of seven rope factories, one of three glass works, both of the Canadian steel mills, and six of the nation's twelve rolling mills.

Although Stairs succeeded in his efforts to have the I.C.R. sugar freight rates reduced,[50] the problem facing the Maritime entrepreneur was not one which could be solved simply by easier access to the larger central Canadian market; its cause was much more complex. In the cotton industry, for example, the Canadian business community had created industrial units with a production potential sufficient to supply the entire national market. In periods of recession

47 J. F. Stairs to J. M. Pope, 10 September 1885, Macdonald Papers, 50080-5, Public Archives of Canada.

48 J. F. Stairs to Macdonald, 5 February 1886, *ibid.*, volume 155.

49 *Monetary Times*, 5 October 1888.

50 *Ibid.*, 12 February 1886.

many American cloth manufacturers were prepared to cut prices on exports to a level which vitiated the Canadian tariff; this enabled them to gain control of a considerable portion of the Canadian market. The problems of the cotton cloth manufacturers could have been solved by a further increase in the tariff — a politically undesirable answer —, by control of railway rates, or by a regulated industrial output.

From a Maritime regional viewpoint the second of these alternatives appeared to be the most advantageous; the limitations of the tariff could then be accepted and, having attained geographic equality with Montreal through a regulated freight rate, the more efficient Maritime mills would soon control the Montreal market. Such was the hope; there was little possibility of its realization. Such a general alteration in railway policy would have required subsidization of certain geographic areas—districts constituting political minorities — at the expense of the dominant political areas of the country, a prospect which the business community of Montreal and environs could hardly be expected to view with equanimity. Apart from the political difficulties of the situation, most Maritime manufactories suffered from two major organizational problems: the continued difficulty faced by community corporations in securing financing in the frequent periods of marginal business activity,[51] and the fact that most firms depended upon Montreal wholesale houses to dispose of their extra-regional exports.[52] Short of a major shift in government railway or tariff policy, the only solution to the problem of markets which seemed to have any chance for success appeared to be the regulation of industrial production, a technique which was to bring into the Maritimes the Montreal interests which already controlled the major part of the distributive function in eastern Canada.

III

The entry of Montreal into the Maritime region was not a new phenomenon. With the completion of the Intercolonial Railway and the imposition of coal duties in 1879, Montreal railway entrepreneurs moved to control both the major rail systems of New Brunswick and the Nova Scotia coal fields. A syndicate headed by George Stephen and Donald Smith had purchased the New Brunswick Railroad from Alexander Gibson and the Hon. Isaac Burpee in 1880,[53] with the intention of extending it to Rivière du Loup. This system was expanded two years later by the purchase of the New Brunswick and Canada Railroad with the ultimate view of making St. John the winter port for Montreal.

In the same year, another Montreal group headed by John McDougall, David Morrice and L.-A. Sénécal acquired from fifteen St. John bondholders, four-fifths of the bonds of the Springhill and Parrsboro Railroad and Mining

---

51 See the problems faced by John Parks and the N. B. Cotton Mills, Parks Family Papers, F, New Brunswick Museum.

52 Montreal *Herald*, 15 October 1883.

53 *Monetary Times*, 8 October 1880.

Company,[54] and followed this up in 1883 with the purchase of the Springhill Mining Company, the largest coal producer in Canada[55]. The following year another syndicate acquired the International Mine at Sydney[56]. The coal mine takeovers were designed to control and expand the output of this fuel source, partially in an effort to free the Canadian Pacific Railways from dependence upon the strike-prone American coal industry. By contrast, the entry of Montreal interests into the manufacturing life of the Maritimes aimed to restrict output and limit expansion.

The first serious attempts to regulate production occurred in the cotton industry. Although informal meetings of manufacturers had been held throughout the mid-1880's, the business depression of 1886 and the threatened failure of several mills resulted in the organization of the first formal national trade association. Meeting in Montreal in the summer of 1886, representatives of sixteen mills, including four from the Maritimes, agreed to regulate production and to set standard minimum prices for commodities. The agreement was to be renegotiated yearly and each mill provided a bond as proof of good faith[57]. The arrangement at least stabilized the industry and the agreement was renewed in 1887.

The collapse of the association the following year was precipitated by a standing feud between the two largest Maritime mills, the St. Croix at St. Stephen and the Gibson at Marysville. Alexander Gibson had long been the maverick of the organization, having refused to subscribe to the agreement in 1886 and 1887. During this period he had severely injured his larger St. Stephen competitor in the Maritime market. By the time Gibson agreed to enter the association in 1888, the St. Croix mill, faced with bankruptcy, dropped out and reduced prices in an effort to dispose of its huge inventory. The Gibson mill followed suit. With two of the largest coloured cotton mills in the Dominion selling without regulation, the controlled market system dissolved into chaos, and the association, both coloured and grey sections, disintegrated[58]. The return to an unregulated market in the cotton industry continued for more than two years. A business upswing in 1889 mercifully saved the industry from what many manufacturers feared would be a general financial collapse. Even so, only the mills with the largest production potential, regardless of geographic location, escaped unscathed; most of the smaller plants were forced to close temporarily.

In the summer of 1890 a Montreal group headed by A. F. Gault and David Morrice prepared the second attempt to regulate the cotton market. The technique was to be the corporate monopoly. The Dominion Cotton Mills Company, with a $5,000,000 authorized capital, was to bring all of the grey cotton

54 *Ibid.,* 15 December 1882.

55 *Ibid.,* 8 June 1883.

56 *Ibid.,* 16 November 1884.

57 *Ibid.,* 13 August 1886; *Canadian Manufacturer*, 20 August 1887.

58 *Canadian Journal of Commerce*, 7 September 1888.

producers under the control of a single directorate. In January 1891, David Morrice set out on a tour of Maritime cotton centres. On his first stop, at Halifax, he accepted transfer of the Nova Scotia Cotton Mill to the syndicate, the shareholders receiving $101,000 cash and $101,000 in bonds in the new corporation, a return of 25 cents on the dollar of their initial investment.[59] The following day Morrice proceeded to Windsor, "to consummate the transfer of the factory there",[60] and from there moved on to repeat the performance at Moncton. Fearful of total bankruptcy and hopeful that this stronger organization would provide the stability that earlier efforts had failed to achieve, stockholders of the smaller community-oriented mills readily acquiesced to the new order. Although they lost heavily on their original investment, most owners accepted bonds in the new corporation in partial payment for their old stock.

The first determined opposition to the cotton consolidation movement appeared in St. John. Here, John H. Parks, founder and operator of the thirty-year old New Brunswick Cotton Mill, had bought the bankrupt St. John Cotton firm in 1886 and had proceeded to operate both mills. Despite the perennial problem of financing, the Parks Mills represented one of the most efficient industrial operations in the Dominion, one which had won an international reputation for the quality of its product. The company's major markets were found in western Ontario, a fact which made the continued independence of the firm a particular menace to the combination. The firm's major weakness was its financial structure. Dependent upon the Bank of Montreal for his operating capital, Parks had found it necessary to borrow more heavily than usual during the winter of 1889-90. By mid-1890 his debts totalled $122,000.[61]

At this point two events occurred almost simultaneously: Parks refused to consider sale of the St. John Mills to the new corporation, and the Bank of Montreal, having ascertained that the Montreal syndicate would buy the mills from any seller, demanded immediate payment in full of the outstanding debts of the company[62]– a most unusual procedure. Claiming a Montreal conspiracy to seize the company, Parks replied with an open letter to the dry goods merchants of greater St. John.

> . . . I have made arrangements by which the mills of our company will be run to their fullest extent.
> These arrangements have been made in the face of the most determined efforts to have our business stopped, and our proprety sold out to the Montreal syndicate which is endeavouring to control the Cotton Trade of Canada . . . . I now propose to continue to keep our mills in operation as a St.

59 Thomas Kenny in Canada, House of Commons, *Debates*, 1893, p. 2522.

60 *Monetary Times*, 16 January 1891.

61 St. John *Globe*, 1 May 1891.

62 E. S. Clouston to Jones, 25 April 1891, Bank of Montreal, General Managers Letterbooks, vol. 8, Public Archives of Canada.

John industry, free from all outside control. I would therefore ask you gentlemen, as far as your power, to support me in this undertaking —

It remains with you to assist the Wholesale Houses in distributing the goods made in St. John in preference to those of outside manufacture so long as the quality and price of the home goods is satisfactory.

The closing of our mills ... would be a serious calamity to the community, and you, by your support can assist materially in preventing it. I believe you will.[63]

Parks' appeal to community loyalty saved his firm. When the bank foreclosed the mortgage which it held as security for its loans, Mr. Justice A. L. Palmer of the New Brunswick Supreme Court placed the firm in receivership under his control until the case was resolved. Over the strongest objections of the bank, and on one legal pretext after another, the judge kept the mill in receivership for nearly two years.[64] In the meantime he forced the bank to continue the provision of operating capital for the mill's operations, and in conjunction with the receiver, a young Fredericton lawyer, H. H. McLean, proceeded to run an efficient and highly profitable business. When the decision was finally rendered in December 1892, the firm was found to have cleared profits of $150,000 during the period of the receivership. Parks was able to use the funds to repay the bank debts and the mill continued under local control.[65]

The St. John experience was unique. Gault and Morrice organized the Canadian Coloured Cotton Company, sister consolidation to the Dominion Cotton Mills, in 1891. The St. Croix Mill entered the new organization without protest early in 1892,[66] and even the Gibson Mill, while retaining its separate corporate structure, agreed to market its entire output through the new consolidation. By 1893 only the St. John Mills and the small Yarmouth plant remained in the hands of regional entrepreneurs.

The fate of the Maritime cotton mills was parallelled in the sugar industry. In 1890 a syndicate of Scottish merchants, incorporated under English laws as the Halifax Sugar Refinery Ltd., bought up the English-owned Woodside Refinery of Halifax.[67] The ultimate aim of the Scottish group was to consolidate the sugar industry into a single corporate entity similar to Dominion Cotton. Failing in this effort because of the parliamentary outcry against combines, they turned their efforts to regional consolidation. With the assistance of John F. Stairs, M.P., they were able, in 1894, to secure an act of incorporation as the Acadia Sugar Refineries which was to amalgamate the three Maritime

63 15 December 1890, Parks Papers, Scrapbook 2, New Brunswick Museum.

64 Clouston to Jones, 13, 22 April, 23 May 1891, Bank of Montreal, General Managers Letterbooks, vol. 8, Public Archives of Canada.

65 St. John *Sun*, 28 December 1892.

66 *Monetary Times*, 18 March 1892.

67 *Ibid.*, 24 October 1890.

firms. Unlike the Cotton Union, the new consolidation worked in the interests of the regional entrepreneurs, the stock holders of all three refineries receiving full value for their holdings. Equally important, the management of the new concern remained in the hands of Thomas Kenny, M.P.

The consolidation movement of the early 1890's swept most of the other major Maritime manufactories. In some cases local entrepreneurs managed to retain a voice in the direction of the new mergers — John Stairs, for example, played a prominent role on the directorate of the Consumers Cordage Company which swept the Halifax and St. John rope concerns into a new seven-company amalgamation in 1890.[68]   On the other hand, the Nova Scotia Glass Company of New Glasgow disappeared entirely in the Diamond Glass consolidation of that same year.[69]   On the whole, saving only the iron and steel products, the confectionery and the staple export industries, control of all mass consumption industries in the Maritimes had passed to outside interests by 1895. Thus, in large measure the community manufactory which had dominated the industrial growth of the 1880's ceased to exist in the 1890's. Given the nature of the market of the period, some degree of central control probably was inevitable. The only question at stake was whether it would be a control effected by political or financial means, and if the latter, from which centre it would emanate.

The failure of any Maritime metropolis to achieve this control was partly a result of geography and partly a failure of entrepreneurial leadership. The fear of being left on the fringes of a national marketing system had been amply illustrated by the frenetic efforts of the St. John and Halifax business communities to promote political policies which would link the Canadian marketing system to an Atlantic structure with the Maritime ports serving as the connecting points.[70]

The question of entrepreneurial failure is more difficult to document. In part the great burst of industrial activity which marked the early 1880's was the last flowering of an older generation of lumbermen and wholesale shippers. Having failed to achieve their position as the link between central Canada and Europe, and faced with the dominant marketing and financial apparatus of the Montreal community, they drew back and even participated in the transfer of control. This failure is understandable in the smaller communities; it is more difficult to explain in the larger. In the latter case it may well be attributable to the perennial failure of most Maritime communities to maintain a continuity of industrial elites. The manufacturing experience of most families was limited to a single generation: Thomas Kenny's father was a wholesale merchant, his son a stock broker. John F. Stairs was the son of a merchant and the father of

68 *Canadian Journal of Commerce*, 22 March 1895.

69 *Monetary Times*, 24 October 1890.

70 *Ibid.*, 12 June 1885, 22 April 1887, 22 August 1902; Minutes of the St. John Board of Trade, 1 December 1879, 8 November 1886, New Brunswick Museum.

a lawyer. Even in such a distinguished industrial family as that of John Parks, a second generation manufacturer, the son attended the Royal Military College and then entered the Imperial service. Commerce and the professions provided a much more stable milieu, and while many participants in both of these activities were prepared to make the occasional excursion into manufacturing, usually as part of a dual role, few were willing to make a permanent and sole commitment to an industrial vocation.

IV

The lesson brought home to the Maritime entrepreneur by the industrial experience between 1879 and 1895 was that geography would defeat any attempt to compete at parity with a central Canadian enterprise. In response to this lesson, the truncated industrial community of the region turned increasingly to those resource industries in which geography gave them a natural advantage over their central Canadian counterparts. In the 1890's the thrust of Maritime industrial growth was directed toward the processing and manufacturing of primary steel and of iron and steel products. In part, since these enterprises constituted much of the industrial machinery remaining in the hands of regional entrepreneurs, there was little choice in this development. At the same time, Nova Scotia contained most of the active coal and iron deposits in the Dominion and had easy access to the rich iron ore deposits at Belle Isle. In any event, most competition in these industries came from western Ontario rather than Montreal, and the latter was thus a potential market.

Iron and steel development was not new to the region. Efforts at primary steel making had been undertaken successfully at New Glasgow since 1882. Yet production there was limited and would continue so until a more favourable tariff policy guaranteed a stable market for potential output. Such a policy was begun in 1887 with the passage of the "iron" tariff. Generally labeled as a Nova Scotia tariff designed to make that province "the Pennsylvania of Canada"[71] and New Glasgow "the Birmingham of the country"[72] the act provided an effective protection of $3.50 a ton for Canadian-made iron, and imposed heavy duties on a variety of iron and steel products.[73] Protection for the industry was completed in 1894 when the duty on scrap iron, considered a raw material by secondary iron manufacturers, was raised from $2 to $4 a ton, and most rolling mills were forced to use Nova Scotia-made bar iron rather than imported scrap.[74]

The growth of the New Glasgow industries parallelled this tariff development. In 1889 the Nova Scotia Steel Company was united with the Nova Scotia Forge Company to form a corporation capable of manufacturing both primary steel

71 *Monetary Times*, 20 May 1887.

72 *The Canadian Journal of Commerce*, 29 April 1887.

73 Canada, Statutes, 50-1 Victoria C. 39.

74 Simon J. MacLean, *The Tariff History of Canada* (Toronto, 1895), p. 37.

and iron and steel products. In the same year, to provide the community with its own source of pig iron, a group of Nova Scotia Steel shareholders organized the New Glasgow Iron, Coal and Railroad Company with a capital of $1,000,000.[75] Five years later, following the enactment of the scrap iron duty, New Glasgow acquired the rich Wabana iron ore deposits at Belle Isle — some eighty-three acres covered with ore deposits so thick they could be cut from the surface. This was followed the next year by the union of the Nova Scotia Steel and Forge and the New Glasgow Iron companies into a $2,060,000 corporation, the Nova Scotia Steel Company. Containing its own blast and open hearth furnaces, rolling mills, forges, foundries, and machine shops, the firm represented the most fully integrated industrial complex in the country. The process was completed in 1900 when the company acquired the Sydney Coal Mines on Cape Breton Island, developed new steel mills in that area and reorganized as the Nova Scotia Steel and Coal Company with a $7,000,000 capital.[76]

The development of the Nova Scotia Steel and Coal corporation had begun under the direction of a cabal of Pictou County Scottish Nova Scotians, a group which was later enlarged to include a few prominent Halifax businessmen. Aside from Graham Fraser, its leading members included James D. McGregor, James C. MacGregor, Colonel Thomas Cantley, and John F. Stairs. All four were third generation Nova Scotians, the first three from New Glasgow. Saving only Cantley, all were members of old mercantile families. Senator McGregor, a merchant, was a grandson of the Rev. Dr. James McGregor, one of the founders of the Presbyterian Church in Nova Scotia; MacGregor was a partner in the large shipbuilding concern of Senator J. W. Carmichael, a prominent promoter of Nova Scotia Steel. Cantley was the only member of the group of proletarian origins. Like Graham Fraser, he spent a lifetime in the active service of the company, having entered the newly established Nova Scotia Forge Company in 1873 at the age of sixteen. Promoted to sales manager of the amalgamated Nova Scotia Steel Company in 1885, he had been responsible for the introduction of Wabana ore into England and Germany. In 1902 he succeeded Graham Fraser as general manager of the corporation.[77]

Aside from its value to the New Glasgow area, the Nova Scotia Steel Company was of even greater significance as a supplier of iron and steel to a variety of foundries, car works and machine mills in the region. Because of its unique ability to provide primary, secondary and tertiary steel and iron manufactures, it was supplying most of the Maritime iron and steel needs by 1892.[78] In this

75 *Nova Scotia's Industrial Centre: New Glasgow, Stellarton, Westville, Trenton. The Birthplace of Steel in Canada* (n.p., 1916), pp. 45-6.

76 *Monetary Times*, 9 March 1900; *Industrial Canada*, 20 July 1901.

77 *WWW*, VI & VII, pp. 927, 1075-6.

78 R. M. Guy, "Industrial Development and Urbanization of Pictou Co., N. S. to 1900" (unpublished M.A. thesis, Acadia University, 1962), pp. 120-3.

respect, the industrial experience of the 1890's differed considerably from that of the previous decade. It was not characterized by the development of new industrial structures, but rather by the expansion of older firms which had served purely local markets for some time and expanded in response to the demand created by the tariff changes of the period.[79]

The centres of the movement were at New Glasgow, Amherst and St. John, all on the main lines of the Intercolonial or Canadian Pacific railroads. At New Glasgow, the forge and foundry facilities of the Nova Scotia Steel Company consumed half the company's iron and steel output. At Amherst, Nathaniel Curry (later Senator) and his brother-in-law, John Rhodes, continued the expansion of the small woodworking firm they had established in 1877, gradually adding a door factory, a rolling mill, a railroad car plant and an axle factory, and in 1893 bought out the Harris Car Works and Foundry of St. John.[80] At the time of its incorporation in 1902, Rhodes, Curry & Company was one of the largest secondary iron manufacturing complexes in the Dominion.[81] Curry's industrial neighbour at Amherst was David Robb. Son of an Amherst foundry owner, Robb had been trained in engineering at the Stevens Institute of New Jersey and then had entered his father's foundry. Specializing in the development of precision machinery, he expanded his activities into Massachusetts in the 1890's and finally merged his firm into the International Engineering Works of South Framingham of which he remained managing director.[82]

If under the aegis of a protective government policy the iron and steel industry of the Maritimes was rapidly becoming a viable proposition for local entrepreneurs, it was also increasingly attracting the interest of both Boston and Montreal business interests. There was a growing feeling that, once a reciprocal coal agreement was made between Canada and the United States, Nova Scotia coal would replace the more expensive Pennsylvania product in the New England market. Added to this inducement was the fact that Nova Scotia provided the major fuel source on the Montreal market — the city actually consumed most of the coal produced in the Cape Breton fields.[83] With its almost unlimited access routes and its strategic water position midway between Boston and Montreal, Nova Scotia seemed an excellent area for investment.

In 1893 a syndicate headed by H. M. Whitney of Boston and composed of Boston, New York and Montreal businessmen, including Donald Smith, W. C.

---

79 *Canadian Manufacturer*, 20 April 1894.

80 *Monetary Times*, 30 June 1893.

81 *Industrial Canada*, March, 1910; *Canadian Men and Women of the Time* (1912), p. 290.

82 *CCB*, II, p. 183; *CBD*, II, pp. 506-7; *WWW*, VI & VII, p. 997; *Canadian Men and Women of the Time* (1912), p. 947.

83 *Monetary Times*, 26 November 1896. The St. Lawrence ports imported 88,000 tons of British and American coal in 1896, and 706,000 tons of Nova Scotia coal. The transport of this commodity provided the basis for the Nova Scotia merchant marine of the period.

Van Horne and Hugh McLennan, negotiated a 119-year lease with the Nova Scotia government for most of the existing coal fields on Cape Breton Island.[84] The new Dominion Coal Company came into formal being in March of that year, with David MacKeen (later Senator) as director and general manager, and John S. McLennan (later Senator) as director and treasurer. The son of a Scottish-born mine owner and member of the legislative council, MacKeen had been an official and principal stockholder in the Caledonia Coal Company which had been absorbed in the new consolidation.[85]   McLennan was the second son of Hugh McLennan of Montreal, a graduate of Trinity College, Cambridge, and one of the very few entrepreneurs who made the inter-regional transfer in this period.[86]   The success of the Dominion Coal syndicate and the growing feeling that the Canadian government was determined to create a major Canadian primary steel industry led Whitney in 1899 to organize the Dominion Iron & Steel Company. The date was significant. Less than two years earlier the government had announced its intention to extend bounty payments to steel made from imported ores.[87]   The $15,000,000 capital of the new company was easily raised, largely on the Canadian stock market,[88] and by 1902 the company was employing 4,000 men in its four blast and ten steel furnace works.[89]   Graham Fraser was induced to leave Nova Scotia Steel to become general manager of the new corporation,[90]   and J. H. Plummer, assistant general manager of the Bank of Commerce, was brought from Toronto as president.

The primacy of American interests in both the Dominion Steel and Dominion Coal companies was rapidly replaced by those of Montreal and Toronto after 1900. The sale of stocks added a strong Toronto delegation to the directorate of the steel company in 1901.[91]   In that same year James Ross, the Montreal street railway magnate, bought heavily into the coal corporation, re-organized its management and retained control of the firm until 1910.[92]

V

The increasing reliance on the stock market as a technique for promoting and securing the necessary financial support to develop the massive Nova

84 *Ibid.*, 3 February 1893.

85 *Canadian Men and Women of the Time* (1912), pp. 698-9; *WWW*, VI & VII, p. 1118.

86 *WWW*, VI & VII, p. 1322.

87 Donald, however, argues that Whitney had been determined to go into steel production even if no bounty had been granted. See Donald, *The Canadian Iron and Steel Industry*, p. 203.

88 Partly, the *Canadian Journal of Commerce* (15 March 1901) suggested, on the promise of the promoters that the Company would receive bonuses of $8,000,000 in its first six years of operation.

89 *Industrial Canada,* May, 1902.

90 J. H. Plummer to B. E. Walker, 3 December 1903, Walker Papers, University of Toronto Archives.

91 *Annual Financial Review*, I (1901), p. 92; III (1903), pp. 158-160.

92 *Monetary Times*, 3 August 1907.

Scotia steel corporations emphasized the growing shift from industrial to financial capitalism. Centred on the Montreal stock market, the new movement brought to the control of industrial corporations men who had neither a communal nor a vocational interest in the concern.

In emulation of, and possibly in reaction to the Montreal experience, a group within the Halifax business and professional communities scrambled to erect the financial structure necessary to this undertaking. The city already possessed some of the elements of this structure. The Halifax stock exchange had existed on an informal basis since before Confederation.[93] The city's four major banking institutions — the Nova Scotia, the Union, the Merchants (which subsequently became the Royal Bank of Canada) and the Peoples — were among the soundest in the Dominion. The development of Halifax as a major centre for industrial finance began in 1894, at the height of the first Montreal-based merger movement, when a syndicate headed by J. F. Stairs founded the Eastern Trust Company.[94] The membership of this group was indicative of the change that was occurring in the Halifax business elite. Although it contained representatives of the older mercantile group, such as Stairs, T. E. Kenny and Adam Burns, it also included manufacturers and coalman, notably J. W. Allison and David McKeen, a stockbroker, J. C. MacKintosh, and lawyers such as Robert L. Borden and Robert E. Harris.

Until his death in 1904, the personification of the new Halifax finance capitalism was John Stairs. It was Stairs who arranged the organization of Acadia Sugar in 1894, who initiated the merger of the Union bank of Halifax with the Bank of Windsor in 1899, and who led the Halifax business community back into its traditional imperium in the Caribbean with the organization of the Trinidad Electric and Demerara Electric corporations.[95] After 1900, it was Stairs who demonstrated to this same group the possibilities for industrial finance existing within the Maritimes. With the assistance of his young secretary, Max Aitken, and through the medium of his own holding company, Royal Securities, he undertook the re-organization of a number of firms in the region, most notably the Alexander Gibson Railroad and Manufacturing Company which was re-capitalized at $6,000,000.[96] The scope of his interests, and the changes which had been wrought in the Maritime business community in the previous twenty-five years, were perhaps best illustrated in the six corporation presidencies which Stairs held in his lifetime, five of them at his death in 1904: Consumers Cordage, Nova Scotia Steel, Eastern Trust, Trinidad Electric, Royal Securities, and Dalhousie University.

93 *Ibid.*, 17 April 1903.
94 *Ibid.*, 23 February 1894.
95 *Annual Financial Review*, XXIII (1923), pp. 682, 736.
96 *Monetary Times*, 5 December 1902.

Yet, while promotion of firms such as Stanfield's Woollens of Truro constituted a fertile field of endeavour,[97]   the major industrial interest of the
Halifax finance capitalists was the Nova Scotia Steel Company. In its search
for additional capital resources after 1900, the entrepreneurial strength of this
firm was rapidly broadened from its New Glasgow base. The principal new
promoters of the company were Halifaxmen, notably James Allison, George
Campbell and Robert Harris. The New Brunswick-born nephew of the founder
of Mount Allison University, Allison had entered the chocolate and spice
manufactory of John Mott & Company of Halifax in 1871, and had eventually
been admitted to a partnership in the firm. He had invested heavily in several
Nova Scotia industries and sat on the directorates of Stanfields Woollens, the
Eastern Trust, and the Bank of Nova Scotia in addition to Nova Scotia Steel.[98]
George Campbell, the son of a Scottish gentleman, had entered the service
of a Halifax steamship agency as a young man and ultimately became its head.
Like Allison he was deeply involved in a number of Nova Scotian firms in-
cluding Stanfields, the Silliker Car of Amherst, the Eastern Trust and the
Bank of Nova Scotia.[99]

By far the most significant figure in the Nova Scotia Steel Corporation after
Stairs' death was Mr. Justice Robert Harris. The Annapolis-born scion of a
Loyalist family, Harris shared the same antecedents as the Moncton and St.
John entrepreneurs of the same name. After reading law with Sir John Thompson, he was called to the Nova Scotia bar in 1882 and rapidly became one of
the leading legal figures in the province. In 1892 he moved his practice to
Halifax and there became intimately involved in the corporate promotions of
the period, ultimately serving on the directorates of thirteen major corporations including the Eastern Trust, Eastern Car, Bank of Nova Scotia, Maritime
Telegraph and Telephone, Acadia Sugar, Robb Engineering, Brandram-Hen-
derson Paint, and held the presidencies of Nova Scotia Steel, Eastern Trust,
Demerara Electric, and Trinidad Electric.[100]

Despite the continuing need for additional capital, the Nova Scotia Steel
Company found little difficulty obtaining most of this support from the Halifax business community.[101]   In turn, the corporation remained one of the most
efficiently organized industrial firms in the country. In striking contrast to the
larger Dominion Steel enterprise, Nova Scotia Steel's financial position remained strong, its performance solid and its earnings continuous. It was gen-

97 *Ibid.*, 22 April 1911.

98 *Canadian Men and Women of the Time* (1912), p. 19; *WWW*, VI & VII, p. 762; *Annual Financial Review*, III (1903), pp. 174-6.

99 *Canadian Men and Women of the Time* (1912), p. 192; *WWW*, VI & VII, p. 803.

100 *Canadian Men and Women of the Time* (1912), p. 505; *WWW*, VI & VII, p. 1107; *Annual Financial Review*, III (1903), pp. 174-6.

101 Most of the stock in this concern was held by Nova Scotians who also bought up two-thirds
of the $1,500,000 bond which the company put out in 1904. L. M. Jones to B. E. Walker, 5 August
1904, Walker Papers; *Monetary Times*, 15 August 1902.

erally credited with being the only major steel company which could have maintained its dividend payments without the aid of federal bounties.[102]

As the first decade of the twentieth century wore to a close, the Halifax business elite appeared to have succeeded in establishing a financial hegemony in the industrial life of an area centred in eastern Nova Scotia and extending outward into both southern New Brunswick and peninsular Nova Scotia. Yet, increasingly, that hegemony was being challenged by the burgeoning consolidation movement emanating from Montreal. The most serious threat was posed in 1909 when Max Aitken, with Montreal now as the centre for his Royal Securities Corporation, arranged the amalgamation of the Rhodes, Curry Company of Amherst with the Canada Car, and the Dominion Car and Foundry companies of Montreal to form the Canadian Car and Foundry Company. The union marked a triumph as much for Nathaniel Curry as for Aitken — he emerged with the presidency and with nearly $3,000,000 of the $8,500,000 capital stock of the new corporation.[103] The move was a blow to the Halifax capitalists, however, as it placed the largest car manufactory in the country, an Amherst plant employing 1,300 men and annually producing $5,000,000 in iron and steel products,[104] firmly in the Montreal orbit of the Drummonds and the Dominion Steel and Coal Corporation. Tension was heightened by the feeling that this manoeuvre was a prelude to the creation of a railroad car monopoly. The reaction was swift. To prevent the takeover of the other Amherst car works, the Silliker Company, a Halifax-based syndicate bought up most of the Silliker stock and organized a greatly expanded company, Nova Scotia Car Works, with a $2,625,000 capital.[105] The following year Nova Scotia Steel organized its own $2,000,000 car subsidiary, the Eastern Car Company.

The contest between Montreal and Halifax finance capitalism reached its climax at the annual meeting of the Nova Scotia Steel Company of New Glasgow in April, 1910. Fresh from the triumph of the Dominion Coal and Steel merger, Montreal stockbrokers Rudolphe Forget and Max Aitken determined to extend the union to include the smaller steel firm, a proposal which the Scotia Steel president, Robert Harris, flatly refused to consider. Arguing that the firm was stagnating and that a more dynamic leadership in a reorganized corporation would yield greater returns, Forget launched a major effort to acquire proxies with a view to taking control from the Nova Scotia directors. Using the facilities of the Montreal Stock Exchange, he bought large quantities of Scotia stock at increasingly higher prices, an example followed by Robert Harris and his associates at Halifax. At the April meeting, Harris offered Forget a minority of the seats on the directorate; Forget refused. In the voting which

102 *Monetary Times,* 9 March 1907.

103 *Ibid.,* 8 January 1910.

104 *Industrial Canada,* August, 1913.

105 *Monetary Times,* 29 October 1910.

followed, the Montreal interests were narrowly beaten. The *Monetary Times*, in a masterpiece of distortion, described this victory as the triumph of "the law . . . over the market place",[106]   and proclaimed that "New Glasgow prefers coal dust to that of the stock exchange floor".[107]   In fact, it marked a victory, albeit a temporary one, for New Glasgow industrial capitalism and Halifax financial capitalism. More important, it marked the high point of a late-developing effort on the part of the Halifax business community to create an industrial region structured on that Atlantic metropolis. It was a short-lived triumph. By 1920 the Halifax group made common cause with their Montreal and London Counterparts in the organization of the British Empire Steel Corporation, a gigantic consolidation containing both the Dominion and the Nova Scotia Steel companies. This event marked both the final nationalization of the region's major industrial potential and the failure of its entrepreneurs to maintain control of any significant element in the industrial section of the regional economy.

VI

The Maritimes had entered Canada very much as a foreign colony. As the least integrated part of the Canadian economy, it was the region most dependent upon and most influenced by those policies designated to create an integrated national state. The entrepreneurs of the 1880's were capable men, vividly aware of the problems involved in the transition from an Atlantic to a continental economy. The tragedy of the industrial experiment in the Maritimes was that the transportation lines which linked the region to its new metropolis altered the communal arrangement of the entire area; they did not merely establish a new external frame of reference, they re-cast the entire internal structure. The Maritimes had never been a single integrated organic unit; it was, in fact, not a "region" at all, but a number of British communities clustered on the Atlantic fringe, each with its separate lines of communication and its several metropolises — lines that were water-borne, flexible and changing. In this sense the railroad with its implications of organic unity, its inflexibility, and its assumption that there was a metropolitan point at which it could end, provided an experience entirely alien to the Maritime tradition. The magnitude of this problem was demonstrated in the initial attempts at industrialization; they all occurred in traditional communities ideally located for the Atlantic market, but in the most disadvantaged positions possible for a continental one.

Central to the experience was the failure of a viable regional metropolis to arise to provide the financial leadership and market alternative. With its powerful mercantile interests and its impressive banking institutions Halifax could most easily have adopted to this role, but its merchants preferred, like their

106 *Ibid.*, 2 April 1910.
107 *Ibid.*, 9 April 1910.

Boston counterparts, to invest their large fortunes in banks and American railroad stocks than to venture them on building a new order. Only later, with the advent of regional resource industries, did that city play the role of financial metropolis.

Lacking any strong regional economic centre, the Maritime entrepreneur inevitably sought political solutions to the structural problems created by the National Policy; he consistently looked to the federal government for aid against all external threats and to his local governments for aid against Canadians. Since the regional politician was more able to influence a hostile environment than was the regional businessman, the latter frequently became both. In many respects the National Policy simply represented to the entrepreneur a transfer from a British to a Canadian commercial empire. Inherent in most of his activities was the colonial assumption that he could not really control his own destiny, that, of necessity, he would be manipulated by forces beyond his control. Thus he produced cotton cloth for the central Canadian metropolis in precisely the same manner as he had produced timber and ships for the British. In so doing he demonstrated considerable initiative and considerable courage, for the truly surprising aspect of the whole performance was that he was able, using his limited community resources, to produce such a complex and diversified industrial potential during the last two decades of the nineteenth century. The inability of the Canadian market to consume his output was as much a failure of the system as of the entrepreneur; the spectacle of a metropolis which devoured its own children had been alien to the Maritime colonial experience. Ultimately, perhaps inevitably, the regional entrepreneur lost control to external forces which he could rarely comprehend, much less master.

L.D. McCANN   Reprinted from Vol. XIII, No. 1
                                        (Autumn 1983)

Metropolitanism and Branch Businesses in the Maritimes, 1881-1931[1]

METROPOLITANISM IS AN OLD THEME in the historiography of the Maritimes, and the sting of the metropolis is felt throughout the region, from the smallest village to the largest city.[2] In the 19th century the locus of metropolitan dominance was based across the Atlantic in Britain. Now it rests in central Canada. Despite our awareness of the metropolis and its impact on the Maritime economy, surprisingly little is known about the *unfolding* of metropolitan dominance across the Maritime region in the years between Confederation and the Great Depression.[3] New evidence on the process of metropolitanism in the Maritimes suggests answers for several basic yet unresolved questions. First, which metropolis dominated the region in the post-Confederation period? Second, which sectors of the regional economy were linked most strongly to the metropolis? And third, what was the geographical sphere of influence of the metropolis?

One of the inherent features of metropolitanism is the extension into the hinterland of economic activities headquartered in the metropolis. Branch businesses may be regarded as the emissaries, so-to-speak, of the metropolis, advancing its economic interests and consolidating its empire throughout the hinterland. Among other activities, branch businesses engage in manufacturing, facilitate the distribution of goods, channel capital flows, and sell and service the

1   Research on branch businesses in Canada has been funded by the Social Sciences and Humanities Research Council of Canada in conjunction with the Historical Atlas of Canada Project. Able research and computer assistance was provided by Janice Milton, Virginia Lieter, and Libby Napper. The cartographic work is the careful labour of Geoff Lester and his staff at the University of Alberta; a grant from Mount Allison University provided for the preparation of the maps and diagrams. A more extended version of this paper was read in 1983 before the annual meetings of the Canadian Historical Association (Vancouver) and the Social Science History Association (Washington, D.C.), and the helpful remarks of Graeme Wynn and Gil Stelter, commentators at these meetings, are gratefully acknowledged.

2   See, for example, J.B. Brebner, *New England's Outpost: Acadia Before the British Conquest of Canada* (New York, 1927), J.M.S. Careless, "Aspects of Metropolitanism in Atlantic Canada", in Mason Wade, ed., *Regionalism in the Canadian Community* (Toronto, 1969), pp. 117-29, and David A. Sutherland, "The Merchants of Halifax, 1815-1850: A Commercial Class in Pursuit of Metropolitan Status", Ph.D. thesis, University of Toronto, 1975. The classic Canadian statement on metropolitanism is Careless, "Frontierism, Metropolitanism, and Canadian History", *Canadian Historical Review*, XXXV (1954), pp. 1-21, but see also N.S.B. Gras, *An Introduction to Economic History* (New York , 1922), pp. 186-240, and L.D. McCann, "The Myth of the Metropolis: The Role of the City in Canadian Regionalism", *Urban History Review*, 9 (1981), pp. 52-8.

3   For a recent interpretation of the regional development of the Maritimes, set within the context

products of the metropolis. Drawing chiefly upon Dun and Bradstreet records, it is possible to build a comprehensive picture of branch businesses operating in the Maritimes in the post-Confederation period. Information on all branch businesses, as well as a ten per cent sample of the composite business structure of the Maritimes, was collected from the *Mercantile Agency Reference Books* of Dun, Wiman and Company and its successor, R.G. Dun and Company, at ten-year intervals from 1881 to 1931. This yielded a computerized data base of more than 11,000 businesses.[4] Analysis of the emergence of different types of metropolitan branch businesses offers an opportunity to measure not only urban dominance and control over different economic sectors, but also the actual process of integrating metropolis and hinterland. Moreover, the geographical patterns of branch businesses in the hinterland identify spheres of metropolitan influence.

The rise of branch businesses gained considerable momentum after Confederation. Overall, as Figure 1 shows, they experienced a fourfold increase in numbers, but their most noticeable advance occurred between 1901 and 1921 when they more than doubled from 416 to 950. During this period of branch development, the composite make-up of the region's business structure had remained remarkably stable. Manufacturing enterprise had fallen back gradually, its losses absorbed by the retail trades, but the relative share of the other sectors deviated little over the 50-year period. When the economy of the Maritimes went into serious decline in the 1920's, forcing a net loss of about 1,100 businesses, branch businesses managed to hold firm, and in so doing gained a greater share of all business activities. Branch businesses were always considerable in the resource, manufacturing, retailing, and banking sectors, but the most appreciable advance occurred in wholesaling and distribution. Over time, the mass distribution of goods was increasingly lost by the Maritime businessman.

This gathering momentum of branch enterprise can also be measured in another way. Not unexpectedly, branch businesses have always been parented by companies of considerable financial strength. In 1931, for example, more than 90 per cent of the branch businesses headquartered outside of the region were backed by companies holding assets of more than $1,000,000. At the same date, less than two per cent of regional firms, including those managing branch businesses, were similarly financed.

As Figure 2 shows, branch businesses based outside of the Maritimes became

of metropolis and hinterland, see Graeme Wynn, "The Maritimes: The Geography of Fragmentation and Underdevelopment", in L.D. McCann, ed., *Heartland and Hinterland: A Geography of Canada* (Toronto, 1982), pp. 156-213. Despite his framework of inquiry, Wynn does not focus specifically on the theme of metropolitan dominance.

4   For each business, the following information was recorded: (1) name of company, (2) type of business, coded according to Statistic Canada's *Standard Industrial Classification Manual* (1970), (3) settlement location, including large urban place (≥2,500 people), county and province; (4) pecuniary strength; (5) if branch business, location of the headquarters of the company; and (6) product lines, if listed. This information was subjected to various statistical

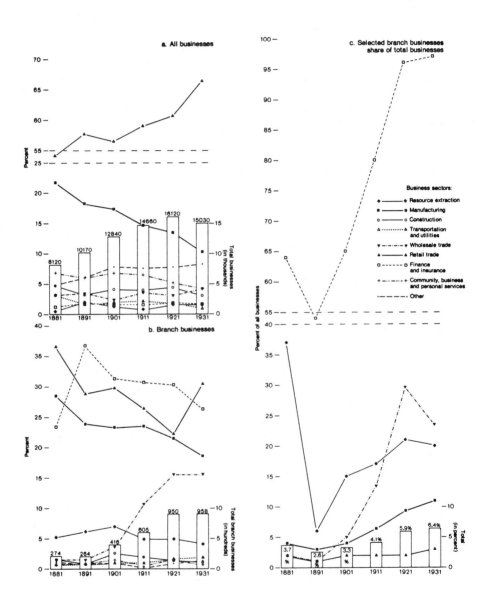

Figure 1:   Changes in the Business Structure of the Maritimes, 1881-1931

increasingly prominent over time, rising from a less than 10 per cent share in 1881 to more than 55 per cent in 1931. Measured by companies holding assets of more than $1,000,000, the external share increased even more dramatically, from 22 to 79 per cent. At the end of the 1920s, nearly half of all branches in the Maritimes traced their chain of command to either Montreal or Toronto; the balance was distributed among more than 400 communities. This was essentially a reversal of the metropolitan pattern that had existed shortly after Confederation when Saint John and Halifax spawned the majority of the region's branches. In fact in 1881 Toronto maintained not one branch in the Maritimes, and Montreal only 13. Expanding only slowly throughout the late 19th century, Montreal's presence was more commonplace by the First World War. Many towns and cities established branch businesses in nearby communities at this time, but none could compare to the prominence of this expanding Canadian metropolis. Through a flurry of merger and takeover activity, particularly in the 1890s and early 1900s, Montreal replaced Halifax and Saint John as the dominating metropolitan influence in the Maritimes. But this leadership was soon challenged by Toronto during the 1910s and 1920s. In 1901, Toronto firms had located only nine branches in the region; by 1931 the total was 228, just one less than Montreal. No other urban centres were nearly as competitive, not even American or British cities, and Halifax and Saint John by this time offered only limited competition.

The metropolitan outreach was facilitated by a number of factors, such as the construction of the national railways across the region during the 1870s (Intercolonial) and the 1890s (CPR), but these advances only partially explain the rise of branch businesses in the Maritimes. Metropolitan interests expanded their operations by responding to more specific factors that affected individual business activities.[5] The spread of branch banks, for example, was directly attributable to government policies, including the Bank Act of 1871, that favoured this type of banking system.[6] The metropolitan domination of this sector, in turn, rested with the growth of central Canadian banks on their own terms, and the eventual centralization of Maritime banks either in Montreal or in Toronto.[7]

analyses to provide the data reported in the text and used in the maps and diagrams. For this paper, we emphasize the aggregate changes in the business structure of the Maritimes, focusing attention on the theme of metropolitan dominance. Data on all branch businesses for all of Canada between 1881 and 1931 have also been collected; they will be the subject of other papers.

5 Branch business development, of course, is one particular strategy related to the growth of the firm. For reviews of this theme which are relevant to an interpretation of the metropolitan outreach, see Alfred Chandler, *Strategy and Structure: The History of the American Industrial Enterprise* (Cambridge, Mass., 1962), Lars Hakanson, "Towards a Theory of Location and Corporate Growth", in F.E. Ian Hamilton and G.J.R. Linge, eds., *Spatial Analysis, Industry, and the Industrial Environment*, Vol. 1 (New York, 1979), pp. 115-38, and H.D. Watts, *The Large Industrial Enterprise* (London, 1980).

6 E.P. Neufeld, *The Financial System of Canada* (Toronto, 1972), pp. 81-9, 97-102.

7 The centralization process took place between 1900 and 1920, and was highlighted by the move-

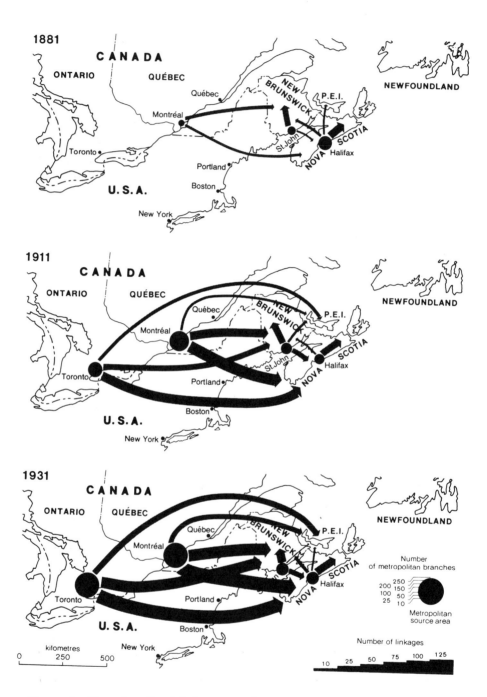

Figure 2: Changing Spatial Patterns of Metropolitan Branch Businesses in the Maritimes, 1881-1931

Metropolitan domination in banking became strongest in the 1910s, when Toronto's banks doubled their branches in the Maritimes (from 63 to 125), challenging strongly the previous and almost complete control of Montreal (Figure 3).

Seeking explanations for the metropolitan involvement in the manufacturing industries of the Maritimes is much more complex, but several basic patterns do prevail. First, metropolitan involvement has been restricted to a limited number of industries. Second, unlike the spillover of American industry into southern Ontario and the construction there of branch plants, branch manufacturing in the Maritimes usually grew when central Canadian firms bought out earlier, community-established companies. Typical of hinterland areas, the Maritime industrial base has always been narrowly focused, emphasizing the primary manufacturing of forest, fish, and iron and steel products.[8] Significant shares of these industries fell under metropolitan control after Confederation, either through takeover and merger activity (in fish processing and iron and steel),[9] or by some new plant construction (in pulp and paper).[10] The force of the metropolis in manufacturing was exerted most dramatically in the 1890s and early 1900s through the takeovers and subsequent dismantling of key manufacturing industries, including cotton textiles, rope and cordage, sugar, glass, and paint — almost all by corporations headquartered in Montreal.[11]

Toronto's failure to participate directly in the de-industrialization of the Maritimes might at first seem surprising, especially considering its national prominence in manufacturing, but this is not to say that Toronto failed to influence manufacturing across the region. It did, and in a way that coincided with the rise of the large industrial enterprise that integrated mass production with mass distribution, and with associated changes in managerial organization.[12] Appear-

ment of the Bank of Nova Scotia to Toronto (1900) and the Merchants' Bank of Halifax (later the Royal Bank of Canada) to Montreal (1904). Of further significance, the Halifax Banking Company was absorbed by Toronto's Bank of Commerce (1903), The People's Bank of Halifax by the Bank of Montreal (1905), and the Union Bank of Halifax by the Royal (1910): *Annual Financial Review*, (1923), pp. 111, 126. See also James Frost, "The 'Nationalization' of the Bank of Nova Scotia, 1880-1910", *Acadiensis*, XII, 1 (Autumn 1982), pp. 29-30.

8   R.E. Caves and R. Holton, *The Canadian Economy: Prospect and Retrospect* (Cambridge, Mass., 1959), pp. 140-94.

9   Fish processing remained controlled largely from within the region, particularly at Halifax, although the Portland Packing Company of Maine held an important share of the industry before World War I.

10 Donald W. Emmerson, "Pulp and Paper Manufacturing in the Maritimes", *Pulp and Paper Magazine of Canada* (December 1947), pp. 129-55.

11 T.W. Acheson, "The National Policy and the Industrialization of the Maritimes, 1880-1910", *Acadiensis*, I, 2 (Spring 1972), pp. 3-29.

12 Alfred Chandler has written persuasively of a managerial revolution in American business, whereby "the visible hand of managerial direction . . . replaced the invisible hand of market mechanisms . . . in coordinating flows and allocating resources in major modern industries". Typical were mass producers of low-priced, semi-perishable, packaged products (e.g. flour and

ing first in the United States during the 1880s, the integrated industrial enterprise made little headway in Canada until after the turn of the century. When it did, however, it was tied inextricably to the American model, and frequently to an American parent company maintaining a Canadian head office in Toronto.

Many Toronto-based enterprises entered the Maritime market not by building manufacturing plants, but by establishing a regional distribution network for their products. This included such industries as food processing (Swift Canadian, Harris Abattoir, and Maple Leaf Milling); agricultural implements (Massey-Harris); business machines (National Cash Register, International Business Machines, and United Typewriter); rubber products (Goodyear and Dunlop); and heavy machinery (Canadian General Electric, Canadian Westinghouse, and Otis Elevator). They appeared mostly in the region's major towns and cities, and accounted for Toronto's rapid surge and dominance in the branch wholesaling sector after 1911 (Figure 3). Such industries, of course, mirrored the capital-intensive and diversified industrial structure of the Ontario metropolis. By contrast, Montreal's wholesaling advance was more limited, emphasizing its national prominence in labour-intensive manufacturing such as tobacco (Imperial Tobacco) and drugs (National Drug), as well as its traditional import-export function in metals, dry goods, and specialized food products.

The visible hand of management also made its mark on retailing, and the growth of branches in this sector also accelerated Toronto's metropolitan outreach. Small retail shops — grocery and general stores, produce and meat markets — were the most numerous activities in the region's composite business structure. Many faced stiff competition from branches originating within the Maritimes, but external competition was limited until after the First World War. Although Maritimers could order catalogue items from the T. Eaton Company of Toronto by the 1890s, it was not until the 1920s that they were forced to make conscious decisions about shopping in a metropolitan-based store. More favourable freight rates for shipping goods into the region, a growing consumer demand for nationally advertised brands, and the growth of national retail chains, all affected the timing of this metropolitan outreach. As a result, the residents of Halifax, Truro, Sydney, New Glasgow, Moncton, or Saint John could, if they so chose, buy groceries at Dominion, shop for novelty items at a Woolworths or Metropolitan store, look for clothes at Tip Top Tailors, try on shoes at Agnew Surpass, or order all of these items from an outlet of T. Eaton and Company. All of these Canadian and American retail

cereals); processors of perishable products for national markets (e.g. meatpacking); manufacturers of new mass-produced machines that required specialized marketing services if they were to be sold in volume (e.g. agricultural implements and business machines); and the makers of high-volume producer goods that were technologically complex but standardized (e.g. electrical equipment). Alfred Chandler, "The United States: Seedbed of Managerial Capitalism", in Chandler and Herman Daems, eds., *Managerial Hierarchies: Comparative Perspectives on the Rise of the Modern Industrial Enterprise* (Cambridge, Mass., 1980), pp. 9, 23. See also Chandler, *The Visible Hand* (Cambridge, Mass., 1978).

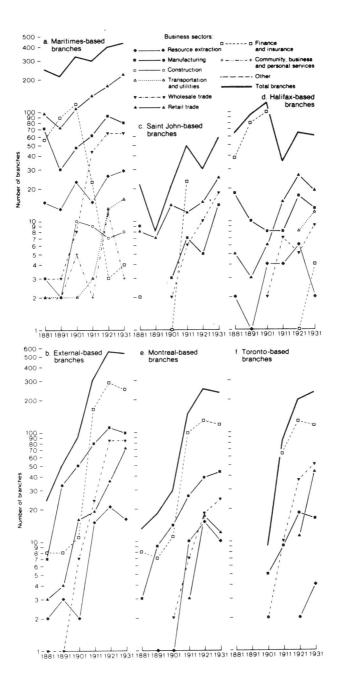

Figure 3: Changes in the Types of Metropolitan Branch Businesses in the Maritimes, 1881-1931

chains were based in Ontario, and except for Agnew Surpass and Metropolitan Stores, all were managed from Toronto head offices. It is difficult to gauge the full impact of these chains, but it is clear that the indigenous retail sector remained largely intact through the 1920s; indeed, there was modest growth in the actual number of local retail businesses (see Figure 1). The fullest impact on retailing would not be felt until after the Second World War, when suburban shopping centres actively sought the national chains as their major clientele. This pattern would also coincide with branch expansion in highly specialized service industries such as national advertising agencies, financial counselling companies, and engineering firms.

To ascertain the spheres of influence of the dominant metropolitan centres throughout the Maritimes, the numbers of Halifax, Saint John, Montreal, and Toronto branch businesses located in the region's counties and large urban places were first tallied. Dominant status was then assigned to the metropolitan centre controlling the greatest number of branches in each county or place. If no clear majority existed, where two or more centres shared the same number of branches, the sphere of influence was recorded as overlapping between two or more centres (see Figure 4). The results of these analyses for 1881, 1911, and 1931 reveal, rather dramatically, the changing geographical relationships between the Maritimes and central Canada.

Confederation is purported to have seriously undermined the economic development of the Maritimes, but even if this was so, the impact was not seriously felt until early in the 20th century. In 1881, regional autonomy still largely prevailed. The region managed its own banks and its merchants had recently rallied to finance a burst of industrial activity.[13] Halifax dominated all of the Nova Scotia counties, those of Prince Edward Island, and even some in New Brunswick. Most large urban places across the region were linked to the Nova Scotia capital. Montreal shared influence in the New Brunswick countryside with Saint John, whose businessmen took an active interest in the forest industry. By 1911, however, Montreal had taken over leadership throughout most of Nova Scotia and New Brunswick, largely because of its control of banking, takeovers in manufacturing, and the quest for industrial materials such as Cape Breton coal. Its bankers and industrialists managed a variety of branches in Halifax, Saint John, Fredericton, and lesser places, while its coal companies were the principal employers in Springhill, Westville, Stellarton, Inverness, and Glace Bay. In "Busy Amherst", the 20th ranking industrial town in the country, Montreal companies had gained control of many industries, including the Canadian Car and Foundry Company, one of the largest of its

---

13 The mercantile-industrial transition is treated in L.D. McCann, "Staples and the New Industrialism in the Growth of Post-Confederation Halifax", *Acadiensis*, VIII, 2 (Spring 1979), pp. 47-79, and "The Mercantile-Industrial Transition in the Metals Towns of Pictou County, 1857-1931", *Acadiensis*, X, 2 (Spring 1981), pp. 29-64.

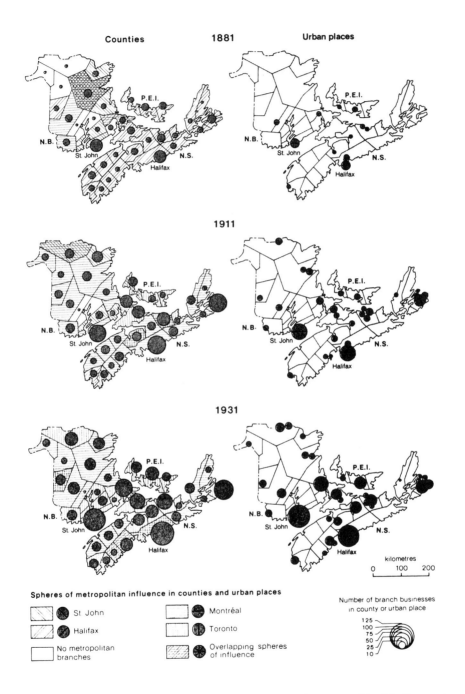

Figure 4: Metropolitan Dominance and Spheres of Geographical Influence in
the Maritimes, 1881-1931

kind in Canada.[14] On the eve of the war years, therefore, the Maritimes was unmistakably a hinterland to Montreal.

Montreal's dominance is acknowledged by most scholars who have written about the economic development of the Maritimes, but less recognized is the build-up of Toronto's influence over the region.[15] As Figure 4 reveals, Toronto in 1931 held complete sway over Prince Edward Island and the important belt of urban and industrial counties in southern New Brunswick and central Nova Scotia, as well as industrial Cape Breton. In fact, Toronto could claim dominance over Montreal and other competing cities in a majority of the region's counties and large urban places. During the 1910s and 1920s, Toronto had beaten out Montreal's leadership in about one-third of these counties and places. Toronto's dominance was based on banking, its considerable interests in wholesale distribution and retail trade, and some manufacturing. In this reshuffling, Montreal continued to hold onto northern New Brunswick, the Annapolis Valley of Nova Scotia, and the coal mining counties outside of industrial Cape Breton. In Montreal's drive for regional hegemony, it had remained largely aloof of the American influence so common in Toronto, but with the development of pulp and paper in northern New Brunswick during the 1920s, Montreal finally also became more active as an intermediary for American corporate enterprise.[16]

Between the post-Confederation period and the Great Depression, the pattern of metropolitanism in the Maritimes was substantially revised at least three times. This reorientation, from a Halifax-centred region, to Montreal's sting, and then to the challenging force of Toronto, coincided with the mercantile-industrial, rural-urban transformation of the region. As the Maritimes shifted away from the Atlantic economy, based on staple trades, slowly integrating with the emerging continental market, focused on the new industrialism, new alliances took form. These alliances were essentially urban in character; they reveal a changing structure of geographical interdependencies or linkages that is important for interpreting urban dominance and economic growth in the region (Figure 5).

Traditionally, until late in the 19th century, the economy of Maritime towns and cities grew largely by success in the staple trades. Most communities went about these trades independently of each other. When local merchants required extra supplies or capital, they were usually serviced directly from Halifax or

---

14 Nolan Reilly, "The General Strike in Amherst, Nova Scotia, 1919", *Acadiensis*, IX, 2 (Spring 1980), pp. 56-77.

15 See, for example, T.W. Acheson, "The Maritimes and 'Empire Canada'", in David Bercuson, ed., *Canada and the Burden of Unity* (Toronto, 1979), pp. 87-114.

16 The development of the pulp and paper industry was led by regional entrepreneurs before the First World War, by American interests in the interwar period, and by a combination of local, American, European, and British Columbian companies after 1960: Emmerson, "Pulp and Paper".

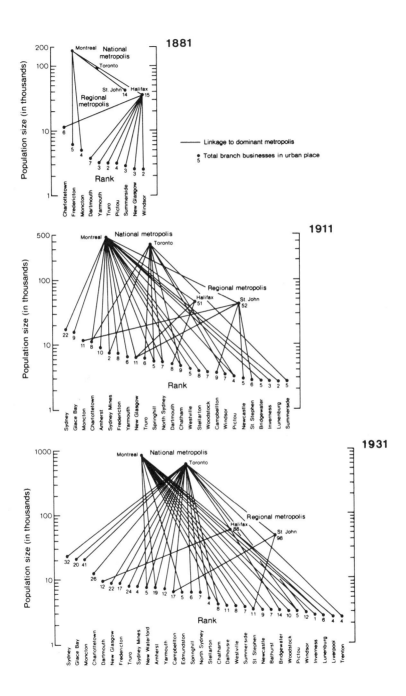

Figure 5: Metropolis and Hinterland: Changes in the Structure of Urban Relationships, 1881-1931

Saint John, or through the branch houses of these centres. The new industrialism in time brought increasing interdependence among cities, forging new
and deeper links with central Canada. As Montreal gained ascendancy, the
numbers of metropolitan branches in urban places became more prominent,
and the population growth of these industrial towns became more dependent on
externally-made decisions. The structure of interdependencies in 1931, however, measures new and stronger alliances focused on Toronto. Indeed,
Toronto's remarkable hegemony over all but one of the region's 16 largest urban
places in 1931, based largely on tertiary economic activities, forces us to recon-
sider the basis of urban growth in many places across the region during the
1910s and 1920s.[17]

Many towns and cities lost population during the 1920s — Amherst, Trenton,
Westville, Sydney Mines, to cite only several. But some of those that actually
gained population — Moncton, Glace Bay, and Truro, for example — grew, it
appears, largely because of changes in the tertiary sector of their economies.
Indeed, increased urban employment was frequently the result of newly established branch businesses engaged in the wholesale or retail trades. A case in
point is Moncton, which grew from just over 11,000 in 1911, to about 17,500 in
1921, and then to some 20,000 in 1931. In the mid-19th century, Moncton pros-
pered briefly as a shipbuilding centre only to decline shortly after Confederation.[18] However, with the arrival of the Intercolonial Railway's headquarters, re-
pairshops, and marshalling yards after 1872, and a revitalized economic climate,
new industries soon appeared (a sugar refinery, a cotton factory, and a woollen
mill). Many of these industries went into decline after 1900, but Moncton's
potential as a distribution centre soon attracted another round of growth, this
time based on branch businesses in the tertiary sector, chiefly in transportation,
wholesaling, financial and insurance activity, and retailing. Massey-Harris
made Moncton their Maritimes distribution centre in 1907, and in 1920, the T.
Eaton Company opened their mail order house for the Maritime provinces, employing more than 750 people.[19] Between 1911 and 1931, Moncton's population
doubled and its total number of businesses climbed from 248 to 370, but its
branch businesses, which now included many of the city's largest employers, increased fourfold, from 11 to 41. Such expansion, nevertheless, did little to lessen
the growing interdependence between Maritime centres and the metropolis; on
the contrary, urban dominance and interdependence had increased appreciably.

17 We lack studies of urban growth in the Maritimes during this period, but for one attempt which
   details data on the population growth of all urban places in Nova Scotia between 1871 and 1931,
   see McCann, "The Mercantile-Industrial Transition".

18 James Appleton, "The Town of Moncton: A Metropolitan Approach, 1880-1889", B.A. thesis,
   Mount Allison University, 1975, and Sheva Medjuck, "Wooden Ships and Iron People: The
   Lives of the People of Moncton, New Brunswick, 1851-1871", Ph.D. thesis, York University,
   1978.

19 Lloyd A. Machum, *A History of Moncton: Town and City, 1855-1965* (Moncton, 1965), pp. 207,
   281.

The presence of a metropolitan branch business in a community is evidence of the economic interdependence between metropolis and hinterland. There are other forms of interdependencies, of course, including cultural and political ties, which are implicit in the concept of metropolitanism. But examination of branch businesses, set within the context of the composite business structure of a region, provides a meaningful indication of the interplay between metropolis and hinterland. As the forces of metropolitanism unfolded after Confederation, Maritimers, like all Canadians, were subjected to an increasingly complex array of changes in the sphere of business. Shortly after Confederation, it was likely that Maritimers deposited their accounts in a regionally-controlled bank or bought groceries from a locally-owned store. At the same time, many of the basic necessities of life — vegetables, furniture, carriages — were produced by themselves or by local craftsmen. By the eve of the Great Depression, however, the savings in their bank accounts were controlled by Montreal and Toronto financiers and groceries could be bought in a metropolitan-based chain store; the new canned foods, mass-produced furniture, and horseless carriages, were produced outside of the region. The sting of Montreal and Toronto penetrated deeply into all sectors and regions of the Maritime economy. By the close of the 1920s, the basic stimuli for urban and regional economic growth in all sectors of the Maritime economy were greatly affected by external forces emanating from the metropolis. Of course, Montreal and Toronto's dominance over the region was also shared indirectly with American enterprise; this was the particular nature of Canadian metropolitanism after the First World War, and it has remained so.[20]

---

20 R. Keith Semple and W. Randy Smith, "Metropolitan Dominance and Foreign Ownership in the Canadian Urban System", *The Canadian Geographer*, 25 (1981), pp. 4-26.

DAVID FRANK

Reprinted from Vol. VII, No. 1
(Autumn 1977)

The Cape Breton Coal Industry and the Rise and Fall of the British Empire Steel Corporation*

Our understanding of regional underdevelopment in Atlantic Canada has been slow to develop. For more than 50 years we have had extensive documentation of the existence of serious regional inequality in Canada. Attempts to explain the reasons for this have been less common. In the 1920s politicians active in the Maritime Rights movement catalogued the "unfilled promises" and "betrayals" of Confederation and demanded increased federal subsidies as compensation.[1] A less subjective interpretation was proposed by S. A. Saunders, C. R. Fay and Harold Innis, who attributed the region's troubles to the new era of industrialism. For the Maritimes it was "prosperity so long as their face was towards the sea, and . . . struggle against adversity when the pull of the land increased". Like an "economic seismograph", the Maritimes registered the shockwaves of a "rising tide of continental forces that were destined to dominate the economy of the Maritime Provinces".[2] Recent studies have questioned this approach: an economic historian has challenged the myth of the "Golden Age"; an historical geographer has traced the domination of the region by outside forces during the colonial era; an economist has pointed out that during a decisive period in the 1830s and 1840s local entrepreneurs neglected the region's industrial potential.[3]

---

*   For their constant support and critical comments, I would like to thank Michael Cross, Judith Fingard, Craig Heron, Gregory Kealey, Don Macgillivray, Ian McKay, Del Muise, Nolan Reilly and David Sutherland.

1   Nova Scotia, *A Submission of Its Claims with Respect to Maritime Disabilities within Confederation* (Halifax, 1926); Nova Scotia, *A Submission on Dominion-Provincial Relations and the Fiscal Disabilities of Nova Scotia within the Canadian Federation* (Halifax, 1934).

2   C. R. Fay and H. A. Innis, "The Economic Development of Canada, 1867-1921: The Maritime Provinces", *Cambridge History of the British Empire* (Cambridge, 1930), vol. VI, pp. 657-71; S. A. Saunders, "Trends in the Economic History of the Maritime Provinces", *Studies in the Economy of the Maritime Provinces* (Toronto, 1939), pp. 245-65.

3   P. D. McClelland, "The New Brunswick Economy in the 19th Century", *Journal of Economic History*, XXV (1965), pp. 686-90; A. H. Clark, "Contributions of its Southern Neighbours to the Underdevelopment of the Maritime Provinces Area, 1710-1867", in R. A. Preston, ed., *The Influence of the United States on Canadian Development* (Durham, N.C., 1972), pp. 164-84; R. F. Neill, "National Policy and Regional Underdevelopment", *Journal of Canadian Studies*, IX (May, 1974), pp. 12-20.

The most important revisionist studies were those published in the early 1970s by Bruce Archibald and T. W. Acheson. In 1971 Bruce Archibald applied a sweeping metropolis/satellite interpretation to the economic history of the region. He argued that the region has "always existed in a dependent relationship with a larger controlling metropolis" and the region must be seen as "the back yard of a dominant economic centre rather than an autonomous but struggling unit". His survey stressed the role of outside exploitation in the underdevelopment of the region: the extraction of resources and capital in response to the needs of outside forces divided the loyalties of local entrepreneurs and produced growing regional underdevelopment.[4] In 1972 T. W. Acheson challenged the view that the Maritimes did not experience economic growth after Confederation; his study found that the Maritimes sustained a significant amount of industrial expansion in the late nineteenth century, as a group of "community-oriented" entrepreneurs transferred capital from traditional pursuits to new industrial investments. By the 1920s, however, this industrial structure had collapsed, mainly because no "viable regional metropolis" had emerged to take leadership and central Canadian business and finance had asserted control over the region's economic life.[5]

In the light of these studies, it seems clear that a new framework is necessary for understanding regional underdevelopment. A tentative approach may be drawn from the Marxist analysis of regional inequalities under industrial capitalism, which explains uneven development between regions as a natural feature of capitalistic economic growth. The continuing search for new economic surpluses, better rates of profit, new raw materials, markets and sources of labour supply, all caused an expansion in the scale of capital accumulation. As part of this process, the operation of the free market system generally led to the concentration and centralization of capital; economic wealth and power tended to become concentrated in fewer hands and centralized in fewer places. Once the structure of an inter-regional market in goods, labour and capital was established, relationships of domination and dependency emerged between regions. As the process continued, regional

4   Bruce Archibald, "Atlantic Regional Underdevelopment and Socialism", in Laurier LaPierre *et. al.*, eds., *Essays on the Left* (Toronto, 1971), pp. 103-20; Archibald, "The Development of Underdevelopment in the Atlantic Provinces" (M.A. thesis, Dalhousie University, 1971); Archibald's work was based on an application of Andre Gunder Frank, "The Development of Underdevelopment", *Monthly Review*, XVIII (September, 1966), pp. 17 - 31.

5   "The National Policy and the Industrialization of the Maritimes, 1880-1910", *Acadiensis*, I (Spring, 1972), pp. 3-28. Similar in approach was J. M. S. Careless, "Aspects of Metropolitanism in Atlantic Canada", in Mason Wade, ed., *Regionalism in the Canadian Community 1867-1967* (Toronto, 1969), pp. 117-29.

disparities deepened and the subordinate communities entered a cycle of capital deficiencies, population losses and economic powerlessness.[6]

By the 1880s industrial capitalism had become well-established in central Canada and began to extend its hegemony over regions and sectors where the growth of industrial capitalism was less advanced. The emergence of this trend towards the concentration and centralization of capital had devastating consequences for economic development in the weaker regions and communities of the country.[7] The concentration and centralization of the Canadian economy affected these regions, especially the Maritimes, in several ways. First, national economic policies under Confederation promoted regional underdevelopment. The political hegemony of central Canada helped shape state policy to aid central Canadian goals and to injure or neglect regional interests, especially in tariff, railway, trade, marine and fisheries matters. The completion of the railway network added a key instrument of national economic integration; the railways brought western goods in and took eastern people out. The creation of a national market in goods undermined local industry as outside competitors conquered the regional market, and the creation of an inter-regional labour market tended to make the region a reserve pool of labour for neighbouring regions. A fourth aspect was the growing division of labour between regions, which often took the form of the export of raw materials and specialized products to the metropolitan market, but also resulted in the location of resource-based and labour-intensive industries to take advantage of raw materials and low wages in the underdeveloped region. A corollary was the emergence of economic sectors, which, because they were not important to the national economy, suffered capital deficiencies (the fisheries) or were absorbed into other economic empires (the forest industries). A fifth aspect of the "Canadianization" of the region was the steady import of central Canadian social and cultural norms; by the time they reached Ottawa, political figures like W. S. Fielding and R. L. Borden readily accepted the assumptions of central Canadian hegemony. Finally, the most effective form of regional subordina-

---

6   Karl Marx, *Capital* (New York, 1967), vol. I, especially ch. XXV; Paul Baran, *The Political Economy of Growth* (New York, 1968); Ernest Mandel, *Capitalism and Regional Disparities* (Toronto, 1970); Henry Veltmeyer, "The Methodology of Dependency Analysis; An Outline for a Strategy of Research on Regional Underdevelopment" (unpublished paper, Saint Mary's University, 1977).

7   Recent work on regional underdevelopment includes E. R. Forbes, "The Maritime Rights Movement, 1919-1927: A Study in Canadian Regionalism" (Ph.D. thesis, Queen's University, 1975); David Alexander, "Newfoundland's Traditional Economy and Development to 1934", *Acadiensis*, V (Spring, 1976), pp. 56-78; see also the contributions by C. D. Howell, Carman Miller, E. R. Forbes and T. W. Acheson to D. J. Bercuson, ed., *Canada and the Burden of Unity* (Toronto, 1977).

tion was the extension of direct metropolitan financial control over the region. Through competition and credit manipulation, and mergers and takeovers in all important industries and financial institutions, the domination of central Canada over the Maritimes was consolidated by the 1920s. Much of the social and political turmoil of that decade expressed the community's response to the crisis of the regional economy.

Nowhere can the results of these developments be seen more clearly than in industrial Cape Breton, where the process of national economic integration was of decisive importance in the exploitation of one of the region's richest natural resources, the coal-fields. At the beginning of the twentieth century, industrial Cape Breton seemed a dynamic and prosperous industrial community. The population of the industrial area, which numbered 18,005 people in 1891, had increased to 57,263 people by 1911.[8] The largest and most valuable in eastern Canada, the Sydney coal-field stretches about 30 miles along the northeastern shore of Cape Breton Island and in the 1920s the field's proven reserves were known to exceed one billion tons. The accessibility and quality of the coal supply gave the Sydney field considerable economic importance. Cape Breton's bituminous coal compared favourably with other industrial coals, although it was no rival for anthracite as a domestic fuel.[9] The inexpensive water route to Quebec enabled Cape Breton coal to penetrate the central Canadian market, and the extensive iron ore reserves at Bell Island, Newfoundland, generated the establishment of an iron and steel industry in Cape Breton; these two markets consumed the bulk of the coal industry's output. By the time of the First World War industrial Cape Breton occupied an important place in the national economy. The coal mines supplied more than 44 per cent of Canada's annual coal production, and the iron and steel industry produced more than one-third of the country's pig iron.[10]

Although the condition of the local economy at the peak of its fortunes inspired widespread optimism, at least one thoughtful observer was troubled by the emerging pattern of industrial development. A Yorkshire mining en-

---

8   D. A. Muise, "The Making of an Industrial Community: Cape Breton Coal Towns, 1867-1900" (paper presented to the Atlantic Canada Studies Conference, Fredericton, 1976), Appendix I.

9   M. J. Patton, "The Coal Resources of Canada", *Economic Geography,* I (1925), pp. 84-5; A. L. Hay, "Coal-mining Operations in the Sydney Coal Field ', American Institute of Mining and Metallurgical Engineers, *Technical Publication No. 198* (New York, 1929), pp. 3-6.

10 F. W. Gray, "The Coal Fields and Coal Industry of Eastern Canada", Canada, Mines Branch, *Bulletin No. 14* (Ottawa, 1917), p. 14; W. J. Donald, *The Canadian Iron and Steel Industry* (Boston, 1915), Appendix B. In 1913 Nova Scotia produced 8,135,104 short tons of coal; of this total the Sydney field supplied 6,313,275 tons. For production data see Canada, *Report of the Royal Commission on Coal, 1946* (Ottawa, 1947), pp. 64-5.

gineer who had immigrated to Cape Breton, Francis W. Gray, lamented in 1917 the underdevelopment of the coal resources:

> Nova Scotia, as a province, has not reached the stage of industrial and manufacturing activity that should have accompanied a coal mining industry 100 years old . . . . It must be confessed that the potentialities of Nova Scotia have been but meagrely realized. Take away the steel industry from Nova Scotia, and what other manufacturing activity has the Province to show as a reflex of the production of 7,000,000 tons of coal annually? . . . . The coal mined in Nova Scotia has, for generations, gone to provide the driving power for the industries of New England, Quebec and Ontario, and has, in large part, been followed by the youth and energy of the Province. For almost a century, Nova Scotia has been exporting the raw material that lies at the base of all modern industry . . . .

"Briefly", Gray concluded, "Nova Scotia has achieved the status of a mining camp, whereas its full stature should be that of a metropolis of industry".[11] Gray's worries proved well-founded. After the First World War, the local economy experienced a crisis from which it has never recovered. In 1921 the British Empire Steel Corporation assumed control of the coal and steel industries in Nova Scotia. The outcome of a well-established pattern of regional underdevelopment in Atlantic Canada, the rise and fall of the British Empire Steel Corporation marked a decisive turning point in the economic history of industrial Cape Breton.

---

11 Gray, "The Coal Fields of Eastern Canada", pp. 13-14. The same question puzzled historians V. C. Fowke, S. A. Saunders and Harold Innis, who briefly examined the coal industry in the 1920s and 1930s. They observed that Canada's coal industry was located at the ends of the country, while most industry was clustered at the centre. They stressed the difficulties in shipping a cheap, bulky commodity like coal long distances to market and lamented the inadequacy of local markets within the region. By failing to attract other production factors to generate industrial growth in its own geographic locale, the coal industry seemed to follow an anomalous growth strategy. To explain this, Innis and his associates began to point out the dominant role of central Canada in the construction of the national economy. This approach was supplemented by economist David Schwartzman and labour historian C. B. Wade, who drew attention to the manipulative and exploitative financial policies of the coal companies. They found that the ideas of O. D. Skelton's "financial buccanneers" had blossomed handsomely in the coal-fields and concluded that the industry's chronic instability and mismanagement stemmed largely from this source. See V. C. Fowke, "Economic Realities of the Canadian Coal Situation — 1929" (M.A. thesis, University of Saskatchewan, 1929); S. A. Saunders, *The Economic Welfare of the Maritime Provinces* (Wolfville, 1932), pp. 30-46; H. A. Innis, "Editor's Foreword", in E. S. Moore, *American Influence in Canadian Mining* (Toronto, 1941), pp. v-xvii; C. B. Wade, *Robbing the Mines* (Glace Bay, 194-; Wade, "History of District 26, United Mine Workers of America, 1919-1941" (unpublished manuscript, Beaton Institute of Cape Breton Studies, Sydney, 1950); David Schwartzman, "Mergers in the Nova Scotia Coal Fields: A History of the Dominion Coal Company, 1893-1940" (Ph.D. thesis, University of California, Berkeley, 1953).

Before the 1860s the growth of the coal industry in Nova Scotia was re-stricted by imperial policy. In 1826, under a royal charter, the General Mining Association (GMA) of London took exclusive control of the mineral resources of Nova Scotia, but advocates of colonial economic development, including Abraham Gesner and Joseph Howe, helped lead a popular cam-paign against the monopoly. In 1858 the Association's rights were restricted and control of mineral rights was vested in the colony. This successful revolt against colonial underdevelopment opened the way for expansion of the coal industry. Numerous mining companies were formed and a brief boom followed. Under the unusual conditions of the 1854 Reciprocity Treaty and the high demand for coal during the American Civil War, Cape Breton coal entered the long-coveted United States market on a large scale. The boom ended in 1867, however, when Congress restored prohibitive import duties.[12]

The collapse of the export trade led to growing protectionist sentiment in the coal industry. The example of British industrial growth, where the coal resources fueled the industrialization of the Black Country, provoked hopes for a large local market based on "home manufactures".[13] But the dominant protectionist impulse was support for a federal tariff to enable Nova Scotia coal to enter the central Canadian market. The idea was influential among pro-Confederates in the 1860s.[14] A short-lived duty in 1870 demonstrated the effectiveness of a coal tariff, and during the 1870s the Cape Breton coal operators campaigned for "the same just and reasonable protection as has been afforded to other Dominion industries".[15] This agitation was successful in 1879 when the National Policy established a 50c per ton duty on coal imports, which was raised to 60c the next year. Nova Scotia's coal sales in Quebec rose sharply, and the local market also became important, as the Maritimes experienced industrial expansion under the National Policy. Based

12   Abraham Gesner, *The Industrial Resources of Nova Scotia* (Halifax, 1849); Richard Brown, *The Coal-Fields and Coal Trade of the Island of Cape Breton* (London, 1871); C. B. Fer-gusson, ed., *Uniacke's Sketches of Cape Breton* (Halifax, 1958), pp. 117-29; J. S. Martell, "Early Coal Mining in Nova Scotia", *Dalhousie Review,* XXV (1945-1946), pp. 156-72; Saunders, "The Maritime Provinces and the Reciprocity Treaty", *Dalhousie Review,* XIV (1934), pp. 355-71; Phyllis Blakeley, "Samuel Cunard", and David Frank, "Richard Smith", *Dictionary of Canadian Biography,* IX (Toronto, 1976), pp. 172-84, 730-2.

13   C. O. Macdonald, *The Coal and Iron Industries of Nova Scotia* (Halifax, 1909), p. 42; G. A. White, *Halifax and Its Business* (Halifax, 1876), pp. 108-9.

14   B. D. Tennyson, "Economic Nationalism and Confederation: A Case Study in Cape Breton", *Acadiensis,* II (Spring, 1973), pp. 39-53; D. A. Muise, "The Federal Election of 1867 in Nova Scotia: An Economic Interpretation", Nova Scotia Historical Society *Collections,* XXXVI (1967), pp. 327-51.

15   J. R. Lithgow, *A Letter to the House of Commons of Canada on Behalf of the Coal Interests of Canada* (Halifax, 1877), p. 9.

on this twin foundation, the coal industry's long expansionist cycle continued until the First World War.

During this expansionist period the growth of the coal industry demonstrated several aspects of the uneven development between regions which characterized the emergence and consolidation of industrial capitalism in Canada. The growing concentration and centralization of capital in the Canadian economy created a national economic structure based on inter-regional linkages and dependencies. National economic policies encouraged the expansion of the coal industry, but did not promote stability or prosperity for the hinterland resource area. The creation of national markets led to a division of labour between regions, which established the Cape Breton coal industry as a source of industrial energy filling the needs of the central Canadian market. With the growth of strong Canadian financial centres, a corporate consolidation movement unified the coal industry into a few large companies and delivered control of the industry into the hands of powerful financial interests in central Canada.

The division of labour between regions established the coal industry in Nova Scotia as an important — but vulnerable — source of industrial energy in Canada. After the 1870s, imports of British coal into Canada declined sharply. Under the tariff, shipments of Nova Scotia coal to the Quebec market grew from 83,710 tons in 1878 to 795,060 tons in 1896 and 2,381,582 tons in 1914. Simultaneously, imports of American coal into Canada increased heavily, from 331,323 tons in 1878 to 1,451,508 tons in 1896 and 18,145,769 tons in 1913. By the eve of the First World War, Nova Scotia supplied 54 per cent of Canada's coal production — but 57 per cent of the coal consumed in Canada was imported from the United States.[16] Although the tariff promoted expansion of the domestic coal industry, it provided only partial protection. The Ontario market remained beyond the economic reach of the industry, and in Quebec Nova Scotia coal continually faced keen competition. Despite protests from Nova Scotia, the tariff on bituminous coal was reduced to 53c per ton in 1897 and remained at this figure until 1925. As coal prices approximately doubled during this period, the effect of the fixed duty, which had amounted to more than 20 per cent in the 1880s, was seriously diminished.[17] Under a national policy that was never truly national, the coal trade occupied a vulnerable position in the Canadian market.

The coal market in the Maritimes also grew during this period, reaching a

---

16 *Importance of the Canadian Coal Industry* (n.p., n.d., probably 1897), pp. 50-5; Canada, Dominion Bureau of Statistics, *Coal Statistics for Canada, 1927* (Ottawa, 1928), p. 27.

17 *Importance of the Canadian Coal Industry*, p. 21. Tariff changes on coal are summarized in *Royal Commission on Coal, 1946*, pp. 575-7.

peak of more than three million tons in 1913,[18] but the key factor in the coal market was a single customer. In 1913 the steel plant at Sydney consumed 1,362,000 tons of coal, more than half the total coal sales in Nova Scotia.[19] A vital customer for the coal industry, the Nova Scotia steel industry suffered from chronic instability throughout its history; dependence on this market was a source of further vulnerability for the coal industry.[20] In general, the industrial structure of the Maritimes was limited in scope and suffered seriously from its own pattern of underdevelopment and deindustrialization.[21]

The second main trend in the coal industry was the growth of a consolidation movement in the coal-fields. Completion of the railway to central Canada in the 1870s was followed by mergers dominated by Montreal interests in the mainland coal-fields in 1884 (Cumberland Railway and Coal Co.) and 1886 (Acadia Coal Co.). Plagued by the insecurities of seasonal operations, distant markets and inadequate capital, the Cape Breton coal operators also turned to mergers. The formation of the Provincial Workmen's Association prompted a short-lived defensive alliance among the coal operators in the early 1880s, the Cape Breton Colliery Association.[22] The battle for "survival of the fittest" continued, however, and of the 20 mines opened in Cape Breton after 1858, only eight remained in operation in 1892. The coal operators welcomed the formation of the Dominion Coal Company.[23]

The Dominion Coal Company played an important part in integrating the Cape Breton coal industry into the national structure of industrial capitalism in Canada, although ironically, this was not the original aim of the company's promoters. The formation of Dominion Coal in 1893 was sponsored by an alliance between Boston financier Henry M. Whitney, who promised to invest capital and revive the lost coal trade to New England, and a group of Nova Scotia coal operators and politicians anxious to expand the coal industry and

---

18 *Report of the Royal Commission on Coal Mining Industry in Nova Scotia* ⌊*Duncan Report*⌋, Supplement to the *Labour Gazette* (January, 1926), p. 13.

19 E. H. Armstrong, untitled manuscript on the coal industry in Nova Scotia, 1921, E. H. Armstrong Papers, Box 41, Public Archives of Nova Scotia ⌊PANS⌋.

20 Basic accounts of the steel industry include Donald, *The Canadian Iron and Steel Industry;* E. J. McCracken, "The Steel Industry of Nova Scotia" (M.A. thesis, McGill University, 1932); W. D. R. Eldon, "American Influence on the Canadian Iron and Steel Industry" (Ph.D. thesis, Harvard University, 1952).

21 Important studies of this process are Acheson, "Industrialization of the Maritimes", and Nolan Reilly, "The Origins of the Amherst General Strike, 1890-1919" (paper presented to the Canadian Historical Association Annual Meeting, Fredericton, 1977).

22 *Canadian Mining Review* (August, 1894), p. 131.

23 Robert Drummond, "Appendix", in Richard Brown, *The Coal Fields and Coal Trade of the Island of Cape Breton* (reprint, Stellarton, 1899), pp. 123-5.

restore dwindling provincial revenues. An experienced promoter, in 1886 Whitney had created Boston's West End Street Railway Company, the first extensive electrified rail system in the country, and energy for the railway was supplied by his coal-burning New England Gas and Coke Company. Whitney's interest in Cape Breton was designed to secure an inexpensive coal supply and improve the financial position of his other companies. The financial arrangements indicate that the formation of Dominion Coal was a typical episode in an age of corporate carpetbagging.[24] Dominion Coal also received considerable encouragement from the provincial government. The legislature approved a 99-year lease on all the unassigned coal resources of Cape Breton and the company was permitted to purchase any others; in return Dominion Coal guaranteed a minimum annual royalty at a fixed rate of 12½c per ton for the duration of the lease. Premier W. S. Fielding predicted the coal industry would grow tenfold as Whitney accomplished "what nature intended . . . the shipment of large quantities of coal to the United States".[25]

The creation of Dominion Coal marked the integration of the coal industry in Cape Breton into a metropolitan network of financial control. The composition of Dominion's first board of directors revealed an alliance of New England, Nova Scotia and Montreal capitalists under Whitney's presidency.[26] The establishment of the merger also marked the triumph of the strategy of exporting the province's coal resources in large volume. Dominion Coal soon acquired control of all the existing operations in the Sydney coal-field, except the GMA's holdings at Sydney Mines. The unification of the south Cape Breton field under one management rationalized exploitation of the coal resource and the new coal company applied a much-needed infusion of

24 Robert Drummond, *Minerals and Mining, Nova Scotia* (Stellarton, 1918), pp. 192-205; *The National Cyclopedia of American Biography*, X (1900; Ann Arbor, 1967), p. 155; *Who Was Who in America*, I (Chicago, 1943), p. 1340; Schwartzman, "Dominion Coal", pp. 109-21.

25 Nova Scotia, *Debates and Proceedings of the House of Assembly*, 1893, p. 15. Conservative Party critics attacked the generous lease provisions and warned that the future of the coal industry would now depend "upon a thousand and one financial considerations . . . and not upon any consideration for the coal mines or for the people of Nova Scotia". One protectionist critic opposed the export of a single ton of coal: "This commodity is essential to our success as a manufacturing centre. If we jealously guard this commodity, the day may yet dawn when Nova Scotia will become to the Dominion of Canada what Manchester is today to England, Ireland and Scotland". *Debates*, 1893, pp. 41-2, 71-3.

26 *Canadian Mining Review* (August, 1894), pp. 131-3. In addition to Whitney, the board included his brother-in-law H. F. Dimock, a Mr. Winsor representing Kidder, Peabody and Company, the Boston investment house, and F. S. Pearson, a Boston engineer employed by Whitney. The Canadians included two local coal operators, J. S. McLennan, who became treasurer, and David McKeen, resident manager, two Halifax lawyers, W. B. Ross and B. F. Pearson, and three Montreal capitalists, Hugh McLennan, Donald Smith and Sir W. C. Van Horne.

capital and technology. Hopes of capturing the New England market were disappointed,[27] but the trade into the St. Lawrence ports continued to grow rapidly and Dominion Coal established an extensive network of railways, shipping piers, coal carriers and coal yards to serve this market.

Control of the coal industry again changed as the integration of the regional economy into the national economic structure accelerated after the 1890s. In 1901 Whitney sold control of Dominion Coal to James Ross, the prominent Montreal capitalist. Dominion Iron and Steel, another Whitney company launched with great fanfare in 1899, was abandoned to central Canadian interests at the same time. Ross and his backers briefly controlled both the coal and steel companies, but in 1903 separate control was established, with J. H. Plummer of Toronto as president of the steel company.[28] Ross and Plummer were both important figures in Canadian business circles: in 1906 Ross held 15 directorships in addition to Dominion Coal, including seats on the Bank of Montreal and Montreal Rolling Mills boards, and Plummer, formerly assistant general manager of the Bank of Commerce, held seven directorships in addition to Dominion Iron and Steel.[29] The two companies quarrelled continually; Ross attempted to take over the steel company in 1907, but in 1910 Plummer triumphed and merged the two companies into the new Dominion Steel Corporation. The merger also took over the Cumberland Railway and Coal Company, but failed to win control of the Nova Scotia Steel and Coal Company, the New Glasgow industrial complex.[30] With Plummer as president and Sir William C. Van Horne as vice-president, Dominion Steel represented a powerful alliance of Toronto and Montreal interests. Closely linked to the Bank of Montreal and the Bank of Commerce, the Dominion Steel directors as a group held more than 179 company directorships.[31] Thus, by the eve of the First World War the Cape Breton coal industry had become not only an important source of industrial

---

27 Reduced in 1894, the U.S. coal duty was restored near full strength in 1897; except for long-term contracts with Whitney's coke company, shipments to the U.S. remained small. Donald, *The Canadian Iron and Steel Industry,* p. 200.

28 *Canadian Mining Review* (March, 1902), pp. 45-6; *ibid* (December, 1903), pp. 241-2. The rapid transfer from American to Canadian control is often overlooked, as in R. T. Naylor, *The History of Canadian Business* (Toronto, 1975), II, pp. 176-7, 210.

29 W. R. Houston, ed., *Directory of Directors in Canada* (Toronto, 1906).

30 Acheson, "Industrialization of the Maritimes", pp. 25-7, discusses the struggle for Scotia.

31 W. R. Houston, ed., *Directory of Directors in Canada, 1912* (Toronto, 1912). In 1912 the Dominion Steel directors included from Toronto, J. H. Plummer, George Cox, Frederic Nicholls, William Mackenzie, James Mason, Henry Pellatt, and from Montreal, W. C. Van Horne, J. R. Wilson, William McMaster, H. Montagu Allan, George Caverhill, Robert MacKay, W. G. Ross, Raoul Dandurand. David McKeen of Halifax was the lone Maritimer. The board of Dominion Coal was very similar; Toronto: Plummer, Cox, Mason, Pellatt, Mackenzie, W. D. Matthews, E. R. Wood; Montreal: Wilson, Van Horne, Dandurand,

energy for the Canadian economy, but also an attractive field of investment for Canadian businessmen. These two aspects of the Canadianization of the region's economic life would contribute heavily to the crisis of markets and corporate welfare which gripped the coal industry in the 1920s.

The emergence of the British Empire Steel Corporation (Besco), which was incorporated in the spring of 1920, was the result of extended manoeuvres for further consolidation of the coal and steel industries in Nova Scotia. By 1917 American financial interests had gained control of the Nova Scotia Steel and Coal Company (Scotia) and were actively pursuing a merger with the much larger Dominion Steel Corporation. The same idea attracted interest in Britain at the end of the war, and in 1919 a syndicate of British industrialists began to buy control of Dominion Steel. At the same time, a third group also appeared on the scene; based in Canada Steamship Lines and led by two Montreal entrepreneurs, J. W. Norcross and Roy M. Wolvin.

The Nova Scotia Steel and Coal Company boasted a strong reputation for cautious management, technical excellence and financial success. From humble beginnings in the 1870s in New Glasgow, the Scotia companies had pioneered the growth of the Canadian steel industry, smelting the first steel ingots in Canada in 1883. In 1899 Whitney had attempted to include Scotia in his new Dominion Iron and Steel Company. In 1900 Scotia entered Cape Breton by taking over the GMA's holdings at Sydney Mines and building a steel plant there. Despite growing links with Toronto interests, especially through customers like Massey-Harris and financial backers like the Bank of Nova Scotia, the company remained dominated by Nova Scotia financiers and industrialists.[32]

MacKay, McMaster, Lord Strathcona (formerly Donald Smith), F. L. Wanklyn. W. R. Houston, comp., *The Annual Financial Review, Canadian* [*Houston's Review*], XII (1912). An important study of the Canadian financial community in 1910 graphically situates Dominion Steel between financial groupings surrounding the Montreal and Commerce banks. The board of Dominion Coal had four or more directors in common with the following: Bank of Montreal, National Trust, Canadian Pacific Railway, Toronto Railway Company, Electrical Development Company, Canada Life Assurance Company, Gilles Piédalue, "Les groupes financiers au Canada, (1900-1930)", *Revue d'Histoire de l'Amérique Française,* XXX (1976), pp. 28-9.

32 J. M. Cameron, *Industrial History of the New Glasgow District* (New Glasgow, 1960), ch. III; Donald, *The Canadian Iron and Steel Industry,* pp. 194-9, 254-6. The Scotia board included J. W. Allison, Robert Harris, Thomas Cantley, G. S. Campbell, Frank Stanfield, G. F. McKay, J. D. McGregor, J. C. McGregor, all of Nova Scotia; W. D. Ross and Robert Jaffray, Toronto; Lorne Webster and K. W. Blackwell, Montreal; Frank Ross, Quebec City; J. S. Pitts and R. E. Chambers, St. John's, Newfoundland. *Houston's Review,* XII (1912). The Scotia board was closely linked to the Bank of Nova Scotia and the Eastern Trust Company, itself also close to the Royal Bank; Piédalue, "Les groupes financiers", p. 28. From 1902-1909 Lyman Melvin-Jones, president of Massey-Harris, was a director of Scotia; according to Cantley, half of Scotia's sales were to agricultural implement manufacturers; Eldon, "The Canadian Iron and Steel Industry", p. 489.

In 1915 a number of steps signaled the closer integration of Scotia into the metropolitan financial structure. President since 1905, Robert Harris, the prominent Halifax financier, resigned to take a seat on the province's Supreme Court. He was replaced as president by Thomas Cantley, Scotia's longtime general manager. W. D. Ross, a native Cape Bretoner active in Toronto financial circles (and ultimately Lieutenant-Governor of Ontario), became financial vice-president, and N. B. McKelvie of New York joined the Scotia board as a representative of the New York investment house of Hayden, Stone and Company. In 1917 McKelvie's group supplied a large investment of working capital for Scotia and secured control of the company. Cantley was replaced as president by Frank H. Crockard, formerly vice-president of a Tennessee coal and steel company, "one of the bright stars of the United States Steel Corporation's galaxy of subsidiary corporations".[33] The New York investment banker, Galen L. Stone, became chairman of Scotia's finance committee. Speculation in the press suggested the giant U.S. Steel Corporation was behind the influx of American investment, but Scotia denied this rumour.[34] President Crockard explored plans for amalgamation with Dominion Steel, which he regarded as "absolutely essential" to develop local resources "along broad lines as followed in the States in the Iron and Steel industry".[35] Efforts to purchase shares in Dominion Steel met resistance and direct negotiations for a merger also failed in the spring of 1918. Dominion Steel President Mark Workman commented favourably on the idea, but insisted that control must remain in Canadian hands.[36] Soon Scotia recruited the general manager of Dominion Steel to its side. A native Cape Bretoner, D. H. McDougall had worked for the Dominion companies for almost 20 years, rising from mechanic's apprentice to general manager, but in 1919 he accepted an appointment as president of Scotia.[37] A mining engineer, McDougall strongly favoured a merger of the coal operations in the Sydney coal-field, as the haphazard distribution of submarine coal

33 *Financial Post* (Toronto), 30 June 1917; *Monetary Times* (Toronto), 22 February 1918, 22 June 1917. The new directors included D. C. Jackling, New York, and W. Hinckle Smith, Philadelphia, capitalists interested in mining investments and associated with Boston banker Charles Hayden, prominent in Kennecott Copper, Utah Copper and the International Nickel Company. *Who Was Who in America,* I, p. 538; II (Chicago, 1950), p. 498; III (Chicago, 1963), pp. 195, 440-1.

34 *Montreal Herald,* 10 July 1917.

35 F. H. Crockard to N. B. McKelvie, 6 February 1918, Thomas Cantley Papers, Box 175, PANS.

36 *Montreal Gazette,* 5 February 1918; *Canadian Annual Review 1918; Monetary Times,* 22 February 1918.

37 *Canadian Mining Journal* (30 April 1919); *ibid.,* (14 September 1923); *Who's Who and Why, 1921* (Toronto, 1921), p. 885.

leases threatened to cause mine closures and costly duplication of effort by the two rival companies.[38]

The next steps towards merger took place within Dominion Steel. In 1916 a Montreal clothing manufacturer, Mark Workman, had succeeded Plummer as president, but otherwise the controlling group remained stable. In October 1919 new merger rumours circulated; the "inside story", denied by Workman, was that Lord Beaverbrook had accomplished a merger of the Scotia and Dominion companies.[39] Soon it was revealed that a British syndicate had purchased a large quantity of Dominion Steel shares and that a London Advisory Committee had been formed to represent the British interests.[40] The London syndicate included a blue-ribbon committee of industrialists from the British steel and shipbuilding industries: Viscount Marmaduke Furness, chairman of the Furness iron, steel and shipbuilding companies; Benjamin Talbot, managing director of the Furness group; Sir Trevor Dawson, managing director of Vickers Ltd.; Henry Steel, chairman of the United Steel Companies of Great Britain; and Sir William Beardmore (soon Lord Invernairn), chairman of the large Glasgow shipbuilding company.[41] The most active members of the London group were Sir Newton Moore and Lt. Col. W. Grant Morden. Prominent in the Australian mining and steel industries, Moore had been active in Australian politics before removing to London during the war. There he sat in the House of Commons and pursued his business interests, especially in General Electric and various empire mining and steel companies. Chairman of the London group was Lt. Col. Morden, a Toronto-born entrepreneur who first came to prominence as promoter of the Canada Steamship Lines (CSL) merger in 1912, which had been backed by Vickers and Furness. Morden himself had moved to London, engaged in industrial espionage in Germany and Switzerland during the war, chaired a British chemical firm and sat in the House of Commons. And according to a sketch in the *Sydney Record*, Morden was also "above all an accountant to the nth

---

38 Dominion Steel resisted accommodation with Scotia and both the provincial government and the Dominion Fuel Controller were forced to intervene in the dispute. Armstrong Papers, vol. II, Folders 3, 4, 5, PANS.

39 *Sydney Post,* 3 October 1919. Evidence for Max Aitken's involvement is circumstantial. In February 1919 Aitken was meeting with both Cantley and Workman in London, and in June 1919 he was accompanied on his trip to Canada by W. D. Ross. "Daily Memorandum Covering European Visit, 1919", Cantley Papers, Box 167, PANS; *Montreal Star,* 25 June 1919. Grant Morden, the main Besco promoter, admitted in a New York interview that he was an associate of Aitken; *Sydney Post,* 13 February 1920. The rhetoric of the Besco promoters reflected Beaverbrook's vision of imperial economic cooperation.

40 *Monetary Times,* 28 November 1919; *Sydney Post,* 15 December 1919, 10 January 1920.

41 *Houston's Review,* XX (1920), p. 166; *Who Was Who, 1929-40; Who Was Who, 1941-1950; Who's Who, 1920* (London, 1920).

degree, lightning-like in his grasp of detail".[42]

During 1919 a third group also displayed interest in Dominion Steel. Led by J. W. Norcross and Roy Wolvin of Montreal, this group appeared to be working independently of the London syndicate. Norcross had started steamboating on Lake Ontario as a youth and eventually became managing director of Canada Steamship Lines. In a bitter battle early in 1919, Norcross insisted on a distribution of common shares dividends and supplanted CSL president James Carruthers. Vice-President of the Collingwood Shipbuilding Company, Norcross was also a director of the Canadian branch of Vickers. Like Norcross, Wolvin was an aggressive young entrepreneur who came to prominence on the Great Lakes. Born in Michigan in 1880, Wolvin became a leading transportation expert in the shipping trade. As early as 1902, when he was working out of Duluth, Wolvin was known in Halifax as "one of the shrewdest shipping men on the lakes" and praised for his efforts to improve the capacity of the St. Lawrence canal system. Later Wolvin established the Montreal Transportation Company and joined Norcross in CSL and Collingwood Shipbuilding.[43] In the wake of the Halifax Explosion, Wolvin was invited by the Minister of Marine to consider the potential for establishing steel shipbuilding at Halifax, long a fond local hope. The result was the formation of Halifax Shipyards Ltd. in 1918 under the control of Wolvin, Norcross and their associates. Events then proceeded rapidly. Wolvin was impressed by the immense advantages of the Nova Scotia coal and steel industries and hoped to link them to his shipbuilding and shipping concerns. Following a chance shipboard conversation with Mark Workman, Wolvin began to purchase shares in Dominion Steel and entered the board as a director in July 1919. At some point during the year, Wolvin later recalled, he established a "a friendly understanding, you might say", with the London interests. In January 1920 Norcross also entered the board and in March 1920 the London group proved their control of Dominion Steel by installing Wolvin as the new president. A "silent revolution" had taken place in the affairs of Dominion Steel.[44]

Plans for creation of the British Empire Steel Corporation were unveiled in a speech by Morden at a meeting of the Empire Parliamentary Association in Ottawa on 14 April 1920. "If we can combine the capital and experience of

42 *Who Was Who, 1929-1940*, pp. 963, 965; clipping, 1920, in Stuart McCawley Scrapbook, p. 6, Miners' Memorial Museum, Glace Bay; *Sydney Record*, 1 May 1920; *Canadian Mining Journal* (March, 1934). Two ships in the CSL fleet reflected the links with Vickers: the *W. G. Morden* and the *Sir Trevor Dawson*, clipping, Cantley Papers, Box 175, PANS.

43 *Monetary Times*, 14 February 1919; *Sydney Post*, 16 October 1919, 31 March 1920; *Monetary Times*, 26 March 1920; H. J. Crowe to G. B. Hunter, April 1902, H. Crowe Letterbook, PANS.

44 Nova Scotia, Royal Commission on Coal Mines, 1925, "Minutes of Evidence", p. 2061; *Sydney Post*, 22 March 1920; *Monetary Times*, 26 March 1920.

the Old Mother Land with the resources of our Overseas Dominions", he explained, "we are going to put ourselves in an economic position that will forever maintain us as the greatest Empire in the world. I have long felt that the so-called 'silken thread of sentiment' should be reinforced by 'golden chains of commerce', but the difficulty was how to do it".[45] In its earliest form, the proposal was to create a $500 million merger which would join Canadian coal, iron and steel resources to the British steel and shipbuilding industries; the frankly predatory design was to use Canadian resources to revitalize British industry in the face of American competition. The proposal involved nine companies. In addition to the Dominion and Scotia companies, the merger would include three companies controlled by Wolvin's group (CSL, Halifax Shipyards and Collingwood Shipbuilding) and four smaller companies (Canada Foundries and Forgings, Port Arthur Shipbuilding, Davie Shipbuilding and Repairing, and the Maritime Nail Company). The book value of the corporation's assets was set at $486 million, including an estimated valuation of the coal and ore reserves at $200 million. The plan was to issue four types of shares, to a total value of $207 million: 8 per cent cumulative first preference ($25 million), 7 per cent cumulative second preference ($37 million), 7 per cent non-cumulative preference ($68 million) and common shares ($77 million). The first class of shares was reserved to raise new capital on the British financial market and the remainder were to be issued at advantageous rates of exchange for the securities of the merging companies.[46]

The proposal generated immediate controversy, including a three-hour debate in the House of Commons on the subject of "cosmopolitan grafters". "Members are afraid that it is some great stock jobbing scheme", reported the *Monetary Times*. "They will have to be convinced that there is no huge watered stock promotion job." Rather than face a threatened investigation, Besco quickly reincorporated in Nova Scotia, where the province was pleased

---

45 *Saturday Night,* 8 May 1920; *Salient Facts of the Steel Merger* (n.p., 1 June 1920); *Press Opinions of 'Empire Steel'* (n.p., 1 July 1920). The crisis of the British economy in the post-war period led to efforts by prominent industrialists to revitalize the national economy, but they could not always rely on the support of the London financial community. For short summaries, see Sidney Pollard, *The Development of the British Economy, 1914-1950* (London, 1962), and John Foster "British Imperialism and the Labour Aristocracy", in Jeffrey Skelley, ed., *The General Strike, 1926* (London, 1976), pp. 3-16. According to Wolvin, the two financiers in the original Besco promotion, Morden and an Austrian banker named Szarvassy, also tried to recruit American support; Duncan Commission, "Minutes of Evidence", p. 2063.

46 *Monetary Times,* 7 May 1920.

to receive a $75,000 fee and granted a charter specifying wide powers.[47] The proposed basis of share exchanges aroused criticism from directors of the Dominion and Scotia companies, who questioned the inclusion of the lesser companies, on which they lacked adequate financial information and on which the promoters of the merger stood to gain substantially through the merger. In response, the organizers made several revisions, dropping Halifax Shipyards and allowing better terms for the Scotia shareholders. But by the time of Dominion Steel's annual meeting in June 1920, a small group of veteran directors were in open revolt against the merger. In addition to Workman and Plummer, the dissident group included E. R. Wood and Sir William Mackenzie of Toronto and George Caverhill, William McMaster and Senator Raoul Dandurand of Montreal. A stormy session followed, as Wood, a Bank of Commerce director, pinpointed irregularities in the Besco balance sheet and protested the dilution of the steel company shares by the inclusion of the weaker companies.[48] Relying on the backing of the British group and his own holdings, Wolvin was able to control the outcome of the meeting.[49] The old board was defeated and only five members were retained on the new board: Wolvin, Norcross, Senator Frederic Nicholls and Sir Henry Pellatt (both vigorous defenders of the merger), and the aging Sir William Mackenzie. New members of the Dominion Steel board included Stanley Elkin, manager of the Saint John Maritime Nail Company, Senators Sir Clifford Sifton and C. P. Beaubien, and three of Wolvin's associates from the CSL, Halifax Shipyards, Collingwood and Davie Shipbuilding group. Three representatives of the London group also entered the board at this time: Moore, Talbot and Furness. In July D. H. McDougall of Scotia and Senator W. L. McDougald of Montreal, both directors of companies involved in the merger, were also added to the board.[50]

Ratified by the three principal companies, the merger was never com-

---

47 Canada, House of Commons, *Debates,* 1920, pp. 1945-67; *Monetary Times,* 7, 28 May 1920. Letters patent authorizing a capitalization of $100,000 were obtained from the federal government on 15 March 1920; the increase to $500 million was obtained in Nova Scotia on 22 May 1920; *Besco Bulletin,* 11 April 1925.

48 *Monetary Times,* 18 June 1920; *Sydney Post,* 15, 16, 18 June 1920.

49 By this time the London group held about 180,000 shares in Dominion Steel; Wolvin held 50,000 himself and as President controlled another 50,000. The dissident directors polled only 3,000 shares against the merger, which received 298,000 votes. Newton Moore to W. L. Mackenzie King, 1 September 1923, W. L. Mackenzie King Papers, Public Archives of Canada [PAC]; *Sydney Post,* 23 June, 16 July 1920.

50 *Monetary Times,* 25 June, 2 July 1920; *Sydney Post,* 23 June, 19 July 1920. The changing composition of the board may be followed in Table I.

pleted.[51] First, an uproar took place over the arrangements with CSL. Cantley suddenly learned that instead of bringing the shipping firm in as one of the merging companies, Wolvin now planned to sign a 25-year lease guaranteeing a fixed return of 7 per cent to CSL shareholders. In effect, this would make dividends to Steamship shareholders a fixed charge on the earnings of Besco, to be paid ahead of returns to other Besco shareholders. Enraged, Cantley protested that Scotia was being "jockeyed out of its property and its resources and earnings" and denounced the lease as a violation of the merger terms; Galen Stone in New York agreed the news was "a tremendous shock" and suggested the merger might be voided as a result.[52] Furthermore, the new corporation encountered great difficulty in raising capital; completion of the merger remained conditional on the issue of the $25 million first preference shares, shown on the balance sheet as available working capital. The London financial market was not receptive. Besco had earned a poor reputation on the London "street". Initially enthusiastic, the *Financial Times* grew exasperated at the repeated revisions in the plans and in July 1920 denounced Besco's "Merger Mysteries". The lack of adequate information on the merging companies revealed that "so far as British investors are concerned, they have been very cavalierly treated" and the editors warned investors to be cautious:

> The efforts of the promoters of the deal seemed to have been concentrated to rush the matter through as quickly and with as little discussion as possible . . . . We do not like this way of doing business, and those interested in Canadian enterprise and anxious to secure the good opinion of the public on this side cannot learn the fact too quickly.[53]

Moreover, the collapse of the postwar speculative boom during the spring

---

50 *Monetary Times,* 25 June, 2 July 1920; *Sydney Post,* 23 June, 19 July 1029. The changing composition of the board may be followed in Table I.

51 W. D. Ross and D. H. McDougall encountered little resistance in gaining approval for the merger from Scotia shareholders. In New Glasgow their argument was that "the merger is going through with or without us", that the smaller company could not withstand the competition and that Scotia needed the capital which would be available through the merger; "Special Meeting, Scotia Shareholders, YMCA Building, New Glasgow, 25 June 1920", Cantley Papers, Box 175, PANS. The controlling interest in Scotia was held by the American investors, but the character of U.S. interest in Scotia had changed by 1920; during the interwar period the American steel industry favoured a policy of retrenchment and did not engage in expansionist policies abroad; Mira Wilkins, *The Maturing of Multinational Enterprise: American Business Abroad from 1914 to 1970* (Cambridge, 1974), pp. 151,153.

52 Cantley to Stone, 21, 26 July 1920; Stone to Cantley, 26 July 1920; Cantley Papers, Box 175, PANS. Also, before entering the merger, CSL shareholders purchased Wolvin's Montreal Transportation Company; *Monetary Times,* 2, 30 July 1920.

53 *Sydney Post,* 28 July 1920; *Financial Times* (London), 23, 24, 29 July 1920, 4 May 1920.

and summer of 1920 caused a contraction of British capital markets and, under an adverse exchange situation, Canadian borrowing in London became more difficult. Wolvin later estimated that the Besco merger "missed the boat" by about two weeks.[54]

A less frenzied pace characterized the reconstruction of Besco in 1921. Wolvin persisted in his plans for the merger by secretly buying Scotia shares on the open market and had gained about ten per cent of the stock before his activity became known. The London shareholders, heavily committed to Dominion Steel, also continued to favour the merger. The London Committee arranged a meeting in London in January 1921, where Wolvin reached an agreement with D. H. McDougall of Scotia.[55] A new merger plan was prepared, under which Scotia enjoyed improved terms and Wolvin was forced to exclude CSL, although Halifax Shipyards was admitted. The terms were approved by the shareholders of all three companies and the merger went into effect smoothly on 15 April 1921. Variously described as a "British" or "Montreal" company, it was difficult to identify Besco with any one geographic locale. The head office was in the Canada Cement Building in Montreal, but in 1922 the board's directors were distributed by residence among six locations: Toronto 4, Montreal 5, Britain 5, Nova Scotia 1, Boston 1, Quebec City 1. The directors fell into several interest groups. The first board was dominated by Wolvin and his partners Norcross and H. B. Smith. Three directors represented the Scotia company: President McDougall, W. D. Ross of Toronto and Galen Stone of New York and Boston. With expansion of the board the following year, there were several changes. Quarrelling with Wolvin over CSL and Halifax Shipyards, Norcross left Besco; Wolvin added J. F. M. Stewart, Frank Ross and Senator McDougald, all associates from shipping firms and coal agencies in Quebec and Ontario. Bank of Nova Scotia director Hector McInnes of Halifax joined fellow director W. D. Ross on the Besco board. And Sir Newton Moore led a group of five members of the London Committee onto the directorate. The changing structure of the Besco board in the 1920s is shown in Table I.

Restricted to three companies, two of them well-known, the creation of the new holding company seemed less open to charges of stockwatering, although the inclusion of Halifax Shipyards reminded one critic of the "family compact element in the original merger that repelled the average investor".[56] The basis of share exchanges in the creation of Besco is shown in Table II. The

---

54 *Monetary Times,* 9 January, 2 July, 1 October 1920, 7 January 1921; Duncan Commission, "Minutes of Evidence", p. 2070.

55 Duncan Commission, "Minutes of Evidence", p. 2062.

56 Clipping, 25 February 1921, Armstrong Papers, Box 674, PANS.

Table I

Directors, British Empire Steel Corporation, 1921 - 1929

	Residence	1921	22	23	24	25	26	27	28	29	30 (Dominion Steel and Coal Corporation)
R M Wolvin	M	P	P	P	P	P	P	P	—	—	
D H McDougall	M	V	V	V	—	—	—	—	—	—	
W Mackenzie	T	X	—	—	—	—	—	—	—	—	
J W Norcross	M	X	—	—	—	—	—	—	—	—	
W D Ross	T	X	X	X	X	X	X	X	—	—	
H B Smith	T	X	X	X	—	—	—	—	—	—	
G L Stone	B	X	X	X	X	—	—	—	—	—	
H M Pellatt	T	X	—	—	—	—	—	—	—	—	
C S Cameron	M							V,S	V,S	V,S	V,S
C P Beaubien	M		X	X	X	X	X	X	X	X	X
Vt Furness	L		X	X	X	—	—	—	—	—	
T Dawson	L		X	X	X	X	X	—	—	—	
N Moore	L		X	X	X	X	X	X	X	X	V
H McInnes	H		X	X	X	X	X	—	—	—	
J F M Stewart	T		X	X	X	—	—	—	—	—	
B Talbot	L		X	X	X	—	—	—	—	—	
Invernairn	G		X	X	X	X	X	X	X	X	X
W L McDougald	M		X	X	—	—	—	—	—	—	
F Ross	Q		X	X	X	X	X	X	X	X	
G S Campbell	H		X	—	—	—	—	—	—	—	
J P B Casgrain	M		X	X	X	X	X	X	X	X	X
J E McLurg	S				V	V	V	V	V	V	
G F Downs	NY				X	X	X	X	X	X	V
R F Hoyt	NY				X	X	X	X	X	X	
L C Webster	M					X	X	X	X	X	X
C B McNaught	T							P	P		P
C J Burchell	M							X	X		X
G H Duggan	M							X	X		X
J H Gundy	T							X	X		X
H S Holt	M							X	X		X
G Montgomery	M							X	X		X
W E Wilder	T							X	X		—
H J Kelley	S										V,G
C B Gordon	M										X
J Kilpatrick	T										X

Key:
B	Boston	P	President
G	Glasgow	V	Vice-President
H	Halifax	X	Director
L	London	S	Secretary and Treasurer
M	Montreal	G	General Manager
NY	New York		
Q	Quebec City		
S	Sydney		
T	Toronto		

Source: *Houston's Canadian Annual Financial Review,* XX - XXXI (1920 - 1931).

Table II

Formation of the British Empire Steel Corporation, 1921

($ = millions)

	Stock issued by merging companies		Stock issued by British Empire Steel Corporation				
	cum pf	cmmn	1st pf A 8% cum	1st pf B 7% cum	2nd pf 7% cum	pf 7% noncum	cmmn
Dominion Steel	6% $7.0	6% $43.0		$7.0	$40.85		$17.2
Dominion Coal	7% $3.0			$3.0			
Dominion Iron and Steel	7% $5.0			$5.0			
Nova Scotia Steel and Coal	8% $1.0	5% $15.0		$1.2	$13.5		$ 6.0
Eastern Car	6% $ .75			$ .75			
Halifax Shipyards	7% $3.0	$ 5.0		$3.0	$3.0		$ 1.25
Sub-totals	$19.75	$63.0	—	$19.95	$57.35	—	$24.45
Total stock Issued	$82.75		$101.75				

Key:	cum	cumulative	Sources:	*Houston's Review,* XXI, XXII
	pf	preference		(1921, 1922); *Duncan Report,*
	noncum	non-cumulative		pp. 25 - 8.
	cmmn	common		

share capitalization of the merging companies amounted to $82.75 million; in the merger this was transformed into $101.75 million, an increase of $19 million in stock value. The capital structure of the various merging companies included previous accumulations of "water" amounting to $38.5 million and the distribution of shares among the various classes of stock also allowed a considerable inflation of stock values. All the cumulative stock of the merging companies was exchanged, mainly on a share for share basis (except where 6 per cent stock became 7 per cent) for Series B first preference cumulative stock. On the other hand, the common stock of the merging companies, which amounted to $63.0 million, mainly at 6 per cent, was translated into a small number of common shares and a large block of second preference shares paying 7 per cent. The creation of this new class of stock was probably the most flagrant aspect of the merger and prompted Eugene Forsey to comment, in 1926: "Bless thee, Bottom, thou art translated".[57] The capital structure of the corporation also allowed the issue of two further categories of stock: 7 per cent non-cumulative preference shares, which would be paid ahead of common stock dividends, and Series A first preference 8 per cent cumulative shares, which would have first priority on the corporation's earnings. The plan was to issue $24.45 million of the Series A stock as soon as possible in order to raise new capital for the merger's operations.

While the Besco merger was before the House of Assembly in 1921, acting Nova Scotia Premier E. H. Armstrong requested an independent opinion of the merger arrangements from Ontario Liberal Party leader Newton W. Rowell. Rowell alerted Armstrong to the dangers the capitalization of the company created. The high authorized capitalization of $500 million might lead to the acquisition of new companies, possibly above their fair value. The lack of working capital in the consolidation might require the issue of further stock, possibly below par value. As the terms of such arrangements could not be foreseen, there was a danger of new water entering the merger at a later date, and Rowell suggested that the province require Besco to seek approval of any stock issues or exchanges. As for the exchanges already outlined, a considerable danger existed: "without any addition to the tangible assets of any of these companies and without providing any additional capital for their operation or development", the share exchanges created a large volume of new stock:

> This change in the character of the securities and this increase in the capital stock issued will undoubtedly involve sooner or later a serious Demand from Directors and Shareholders for a substantial increase in the earnings of the coal companies in order to pay dividends on these huge blocks of stock. These dividends can only come from increased efficiency in operation or an increase in price of coal over what would be necessary to pay a reasonable dividend on the old capitalization.[58]

Despite this warning, Armstrong loyally backed the merger, speaking out strongly against "any action that would intimidate capital from embarking in Nova Scotia enterprises at such a critical time as the present".[59]

The British Empire Steel Corporation commenced operations in the unstable economic conditions of the early 1920s. Hopes for an enhanced level of profits were soon defeated, as were visions of new markets for the output

57   Eugene Forsey, *Economic and Social Aspects of the Nova Scotia Coal Industry* (Montreal, 1926), p. 40.

58   N. W. Rowell to E. H. Armstrong, 9, 12 May 1921, Armstrong Papers, Box 663, PANS.

59   *Sydney Post,* 28 May 1921.

of the Nova Scotia coal and steel industries. Throughout its short history, the British Empire Steel Corporation remained in financial crisis. The corporation's financial structure required minimum earnings of about $3 million a year to meet fixed charges. Dividends on the first preference stock required an additional $1.3 million. To make payments on the cumulative second preference stock would require about $4 million annually. Thus Besco required an annual operating profit of more than $8 million in order to meet financial commitments. Additional profits would be needed to build a reserve against less profitable years, to establish a surplus for capital expansion, or to pay dividends on the common stock. As Table III shows, Besco never met these expectations. No dividends were ever paid on the common or second preference shares. About $3.6 million was distributed in first preference dividends, until payments were suspended in early 1924. In 1924 and 1925 profits were too meagre to meet fixed charges and the corporation turned to bank loans and prior surpluses to meet these payments. By the end of 1925 Besco had accumulated a deficit of $5.7 million. Burdened with the unrealistic expectations embodied in Besco's corporate structure, Wolvin and his directors pursued an increasingly desperate strategy of corporate survival during the 1920s. As the industry's traditional markets were thrown into crisis during this period, Wolvin and his directors pursued two central goals: to reduce the cost of labour power in the coal industry and to recruit state support for the coal and steel industries in the national market.

Table III

Financial Statements, British Empire Steel
Corporation, 1921 - 1926

($ = millions)

	1921	1922	1923	1924	1925	1926
Operating profit	4.416	6.917*	4.444	.924	-1.133	4.424
Sinking funds and depreciation	1.501	3.628	1.113	1.113	1.342	1.462
Bond and debenture interest	1.182	1.677	1.978	2.024	1.936	1.824
Net profit	1.734	1.613	1.354	-2.213	-4.411	1.138
Dividends	.978	1.344	1.347	.145	—	—
Net surplus	.756	.268	.007	-2.358	-4.411	1.138
Balance	.756	1.024	1.031	-1.327	-5.738	-4.600

* including $4 million settlement from the federal government

Sources: *Houston's Review*, XX-XXX (1920 - 1930); *Monetary Times*, 1920 - 1928.

Firmly convinced his corporation possessed "the greatest known deposits of coal and iron ore, splendidly situated", Wolvin hoped to implement a programme of capital expansion and enlarge the scope and capacity of the steel industry at Sydney.[60] Under Besco in 1922 the Sydney steel plant for the first time in its history made a brief entry into foreign markets for finished steel.[61] Symbolic of the steel industry's aspirations for diversified production was the opening of Canada's first ship plate mill in February 1920; producing steel plate for shipbuilding, the mill represented a key addition to the industrial structure of the Maritimes. The federal government encouraged establishment of the mill during the war by contracting advance orders and in 1920 the new mill had some success in selling plate to British yards. But in 1920 the federal government cancelled its orders and a long dispute ultimately yielded Besco a $4 million settlement. The plate mill closed and was forgotten for 20 years.[62] Another desultory symbol of Besco's expansionist hopes was an unfulfilled agreement to construct a steel plant in Newfoundland by 1926.[63] Demand for the output of the Nova Scotia steel industry fell sharply after 1919. During the 1920s the steel industry at Sydney eked out a hand-to-mouth existence as it lobbied for orders to keep the plant open for months at a time. The smaller Scotia plant at Sydney Mines, though equipped with a new blast furnace at the end of the war, was closed in November 1920 and never reopened. Pig iron production at Sydney dropped from a near-capacity output of 421,560 tons in 1917 to 296,869 tons in 1920 and 120,769 tons in 1922; production then rose slowly but did not exceed 250,000 tons again until 1928. In 1922 the export to the Ruhr of more than 720,000 tons of iron ore, about three-quarters the annual production of the Bell Island mines, signified clearly the failure of Besco's hopes for expansion of the local steel industry.[64]

The coal industry also suffered seriously at the end of the war. The sharp drop in steel production curtailed the coal industry's largest single market; by the end of 1920 the Sydney steel plant's consumption of coal had fallen from more than 100,000 tons per month to 40,000 tons.[65] The war itself had also

60 *Monetary Times,* 2 July 1920.

61 *Ibid.,* 14 July 1922.

62 McCracken, "Steel Industry", pp. 154 - 66; *Monetary Times,* 17 September, 26 November 1920.

63 *Monetary Times,* 9 June 1922.

64 *Monetary Times,* 13, 27 May 1921; McCracken, "Steel Industry", Appendix; *Houston's Review,* p. 180. Overexpansion, competitive disadvantages and deteriorating tariff protection caused a general problem of excess capacity in the Canadian steel industry during the 1920s; the hinterland steel plants at Sydney and Sault Ste Marie, specializing in basic steel and rails and located at a distance from the industrial heartland, suffered the greatest contraction; Eldon, "The Canadian Iron and Steel Industry", p. 132.

65 Armstrong, untitled manuscript, 1921, PANS.

disrupted the traditional pattern of markets for coal. The loss of the coal fleet to war service closed the St. Lawrence market, though this loss was compensated during the war by the vigorous local demand and the wartime shipping trade. When the war ended, readjustment was necessary. The return of coal vessels was slow and the Quebec market could not be entered aggressively until the 1921 season. Always costly, the alternative of rail shipments was uneconomic and the capacity of this route was limited by the Canso Strait. Also, high prices in the postwar bunker trade and potential export markets in France, Belgium and Britain tempted the coal operators more than the resumption of sharp competition in Quebec.[66] Recapturing Nova Scotia's share of the Quebec market took place slowly and with difficulty. The most formidable obstacle was the entrenched position of American coal suppliers, who shipped more than 3.5 million tons of coal to Quebec in 1920. Overexpansion of the U.S. coal industry during the war had led to the entry of large quantities of cheap coal into the Canadian market and the Nova Scotia coal industry did not regain its former share of this market until 1927.[67] In the Sydney coal-field, where production had reached a peak of 6.3 million tons in 1913, output fell to 4.5 million tons in 1920. The number of man-days worked in the coal industry plunged by one-third, from a peak of 4.5 million man-days in 1917 to 3.0 million in 1921; for the next two decades the level of activity never exceeded 3.3 million man-days per year and the industry was marked by irregular employment and a declining work force.[68]

Wage reductions in the coal industry promised substantial savings for Besco. The coal industry remained surprisingly labour-intensive and the potential for generating surpluses from the coal operations without new capital investment or a large amount of working capital, was attractive. Furthermore, since Whitney's time the coal operations had supplied hidden subsidies to allied companies, through below-cost contracts for coal (which the New England Gas and Coke Company and the Sydney steel plant enjoyed) or through the transfer of credits and surpluses within mergers (which took place within Dominion Steel after 1910).[69] Wolvin made no secret of the

66 *Sydney Post,* 28 November 1919, 26 February, 27 March 1920.

67 The Quebec market normally obtained two-thirds of its coal supply from Nova Scotia, but in 1920 Canadian coal accounted for only 250,880 tons; by 1923 Canadian coal accounted for 1,540,284 tons and U.S. coal 2,922,991; by 1927 the more normal proportions were reestablished: Canada 2,307,185, U.S. 1,572,692 tons. As late as the 1940s, central Canada continued to derive half its energy needs from coal. See Canada, DBS, *Coal Statistics for Canada,* 1922, pp. 23 - 4; *ibid.,* 1927, pp. 22 - 7; J. H. Dales, "Fuel, Power and Industrial Development in Central Canada", *American Economic Review,* XLIII (1953), pp. 182-3.

68 Nova Scotia, *Journals of the House of Assembly,* 1940, App. 9, p. 148.

69 Donald, *The Canadian Iron and Steel Industry,* p. 257; Schwartzman, "Dominion Coal", pp. 113, 125 - 37.

fact that he regarded all assets within the merger as common ones and the transfer of earnings or materials from one to the other was the equivalent of changing money from one pocket to the other.[70] The Duncan Commission criticized this policy in 1926 and revealed that Dominion Coal had remained a profitable operation during most years in the early 1920s, in spite of Besco's claims that losses had required wage reductions.[71] David Schwartzman has reconstructed a series of estimates to show the financial position of Dominion Coal during the period when Besco did not issue separate reports for its constituents. When set beside the corporation's financial record, these figures reveal that in the merger's first years the coal operations contributed profits to the merger; by 1923, however, Besco could no longer lean on the coal operations to sustain the corporation.[72]

The coal miners' resistance to Besco's campaign of wage reductions made it impossible for Besco to implement this strategy of survival. In 1920 Wolvin reluctantly signed an agreement for substantial increases for the coal miners. When this contract ended, Besco began its campaign to reduce wages. In 1922 the corporation sought a reduction of about one-third, but after a dramatic struggle was able to win only half this amount. In 1924 and 1925 Besco sought 20 per cent reductions; in 1924 the coal miners won a small increase and in 1925, after a long and bitter strike, a royal commission allowed the corporation a ten per cent reduction. The outstanding feature of industrial relations in the coal-fields in the 1920s was the tenacity of the coal miners' resistance to wage reductions. Besco's notorious labour policies did little to endear the corporation to public opinion and the coal miners' determined resistance placed an insuperable obstacle in the path of Besco's survival.[73]

To improve the competitive position of the coal and steel industries in the national market had long been a goal of the coal industry in Cape Breton.

70 Canada, Special Committee of the House of Commons on the Future Fuel Supply of Canada, *Official Report of Evidence* (Ottawa, 1921), p. 137.

71 *Duncan Report*, p. 15. The financial data convinced the commissioners that no reduction of miners' wages was justified in 1922, that a reduction in 1923 would have been suitable, that the 1924 increase was not unjustified and that a ten per cent reduction was appropriate in 1925.

72 Schwartzman, "Dominion Coal", p. 182, estimates that for the year ending March 1921 Dominion Coal's profits were $4.2 million gross ($2.9 net), for December 1921 $3.4 million gross ($2.4 net), for December 1922 $2.6 million gross ($1.3 net), for December 1923 $1.4 million gross ($.1 net), for December 1924 $.7 million gross ($-.6 net).

73 Don Macgillivray, "Industrial Unrest in Cape Breton, 1919 - 1925" (M.A. thesis, University of New Brunswick, 1971); David Frank, "Coal Masters and Coal Miners: The 1922 Strike and the Roots of Class Conflict in the Cape Breton Coal Industry" (M.A. thesis, Dalhousie University, 1974); David Frank, "Class Conflict in the Coal Industry: Cape Breton 1922" in G. S. Kealey and P. Warrian, eds., *Essays in Canadian Working Class History* (Toronto, 1976), pp. 161 - 84, 226 - 31.

The coal duty never provided effective protection for a national market in coal. Wartime shortages alerted central Canadian consumers to the vulnerability of their fuel supply, as did postwar disruptions in the coal trade. Sentiment for an all-Canadian coal market rose high during the early 1920s, but had little impact on public policy.[74] After a thorough review of proposals for more protection for coal, the *Monetary Times* concluded that higher duties would "restrict the operation of Ontario and Quebec industries and increase general living and production costs throughout these provinces."[75] In Nova Scotia improved protection for coal was a major theme of the Maritime Rights movement, a coalition which harnessed various regional grievances to the political ambitions of the Nova Scotia Conservative Party. The main demand was for an increase of the 14c per ton duty on slack coal to the general level of 53c and for a programme of subsidies to help Nova Scotia coal penetrate deeper into the central Canadian market.[76]

The relationship of Besco to this agitation was a complex one. In 1924 and 1925 the corporation did not participate in the large Maritime Rights delegations which visited Ottawa. In February 1925, however, Besco commenced publication of the *Besco Bulletin,* which campaigned for a "Bluenose tariff" to protect local industry. Besco's campaign grew most active in 1926, when the federal government appointed a tariff board to consider changes in protection for iron and steel. Wolvin in 1926 appealed for a 75c duty on coal and blamed the deteriorating protection for primary iron and steel over the previous two decades as the chief difficulty facing his corporation.[77] Yet Besco's

74 *Monetary Times,* 3 January 1919, 15 September 1922. "Canada can only be politically independent so far as she controls and supplies her own bituminous coal", warned F. W. Gray; by his estimate Nova Scotia was producing two million tons less than capacity during the 1920s and with adequate capital investment could supply 10 million tons of coal per year. F. W. Gray, "Canada's Coal Supply", Canadian Institute of Mining and Metallurgy and the Mining Society of Nova Scotia, *Transactions,* XXIII (1920), pp. 300 - 1, 304; Gray, "Canada's Coal Problem", *ibid.,* XXV (1922), pp. 293 - 300.

75 *Monetary Times,* 6 March 1925. To economic historian J. H. Dales, the coal tariff "appears to be nothing but a mischievous hidden tax on Canadian manufacturing" whose effect was to "retard the industrial development" of central Canada; Dales, "Fuel, Power and Industrial Development in Central Canada", p. 183.

76 Forbes, "The Maritime Rights Movement", pp. 147 - 9, 222 - 7, 280 - 2; Associated Boards of Trade of the Island of Cape Breton, *Memorandum with Regard to the Conditions Presently Existing in the Coal and Steel Industries of the Province of Nova Scotia* (n.p., 1925). Slack coal provided 1/5 of imported coal in 1920, but almost 2/5 in 1923. The lobby also sought abolition of the 99 per cent rebate on the coal duty allowed since 1907 to consumers using coal for steelmaking. Cantley favoured a duty of $1.50 per ton; *Monetary Times,* 10 February 1928.

77 *Besco Bulletin,* 6 June 1925; *Houston's Review,* 1926, pp. 165 - 6; Canada, House of Commons Special Committee Investigating the Coal Resources of Canada, *Minutes of Proceedings and Evidence* (Ottawa, 1926), pp. 105 - 23.

enlistment in the ranks of Maritime Rights did not present a credible appearance. "At once the giant and the ogre of the Maritimes", Besco earned frequent attacks from local politicians and small businessmen who regarded the corporation as an embodiment of the outside exploitation which had destroyed the region's economy.[78] When Arthur Meighen came out "flat-footed for protection" for the coal industry in February 1925, he provoked dismay among party leaders in Nova Scotia. Gordon Harrington, the Glace Bay lawyer and future premier, warned Meighen that it would be unwise to become associated with protection for Besco, "until some very severe restrictions are placed upon it in the handling of the monopoly it has obtained of the industries based on the natural resources of our country. The absurdity of this corporation asking for tariff concessions on the one hand, and the reduction in already too meagre wage scales on the other hand, must be apparent. Further, the corporation appears to be financially hopelessly unsound and its direction is beyond comment".[79]

The campaign for state intervention in the coal industry did meet some success by the end of the 1920s. In 1924-25 a limited system of rail subventions was tested, but abandoned. The intense lobbying in the winter of that year, the bleakest and most desperate months in the coal-fields in the 1920s, caused the Liberal government that spring to standardize the duty on all bituminous coal at 50c per ton. While the Duncan Report failed to endorse tariff changes or subsidies, it called for wider use of Canadian coke in central Canada. The report concluded with an eloquent personal appeal by commissioner Hume Cronyn, a native Maritimer and Ontario businessman, who called on residents of Ontario and Quebec to make sacrifices to help this important Maritime industry. In the comfort of a steamship en route to Nassau that winter, Cronyn also penned a second addendum to the report in a private letter to Sir Robert L. Borden:

> There are two main difficulties in Nova Scotia which could not be set forth openly in a public document. In the first place the industry is economically unsound and must remain so until the cheaper Virginian and Kentucky coals cease being dumped on our market. Next (quite confidentially) the company (Besco) is in the wrong hands. If it could be re-organized under a new President and staff and could obtain some relief by way of duties or bounties there would be hope for the future. Otherwise I can see nothing ahead but liquidation with all its attendant distress and loss.[80]

78   *Monetary Times,* 25 March 1927; *Halifax Herald,* 14 March 1924.

79   G. S. Harrington to Arthur Meighen, 16 March 1925, Arthur Meighen Papers, PAC.

80   Duncan Report, pp. 30 - 1; Hume Cronyn to R. L. Borden, 14 February 1926, Robert L. Borden Papers, PAC.

As a result of the tariff board hearings, protection for iron and steel was raised substantially in 1930 and 1931, and the coal duty was increased to 75c in 1931. Railway subventions were renewed in 1928 and soon became a large factor in the transportation of coal to central Canada.[81] But these important changes came too late to help Besco, and too late to rescue industrial Cape Breton from a condition of economic dependency and decline.

At stake in Besco's strategy of corporate survival was the corporation's inability to raise new capital or to return a satisfactory profit. As Besco's fortunes deteriorated, internal tensions grew. To one observer, Besco in the 1920s was "a vicious circle of ancient rivalries and new antagonisms".[82] The battle on the board of Dominion Steel in the summer of 1920 was followed by new manoeuvres two years later, at Besco's first annual meeting. The most powerful financial figure in Canada, Royal Bank President Sir Herbert Holt, was reportedly ready to assume the presidency of Besco and provide the financial backing the corporation needed. Besco stock values rose with this speculation, but the London group continued to support Wolvin and retained control of the corporation for him.[83] In November 1922 Wolvin raised new capital by issuing Dominion Iron and Steel mortgage bonds worth $4.6 million, which were financed by director Galen Stone's investment house.[84] At the next annual meeting, in an effort to make the corporation more attractive to investors, Wolvin reduced the corporation's authorized capital by half to $250,000.[85] The intense labour conflict of the summer of 1923 created more anxieties for the corporation. The popular vice-president and general manager, D. H. McDougall, resigned and was replaced by E. H. McLurg, general manager of Halifax Shipyards.[86] The most influential of the directors, Moore and Stone, remained active behind the scenes attempting to raise capital. In September 1923 Moore pleaded with Prime Minister Mackenzie King not to obstruct their efforts by appointing a royal commission to investigate the summer's labour strife. Moore sounded a plaintive note:

A good many of us have put the savings of years into this Canadian enterprise and have been bitterly disappointed that the Company has not been

81 Eldon, "The Canadian Iron and Steel Industry", p. 366; F. W. Gray, "The History of Transportation Subventions on Nova Scotia Coal" (unpublished manuscript, Miners' Memorial Museum, Glace Bay, 1944); O. J. McDiarmid, *Commercial Policy in the Canadian Economy* (Cambridge, 1946), p. 276.

82 *Canadian Mining Journal* (26 August 1927).

83 *New York Times*, 21, 27 June 1922; *Financial Post*, 30 June 1922; *Financial Post Survey*, 1927, pp. 233, 235.

84 *Monetary Times*, 8 December 1922.

85 *Monetary Times*, 30 March 1923.

86 *Houston's Review*, 1924, p. 175.

able to return some interest on the capital invested . . . the present market value of our shares represents only 1/4 of the amounts of the purchase money.[87]

The turning point in the rise and fall of Besco was evident in the record of financial success. Operating profits fell sharply from $4.4 million in 1923 to $.9 million in 1924, when the corporation lost $2.3 million. In March 1924 the directors suspended dividend payments on all stock. Though additional capital was secured through the issue of Dominion Coal bonds, the year ended with a net loss of $1.3 million.[88] Besco's dividend policy awakened shareholder dissatisfaction. Wolvin received a "great many" letters criticizing the non-payment of dividends on the second preference stock and with the suspension of all payments, complaints multiplied.[89] The condition of Besco grew worse in the winter of 1924-1925, and the hardship and suffering of the local community starkly dramatized the plight of the coal industry. After the annual meeting in March 1925, a dejected Besco shareholder and director, *Montreal Herald* publisher Senator J. P. B. Casgrain, poured his heart out to Mackenzie King:

> I am a director of the British Empire Steel Corporation, and an unfortunate shareholder for a very large amount. I have never had one cent of dividend on that merger-stock. However, that is my own affair . . . . I do not plead for myself — although since the merger I have very foolishly invested, in money, in that enterprise $123,000. My wife, 25 years ago, after a visit to Sydney with Sir Laurier, Lady Laurier and myself, invested of her money $40,000. I know all this has nothing to do with the question of bounties and duties and it is not for that that I write. Forget about us but think of the 22,500 men who will be out of work when we close up. With their families, there will be over 100,000 who will probably have to leave Nova Scotia.[90]

Wolvin's intransigence in the 1925 strike, when he and McLurg refused to meet union leaders and closed company stores, further damaged the corporation's reputation. In July 1925 the Liberal government was overwhelmingly defeated in a provincial election, partly as a result of their association with the corporation.[91] Tory premier E. N. Rhodes, who had promised to settle the five-month strike, now found it impossible to deal with

87   Newton Moore to W. L. Mackenzie King, 1 September 1923, King Papers, PAC.

88   *Monetary Times,* 4 April, 29 August 1924. See Table III.

89   Roy Wolvin to E. H. Armstrong, 4 March 1924, M. C. Smith to Br Emp S Co [sic], 1 March 1924, Armstrong Papers, PANS.

90   J. P. B. Casgrain to W. L. M. King, 19 March 1925, King Papers, PAC.

91   Paul MacEwan, *Miners and Steelworkers* (Toronto, 1976), p. 145.

Wolvin; "Wolvin is, I think, the most stubborn man with whom I have ever come in contact", he complained to Borden, "and his stubborness [sic] is increased by the fact that his Companies are almost bankrupt".[92] E. R. Forbes has found that Wolvin finally came to terms as a result of financial pressure from Bank of Commerce chairman Sir Joseph Flavelle, whose bank threatened to deny short-term money to Dominion Coal.[93] The strike ended with a temporary agreement and the appointment of a provincial royal commission, which, under the chairmanship of British coal expert Sir Andrew Rae Duncan, vice-president of the British Shipbuilding Employers' Federation, criticized Besco's unrealistic capital structure and financial policies.[94]

In the spring of 1926 the Bank of Commerce and Bank of Montreal refused Besco additional short-term financing, and Wolvin resolved to allow Dominion Iron and Steel, the weakest part of the merger, to go into receivership. In July 1926 Dominion Iron and Steel defaulted on bond payments and National Trust, closely linked to the Bank of Commerce, was appointed receiver for the company. No surprise, the collapse nevertheless caused a sharp fall in Canadian bond prices that summer and marked the beginning of Besco's disintegration.[95] Bondholders' committees were appointed to guard the interests of various investors, and early in 1927 National Trust began court proceedings for the winding up of Besco and Dominion Steel.[96] The Supreme Court of Nova Scotia refused to wind up Besco, but agreed to the liquidation of Dominion Steel, appointing Royal Trust, which was allied to the Bank of Montreal and the Royal Bank, as the receiver. In July 1927 Wolvin submitted a reorganization scheme to his shareholders, but could not win their support.[97] Soon Wolvin agreed to sell his holdings to Herbert Holt and a group of his Royal Bank associates. At the annual meeting in January 1928 Wolvin resigned as president of Besco.[98]

Wolvin's successor as Besco president was C. B. McNaught, a Toronto director of the Royal Bank. With the entry of seven new directors onto the Besco board in 1928, the coal and steel industries passed into the hands of a

---

92   E. N. Rhodes to R. L. Borden, 3 August 1925, Borden Papers, PAC.

93   Forbes, "The Maritime Rights Movement", pp. 263 - 8.

94   *Who Was Who, 1951 - 1960,* p. 326; Duncan Report, pp. 26 - 8.

95   Forbes, "The Maritime Rights Movement", pp. 392 - 7; *Monetary Times,* 11 June 1926; *Houston's Review,* 1926, pp. 165 - 6; *Financial Post Survey,* 1927, p. 233.

96   *Monetary Times,* 10 September 1926, 25 March 1927.

97   *Houston's Review,* 1928, pp. 216 - 7; *ibid.,* 1927, pp. 182 - 3; *Monetary Times,* 28 October 1927.

98   *Monetary Times,* 3 February 1928. Wolvin re-established himself in the Canadian shipping and shipbuilding industry and on his death was chairman of the executive board of Canadian Vickers Ltd.; *New York Times,* 8 April 1945.

financial grouping dominated by the Royal Bank. The group began plans to reorganize the corporation. McNaught and J. H. Gundy visited London to reach agreement with the British investors. In March 1928 the group incorporated a new holding and operating company, the Dominion Steel and Coal Corporation, which was capitalized at $65 million and took over the Besco properties.[99] With the completion of this transfer in May 1930, the British Empire Steel Corporation ceased to exist. The new company represented an alliance of old and new interests. The Royal Bank group held half the seats on the Dosco board, but Sir Newton Moore and Lord Invernairn remained as directors to represent the continued British interest; Moore served as vice-president and from 1932 to 1936 was president of the corporation. The new company ended a decade of financial turmoil and disappointment and placed the corporation in a strong position to weather the troubles of the 1930s.

As an episode in Canadian economic history, the development of industrial Cape Breton between the 1880s and the 1920s revealed a pattern of rapid growth culminating in severe crisis. Far from a backwater of economic inactivity, industrial Cape Breton performed important and useful functions for the national economy. Through the coal industry, the region supplied a basic industrial raw material, supported the local iron and steel industry and provided a lucrative arena for the financial wizardry of various investors. But industrial capitalism could not provide balanced and harmonious economic growth between regions; on the contrary, the national economic structure which emerged in Canada during this period promoted uneven development and regional dependency. This pattern of uneven development led to the crisis of markets and corporate welfare in the coal industry during the 1920s. Vulnerable in its distant markets and unable to rely on a stable local market, the importance of the Cape Breton coal industry declined. At the same time, the metropolitan search for economic surpluses continued, and in the case of Besco, reached unrealistic proportions. After the 1920s, the main functions of industrial Cape Breton in the national economy changed; the community was now called upon to provide a large pool of labour for the national labour market, and, in time of need, to supply reserve capacity for the national energy and steel markets. The rise and fall of the British Empire Steel Corporation provided the occasion, though not the root cause, for a structural turning point in the economic history of industrial Cape Breton.

The growth of the coal industry in Cape Breton expressed above all the financial opportunism of its successive owners, rather than any commitment to principles of regional economic welfare. Spokesmen for the coal industry from Richard Brown to Roy Wolvin endorsed local industrial development as a strategy for utilization of the local coal and iron resources, but in prac-

99 *Monetary Times,* 30 March, 18 May 1928.

tice they sought trading links with distant markets and pursued policies of rapid resource depletion. The local business class offered no effective resistance to the integration of the coal industry into the national economy; native Cape Bretoners like D. H. McDougall and W. D. Ross were capitalists foremost and proved no more loyal to the region's welfare than Whitney, Ross, Plummer or Wolvin. The experience of industrial Cape Breton also suggests that in the period between 1890 and 1930 Canadian capitalism featured a powerful and aggressive business class, associated in common purposes although often divided by rivalries. The resources of industrial Cape Breton attracted the interest of American and British investors, but except for the frustrated intentions of Whitney in the 1890s and the London syndicate in 1920, they preferred to leave direct control in Canadian hands. The passage of control over the coal industry from Bank of Montreal circles to a Bank of Montreal-Bank of Commerce alliance before the war, and ultimately to the Royal Bank in the 1920s, paralleled the successive domination of Canadian capitalism by these financial groupings. The route from Van Horne and James Ross to Sir Herbert Holt was interrupted in the 1920s by the intervention of Roy Wolvin and his allies on the Great Lakes and St. Lawrence and in London. But the extreme brevity and catastrophic failure of their regime during the 1920s indicated the distance that separated this group from the real seats of power in Canadian capitalism.

The most important conclusions to this episode in Canadian economic history were those reached by the local community in industrial Cape Breton. At a time when the labour movement was on the defensive across the country, the resistance of the coal miners to the British Empire Steel Corporation caused the eventual collapse of that enfeebled enterprise. The emergence of a militant labour movement in Canada helped begin a new stage in the history of Canadian capitalism. After the 1920s and 1930s, an ever closer collaboration between state and capital was needed to maintain the essential structure of the national economy. In industrial Cape Breton the deteriorating local economy would be propped up by government subsidies, enabling private capital to continue profitably to exploit the region's economic assets, while the deepening underdevelopment of the region would drive Cape Bretoners to leave their homes and enter the national labour market. The local working class continued to resist the progressive destruction of their community by campaigning for improved social standards and equitable national policies, and for public ownership of the coal and steel industries, which was achieved in 1968. In 1928 hopeful members of the Cape Breton Board of Trade celebrated the arrival of the new Besco president, C. B. McNaught, with a ceremonial banquet. But the rise and fall of the British Empire Steel Corporation left most Cape Bretoners with a permanent distrust of outside capitalists.

IAN McKAY

Reprinted from Vol. XIII, No. 1
(Autumn 1983)

Strikes in the Maritimes, 1901-1914

AS JAMES PENDER SAT AT HIS DESK on 6 November 1912, he was thinking about the traumatic events of the last few months and their ominous implications. Just one month before, the machinists in his nail factory in Saint John had presented a request for a wage increase and the nine-hour day, and they later refused to work on a Saturday afternoon at the rate normally paid during the week. On 7 October, three machinists, including two who had represented the workers in negotiations with Pender, were dismissed, and the remaining men went on strike in support of their shop mates. Like so many other employers in the Maritimes, Pender found himself in the middle of a difficult industrial conflict.[1]

Pender exemplified many of the features of the age of consolidated capitalism. He doubtless saw himself as the Saint John *Sun* described him, as a "progressive business man" and a "most excellent citizen". He had responded with anger to attempts by the U.S. Steel Company to force Canadian wire nail manufacturers into dependence, pledging his support instead to the Dominion Iron and Steel Company and its new rod mill in Sydney. Predictably Pender supported protection for the wire industry, and he also supported the Liberal Party, whose policies toward the steel industry had allowed it to reap the benefits of protectionism without formally rejecting its free-trade heritage. When he ran as a candidate for the party in 1908, 55 workers in his factory signed a letter praising him as "the friend of labor and the unswerving and outspoken advocate of everything pertaining to the welfare of our city". Sixteen of these workers had been employees of Pender for more than 15 years. Pender at once represented both the old competitive capitalism, for the nail industry in Saint John had been one of the conspicuous triumphs of the National Policy, and the new monopoly capitalism, for the Pender enterprise was soon to be little more than a bookkeeping entry in the consolidated balance sheet of the Dominion Steel Corporation.[2]

Perhaps he had been stung by the attacks upon his use of "Homestead tactics" and upon his rudeness to the men's committee. (A poem in the labour press on this strike noted, "Next day he sent for the committee,/ said he dident

1   *Standard* (Saint John), 8 October 1912, *Eastern Labour News* (Moncton), 12 October 1912. An earlier version of this paper was delivered to the Atlantic Workshop in Halifax in 1981. Since that time I have received support and criticism from many colleagues, for which I am very grateful. I thank Doug Cruikshank for sharing his own research on strikes with me, and Linda Baggs and Pat Burden for research assistance.
2   *Sun* (Saint John), 7, 8 April 1904, 19 September 1908.

[sic] give a damn,/ He would'nt [sic] be dictated to/by any union man").[3] Whatever the reason, Pender took the unusual step of writing a heartfelt polemic on the subject of strikers and labour organizers to the Department of Labour, denouncing labour organizers and the foolish workers who listened to them:

> We think it an outrage on Canadian Industries that lazy adventurers from the United States should be permitted to come into this country & organize Unions & collect dues from Confiding dupes who Know little or nothing about the way their dues are wasted by these loafing promoters who bask in the sunshine of these dues contributed by their confiding dupes who thus loaf a soft & easy living and live in affluence on the mischief they create between men & their employer by playing on the feelings & prejudices of the men & who make them believe that they are abused & badly used when such is not the case We think they should be jailed or deported whenever they show their mischievous presence in Canada & we hope to see legislation ere long that will deport them same as lepers.[4]

From Pender's point of view, the strike was the result of foreign agitators who had somehow undermined the relations of men and employers by appealing to irrational feelings. (In fact, the "lazy adventurer" in question was the Canadian vice-president of the International Association of Machinists, and Pender's solution of erecting a protective barrier against foreigners would not have stopped him). Pender thought the vital nucleus of the problem was the contamination of his naive workers, those confiding dupes who just four years before had pledged they would forever be "willing and anxious to fight the battles of our generous employer". Now they seemed to be fighting against him. The workers thought the problem stemmed from the impact upon Pender of his dependence upon the growing monopoly in the steel industry. Noted the *Eastern Labour News:* "Mr. Pender is not altogether to blame for this matter. He has generally been fair, but the heads of the great steel trust at Sydney, who own the Pender Plant with one Douglas as chief executive, are the people to blame for the present trouble in a usually peaceful house".[5] Monopoly capitalism, this analysis seemed to suggest, had created a new type of employer. What is so fascinating about these comments is that both sides thought that a previously peaceful situation had been transformed by the new structures of Canadian capitalism. Their angry responses brought out the bewilderment and uncertainty felt by men in a difficult new situation.

3 *Eastern Labour News,* 23 November 1912.

4 Strikes and Lockouts Files, Vol. 300, file 3605, Department of Labour Records (RG 27), Public Archives of Canada [PAC].

5 *Eastern Labour News,* 26 October 1912.

Recent studies have illustrated the strength and significance of working-class movements in the Maritimes during the late 19th and early 20th centuries. Other work has emphasized the organization of local and international unions and the emergence of the socialist movement in the region.[6] A study of strikes in the Maritimes can help provide a regional context for such work, and also help correct the regional imbalance in national historiography. Strikes themselves were crucial events, and no historical interpretation of the region in this period can safely overlook them. By studying the vigorous response of the region's workers to the new political economy of the early 20th century, we can start to understand the human implications of economic change. For these reasons, it is worth our effort to describe and analyze the general pattern of strikes, often in quantitative terms. This general pattern can then be related to the region's economic structure and help broaden our understanding of the economic revolution which transformed the region from the 1880s to the 1920s. In particular, two major themes emerge from this analysis: the transformation of the labour market and the revolution in the workplace. In important ways, then, this study can help us grasp the complex and profound changes taking place in the Maritimes, a society too often written off as a peripheral backwater where deferential and isolated workers were sporadically aroused by organizers for international unions. A history of the strikes of 1901-1914 helps us replace this condescending approach with a more complex understanding of the strengths and weaknesses of the working-class movement in the Maritimes in a decisive period of class awakening. It shows us how widespread was the movement of resistance which had so shocked and offended Pender.

The Maritime Provinces were dramatically transformed in the years between 1870 and 1914. Initially dependent upon exports of timber, lumber products, ships and fish, the Maritimes experienced rapid industrial growth in the decade following the introduction of the National Policy in 1879. In the first phase of industrialization, the region was characterized by locally-controlled secondary manufacturing located in widely-dispersed centres. In the 1890s and early 20th century, a widespread movement of economic consolidation brought most of these consumer-goods industries under the control of Montreal finance capital,

6 Recent publications in Maritime working-class history include Robert Babcock, "The Saint John Street Railwaymen's Strike and Riot, 1914", *Acadiensis*, XI (Spring 1982), pp. 3-27; Peter DeLottinville, "Trouble in the Hives of Industry: The Cotton Industry Comes to Milltown, New Brunswick, 1879-1892", *Historical Papers 1980*, pp. 100-15; Judith Fingard, *Jack in Port* (Toronto, 1982); David Frank, "Company Town/Labour Town: Local Government in the Cape Breton Coal Towns, 1917-1926", *Histoire sociale/Social History*, XIV (May, 1981), pp. 177-96; Donald Macgillivray, "Military Aid to the Civil Power: the Cape Breton Experience in the 1920s", *Acadiensis*, III (Spring 1974), pp. 45-64; Nolan Reilly, "The General Strike in Amherst, Nova Scotia, 1919", *Acadiensis*, IX (Spring, 1980), pp. 56-77; Allen Seager, "Minto, New Brunswick: A Study in Class Relations Between the Wars", *Labour/Le Travailleur*, 5 (Spring 1980), pp. 81-132. See David Frank and Nolan Reilly, "The Emergence of the Socialist Movement in the Maritimes, 1899-1916", *Labour/Le Travailleur*, IV (1979), pp. 85-113, for an article which parallels the present study in periodization and regional focus.

Trad. rays not stagnant not a backwater

the major seaports into the Canadian transportation system, and the separate communities of the Maritime Provinces into closer association with each other and with Montreal, the metropolis. A second phase of industrialization, focused on the coal and steel industries, emerged strongly in the same period. The advent of monopoly capitalism coincided with both the industrialization and subordination of the region. The consequence was highly paradoxical, for while the rapid loss of control over the regional economy by its indigenous capitalists accentuated underdevelopment in the long term, its short-term effect was to help overcome the problem of fragmentation and enable Maritimers to build more coherent class and regional traditions.[7]

Throughout the period 1901-1914 workers in the Maritimes faced an economy and society of striking variety. The greater part of the region was dominated by the rhythms of rural life, whether this was the agriculture of Prince Edward Island and the Annapolis Valley or the fishing economy of the coastal villages from Passamaquoddy to Cape North. If we remove the metal and coal towns of the region's north-east (the band of communities from Moncton to Glace Bay) and the two large seaports, we find in the remainder of the region only three communities with more than 5,000 people in 1911: two capital cities (Fredericton and Charlottetown) and the venerable old port of Yarmouth. In the remaining 20 centres in this zone, the average population was 2,469. Here was a zone of slow growth and outright population losses. The first, dispersed phase of industrial growth had left its mark; there were still cotton factories in Windsor, Milltown and Marysville, among other legacies of the National Policy. But the greater part of this area was dominated by primary production. Working-class life took place in small towns or villages, and only a few of these developed large labour movements. Paternalism could find its natural habitat here, in communities small enough to permit the personal sway of the capitalist to carry into many spheres of life.

Halifax and Saint John were different places altogether. Retaining many industries founded during the National Policy, they also faced the massive restructuring required by the growth of a national transportation system. The redevelopment of both cities as the winter ports of the Dominion suggested the consolidating logic of the new age. Workers here lived in variegated urban centres. In the early 20th century both cities were undergoing rapid changes which tended to conflict with their modest growth of population. In Saint John

7   See T.W. Acheson, "The National Policy and the Industrialization of the Maritimes, 1880-1910", *Acadiensis*, I (Spring 1972), pp. 3-28; Larry McCann, "Staples and the New Industrialism in the Growth of Post-Confederation Halifax", *Acadiensis*, VIII (Spring 1979), pp. 47-79; Robert Babcock, "Economic Development in Portland (Me.) and Saint John (N.B.) During the Age of Iron and Steam, 1850-1914", *The American Review of Canadian Studies*, IX (Spring 1979), pp. 3-37; David Frank, "The Cape Breton Coal Industry and the Rise and Fall of the British Empire Steel Corporation", *Acadiensis*, VII (Autumn 1977) pp. 3-34; Elizabeth W. McGahan, *The Port of Saint John*, Vol. 1, *From Confederation to Nationalization 1867-1927* (Saint John, 1982).

5,270 employees worked at 177 major establishments in 1911; in Halifax-Dartmouth 4,490 workers found employment at 123 establishments. These estimates do not include the many men who found employment on the waterfront and who formed the natural core of the labour movement in both cities.

Finally, in the region's eastern and northern section, was found the belt of heavy industry and the coalfields, which from Moncton to Glace Bay formed the dynamic heart of the second wave of industrialization. The coalfields posted a 93 per cent increase in production in the first decade of the 20th century, and the number of employees rose from 9,184 to 14,977. Even more impressive were the huge population increases in Amherst and Sydney. Unified by the railway system, dominated by the bankheads belching smoke and by dirty duff banks, and dotted with the heavy industry spawned by the age of the railway — from car works at Trenton and Amherst, to the new steel mills themselves at Sydney and Sydney Mines — this zone had an ambience quite different than that of Halifax or the rural Maritimes. Workers here lived in the front ranks of the great economic transformation, and they experienced its opportunities and difficulties at first hand. Often they lived in instant communities, built for the sole function of servicing the great empire of steel and coal whose conquests were the pride of the local boosters. This was the heartland of monopoly capitalism.

Speaking in round figures — it would be pretentious, given the highly flawed statistics, to do anything else — of the region's 45,000 industrial workers in 1911, 61 per cent lived in the highly industrialized zone from Moncton to Glace Bay, 22 per cent in the great seaports, and 18 per cent in the semi-rural remainder of the region.[8]

Where do we find significant working-class protests in this period? Almost everywhere. In Halifax and Saint John, workers increasingly supported international unions and resurrected trades and labour councils; labouring men mounted campaigns for political representation; labour issues were debated in the churches and in the newspapers. Labour movements here were often divided. Longshoremen, because of the enduring effects of casualism, often fought each other as strenuously as they fought their employers; only after the International Longshoremen's Association installed itself on the docks did a degree of unity replace division. Skilled craftsmen might well regard unskilled workers as potential enemies who stood ready to help employers undermine their position. The many women who found employment in the two major cities were generally left outside the ranks of organized labour (although there were significant exceptions) and little effort was made to organize the juveniles who delivered messages and performed countless other functions in the urban economy. Trade

---

8 The data in the preceding paragraphs are drawn from the *Census of Canada, 1911*, Vol. III, Tables XI, XII, XXXV. It should be noted that census statistics are approximate because establishments with fewer than five employees were not counted, and many seasonal industries were also missed.

unionism in the two major cities had made important and decisive gains, and the "foreign agitators" so roundly denounced by Pender had effected a shift towards international affiliation — but it did not challenge the traditional divisions within the working class nor the political order very aggressively.[9]

It was a far different story in the railway, metal and coal towns of the industrial core. There one found many powerful and cohesive trade unions which within their communities exerted an impact far beyond the workplace. The most important union of all was the Provincial Workmen's Association, perhaps the most misunderstood and misrepresented of all Canadian trade unions. Frequently labelled a "company union" by its critics, the PWA united workers in the coalfields throughout Nova Scotia and made significant and controversial inroads into the transportation sector. Because the PWA had changed its structure at the end of the 19th century to one in which many important powers were wielded by district sub-councils, the workers within the union were rarely discouraged from going on strike. More strikes were waged by the PWA in this period than by any other union. Decentralization aided local militants, who in many cases sympathized with socialism. Much of the rhetoric of the local activists was tinged with a syndicalist spirit, in stark contrast to the moderate language of the union's leadership. The PWA absorbed many of the energies unleashed by the "new unionism" of the 20th century, and like many of the trade unions discussed by David Montgomery, this aggressive local pursuit of workers' power coexisted with a moderate provincial leadership. International unionism made headway in Moncton, Sackville and Sydney, but until 1908 the PWA exerted an unquestioned sway over the coalfields. Only when a conservative rump attempted to undermine a majority decision to affiliate with the United Mine Workers of America did the PWA lose its credibility as the fighting arm of the miners.[10]

The rest of the region is something of an enigma. International unions were influential in St. George, Fredericton, the Hants County gypsum district, and elsewhere. Local organizations surfaced in surprising places. Pugwash had its own longshoremen's union, and the workers of Sussex, New Brunswick, united behind a local Nine Hours League. From some sectors of the rural Maritimes there is silence: whether because of the partial nature of our sources or a genuine absence of working-class mobilization, there is next to nothing indicating organization in the lumber camps, the great majority of the fishing communities, or in agriculture. Fishermen in Nova Scotia belonged to the Fisher-

9 See Robert Babcock, *Gompers in Canada: A Study in American Continentalism Before the First World War* (Toronto, 1974), pp. 119-123 for a description of the activities of the American Federation of Labor in the Maritimes; earlier organizational history may be found in Eugene Forsey, *Trade Unions in Canada 1812-1902* (Toronto, 1982).

10 The union's early history is described by Sharon Reilly, "The History of the Provincial Workmen's Association, 1879-1898", M.A. thesis, Dalhousie University, 1979.

men's Union of Nova Scotia, which was a union in name only.[11] However, sardine fishermen in Charlotte County and lobster fishermen at Gabarus and Main-a-Dieu in Cape Breton organized active protests against canneries which suggest something more than spontaneous, unorganized outbursts. Many small communities of the rural Maritimes witnessed serious strikes by workers who, at least formally, had no organization. In Shelburne, Bridgetown, Woodstock, and Parrsboro — to name only a few places — we find strikes organized by men who made coherent demands and fought in an organized way. The many ties of kinship and community binding workers together in these centres may have helped them fight successfully without formal union organization. In the rural Maritimes, supposedly dominated by an ancient paternalism and an absence of class conflict, we find instead a number of interesting experiments in purely local working-class mobilization.

The workers of the Maritimes faced a wide variety of conditions and created an astonishing diversity of organizations, but certain things were commonly experienced. No one stood completely apart from the dynamic expansion of the economy. Throughout the record of strikes, we find navvies and construction labourers, from the new sewers of Springhill and Amherst and Fredericton, the buildings of Dalhousie University in Halifax and the churches of Sydney, to the waterworks extension in Saint John and railway construction near Campbellton. The new economy entailed a massive expansion in the physical capital of the state apparatus. Everywhere we find the same complaint: "Labour is scarce". There are no reliable unemployment statistics for this period, but the consistency with which the scarcity of labour is referred to suggests that the workers' movement faced no great shortage of jobs. Although no studies of the standard of living have been completed of the calibre of those for other regions, it appears that Maritime workers all faced an economy in which wage increases did not keep pace with inflation. The record of the strikes brings to the fore the pervasive fear that earnings were slipping beneath what workers thought an acceptable level. Prices of food, fuel and other necessities in Maritime cities rose between 31 and 43 per cent, and rents from 36 to 56 per cent: lower increases than reported elsewhere in Canada, but enough to make the workers of the Maritimes very anxious. Local construction booms, such as the one in Sydney between 1901 and 1904, sent prices and rents skyrocketing.[12] Everywhere we find evidence that the region was increasingly being unified by the railway system and the emergence of much larger employers. The rail yards of Halifax gave

11 L. Gene Barrett, "Underdevelopment and Social Movements in the Nova Scotia Fishing Industry to 1938", in Robert Brym and R. James Sacouman, eds., *Underdevelopment and Social Movements in Atlantic Canada* (Toronto, 1979), pp. 127-160, provides the essential background for fishing.

12 As the *Chronicle* (Halifax), 18 June 1901, remarked during a strike of steamer firemen in 1901: "There is a scarcity of firemen here, and in consequence the men are very independent". For the cost of living, see Canada, Department of Labour, Board of Inquiry into the Cost of Living, *Report* (Ottawa, 1915), Vol II, pp. 76-7, 377, 382, 1063

work to men from Memramcook, unemployed fishermen found work in Halifax and Saint John, and the great building boom in Sydney caused a shortage of skilled workers in Halifax and a reorientation of agricultural production in the surrounding countryside. Coal strikes were regarded with utmost seriousness because they could bring to a halt industries throughout the region. A strike in Springhill caused real fears of fuel shortages in Saint John, Amherst, and Moncton. Longshoremen were reminded of the wide ramifications of their militancy by no less a personage than Israel Tarte, who warned Saint John longshoremen that their excesses would drive their port into the same ruin which had befallen Quebec, all to the benefit of Montreal and Halifax.[13]

There were isolated strikes in this period, strikes waged by men whose actions had little possible bearing on workers elsewhere in the region. But such isolated strikes loom less large than the strikes which affected parts of the region far removed from the site of the conflict. In an economy dependent on coal, railways, and steamships, workers derived tremendous power from the interlocked character of production. A 19th century coal strike was a nuisance; a large coal strike in the 20th century was a calamity. A new dynamism could be found in this economy, and here lies the key to the militancy of these years. Workers enjoyed the unusual position — in the Maritimes, at any rate — of being able to take advantage of their scarcity value in the labour market. The rapid expansion of the economy masked serious structural weaknesses and allowed contemporaries to confuse growth with genuine development. But it did give workers a rare chance to make their power felt in this society, and this chance was seized with real enthusiasm.

Workers in the Maritimes fought at least 411 strikes from 1901 to 1914, accounting for 1,936,146 striker-days. It is difficult to place this statistic in national context, because it is derived from sources different than those customarily cited. (The official data for the Maritime region are highly defective). The highly ambiguous statistics we do possess hint that this level of militancy was comparatively high.[14] It is also not altogether easy to place this finding in temporal perspective. Only a few places have been researched on the same level from the 19th to the early 20th centuries. In Halifax from 1901 to 1914 there were more strikes (54) than in the half century before 1900 (42), and in the two Cumberland coalfields there were more strikes in the first 14 years of the 20th century (37) than in the preceding 21 years (36). Impressionistic evidence

13 *Chronicle*, 5 June 1901, 30 May 1903, *Herald* (Halifax), 17 June 1904, *Sun*, 24 October 1907, 24 November 1905.

14 The number of striker-days is calculated by multiplying the number of strikers by the working days involved. All strike statistics in this paper are drawn from a computer file compiled from three sources: (1) the published works of the Department of Labour, notably the *Labour Gazette* and the *Report on Strikes and Lockouts in Canada 1901-1916* (Ottawa, 1918), (2) unpublished reports on strikes prepared by the Department of Labour in the strikes and lockouts files, and later departmental revisions [RG 27, PAC], (3) newspapers of the region, notably daily newspapers in the two major cities throughout this period (the *Sun, Standard* and *Globe* in Saint John

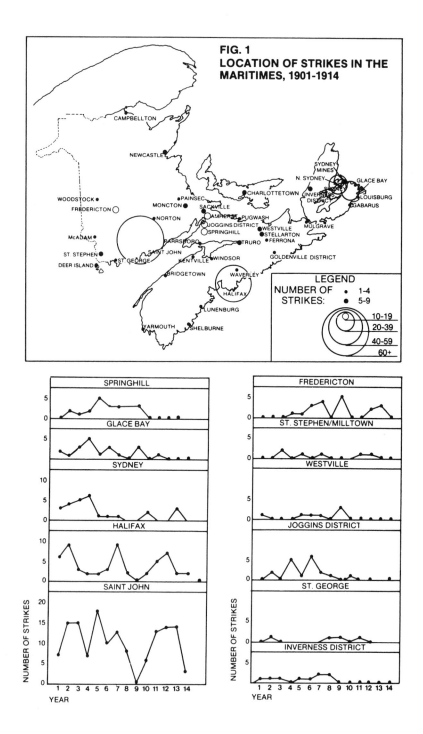

FIG. 1
LOCATION OF STRIKES IN THE MARITIMES, 1901-1914

from Saint John in the 1880s suggests that the high level of militancy in the early 20th century might also be seen as a break with the past.[15]

There is an abundance of evidence which suggests that contemporaries perceived the strikes of the early 20th century as a departure from tradition. In Lunenburg, the workers of the Smith and Rhuland shipyard launched in November 1910, what the local correspondent called "the first strike in the era of our commercial enterprizes . . . ". The strike of workers at the Eastern Hat and Cap Company in Truro was reported under the headline, "Truro Has Had Its First Taste of a Real Genuine Strike With Modern Accompaniments", and after enumerating such signs of local progress as paved streets and a new railway station, the writer concluded, "Now the sight of strikers on our streets gives the finishing touches to all that goes to make up the daily routine of the biggest city in the world". The general strike of skilled and unskilled workmen in Shelburne, which in 1912 closed down the shipyards, boat shops and other establishments of the town, was thought to be the community's first major strike. It was believed that the workers of the Hartt Boot and Shoe Factory in Fredericton had launched the factory's first strike when they walked out in 1907.[16] Even in the coalfields and major ports, where large strikes had been noted since the mid-19th century, contemporaries noted a new intransigence. In Springhill, a town which more than any other symbolized the class polarization of the age, it was said that "wars and rumours of wars are practically our daily portion in this town". The Halifax *Chronicle* conveyed the same sense of alarm when it commented in 1901, "Local labor circles are agitated just now and it is not known where the end will be".[17]

and the *Herald* in Halifax), supplemented by the *Eastern Labour News*, the *Maritime Mining Record*, and a wide variety of local papers which were consulted if other sources indicated industrial unrest. The official strike statistics compiled by the Department of Labour are highly unreliable. According to *Strikes and Lockouts in Canada* there were 153 strikes in the Maritimes from 1901 to 1914; our evidence suggests this estimate is based on only 37 per cent of the strikes known to have occurred in the region. Moreover, the departmental estimates of individual strikes generally had to be recalculated. Inter-regional strikes are excluded from this analysis. The grave problems associated with official statistics suggest that inter-regional comparisons will have to wait until historians recalculate the strike statistics for other regions: there is at present no sound statistical base for such an enterprise. For seminal work on strike patterns in other countries, see Edward Shorter and Charles Tilly. *Strikes in France, 1830-1968* (Cambridge, 1974), James E. Cronin, *Industrial Conflict in Modern Britain* (London, 1979), and Michelle Perrot, *Les ouvriers en grève: France 1871-1890*, 2 tomes (Paris, 1974), probably the best study to date.

15 See Ian McKay, "The Working Class of Metropolitan Halifax, 1850-1889", Honours Thesis, Dalhousie University, 1975; Babcock, "Saint John Street Railwaymen", p. 10, and James Richard Rice, "A History of Organized Labour in Saint John, New Brunswick, 1813-1890", M.A. Thesis, University of New Brunswick, 1968 — although this last work reminds us of the more militant period in Saint John of the 1870s.

16 *Herald*, 22 November 1910; *Colchester Sun* (Truro), 23 October 1912; *Evening Mail* (Halifax). 14 May 1912; *Globe* (Saint John), 4 July 1907 and *Daily Gleaner* (Fredericton), 11 July 1907.

17 *Herald*, 7 August 1907; *Chronicle*, 3 June 1901.

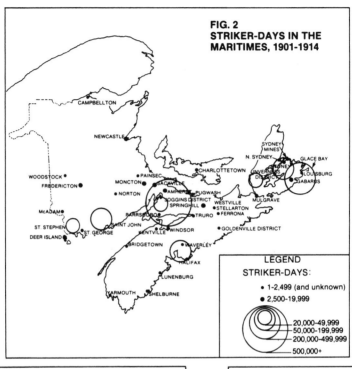

FIG. 2
STRIKER-DAYS IN THE
MARITIMES, 1901-1914

LEGEND
STRIKER-DAYS:
• 1-2,499 (and unknown)
● 2,500-19,999
20,000-49,999
50,000-199,999
200,000-499,999
500,000+

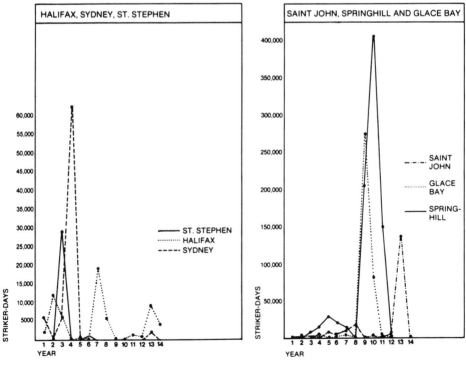

The strikes were found throughout the region. The greatest number were found in the seaports (198), followed by 143 strikes in the region of heavy industry and 70 in the widely-dispersed industrial and resource communities elsewhere. Table One lists the Maritime centres which recorded more than 10,000 striker-days in the period 1901-1914. Of these 11 locations, five were dominated by the coal-mining industry. Other important strike locations included Sydney Mines (8 strikes), Moncton (5), Fredericton (19), Amherst (11), and Newcastle/Chatham (8). One may read the evidence in two ways. If one is anxious to stress the peculiar militancy of the coal miners, one should note that 69 per cent of the striker-days in the region can be placed in Glace Bay and Springhill. More than half the total striker-days can be attributed to the coal miners' strikes in Inverness, Glace Bay and Springhill in 1909-11 for recognition of the United Mine Workers of America. On the other hand, Saint John was by far the regional leader in the *number* of strikes, and the two port cities together accounted for 48 per cent of the region's strikes. An approach to the region's workers, such as that championed by Stuart Jamieson, which emphasizes the

Table One

Strike Centres in the Maritimes, 1901-1914

Place	Number of Strikes	Striker-Days	Active Workers
Springhill	19	978,664	Coal miners, railwaymen, trapper boys
Glace Bay	20	363,382	Coal miners
Saint John	144	199,025	Longshoremen, construction labourers, civic labourers, building trades, metal trades
Sydney	26	80,487	Building trades, steelworkers, construction labourers
Halifax	54	64,185	Longshoremen, building trades, metal trades
Inverness District	9	39,970	Coal miners
St. Stephen/Milltown	6	29,800	Cotton factory workers
St. George	4	24,278	Granite cutters, pulp mill workers
Joggins District	18	20,223	Coal miners
Westville	7	18,760	Coal miners
Sackville, N.B.	5	16,948	Metal trades

"low incidence of strikes or other overt expressions of industrial conflict", outside the coal mining industry, falls wide of the mark. The coal miners were exceptional not because they decided to go on strike more often than other workers but because their strikes were far larger in terms of numbers and duration.[18]

The strikers could be found in a wide range of occupations. Messenger boys, waitresses, actors, professional hockey players, attendants at bowling alleys, paid members of church choirs, and firemen comprised some of the less usual strikers, whose 24 strikes are classified under "miscellaneous". Coal miners waged 82 strikes, unskilled labourers 140, factory workers 62, and skilled craftsmen 103. These data are somewhat startling, because they disagree sharply with the pattern in central Canada, where skilled craftsmen dominated both the labour movement and the history of industrial conflict. The most active single group were the labourers — including longshoremen, haypressers, freighthandlers, construction labourers, — and if we add to their number the factory workers, men who rarely were considered skilled, we arrive at the surprising conclusion that close to half the strikes were waged by those without generally recognized skills. As soon as we examine striker-days, however, the coal miners once again assert their dominance, accounting for fully 74 per cent of the striker-days (as compared with 3 per cent for unskilled labourers, 14 per cent for factory workers, 7 per cent for skilled craftsmen, and 2 per cent for other workers).

Particular groups within each occupational category emerge from the analysis as leaders of strikes. A surprising number of strikes (18) were fought by boys who worked in the coal mines, an indication of the power wielded by these young workers who minded ventilation doors, drove the horses, and often helped load the coal. More than half the craft strikes were found in the building trades, centred in such places as Halifax, Saint Johh, Sydney and Fredericton, and more than two-fifths were concentrated in the metal trades. Sackville, Moncton, and Amherst stand out particularly in this revolt of the skilled metal trades, a battle made all the more bitter by the intransigence of such employers as the Record Foundry in Moncton and the Fawcett Foundry in Sackville. The strikes of craftsmen were concentrated in the two economic spheres most closely integrated with the new capitalism — construction and heavy industry. There were very few strikes to be found among other craft groups, although such ancient trades as printing and caulking accounted for a few. The labourers are perhaps the most interesting group. Some of them, such as the longshoremen of Saint John and Halifax, were in the process of creating controls over the waterfront that stood comparison with the exclusivism of the crafts. Other labourers, such as the civic labourers in Saint John, were able to count on the old traditions of patronage and the political benefits of winning favour with a visible component

18 Stuart M. Jamieson, *Times of Trouble: Labour Unrest and Industrial Conflict in Canada, 1900-66* (Ottawa, 1968), p. 100.

of the working-class movement. These labourers, while they had few marketable skills, could use other means to defend their interests in the labour market. Many others were not so fortunate. A surprisingly large amount of the heavy construction work was done by foreigners. Hungarians and Italians helped build the Sydney steel mill, and Italians laid new sewers in Fredericton and built the railway in northern New Brunswick. Such men, provided to local contractors through intermediaries in Quebec or the United States, had only the most rudimentary ways of defending their interests. Isolated from the rest of the society, and confronted with contractors who always seemed on the verge of bankruptcy, these foreigners faced problems quite different in scope from the unskilled labourers of the cities. Twenty-six strikes were fought exclusively by foreign workers, whose most common fate was to be immediately replaced by another gang.

Although many critics of the working-class movement placed the blame for insurgency on the shoulders of meddling organizers, the record of the strikes does not support their contention. Out of 384 strikes for which information on union status is available, 164 involved non-unionized workers, 112 members of international unions, and 108 members of regional or local bodies. The PWA alone accounted for 65 strikes, many waged by local lodges without central approval. Of course the workers of the Maritimes did not live in isolation, and

Table Two

Yearly Levels of Strikes in the Maritimes, 1901-1914

Year	Number of Strikes	Striker-Days	Largest Strikes
1901	26	16,489	Pictou coal miners
1902	41	37,303	Moncton moulders
1903	39	56,449	Milltown cotton workers
1904	37	96,065	Sydney steelworkers
1905	39	58,696	Springhill coal miners
1906	38	41,015	Springhill coal miners
1907	44	190,418	Springhill coal miners
1908	20	47,501	St. George granite workers
1909	21	543,320	Glace Bay coal miners
1910	14	479,689	Springhill coal miners
1911	21	164,281	Springhill coal miners
1912	32	17,339	Moncton moulders
1913	32	172,324	Saint John mill workers
1914	7	15,257	Amherst machinists
Totals	411	1,936,146	

ideas and methods of both American and British trade unions were followed with interest. But few strikes can be blamed on the relatively infrequent visits by American organizers, and local workers lacked neither the will nor the reasons for going on strike.

The decision to go on strike was influenced by many factors. Table Two summarizes the annual strike record for the region, and suggests the impact of the business cycle. In the boom years of 1901-1907 there was a tight labour market and about 32 strikes a year. The recession of 1908 reduced the number of strikes, and only in 1912 and 1913 did strikes regain previous levels. By 1914 an economic reversal and the coming of the war brought strikes to their lowest point in this period. The pattern evident in the number of strikes supports the classic view that strikes were most common in times of prosperity.[19]

If we look more closely at the individual communities, as Figures One and Two allow us to do, we discover a more complex picture. Each community had its own pattern. The most violent fluctuations were evident in Saint John, where no fewer than 18 strikes were fought in 1905 (the peak of any location in the Maritimes in a single year) and where no strikes have surfaced in 1909. In Halifax where the peaks were lower, the city's maximum totals were found in 1902 and 1907 (nine strikes). In both cities, there was a drastic reduction in the years 1908-1910, and recovery afterwards, with Saint John experiencing a major wave of strikes in the years 1911-1913 in response to the expansion of the port. These cities most closely resembled the Ontario pattern described by Craig Heron and Bryan Palmer. In Sydney, strikes were concentrated in the first four years of the period, and were sharply reduced after the defeat of the steel strike waged by the PWA in 1904. The coalfields possessed their own pattern. The years leading up to 1909 were exceptionally militant; there were no fewer than five strikes in Springhill in 1905 alone. In 1909 to 1911 the coal miners went against the regional trend by waging the region's largest strikes, and they fell almost silent after their defeat. Were one to rely on the statistics of striker-days, one would discover a positive correlation between economic recession and militancy — because the coal miners were counter-cyclical, waging their most impressive struggles in the depths of recession.

Workers went on strike for a wide variety of reasons, and there are a number of ways of analyzing the general pattern. Adopting the categories used by Heron and Palmer, with minor additions for the regional context, Table Three suggests the importance of wage struggles in the working-class movement. (Because a strike involving two issues is counted twice, the total of issues raised does not correspond with the total number of strikes). About 46 per cent of the issues raised in strikes focused on the level of wage payment, while strikes in Category II, which turned broadly on questions of control, made up 50 per cent of the

19 Compare with Craig Heron and Bryan D. Palmer, "Through the Prism of the Strike: Industrial Conflict in Southern Ontario, 1901-1914", *Canadian Historical Review*, LVIII (December, 1977), pp. 425-6.

Table Three

Strike Issues

Category I

For higher earnings	204
Against wage reductions	22

Category II

For recognition of union	14
For shorter hours	46
Defence of trade unionism	7
Sympathy	7
Apprenticeship control	2
Objection to new system of work	12
Change in conditions of work	31
Objection to employment of particular persons	36
Adjustment of procedures of wage payment	44
Against dismissal of worker or supervisor	43
Improvement in housing conditions	3
Political demands	2
Other/Unknown	21

issues raised. It might be objected, however, that this minimizes the impact of economic issues involved in strikes by counting as demands for "control" essentially economic issues. By dividing the strikes between economic and non-economic on the strict criteria of whether or not the strikers would obtain immediate economic advantages if they won the strike, we find 280 "economic" strikes, 115 "control" strikes, and 16 which cannot be classified. Table Four outlines the yearly fluctuations of these strictly demarcated control" strikes. Both estimates of the issues raised in strikes make the same point. It would be misleading to present the strike as a simple response to "bread-and-butter" issues. Whether we define control broadly, as in Table Three, or very narrowly as in Table Four, we find control strikes accounting for between 28 and 54 per cent of the total. By either measure, we find workers were determined to defend certain basic controls over their jobs, such as the right to control the discharge of individuals and the character of supervision. David Montgomery's pathbreaking work on American control strikes suggests that such strikes at the turn of the

Table Four

Strike Issues

	Improved Earnings	Control	Not Classified
1901	20	6	0
1902	29	11	1
1903	28	10	1
1904	21	16	0
1905	26	11	2
1906	29	8	1
1907	29	12	3
1908	14	6	0
1909	12	9	0
1910	8	4	2
1911	16	4	1
1912	21	7	4
1913	23	9	0
1914	4	2	1
Totals	280	115	16

century generally involved craftsmen seeking a firm hold within the congealing structure of monopoly capitalism.[20] The experience of the workers of the Maritimes may have been somewhat different, for the craftsmen did not account for most of the control strikes, nor did traditional craft issues (such as limitation of the number of apprentices) loom very large. The heartland of the control strike was the coalfields. Of the 115 "pure" control strikes, 41 were fought in the coalfields, 30 involved labourers, 13 factory workers, 22 craftsmen, and 9 other workers.

Finally, some assessment should be made of the success rate of the strikers. Table Five outlines the essential data on a yearly basis. The strike was clearly something of a gamble, and the chance of winning varied with the business cycle. The bottom had fallen out of the workers' movement in the recession of 1908, for example, when 55 per cent of the strikes were defeats. When we analyze the successes of workers by occupation, we find two distinct patterns. For the coal miners and the skilled craftsmen, the strike often paid off. Coal miners won 35 per cent of their strikes outright, and lost 23 per cent; the corresponding statis-

20 David Montgomery, "The 'New Unionism' and the Transformation of Workers' Consciousness in America, 1909-22", in *Workers' Control in America: Studies in the History of Work, Technology, and Labor Struggles* (Cambridge, 1979), p. 98.

Table Five

The Results of Strikes

Year	Workers Succeed	Employers Succeed	Compromise	Indeterminate	Unknown
1901	4	4	8	5	5
1902	12	11	8	2	8
1903	8	11	8	0	12
1904	13	14	4	1	5
1905	12	17	3	0	7
1906	11	12	7	1	7
1907	12	17	8	2	5
1908	5	11	1	2	1
1909	2	8	2	0	9
1910	2	4	2	2	4
1911	8	4	2	0	7
1912	7	8	8	1	8
1913	9	8	7	1	7
1914	1	3	2	0	1
Totals	106	132	70	17	86

tics for craftsmen were 34 and 26 per cent respectively. For less well-protected workers, however, the failure rate was crushing. Labourers lost 38 per cent of their strikes, winning only 19 per cent outright; factory workers lost 37 per cent and won 19 per cent; and miscellaneous workers lost 41 and won only 17 per cent. However, these estimates may be somewhat misleading, because they do not register variations over time. The most dramatic change was experienced by the most powerful workers, the coal miners. Before 1907 the coal miners endured only eight defeats, a failure rate of just 15 per cent; after 1907 they lost 19 strikes, including the 22-month strike in Springhill, for a failure rate of 55 per cent. These strikes illustrated the rapid ebb and flow of working-class power, especially in an age in which the state aggressively restructured labour relations and capital mobilized with resolute swiftness to keep the coal mines working.

The workers of the Maritimes clearly responded with tremendous force to the new realities of monopoly capitalism. Apart from places where no large proletarian population existed, the strike was at home everywhere: in the mines, on the docks, in the factories. The statistics reveal a differentiated working class making a wide range of demands. In order to grasp their full meaning and the structures underlying them, we need to consider closely the transformation of

the labour market and the revolution in the workplace which were the precondi-
tions for this pattern.

Economic historians have established that a marked consolidation of capital
took place in the late 19th and early 20th centuries, evident in the "nationalization" of Maritime banks and the "internationalization" of stock promotions. It
has been less frequently observed that the same period witnessed a consolidation
of the labour market of equal scope and significance. The capitalist labour
market, whose emergence in central Canada in the 1850s and 1860s was analyzed so brilliantly by H.C. Pentland, had not really demolished regional and
national barriers between various local labour markets in the 19th century.[21] The
massive expansion of the economy in the early 20th century demanded just such
a demolition of barriers to the free circulation of labour power. Employers
might debate the exquisite intricacies of incidental protection and unrestricted
reciprocity with great enthusiasm, but on the subject of the need for a free
labour market they were united to a man.

Centralized production and the interpenetration of finance and industrial
capital made it possible for employers to gain access to far larger labour pools,
within the region and outside it. This creation of a much larger labour market
destabilized the working-class world, but at the same time it created new opportunities for mobilization. In the new economy, workers were informed about the
going rate in the region and the country as a whole and were quite prepared to
demand it. The broadening of the labour market provided them with a rapid
education in the new "rules of the game", and employers were soon complaining, with perennial inconsistency, that the workers were playing very capably in
the impersonal world of the capitalist labour market. One of the most important
victories of the workers was the large increase in wages secured in the major
coalfields in this period — a wage increase which took account of the rising price
of coal. What was most impressive about this was that for the first time the
PWA had bargained for a wage increase in a unified way, a dramatic break with
the somewhat uncoordinated activities of the union in the 19th century.[22]

Workers could use the new structure to their own advantage. Many of the
defeats of unskilled construction labourers have to be placed in the context of
the high international demand for their services. Like 19th century Irish railway
navvies, the Italian labourers who worked at Loch Lomond near Saint John on

21 For economic consolidation see James Frost, "The 'Nationalization' of the Bank of Nova
Scotia, 1880-1910", *Acadiensis*, XII (Autumn 1982), pp. 3-38, and Christopher Armstrong,
"Making a Market: Selling Securities in Atlantic Canada before World War I", *Canadian
Journal of Economics*, XIII (August, 1980), pp. 438-54. Pentland's major work is *Labour and
Capital in Canada, 1650-1860* (Toronto, 1981).

22 The wage struggles of the PWA are documented in the *Amherst Daily News*, 4 January 1901,
Sun, 1 January 1901, *Chronicle*, 1, 2, 4, 7 January 1901; J.R. Cowans to M.R. Morrow, 17
April 1900, Exhibit H/33, Record of Proceedings, Rex v. Cowans and Dick, Vol. 328, Series
"A", RG 21, Public Archives of Nova Scotia; John Moffatt, *Coal Cutting Rates in Nova Scotia*
(Stellarton, n.d.).

Librarians

the city's new waterworks extension endured conditions of unimaginable hardship — often they worked with cold water up to their knees and lived in primitive
shanties — and they fought, along with "Galicians" and other unskilled labourers, many unsuccessful strikes. But while their situation was one of dire helplessness in some respects, it in fact provided them some power. As the *Globe* reported, the labourers believed themselves to be "masters of the situation"
because of the project deadlines and the contractor's concern that rains might
jeopardize the project. Even more to their advantage was the existence of many
jobs throughout North America in a period of rapid urban development. After
one strike, the Italians were reported to be bound for "Boston, Montreal or any
other place at which they have reason to believe work may be obtained", and the
project was left looking for more workers. Such labourers would come, go on
strike (often with a hint of violence), and leave: the "defeats" of their strikes
were spurs to their rapid departure. Austrians and Italians at work on the Fredericton sewers merely returned to the immigrant "colony" in Quebec or to
Boston; as they informed the *Gleaner*, there would be no trouble in obtaining
work elsewhere. These foreigners embodied the ambivalence of the international
labour market, which brought them harsh conditions but also opportunities for
direct action. But emigration was not the prerogative of itinerant workers alone.
St. George granite cutters left for employment in Newfoundland during their
strike in 1902; Halifax moulders, from the anti-union Hillis Foundry, emigrated
to Haverhill, Massachusetts, during a strike in 1905; when Sackville moulders
emigrated to the United States, a reporter lamented that Sackville would thereby lose "a number of good citizens", thanks to the participation of Enterprise
Foundry in an open-shop drive. For many skilled workers, one of the great
attractions of holding a card from an international union was the flexibility it
allowed in such times of trouble. Coal miners found employment in other coalfields during strikes; miners in the Joggins coalfield complained during the long
strike of 1909-11 in Springhill that Springhill miners were flooding the local
labour market. Many coal miners went west when big strikes shut down the
Nova Scotia industry.[23]

The new conditions of the labour market gave the workers advantages as well
as undermining their traditions of local protection. In a minority of strikes the
working class can be seen trying to restore such local protection by means of excluding workers of other races and nationalities, or by aligning with other
classes against "outsiders". Maritimers faced daunting problems of fragmentation, and it would be unrealistic to believe that class allegiance automatically
overcame deeply-rooted ethnic and religious divisions. Blacks were not propor-
tionately represented in the crafts, and it is probable that the practice of the
closed shop served to perpetuate their exclusion. Saint John machinists, for

23 *Globe*, 7 September 1905, 11 July 1905, 23 May 1905; *Gleaner*, 18 June 1906; *Sun*, 17 June 1902;
Herald, 2 November 1905; *Amherst Daily News*, 21 September 1905; *Herald*, 28 August 1909;
Herald, 15 September 1909.

example, went on strike at one foundry in the city to force the discharge of a black man, who later commented that "he was a British subject and proud to live under the Union Jack, but . . . the action of the foundry hands had made him almost ashamed that the Union Jack floated over St. John". A later strike of woodworking employees in Saint John in 1913 raised the same issue of ethnic division, although in a different way. The city's carpenters were faced with the problem of whether they would work with non-union materials coming from the woodworking factories. Although some of them supported this act of solidarity, and the international union gave its blessing to a sympathy strike, the local carpenters demurred and the woodworkers' strike was subsequently broken. As the local correspondent of the *Labour Gazette* saw it, one weakness of the strikers had been ethnic division: "The strike was not popular with native workmen. The leaders were principally new commers [sic] to the city (englishmen) labor agitators".[24] The waterfront was particularly prone to this kind of division. The divisiveness of the Saint John waterfront was legendary: divided along geographical, religious and economic lines, the city's longshoremen typified the survival of localism. Labour struggles in Pugwash pitted unionized full-time longshoremen against non-union farmers who were supplementing their normal income. The workers of the Miramichi responded with violence to the incursions of millmen and other labourers from Saint John.[25]

Even in the coal and steel centres one finds strikes which suggest ethnic and other divisions. About 300 Italian labourers went on strike in Sydney in March 1903 against the Dominion Iron and Steel Company, alleging that they were not treated as well as native workers and that the latter were given the preference in the allocation of work. The labourers also charged that they had been brought from Montreal on the understanding they were to receive $1.50 per day; their actual pay had been reduced to $1.35. A crowd of agitated foreigners armed with heavy clubs, picks, shovels, and iron bars assembled at both the open hearth and coke oven entrances. As native workmen passed the strikers, the Italians began to shout and lift their weapons threateningly: "The police waited no longer and started to disperse them by force. After the police did considerable clubbing and arrested one or two they succeeded in quelling the crowd". Some Hungarians and Newfoundlanders had joined the agitation, but the majority of the native workers did not take part. Nor did they protest when the Italian ringleaders of the strike, who had waved a red flag and claimed membership in an "Italian union", were dismissed.[26] Ethnic divisions also surfaced in the mines: when Newfoundlanders demanded the same pay as experienced miners but failed to get it; when coal miners in Dominion No. 6 mine com-

24 *Sun*, 25 April 1907; report of Fraser Gregory, Vol. 302, file 13 (67), RG 27.

25 McGahan, *Port of Saint John*, pp. 180-187; *Amherst Daily News*, 16 August 1907; *Sun*, 17 May 1904.

26 *Daily Post* (Sydney), 3 March 1903; *Amherst Daily News*, 3 March 1903; *Chronicle*, 3 March 1903; *Herald*, 5 March 1903.

plained that longwall positions were unfairly given to outsiders in preference to native workmen; when the miners of Reserve complained that "Old Country" miners had been given all the best places in the mine; and in the separate strike waged by Newfoundlanders against an increase of board for the "big shacks" of the Dominion Coal Company. When the miners of Golden Rule Lodge attempted to secure the closed shop for the PWA in Bridgeport, they encountered serious resistance from the "old countrymen" and Newfoundlanders, in surprising contrast with immediate support from the Italians.[27]

But there was another aspect to the growing prominence of immigrant workers. The immigrant often helped to bring Maritimers in contact with new ideas. At the most modest level, immigrants (or Maritimers returning from a stint outside the region) imported standards for jobs and wages. When Halifax electrical workers, during their strike of 1907, reported themselves to be in touch with "Toronto, Ottawa and Montreal", where standards were far better than in Halifax, they merely confirmed a pervasive regional pattern. Coal miners were fond of comparing their wage rates with those of the western coal miners (not always mentioning in the same analyses the higher western cost of living). The strike of Halifax boilermakers in 1907 provided a classic instance of the unintended consequences of importing workers. Confronted with a determined union anxious to enforce shop rules, the employers turned to England for a foreman and some new workers. John O'Toole of the boilermakers gave as the reason for the strike, "Men being imported from England to break our rules...". But the English workers, discovering that Halifax rates and standards were lower than those in England, promptly joined the union and fought to bring Halifax standards up to an English level.[28]

It would probably be a mistake to insist too strongly on the divisive consequences of ethnic divisions. Acadian workers from Memramcook and other points in New Brunswick aroused considerable public sympathy when they went on strike in the Halifax rail yards in Richmond in 1912, and they fought side by side with local men. The case of the Scottish girls brought to work for the Christie Fish Company in Dartmouth became a *cause célèbre* in reform circles in Nova Scotia. A reporter for the Halifax *Daily Echo* found that the girls (who were required to gather seaweed, periwinkles, and cord wood, nail boxes, and perform other tasks from 7 a.m. to 6:30 p.m. for $4.00 per week) lived under close supervision and were forced to do without coal. The Chief of Police and the Society for the Prevention of Cruelty managed to win somewhat better conditions for them. Immigrants also became members of the PWA, and Scottish, Belgian and Welsh miners distinguished themselves in the long struggles for the UMW. It would appear that the "vertical" consciousness of some workers, who defended their position in the labour market by erecting barriers to strangers,

27 *Maritime Mining Record*, 27 April 1904; *Herald*, 13 June 1906; *Herald*, 2 May 1906; *Maritime Mining Record*, 17 April 1901; *Herald*, 21 March 1907.

28 *Herald*, 4 July 1907; Vol. 295, file 2997, RG 27.

was of less significance than an emergent "horizontal" consciousness based on a common class position.[29]

Perhaps the most visible sign of the new economy of labour was the pervasive influence of strikebreaking, which represented the forceable breaking down of barriers to a free labour market. The emergence of mass strikebreaking presupposed a certain consolidation of employers, who could blacklist employees, oppose restrictions to the hours of labour, and collaborate in setting prices. Strikebreaking represented a logical outcome of the consolidation of capital, because the massive scale on which it was practised in this period required both companies big enough to have access to large pools of labour, and the active involvement of the state. The recruitment of strikebreakers was not altogether a new phenomenon; at least as early as the 1880s one reads of the importation of men for the purpose of taking strikers' jobs. But there is nothing in the 19th century to compare with the scope of the strikebreaking drive in the early 20th century.[30]

For many unskilled workers, of course, automatic replacement by others in the course of a strike was an unavoidable fact of life. The gas-house employees who went on strike in Saint John in 1905 for a modest wage increase included employees of 31 years standing. The management had no qualms about replacing such old employees by unemployed labourers thoughtfully recruited by the Saint John police department. Countless strikes could be given the epitaph of a Saint John labourers' strike of 1902: strikers fired, "men hired indiscriminately". "Others have taken their places and the work continues without any interruption", was the description of the termination of a railway labourers' strike near Sydney Mines. Such strikers faced the brutal dehumanization of the capitalist labour market.[31]

But the new mass strikebreaking represented an effort to generalize their condition to all the workers and remove the worker's proprietary interest in his job. In this age it was systematized and perfected, not "naturally", but by an active process in which the key element was physical force. Systematic, mass replacement of a striking workforce was attempted in 23 strikes. No strata of the working class were protected: the skilled were as jeopardized as the unskilled, and may indeed have sustained heavier losses. Thus the record of strikebreaking includes threats of replacement against Saint John ship carpenters, the replacement of Halifax carpenters by men from outside districts during a strike in the summer of 1903, and the replacement by American strikebreakers of Saint John tailors in 1904. The printers of the two port cities faced tough employers, and

---

29 *Herald*, 30 August 1912; *Daily Echo* (Halifax), 30 April, 2 May 1910; for the admission of immigrants to the PWA, see Minutes of Holdfast Lodge of the PWA, Joggins, 29 August 1896, Dalhousie University Archives.

30 For an example, see Robert Drummond, *Recollections and Reflections of a Former Trades Union Leader* (n.p. [Stellarton] n.d. [1926]), p. 39.

31 *Sun*, 27, 31 May 1905; *Sun*, 22 April 1902; *Daily Post*, 3 May 1902.

Montreal strikebreakers were used against Saint John printers of the *Telegraph* and *Times*; advertisements for strikebreakers were inserted in newspapers as far away as London and Manchester. Fredericton plumbers were replaced with men imported from Quebec, Saint John machinists by renegade craftsmen from Amherst, and Halifax plumbers by English plumbers who came to the city via Montreal.[32] Workers in the mills and factories suffered the same fate. Employers were generally attracted to recruitment of foreign or Québécois workers, because such men would be desperate enough to agree and because they could not easily communicate with the strikers. This tactic was not foolproof. Italian strikebreakers brought in to break the Sydney steel strike in 1904 were met at the gates by Italian members of the PWA. Given the past record of the Sydney Italians, who earlier had posted notices that anyone going to work would be killed, one imagines many spirited conversations at the entrance. The management of the pulp mill in St. George, New Brunswick enjoyed greater success in recruiting strikebreakers ("anything and everything . . . that might pass for a man", wrote the spokesman for the union), particularly from Weymouth, Nova Scotia.[33]

Throughout the region strikebreaking threatened militant workers and brought home the lessons of the new labour market. But the coalfields and the docks were in a league by themselves. Strikebreaking on the waterfront was facilitated by the presence of crew members, who could be coerced or cajoled into doing the work of the longshoremen themselves. Longshoremen in Saint John in 1905 derived a certain amount of enjoyment from watching the awkward efforts of crew members unloading a valuable cargo of bricks:

> The Longshoremen who were on the McLeod wharf yesterday morning when the crew of the Alcides were trying to get some bricks unloaded were much amused when one after another the contents of three tubs were emptied into the harbor, owing to the awkward manipulation of the unloading apparatus. These bricks were worth seven cents apiece, and about forty-five dollars' worth went over the side of the vessel.
> The longshoremen are talking of making information against these men for throwing refuse into the harbor.

This was a light-hearted moment in an otherwise difficult war. Like all other employers, the steamship lines could exploit ethnic divisions in strikes on the waterfront (although Halifax blacks refused to play along in 1902 and Italians were to prove difficult in Saint John in 1905). But they enjoyed additional

---

32 *Sun*, 17 March 1902; *Labour Gazette*, August 1903, p. 106; *Sun*, 24 May 1904; *Sun*, 6, 9 April 1908; Vol. 299, file 3507, RG 27; *Standard*, 28 October 1912; *Chronicle*, 27 June 1914 and Vol. 303, file 14 (17), RG 27.

33 *Herald*, 4 June 1904, *Chronicle*, 2 March 1903; Christopher Wren to F.A. Acland, 9 September 1912, Vol. 298, file 3341, RG 27, and *Standard*, 8 June 1911.

advantages thanks to the integration of the Canadian transportation system, which allowed them easy access to the vast casual labour market of Montreal. This was the key factor in the smashing of the Saint John strike in 1905. The Shipping Federation, with its headquarters in Montreal, used the services of The General Labor Company, Limited, a professional strikebreaking outfit, and this company recruited men for a period of two weeks or longer. Since the negotiations were generally carried out in English, many of the foreigners were not fully aware of the function they were really performing. The Saint John longshoremen were highly creative in their response, putting up many of the strikebreakers as guests and encouraging many others to quit work, but the strikebreaking tactic ultimately did succeed in defeating them.[34]

The coalfields provided the most unforgettable instances of the new economy of labour. There was no precedent for the importation of 3,000 strikebreakers into Cape Breton and several hundred into Springhill. Once again Montreal-based companies secured the services of a strikebreaking outfit, this time the Reliance Labor Exchange, housed, appropriately enough, on St. James Street. Once again the employers advertised far and wide for men, and company recruiting agents scoured Newfoundland. One was unwise enough to look for recruits in Cumberland County, and was relieved of 25 strikebreakers in Amherst by UMW sympathizers and encouraged to leave Springhill by a crowd of between 200 and 300 men. Further problems were presented by English miners who baulked at living in prison conditions behind the barbed-wire fences provided for the strikebreakers in Cape Breton. The general manager at Springhill, J.R. Cowans, had rhapsodized about the wonderful future his company would face if only he could get rid of his rebellious workers and replace them with Europeans or Chinese; his strikebreakers, who arrived in 1910, proved to be disappointingly preoccupied with fighting among themselves.[35]

Strikebreaking involved such difficulties and problems, and it was a tactic guaranteed to escalate labour disputes into miniature civil wars. Like the Saint John longshoremen, the Cape Breton miners commented on the shoddy work of the men who had replaced them. When Dan McDougall, president of the United Mine Workers of America in Nova Scotia, was asked how he thought the imported workmen compared with the striking miners, he replied, "I don't consider them in the same class with our men, either physically or morally. The men on strike, by the company's own admission, comprise the pick of skilled Cape Breton miners, and it is practically impossible to duplicate them anywhere".

34 For a discussion of the 19th-century pattern, see Judith Fingard, "The Decline of the Sailor as a Ship Labourer in 19th Century Timber Ports", *Labour/Le Travailleur*, II (1977), pp. 35-53; *Sun*, 25 November 1905; *Herald*, 3 April 1902; *Sun*, 29 November 1905; *Sun*, 24, 25 November 1905.

35 *Herald*, 13 July 1909; *Herald*, 27 July 1909; *Herald*, 18 August 1909; *Herald*, 4 July 1909; *Sun*, 10 December 1909 and *Herald*, 21 April 1910. For disturbances among the strikebreakers, resulting in the death of one man, see Peter Owen Carroll, *Life and Adventures of Detective Peter Owen Carroll* (n.p., n.d. [c.1924]), p. 68.

Such men would fight strikebreakers with determination. One report from Cape Breton in 1909 dramatized the battle for control over the labour market:

> There is a steady tug of war between the Dominion Coal Company and the U.M.W. as to who is to control the new-comers looking for work. Tonight the U.M.W. rounded up one hundred men for a Moncton contractor and shipped them off to Sydney in a special car. The car had just left the big town when a special train from Louisburg came in over the company's road with over one hundred men who are ready to work at daylight. The U.M.W. pickets claim that they will have half of these by tomorrow night and it is only a matter of time until they get the others. U.M.W. pickets are stationed at all points and it is practically impossible for a stranger to enter town without being held up, and once it is learned he is looking for work the U.M.W. and the company representatives both endeavour to get control of him and it is a case of the best men winning.

Besides such mass mobilization in the streets, the UMW sent representatives to Newfoundland to counteract the recruiting efforts of the company and published advertisements (later the subject of criminal proceedings) in the Montreal French-language press. J.B. McLachlan of the UMW even wrote to Samuel Gompers of the American Federation of Labor to persuade him to write to the leaders of Belgian labour to stop strikebreakers from leaving that country.[36]

Workers also appealed to the law. Saint John printers appealed to the Alien Labour Act, which had been passed in 1897 in retaliation against American alien labour legislation. The city's longshoremen attempted to take advantage of the labour licensing system which imposed a tax of $7.50 on outsiders who came to the city to work. Had this embodiment of local protectionism served their purposes, mass strikebreaking would have been expensive indeed. In the 1907 longshoremen's strike, however, the shipping companies managed to have their investment in the labour licences returned. Against the efforts of the Canadian Shipping Federation, the Trades and Labour Council and the *Eastern Labor News* continued to fight for the licensing system, seeing in it an element of protection against the new labour economy, but that system had clearly failed to protect the longshoremen from the army of strikebreakers the shipping companies held in reserve. Similarly, Halifax electrical workers cited municipal bylaws governing the certification of wiremen, and plumbers reported to the Board of Health those strikebreakers lacking proper qualifications. There were really very few laws, however, which could stand against mass strikebreaking, and the trend of legislation was running strongly in the other direction.[37]

---

36 *Herald*, 28 March 1910; *Herald*, 9 July 1909; for attempts to stop Belgian strikebreaking, see Gompers to Bergmans, 30 March, 1 April 1910, Gompers to J.B. McLachlan, 1 April 1910; National Union Files, Reel No. 7, AFL-CIO Library, Washington, D.C.

37 *Sun*, 18 July 1908; *Sun*, 9 January 1902, 29 July 1904, 26 December 1906, 10, 20 February 1908;

Strikebreaking was very successful, and all the workers' efforts to combat it failed. From the pacific tactics of the PWA in the 1904 steel strike, during which union sentinels were posted in Truro, Halifax, Saint John and other points to watch stations and report upon incoming labourers,[38] to the legal challenges mounted by the Saint John longshoremen and the Halifax craftsmen, the record of failure was consistent. Strikebreakers were given the protection of the militia and police, and in the four great strikes dominated by hundreds of strike-breakers, nothing could match the combined force of capital and the armed servants of the state.

Monopoly capitalism entailed far-reaching changes in the labour market, but it also entailed a dramatic transformation of the labour process. Tables Three and Four have already suggested the broad range of issues which sparked strikes, and established that by both liberal and conservative measures, strikes over questions of job control were central to the pattern as a whole. Such "control" struggles took place in the context of dynamic new philosophies of work, which might broadly be subsumed under the heading "scientific manage-ment".[39] As a specific ideology and practice associated with F.W. Taylor and his disciples, scientific management had very limited relevance to the Maritimes, where so many workers were employed in such unsuitable industries as long-shore and coal mining. But taken in its broadest sense, scientific management — a systematic effort to obtain greater productivity from workers by exerting greater managerial discipline — had great relevance to the region, and its impact can be seen in many of the workers' struggles. We can explore the struggle for control more fully by examining several crucial dimensions of such control struggles, particularly hiring, discharge, supervision, and production techniques, as well as more general issues of control.

The ability of workers to influence the labour market through placing limits on hiring was possibly the most crucial. In the 19th century the vital battle-ground for this kind of struggle was the enforcement of apprenticeship rules. Although the painters of Saint John were able to defend apprenticeship tradi-tions in 1903, one has the distinct impression that apprenticeship had long since ceased to be an effective safeguard against the dilution of the crafts. The ex-perience of the moulders of Sackville is instructive. The moulders of the Fawcett Foundry failed to win any of their demands regarding shop management, and

---

Sun, 4 December 1907; *Eastern Labour News,* 12 August 1911, 26 October 1912; *Eastern Labour News,* 27 May, 28 October 1911; *Herald,* 5 July 1907.

38 *Herald,* 4 June 1904.

39 For discussions of scientific management, see Harry Braverman, *Labor and Monopoly Capital: The Degradation of Work in the Twentieth Century* (New York, 1974), and Richard Edwards, *Contested Terrain: The Transformation of the Workplace in the Twentieth Century* (New York, 1978), among many other titles. Michael Burawoy provides an exciting analysis of the literature concerning the workplace in "Towards a Marxist Theory of the Labour Process: Braverman and Beyond", *Politics & Society,* VIII (1978), pp. 247-312.

their employer filled the shop with apprentices. On the other hand, coal miners managed to enforce a form of apprenticeship through safety legislation which imposed a waiting period on new miners before they could advance "to the picks" and become fully-fledged miners. They were not able, however, to impose effective legal restrictions upon the new machine runners who played an important role in the Cape Breton mines.[40]

A second sort of control over entry to the labour market was the demand for union recognition and the related (but not identical) insistence upon the exclusive employment of union members (the "closed shop"). The craftsmen of the Maritimes were rather surprisingly not prone to press closed-shop demands. Such strikes were mounted by Truro painters in 1904, Saint John painters in 1905, and the Halifax building trades in 1914 (in sympathy with plumbers faced with strikebreakers), but with mixed results. The most dramatic failure occurred in the Halifax printing trades, when the composing room staff of the Halifax *Chronicle* and *Echo*, from the foreman to the boys, went on strike to protest the employment of a non-union machinist on their monolines. This strike failed, as did an attempt by Saint John carpenters to enforce the city-wide closed shop in 1907. This record seems to correspond with other evidence suggesting a weakening of the craftsmen's position in the region during this period.[41]

By contrast, both longshoremen and coal miners made significant advances. In 1907, Halifax longshoremen scored a signal victory when they went on strike to lend some weight to a "distinct understanding" that non-union men were not to be employed. Their success in this strike marked the culmination of a sporadic campaign to control hiring that went back to 1884. The coal miners in the PWA staged an impressive province-wide struggle for the closed shop from 1905-1907 — a campaign which strengthened the union immeasurably after its defeat in Sydney in 1904. In Westville, for example, the coal miners simply posted notices about the works to the effect that they would not work with non-union men after 5 November 1906. As a result of the notice, 100 non-union men joined Ladysmith Lodge of the PWA. A similar struggle in Chignecto (which began as a wage dispute but escalated into a demand for the closed shop and union recognition) forced the resignation of the general manager, James Baird.[42]

Secondly, workers defended their rights to job control by limiting management's right to dismiss employees. Some of these strikes were poignant reminders of the helplessness of many organized and unskilled workers in the face

40 *Sun*, 23 April 1903; *Amherst Daily News*, 3 May 1902, *Herald*, 12 July 1902. For an analysis of the weakening of the miners' resistance to the employment of machine runners without the training period, see Donald Macleod, "Miners, Mining Men and Mining Reform: Changing the Technology of Nova Scotian Gold Mines and Collieries, 1850 to 1910", PhD Thesis, University of Toronto, 1981, pp. 538-45.

41 *Herald*, 19 July 1904; *Sun*, 1 June 1905; Vol. 303, file 14 (28) RG 27; *Sun*, 6 August 1902; *Sun*, 28 March 1907 and Vol. 294, file 2838, RG 27.

42 *Herald*, 7 August 1907; Vol. 295, file 2989, RG 27; *Herald*, 5, 12 February 1907; *Herald*, 7 November 1906; *Herald*, 11 April 1906.

of arbitrary employers. The boys who worked at the Victoria Bowling Alley in Saint John went on strike to protest the dismissal of another boy who had had the misfortune to get sick. About 300 workers at the Nova Scotia Car Works in Halifax went on strike in 1911 after the management fired their unofficial representative, who had tried to interview the employer about new rules being enforced by the company. Gold miners at the Boston-Richardson mine in Goldboro were incensed when the management fired miners who had had the temerity to take time off to vote in an election, but the workers were not reinstated. In such situations, the unorganized workers were at the mercy of the employers.[43]

Once again, the heartland of control lay in the coalfields, the antithesis of the authoritarian world of the unskilled labourer. It seemed, to weary newspaper editors and irate mine managers, that the coal miners would protest if anyone was ever discharged from a coal mine. There was criticism of the miners of Westville, for example, who tied up their mine from 3 April to 25 April 1905 over a discharge of a man accused of improperly grooming the horses. Should a major industry be tied up by so trivial an issue? But for the miners the issue concerned not only whether the hostler involved should be fired but whether the union could claim him as a member. As the men's committee explained its position: "The company say there must be discipline, the men say granted, but let it be tempered with mercy". The employee was reinstated.[44] So often in the coal mines of this period we find the clash of two irreconcilable rights, the right to independence and work, and the right to discipline and fire. As the press noted with regard to a strike of boys in Springhill in 1906, "With the company it is a question of regulation, and with the boys it is a question of upholding the right of a person to keep his own job if he so desires provided there is no breach of discipline". But where did the boundaries of just discipline lie? In 1906, according to the coal boys of Springhill, they did not enclose such vital issues as dismissal or the allocation of work within the mine. In November of that year they went on strike because a trip runner formerly on the 2,600-foot level was moved up to the 3,200-foot level, and the runner from the latter level placed at inferior employment. This was considered unjust. They also insisted on the reinstatement of a loader who had been dismissed for loading boxes without the proper weight. The strike ended in a compromise which suited the boys, and prompted the general manager to comment, "We own the works, we pay the wages; we have some right to say where and how our employees shall work". These strikes by the lowliest workers of the mine suggest the industrial freedom its other workers must have enjoyed, in marked contrast to the harsh discipline of so many factories and construction sites.[45]

43 *Eastern Labour News*, 5 February 1910; *Eastern Labour News*, 9 September 1911; *Evening Mail* (Halifax), 19, 22, 25 March 1904.

44 *Herald*, 10, 12, 25 April 1905.

45 *Herald*, 29, 30 November 1906; see also *Amherst Daily News*, 7 December 1906, and *Herald*, 15 December 1906.

The question of supervision surfaces with frequency in the record of the strikes. The selection of foremen was generally conceded to be the exclusive prerogative of management, and only in the case of the printers and a few very minor officials in the coal mines were supervisors included within the union. But workers occasionally influenced the selection process. The Intercolonial trackmen of Saint John and district forced the resignation of their sub-foreman as an act of solidarity with their brothers on the Canadian Pacific system. This subforeman had worked as a strikebreaker during a recent strike, and the unionized trackmen described his appointment as an insult. There was something of a tradition of this in Charlotte County. Workers in Milltown appealed to an entrenched local hostility to the foreign owners of the cotton factory when they fought the selection of a new foreman in 1902. Since the arrival of the new foreman, an American, a number of local overseers had been discharged and their places filled with newcomers from other mills. The community and employees were outraged. The community felt that the company was betraying an informal agreement that it would give preference in promotion to citizens of Milltown, an offence which seemed particularly heinous in light of the large tax concessions made to the company. Workers urged that the Alien Labour Law be applied against the "small army" of men and women who worked in the New Brunswick mill from Calais, Maine. The upshot of this agitation was the resignation of the "Arrogant Yankee Cotton Mill Superintendent" and his replacement by a native of Milltown, whose elevation was said to have given "very general satisfaction among all classes". Two months later, however, weavers at the same mill went on strike against the dismissal of a popular overseer in the weave room. which suggests the debate over foremanship had not been completely resolved. Even in Ganong's candy factory in St. Stephen, that fortress of paternalism, women workers fought against the appointment of an unpopular supervisor.[46]

Workers throughout the region fought a surprising number of strikes against the dismissal of popular foremen, and this suggests the pivotal (and ambiguous) role the foreman was asked to play in the transformation of work. Sydney machinists went on strike on behalf of a foreman who had merely had a fistfight with the superintendent. Cotton factory workers in Saint John, car workers in Amherst, and coal drivers in Glace Bay all fought strikes on this issue. Workers in fact did influence the foremen whose day-to-day supervision placed them on the front lines of any transformation of work. The way in which supervision was carried out was often cited as an issue in strikes. Halifax boilermakers cited the constant "nagging" of supervisors in the Halifax Graving Dock Company as one of the primary reasons for the strike of 1907; they were continually being told to hurry up and hated what they called the "continual fault-finding" with their work. The pipefitters in the employ of the Nova Scotia Steel and Coal Company at Sydney Mines went on strike for overtime on Sundays, but they

46 *Sun*, 11 September 1901; *Sun*, 12 January, 9 February, 14 March 1903; *St. Croix Courier*, 13 April 1911.

cited the quality of supervision as an important contributing factor. "The men also claim that there were too many bosses over them, the majority of whom did not understand their business", noted the Sydney *Daily Post*. The coal mines provided the classic location for such foremanship struggles. Coal mines could be thrown into an uproar by an official who disregarded longstanding traditions or treated colliers in an offensive manner. A strike at Dominion No. 2 in Glace Bay was caused by the peremptory decision to change the basis on which drivers had been paid, a case, noted the *Herald* correspondent, "of dissatisfaction among employees that on the appointment of a new official, sweeping changes may be looked for, and which are generally so distasteful to them as to result in a strike . . .". Similarly, the abrasiveness and lack of courtesy of supervisory staff at the Springhill mines were a crucial factor in the town's many labour battles.[47]

Often the workers' dissatisfaction with working conditions crystallized in attacks upon individual foremen, and the more general debate over the nature of work was thereby overshadowed. Yet there were such general debates. While no major figure in the Maritimes came forth to advocate a fully-fledged programme of scientific management, the creation of Dominion Coal in 1893 was based on the assumption that local coal producers would attain American standards of efficiency. Local mining men, faced with the pressures of high demand and growing concentration in their industry, had every incentive to reduce their costs of production and increase productivity. While they could turn to mining machines and greater efficiency in the bankhead, most of the classic solutions of scientific management theory were wholly inappropriate for the mining environment. Many of the struggles over authority in the workplace were related to "scientific management", and stemmed from a largely frustrated attempt to make the mines into efficient factories.[48] In Springhill, for instance, coal miners and management fought each other implacably over such issues as the proper weight of a box, how much the company should penalize workers for loading stone in the boxes, whether the amount of coal produced by the worker should be measured at the top of the chute or on the surface — all issues which detailed investigation shows were connected with a broadly-conceived modernization programme. Nobody outside the coal mines really grasped why the town was so frequently engulfed in conflicts over such arcane issues, but both labour and

47 *Herald*, 23 October 1902; *Globe*, 4 December 1902; *Amherst Daily News*, 14 January 1904 and *Herald*, 15 January 1904; *Maritime Mining Record*, 18 June 1902; *Herald*, 24 October 1907;*Herald*, 23 September 1905 and *Daily Post*, 21 September 1905; *Herald*, 11 February 1904; *Herald*, 17 June 1905. The question of foremanship is discussed effectively in Joseph Melling, " 'Non-Commissioned Officers': British Employers and Their Supervisory Workers, 1880-1920," *Social History*, V (May, 1980), pp. 183-221.

48 See Hugh Archbald, *The Four Hour Day in Coal* (New York, 1922), Carter Goodrich, *The Miner's Freedom: A Study in the Working Life of a Changing Industry* (Boston, 1925), and Keith Dix, *Work Relations in the Coal Industry: The Hand-Loading Era, 1880-1930* (Morgantown, W. Va., 1977).

capital realized their importance for the miners' wages and the management's development programme. When labour legislation required the intervention of third parties, the imbroglio was complete — mystified judges were hardly able to catch up on the intricacies of coal mining in a few days. Coal miners knew the mining context inside out, and nothing could be more comprehensive than their critiques of past mismanagement and their programmes for reform. A good example is provided by the coal miners of Inverness, who outside the heroic years of 1909-11 were relatively quiet. Yet pushed into a strike by the institution of a new dockage system in 1906, they produced an impressive ten-point programme for the reform of their mine, which included new rates for track-laying, pushing boxes, shovelling down coal in heads and balances, brushing roof, and shot-firing. It was a "bread-and-butter" strike, but the mine management correctly interpreted it as an attempt to tell them how they should run the mine.[49]

The coal miners were in the vanguard of such general assaults on managerial authority. Much of this had to do with the particular circumstances of their work. Safety strikes loomed far larger in the coal mines than elsewhere. Coal miners were convinced that their own safety standards were at least as rigorous as those of the state or management. The miners of Chignecto, for example, refused to go down into their pit unless the company agreed to send down their picks together in the morning instead of leaving it up to each man to take down his own. Middle-class commentators thought this was a prime example of mindless militancy, the demand being "so trivial . . . that outsiders cannot believe a settlement will be long delayed". Such comments reflected ignorance of mining conditions in Cumberland, where steeply-pitching coal seams made carrying picks a tricky and sometimes even fatal business. The miners of Joggins were equally stubborn in waiting to re-enter their mine until they were guaranteed that a recent fire had been extinguished, and those of Port Morien in refusing to go back unless ventilation was improved. Since the miners had a written code of safety regulations and a secure trade union, they could more often wage struggles for safety that lay beyond the reach of other workers — who were left struggling, with some effect, for workmen's compensation and factory inspection.[50]

Scientific management is a sub-text of the history of strikes in this period, and rarely surfaces explicitly, either in resistance to new time-keeping measures or mechanization. Workmen at Cushing's mill at Union Point fought against a new time-marking machine in 1903, principally because it caused such crowding and crushing of men that the "strong got ahead of the weak"; it was noted that "dislike of the scheme has grown intense". J.B. Snowball told his mill workers in Chatham that they could easily be replaced by a new carrier system, and hod

49 *Chronicle,* 3 December 1903, *Amherst Daily News,* 2, 3 December 1903; *Sun,* 4, 7 December 1903 detail one such Springhill dispute; *Herald,* 19 March 1906.

50 *Herald,* 14 January 1904; *Herald,* 1 February 1904; *Chronicle,* 24 January 1903.

men were replaced with a steam carrier in a Saint John dispute in 1907. Far more common were new methods of calculating wages which entailed speeding up the performance of work. A classic instance of this was the strike at the Hartt Boot and Shoe Company in Fredericton, sparked by the attempt of an American manager to introduce piece work for the cutters. It appears that this "reform" was successfully resisted. A new bonus system was the cause of a strike at Pender's nail factory in 1911, and nailworkers also protested the adoption of the system at the Maritime Nail Works in 1914.[51] Other workers were incensed by production speed-ups, which often contradicted well-established notions of "a fair day's work". In Chatham workers refused to work in gangs of six instead of seven, arguing that "the work is heavy enough as it is with seven". Perhaps the most interesting struggle against intensified working schedules — and incidentally the one documented case of a "strike on the job" in this period — comes from the workers of a cotton factory in Saint John:

> The weavers state that they are paid by the piece, or cut, as it is technically called, getting from 37 to 45 cents per cut. A cut, in the past, was sixty yards, and on this basis the men were paid. Some time ago the manager of the mill increased the cut to sixty-five yards, and as no action was taken by the men, a further increase of five yards was made more recently. The weavers state that they were thus expected to make seventy yards of cloth for the same money as they had previously received for sixty yards . . . They say that they objected to this increase in the length of the cut, and complained, but as no remedy was provided, they of their own accord cut the cloth at the old sixty yard mark. This was discovered, and the men were warned to desist.

The strike resulting from this conflict lasted only one hour, but it was obviously part of a protracted struggle through which the workers had sabotaged the company's speeding up of production.[52]

We find a general attempt to change old rhythms of work, to speed things up and get more effort from workers. Steelworkers in Sydney, ferry engineers in Dartmouth, coal miners everywhere suggested that this was the new reality they faced. In a rare attempt to spell out the general implications of this question, a commentary on a strike of Springhill coal boys against dockage linked this very particular struggle to more general debates over the intensity of labour: "The men, and many of the most thoughtful ones too, consider that a workman should do a fair day's work and make a fair day's pay, but when he works early and late, and slaves between to produce big pay, they consider him unreason-

51 *Globe*, 6 March 1903; Vol. 294, file 2913, RG 27; *Labour Gazette*, VII (1905), p. 951; *Daily Gleaner*, 13, 31 May 1909, *North Shore Leader* (Newcastle), 4 June 1909; Vol. 298, file 3436 and Vol. 303, file 14 (36) RG 27; *Sun*, 28 May 1907 (Chatham).

52 *Sun*, 7, 8 March 1905.

able, and an enemy to his fellows, because he has created conditions which an average steady worker, who properly respects the constitution God has given him, cannot produce the amount he should receive".[53]

David Montgomery has observed that the struggles waged by workers in the United States in the early 20th century to establish collective control over their conditions of work were less richly rewarded in their long-term effects than such general campaigns as that for the eight-hour day. Workplace issues were hard to generalize. Only in some of the coal strikes did workers take their demands for workplace reforms and transform these into demands for workers' control of industry. Such writers as Carter Goodrich have recognized the distinction between "negative" responses to new systems of work and "positive" demands for general workers' control.[54] Most of the control struggles of this period were defensive. Many were sparked by the workers' dislike of bad manners, high-handed autocracy and favouritism. Among the many items on the indictment brought against J.R. Cowans of Springhill by his workmen were his absolute lack of tact and his inability to "receive a committee of men in a gentlemanly manner". As one Halifax bricklayer explained in a strike for the eight-hour day: "What we object to . . . is the autocratic way in which the bosses grant the eight-hour day when they like and refuse to grant it when they don't like". There was a general social critique in such remarks. As the miners of Springhill argued: "The manager in charge at Springhill cannot appreciate that a man working in his mines at Springhill is STILL A MAN, and after 18 years of experience has not yet learned that the miners are rational, intelligent, human beings, with more than ordinary amount of general information, and education, and while they are amenable to reason, will not be dogged or driven". "It's not money they want", James Pender wrote of his militant workers in 1911, "they want to browbeat us, in other words, want to run the show". Not many employers would have shared his alarm, but in the coalfields some would have agreed with him. Struggles for job controls, if conducted in a certain way and in a disciplined manner, did carry the risk of developing into battles for workers' control. As one Springhill miner urged in 1909, the struggle for the workplace could be expanded into a critique of all autocracy: "[A] time comes in the life of nations, it comes in the life of communities, and in the life of organizations when THEY CANNOT ENDURE ANY LONGER THE IMPOSITIONS FORCED ON THEM BY AN AUTOCRATIC AND OVERBEARING SPIRIT".[55]

The questions remain, what difference did the strikes of 1901-1914 really make to the evolution of regional society? Did they really represent a moment of

53 *Chrinicle*, 2 October 1903; *Evening Mail*, 24 June 1908; *Amherst Daily News*, 29 March 1901; *Herald*, 4 July 1906.

54 Montgomery, "New unionism", p. 98; Carter Goodrich, *The Frontier of Control: A Study in British Workshop Politics* (London, 1975 [1920]), p. 258.

55 *Herald*, 2 November 1909; *Herald*, 6 May 1908; *Herald*, 22 August 1907; Vol. 298, file 3436, RG 27; *Herald*, 17 August 1909.

possibility for critics of capitalism? Why was the system able to contain them? What do they tell us about the working class of the region and the level of working-class consciousness?

There can be no doubt that workers struggled against heavy odds and suffered crushing defeats. The coal miners, after nearly two years and expenditures nearing a million dollars, were denied the union of their choice and returned to work under humiliating conditions. Millmen in Saint John and moulders in Moncton and Sackville had suffered reverses. No strong regional labour movement emerged and workers were still without political representation. If the strike movement could be seen as a social challenge, this challenge was contained.

But we need to examine more closely the way in which this containment took place. This means looking more closely at the place of politics, and at the measures taken by the state. It must be remembered that workers enjoyed certain natural advantages in struggles with capital. A crowd of strikers could be assembled in a picket line that could stop production; sympathizers could make life intolerable for strikebreakers; workers could go on strike without warning to obtain redress for their grievances — which in many industrial contexts, particularly coal mining, meant that the companies either gave in or ran the risk of losing their investment. Nothing had happened in the labour process which had destroyed many workers' capacity for autonomous action. All of these considerations lead us to the state as the crucial new force which contained labour's challenge to capital.

The strike was frequently represented as a threat to public order and civilization itself, but violence was extremely rare and confined to very particular circumstances. Of the 22 strikes which were reported to involve some physical force (fist-fights, stone-throwing, riots), 15 involved foreign workers. No one was killed as a direct consequence of labour disputes, which suggests the generally peaceful character of strikes in the region as compared with many parts of the United States. The Saint John *Sun* "explained" the foreigners' violence by referring to the "passionate and unreflecting races from southern and southeastern Europe," but it is more plausibly viewed as the logical response of isolated construction workers, who saw forceable action as the only means of negotiating with contractors. "Collective bargaining by riot", to use E.J. Hobsbawm's useful phrase, was a predictable consequence of their conditions of employment.[56] At Hubbard's Cove in 1902, Italians employed on the Halifax and South Western Railway surrounded the house occupied by the timekeeper and started to burn it down, but were discouraged by their foreman. Later the same day the workers, armed with revolvers and axes, approached the house and began to demolish it. Once they obtained the timekeeper's books and confirmed their suspicion that they had been cheated of their wages, they dispersed, having been promised the wages due them. New Brunswick rang with large disturb-

---

56 *Sun*, 3 June 1904; E.J. Hobsbawm, "The Machine Breakers", in *Labouring Men: Studies in the History of Labour* (London, 1974), p. 16.

ances mounted by railway labourers in this period. Near Moncton, Italian, Austrian and Bulgarian workers demanded a wage increase. They paraded behind a "huge red flag", carrying clubs and firearms. They marched to the offices of the Grand Trunk Pacific in Moncton, where three were arrested. More than 800 Italians near Campbellton mounted a similar protest, also flourishing weapons and a red flag. Railway labourers working near Windsor Junction sent their foreman to hospital in 1904, and Hungarians labouring at the steel mill demolished the residence of a strikebreaker.[57] Apart from these construction disturbances, so reminiscent of the 19th century, disorder was found in the two major tramway strikes in Halifax (1913) and Saint John (1914), the Sydney steel strike of 1904, and the three large strikes in the coalfields in 1909-11. In Cape Breton in 1910 company police and UMW supporters clashed, shots were fired, and two men were injured. Ten arrests were made, five on a charge of unlawful assembly and five for carrying concealed weapons. The front porch of Robert Simpson, manager at Reserve Mines, was blown up; responsibility for this act was never fixed. There were also clashes between strikebreakers and strikers in Springhill.[58]

Condensed in this way, it may appear that the record of strikes was highly violent, but given the much larger number of peaceful strikes, the absence of fatalities, and the presence of armies of detectives and militia, one is left wondering why so few disturbances occurred. Part of the reason appears to have been labour's consistent policy of non-violent protest. The PWA in 1904, facing the mass mobilization of Sydney steelworkers, hastened to reassure Nova Scotians that the strike would bear no resemblance to strikes in Europe and the United States, where "lawlessness, growing out of ignorance and vindictive spite, reign supreme". When non-unionized Italians attacked a policeman, the PWA appointed a committee to assist the city police in maintaining order among the immigrants living near the steel plant. The union dramatized its devotion to law and order by giving the militia hearty cheers on its return to Halifax, and "soldiers just as heartily returned the cheers". The PWA was pleased to announce that it had done "all they could to save the country the disgrace of having the riot act read", and the *Herald*, drawing the intended moral, remarked that "Such behavior is certainly not that of men imbued with the spirit of lawlessness and brute force".[59]

For a strike lasting 22 months and broken with troops and strikebreakers, the great Springhill strike of 1909-11 was a triumph of law and order. The strikers knew the propaganda value the company would extract from a show of disorder. (Four years earlier J.R. Cowans had described the beginning days of a strike as an "orgy" and the "biggest drunk ever witnessed in Springhill", although no-

57 *Herald*, 24, 29 December 1902; *Sun*, 3, 4 August 1908, and *Amherst Daily News*, 5 August 1908; *Sun* , 12 August 1908; *Herald*, 9 August 1904; *Herald* and *Sun*, 3 May 1904.

58 *Herald*, 11 January 1910; *Herald*, 17, 28 July 1909; *Sun*, 1 March 1910.

59 *Herald*, 28 June 1904; *Sun*, 16 June 1904; *Herald*, 12 July 1904.

body else seems to have noticed any disturbance). The UMW collaborated with the mayor to protect the town against fire, and urged members not to give the company "a point against them, but still maintain the same silent and determined struggle they have carried through for over a year". Victory would come only through endurance, patience and self-control. The records of the local UMW document the union's preoccupation with keeping the peace.[60]

The labour movement advocated non-violent and passive strikes. But both the state and capital championed far more aggressive and forceful approaches. Troops, detectives, spies, special constables: on a scale never before imagined, these were the *dramatis personae* of these years. Employers used spies in Halifax in 1907 during a longshoremen's strike, and detectives and company police were everywhere in the coalfields. It was difficult to tell where the public police stopped and capital's private army began. Saint John police refused to arrest strikebreakers who attacked strikers in 1905, and even helped to recruit strikebreakers on another occasion. Such modest efforts paled beside the great show of force brought to bear upon the strikers in the coalfields. Those who watched the scene thought instinctively in military metaphors, as we find in one sensitive portrait of Glace Bay's deserted company houses:

> When a man is evicted from his house by the Dominion Coal company, because he has refused to work, no time is lost by the officials in putting their mark upon the empty dwelling. White boards are nailed tightly over the glass. No pains are taken to do the job artistically. All that is wanted is to make the job secure. So all over town are seen those windowless houses, not the sign of martial encounters, but the mark of an industrial struggle unparalleled in the determination of the contending armies to fight to a finish and which, tho' bloodless, is no less fierce than if the march of war-like men were seen and the roar of artillery heard.

Nobody could quite understand why the troops had been brought in, nor why they came with such fire-power. Nearly a quarter of Canada's fighting men were in Cape Breton by July 1909. Puzzled citizens wondered at the necessity of a "force which is of greater dimensions than many a punitive expedition against African tribes", combined with seven or eight hundred special constables. If all this were primarily an "aid to the civil power", it seemed odd that the representatives of civil power most concerned, the mayors of Springhill and Glace Bay, were against the coming of the troops.[61]

60 *Herald*, 21 June 1905; *Herald*, 12 August 1910; Minutes of UMW Local Union 469, Springhill, entry for 6 January 1910, Angus L. Macdonald Library, St. Francis Xavier University, Antigonish, indicates the miners' active interest in suppressing drinking and disorder.

61 John Bell, ed., "On The Waterfront: A Glimpse into Company Espionage", *Bulletin of the Committee on Canadian Labour History*, I (1976), pp. 8-9, documents the use of spies in Halifax; *Sun*, 28 November 1905; *Herald*, 20 October 1909; *Herald*, 14 July 1909. For the use of local spies at Acadia Coal, Westville, see John Higston to C. Evans, 30 May 1913, RG 21,

The troops were not required to preserve public order, but they were needed if the strikebreakers were to continue to keep the mines open. They were the embodiment of the new economy of labour, the free labour market carrying a gun. The state, through violence, safeguarded the achievement of the new consolidated economy of labour and prevented workers from erecting effective barriers against it. It also moved decisively to change the terms of power within the workplace.

Trade unions of this period enjoyed few formal rights, and many doubts existed as to what they could or could not do. Incorporation of trade unions, legislation on arbitration, and their daily participation in local communities, all provided trade unionists with a certain legitimacy, but without many guaranteed legal rights. The dominant trait of Canadian labour law was an emphasis on "fire-fighting", that is, asserting "the public interest" strictly at the point of actual or apprehended conflict (and not at the point of maintaining trade-union rights in bargaining nor making sure the bargain was kept once arrived at). The Industrial Disputes Investigation Act (1907), the most important piece of federal legislation in this period, was intended to operate in utilities, railroads and coal mines, and required compulsory investigation before a strike or lockout began. The terms of employment would be frozen, and an attempt to reach an agreement was to be made by a conciliation board; if this didn't work, the board's report became public and both workers and employers were restored to their common-law rights and duties. No protection was given to unions, and even a collective agreement reached under the Act had no status in law.[62]

The IDIA is often seen as a fairly mild act, which may even have narrowed the possible scope of state intervention by hiving off a particular sector of the economy for special treatment. From the point of view of the Maritimes, however, the IDIA appears to have been a major revolution in the region's most militant workplaces, the waterfronts and the coal mines. The Act must be placed within the context of the state's use of massive displays of force to crush strikes. The Act provided no guarantees that employees would not be dismissed before or after the period of compulsory investigation, and thus ensured that employees could be victimized with impunity. Especially in the coal mines, the results were dramatic: miners could no longer conduct their swift strikes on control issues, which had won them so much direct power in the period 1901-1907; instead, they had to wait and give management as much time as it required to undermine dissidents by any number of means. Workers lost the advantages of speed and sur-

Series "A", Vol. 39, No. 38, PANS. The company was kept abreast of developments within the UMW by the Thiel Detective Agency. For a general interpretation, see Desmond Morton, "Aid to the Civil Power: The Canadian Militia in Support of Social Order", *Canadian Historical Review*, LI (1970), pp. 407-425.

62 A.W.R. Carrothers, *Collective Bargaining Law in Canada* (Toronto, 1965), p. 32; the emergence of the IDIA is described by Paul Craven, *'An Impartial Umpire': Industrial Relations and the Canadian State 1900-1911* (Toronto, 1980).

prise, but employers lost no real power whatever. Ideologically, the IDIA was a heaven-sent weapon for capital. Manipulating the near-universal respect for the law, which the non-violent character of the labour movement reveals so well, the Act cast a suspicion of illegality and unreason over the pursuit of collective rights. The long history of conciliation in Springhill from 1907 to 1909 confirmed the usefulness of the Act for management, as board after board tried to understand mining issues, contradicted one another, issued confusing judgments, and muddied the issues beyond belief. The management broadcast far and wide the decisions of boards in its favour, but 'when one board (for once including some knowledgeable mining men) criticized the treatment of the coal miners, the company treated its finding as a joke. When a conciliation board ruled that the miners of Springhill had no right to affiliate with an international union because this would imperil local interests, its ruling was popularly seen as an edict based on the law itself, and not the verdict of a few opinionated individuals.[63]

The example of the dispute in Inverness, the second of the three great strikes of 1909-11, highlights the effects of the new legal structure. The mine at Inverness was controlled by those archetypical creatures of the new age, Mackenzie and Mann, and employed 600 men. In a referendum leading up to a split within the PWA, supporters of the UMW numbered only 96, but the international union gradually won over three-quarters of the mineworkers. The PWA had negotiated a check-off of union dues with the company in 1906, and the company refused to stop the collection of dues for the PWA even after a majority of the miners turned against the old union. Then the company circulated typewritten cards to individual miners, which ostensibly allowed individuals to stop the deduction of PWA dues from their pay, and many miners signed these cards. Then, one by one, the company discharged every miner who had done so. Despite appeals from the UMW, it refused to change its policies, and on 9 July 1909 the coal miners came out on strike. Two days later the troops arrived, to protect new strikebreakers and the small number of "loyal" workers. Now the real genius of the IDIA was revealed. Although the miners had been individually fired and the "strike" called by the union was very much only a formal recognition of their dismissal, the union had not taken the precaution of consulting with the Department of Labour and going through the conciliation procedure. The coal miners' strike was therefore illegal. The UMW could be prosecuted for providing food for the strikers' families, since under Section 60, Chapter 20 of the Act, supplying provisions to a striker prior to reference of a dispute to a Board of Conciliation and Investigation was illegal. The Supreme Court of Nova

---

63 For the confusion surrounding conciliation in Springhill, partly caused by a complex decision by a judge who interpreted his own ruling differently than everybody else — and announced his revision after a strike of two and a half months — see *Amherst Daily News*, 20 October 1907; criticisms of the conciliation process were made by workers (*Herald*, 7 October 1907) and newspaper editors (*Sun*, 24 October 1907); for the use of the conciliation board reports by the company for propaganda, see the *Herald*, 23 October 1909.

Scotia, which heard the case on appeal, thought it self-evident that giving food to hungry strikers fell within the sphere of prohibited support under the Act. "It is difficult to conceive any more effectual means of aiding strikers than those found in the present case", noted the Court. "It is of course precisely the aid wanted to enable tthe [sic] strikers to live during the pendency of the strike, and it hardly needs comment to show that the defendant as an agent of the United Mine Workers of America so gave the aid with the express and sole purpose of enabling the strikers to stay out until their demands were complied with". The "conciliatory" legislation of 1907 had revealed its coercive essence: under the IDIA the company was allowed to train the physical weapon of starvation and distress against its employees and their children. It was small wonder that coal miners despised the Act.[64]

The IDIA was only one aspect of the legal offensive against labour. Great progress was made in the art of issuing injunctions against picketing and in applying the doctrine that trade unions could be held liable for economic costs imposed on employers. In another case, defendants against whom no evidence had been brought, were nonetheless forbidden to "watch and beset", because the "balance of convenience" dictated that "No injury surely can be suffered by defendants by being restrained from committing alleged illegal acts which they deny". Canadian labour law was profoundly influenced by such cases as "The Cumberland Railway and Coal Co. v. McDougall et al.", which helped place the injunction at the centre of reactions to strikes.[65]

As a force for labour peace, the IDIA was a disaster. As a response to the dependence of an increasingly interconnected economy upon fossil fuels, and as a fillip to the emergence of an aggressively authoritarian state apparatus, the Act was a stroke of genius. Combined with the existing laws against combination and disorder, and the para-military paraphernalia of barbed-wire compounds and armed strikebreakers, the IDIA served to guarantee the preservation of the free labour market. At the same time it removed most important direct powers from the coal miners. It thus represented a victory for capital in both the new labour market and in the subordination of labour in the workplace.[66]

---

64 *Herald*, 10 July 1909; "Rex v. Neilson" (1910), *Eastern Law Reporter*, Vol . IX (1910), pp. 210-213.

65 "Dominion Coal Co. Ltd. v. Bousfield et al.", *Eastern Law Reporter*, Vol. VIII (1909), pp. 145-149; "Cumberland Railway and Coal Co. v. McDougall et al.", Nova Scotia *Reports*, Vol. XLIV (1909-1910), p. 544. The importance of this latter case was underlined by A.C. Crysler, *Labour Relations and Precedents in Canada: A Commentary on Labour Law and Practice in in Canada* (Toronto, 1949), p. 32. For a less famous court case, in which a PWA lodge was held to have violated the rights of an individual by insisting upon the closed shop at Westville, see *Maritime Mining Record*, 26 August 1903.

66 The dramatic regional impact of the IDIA is revealed in the estimate of F.A. Acland of the Department of Labour, that three-fourths of the miners of Nova Scotia in 1909 were working under terms recommended by a conciliation board, or arranged while a conciliation board was being established: Department of Labour, *Report of the Deputy Minister of Labour on*

In Springhill and Cape Breton, the limits beyond which the pursuit of conciliation and consensus no longer applied were unforgettably exposed. On 31 July 1909, large numbers of UMW men and their supporters gathered at the Athletic Grounds in Glace Bay. They were about to march to Dominion to protest against the coal company. They marched peacefully, carrying the Union Jack. As they neared a Catholic church at the boundary of Glace Bay and Dominion, they were startled by something new: a machine gun nest and a group of artillerymen, who seemed ready to mow them down if they tried to proceed to their destination. As they returned to Glace Bay, the marchers must have reflected on the new realities of state power and the limitations these imposed upon public assembly and freedom of speech. Whatever William Lyon Mackenzie King's impenetrable doctrines of conciliation amounted to, they barely concealed the crucial fact that, in defence of capitalism, the state was prepared to kill.[67]

However we evaluate the social challenge represented by the strikes of these years, we should remember that the state regarded them with utmost seriousness. Maritime workers failed to remake their society, but they faced very powerful enemies at a time when their awareness of themselves was only just developing. The system did not survive only through the creative response of the state. Workers themselves were not prepared to endorse a coherent alternative to the system. In the great coalfields' strikes women turned out *en masse*, but only a small minority of women workers ever fought strikes, and there was little challenge to traditional family roles in the working class. Only occasionally did strikers make connections between industrial actions and politics. Many pointed critiques of bonussing, for example, were made during the course of strikes, and sharp words were directed against state subsidies by the men who fought the steamship lines. Local politicians were subject to sharp criticisms during some strikes, but only in Cape Breton in 1904 (when a labour party was formed immediately in the wake of the defeat of the steel strike) and in the coalfields in 1909-11 (that "harvest time for socialists"), can we make a direct connection between strikes and radical ideological shifts. Part of the ambiguity was the ability of the mainstream politicians to absorb radical rhetoric and even concede working-class demands. There could be no better example of this responsiveness than the progressive policies followed by the Nova Scotia Liberals, who constructed an alliance with the PWA to help consolidate their long hold on provincial political power.[68]

If we measure class consciousness solely by the number of socialist ballots

---

Industrial Conditions in the Coal Fields of Nova Scotia (Ottawa, 1909), p. 32. The IDIA was also used to settle disputes of Halifax freighthandlers, Halifax plumbers, and Saint John longshoremen.

67 See Danny Moore, "The 1909 Strike in the Nova Scotia Coal Fields", unpublished research essay, Carleton University, 1977, p. 97, for a good description of this incident.

68 For the aggressive tactics of women in coal strikes, see the *Herald*, 7, 13 July 1909; for an attack

cast, the workers of the Maritimes appear to have made only slight gains in this period. Yet this pessimistic view is too static, especially in any description of something as fluid and dynamic as consciousness. The evidence of the strikes reveals a more complex portrait. One of its most interesting aspects is the evident interest taken by workingmen in religion. It is a commonplace of Canadian social history that the first decades of the 20th century witnessed the emergence of the "social gospel" as a theological response to industrialism, but from the evidence of the strikes one gains an impression of workingmen themselves fighting for the social gospel and bringing pressure to bear against their churches. The *Eastern Labour News* covered the emergence of the new theological positions with energy and competence. Maritime workers were adamantly Christian, notwithstanding the heroic efforts of Marshall Govang, the region's first labour historian, who lectured car workers in Moncton on the benefits of Free Thought.[69] When Cape Breton mining families withdrew their children from Sunday School classes taught by company officials, or when the Salvation Army chaplain denied use of the church to strikebreakers in Springhill, they were taking important and dramatic steps. Letters to the *Herald* bristled with quotations from John Bunyan and Isaiah and demanded the Presbyterian church denounce the system of modern industry and its selfishness of spirit. We find clergymen taking emphatic steps to support local strikes. That a minister who sided with capital faced mixed reviews was illustrated by Rev. R.W. Norwood of Springhill, who denounced workers of Springhill for listening to revolutionary socialists. Not coincidentally, it was his valedictory sermon. He was attacked mercilessly by workingmen in the press. We confront a large array of evidence which suggests that workers were seeking a reconciliation of their religious beliefs with the realities of industrial conflict. In 1909 the *Herald* carried a dramatic story which illustrated this difficult situation. When a number of the wives of the strikers in Cape Breton were prevented from "interfering" with the strikebreakers and had no other way of manifesting their opposition, "they knelt down on the road and appealed to God with genuine fervour to cause the rocks in the pit to fall upon the objects of their hatred". Everywhere we find indications like this, of men and women looking for something — some confusedly, others entirely lucidly — a theological framework suited to the changed condi-

on steamship subsidies by a supporter of the longshoremen, see the *Herald*, 29 May 1907; the political impact of the 1904 steel strike is discussed by Ronald F. Crawley, "Class Conflict and the Establishment of the Sydney Steel Industry 1899-1904", M.A. thesis, Dalhousie University, 1980, pp. 121-2; the PWA/Liberal relationship is explored by Joe MacDonald, "The Roots of Radical Politics in Nova Scotia: The Provincial Workmen's Association and Political Activity, 1879-1906", B.A. thesis, Carleton University, 1977; Frank and Reilly, "Socialist Movement," pp. 99-101, discuss the political impact of the strike of 1909-11 in Springhill.

69 Colin McKay, the region's first radical sociologist, published important essays on the social gospel in the *Eastern Labour News* (see, for example, his study of new theology in the issue of 1 February 1913); for Govang and the Moncton Truth Seekers Association, see *Eastern Labour News*, 24 April, 1, 8 May 1909.

tions of social life.[70] It is not a portrait of religious stagnation that emerges from this evidence, nor can we infer political stagnation from the continuing hold of old parties without knowing more about the concessions they offered and the political imagery that they used.

The record of strikes cannot give us a portrait of the class, for there is a vast amount of additional evidence to consider before any definitive judgements are made about the general contours of Maritime working-class history. But insofar as this partial evidence allows us to reach some initial hypotheses about class consciousness, one can easily see that it undercuts the stereotype of "regional conservatism". The slow development of regional labour historiography denies us the pleasure of criticizing a "traditional interpretation" of Maritime workers. But one can well imagine what such a "traditional interpretation" might amount to. Denied large-scale immigration and demoralized by high levels of unemployment, the argument might run, Maritime workers inhabited small, isolated worlds, where paternalist employers provided the focus of life. Growing up in the isolated and stagnant communities of a traditional region, workers would not demand many changes in a time-honoured way of life. Cut off from the main traditions of North American trade unionism by their own isolation and the domination of the PWA, that "company union", the workers of the Maritimes lived in a social as well as economic hinterland, and only a few immigrants or peripatetic organizers helped to alleviate the "feudal" conditions of their oppression.[71]

The interpretation of working-class mobilization in 1901-1914 offered here contradicts such analysis. Nothing seems backward about the workers of the Maritimes in this period — not their struggles for job control, their eagerness to press for such general objectives as nine (or even eight) hours, their rethinking of religious traditions. Most of the issues raised in the workplaces of the Maritimes could as easily have been raised in England. Whatever the scope of paternalism in the 19th century, it was a waning force in this period. Living in a dynamic region with an abundance of jobs in construction, coal mining, and manufacturing, workers were making new contacts with their brothers in North America. Even more crucially, they were painstakingly developing a regional framework of class awareness, as seen in the new regional labour press, the work of Maritimes-based organizers in other parts of the region, and the inspiration drawn by workers from other regional strikes. When pulp workers in St. George, New Brunswick tried to justify their three-year struggle to themselves, they thought

---

70 *Herald*, 31 July 1909; *Herald*, 15 April 1910; *Herald*, 17 July 1909; *Herald*, 4 September 1909; *Herald*, 31 July 1909.

71 An interpretation which comes close to this stereotype is that of John Mellor, *The Company Store: James Bryson McLachlan and the Cape Breton Coal Miners, 1900-1925* (Toronto, 1983); see the effective critique by Don Macgillivray, "Cultural Strip-Mining in Cape Breton", *New Maritimes* (September 1983), p. 16.

of the long battles waged by the miners of Cape Breton and Springhill.[72]

One comes away from the strikes of 1901-1914 with two conflicting impressions. The first is that of monopoly capitalism reshaping the region and the working-class world, of a remorseless and inexorable process of consolidation. The second is that of a dynamic working-class movement, posing a real challenge to capital and to the traditional ruling classes of the Maritimes. It was a period of both defeat and awakening, a period in which both capital and labour were attaining greater strength. Perhaps this evidence suggests that working-class traditionalism in the Maritimes, like many other regional traditions, is of relatively recent vintage — a product of the economic collapse of the 1920s.

In Springhill in 1910, the workers displayed all the contradictory features of the new age. On 10 August 1910, a parade and picnic were held to mark the end of the first year of the Great Strike. It was a sign of the harsh defeats faced by workers in this new situation: on the very day of the parade, the company hoisted 641 tons of coal by using strikebreakers protected by the state. It would take another ten months to break the strike completely, but already the workers were fearing the worst. But was it not also a sign of the new consciousness and new discipline of labour? The procession formed up at Pioneer Hall, which had once rung to the mass meetings of the PWA, and then started down Main Street. First came the town band and a body of miners, then the band of the 93rd regiment, and then the children from the Socialist Sunday School, carrying small red flags. They were followed by another delegation of socialists, numbering about 100, who carried a large red flag. As the parade wound through Springhill, it passed house after house bedecked with red flags and banners. The parade finally reached the picnic grounds, where more than 4,000 people were gathered.[73] We know the marchers were also moving toward defeat, but their parade suggests the hopes of men and women, high in one colliery town, for a new social world. By raising high the banner of the modern enlightenment, they live on in our minds, symbols of an age of struggle and aspiration.

72 Christopher Wren to F.A. Acland, 9 September 1912, Vol. 298, file 3341, RG 27.
73 *Herald*, 11 August 1910.

E. R. FORBES

Reprinted from Vol. I, No. 1
(Autumn 1971)

Prohibition
and the
Social Gospel
in Nova Scotia

The success of the Prohibition movement in Nova Scotia in 1921 was a result of the transformation of a narrow nineteenth century temperance crusade, based upon rural values and ideas of personal salvation, into a broad campaign for progressive reform. Armed with a new idealism, leadership and greatly expanded institutional support, prohibition became politically irresistable. The change was brought about largely through the churches, in which development of a collectivist, reform theology accompanied the rise of progressive ideology in secular thought. As influential elements among the clergy became committed to the social gospel, as the new theology was called, they provided both an agency for the propagation of reform ideas and the leadership for their implementation[1]

Viewed in this context, the popular image of the prohibitionists as frustrated puritanical zealots bent on suppressing the pleasures of others rapidly breaks down. A detailed examination of the prohibition movement in Nova Scotia suggests that the prohibitionists were motivated primarily by a desire to eliminate the roots of human unhappiness. They wanted to create a new society in which crime, disease and social injustice would be virtually eliminated. Their success in committing society to these goals would be reflected both in the victory of prohibition in Nova Scotia and in its ultimate defeat.

1 Richard Allen's pioneering study of the social gospel provides the key to an understanding of the prohibition movement in Canada. Although more concerned with the impact of the social gospel in moulding attitudes towards labour, Allen devotes a chapter to prohibition and indicates the leading role played by the social reformers in the temperance movement. The Maritime Provinces, however, are largely neglected in this general study. A. Richard Allen, "The Crest and Crisis of the Social Gospel in Canada, 1916-1927" (unpublished Ph.D. thesis, Duke University, 1967). Also valuable are his "Salem Bland and the Social Gospel in Canada" (unpublished M.A. thesis, University of Saskatchewan, 1961); "The Social Gospel and the Reform Tradition in Canada, 1890-1928", *C.H.R.*, XLIX (1968), pp. 381-399; and "The Triumph and Decline of Prohibition" in J. M. Bumsted, *Documentary Problems in Canadian History* (Georgetown, Ontario, 1969).

The Nova Scotia crusade for prohibition rested upon a strong temperance tradition. In 1827, the community of West River, Pictou County, established what was later claimed to be the first organized temperance group in North America? The extension of an American fraternal Order, Sons of Temperance, to Nova Scotia in 1847 gained immediate acceptance and the colony served as a point of export for this item of North American culture to Great Britain? A similar group, the Order of Good Templars, entered the province in the early fifties. By 1900 other "total abstinence" groups included the Women's Christian Temperance Union, the Church of England Temperance Association and the Roman Catholic League of the Cross.

The agitation for prohibition dated from the mid-nineteenth century. It seems to have been spearheaded by the fraternal groups and actively supported by the evangelical churches. By the end of the century the movement had made some progress towards regulating and restricting the sale of alcoholic beverages. The *Report of the Dominion Royal Commission on the Liquor Traffic* in 1895 described Nova Scotia as "a strong temperance province."[4] It noted that liquor could be legally sold only in Halifax City and the two counties of Halifax and Richmond. Of the remaining sixteen "dry" counties, sales were prohibited in twelve under the Canada Temperance Act (Scott Act) of 1878 and in the other four by a stringent provincial act which required an annual petition by two-thirds of the local electorate to permit the renewal of liquor licences. Strong popular support for prohibition appeared to be indicated by the plebiscites of 1894 and 1898 which yielded majorities of more than three to one in favour.[5]

Yet one could easily exaggerate both the extent of prohibition and the sentiment supporting it in Nova Scotia before 1900. Certainly the people had never experienced nor, perhaps, did many of them yet envision, the "bone dry" legislation which would later be attempted. While it is true that the saloon had largely disappeared from rural Nova Scotia, there was nothing in the existing legislation to prevent an individual from ordering liquor from legal outlets. Shipments were regularly sent out by mail coach or train, frequently under the guise of groceries and other merchandise. To facilitate matters, the Halifax merchants deployed agents to take orders and make deliveries. In several towns, sales persisted as local councils, which were

2 *Report of the Royal Commission on Liquor Traffic* (Ottawa, Queen's Printer, 1895), p. 770. See also R. Elizabeth Spence, *Prohibition in Canada* (Toronto, The Ontario Branch of the Dominion Alliance, 1919), p. 38. Spence mentions similar claims by Montreal and Beaver River, N. S.

3 *Centennial Book of the Order of the Sons of Temperance of Nova Scotia, 1847-1947* (n.p., 1947), p. 22 and the *Sons of Temperance of North America Centennial* (n.p., 1942), p. 169.

4 *Report,* p. 661.

5 *Debates and Proceedings of House of Assembly of Nova Scotia,* 1907, pp. 308-309, and E. Spence, *op. cit.,* p. 218. In 1894 the vote was 42,756 to 12,355 in favour; in 1898, it was 34,678 to 5,370.

sponsible for enforcing the Scott and License Acts, arranged "deals" with retailers by which certain periodic fines served to replace the inconvenience of the licencing system.

It is clear that the prohibitionists of the nineteenth century had, to some degree, persuaded governments to regulate and remove the more blatant features of the liquor traffic. By the end of the century, however, it became evident that the politicians were unwilling to go farther. Both federal parties, after stalling by means of royal commissions and plebiscites, made it clear that action could not be expected from them. The Liberal government of Nova Scotia, under the leadership of George Murray, not only rejected any further extension of prohibition but in 1905 appeared to move in the other direction. In that year the government legalized the on-the-premises consumption of liquor in Halifax hotels and extended the hours of sale for that city. It is doubtful if the prohibition movement would have had any greater impact on Nova Scotia had there not been in motion at this time a fundamental change in the social theology of the churches which directly affected their attitude towards prohibition.

In broad terms this change might be seen as part of the growth of a collectivist trend in social thought. In the 1870's, Herbert Spencer's widely publicized portrayal of society as an evolutionary organism governed by the law of the "survival of the fittest" was initially employed as a doctrine justifying poverty and laissez-faire capitalism. But it soon produced a strong progressive response. Henry George in *Progress and Poverty* and Edward Bellamy in *Looking Backwards,* for example, both accepted organic and evolutionary concepts, but made them the basis for an optimistic projection of social progress and reform.[6]

Collectivism in secular thought was closely paralleled in theology by a similar movement which became known as the social gospel. In the United States, Washington Gladden, Richard Ely and Walter Rauchenbush developed theories of an organic and dynamic society.[7] It was a society which might ultimately be perfected on the principles of the fatherhood of God and the brotherhood of man as expressed by Jesus in the "Sermon on the Mount" and elsewhere. Such a belief transformed the social attitude of many churches. No longer could the primary emphasis be placed on individual salvation. If "Christ . . . came to save society" as the Nova Scotia Methodist

6 See Richard Hofstadter, *Social Darwinism in American Thought* (rev. ed., New York, 1959), pp. 42, 108 and 112-113, and Daniel Aaron, *Men of Good Hope* (New York, 1961), pp. 72, 103.

7 For a discussion of the origin and nature of the social gospel in the United States see Charles H. Hopkins, *The Rise of the Social Gospel in American Protestantism, 1865-1915* (New Haven, 1940) and P. A. Carter, *The Decline and Revival of the Social Gospel* (Ithaca, 1956).

Conference claimed in 1907,[8] the churches were obligated to follow his example.

Both the secular and religious movements for reform owed much of their popular appeal to the serious social problems which confronted the people. In Canada the rapid industrialization and urbanization of the Laurier era created or threw into sharp relief a host of social ills. Red light districts abounded in the towns and cities, alcoholism increased sharply, the exploitation of workers became blatant and the failure of traditional institutions to provide security for the less fortunate was increasingly manifest.[9] Rural residents were alarmed not only by the moral and social problems of the cities and towns but also by the depopulation of their own communities. Nova Scotians, who were noted for their strong church allegiance,[10] tended to look to the clergy for leadership in solving their problems. The latter proposed as a general solution implementation of the social gospel — a fundamental reform of society on the basis of Christian principles.

In the latter half of the nineteenth century, the official attitude of most of the Nova Scotia churches towards intemperance was one of personal sin. This provided the basis for their limited support of prohibition. In replies to the survey by the Royal Commission of 1892-4, a spokesman for the Methodist Church based his advocacy of prohibition upon the Church *Discipline* which contained a "footnote" including intemperance among such "sins" as dancing and playing cards. The Presbyterians, although admittedly divided on the question of prohibition, denounced intemperance as "sinful". The Anglicans and Roman Catholics commended personal abstinence, but showed no sympathy for prohibition directly on humanitarian grounds.[11]

The acceptance of the new theology by the churches had profound implications for the prohibition movement. Firstly, the social gospel tended to justify or even compel a church's interference in politics. If society were

8 *Minutes of the Nova Scotia Conference of the Methodist Church* (hereafter cited as *Minutes, Methodist*), 1907, p. 78; from the Report of the Committee on Temperance and Moral Reform as adopted by the Conference.

9 For a brief description of conditions in one Nova Scotian city see *Sydney, Nova Scotia: The Report of a Brief Investigation of Social Conditions by the Board of Temperance and Moral Reform of the Methodist Church and the Board of Social Service and Evangelism of the Presbyterian Church* (n.p., 1913).

10 W. S. Learned and K. C. M. Sills, *Education in the Maritime Provinces of Canada* (New York, 1922), p. 14.

11 *Report of the Royal Commission on Liquor Traffic*, 1895, pp. 81-82, 684. This is not to say that social concern was not behind the church's pronouncements on intemperance. But the language used in condemning intemperance appeared to be primarily that of personal censorship on moral grounds. Perhaps the most striking example of the change was the removal in 1911 of the list of "sins" which had been included in a footnote to the Methodist Discipline in 1886. See Marion V. Royce, "The Contribution of the Methodist Church to Social Welfare in Canada" (unpublished M.A. thesis, University of Toronto, 1940), pp. 263-265.

capable of regeneration along Christian lines, a heavy responsibility rested with the churches to employ every means in bringing this about. To those firmly imbued with the reforming vision, traditional methods of teaching and preaching appeared too slow. Legislation and government activity represented the obvious method of implementing large scale reform. Secondly, the social gospel changed the emphasis and strengthened the motivation in the churches' advocacy of prohibition. It was understandable that progressive churchmen, as they surveyed the ills of their society, should emphasize the problem of intemperance. Not only was alcoholism a serious social problem in itself, but it was thought to be an important contributory cause to a host of other ills, including poverty, disease, the disintegration of the family, and traffic and industrial accidents. Prohibition thus became an integral part of a sweeping programme for social reform. In this form it exerted a much wider appeal particularly among the young and idealistic than under its previous image of a mere crusade against sin. Finally, in accepting the principle of an organic society, the church was subtly undermining the primary grounds for opposition to prohibition — that of the infringement of personal liberty. If Christ died to save society, individual whims and wishes would have to be sacrificed for the same goal. The reformer only need prove that society was being harmed by a certain abuse and it was the duty of the Christian to support its removal, individual "rights" notwithstanding.

If the social gospel contributed to prohibition, the question of prohibition played a key role in the transition of the churches to the social gospel. This was one issue on which religious conservatives and progressives could readily unite. It was thus no accident that the social gospel made its initial appearance in the churches by way of the temperance committees. These in fact served as useful agencies through which the social gospel ethic might be spread in each church.

The Methodists appear to have been among the first in Canada to accept formally the implications of the new ideas. A move in that direction was indicated by the change in name of the Committee on Temperance to that of Temperance, Prohibition and Moral Reform at the Canadian Conference of 1898. This committee became a permanent board in 1902 and Dr. S. D. Chown was appointed its full time secretary. In the Nova Scotia Conference, the change in name of the committee was accompanied in 1903 by what appeared to be a general acceptance of the social gospel. The report of the committee which was adopted by the 1903 Conference declared in its opening sentence that it was the "intention of the Lord that . . . through his faithful ones the principles of the gospel of Christ are to be made supreme in all departments of human activity."[12] The report went on to discuss tactics for the defeat of intemperance, cigarette smoking by the young, commercial dishonesty, social

---

12 *Minutes, Methodist,* 1903, pp. 80-81.

vice and political corruption. In the next three years, other abuses singled out for attack included the opium traffic, race track gambling, prize fighting and in 1906 the committee expressed its wish to investigate "any forms of commercial or industrial oppression affecting our people."[13] As part of their programme for social reform, the members of the Conference in 1905 endorsed the policy of provincial prohibition and pledged themselves to vote only for men who would support this measure in the Legislature. Ministers were urged to promote the cause of "temperance" in the pulpit and the church appointed delegates to attend a Temperance Convention in Truro called to organize a province wide campaign.[14]

More dramatic was the simultaneous adoption of the cause of prohibition and the social gospel by the Maritime Synod of the Presbyterian Church. The convener of the Temperance Committee which proposed the acceptance of the social gospel was H. R. Grant, the man who would dominate the prohibition movement in Nova Scotia for the next thirty years. A native of Pictou County, Grant had undertaken his theological studies at Queen's University where the new theological trends appear to have received full consideration under the principalship of George Monro Grant.[15] After further study at Edinburgh and experience in mission work in Manitoba and New Brunswick, H. R. Grant returned to take charge of the congregation of Trenton in his home county. Keenly interested in temperance and social reform, he served as convener of the Temperance Committee of the Maritime Synod from 1902 to 1907. In 1904 he resigned his charge in Trenton to undertake full time the task of temperance organization in Pictou County. In 1906 Grant participated in the formation of the Nova Scotia Temperance Alliance of which he became general secretary in 1907. He held his post until 1917 when he assumed a similar position in the Social Service Council of Nova Scotia.

In delivering the report of the Temperance Committee to the Maritime Synod in 1907, Grant rejoiced at the "advanced ground" which the General Assembly had taken in creating a committee to investigate such questions as the relation of the church to labour, political and commercial corruption, gambling and the liquor traffic. He then went on to present a clear statement of the principles of the social gospel.

> Public affairs, the social and political business of the country must be brought under the ten commandments and the sermon on the mount . . . the pulpit must have an outlook on the every day life of men . . . the state as well as the individual has a character and the social and political life of the state must obey the . . . teaching of Christ . . . temperance [is]

13 *Ibid.*, 1906, p. 83.
14 *Ibid.*, 1905, pp. 76-77.
15 H. H. Walsh, *The Christian Church in Canada* (Toronto, 1956), p. 330. See also A. Richard Allen, "Salem Bland and the Social Gospel in Canada," pp. 30-32.

but one of the social, we might say national, questions which the church must consider . . . . Abuses must not only be discovered but reformed as well.[16]

In the following year, the new committee on moral and social reform submitted a series of resolutions calling for the formation of moral and social reform councils and a direct commitment by the Synod to prohibition and other social measures. The resolutions went much further than those hitherto entertained by the General Assembly. One called for the Synod to express its "cordial sympathies with the workingman in all their just and worthy efforts to improve the conditions under which they live and labour" and denounced child labour, "undue long hours of labour" among adults and "conditions associated with the sweating system". Another demanded the adoption of a penal system designed to reform rather than punish.[17]   The resolutions appear to have implied too sharp a transition for some members of the Synod and were referred to the presbyteries for further discussion. The next year they were introduced again in the same form, and after an amendment favouring local option had been defeated by "a large majority", passed *in toto*.[18]

The Baptists seem to have pursued a similar course in the direction of the social gospel. In 1903 the Temperance Committee of the Maritime Baptist Convention under the chairmanship of W. H. Jenkins submitted a report which clearly viewed the temperance problem in terms of the social gospel. Christ's "mission", it stated, was both "to save souls" and "to save society". Christ was "the greatest social reformer that the world has ever seen". "Loyal hearts" were needed "to battle boldly with that monster iniquity, the liquor traffic which . . . gathering under its banner all the supreme ills that afflict the people . . . stalks forth to challenge Christianity to mortal combat".[19]   In 1908, a resolution of the Convention urged Baptists to "rise above party in voting on questions of temperance and moral reform" and denounced the idea of government control as "complicitly with the drink traffic."[20]

The Church of England, lacking a strong temperance tradition and proud of its conservative stance, responded more slowly to the new ideas. Yet respond it did. Some Anglicans seemed prepared to accept them on the grounds that if members did not find them being implemented in their own church, they might go elsewhere. This was the argument used by the Temperance

16 *Presbyterian Witness,* 19 October 1907, p. 34.

17 *Minutes of the Maritime Synod of the Presbyterian Church of Canada,* (hereafter cited as *Minutes, Presbyterian),* 1908, p. 25; from the Report of Committee on Moral and Social Reform. Compare with the Report of Committee on Temperance and Moral Reform in *The Acts Proceedings of the General Assembly of the Presbyterian Church of Canada,* 1908, pp. 248-252.

18 *Minutes, Presbyterian,* 1909, pp. 28-29.

19 *Year Book Maritime Baptist Convention,* 1903, p. 22. Jenkins later became a staunch supporter of J. S. Woodsworth's Labour Party.

20 *Wesleyan* (Methodist), Halifax, 23 September 1908, p. 1. Taken from the *Maritime Baptist.*

Committee of 1902 in urging the need for a temperance organization in every parish.[21]   Others such as Rev. D. V. Warner of Shelburne, advocated the acceptance of a new social ethic on theoretical grounds and pointed to a social gospel tradition within the Church of England itself. Warner in 1909 published a pamphlet entitled *The Church and Modern Socialism* in which he referred specifically to the tradition of "Christian Socialism" set forth in the writings of the nineteenth century English cleric, Charles Kingsley. By analyzing Christ's teachings as illustrated in the "Sermon on the Mount", the "Lord's Prayer" and other selections from the New Testament, he sought to prove that socialism was closer to "practical Christianity" than was the practice of the Church.[22]

The Anglican debate on the social gospel appeared to reach a climax in the Nova Scotia Synod of 1912. The conservative position was strongly stated in the opening address of Bishop C. L. Worrell. Worrell expressed his alarm that "some of the clergy . . . have endeavored to take up the socialistic tendency of the time" and cautioned against "undue playing with this dynamic force". While it might be proper for individual churchmen to take the lead in movements which tended to the "purity, sobriety and thrift" of the people, it was not the Church's duty to devote its attention to the social problems of the day "except through the general instruction of Christian principles." In conclusion he quoted the dictum of Dean Inge that "political agitation is not the business of the clergy".[23]   The Synod disagreed. Its "Report of the Bishops Charge" opened with a reference to the "Sermon on the Mount" and argued that "The Church of God exists for his glory and the true happiness and well being of his children, the sons of men, and therefore anything which emphasizes this aspect of his kingdom is to be fostered and strengthened".[24]   By 1914 this creed had been translated into practical action with the formation of a Diocesan Commission of Social Service. A year later the Synod passed a resolution calling for the "fullest possible measures" by Dominion and Provincial legislatures to prevent the sale and use of intoxicating beverages in Nova Scotia.[25]

The Roman Catholic Church in Nova Scotia also reacted favourably to the new ideas. The papal encyclical, *Rerum Novarum* of 1891, had paved the way by its rejection of economic liberalism and condemnation of the exploitation

21 *Journals of Nova Scotia Synod, Church of England,* Appendix N, printed in the *Year Book* (hereafter cited as *Year Book, Church of England*), 1901-1902, p. xxxi.

22 D. V. Warner, *The Church and Modern Socialism* (Truro, N. S., 1909).

23 *Year Book, Church of England,* 1911-1912, pp. 111-113.

24 *Ibid.,* Appendix Q, pp. xxvi-xxvii.

25 *Ibid.,* 1914-1915, pp. 149 and 320. The Nova Scotia Conference seems to have been acting in advance of the rest of the Church in urging prohibition as the National Synod remained uncommitted. See *The General Synod of the Church of England in the Dominion of Canada,* 1915, p. 268.

of workers by employers. The Antigonish *Casket,* a spokesman for Celtic Roman Catholicism in the eastern half of the province, displayed an increasing interest in the problems of labour, particularly in the mining areas. In 1909, the Rev. Dr. Thompson of St. Francis Xavier University represented the reform wing of the church in calling for the creation of a strong public opinion, which would empower governments to interfere in the "liberties" of persons and corporations and "put an end to the strikes and lockouts in the most effective way . . . i.e. by removing the causes which produce them." [26]

The Roman Catholic view of prohibition seemed ambiguous. The Antigonish *Casket* conceded that the liquor traffic should be suppressed, but argued that public opinion was opposed and advocated a generous licensing law providing for "drinking on the premises" but limiting licenses to 1 per 750 of population.[27]   The *Casket* also suggested that the activities of the League of the Cross, the Roman Catholic temperance organization, should be limited to converting people to temperance through teaching. Yet as early as 1903 the League was reported to be nominating candidates in the municipal elections and in 1907 was campaigning for the repeal of the Scott Act so that the more stringent License Act might apply in Cape Breton County. In that year its president reported a membership of 2108 in 29 branches.[28]   While the motivation of the League is unclear, from its actions it would appear that at least some of its leaders were fired by the reform spirit of the age.

Against this background of changing opinion and demand for reform by the churches, a political agitation was building up which would make the passage of prohibition almost unavoidable. But the Liberal administration of Premier George Murray did everything it could to keep from having to act on the question. In fact the story of the struggle for prohibition between 1904 and 1916 is largely the story of a political duel between the temperance forces led by H. R. Grant and the provincial government led by George Murray. On one side were the churches, leading moulders of public opinion in the province, on the other the Liberal Party, holding every seat but two in the Assembly and having as its leader one of the wiliest politicians in the country.

The object of the struggle soon became clear. The Liberals wanted to avoid taking a definite stand on the controversial issue of prohibition. The pro-

---

26 *Casket,* 12 August 1909. Students of the social gospel including A. R. Allen, C. Hopkins and P. Carter, have ignored the impact of its ideas on the Roman Catholic Church. That their influence was important is suggested most spectacularly by the leading role played by such reform minded priests as Fathers "Jimmy" Tompkins and M. M. Coady in the development of the co-operative movement in Nova Scotia in the latter part of the 1920's. Coady's later justification of the Church's role in this movement would appear to differ little from some Protestant versions of the social gospel. See M. M. Coady, *Masters of their own Destiny* (New York, 1939), pp. 144-148.

27 *Casket,* 29 August 1907, p. 4.

28 *Ibid.,* 31 January 1907, p. 6; 15 January 1903, p. 4; 8 August 1907, p. 2; and 12 September 1907, p. 2.

hibitionists were determined to manoeuvre the government into a position where it would be compelled to act or publicly demonstrate its disdain for the stated wishes of a large element of the population.

Each year between 1902 and 1905, a bill was introduced to prohibit or render more difficult the sale and shipment of liquor into the dry areas of the province.[29] For the first three years, these were debated briefly and unceremoniously rejected. In 1905, when R. M. McGregor, Liberal M.L.A. for Pictou County, introduced a bill prepared by H. R. Grant and the Pictou County Temperance Association, the members showed greater discretion. The bill, which provided for both the prohibition of the shipment of liquor into the "dry" areas and provincial enforcement of existing legislation, appeared to receive sympathetic consideration from the House. Government members vied with the opposition in expressing their admiration of temperance and "Temperance people". Premier Murray's enthusiasm, however, was tempered somewhat by statements to the effect that his government was not united on the issue and that such a law might be unconstitutional.[30] The bill was approved in principle and then disappeared into committee where it was effectively chopped to pieces.

The churches voiced their anger in unmistakeable terms. In the Presbyterian Synod, the Temperance Committee condemned the legislature for its encouragement of the liquor traffic and called for "more definite, united and aggressive action".[31] The report adopted by the Methodist Conference pledged its members to secure "by voice, influence, and vote the defeat of that portion of the Legislature that stood for the liquor traffic against the moral and material welfare of our people". It concluded:

> If we are to do permanent work we must enter the field of politics as our opponents the liquor interests have done and fight this battle for God and our homes.... [We] express the hope ... [that] the curse of blind partisanship may be done away with and all our people... may rise in the strength of God and by the exercise of that God given privilege — the Ballot — smite the liquor traffic to the death.[32]

With an election planned for June of 1906 and the Conservatives committed to a promise of provincial prohibition,[33] Murray decided that an appropriate gesture to the churches would be in order. In the 1906 session, the government introduced a bill prohibiting the shipment of liquor from "wet" to "dry"

29 For a brief sketch of these early attempts see E. Spence, *op. cit.*, pp. 330-333.

30 *Debates*, 1905, pp. 311, 85-86.

31 *Minutes, Presbyterian*, 1905, p. 31.

32 *Minutes, Methodist*, 1905, p. 78.

33 See below n. 35.

areas of the province. In general, the bill was similar to those advocated by prohibitionists in previous years. But a large "joker" had been added by the phrase restricting the application of the bill to liquor "to be paid for on delivery".[34]   The effect of the bill was merely to require people in rural areas to order their liquor prepaid rather than C.O.D. The Conservatives strove valiantly to make this fact clear, while demonstrating their own championship of prohibition with an amendment designed to restore the restrictive intent of the legislation. Government members replied by strongly denouncing those who would make the "sacred" cause of prohibition a party issue. Only two Liberals broke party lines on the amendment which was defeated eighteen to four.[35]

In the election campaign which immediately followed, prohibition played a prominent role. The Conservatives included in their platform a promise of provincial prohibition within a year of a successful plebiscite on the question. At Pictou, Conservative Leader Charles Tanner issued a reform manifesto which called for prohibition, purity in elections, public interest as opposed to corporate power and betterment of the working classes.[36]   In most counties, temperance groups attempted to pledge their members to support prohibitory legislation. The Methodist Conference even went so far as to endorse formally two independents in Kings County.[37]   But the Government's last minute "prohibition" bill had helped to blur party divisions on the question and in the constituencies candidates adopted positions which were locally popular. In rural areas where temperance sentiment was strong, such as Yarmouth County for example, all candidates pledged themselves to support prohibition.[38]
In Halifax, with its military and seafaring traditions, opposition to prohibition was predominant. Here local Conservative newspapers left the prohibition plank out of the party platform, while Liberal Premier Murray promised the inhabitants that his government would not impose prohibition upon the city without their consent.[39]   Thirty-two Liberals, five Conservatives and one "Methodist" Independent were elected.

The Liberals had apparently suffered little on the issue, but the prohibitionists had gained in the election a solid corps of M.L.A.'s pledged to support their demands. Meanwhile, the temperance groups of the province co-ordinated their efforts in the formation of the Nova Scotia Temperance Alliance. As secretary of the new organization, Grant stationed himself in the gallery

34 *Debates*, 1906, p. 309.

35 *Ibid.*, pp. 312, 330-331.

36 J. Castell Hopkins, *The Canadian Annual Review*, 1905, p. 331 and 1906, p. 393 (hereafter cited as *C.A.R.*).

37 *Minutes, Methodist*, 1906, p. 81.

38 *Debates*, 1907, pp. 313 and 372.

39 *Ibid.*, pp. 313 and 400.

of the Legislature to direct the strategy of the temperance forces.[40] The first step was the introduction of a prohibition bill by E. H. Armstrong of Yarmouth, a young Liberal M.L.A. pledged to the cause in the election. Armstrong made clear that he was serving as the mouthpiece of the Alliance and that he himself had nothing to do with the drafting of the measure.[41] The bill called for the prohibition of the sale of liquor throughout the province and enforcement by provincial inspectors.

The bill was immediately rejected as unconstitutional by the Premier on the grounds that only the government could introduce bills which encroached upon the revenue of the crown. Armstrong was prepared for this development and at once gave notice of a resolution requiring the introduction of the bill by the government.[42] Obviously Grant had manoeuvered the Government into the position he wanted. The resolution could only be debated on the open floor of the House. Members would have to take a definite stand which could be identified by their constituents. Meanwhile, as the debate proceeded, the Legislature was bombarded with over thirty petitions in favour of the legislation and resolutions of support from the Synods and Conferences of the Presbyterian, Methodist and Baptist churches, the Sons of Temperance, the Order of Good Templars and the Grand Orange Lodge.[43]

Armstrong's speech in introducing his resolution clearly reflected the characteristic social gospel approach to prohibition. The measure was necessary as a basic social reform. Problems of poverty, neglect of wives and children, disease, and accidents could be traced in large measure to intemperance. Its influence was both direct, as people on "sprees" caught pneumonia or were injured, and indirect, since in spending their money on "drink", men failed to provide the care and nourishment for themselves and their families necessary to ward off diseases such as typhoid fever or tuberculosis. Armstrong quoted a Dr. Reid who estimated that "90% of the cases in our hospitals are directly or indirectly due to the evil effects of intemperance" and suggested that prohibition might even put the hospitals out of business.[44]

In anticipating possible objections from the critics of the Bill, Armstrong's arguments reflected the growing collectivism of the period. Opponents of prohibition frequently argued that "prohibition was a curtailment of personal liberty". According to Armstrong this view might have some relevance in the "classic past" but not in the twentieth century. "The organic unity of society",

40) Speakers frequently gave H. R. Grant credit for supplying the information with which they "corrected" statements of the opponents of prohibition. See for example, *Debates*, 1916, p. 180.

41 *Debates*, 1907, p. 301.

42 *Ibid.*, pp. 224, 227.

43 Nova Scotia, *Journals of the House of Assembly* (hereafter cited as *J.H.A.*), 1907, various references pp. 45-154 and *Debates*, 1907, p. 310.

he stated, "is a principle political science recognizes at the present time".[45]
It was only a question of whether the social weakness at issue was great enough
to require a stringent measure of reform.

Armstrong went on to deal with the constitutional argument, which had
hitherto been one of the government's favourite means of escape. Reviewing
the ancient controversy over whether Dominion or provincial governments
had the power to impose prohibition, he cited various decisions of the Judicial
Committee of the Privy Council to establish the limits of each level's authority.
While it was true that only the federal government had the power to prohibit
the shipment of liquor from outside of a province, provincial governments,
as had been clearly determined in 1901 in the case of Manitoba, could legally
prohibit the sale or shipment of liquor within the province. It was this and no
more that the Alliance's Bill proposed to do.

But once again, the members of the Legislature were saved from having to
declare themselves unequivocally on the issue. Liberal M.L.A., C. F. Cooper,
Baptist clergyman from Queens County, proposed an amendment calling for
an address to the Dominion Parliament to request legislation banning the
importation of liquor into "dry" counties from other provinces. When this
was achieved, provincial legislation could then be secured to prevent its importation from areas of the province where liquor was legally sold. This,
according to Cooper, was a much greater step towards prohibition that the
measure proposed by the Alliance.[46]

Certainly Premier Murray was much happier with the latter proposal. The
imposition of prohibition in Halifax would be in Murray's words "a dangerous
experiment." Nova Scotia was already far in advance of other provinces in
temperance legislation and "fully up [to], if not in advance of what public opinion demands".[47]   Nevertheless, Murray quite agreed with Cooper's idea of an
address to the federal parliament. To Murray the ideal solution was Dominion
legislation enforced by municipal authorities.

After a long and tedious debate which filled nearly one hundred pages in
the official record, the amendment was carried twenty-two to twelve. The
Liberal strategy had worked; the members of the party who wished could still
pose as champions of prohibition. Nevertheless, the vote did reveal the friends
of the Alliance, as in addition to the Conservative opposition, five Liberals
and the independent member opposed the amendment.[48]

---

44 *Debates,* 1907, p. 304. This was probably Dr. J. W. Reid, M.D. of Windsor, N. S., who was
elected to the House in 1911 and therafter gave strong speeches in support of prohibition which
were crammed with similar statistics. See for example, *Debates,* 1916, p. 170.

45 *Debates,* 1907, p. 306.

46 *Ibid.,* p. 317.

47 *Ibid.,* p. 385.

48 *Ibid.,* p. 400.

At its annual meeting of 1908, the Alliance outlined more clearly the goals which genuine prohibitionists would be expected to support. It wanted to replace the existing jungle of temperance legislation with a federal measure outlawing the importation and manufacture of alcoholic beverages, and a provincial law prohibiting their sale. Both would be enforced by provincial officers. These proposals were presented to an unsympathetic Premier Murray by a delegation from the Alliance led by H. R. Grant. Murray explained that it was government policy to seek an amendment to the Scott Act which would prevent the importation of liquor into the province. Grant refused to be associated with any such legislation, which would apply only to areas where the Scott Act was in effect and merely serve to increase the confusion.[49]   In the legislature in 1909 Premier Murray described as "incomprehensible" the Alliance's repudiation of the Government's proposal and suggested that this could only arouse "suspicions" as to the motives of the organization. In a remarkable reversal E. H. Armstrong opposed the prohibition measure introduced by Independent M.L.A., C. A. Campbell, and suggested that the Alliance was plotting with the Tories.[50]

The Liberal concern was understandable. Far from keeping the "sacred" cause of temperance out of politics, prohibitionists appeared to be using every opportunity to embarrass the government politically and force them to adopt the Alliance programme. Speakers imported from other regions added their testimony to the failure of the government. For example, Dr. J. G. Shearer, secretary of the Committee on Temperance and Moral and Social Reform of the General Assembly of the Presbyterian Church, denounced the lack of law enforcement in Halifax claiming that "sixty-four bar-rooms, with shop licenses which expressly forbid selling for consumption on the premises, are doing business in direct violation of section 63 of the Licence Act".[51]

The prohibition forces were operating from an ever-expanding base. In January of 1909, H. R. Grant represented the Alliance in the creation of the Social Service Council of Nova Scotia, which included representatives of all the major churches, the farmers' associations, organized labour and boards of trade. The provincial organization was to be supplemented by similar councils in the municipalities. Intemperance was listed as one of the primary social problems with which the council proposed to deal and the solution advocated was education and prohibitory legislation.[52]

In 1909 and 1910, by-elections were fought in five counties. In two, Queens and Hants, Conservatives were elected on platforms including provincial

49 *C.A.R.,* 1908, pp. 426-427, 108.

50 *Debates,* 1908, pp. 334, 374.

51 *C.A.R.,* 1908, p. 427.

52 Halifax *Herald,* 22 January 1909, p. 6.

prohibition.[53]   With a general election approaching, the worried Liberals introduced a bill in the session of 1910 providing for provincial prohibition. The bill forbade the sale of intoxicating beverages (those containing more than 3% alcohol) in the province outside the city of Halifax. The only exception was for medicinal, sacramental, art trade and manufacturing purposes. "Spirits" for these uses would be supplied by specially authorized vendors. Liquor might not be shipped from Halifax to any other part of the province unless actually purchased in the city for personal or family use. In the capital city, the number of licenses was reduced from 90 to 70 with further reductions promised. The act was to be enforced by municipal officers under the supervision of a provincial inspector-in-chief. Early in 1911, with an election still pending, the Act was tightened to include all beverages containing alcohol, to prevent societies and clubs from keeping such beverages on their premises and to provide mandatory sentences of three month imprisonment for second offenders. At the same time the Legislature passed a resolution urging the federal government to prohibit the transportation of liquor into the province.[54]

The Alliance had attained a large portion of its demands. The obvious reason for its success was political. The Liberal Government was acting to satisfy an aroused public opinion before the election — a public opinion which had been largely moulded by the influence of the churches under the impact of the social gospel. The weight of this opinion was responsible not only for prohibition. In fact the latter was only one item in a broad slate of reform legislation passed by the Murray Government in 1909 and 1910. Other measures included workmen's compensation, factory legislation, stricter limitations on child labour and a system of contributory old age pensions. In a relatively prosperous economy the vision of a transformed society was yielding practical results. The churches expressed their appreciation to the Government,[55]   and in the election of 1911, the Liberals were returned by a comfortable majority of sixteen seats.

The Alliance's pressure on the government was not eased for long. H. R. Grant soon declared that prohibition must be extended to Halifax, both to save the young men of that city from destruction and to cut off a major source of supplies for illicit sale in the rest of the province.[56]   In 1912 the Liberals sought to divert attention from this issue by "packing" the annual meeting of the Alliance with government supporters. E. R. Armstrong, by this time a member of the Cabinet, requested several M.L.A.'s to have their friends attend the meeting of the Alliance to block "unsound" proposals and the efforts of those who

53 E. Spence, *op. cit.*, p. 339; *C.A.R.*, 1909, p. 432, and 1910, p. 459. In the latter constituency this was reputed to be the first election of a Conservative in thirty years.

54 *C.A.R.*, 1911, p. 551.

55 *Minutes, Presbyterian*, 1910, p. 29. *Minutes Methodist*, 1910, p. 89.

56 E. Spence, *op. cit.*, pp. 341-342.

would "complicate the situation as far as the local government is concerned".[57] This attempt was a failure. The following year, Conservative leader C. E. Tanner openly championed the Alliance's cause by introducing an amendment to the Nova Scotia Temperance Act to extend the application of its prohibitory clauses to Halifax. This was defeated eighteen to thirteen. In May of 1914 a similar proposal was lost fourteen to thirteen and in 1915 the measure was defeated only by the vote of the speaker. Early in 1916, with another election just months away, a similar amendment by Conservative H. W. Corning passed with only the three members from Halifax in opposition.[58]

The War was an obvious factor in overcoming resistance. In the final debate, several of the members mentioned the endorsement of prohibition by the Nova Scotia Synod of the Church of England as influencing their decision on the question.[59] Although a prohibition resolution had been submitted to the Synod before the outbreak of war, the matter had been referred to the Social Service Commission for further study. Canon C. W. Vernon, who moved the resolution of 1915, was quoted as saying that he himself had been converted to prohibition by the needs of the war effort and that without the War his motion would never have passed.[60] The need for conservation created by the War was mentioned by some speakers and the need for sacrifice by others. Premier Murray, still very sceptical of the measure, called it "experimental legislation" which the province might afford in "days of strain and stress . . . as we perhaps could not do under more normal conditions".[61] The emotional climate in which the bill was passed was further illustrated in Corning's concluding speech in which he appealed for a moral regeneration of the Empire and quoted Admiral Beatty on the need for a religious revival as a necessary prelude to victory.[62] Amid this climate of idealism and sacrifice the standard objections to prohibition as an infringement of personal liberty appeared to carry little weight.

Yet one should not exaggerate the influence of the war on the prohibition movement in Nova Scotia. The major break-through had taken place in 1910 when the government, protesting that the Alliance's policy of pledging members was "unfair and indecent",[63] had nevertheless enacted a major part of the prohibitionists' demands. In 1914, before the outbreak of the War, prohibition for Halifax had been defeated by only one vote. With the Conservative party becoming clearly identified as the champions of prohibition, it is difficult to see how Murray could have avoided making this concession to the

57 Armstrong to Dr. J. W. Reid, 15 February 1912 and Armstrong to W. M. Kelly, 15 February 1912, E. R. Armstrong Papers, P.A.N.S.

58 *Presbyterian Witness*, 4 March 1916, p. 5 and *Debates*, 1916, p. 225.

59 *Debates*, 1916, p. 176.

60 *Ibid.*, p. 143.

61 *Ibid.*, p. 206.

62 *Ibid.*, p. 258.

63 E. Spence, *op. cit.*, p. 341.

temperance interests before another election. He had acted to disarm his opponents on the issue before each of the previous elections and it is doubtful if he would have acted differently on this occasion. As it was, the Conservatives tried to make Murray's alleged fondness for the liquor interests a major issue in their campaign.[64]

Where the influence of the war did prove decisive, however, was in convincing the federal government to adopt prohibition. In 1916 the Dominion Temperance Alliance called for prohibition for the duration of the war and a three year reconstruction period thereafter. In January, H. R. Grant was a member of a delegation that called upon Robert Borden to press for Dominion prohibitory legislation. In March, the so-called Doherty Bill banned the importation of intoxicating beverages into provinces where provincial legislation was in effect. Since they still might be imported for personal use, this had little effect in Nova Scotia. In December, 1917, as a part of the war effort, the importation of intoxicating beverages was prohibited for the whole country. This still left the door open for Nova Scotians to order, legally, in unlimited quantities, liquor for personal use from Quebec.[65] Finally in March of 1918, by an Order-in-Council under the War Measures Act, the manufacture and sale of intoxicating beverages was prohibited throughout the whole country. Thus "bone-dry" prohibition came to Nova Scotia for the first time.

Thereafter attention shifted to the problem of enforcement. In 1917 the temperance forces of Sydney organized a citizen's league which campaigned in the Municipal elections and overturned a council which it claimed had failed to enforce the Act.[66] Inspector-in-chief J. A. Knight stated that "on the whole" prohibition in Halifax had been a success.[67] On this occasion Knight's opinion appeared to be supported by statistics, as the number of arrests for drunkenness in the province, which had reached 3614 in 1916, dropped to 2546 in 1917.[68] Evidence of improvement in restricting consumption of alcoholic beverages came from other sources as well. Sixty-nine per cent of the Anglican clergy of Nova Scotia who responded to a poll by the Council for Social Service of the Church of England in 1919, testified to the success of prohibition in their province.[69] Perhaps even more indicative of the drying up of traditional sources of supply was the Inspector-in-chief's report of

64 See Halifax *Herald,* 10 June 1916, p. 6.

65 See Report of the Inspector-in-chief for 1919, *J.H.A.,* 1920, Appendix 26, p. 1.

66 *Year Book, Church of England,* 1916-1917, p. 146.

67 Report of Inspector-in-chief, 1917, *J.H.A.,* 1918, Appendix 26, p. 1.

68 *The Control and Sale of Liquor in Canada* (Ottawa, Dominion Bureau of Statistics, 1933), p. 9, Table 5.

69 Compared with only 48.3% who were of a similar opinion in 1917. See *Prohibition II* (Kingston, 1919), p. 9. and *Prohibition I* (Kingston, 1917), p. 6. (Bulletins of the Council for Social Service of the Church of England).

1919, which for the first time mentioned smuggling and moonshining.[70] It was apparent that prohibition was beginning to make a significant impact upon the province.

On December 31, 1919, the Orders-in-Council prohibiting the importation of liquor were repealed in favour of an amendment to the Canada Temperance Act, providing for provincial plebiscites on the question. A simple majority vote in favour of prohibition would result in the extension of the necessary federal legislation to the province concerned. In Nova Scotia the plebiscite was scheduled for October 25, 1920, after the provincial election of that year. Meanwhile, the people quenched their thrist and stocked up for the dry years to come.

By the time of the plebiscite, prohibition had acquired new enemies and friends. Organized labour made unsuccessful representations to the legislature to plead for the exemption of beer from prohibitiry legislation and thereafter became increasingly hostile.[71] Organized farmers took the opposite view and in 1920 the newly-formed United Farmers' Party campaigned on a platform advocating "bone-dry" liquor legislation.[72] Nevertheless, with the plebiscite already scheduled, it is doubtful if prohibition played a major role in the election of 1920. Challenged by the new farmer and labour parties, but taking full advantage of the division among its opponents, the Murray Government remained in power on a minority of the popular vote and lost only one seat from its majority in the House.[73]

The most important accession to the temperance forces was the direct support of the Roman Catholic Church, the largest denomination in the province. During the campaign for the plebiscite, the Antigonish *Casket* came out strongly for prohibition claiming it "has done wonders but it has not yet had time to do its best". This was supported by a letter from Bishop James Morrison of Antigonish which concluded ". . . let me say once more than *(sic)* the adoption of the prohibitory law has my strongest word of approval, and let us all hope it will be given a fair trial in this province."[74] In the plebiscite, Nova Scotians declared for prohibition 82,573 to 23,953, the largest support for prohibition ever recorded in the province.[75] Every county yielded a majority except Halifax, whose people still appeared to resent the fiat imposed upon them in 1916.

70 Report of Inspector-in-chief, 1919, *J.H.A.*, 1920, Appendix 26, p. 9.

71 *C.A.R.*, 1919, p. 703; Halifax *Citizen*, 30 May and 22 August 1923.

72 *C.A.R.*, 1920, p. 678.

73 See J. M. Beck, *The Government of Nova Scotia* (Toronto, 1957), p. 162 and Anthony MacKenzie, "The Rise and Fall of the Farmer Labour Party in Nova Scotia" (unpublished M.A. thesis, Dalhousie University, 1969), p. 77.

74 *Casket*, 14 October 1920, pp. 1 and 6.

75 *Presbyterian Witness*, 20 November 1920.

The overwhelming victory of prohibition in the plebiscite again reflected the strength of the social gospel sentiment which seemed to reach its climax in Nova Scotia after the War. As in the rest of the country, however, other reform measures associated with the movement did not enjoy similar success. All provinces faced the problem of lack of revenue which most reforms required. The aging Murray Administration was prepared neither to incur the odium of increased taxes nor to offend corporations with fundamental changes in labour legislation. Its sole gesture to the mounting demands for reform immediately prior to the election of 1920 was the appointment of a Royal Commission to consider "mother's allowances".[76] That this was much less than the people demanded is indicated both by the appearance in the election of the new farmer and labour parties and the support of 55 percent of the voters for the hastily-assembled and divided opposition.

The prohibition movement had reached its zenith by 1921 and thereafter began a gradual decline. The social gospel ideology on which it was based was approaching a crisis which would undermine its position of influence within the churches. Already it had been compromised to some extent by the Russian Revolution. In urging a fundamental reconstruction of society most social gospel reformers were forced to distinguish after 1917 between the right and wrong kinds of revolution. Many clergymen apparently judged from the newspaper reports available in Nova Scotia that the Winnipeg General Strike of 1919 was a dangerous experiment of the wrong kind. The focus of Communist activity in Cape Breton in the early 1920's — especially the activities of J. B. McLachlan, leader of the largest union in the province (District 26 United Mine Workers), in promoting "Bolshevist" doctrines and attempting to affiliate his union with the Red International[77] — tended to confirm their fears and strengthened the conservative element in the churches. The dilemma of the social gospel wing was reflected in the churches' initial failure to support labour in its critical struggle with the British Empire Steel Corporation. Not until International President John L. Lewis dismissed McLachlan and his radical executive in 1923 did the assistance materialize which one might expect from a socially committed clergy.[78]

76 *C.A.R.*, 1920, p. 673.

77 See William Rodney, *Soldiers of the International* (Toronto, 1968), p. 111. Rodney portrays a variety of Communists in this period optimistically channelling their energies into work in the industrial areas of Cape Breton.

78 The *Casket*, while bitterly denouncing agitators such as McLachlan, was equally critical of Besco (British Empire Steel and Coal Corporation) and suggested the problem might be solved by nationalization of the coal fields. *Casket*, 21 October 1920, p. 1. The Methodist *Wesleyan* in 1923 denounced the "nest of anarchists" in Cape Breton and suggested that the "firebrands" be eliminated from the country. *Wesleyan*, 4 July 1923, p. 1. By 1925 although still critical of labour's resort to violence, it was directing its fire against the Corporation and demanding relief "for the labourer who grinds his face to produce dividends for stocks for which no single dollar has been paid." *Wesleyan*, 1 April 1925, p. 4. In that year the clergy played an important role in providing relief for the families of the striking miners and in 1928 the Ministerial Association of Sydney petitioned the Tariff Advisory Board that the Corporation should not be given tariff or other subsidy until it had substantially improved the labouring conditions of the steelworkers. Papers of the Advisory Board on Tariffs and Taxation, Vol. 9, P.A.C.

The re-imposition of Federal prohibitory legislation on Nova Scotia in February of 1921 did mark the beginning of a "new era" in the province, but it turned out to be the era of the "rum-runner". In January 1920, the Volstead Act prohibited the importation of liquor into the United States. An elaborate system of smuggling quickly evolved in which the Nova Scotian fisherman and ship owners came to play a prominent role. With the return of prohibition to Nova Scotia the new techniques were applied at home.

Attempts to enforce the legislation led to co-operation between Custom officers attempting to prevent smuggling, the Department of Revenue officers hunting for stills and the Temperance inspectors trying to suppress bootlegging. Assisting all three were the prohibitionists, operating on their own initiative in an attempt to make effective the legislation for which they had worked so hard. Thus in 1921, these groups began a game of "cops and robbers" with the smugglers, bootleggers and moonshiners which would continue until the end of the decade.

It was a game which before long the ill-equipped, untrained and quite inadequate municipal and provincial officers were obviously losing. In 1925, a discouraged Inspector-in-chief, J. A. Knight, gave the following assessment:

> So much liquor is now smuggled and distributed throughout the Province in motor cars and by bootleggers that the closing of bars and blind pigs does not have much effect on the total consumption. It is beyond the power of local inspectors to control smuggling or even check it to any appreciable extent. Dominion Officers, whose duty it is to deal with smuggling, are few in number and quite unable to keep an effective watch on all parts of the coast where liquor may be landed . . . Owing to the prevalence of home manufacture, the consumption of intoxicating beer in some country districts, probably, has been greater in recent years than it was under the old licence law.[79]

He might have added that in the three years between 1922 and 1924, the government had received over a million dollars in revenue from the sale of liquor for "medicinal, sacramental and scientific purposes".[80]

Despite the manifest difficulties of enforcing the law, which received such prominence in the daily press, there was some evidence that prohibition was fulfilling its main objective. Liquor was expensive, not always easily obtained and, by the time it had passed through the hands of several bootleggers, not very strong. This was reflected in the arrests for drunkenness which had risen steadily in Nova Scotia from 1,255 in 1900 to a high of 3,999 in 1914. With the resumption of federal prohibition they declined from 3,140 in 1920 to a low of 1,392 in 1923. In 1925 they were still only 1,466.[81]

79 Report of Inspector-in-chief, 1925, *J.H.A.*, 1926, Appendix 18, pp. 5-8.
80 *The Control and Sale of Liquor in Canada*, p. 8, Table 4.
81 *Ibid.*, p. 9.

In July of 1925 a Conservative government came to power in Nova Scotia. Murray had retired from politics in 1923 leaving the reins of government to the one-time prohibition advocate E. H. Armstrong. The luckless Armstrong was left to face a critical depression, disastrous strikes in the major coal and steel industries, mounting costs of government and dwindling revenues. The result of the election of June 25, 1925 was almost a foregone conclusion as the Conservatives under the leadership of E. N. Rhodes won 40 of the 43 seats in the Assembly.[82]

Rhodes appeared to have viewed the termination of prohibition as a potential solution to the critical problem of government deficits. By 1925 the four Western Provinces and Quebec had abandoned prohibition for a system of so called "government control," that is, government sale of liquor. It was proving an extremely lucrative business for the provinces involved. British Columbia for example in 1923 realized a net profit from liquor sales of over three million dollars,[83] an amount equal to three-fifths of the entire Nova Scotia budget. In 1926, Rhodes reported to Sir Robert Borden that he detected: "a marked swing towards Government control of liquor. This will probably be accelerated by our financial position as we are faced during the current year with a deficit of $1,050,000."[84]

Nevertheless, Rhodes was in no position to abandon prohibition. Temperance sentiment was still strong and well organized. Rhodes was also cognizant that a large element of his party's support in the election of 1925 had come from the reform element in the province. His personal manifesto and the party platform had contained promises of "mothers' allowances", a less partisan government, and full scale investigations of labour problems and rural depopulation — all of which had been urged by the churches and the Social Service Council. Although prohibition had not been mentioned in the platform, party candidates in rural areas had been strong in their denunciation of Liberal deficiencies in enforcement.[85] Within the first six months of coming to office his government was presented with petitions supporting prohibition from nearly five hundred organizations in the province — temperance societies, church groups, women's institutes and agricultural clubs. In September, 1925, the Maritime Conference of the newly created United Church endorsed prohibition by an "unanimous standing vote".[86] Early in 1926, Rhodes adopted a policy intended to reassure reform elements of his sincerity

82 See E. R. Forbes, "The Rise and Fall of the Conservative Party in the Provincial Politics of Nova Scotia, 1922-1933" (unpublished M.A. thesis, Dalhousie University, 1967), chapter 2.

83 *The Control and Sale of Liquor in Canada*, p. 8.

84 Rhodes to Borden, 1926, Rhodes Papers, P.A.N.S.

85 In Shelburne a Conservative convention even went as far as to nominate an "independent" candidate to run on a prohibitionist platform. Halifax *Herald*, 10 June 1925.

86 Rhodes Papers, P.A.N.S., vol. 81 and *Minutes of the Maritime Conference of the United Church of Canada*, 1925, p. 23.

in enforcing prohibition while leaving the door open for its subsequent abandonment. He pledged his government to a determined effort to enforce the prohibition laws, but if, after a reasonable time, this proved impossible he would introduce a program for government control. Lest any should doubt his sincerity in enforcing prohibition he appointed as his inspector-in-chief Rev. D. K. Grant, a lawyer, clergyman and prohibitionist. It was an appointment which won the immediate and grateful approval of the United Church.[87]

D. K. Grant promised no miracles in enforcement. In his first report, after six months in office, he stressed the difficulties of reforming a situation which had become entrenched after "years of administrative neglect and indifference on the part both of the Federal and Provincial authority". The problem was also aggravated by "the fact of a sharply divided public opinion, a large element of society, including the magistry *(sic)* itself being either openly antagonistic or passively resistant to the present law".[88]

Nevertheless, Grant set to work in a burst of energy to increase the size of the provincial force, raise the wages of the municipal inspectors and propose fresh amendments to the Nova Scotia Temperance Act. Assisted by the newly created Dominion Preventive Force of the Department of Customs and Excise, Grant and his inspectors launched a determined assault upon illicit liquor traffic. During his first year in office, arrests, seizures and convictions by provincial inspectors more than doubled, while successful prosecutions by both provincial and municipal inspectors increased from 716 for 1926 to 938 for 1927.[89] This increased activity was far from appreciated by influential elements in both political parties. The Conservative Halifax *Herald* began a campaign against Grant for his "arbitrary" methods of prosecuting offenders.[90] Some Liberals indicated their displeasure by securing the dismissal of the federal Preventive Officer at Glace Bay for being "too active in his duties."[91]

In fact, despite Grant's best efforts at enforcement there was evidence of a gradual decline in support for prohibition and an increase in the consumption of alcohol. In 1926 there were 1,898 arrests for drunkenness, 2,053 in 1927 and 2,176 in 1928.[92] There also appeared to be an increased reluctance on the part of juries to convict bootleggers, especially in the case of second offenders for whom jail terms were mandatory.[93]

The resistance to prohibition as usual was strongest in Halifax. The Conservative M.L.A.'s from the city found it expedient to show their opposition by

87 *Minutes, United Church,* 1927, p. 27.

88 Report of Inspector-in-chief for 1926, *J.H.A.,* 1927, pp. 5, 12.

89 *Ibid.,* 1927; *J.H.A.,* 1928, pp. 6, 15.

90 Halifax *Herald,* 1 March 1928.

91 "Memorandum Re: N. S. Affairs," 1927, vol. 7, Col. J. L. Ralston Papers, P.A.C.

92 *Control and Sale of Liquor in Canada,* p. 9, Table 5.

93 Report of Inspector-in-chief for 1927, *J.H.A.,* 1928, Appendix 8, p. 10.

resolutions in the House. These Rhodes deflated with amendments to the effect that the law would not be changed without a referendum. Such signs of growing hostility stimulated a flexing of muscles by the prohibitionists. On January 1, 1928, H. R. Grant announced that the Social Service Council, the Women's Christian Temperance Union and the Sons of Temperance were joining forces to prevent any changes in the Temperance Act.[94]

The pressure upon the provincial administration to resort to government control was substantially increased in 1926 by the federal government's announcement of an old age pension scheme, the costs of which were to be shared equally by the provinces and the Dominion. While such a plan might be within the reach of the western provinces and their relatively young population, it was totally beyond the resources of the Nova Scotia government with its much larger percentage of potentially eligible recipients.[95]   In 1928, Rhodes appointed a Royal Commission to explore methods of financing old age pensions and called an election before the Commission was due to report. During the campaign he reiterated his promise not to abandon prohibition without a plebiscite but gave no indication when such a referendum would be held.[96]

The election nearly proved disastrous for the Conservatives as their majority shrank from 37 to 3. Both prohibition and old age pensions were issues in the campaign. Discontent over the former was probably a factor in Halifax where Conservative majorities of over 7,000 in 1925 melted away and three of the five Conservative candidates were defeated.

After the election the Royal Commission presented its report. To the surprise of no one, it recommended government control of liquor sales as a possible source of revenue for old age pensions.[97]   Shortly thereafter, Rhodes scheduled a plebiscite on the question of prohibition versus government control for October, 1929. Armed with the ammunition supplied by the Commission and with the tacit encouragement of the provincial government, a new Temperance Reform Association was organized in Halifax in September, 1929. Its President, J. A. Winfield, attacked the Nova Scotia Temperance Act for its adverse effect on youth and claimed that his Association was seeking through "moral suasion" and education the most effective means of encouraging temperance in Nova Scotia. This claim was scouted by the editor of the *United Churchman,* who pointed to the rapid disappearance of similar groups in other provinces once the prohibitory system had been destroyed.[98]

94 Halifax *Herald,* 1 January 1928.

95 4.7% of Nova Scotia's population was over 70 years of age compared with 1.2% to 1.8% for the four Western provinces. Report of the Royal Commission on Old Age Pensions, *J.H.A.,* appendix No. 29, p. 43.

96 Copy of speech delivered at Windsor, 8 September 1928, Rhodes Papers, P.A.N.S.

97 *Report of the Royal Commission on Old Age Pensions,* p. 41.

98 *United Churchman,* 25 September 1929, p. 4.

As the campaign increased in intensity, it became evident that the pro-hibitionists had lost many of their allies of 1920. The Anglican *Church Work* was conspicuously silent before the plebiscite and expressed its "relief" when it was over. The *Casket* went to considerable pains to explain that the Roman Catholic Church had never endorsed more than personal abstinence and that membership in the League of the Cross did not convey any obligation to vote for prohibition.[99]

The Rhodes administration apparently did everything possible to aid the campaign for government control. Rhodes, particularly, seems to have seen the future of the government riding on the question. His jaundiced explana-tion of the opposition to government control is perhaps more revealing of his own commitment than of the forces described. According to Rhodes, three elements were fighting for retention of prohibition: the Liberals, on the prin-ciple that "if government control carries, Rhodes is in power for twenty years", the towns, "because of the revenue from fines", and the bootleggers "who were practically solid against us and the rum-runner as well".[100]

Government control won a decisive victory in the plebiscite, 87,647 to 58,082. It received a majority in every county but six. Only the rural counties of Shelburne, Queens, Kings, Hants, Colchester and Annapolis — counties in which the Baptist and United Churches were predominant — did prohibition retain a majority.[101]

The government lost no time in implementing the wishes of the people. The old Act was quickly repealed and a Liquor Commission was set up with a complete monopoly of liquor outlets in the province. Sale by the glass was to be limited by local option; otherwise Commission sales would be unrestricted. Within less than a year the Commission had established a store in every town and city in the province plus a special mail-order agency in Halifax for the convenience of rural customers.

The prohibitionists were bloodied but unbowed; the Social Service Council and its indomitable secretary, H. R. Grant, denounced the Government for its "complicity" in the socially demoralizing liquor traffic, a position endorsed by the United Church.[102] Within a year Grant and other temperance workers were to be found hard at work in a vain effort to pledge members of the Legis-lature to support a measure for local option on a county basis.[103]

A number of obvious factors might be mentioned in explaining the defeat of prohibition in Nova Scotia. The *United Churchman* claimed that the lack of enforcement discredited the movement among its friends and led to the

99 *Church Work,* December 1929, p. 3 and *Casket,* 16 May 1929.
100 Rhodes to J. Philip Bell, 4 November 1929, Rhodes Papers, P.A.N.S.
101 *J.H.A.,* 1929, Appendix 27, p. 38.
102 *United Churchman,* 1 January 1930.
103 Halifax, *Chronicle,* 14 November 1929.

desire to experiment with government control.[104]   This raises the question of whether enforcement was possible, given the opposition to the law by such a determined minority. The answer would appear to hinge on the goal desired. Even with the relatively lax enforcement of the early 1920's, the arrests for drunkenness had been halved throughout the period from 1922 to 1926. Still it is doubtful if even the most rigorous enforcement would have ended the accounts of smuggling, illegal manufacture and related crimes which filled the press of the period. And it was these which made many Nova Scotians wonder if the prohibition cure were not worse than the disease. Such doubts must have become more acute as the prohibitionists saw their cause abandoned by every other province but Prince Edward Island. Then came a positive factor in the Province's need for additional revenue, which the demand for other reforms made crucial. This was certainly the main consideration for the Rhodes' Government, and after the report of the Royal Commission on old age pensions, the issue apparently achieved a similar clarity for the people of Nova Scotia. They were given a choice between prohibition and old age pensions and opted decisively for the latter.

There were more fundamental reasons for the rejection of prohibition in 1929. In the early twentieth century, the movement had rapidly increased in strength, rising upon the tide of optimistic, idealistic reform which accompanied the churches' conversion to the social gospel. As the tide began to ebb, prohibition suffered accordingly. The reform movement of the social gospel reached a climax in Nova Scotia immediately following the World War. People had confidently prepared to create the new and better society which they expected would be within their reach. But conditions in Nova Scotia in the 1920's were conductive neither to optimism or reforms. Instead of the anticipated triumph of humanitarian justice, there came a critical and lingering depression, bankruptcy, wage-cuts, strikes, violence and emigration. In the industrial sphere, proposals for social reform were blocked by the financial difficulties of the corporations on one side, and compromised by the strident voice of radical Marxism on the other. Little could be expected in the realm of legislation from a Government whose economic difficulties precluded the social welfare legislation which seemed to be required as never before.

It is nor surprising under such circumstances, that some churchmen apparently re-examined their consciences and concluded that the church was more useful in consoling suffering mortals, than in shattering lances against an unrepentant society. Disillusionment, however, was avoided by many, who apparently saw as the impediment to the attainment of their goals, nothing more invulnerable than an inept provincial administration, and a federal government whose policies accentuated regional injustices under which their their province suffered. Their reform enthusiasm, retaining some of the rhetoric of the social gospel, became channeled into a broadly based movement

104 *United Churchman,* 6 November 1929.

to rehabilitate the region economically from within, while securing economic "justice" from without. Yet for those who looked with exaggerated hopes to the success of "Maritime Rights" candidates in provincial and federal elections, disillusionment was perhaps but the more severe for being deferred.

The decline of prohibition to some extent paralleled that of the general reform movement. As partially a utopian reform, it had suffered on implementation from the inevitable reaction. It did not yield the results predicted by its proponents. There was apparently no spectacular decline in disease, mental illness, poverty or crime in the province. On the contrary, prohibition was blamed by its opponents for much of the crime which did occur. For a time, many of its supporters maintained faith in their programme by attributing its deficiencies to the obvious lack of enforcement by the Murray-Armstrong administration. Then came the expected transition in government and with it the ultimate disillusionment of the prohibitionists, as one of their own number was no more successful in securing the desired results from prohibition than his predecessors.

Still another factor contributed to the decline in popular enthusiasm for prohibition. In the long battle for enforcement, the goals of reform appeared to receive less and less discussion. Harassed clergymen in their pre-occupation with the struggle began to denounce rum-running and bootlegging as "sins". Unconsciously, the prohibitionists were reverting to the language of the nineteenth century movement. Prohibition was becoming divorced in the mind of the public from the main stream of social reform. Gradually it was acquiring the image of censorious fanaticism, which, exaggerated by its opponents, it has retained to the present day.

There was a note of irony in the defeat of prohibition in 1929. Prohibition had acted as mid-wife at the birth of the social gospel in Canadian Churches. The two had been closely linked in the flowering of the reform movement. But the latter, in creating the public demand for social welfare legislation, contributed significantly to the economic pressure providing the immediate cause for the defeat of the former. It was a measure of the success of the social gospel that as one dream was being destroyed, others, perhaps more realistic, were gaining a hold on public opinion. J. S. Woodsworth's victory in forcing the Mackenzie King government to adopt old age pensions had contributed to the fall of prohibition in Nova Scotia. Yet it also symbolized a future victory of the social gospel ideals in secular society, the ultimate goal of the leaders of the prohibition movement in Nova Scotia.

G.A. RAWLYK

Reprinted from XVII, No. 1
(Autumn 1987)

Fundamentalism, Modernism and the Maritime Baptists in the 1920s and 1930s

MANY ENGLISH-CANADIAN HISTORIANS FIND IT embarrassingly difficult to take religion seriously. As they comb the past for relevance they are keen to avoid any confrontation with spiritual and religious realities. Perhaps they are uncomfortable thinking about such issues. Perhaps, because of the older Whig political bias of so much Canadian historical writing and the newer bias of secular social history, they are determined to float in the mainstream of historiography and not be lost in some shallow cul-de-sac. This somewhat unfair caricature of the Canadian historical profession underscores some of the basic problems confronting the writing of religious history in English Canada in the 1980s. When compared with American historians, English-Canadian historians have significantly downplayed the importance of religion as a formative force in national life. Canadian historical writing, especially that of post World War II period, reflects the devastating impact of what has been referred to as "that process of separation and individualism that modernity seems to entail".[1] A sensitive reading of Canadians' collective religious past should bring what Stephen Toulmin has called a degree of "cosmic interrelatedness" back to scholarly investigation.[2] Of course, a revived and Americanized Canadian religious history is not the only way to accomplish this end. But if Canadians could begin to discuss critically and openly issues about religion, values, community, individualism, space and time "in ways that did not disaggregate them into fragments", it might still be possible "to find connections and analogies with the older ways in which human life was made meaningful".[3]

Ironically, within the larger context of the recent historiography of the Maritime Provinces, religious history has not been pushed off into some dark corner of irrelevance, inconsequence, and scholarly oblivion. Since at least the early 1970s the writing of religious history has become "probably the most active and exciting field of historical scholarship in the Maritimes today".[4] Post Revolutionary Maritime history, with its emphasis on the significant influence of the Allinite-New Light legacy, has now found itself on what is to some historians

1 See R.N. Bellah et al., *Habits of the Heart: Individualism and Committment in American Life* (Berkeley, 1985), p. 275.

2 S. Toulmin, *The Return to Cosmology: Postmodern Science and the Theology of Nature* (Berkeley, 1982), pp. 228-9.

3 Bellah, *Habits of the Heart*, p. 283.

4 David Bell, "All Things New: The Transformation of Maritime Baptist Historiography", *Nova Scotia Historical Review*, 4, 2 (Spring 1984), p. 70.

the leading edge of the discipline in Canada.[5] A caustic critic might simply comment that taking into account the sad state of contemporary Canadian religious writing, such a claim is indeed a modest one. Another might respond that the peripheral nature of so much Maritime historical writing is merely underscored by the fact that what is seen as a scholarly *cul de sac* by the Central Canadian opinion-makers is viewed as the mainstream and cutting edge by scholars in or of the region. There is a ring of truth, moreover, in the argument of Professor Terrence Murphy that religious developments in the Maritime region in the immediate post-Revolutionary period have already received adequate scholarly attention. He correctly urges historians to abandon an obsession with the Revolution and Henry Alline and to examine 19th and 20th century religious leaders, movements, and ideology.[6] In fact, although there are a number of very good studies dealing with Roman Catholicism, especially the Antigonish Movement, little of real significance has been published about Protestantism in the Maritimes in the 20th century apart from Professor Ernie Forbes' fine article dealing with "Prohibition and the Social Gospel in Nova Scotia".[7] Thus the 20th century beckons the historian interested in virtually any aspect of Protestant religious development in the Maritimes. There is no fear of being criticized as a nasty revisionist. There is almost nothing to revise.

One group of Protestants that merit immediate study would be the Maritime Baptists. In no other part of Canada do Baptists form such a large proportion of the population nor have they had such a profound influence on the existing popular culture. Although the Baptist Church was never an important force, on Prince Edward Island, in 1901, taking Nova Scotia and New Brunswick as a single entity, the Baptists were the largest Protestant denomination in this area. Twenty years later the Baptists in New Brunswick and Nova Scotia were still the largest Protestant denomination. But in 1931 they were pushed to second place by the United Church and in 1961 to third by the Anglicans.[8]

By the 1920s almost every Baptist in the Maritimes belonged to the United Baptist Convention of the Maritime Provinces, which had been created in 1906 when the Regular or Calvinist Baptists of the region had joined with the Free Baptists or Arminians. Acadia University in Wolfville was the Convention's institution of higher learning and the administrative arm of the Convention was

5 See, for example, D.G. Bell, ed., *New Light Baptist Journals of James Manning and James Innis* (Hantsport, 1984); G.A. Rawlyk, ed., *The New Light Letters and Spiritual Songs* (Hantsport, 1983) and G.A. Rawlyk, *Ravished by the Spirit: Religious Revivals, Baptists and Henry Alline* (Montreal, 1984); J.M. Bumsted, *Henry Alline, 1748-1784* (Toronto, 1971); M.W. Armstrong, *The Great Awakening in Nova Scotia, 1776-1809* (Hartford, 1948); Gordon Stewart and George Rawlyk, *A People Highly Favoured of God: The Nova Scotia Yankees and the American Revolution* (Toronto, 1972).

6 Terrence Murphy, "The Religious History of Atlantic Canada: The State of the Art", *Acadiensis*, XV, 1 (Autumn 1985), p. 173.

7 *Acadiensis*, I, 1 (Autumn 1971), pp. 11-36.

8 See Rawlyk, *Ravished by the Spirit*, pp. 170-2.

located in Saint John. During the late 1920s, however, the unity of the Convention was increasingly threatened by the rising tide of Fundamentalism which began to spread into the region from Central Canada and the United States.

In Central Canada and the West the division between Fundamentalists and Modernists split the Baptist conventions.[9] A principal actor in the so-called Fundamentalist-Modernist controversy in both regions was the Reverend Thomas Todhunter Shields — the influential and controversial Baptist Fundamentalist leader who was minister of the Jarvis Street Baptist Church in Toronto from 1910 to 1955.[10] There was no Maritime Fundamentalist leader whose influence was comparable to that of Shields but the United Baptist Maritime Convention did experience a less serious challenge to its authority from the Reverend John James Sidey.[11] Sidey became the most outspoken critic of the leadership of the Convention, but he was not able to attract to his Separatist, Baptist, and Fundamentalist movement an appreciable number of Convention Baptists. The interesting question is why Sidey was not more successful in his sectarian offensive in the Baptist heartland of Canada. Why did Sidey's schismatic movement remain relatively weak during a period when the Baptist leadership in the Convention was moving off in what to many rank and file Baptists was a liberal direction?[12]

John James Sidey was born in Portsmouth, England on 28 December 1891. His father, the Reverend Charles J. Sidey, was a Wesleyan Methodist missionary-minister in Newfoundland, where the young John spent some of his early years.[13] After this sojourn in Newfoundland, Sidey and his mother returned to England. Sidey's mother, Sarah, was a pious Methodist but her marriage was not a happy one and she separated permanently from her husband when she set sail from Newfoundland for Portsmouth. Consequently, it would be his mother,

9   See W. Ellis, "Social and Religious Factors in the Fundamentalist-Modernist Schisms Among Baptists in North America, 1895-1930", Ph.D. thesis, University of Pittsburgh, 1974; M.B.R. Hill, "From Sect to Denomination in the Baptist Church in Canada", Ph.D. thesis, State University of New York at Buffalo, 1971; G.H. Poucett, "A History of the Convention of Baptist Churches of British Columbia", M.Th. thesis, Vancouver School of Theology, 1982; J.B. Richards, *Baptists in British Columbia* (Vancouver, 1976).

10 L.K. Tarr, *Shields of Canada* (Grand Rapids, 1967); C.A. Russell, "Thomas Todhunter Shields, Canadian Fundamentalist", *Foundations*, XXIV, 1 (Winter 1981), pp. 15-31.

11 A somewhat uncritical and superficial biography of Sidey has been written by one of his followers, Gertrude A. Palmer, *The Combatant* (Middleton, 1976).

12 See, for example, *Maritime Baptist*, published in Kentville, and *The United Baptist Year Book*, printed in Truro, for this period.

13 The biographical material is based upon Sidey's letter of 5 September 1934 to the editor of the *Middleton Outlook* and upon Sidey's testimony in the famous 1935 Kingston Baptist Parsonage case. The *Outlook* letter is in the possession of Mrs. George Moody, Wolfville, Nova Scotia. A copy of the official transcript of the trial is to be found in the Acadia University Archives. Hereafter, the transcript shall be referred to as "Court Records". I have not yet been able to find the original transcript of the trial.

not his father, who would significantly influence, at its formative stage, Sidey's spiritual and emotional life.

At the age of 14, John Sidey was converted and he soon became an active member of the Pembrook Road Methodist Church, serving as a lay preacher. Encouraged by his mother, Sidey became a dentist's apprentice in Portsmouth. Because of financial problems, and the fact that he had injured his right hand and therefore felt his future as a moulder of false teeth was very limited, he decided to emulate his father and become a Methodist missionary to the New World. But when he left Portsmouth for Nova Scotia in the early summer of 1911, the 19-year old Sidey was still uncertain about his future. He was not ordained; he was not an official recruit of a Methodist Missionary Society; and he was not responding to a specific call from a Nova Scotia Methodist Church. Soon after arriving in Halifax, Sidey made his way to his uncle, the Reverend James Heil, a Methodist minister then living in Windsor. In the summer of 1911, despite what he would write in the 1930s and 1940s, Sidey was disoriented and, as one of his most ardent followers has put it, "Uncertain of many things".[14] Assisting his uncle obviously did not satisfy the young Sidey who resolved in 1916 to move to the United States to enroll in two Methodist Episcopal institutions in the Chicago area — Northwestern University and Garrett Biblical Institute.

It has been argued that Sidey went to the United States because he had discovered that "the Nova Scotia institutions were becoming infiltrated" with "a humanistic higher criticism".[15] There may, however, have been other reasons for Sidey's decision in 1916 to emigrate to Illinois. He may have been looking for new worlds to conquer — for a greater challenge than that provided by the relative backwater of Windsor. Or it may have been that the young Methodist did not want to fight for the British cause in Europe. Conscription would not come to Canada until 1917 but Sidey must have felt intense community pressure, especially in 1915 and 1916, to join in the Christian crusade to eradicate the Germanic anti-Christ. Sidey, who was always more positively inclined to maternal influence than fatherly-like pressure, may also have wanted to be independent of his uncle. He therefore saw in his move to Chicago a heaven-sent opportunity to resolve a number of difficult personal and career problems.

While attending Northwestern and Garrett, Sidey supported himself financially by accepting a student pastorship associated with the Rock River Methodist Episcopal Conference and he served three Methodist congregations in South Chicago, Calumet Heights and Langley Avenue. But a year at Northwestern and Garrett with their "modernistic teaching" was more than enough for Sidey who transferred to Union Theological College — also located in Chicago — in 1917.[16] Union was basically controlled by the Congregational-

14 See Palmer, *The Combatant*, p. 25.

15 *Ibid.*, p. 26.

16 *Ibid.*, p. 27. I have a copy of Sidey's Garrett academic record in my possession.

ists and here Sidey found that his Methodist Arminian views were challenged by a tough-minded Calvinism. While studying at Union, and serving as a student pastor in southern Chicago, Sidey also found time "to take up Y.M.C.A. work" and near the end of the war he assisted the senior chaplain at Fort Sheridan as part of his Methodist pastoral work.[17] While serving the Rock River Methodist Episcopal Conference and the American Army and while still studying at Union Theological College, Sidey decided to work for a Doctor of Divinity degree at the Oriental University, located in Washington, D.C. After a "seven or eight months" association with Oriental University — only via correspondence — Sidey was awarded the M.A. and D.D. degrees for a short thesis entitled "Immortality, the Inevitable Result of a Progressive Universe".[18] A short time after Sidey received his D.D. in 1921, Oriental University was declared a fraudulant degree-mill and by court order its doors were permanently closed, or more accurately its mail-box permanently sealed. In 1921, at the same time as Sidey became a Doctor of Divinity (Oriental University), he received the Bachelor of Theology degree from Union and was ordained a Methodist Episcopal minister.[19]

Three years earlier Sidey had travelled to Nova Scotia to marry Edna Card, a teacher then residing in Hants County. The young couple returned to Chicago where both of them had a great deal of difficulty dealing with urban life and the new ideas that seemed to be bombarding the Methodist Church in the immediate post war period. Though apparently successful at Fort Sheridan, Sidey experienced the deep despair of doubt, and morbid introspection seemed to immobilize him. Finally, after much spiritual turmoil, and greatly influenced by two female Salvation Army officers, Sidey found peace of mind as he jettisoned what he was learning in the class room and replaced it with a renewed personal relationship with Christ. "It was a terrific battle", he once observed, "to rid myself of the new ideas that had been, by study and by teaching, superimposed upon the experience of my youth".[20]

While still associated with Fort Sheridan, and spurred by a new sense of evangelical zeal, Sidey and his wife became active in the Soul Winner's Gospel Association which had its headquarters in the St. Paul Methodist Episcopal Church in Chicago. Using his considerable musical skills, Sidey conducted his first evangelistic crusade for the Soul Winner's Association in June 1920, at Diamond Lake, Illinois. The publicity for the crusade, which he probably prepared, described Sidey as "a man, who, while college trained, has evidently learned to think for himself. Although he has not yet acquired a reputation as a flowery orator, he has the faculty of forcefully presenting ideas that start and keep you thinking. His addresses are sure to be of uncommon interest to all those

17 "Court Records", Acadia University Archives.
18 Quoted in Palmer, *The Combatant*, p. 32.
19 "Court Records", Acadia University Archives.
20 Quoted in Palmer, *The Combatant*, p. 31.

who enjoy the exercise of thought". Yet, the crusade was something of a disaster for Sidey who, because of his lack of success, felt a desperate need for "the baptism of power of the Holy Spirit".[21] Disheartened and disillusioned, Sidey decided to revitalize his faith by attending a Prophetic Bible Conference at Moody Bible Institute in Chicago. While staying at Moody, Sidey discovered the influential premillennial tract, *The Second Coming of Christ*. Almost immediately Sidey and his wife saw their Christian faith in a radically new light.[22] The imminent return of Christ, the rapture, the emphasis upon the Dispensational view of the past, the present and future, all now made marvellous sense. According to the premillennial view, the world was becoming increasingly corrupt and the return of Christ was immine..: in order to bring the New Testament Dispensation or age to its glorious end. Just before His return, however, all true Christians on earth were to be "raptured" — that is removed temporarily from earth — so that they would not have to endure the bloody and cataclysmic final battle of Armageddon. They would return with their Christ to rule the earth, from Jerusalem, for a thousand year period. Premillenialism obviously provided Sidey with a new sense of purpose and direction in his life. His favourite verse from the Bible — and this tiny portion of the Scriptures would eventually be chistled on his gravestone — came from I Thessalonians 4.16 "Waiting until the trumpet of the Lord shall sound". Sidey, however, was not satisfied with merely waiting passively for the Lord to return. His premillennialism did not immobilize him. He was determined to help prepare the way for Christ's return by preaching the gospel with zeal and conviction; moreover, he desperately wanted to ensure that as many people as possible were, in fact, raptured before the terrible bloody battle of Armageddon.

In late 1920 and early 1921, a revitalized Sidey continued his work with the Soul Winner's Association of Illinois. His publicity brochure now had a somewhat different emphasis:

> Impressed by the vital need of spiritual life in the individuals who compose our civilization in this age, he with others, has decided to spend his life at the call of the Holy Spirit, in this tremendous field of evangelization. Mr. Sidey brings to the work a modern point of appeal of the Bible. The challenge "Back to the Bible" is the clarion call of his message. He believes in conversion, real regeneration, not hand-shaking or card-signing; but definite inquiry work followed by the witness of the Holy Spirit. On the other hand, the approach to all this is modern, not fanatical or highly emotional; simply an emphasis upon the Biblical spiritual realities as they have been shown to identify themselves with human nature.[23]

21 Quoted in *ibid.*, p. 39.

22 For a fuller discussion of this phenomenon see D.W. Frank, *Less Than Conquerors: How Evangelicals Entered the Twentieth Century* (Grand Rapids, 1986), pp. 66-75.

23 Quoted in Palmer, *The Combatant*, pp. 40-1.

In a period of a few months, Sidey's essential message for the Soul Winner's Association had undergone a fundamental change. There was now a concern about "conversion" and not about "ideas"; there was a new emphasis upon "Back to the Bible" and the "witness of the Holy Spirit" rather than "the exercise of thought". Sidey had, in a sense, become a Conservative Evangelical; he was not yet, the evidence suggests, a Fundamentalist. What seemed to separate these two positions was a certain degree of "violence in thought and language" which characterized the Fundamentalist mind but not the Conservative Evangelical.[24] In other words, the former viewed God as a close-minded judge while the latter saw the Almighty as a loving parent. Moreover, for the Fundamentalist, confrontation was to be preferred to any form of Evangelical accommodation with modernity. By late 1920, however, Sidey was certainly quickly moving in the Fundamentalist direction — towards and beyond Moody Bible Institute and light years away from the University of Chicago Divinity School. The latter institution, for Sidey and his Chicago friends, had become the bastion of all the insidious and evil forces of Modernism and Liberalism then spreading across North America.

Despite the fact that she had two small children to be concerned about, Edna Sidey played a key role in her husband's two Soul Winner's evangelistic campaigns. A vigorous and dynamic woman, intelligent, shrewd and persuasive, she did not enjoy living in the United States and was keen to go back to her beloved Nova Scotia. When her husband's academic work had finally been completed at Union in 1921, and after his ordination, she persuaded him to return to her home in Burlington on the Avon River in Hants County. Soon after their return, Sidey was baptized by immersion by the Reverend Neil Herman, minister of the Emmanuel Baptist Church in Truro, a leading Nova Scotia Fundamentalist, whom Sidey had met in 1916 while spending a summer at Brunswick Street Methodist Church in Truro.

In 1921 Sidey showed little interest in finding a pastorate in a Methodist Church. Instead he resolved to introduce into his adopted province the evangelistic approach he had learned with the Illinois Soul Winner's. His mission was to bring the gospel of Christ to the isolated backwaters of Nova Scotia. His Soul Winner's Association of Nova Scotia became an official branch of the Soul Winner's Association of Chicago.[25] At its first convention held at Cambridge, Hants County, on 1 July 1922, a programme was adopted which stressed that the central thrust of the organization was "soul winning" in the rural, largely unchurched areas of the province. It was explicitly stated that the new group was interdenominational and a faith mission — that is, all financial

---

24 N. Furniss, *The Fundamentalist Controversy, 1918-1931* (New Haven, 1954), p. 36. This theme is superbly developed in C. Johnston, *McMaster University: The Toronto Years*, vol. I (Toronto, 1976), pp. 170-203.

25 For information about the Soul Winner's Association, see its Nova Scotia publication, *The Challenge*, to be found in the Public Archives of Nova Scotia.

support would come from concerned supporters — and that all of Sidey's followers were to be completely dependent upon the "outpouring of the Holy Spirit" and they were not to forsake the "kindred fellowship with other Christians".[26] Sidey organized a small team of dedicated workers and by the spring and summer of 1922 he saw scores of people, especially in Hants County, converted to his brand of Evangelical Christianity. In late 1922 and 1923, Sidey's "Evangelistic Band" travelled to Hammonds Plains, near Halifax and then to the Eastern Shore and Guysborough County.[27] In the Jeddore area, Sidey's team worked very closely with local Baptists. One of the Eastern Shore residents wrote to Sidey on 22 January 1923 that "The work is still growing. Most every person you meet now has something to say about the goodness of God. The men who have gone away to the woods send us beautiful letters telling us how God stands by them in their temptations". On 6 June 1923, it was reported from Jeddore that the revival fires were still burning: "I was down for a month from Lunenburg and it was to me the happiest month I have ever spent in my life. I really felt sorry when I had to leave them.... I said to Mother when I went home that it seemed everybody was better looking. Mother said, 'That's happiness', and I thank God that through Mr. Sidey and his workers that this change has come".[28]

The 1922-23 Eastern Shore Revival, which eventually spread into Guysborough County, was the means whereby hundreds of residents of a string of isolated settlements stretching from East Jeddore to Canso experienced the intensely satisfying and intensely pleasurable feeling of Christian fellowship as the "ecstasy of spontaneous communities" almost overwhelmed them.[29] In Guysborough County in 1923 and 1924, Sidey received enthusiastic support from the Reverend E.W. Forbes, an influential Methodist minister, who would remain close to Sidey throughout the 1920s and 1930s. During the 1923-4 Guysborough County campaign Sidey "preached 105 sermons (one every night) without a break and never preached the same sermon twice".[30] Yet despite the spiritual revivals he and his team had helped coax into existence, Sidey by late 1924 and early 1925 had become rather disillusioned with the work of the Nova Scotia Soul Winner's Association. Even the publishing of his own monthly newsletter *The Challenge*, which began in 1923, did not dispel Sidey's gnawing doubts about his evangelistic work. Sidey and his team realized that it was one thing to help people experience the "New Birth". Hundreds of Nova Scotians

---

26 "Daily Programme of the Soul Winner's Festival, 1 July - 10 July, 1922", to be found in the Public Archives of Nova Scotia. The P.A.N.S. has on microfilm some of the printed material used by Palmer in her study of Sidey.

27 See *The Challenge* for 1923.

28 Quoted in Palmer, *The Combatant*, p. 54.

29 See Victor Turner, *The Ritual Process: Structure and Anti-Structure* (Ithaca, 1979), pp. 139-40.

30 Quoted in Palmer, *The Combatant*, p. 56.

and other Maritimers had been converted in the 1922-4 period through the ministry of the Nova Scotia Soul Winner's Association. Yet once the team left the community and the revival ended, the new converts often found themselves without adequate spiritual nurturing or bitterly divided over which church in the community was the true instrument of the Almighty. A disheartened and disillusioned Sidey observed that "My experience has taught me that, while God has given some pastors a greater gift as evangelists than others, yet, this office would be exercised as among brethren within the framework of the church or denomination to which such men adhere".[31]

After sacrificing four years of his life for the Nova Scotia Soul Winner's Association, Sidey had come to the conclusion that his itinerating evangelistic work may have created more problems than it had resolved and he felt that the time was propitious for him to pastor a single church. He and his wife desired the stability, the regular income, and the peace of mind that they hoped might come from a settled ministry. Preaching 105 different sermons on 105 consecutive days was not something a normal father with a wife and two young children would want to do for the rest of his life. As he entered his mid 30's, J.J. Sidey obviously needed a major change of pace; he needed a church to pastor. But as he looked at his ministerial options in Nova Scotia, he saw few doors open to him. He could not return to the church of his father or to the church in which he had been ordained since both had become part of the United Church of Canada in 1925 and Sidey was opposed to that Church because its theology was too Modern and its leadership too Liberal. Presbyterians opposed to Union had no desire to have him nor did the Anglicans. But some of Sidey's most ardent supporters in the Soul Winner's Association were Maritime Baptists and the Reverend Neil Herman, who had baptized him, urged him to join the Maritime Baptist Convention. The Reverend T.T. Shields, whom Sidey had first met in Halifax in 1924, supported the pro-Baptist argument put forward by Herman. Since Sidey had conducted evangelistic campaigns in Prince Edward Island in 1923 and 1924 and had been particularly successful in the Bedeque area, it should not be surprising that in 1925 the Central Bedeque United Baptist Church asked him to be their temporary supply minister. No other Baptist church in the Maritimes indicated any interest in issuing a call to Sidey, an ordained Episcopal Methodist minister who had had no previous official contact with the Maritime United Baptist Convention. He therefore became a temporary supply minister in a tiny, peripheral Convention church.

Sidey's less than five-year Bedeque sojourn helped to transform him into a committed Fundamentalist. Fundamentalism's militant and extreme "opposition to modernism, both as a theology and a cultural secularity, distinguished it from earlier evangelical traditions".[32] As Ernest R. Sandeen and George S.

31 Quoted in *ibid.*, p. 58.
32 J. Carpenter, "The Revival of American Fundamentalism", Ph.D. thesis, Johns Hopkins University, 1984, p. 5.

Marsden have argued, Fundamentalism in the early 20th century in North America stressed the importance of certain distinctive beliefs — notably premillennialism and the verbal inerrancy of the Bible as well as the revivalistic tradition of Dwight L. Moody, the great 19th century American evangelist.[33] In addition, its belief core included a largely traditional Calvinist theology, and an emphasis on the substitutionary atonement theory — that Christ had died in the place of all truly redeemed sinners. Fundamentalists also stressed that the true church consisted only of those who had been genuinely converted. For Sidey, the inerrancy of the scriptures, substitutionary atonement, and premillennialism as well as Calvinism would be the most important Fundamentalist tenets.

While at Bedeque, Sidey became very closely associated with the controversial Reverend John Bolton Daggett, minister at the nearby Tryon United Baptist Church, who would be Sidey's confidant, aide and intimate friend until Daggett's death in 1939. A native of Grand Manan Island, Daggett was educated at Colby College, Maine and was ordained in 1894 as a Free Baptist minister. He played a key role in pushing the somewhat reluctant Free Baptists into union in 1906 with the much larger Regular or Calvinist Maritime Baptist Association. In 1911 he left the United Baptist ministry to become a deputy minister in the New Brunswick Department of Agriculture and served in this capacity until 1917 when he was implicated in the notorious Valley Railroad and Patriotic Potato Scandal. It was charged that Daggett had not only been the conduit for transferring large sums of money into and out of the hands of Conservative Party supporters but also had lied during the McQueen Commission hearings held in 1918.[34] Driven from the Department of Agriculture, Daggett served as pastor of the Marysville, New Brunswick United Baptist Church, until being called to the Tryon, P.E.I. United Baptist Church, where he ministered until 1926 when he moved to the Kingston, Nova Scotia United Baptist pastorate.

Sidey and Daggett were a remarkable team. In many respects very different, their respective strengths complemented one another. Sidey was a tall and robust man, full of vigour and seldom sick. His penetrating grey-blue eyes were often full of fun and he loved to laugh. Daggett, on the other hand, was sickly, small in stature, and very serious. Unlike Sidey, who carefully hid his emotions from public view, Daggett was a feisty, peppery individual whose quick temper often manifested itself in cutting remarks. He was a battler by nature and, like many others who have also suffered from tuberculosis, he was very mercurial, almost a kind of manic-depressive. When Daggett lived near him, Sidey was far more aggressive and closed-minded and Daggett helped greatly in making Sidey "The Combatant".[35]

33 E.R. Sandeen, *The Roots of Fundamentalism: British and American Millennarianism, 1800-1930* (Chicago, 1970); G.M. Marsden, *Fundamentalism and American Culture: The Shaping of Twentieth-Century Evangelicalism 1870-1925* (New York, 1980).

34 A.T. Doyle, *Front Benches and Back Rooms* (Toronto, 1976), pp. 85-97.

35 See Palmer, *The Combatant*, pp. 78-88.

Even before Sidey had had time to settle into his new Bedeque charge, he found himself a principal actor in the creation of the Maritime Christian Fundamentalist Association. All Maritimers — and not just Baptists — interested in battling against Modernism were invited to a special Conference held in Truro, in August 1925. The Truro Fundamentalist Conference was hosted by the Immanuel United Baptist Church and the guest speaker was T.T. Shields, the so-called "Spurgeon of Canada" and in the 1920s Canada's leading Fundamentalist. He had already helped to split the Ontario and Quebec Baptist Convention into two warring factions — a split that would be formalized a few years later. At the Conference the earlier friendship between Shields and Sidey "was further strengthened" as the former "was used to groom God's man for His job in the Maritimes".[36] Moreover, much to the satisfaction of Shields, a key resolution was adopted that "this meeting having a clear understanding of the issues involved, and realizing that the fundamentals of the gospel are in danger of being obscured in these days, through the widespread acceptance of modern ideas of the Bible, does hereby register its protest, and propose that an organization for the purpose of spreading information as to the real issues involved be formed and shall be known as *The Maritime Christian Fundamentalist Association*".[37] Daggett was elected the Interim President of the new Association and Sidey, the Interim Secretary.

The two Island ministers, spurred on by Shields, organized a special Conference on Christian Fundamentals at Tryon United Baptist Church, from 3-5 November 1925. It was hoped that the Conference would attract interested Fundamentalists from a wide spectrum of Maritime Churches. The main speaker was the Reverend Edward Morris, Rector of St. Matthias Anglican Church, Halifax and a committed premillennialist. A graduate of Wycliff College in the University of Toronto, Morris had become the Maritime spokesman of the premillennial point of view.[38] Morris did not, however, breathe much life into the Maritime Christian Fundamentalist Association. By January 1926 the organization was dead after a life of only a few months. It is hard to see how the Fundamentalist Association hoped to expand from its tiny Baptist base in Prince Edward Island. It needed leadership and support from the New Brunswick and Nova Scotia Baptist mainstream, as well as from key sectors of the United Church, the Presbyterian Church and the Anglicans. In 1925 the United Church had serious organizational problems to worry about and those Presbyterians who had refused to become part of the United Church were

---

36 *Ibid.*, p. 74.

37 Quoted in *ibid.*, p. 74.

38 Some of the manuscript papers of the Reverend Morris are in the possession of Professor Barry Moody, Acadia University. Professor Moody purchased these and other Morris material at an auction. Other Morris material has recently surfaced in the Hamilton Ontario region. Interview with a group of Fellowship Baptist Ministers in Stanley Avenue Baptist Church, Hamilton, 9 April 1987.

preoccupied with denominational survival. There were only a few Evangelical Anglicans and they were not eager to join an organization dominated by premillennialists and those whom they must have regarded as Bush-league Baptists. Most Maritime United Baptist Convention clergy saw no need for such an organization. Their denomination was already sympathetic to certain key elements of the Fundamentalist cause and some of them must have had serious reservations about the leadership of Sidey and Daggett — one an outsider and the other a person with an unsavoury reputation.

The sudden collapse of the Maritime Christian Fundamentalist Association meant that Sidey had more time and energy to devote to his Bedeque Church and to the Maritime United Baptist Convention. In 1926 Sidey officially became a Baptist by becoming a member of the Central Bedeque United Baptist Church. The following year his church asked the Maritime United Baptist Convention Examining Council for Ordination that "their Pastor Rev. J.J. Sidey, formerly a regularly ordained minister of the Methodist Episcopal body, but now a member of the Bedeque Church, be registered as a regularly ordained Baptist Minister". Together with a former Seventh Day Adventist minister, Sidey was examined by the Council for Ordination. After hearing "a frank statement" of his "doctrinal views", the Council resolved that Sidey's name "be added to our official list". He was listed "Sidey, J.J., M.A. D.D. Central Bedeque, 1927".[39]

Sidey loved to write, direct and produce ambitious religious pageants and he tried to use these pageants to consolidate his position in the Convention. His first production, written in 1926, *The Victory of the Gospel*, was based upon the "Wandering Jew" theme. In his foreword Sidey described cogently the essential story. The "Wandering Jew", in

> roaming through the earth in course of time reaches America, and finally Prince Edward Island. He finds the Island simply virgin forest, inhabited by a few savages. While musing one day in a sheltered glade, he is visited by an Angel, who rebukes him for his pessimistic outlook upon the future of the island, and promises to return at the end of each hundred years, to compare with him the results of the preaching of the Gospel of Calvary, in its effect upon the development of the Island.

In 1927 Sidey's *Supplanter*, based on the life of Jacob, was performed at Bedeque and in the following year *The Pilgrim or the Torch of Truth*. This latter pageant tried to describe the history of the "Maritimes Home Missions" from its beginnings in 1814. In the "Final Tableau", all the cast joined "in ascribing praise to the King of Kings, the World's Redeemer", while the Congregation joined "in the singing of 'Crown Him with Many Crowns'".[40] Sidey evidently hoped that

39 *United Baptist Year Book 1927* (Truro, 1927), p. 14.

40 The material about these pageants are to be found in the Sidey Papers, in the Acadia University Archives.

this production would travel the United Baptist Convention circuit and thrust him a little closer to the centre of Convention power and influence. The Reverend E.S. Mason, Superintendant of Home Missions for the Convention, was enthusiastic about the production, but he could not, because of the costs involved, put it on the road.[41]

Although his productions could not be easily transported to the mainland, Sidey and his family could — merely by moving there. In July 1930 he followed his dear friend J.B. Daggett to Kingston, Nova Scotia. Daggett's ill health had forced him to resign as pastor of the Kingston-Melvern Square-Lower Aylesford United Baptist Churches. He persuaded his church to issue a call to Sidey who was eager to leave the Island, having — as Daggett delicately expressed it — "been unfortunate in his investments".[42] Certain persistent Island creditors were pressuring Sidey hard and he was keen to escape the embarrassment and ill will produced by his unsuccessful business ventures in silver fox farming, especially as the dark gloom of the Great Depression engulfed the Island. Moreover, he and his wife Edna were a little bored with their Island ministry.

Less than a month after being inducted as pastor of the Kingston-Melvern Square-Lower Aylesford United Baptist Churches in the summer of 1930, Sidey organized the second annual "Baptist Evangelical Bible Conference", which was held in his Kingston Church. The stated purpose of the Conference was "an outpouring of the Holy Ghost for power in soul winning upon the churches of the United Baptist Convention in the Maritime Provinces and upon every individual attending the Conference".[43] Among the Baptist ministers attending the Conference were R.W. Lindsay, Upper Canard, Allan Tedford, of Woodstock, William B. Bezanson, Glace Bay, Henry T. Wright, Truro, and Horace L. Kinsman of Port Lorne. None of these ministers, it is important to note, had graduated from Acadia University and only Bezanson had a B.D. degree.[44] At the 1931 Conference, the third one held at Kingston, Sidey, as principal organizer, was responsible for shifting the emphasis away from the "Baptism of the Holy Spirit" toward premillennialism. As Sidey put it in his official "Greetings" to the delegates, he was "daily looking forward to that Blessed Hope, the Rapture of the Church".[45] As had been the case in 1930, the Reverend Edward Morris, the Anglican Evangelical from Halifax, was the key-note speaker and among the Convention Baptist Ministers who had attended the

41 Mason would play a key role in orchestrating the anti-Sidey movement in the Convention in the 1930s.

42 *Gospel Light*, Kingston, October 1934.

43 Information about these Conferences are to be found in the Sidey Papers, Acadia University Archives.

44 None of these men is mentioned in *The Acadia Record 1838-1953* (Wolfville, 1953). I have discovered some relevant material in *The United Baptist Year Book 1929* and *The United Baptist Year Book 1930*.

45 See the programme for the 1931 Conference to be found in the Sidey Papers in the Acadia University Archives.

1930 conference, only Reverend Wright from Truro, who had left the region, was not there in 1931. The four other ministers, Lindsay, Tedford, Bezanson and Kinsman, were joined by the Reverends F.C. Haysmere of Clementsvale, Alexander G. Crowe of Bedeque, J.H. Copeland of Nictaux and T.A. Meister of Westchester. Most of these men would join Sidey and Daggett soon after they had left the Convention in 1934.

Because of the "smouldering concern" of the Conference delegates "for their denomination's veracity in the handling of the Scriptures" and their conviction that Acadia University, like McMaster University in Ontario, was a Liberal-Modernist stronghold, it was decided to establish the Kingston Bible College.[46] The College, like scores of other Fundamentalist schools built throughout North America during the interwar years, was designed to protect what was regarded as the true "Biblical faith".[47] Sidey was named the first President of Kingston Bible College and he was to be assisted by Kinsman, Haysmere, and Daggett. The College was defined as an interdenominational rather than as a Baptist institution, probably in order to appeal to a wider cross section of potential students, but there were only three full-time students during the first year of the College's existence.[48]

Thus by the autumn of 1931 Sidey, with Daggett's assistance, had created a parallel Baptist Convention. They had their own publication *The Gospel Light* — established in 1931 — to compete with the *Maritime Baptist*. They had the Kingston Bible College to train their men and women for their special evangelistic work in the region. Sidey and Daggett had their annual "Baptist Evangelistic and Bible Conference", although Sidey was supported by fewer than a half-dozen Baptist congregations while the Convention could count on well over 500. Nonetheless, by 1932 all that Sidey needed was a little push to persuade him to leave the Convention. The push may have been provided by T.T. Shields and his former supporters in Ontario, who made it very clear that their continued financial support to Sidey was dependent on his quitting the Convention. Furthermore, Sidey's Maritime followers were pushing him toward secession. They had had enough of what they regarded as the Modernist Convention and they were disgusted with what they heard was going on at Acadia. According to them, Divinity students were being taught that the Bible was not inerrant; it was like any other book. Their professors openly scoffed at the "divinity of the Lord", and at the Genesis view of creation. Evolution was taught as the inspired gospel of the new scientific elite. And, to make matters even worse, dancing took place "regularly within Acadia's walls".[49] According to

46 Court Records, Acadia University Archives.

47 This is a very important theme in Carpenter, "The Renewal of American Fundamentalism". See also V.L. Brereton, "Protestant Fundamentalist Bible Schools, 1882-1946", Ph.D. thesis, Columbia University, 1981.

48 Palmer, *The Combatant*, p. 95.

49 *Gospel Light*, October 1934. See also the *Maritime Baptist*, 13 June 1934.

Daggett, his and Sidey's complaints about Acadia had fallen upon deaf ears. "We are looked upon as cranks and fanatics", he observed, rather than as committed disciples of the Lord. To underscore further the Modernistic and even "Unitarian influences" which controlled the Convention and Acadia, Professor Shirley Case, a graduate of Acadia in 1893, the scourge of Fundamentalism in the United States, Professor of Divinity at the University of Chicago, and eloquent advocate of theological Liberalism had been awarded the honourary D.C.L. by Acadia University in 1928. According to Daggett, who knew Case personally, the native of New Brunswick was "on the staff of the greatest infidel factory in America". By awarding Case the honourary D.C.L. degree, Acadia and the Convention had "stamped approval upon the most rampant Modernistic Institution on the Continent of America".[50]

By the summer of 1933 it was obvious that the Convention leaders had had enough of Sidey, Daggett, Kingston Bible College, and the intensifying attacks on their so-called "unadulterated Modernism".[51] The 1933 Convention therefore decided to investigate various charges brought against Sidey. On 10 or 11 November 1933, Sidey obviously decided to jump ship before being thrown off and he wrote "a letter of resignation" to the Convention.[52] By the middle of March 1934 his resignation was accepted by the Kingston and Lower Aylesford United Baptist Churches but not by Melvern Square. A majority of members of the latter church and significant minorities from the two former ones left their Churches with Sidey to form the Independent Baptist Church. At their 1934 Convention the United Maritime Baptists accused Sidey of using "a bogus D.D. degree" and of permitting "checks issues by him to be dishonoured by the bank on which they were drawn" and misapplying "denominational funds collected on the circuit at Kingston". In the judgment of the Examining Council, Sidey was felt "no longer worthy to have his name retained on the list of ordained ministers". The Convention also authorized its Executive Committee "to conserve the United Baptist interests at Malvern Square, Lewis Head Shelburne County and whenever necessary throughout the Convention". Daggett's name was striken from the "list of ministers for cause" as was that of the Reverend F.S. Haysmere, the Baptist minister at Lewis Head, who was one of Sidey's Nova Scotia lieutenants.[53] In 1934 the Convention formally accepted that Sidey, Daggett, Haysmere and many of their followers had already quit the Convention. Thus secession became expulsion and the Maritime United Baptist Convention indicated that it was prepared to fight the Sidey group in order to keep the schism in check.

Although the Kingston Bible College was forced to leave the Kingston United Baptist Church building, Sidey stubbornly held on to the parsonage. After a

50 *Gospel Light*, October 1934.

51 *Ibid.*

52 Court Records, Acadia University Archives.

53 *Maritime Baptist*, 12 September 1934.

bitter court case in May 1935, the Convention forced him out of the parsonage. The Kingston Baptist Parsonage Case, conducted in the Nova Scotia Supreme Court, Kentville, from 21 May to 25 May 1935, captured the attention of the entire province. It was not really a case about the ownership of a parsonage; rather it was a remarkable confrontation between two groups of Baptists, two ideologies, and two ways of life. It was essentially a battle between Fundamentalism and a more accommodating spirit — what has been referred to as "a new hermaneutic" based on "a double commitment: to the Biblical faith on the one hand and to the modern outlook on the other".[54] This is not to suggest that the entire United Baptist Convention of the Maritime Provinces was Modernist; it obviously was not. Yet some of its leadership was certainly affected by the so-called "Modernist impulse" and so were a surprising number of its members.[55] And throughout the 1930s the Convention's major mouthpiece *The Maritime Baptist* was far more Liberal than it was Conservative, far more sympathetic to "Modernism" than "Fundamentalism".[56] There appeared to be a serious problem in the Convention; Sidey was determined to do something about it — even if it meant destroying the Maritime United Baptist Convention.

The "Kingston Baptist Parsonage Case" was heard by Mr. Justice Humphry Mellish in the Supreme Court of Nova Scotia during the May 1935 term in Kentville. Over a four day period, from 21 May to 23 May and on 25 May, "No less than 50,000 words of evidence including testimony from as far back as 300 B.C." was heard. For the *Halifax Herald* reporter the packed courtroom, "crowded with members of the clergy, church officials, and prominent laymen, resembled more the place of an important church meeting than a Supreme Court trial". Not to be outdone, the *Halifax Chronicle* special correspondent maintained that the "intense interest" generated by the trial was "reminiscent of" that "at a murder trial".[57]

Sidey, from the beginning, realized that, as he put it, the "real issue fought out in the Supreme Court of Nova Scotia was the issue between Modernism and Fundamentalism".[58] The question of the ownership of the Kingston parsonage was only the excuse for Sidey and his supporters to confront all Convention Baptists with the awful truth that "the Convention" was "no longer Baptist but Unitarian, and in some cases, infidel".[59] Like Fundamentalist leaders such as J. Gresham Machen — the Princeton Presbyterian theologian — and T.T. Shields,

---

54 See C.H. Pinnock, "The Modernist Impulse at McMaster University, 1887-1927", in J. Zeman, ed., *Baptists in Canada* (Burlington, 1980), p. 195.

55 *Ibid.*, pp. 204-5.

56 This conclusion is based on a careful reading of the *Maritime Baptist* during the 1918 to 1939 period. See also *The United Baptist Year Book* for the same period.

57 *Halifax Herald*, 22, 27 May 1935; *Halifax Chronicle*, 18 September 1935.

58 *The Question*, June 1935.

59 *Ibid.*, October 1935.

Sidey was determined never to "bow the knee to the Baal of Modernism".[60] Scores of his supporters pushed themselves into the courtroom carrying with them their Bibles and their conviction that they were indeed supporting the Lord's anointed against the despised Convention anti-Christ. The trial was their trial as well and they desperately wanted the world to know where they stood. There were also the Convention officials and supporters, not as intense and not as alienated as their opponents, and not carrying proudly in their hands the badge of their Fundamentalism — the Scofield Bible — the influential textbook of premillenialism.[61]

When Mr. Justice Humphry Mellish entered the crowded courtroom he was met by what the *Halifax Chronicle* called "Batteries of leading legal talent".[62] Representing the Convention plaintiffs were B.W. Roscoe, K.C. of Kentville and George C. Nowlan, the former Tory M.L.A. and former Convention, Baptist Young People's Union (B.Y.P.U.) President. Opposing them and representing the trustees of the Kingston and Melvern Square Independent Baptist Churches were T.R. Robertson, K.C. and J.E. Rutledge, K.C., both of Halifax, and R.E. Boylan of Berwick. Roscoe and Nowlan argued that the trustees of the Kingston and Melvern Square United Baptist Churches, which had originally and jointly built the parsonage, still owned the building, thought to be worth $3,800 in 1935. Robertson, Rutledge and Boylan, on the other hand, contended that the Independent Baptists were the true Baptists — the ones who still preached and practised what they called "Baptistic principles" — and they therefore had the right to the parsonage. Their clients, however, had to admit that they had seceded from the United Baptist Church and created a new Church — the Independent Baptist Church. This admission, in the final analysis, would completely destroy their case.

With the parsonage detail out of the way, Sidey and Daggett were now ready to strike hard at the Convention — their principal objective. They naively thought that if they could prove, to their own satisfaction, that the Convention, and especially Acadia University, was not orthodox that thousands of Maritime Baptists would rally to the Fundamentalist cause. There was a peculiar sense of hubris and self importance permeating the testimonies of Sidey and Daggett. They were absolutely convinced of the rightness and righteousness of their cause; moreover, they felt that they were special instruments of the Almighty divinely chosen to return Maritime Protestantism to true Christianity. Feeling a tremendous sense of alienation from society because of the way in which the forces of modernity were altering their world, and experiencing both an acute

60 *Ibid.*, June 1936.
61 C.I. Scofield (1843-1921), an American lawyer and Congregational minister, whose *Scofield Reference Bible* was published in 1909. The extensive notes in the *Reference Bible* developed at great length and great detail Scofield's premillennial views. The *Scofield Reference Bible* profoundly affected the 20th century Fundamentalist movement.
62 *Halifax Chronicle*, 18 September 1935.

collective paranoia and garrison mentality, they saw in the pure church ideal the organizational means to deal with what they perceived to be the grim realities of 20th century life. J.B. Daggett declared in 1935 that "We are rushing with lightning speed toward the crisis, vividly foretold in the Book of Books. It behooves the Church of God to separate herself completely from the world, and the things of the world, and to be busy without holidays".[63] For Sidey, if Maritime Baptists did not abandon the "New Paganism" for "Fundamentalist separation and purity", they would be "the human cycle for the religion of Anti-Christ".[64]

Sidey was first questioned on Wednesday, 22 May by his lawyer T.R. Robertson — about his education, his preaching call, and what had transpired in the Kingston and Melvern Square United Baptist Churches in the 1931 to 1934 period.[65] Sidey argued that his Independent Baptist Church alone espoused "the historic Baptist position" concerning Church polity and that by leaving the Convention, his church had become the true Baptist church, while the Convention had, by betraying Baptist independence, become non-Baptist. Sidey's cross examination by George Nowlan did not go as smoothly as had his questioning by T.R. Robertson. Nowlan was a peculiar mixture of sophistication and almost bucolic opaqueness. Sometimes he could cut quickly and deftly to the heart of an issue; at other times he ponderously circled further and further away from the point being considered until the thrust of his questioning appeared to be totally irrelevant. Nowlan obviously disliked Sidey and Daggett and his questioning and his comments made outside the courtroom underscore this point.[66] He wanted to paint Sidey in a bad light and his questioning had little to do with the actual merits of the case involving the Kingston parsonage. Nowlan asked Sidey about Oriental University — "What was that?" "It purported to be a correspondence school, a University" Sidey replied. "You got in touch with them for what purpose?" "To see if I could do further work. I wanted to continue my work. I did seven or eight months work there. I got my M.A. degree for the thesis I submitted; I received my D.D.". The courtroom was deathly quiet as Nowlan pressed the alumnus from Oriental University even further. "It was under charter? Why was it restrained?" he asked. "It was under charter and certain work being done but I understood the restraining order was issued because it was not living up to its printed obligations" was the embarrassed reply. "It was fraudulent and the court stopped it!" Nowlan snapped at Sidey. "Did you ever see the institution?" "No, it was a correspondence course", Sidey answered.

Nowlan also questioned Sidey about his obtaining his "ordination certificate"

63 *The Question*, July 1935.

64 *Ibid.*, August 1935.

65 Unless otherwise noted all of the quotations used in this section about the Kentville trial are from the Court Records, Acadia University Archives.

66 See, for example, *Halifax Herald*, 24 May 1935.

from the United Baptist Convention after enduring a 15-minute period of questioning by an Examining Council chaired by Professor Dr. Simeon Spidle, Dean of Theology at Acadia University. Sidey now contended that his 1927 decision to go before the Convention's Examining Council was, in fact, "unBaptistic". He also stressed that the Convention had abandoned the key Baptist belief that the scriptures, in their original form, were divinely inspired and inerrant. The questioning continued:

> Q. Where are the original writings? A. In the various copies of the New Testament.
> Q. Where are the original writings? A. Some in the British Museum and other libraries throughout the world.
> Q. The original writings? A. The earliest copies we have.
> Q. I am asking where the original writings are. A. I don't know.
> Q. Do you know of any record of them ever being found? A. I don't know. There are translations.
> Q. From what date? A. 325, 350 A.D.
> Q. That would be some three hundred years after some of the events they detailed? A. Certainly.
> Q. And these manuscripts are in what? A. Greek and other oriental writings.
> Q. They in turn have been translated into ours? A. Yes.
> Q. How old are the oldest documents in the Old Testament? A. 200 years B.C., I could not say; 300 B.C. translated into Hebrew; I think the Latin is the oldest and that is 380 B.C.
> Q. And that records historical events that happened long ago? A. It contains writings inspired by God.
> Q. ...You say it is necessary to accept that? A. I say the Holy Spirit of God gave these writings to the world, inspired men to write them, and the same Holy Spirit that gave has guarded and kept that word so we can follow it as God intended.
> Q. You say it is necessary to accept this? A. Absolutely.
> Q. You make that an absolute precedent to entering the church? A. ...That is the condition of membership. I say that would be a condition of membership in any church of which I was pastor.

In this toe-to-toe confrontation, Sidey probably got the better of Nowlan, since Sidey was able to present a moderate Fundamentalist position, and Nowlan did not ask the most important question: what is the so-called traditional Baptistic position vis-à-vis the inspiration of the Scriptures and Church membership?

Nowlan then turned to the Kingston Bible College and forced Sidey to admit that there might have been a connection between his leaving the Convention and the promise of financial assistance for the College from anti-Convention

Baptists in Toronto. This was an important admission and one that must have delighted Convention officials. Nowlan then immediately pressed his advantage by asking Sidey "You did make the suggestion that you would like to teach evangelism at Acadia at one time?" "I deny it", answered Sidey:

> I was talking to Dr. Spidle about the advisability of an evangelistic Bible school. As for my going on the faculty of Acadia I was not expecting it; my work is in the field. If it was mentioned the wrong construction was put on it. I remember talking it over purely from that standpoint; I had no thought of what you suggest. I did suggest a good Bible school in connection with the Convention would be a good thing.

There was enough in Sidey's response to suggest that he was something of a sore loser.

Nowlan ended his examination of Sidey with a series of questions concerning the latter's fundamental beliefs and then B. W. Roscoe took over from a flagging Nowlan. He asked Sidey how he had dealt with the "allotment of contributions to the funds of the Convention". Sidey had to confess that his three churches had, in fact, raised $290.75 for Convention purposes but that he had only sent $150.00 to the Convention. Roscoe then asked Sidey "Will you tell the court if that is not one of the reasons for your retiring from the United Baptist Convention?" "No sir", was the answer — nothing more nothing less. But another seed of doubt had been planted in Kentville.

Daggett was put on the witness stand on Thursday, 23 May, by J.E. Rutledge, one of his lawyers. The former Free Baptist minister was confident, aggressive and impressive in his performance — far more so than Sidey had been. According to Daggett, even before leaving the Convention, he had often declared that "the students at Acadia were filled up with unBaptistic teaching, especially the hypothesis of evolution". Moreover, Acadia "conferred honourary degrees" on the most "unBaptistic" of men. Daggett again emphasized the importance of the independence of the local church and the evils of any form of interdependence. In addition, he condemned dancing and card playing. As for his "scriptural authority" for such a stance and for his anti-Acadia feelings, Daggett declared, as he thumbed quickly through his Bible:

> I would like to close with a word of scripture in this connection. We will turn to First John, second chapter and 22nd verse "Who is a liar but he that denieth that Jesus is the Christ? He is anti-Christ that denieth the Father and the Son"; then First John 4th Chapter, beginning at the second verse "Hereby know ye the Spirit of God: Every spirit that confesseth that Jesus Christ is come in the flesh is of God"; and turn to Second John 7th verse, "For many deceivers are come into the world who confess not that Jesus Christ is come in the flesh. This is a deceiver and an anti-Christ". Our

> Convention has received men and honoured them who deny in the most blasphemous manner that Jesus Christ is the son of God. Then I dare not stay in the Convention lest I become a partaker in their evil ways.

In his cross examination Nowlan wondered why Daggett's earlier Free Baptist view of the importance of the "Ordination Councils" had changed and Daggett had to admit that since the creation of the United Maritime Baptist Convention this had been Convention policy and that he had played a key role in pushing the Convention in this direction. Nowlan then asked Daggett to explain "the Fundamentals". Daggett insisted that "verbal inspiration" of the Bible was the key Fundamentalist tenet. "What are the other fundamentals?" he was asked. "Belief in the scriptures as verbally inspired" he stressed,

> that all scripture was given by the Holy spirit and is not open to any private interpretation; that it is the word of the living God; we believe that Jesus Christ was God revealed in the flesh; that he was God's special gift as a mediator between himself and man, and upon the cross He bore our sins and that his blood cleansed us of all sins if we confess our sins, cleanses us of unrighteousness; next that he rose from the dead physically that he ascended on high physically; that he is to-day our advocate at the right hand of the Father. We believe his physical body's not moved by blood but by the spirit.

Daggett also described his premillennialist view that before Christ "returns to the world to rule the nations of the earth his voice will be heard and the dead in Christ shall rise first" and proclaimed that "No man can be a Christian who does not accept God manifest in the flesh in Jesus Christ, and a man to be a real member of the church must be born again of the Holy Ghost".

B.W. Roscoe's cross examination stressed Daggett's involvement in the 1917 New Brunswick Potato and Railway Scandal and threw at Daggett the charge that had been reverberating throughout Nova Scotia and New Brunswick for months. "Is it right to deposit monies in a name other than your own to the extent of thirty-five thousand dollars? That is what you did when you were Deputy Minister of Agriculture in New Brunswick?" "Under what name?" Daggett asked. "William Thompson, was it not?" came the reply to which Daggett could only respond "Yes, I did, and it was perfectly legitimate too". The feisty, combative preacher was unrepentant and when given an opportunity later in the day to clarify his involvement in the Scandal, Daggett emphasized that he had been duped by the "chief manipulator of the Conservative party". To protect himself from any possible charges of theft, Daggett had deposited $35,000 in a bank under an assumed name. He believed the McQueen Commission Report had completely exonerated him and thundered that "no one but a slanderer and a rascal would bring it up".

On Saturday, 25 May, the Convention decided to put forward its case against the Sidey-Daggett Fundamentalist critique. Two men were selected for this important task, Dr. G.C. Warren, editor of the *Maritime Baptist*, and Dr. Simeon Spidle, perhaps the most powerful and influential person in the Convention. Warren testified first.[67] Born in 1884 on Prince Edward Island, Warren was educated at Prince of Wales College, Charlottetown, at Acadia University and Newton Theological Seminary, Massachusetts, from which seminary he received his B.D. degree in 1912. He pastored Baptist Churches in Bridgetown and at Brunswick Street, Fredericton. In 1929 he was appointed Editor of the *Maritime Baptist*. In 1936 he became a member of the Faculty of Theology at Acadia and in 1942 its Dean. As editor of the *Maritime Baptist*, Warren was far more sympathetic to the so-called Modernist side than to the Fundamentalist. He regularly reprinted articles written by very Liberal theologians from England and the United States — men like Nathaniel Micklem, L.H. Marshall and Shirley Case — but never printed any material authored by any key North American Fundamentalist.[68] Under questioning, Warren contended that Baptist congregational independence was always balanced by associational interdependence and he particularly stressed the crucial role played by the Convention in the ordination process. In his concluding testimony Warren maintained that "As soon as the Baptists developed they said: We are not isolated entities, there is fellowship, and they formed the Association in Nova Scotia in 1800".

Simeon Spidle followed Warren to the witness stand.[69] Spidle was born in New Cornwall in 1867. After graduating from Acadia with a B.A. degree in 1897, he served two Baptist pastorates, in Cape Breton and at Falmouth. In 1903 he received his B.D. from Newton Theological Seminary and in 1911 his Ph.D. in Philosophy from Clark University in Worcester, Massachusetts. In 1911 he was also appointed Professor of Philosophy, Systematic Theology and Church History at Acadia and in 1922 its Dean of Theology until 1936, when he retired. Spidle was the general factotum in the Convention in the 1920s and early 1930s. He was a key member of the Examining Council and almost singlehandedly determined who would and who could not be ordained as ministers in the Convention. An ardent believer in the importance of an educated ministerial elite, he attempted, often without much success, to impose his high academic standards on the Convention. Spidle was neither a Fundamentalist nor a Liberal but rather what might be termed a Liberal Evangelical. He accepted much of the critical Biblical scholarship but without abandoning his belief in the divinity of

67 *Acadia Bulletin*, January 1957.

68 These three men, all of whom had connections with Canada, were widely regarded as leading Liberal theologians.

69 *Acadia Bulletin*, November 1954. See also S. Spidle, *An Outline of Theology*, 2 volumes (privately published, 1953). These lectures were privately printed by Spidle and a copy is available in the Acadia University Archives.

Christ, regeneration, miracles and immortality. As a scholar, he refused to see things solely in black-white terms but rather frequently saw huge grey patches. He did not perform particularly well in Kentville on 25 May 1935, perhaps because of his tendency to avoid meeting certain questions directly and honestly.

George Nowlan asked Spidle to comment on Sidey's contention that "verbal inspiration of the scriptures" was "a pre-requisite to membership in the Baptist church in the Maritime Provinces". "To make it a pre-requisite" or a belief in any form of millennialism, Spidle answered, "is entirely an unbaptistic procedure".

Rutledge's cross-examination was a little more contentious than Nowlan's probing. He zeroed in on Spidle's theology. What did Spidle mean when he stated that the "Old and New Testament Scriptures were written by men divinely inspired — by whom?" "By the spirit of God", Spidle responded. "Is that not, in all fairness, the doctrine of verbal inspiration?" he was asked. "No, not by any means", Spidle replied. "I say verbal inspiration means this, that the very words and ideas were dictated to the minds of the writers; that the writers themselves had nothing to do with creating the ideas or the language". Rutledge then asked Spidle whether he believed there was an actual "dictation to Moses". "Cite the case" Spidle retorted. "What I have reference particularly to is the making of the ten commandments". "There's nothing said there about dictation", was the curt reply. Spidle was urged by Rutledge to clarify his view of inspiration. "Do you accept the scriptures from Genesis to Revelation as being verbally inspired and of God yourself?" "No, certainly not", Spidle answered. "What do you say?" "I hold to the historic theory of the inspiration of the Bible", Spidle replied. "How do you define that?" Acadia's Dean of Theology quickly retorted: "Co-operation of the spirit of God and the mind of man arriving at the religious truth incorporated in the Bible". Rutledge also asked Spidle whether he believed "that Christ was divine". "I certainly do", answered the Acadia Dean of Theology.

> Q. Do you believe and teach he was the Deity? A. He was divine in the sense that there was in him the divine quality of life....
>
> Q. The efficacy of the Blood Atonement — what is generally meant by that? A. It is spoken of in the usual way as the substitution of Christ for the sinner; I don't know if that is what they mean by blood atonement.
>
> Q. Do you believe that the death of Christ upon the cross was by way of atonement of sins? A. I surely do, but you must remember there are no fewer than twelve different theories. The substitution is one of them, which is that the sufferings of Christ were a punishment inflicted on Christ the innocent in place of the guilty; that the innocent was punished for the guilty and the guilty were allowed to go free....
>
> Q. The bodily resurrection of our Lord: Do you teach and preach a physical resurrection? A. I think there is no doubt about the New Testament preaching that; I have no quarrel with the teachings of the New Testament.

Q. Do you believe in the physical return of Jesus? A. That is a doctrine that is held by Baptists, that there will be a return of Christ to this earth.

It was clear to everyone in the courtroom that Spidle had tried to avoid the question. So Rutledge asked again "Do you preach and teach a physical return?" "I never use that in any of my preaching because I don't think it is an important matter to emphasize in teaching; our business is to carry on the work and when the time arrives he will come".

Spidle was also asked on a number of occasions to define Modernism and Fundamentalism, but he stubbornly refused to do so. When asked whether he considered the University of Chicago theologian Dr. Shirley Case a "modernist or a fundamentalist", he shot back "I am not labelling any man"! Spidle was forced to listen to a statement to be found on page 80 of Case's *Jesus Through the Centuries*:

> The spark that ignited the tinder of a new faith for Peter was the need felt within himself during the crucifixion, for his former leader's reinstatement in divine favor. The notion of Jesus' apotheosis, so readily suggested by popular Gentile religions in Peter's environment, brought to him too valuable a relief from his perplexity and too vivid an assurance of future help to leave any room for questioning the propriety of his procedure. Peter did not actually believe that a deceased man had become a god. No Jew however unschooled, could have assented to any such affirmation. It remained for his Greek successors in the new religion to recognize in Jesus a full fledged Christian deity.... Strictly speaking, this risen Jesus was not an absolute deity; he was only a messianized hero.

"Would you say that was in any way fundamentalistic?" Rutledge asked. "I will let the fundamentalist say whether it is or not", was the curt reply. When Rutledge wondered how any orthodox Baptist university could confer an honourary degree on a person like Case whose Modernist views were so well known, Spidle stressed that "The degree was not conferred upon him for his theological views but because he was a teacher in the academy whose centenary was being celebrated". Again, Rutledge endeavoured to pressure Spidle into admitting that Case was a Modernist. "Do you mean seriously to say, as an educationist of this province, you do not care to answer a simple question in regard to extracts I have read as being the work of a fundamentalist or modernist?" "I make no pronouncements on the matter" was Spidle's response. The final question from Rutledge was: "Does Acadia, as a university, teach organic evolution?" "That belongs to the Department of Biology. I am not a member of that Department", answered Spidle. This was not Dean Spidle's finest hour. Perhaps his defensiveness is understandable; but his stubborn refusal to admit the obvious — that Case was a Modernist — is almost incomprehensible.

The final arguments were presented to Mr. Justice Mellish in Halifax on 26 June 1935. Robertson and Rutledge argued that the Melvern Square Independent Baptist Church should receive $1450 from the sale of the parsonage and $2350 should go to the Kingston United Baptists. Nowlan and Roscoe contended that the entire sum should go to the two United Baptist congregations, since the Independents had seceded and had no right to the property which still belonged to the Convention Churches. On 16 September Mr. Justice Mellish declared in favour of the Convention Baptists. As far as costs were concerned, which according to Judge Mellish, "have been considerable when considered in relation to the value of the property involved", judgement was reserved.[70] In late 1935 Mellish awarded the Convention Baptists $548 for "Court expenses", rubbing more salt in the wounds of the Independents.[71]

Even while Judge Mellish was preparing his judgement in the summer of 1935, Sidey was receiving reports from missionaries he had sent out to all corners of the Maritimes and even Newfoundland under the auspices of the International Christian Mission which he established in March 1935. He named himself Chief Commissioner and editor of the I.C.M.'s monthly publication, *The Question*. Daggett continued to edit the *Gospel Light*. Sidey announced in the March 1935 issue of *The Question* that "denominationalism as such through its organizations and ecclesiastical control has had its day and like many other institutions hoary with age, it is now practically a wreck on the shores of time, devoid both of spiritual power and truth". The Mission, he proclaimed, "is not a church but rather a soul saving, Bible teaching, witnessing organization". The College was to train Sidey's missionaries who then would establish congregations of true Christian believers in all parts of the Maritimes and also in "Foreign lands". Expecting an imminent rapture of the Saints, Sidey and Daggett were determined to do all in their power to telescope the last days into a brief apocalytic moment.

Two young men, William Freeman and Hilbourne Redden, were sent to the Canso area, two others, Eric Monevan and Henry Crocker, to Hants County; four women, Mildred Neily, Ethel Skarling, Ethel Thompson and Kizbro Dulliver, to the Yarmouth region and Margaret Tedford to Carleton County; Julian Green was located in Kings County, Nova Scotia, Nancy Nelson and Winona Beylea, in Moncton and William Norton in Kentville. These young men and women associated themselves with Independent Baptist ministers, such as Maxwell Bolser and Orden Stairs in Shelburne County, Russell Lynds and T.A. Meister in Colchester County and Clifford Barkhouse in Cumberland County, Sadie Reid on Prince Edward Island, and Allen Tedford in Truro. All of these young men and women had close connections with Sidey and his Baptist supporters, especially those in Nova Scotia.

Excluding his Kingston team, Sidey had no fewer than 20 ardent disciples

70 *Maritime Baptist*, 25 September 1925.

71 See *The Question*, December 1935.

working for his cause in the three Maritime provinces in the summer of 1935. Financial support for the work came not only from the region but also from Central Canada and the United States. There was also Velma Crummie preaching the Sidey-Daggett gospel in Conception Bay, Newfoundland. Faced with all these Independent Baptist ministers and I.C.M. missionaries at work in the region, Convention Baptists became increasingly concerned and the Convention leaders began a well-planned counter-offensive at the grass-roots level, against what they spitefully referred to as "tramp preachers". At the Eastern United Baptist Association meetings held in Sydney in July 1935 these outsiders were condemned for "endeavouring to poison the minds of our people and destroy their faith". All Convention ministers were urged "to inaugerate a campaign in our churches, which will educate to a greater degree than exists today the rank and file of our members and adherents as regards the origin, principles and polity of Baptist people".[72] At the August 1935 United Baptist Convention, the Home Missions Committee of the Convention reported that "Disturbing agencies are busy in an effort to undo the work of the Christian Church". "Men who have no connection with our body", it was observed, "are brazenly appearing in our churches and whether locally received or rejected carry on a campaign well calculated to destroy the church life". Particularly in the Canso area and in Shelburne County, "such a campaign assumes the nature of a house to house canvass in an attempt to have our Baptist people withdraw from our Baptist work and fellowship".[73]

The Convention counterattack was particularly successful in New Brunswick and the Yarmouth region. Sometimes with the assistance of the local police, Convention leaders expelled certain Sideyites from Convention churches and pushed back the Sidey forces to key bridge heads in the Canso area and in Shelburne County. These were the areas where the Sideyites had their greatest strength outside the Kingston region in the late 1930s and 1940s. The Reverend Tedford was to be forced out of the Emmanuel Baptist Church Truro to be replaced by the dynamic and Conservative Evangelical supporter of the Convention, Abner Langley. The Herman brothers, Neil and Arthur, were the two other outspoken Sidey supporters in the Convention. In 1936 Neil was eased out of West End, Halifax and in that same year became the Field Secretary for the anti-Acadian "English-speaking League of New Brunswick". Three years later he emigrated to Florida. His brother, who was the minister at Highfield Street, Moncton, remained in his church until 1938, sullen, critical, yet unwilling to leave the Convention.[74]

The Sidey schism did not result in a significant haemorrhage of members from Convention Churches. In 1934 the New Brunswick resident membership was

72 Minute Book of the Eastern Baptist Association of Nova Scotia, Sydney, 4 July 1935, Acadia University Archives.

73 *United Baptist Year Book, 1935*, p. 145.

74 *The Acadia Record 1838-1952*, p. 54.

21,090, the non-resident 7,357; the Nova Scotia membership, including the Black churches, 20,856 residents and 7,953 non-residents; and Prince Edward Island 1,542 and 479. In 1936, the New Brunswick resident membership had risen to 21,103 and non-resident to 8,025 and in Nova Scotia the resident to 21,179, while the non-resident had dropped to 7,793 non-residents. In Prince Edward Island, there was a slight increase in both categories to 1,620 and 481. In 1936, 1,736 baptisms were reported while in 1934 there had only been 1,368 and in 1935, 1,377. In 1936, 672 members had been dismissed by letter compared to 590 in 1935 and 546 in 1934, but most of the increase was not due to the Sideyite secession movement. In 1933 before the Sidey-Convention confrontation, no fewer than 736 members had been "dismissed by letter" and in 1941, a few years after, 635. The Depression and its immediate result, emigration, as well as World War II would have a far more significant immediate and long-term impact on the Convention than J.J. Sidey.[75]

Why was the Maritime Baptist Convention able to deal so effectively with the Sidey secessionist threat? In other regions of Canada and in the Northern United States the confrontation first disoriented and then immobilized the Baptists. But even though there was probably a "cosmopolitan/local" polarization in the Maritime Convention in the late 1920s and early 1930, this polarization did not lead to a major split as it had in Ontario, British Columbia and the Northern United States. When a split did occur in a specific congregation, there is no evidence to suggest that class tension was at the core of conflict. What was most important was how specific people reacted to Sidey as a person.

The Convention was a heterogenous mix of people and theologies. On the extremes of the theological spectrum were to be found Fundamentalist and Modernist groups and then moving from the former to the latter, there would be important groups of Conservative Evangelicals and Liberal Evangelicals. The Conservative Evangelicals felt as strongly as the Fundamentalists about the so-called fundamentals of the faith but on two key issues they differed and these two issues created the necessary theological space — what Freud called the narcissism of small differences — between the two groups. Most United Baptist Conservative Evangelicals did not accept the central importance of premillennialism nor did they feel particularly at home within the context of the powerful anti-cultural and anti-societal viewpoints of the Fundamentalists. In other words, the Conservative Evangelicals were not as alienated from societal norms as were the Fundamentalists and they saw little psychological and spiritual need to retreat from Maritime and Canadian society to the safety of sectarian purity. Liberal Evangelicals tried to balance Evangelical spirituality and Liberal learning; theirs was a religion of the heart and head. They refused to abandon the revivalist traditions of the Baptist Patriarchs, but they also refused to close their eyes and their ears to modern scholarship. Of course, most Maritime Baptists, whether members of the United Baptist Convention or merely adherents, did not

75 See the *United Baptist Year Book, 1931, 1932, 1933, 1934, 1935, 1936, 1937, 1939, 1940, 1941.*

spend much time or energy making fine theological distinctions. They were very much part of the Maritime Baptist mainstream — stretching back to the late 18th century — which had always placed far more emphasis on "promoting a good Work" than upon theological "Principles".[76] For these people, continuity was far more appealing than abrupt change as was a certain degree of liberal openness over against an almost paranoid restrictiveness.[77] As a result, Sidey found it extremely difficult to strike a responsive chord in the Convention.

Moreover, Sidey was an outsider to the Convention. He was certainly not the kind of person one might have expected would try so valiantly to return 20th century Maritime Baptists to the purity of their early 19th century Calvinist and Evangelical past. He was not really familiar with the Maritime Baptist historical and religious legacy and the 19th century heroes of the Maritime Baptists — the Patriarchs like Edward and James Manning, Harris Harding, Theodore Seth Harding, and Joseph Dimock, among others — were not part of his religious heritage. Consequently he was neither successful nor effective in his attempt to make his schismatic movement into a 20th century version of an Allinite-Manning Church. Nor was Sidey able to strike a responsive chord with fellow Maritimers at a time when they were experiencing the white heat of the Maritime Rights Movement, for Sidey was not a Maritimer. He was British-born, educated in the United States, and in most respects an outsider. Not only was he an outsider, he was not even an ordained Baptist minister, since he had originally been ordained as an American Methodist Episcopal minister and only became a Baptist minister after permanently settling in the Maritimes and after the creation of the United Church of Canada in 1925. His Methodist ordination was simply accepted in 1925 by his new Prince Edward Island Baptist congregation and Sidey never felt the need to be re-ordained. Not in any significant way an integral part of the Maritime Baptist mainstream in the 1920s and 1930s, Sidey was not an especially brilliant organizer nor was he widely perceived as a charismatic leader, although he was enthusiastic and committed, a very effective preacher, a persuasive polemicist and ardently committed to the Fundamentalist point of view.[78]

Another possible reason for Sidey's failure to become the Shields of the Maritimes was his inability to harness New Brunswick discontent with the Convention and to direct it against the Nova Scotia Convention leaders. Since the early 19th century, the ethos of the New Brunswick Baptists was quite different from that of the Nova Scotia Baptists and for decades they had

76 See the "Records of the Church of Jebogue in Yarmouth", in the Public Archives of Nova Scotia.

77 See Marlene Shore, "Carl Dawson and the Research Ideal: The Evolution of a Canadian Sociologist", *Historical Papers* (1985), p. 73.

78 His wife, Edna, also caused her husband great difficulty and heartache. An independent woman of great ability, Edna Sidey was never intimidated by her husband and on at least one occasion left him — and left him humiliated and angry. This kind of marital discord did little to help the Fundamentalist cause in the Maritime Provinces.

resented the hegemony the Nova Scotians imposed upon the Convention. Yet Sidey had no effective base in New Brunswick; his New Brunswick-born lieutenant, Daggett, was a source of weakness and not of strength, because of his involvement in the notorious 1917 Scandal. Whenever Sidey tried to send his missionaries to New Brunswick they confronted strident opposition. The New Brunswick Baptist leaders had a greater fear and suspicion of Sidey than they did of the Convention leaders in Nova Scotia, especially those at Acadia University. They had considerable freedom within the Convention and even though they might criticize the Liberalism of Acadia they saw no good reason to quit the Convention, in which they still exerted a powerful influence. In New Brunswick, the Sidey forces not only confronted opposition in the Convention — from Fundamentalist, Conservative and Liberal Evangelicals and Modernists — but also from other sectarian Baptist groups like the Reformed Baptists, the Primitive Baptists and some Free Baptists — groups with roots thrust deep into New Brunswick life and society. The Sideyites were no match for these New Brunswick sectarian Baptists. Nor could they compete with the growing Pentecostal movement.

A further reason for Sidey's relative lack of success was the vigorous counter-offensive mounted by Convention leaders such as Spidle, Warren and Dr. E.S. Mason, Superintendent of Home Missions. First, they met the theological challenge posed by the Sidey group by persuading the Convention to accept publically in 1934 "its unshaken loyalty to the historic principles of our Denomination including the Lordship of Christ, the inspiration of the Scriptures, the separation of church and state, the necessity of a regenerative life, and exemplary character and the autonomy and co-operate fellowship of the individual churches".[79] At the local level, especially at the Association level, the Convention leaders urged their followers to battle against Sidey's "tramp evangelists". The implicit argument made to the Convention ministers was a compelling one during the difficult depression years. If the Sidey evangelists were successful, Convention ministers would no longer have churches to minister to and therefore no salaries. Economic survival as well as community prestige energized them in their determination to push back the sectarian invaders and the Kingston Parsonage Case, when won by the Convention, seriously weakened the Sidey forces. Sidey reluctantly admitted this fact in the fall of 1935 when he witnessed a significant downturn in the number of students at the Kingston Bible College as well as widespread concern, even among his most ardent followers, that the Independent Baptist had been relegated to the status of an "illegal church".[80] Making very effective use of local newspapers, Spidle and others viciously and personally attacked Sidey and Daggett, describing them as dishonest, selfish and unChristian leaders.[81] Some of these

79 Quoted in *The Maritime Baptist*, 12 September 1934.

80 *The Question*, December 1935.

81 *Gospel Light*, October 1934.

charges, however unfair, accomplished the desired end, as did the expulsion from the Convention of unrepentent pro-Sidey ministers. Finally, in order to reassert its position at the evangelical core of the Baptist cause in the region, the Convention in the post 1934 period placed a great deal of stress on "Evangelization". Over and over again, on the pages of the *Maritime Baptist*, local congregations were urged not only to pray for a revival but to work diligently for one. Articles and editorials entitled "Need of Revival", "Revival Needed", and "Evangelism Needed" were printed and reprinted. Attempts were made to link the Maritime Baptists of the late 1930s with Henry Alline and the region's First Great Awakening.[82] Sidey never even tried to use the Baptist historical heritage to infuse his movement in the 1930s with pride, respectability, and tradition. As an outsider he could never really understand the "Conservative ethos" of the Maritime Provinces.

A final reason for Sidey's failure to split the Convention was the fact that Baptist mainstream theology in the Maritimes had always been basically syncretic, placing particular stress on personal religious experience and not on a specific religious ideology. It was the religion of Henry Alline and Harris Harding and not that of Gresham Machem or T.T. Shields. Most Maritime Baptists in the 1920s and 1930s could not really empathize with the main North American Fundamentalist or Modernist propagandists because they perceived religion in a radically different manner. Unlike many of their Baptist cousins in Central Canada and the West, they had not, as yet, experienced the profound Americanization of their popular culture and were quite successful in the interwar years in resisting the Fundamentalist-Modernist bombardment from the South. Is it surprising that the two Baptist Conventions in Canada, most greatly influenced by the osmosis of Americanization, were the two Conventions most significantly affected by the Fundamentalist-Modernist controversy? In the final analysis, Sidey may have not been able to emulate Shields because he was too American for Maritime tastes. He had accommodated, too much, the habits of his mind to the Manichaen theological world of Chicago in the immediate post World War I period.

By late 1935, Sidey realized that his attempt to split the Convention had failed. Yet he refused to be immobilized by the events of 1934 and 1935. He seemed even more enthusiastic about his Kingston area churches, more committed to his Bible College and the International Christian Mission. He became increasingly active in the Nova Scotia Sons of Temperance as well as the Canadian Protestant League. Yet, despite his energy and sense of commitment, he was not able to deal successfully with the forces of sectarianism he had helped to unleash in the Kingston area. His College experienced a number of painful schisms as faculty members left outraged at Sidey's enthusiasm for Pentecostalism, one year, or his obsession with British Israelitism during another.[83] They felt that he

82 *The Maritime Baptist*, 22 June 1938.

83 See some of the criticism of Sidey in the Sidey Papers, Acadia University Archives.

was betraying his Fundamentalist principles. Some of his Independent Baptist followers stubbornly refused to toe his line and attacked his College and the I.C.M. because they were not Baptist organizations. These people felt that Sidey had too readily sacrificed his Baptist principles on the altar of interdenominationalism. Although he had played a key role in organizing the Independent Baptist Churches in the Cape Sable area of Shelburne County, in Guysborough County and in Westchester, Cumberland County, as well as in the Bedeque area of Prince Edward Island, by 1939 most of the Nova Scotia Independent Baptist Churches had split away from Sidey. It was ironic that Sidey should have experienced a far worse split in the 1930s than did the United Baptist Convention.

When Sidey formed the Maritime Fellowship of Independent Baptists in 1940, in order to "provide a way whereby the Baptists (Ind) of the Maritime Provinces may find fellowship together",[84] he could only attract to the organization his Kingston area Independent Baptist Church and the tiny Coddle Harbour Baptist Church from Guysborough County. In September 1968 the Fellowship was formally disbanded; Sidey had been unable to keep even a tiny fragile Fellowship together. In 1962, his own Melvern Square Independent Church split, with the secessionist group — including his wife Edna — forming a Fellowship Baptist Church. Four years later, Sidey, a largely spent force, died. He had seen his Independent Baptist world collapse around him; his College was still in reasonable shape despite a tragic fire in 1962 but his I.C.M. was little more than a postal address — a paper missionary society.

Soon after Sidey's death on 23 May 1966, he was described by Pastor Perry F. Rockwood, a former Presbyterian and a Fundamentalist preacher in Nova Scotia, as "probably the pioneer separationist of the Maritimes".[85] One of his faithful Deacons and dear friend, E.E. Skaling from Greenwood, praised Sidey as "a man of faith, a man who knew how to get answers to a prayer, a good friend and a Christian gentleman".[86] J.J. Sidey, in the 1930s, it may be argued, represented the way the mainstream of the Maritime Baptists could have, but did not follow. Ironically, in the short run Sidey may have been the loser but in the long run, as the Maritime Baptist Convention and the Acadia Divinity College became increasingly Conservative in their orientation, as the 1960s blurred into the 1970s, he may well have been the winner after all.

84 Quoted in Palmer, *The Combatant*, p. 160. I have learned a great deal about Sidey's latter years from Mrs. George Moody of Wolfville and from Professor Barry Moody of Acadia University.

85 Quoted in Palmer, *The Combatant*, p. 195.

86 *Ibid.*, p. 196.

JOHN G. REID

Reprinted from Vol. XIV, No. 1
(Autumn 1984)

Health, Education, Economy: Philanthropic Foundations in the Atlantic Region in the 1920s and 1930s

THE EXPERIENCE OF THE CARNEGIE CORPORATION of New York in the Maritime Provinces and Newfoundland during the period between the two World Wars was unorthodox. Or at least that was the feeling of Morse A. Cartwright, Director of the American Association for Adult Education, when he wrote to Carnegie Corporation president F.P. Keppel in 1936 to thank Keppel for showing him copies of letters received from the president of St. Dunstan's College. Cartwright, a frequent adviser of the Corporation in its programmes of support for adult education, went on to elaborate his view in some detail:

> I have one comment to make, namely, that most of the adult education from that part of the world (due no doubt to the success of the Antigonish experiments) seems to be confused as to objective. It seems quite impossible to separate the educational and the economic goals. Perhaps in a pioneer and poverty-stricken country it is not desirable that they be separated and hence my comment is not one of criticism but merely of notation. It does not shock me in the least that oyster culture and religion and art in the home should all be combined in one program as they are on Prince Edward Island, but on the other hand I think that this mixture is in a sense evidence that the Maritime Provinces and Newfoundland are exceptional and quite unlike the situations that ordinarily would be met in the United States. The economic urge is exceedingly strong and I am not at all sure that the interest manifested in education is not largely a reflection of the enlightened self-interest of the people translated into terms of bettering themselves materially.[1]

Cartwright's perception of the Maritimes and Newfoundland as "a pioneer and poverty-stricken country" was one that was at times reflected in the views of officials of the other major U.S. philanthropic foundation that was active in these areas during the 1920s and 1930s; that is, the Rockefeller Foundation.

1 Morse A. Cartwright to F.P. Keppel, 24 April 1936, St. Dunstan's College File, Carnegie Corporation Archives [CCA], New York. The research for this article was funded by the Small Towns Research Project of Mount Allison University, with the support of the Social Sciences and Humanities Research Council of Canada. The author wishes to thank the Carnegie Corporation of New York and the Rockefeller Archive Center for providing access to archival material.

When, for example, the Rockefeller Foundation voted in 1929 to cooperate with the government of Newfoundland in the launching of a public health scheme, it cited the scattered distribution of population and the absence of organized local governments as factors that complicated a health situation characterized by high rates of tuberculosis, nutritional diseases, and high infant and maternal mortality rates.[2] When assessed in worldwide terms, moreover, the Rockefeller Foundation's public health initiatives in the Maritimes and Newfoundland were considered to lend themselves to comparisons with similar projects undertaken far from North American shores. A 1939 report on the foundation's public health activities in Nova Scotia, for example, commented that "the Nova Scotia project represents a type of service that the Foundation has often been called upon to undertake in...Brazil and other countries of South America, in Czechoslovakia and other countries of Europe, in India and other lands of the Orient . . .".[3]

Yet if in some respects the interventions of the two philanthropic foundations in the Maritime provinces and Newfoundland were perceived as excursions into underdeveloped areas, in other ways these regions were treated as part of the North American mainstream. Both foundations made substantial grants to higher education institutions for purposes of endowment. In the field of medical education, for example — and notably in the case of the $500,000 granted in 1920 to the Dalhousie University medical school — the Maritimes and Newfoundland were expressly put in a North American context by the Rockefeller Foundation. Following the setting aside of $5 million earlier in 1920, at the request of J.D. Rockefeller, for the promotion of medical education in Canada, the foundation had set about formulating "a Dominion-wide policy", including support for strategically-placed medical schools. Dalhousie, concluded the foundation's Division of Medical Education in recommending the grant, "is the medical centre of the Maritime Provinces...and includes in its territory Newfoundland. The nearest medical schools are McGill to the west and Dartmouth, Portland and Vermont to the south".[4]

Each of these different perceptions contributed to the reasons that prompted the Carnegie Corporation and the Rockefeller Foundation to spend a combined total of more than $4 million in the Maritimes and Newfoundland between 1918 and 1940. Indeed, when the two perceptions are considered together, a strong case could be made for regarding these regions as an ideal testing ground for new ventures. Of the Carnegie Corporation's involvement in the establishment

2 Proposal for Aid to Newfoundland, 1929, RG2, Series 427, Box 26, Folder 212, Rockefeller Foundation Archives [RFA], Rockefeller Archive Center, North Tarrytown, N.Y.

3 Report on Public Health Progress in Nova Scotia, 1939, RG1.1, Series 427, Box 23, Folder 218, RFA.

4 Records of Development of Medical Education in Canada, 1919-1925, pp. 2, 4-6, RG1.1, Series 427, Box 4, Folder 33, and History of Rockefeller Involvement with Dalhousie Medical School, 1919-1927, pp. 8-10, RG1.1, Series 427, Box 4, Folder 34, RFA.

of Memorial University College in Newfoundland, for example, Morse Cartwright wrote in 1927 that "the whole Newfoundland venture is a most interesting adult education (as well as a regularized education) experiment in a peculiarly pioneer field". Similarly, in recommending Rockefeller Foundation support for the founding of the Institute of Public Affairs at Dalhousie University in 1936, the foundation official Stacy May saw the project as "a control experiment against which to measure experiments supported in the United States", involving "sufficient variables...to serve as an interesting contrast and not so many (as in Europe) as to make the experiment irrelevant".[5] Yet whether informed by one or the other perception, or the combination of both, the actions of the two foundations also depended upon the policies and methods which they had evolved since being established earlier in the century.

When the Carnegie Corporation became in 1911 the latest of several philanthropic trusts established by Andrew Carnegie, its aims were avowedly educational: "to promote the advancement and diffusion of knowledge among the people of the United States". Shortly afterwards, the corporation was empowered by Carnegie to appropriate part of its annual income for similar purposes in Canada and in British overseas territories.[6] The aims of the Rockefeller Foundation, formally established in 1913, had been enunciated by Rockefeller as early as 1909: "to promote the well-being and to advance the civilization of the peoples of the United States and its territories and possessions and of foreign lands in the acquisition and dissemination of knowledge, in the prevention and relief of suffering, and in the promotion of any and all of the elements of human progress". Although this declaration was phrased generally, the specialization of the foundation in health-related activities was quickly established under the influence of Rockefeller's close adviser, the Baptist minister Frederick T. Gates.[7] As philanthropic agencies, therefore, the chief interests of the Carnegie Corpration and the Rockefeller Foundation diverged. More minor differences also emerged over time. The Rockefeller Foundation, according to the opinion expressed in 1930 by F.P. Keppel, tended to have a larger full-time professional staff; Keppel attributed the difference to Andrew Carnegie's original business practice of working with a small staff, as opposed to Rockefeller's continuous

5 Morse A. Cartwright to F.P. Keppel, 4 March 1927, Memorial University of Newfoundland File, CCA; Stacy May, Notes on Dalhousie Project, 3 May 1936, RG1.1, Series 427, Box 33, Folder 345, RFA. For breakdown of the total grants by the two foundations, see Tables One and Two; these figures may be put in an overall Canadian context by reference to Robin S. Harris, *A History of Higher Education in Canada, 1663-1960* (Toronto, 1976), pp. 343-8.

6 Robert M. Lester, *Forty Years of Carnegie Giving: A Summary of the Benefactions of Andrew Carnegie and of the Work of Philanthropic Trusts Which He Created* (New York, 1941), pp. 57-8; Howard J. Savage, *Fruit of an Impulse: Forty-five Years of the Carnegie Foundation, 1905-1950* (New York, 1953), pp. 27-8; Stephen H. Stackpole, *Carnegie Corporation: Commonwealth Program, 1911-1961* (New York, 1963), pp. 3-4.

7 Raymond B. Fosdick, *The Story of the Rockefeller Foundation* (New York, 1952), pp. 14-21.

reliance on expert advisers and organizers.[8] The Rockefeller Foundation also had closer and more frequent contacts with public authorities than did the Carnegie Corporation, largely because its public health work necessarily included cooperation with governments.[9]

Despite these differences between the two foundations, the characteristics that they had in common were more striking. Both depended for their endowments upon the wealth gathered by their founders during the late 19th century period of industrialization in the United States. Both were profoundly influenced by the "gospel of wealth" propounded by Andrew Carnegie in an essay in the *North American Review* of 1889. For Carnegie, any effort to reverse or to subvert through revolution the achievements of capitalist society constituted an attack on "the foundation upon which civilization itself rests". Yet the concentration of wealth in the hands of a few successful industrialists presented a moral and political difficulty if such wealth were selfishly used. Rather, argued Carnegie, wealth was to be regarded as a trust, and the wealthy individual as "the mere trustee and agent for his poorer brethren".[10] Both foundations had then had their high motivations publicly challenged in 1915 by the Congressional Commission on Industrial Relations, on the ground that they were essentially tools of corporate interests from which they sprang, and were able through their grants of funding to exercise a dangerous and irresponsible influence in such important areas as education and social services.[11] Both had responded in later years by recognizing the obligation of foundations as tax-exempt bodies to allow public scrutiny of their finances and activities, by denying that they wielded power other than a power to assist progressive causes, and ultimately by reaffirming a faith in the progress of human civilization regardless of class conflicts. In 1922, for example, the acting president of the Carnegie Corporation, Henry S. Pritchett, commented in his annual report that "the method that the founder emphasized is not that of the establishment and support of agencies operated under the direction of the trustees, but rather the intelligent and discriminating assistance of such causes and forces in the social order as seem to promise effective service...[in any] direction that ministers to the advancement of civilization".[12]

8   F.P. Keppel, *The Foundation: Its Place in American Life* (New York, 1930), pp. 69-70.

9   *Ibid.*, pp. 43-4.

10 Andrew Carnegie, "The Gospel of Wealth", in Carnegie, *The Gospel of Wealth and Other Timely Essays*, ed. Edward C. Kirkland (Cambridge, Mass., 1962), pp. 14-49. On the influence of Carnegie on Rockefeller, see Fosdick, *Rockefeller Foundation*, pp. 14-21, and Keppel, *The Foundation*, pp. 20-1.

11 *U.S. Commission on Industrial Relations: Final Report and Testimony*, Vol. I, pp. 80ff., U.S. 64th Congress, 1st Session, Senate Documents, No. 415; Keppel, *The Foundation*, pp. 26-9. On the work of the commission, see also Graham Adams, Jr., *Age of Industrial Violence, 1910-15: The Activities and Findings of the United States Commission on Industrial Relations* (New York, 1966).

12 Carnegie Corporation of New York, *Report of the Acting President* (New York, 1922), pp. 7-8. For further discussion of Pritchett's concept of social progress, see Ellen Condliffe Lagemann,

The Carnegie Corporation and the Rockefeller Foundation can be closely compared not only in the general matter of their origins, but also in the origins of their interest in the Maritime Provinces and Newfoundland. The 1920 plan of assistance to the Dalhousie medical school was in effect a joint project of the two foundations. As early as 1910, the Carnegie Foundation for the Advancement of Teaching — a separate agency from the Carnegie Corporation, but closely related — had intervened vigorously in the current debates over the future of medical education in North America by publishing an exhaustive study of the subject that it had commissioned from Abraham Flexner. Flexner's report had made sweeping recommendations for rationalization of medical education along lines that emphasized scientific medicine, and henceforth this was one area where the interests of the Carnegie Corporation and the Rockefeller Foundation overlapped.[13] Thus, by the time the Rockefeller Foundation voted its $500,000 to Dalhousie on 26 May 1920, the Carnegie Corporation had resolved to contribute a further $500,000 conditional on the provision of the same amount by the Rockefeller Foundation. Dalhousie would thus provide a strong central medical school for the Maritimes and Newfoundland, just as — so the relevant minute of the Rockefeller Foundation implied — Dalhousie as a university might ultimately be a central institution at least for all Nova Scotia: "although it [Dalhousie] is non denominational it receives no state aid...on account of the jealousies of the other colleges of Nova Scotia, all of which are practically denominational. It has made every effort to be considered the Provincial University but for the reason stated, thus far without success".[14]

The funding of the Dalhousie medical school was not the first involvement of either foundation in the Atlantic region. The Rockefeller Foundation had responded to an appeal for assistance at the time of the 1914 Newfoundland sealing disaster by recommending that a personal donation be made by Rockefeller; the foundation had also been involved in an advisory capacity in relief work following the Halifax Explosion and in the ensuing public health work of the Massachusetts-Halifax Health Commission.[15] The Carnegie Corporation, meanwhile, had already made grants to Dalhousie University amounting to some $45,000, and had also in 1919 granted $50,000 to St. Francis Xavier University for the endowment of a professorship in French, at the behest

---

Private Power for the Public Good: A History of the Carnegie Foundation for the Advancement of Teaching (Middletown, Conn., 1983), pp. 21-36.

13 Savage, *Fruit of an Impulse*, pp. 105-7; E. Richard Brown, *Rockefeller Medicine Men: Medicine and Capitalism in America* (Berkeley, 1979), pp. 142-56.

14 History of Rockefeller Involvement with Dalhousie Medical School, 1919-1927, p. 8, RG1.1, Series 427, Box 4, Folder 34, RFA; H.S. Pritchett to R.M. Pearce, 21 May 1920, Dalhousie University File, CCA.

15 E.H. Outerbridge to S.J. Murphy, 20 April 1914, RG1.1, Series 427, Box 3, Folder 25, RFA; Jerome D. Greene to J.D. Rockefeller, Jr., 27 April 1914, *ibid.*; on the Rockefeller Foundation's involvement in Halifax relief work and the Massachusetts-Halifax Health Commission, see the extensive files in RG1.1, Series 427, Box 2, Folders 14-21, RFA.

of the university's vice-president, J.J. Tompkins.[16] Nevertheless, the large grants to the Dalhousie medical school were for both foundations by far their most important interventions, and furthermore established centralizing principles that were once again to be brought forward by the Carnegie Corporation in the following year. It was in May 1921 that the Carnegie Corporation approved the sending of a small commission "to examine and report upon the educational situation in Newfoundland and the Maritime Provinces of Canada, in order that the Corporation may have reliable data upon which to base any action looking toward appropriations for educational institutions in the region mentioned".[17] The president of the corporation, J.R. Angell, was not sure that the Maritimes and Newfoundland did in fact constitute a single region; in Newfoundland, he believed, the corporation itself might well intervene directly to institute a system of higher education, whereas in the Maritimes the existing institutions could be supported, provided they could be encouraged to adopt "any practicable forms of co-operation".[18] In the event, the commission — consisting of W.S. Learned of the Carnegie Foundation for the Advancement of Teaching, and K.C.M. Sills, Nova Scotia-born president of Bowdoin College, Maine — directed its recommendations chiefly at the Maritimes. The Maritime colleges, they recommended, should be centralized in a federation located in Halifax. They envisaged too that the new institution, supplemented by a junior college in St. John's, would draw students from Newfoundland, and would "furnish this remote population the best of service".[19]

Thus far, the interventions of the Carnegie Corporation and the Rockefeller Foundation in the Maritimes and Newfoundland had been closely comparable. Remote and backward as these regions might be considered to be, the two foundations were convinced that large-scale centralizing schemes aimed at the modernization of medical education and of higher education as a whole were capable of bringing standards into conformity with those prevailing elsewhere in North America. Nevertheless, the roles played by the respective foundations were to differ in the ensuing years, for reasons that lay chiefly in the diversity of perceptions within the provinces themselves as to their needs. The Carnegie Corporation and the Rockefeller Foundation ultimately established their closest contacts with, and drew their most influential advice from, different groups within the social and intellectual milieu of the Maritimes and Newfoundland.

The Rockefeller Foundation was the simpler case, for its activities in the

---

16 Robert M. Lester, *Review of Grants in the Maritime Provinces of Canada and Newfoundland, 1911-1933* (New York, 1934), pp. 31-4; J.J. Tompkins to J. Bertram, 3 December 1919, St. Francis Xavier University File, CCA.

17 Lester, *Review of Grants*, p. 8.

18 J.R. Angell to H.S. Pritchett, 10 August 1921, Maritime Provinces Educational Federation File, CCA.

19 William S. Learned and Kenneth C.M. Sills, *Education in the Maritime Provinces of Canada* (New York, 1922), p. 48 and passim.

Maritimes and Newfoundland continued to be directed at the development of health-related programmes at Dalhousie University, and at working with provincial governments in the field of public health.[20] For the foundation, these were conventional lines of operation, and in the case of the relationship with Dalhousie they proceeded smoothly and successfully. The original grants of 1920 were supplemented in 1921 by a further allocation of $50,000 from the Rockefeller Foundation (matched by a similar grant from the Carnegie Corporation) to enable the Salvation Army to complete the construction of its Grace Maternity Hospital in Halifax, which was to serve as part of the clinical facilities of the medical school. Smaller grants of $5,000 were made in 1928 and 1929 to supplement the teaching staff in the Department of Hygiene, and then in 1933 an allocation of $44,000 was made to be used over a five-year period for teaching in public health and preventive medicine. This grant was supplemented by a further $21,400 voted in 1938 to be payable over three years.[21] Finally, in a venture that went outside the confines of the medical school, although still retaining a connection with public health, the Rockefeller Foundation agreed in 1936 to fund a programme of training and research in the field of public administration. Leading to the establishment of the Institute of Public Affairs at Dalhousie, this was the first initiative of the foundation in the public administration field outside of the United States.[22] The programme not only led, according to Dalhousie president Carleton Stanley, to immediate success in "breaking down the artificial barriers between department and department and faculty and faculty", but also to sponsorship of province-wide conferences and courses in areas such as industrial relations and municipal administration.[23] The continuing connection with the field of public health was reaffirmed in 1937 and 1938 when major studies were initiated of death rates and the availability of medical services in Cape Breton and in Yarmouth.[24]

Appraisals by the Rockefeller Foundation of the results of its grants to Dalhousie University were consistently favourable. The programme of teaching in the field of public health, with the establishment at the university of a Public

20 Not included here are the substantial personal gifts of John D. Rockefeller, Jr., to Acadia College; see the correspondence in J.D. Rockefeller, Jr., Papers, RG2, Educational Interests, Acadia University, Folders 123, 124, Rockefeller Archive Center.

21 History of Rockefeller Involvement with Dalhousie Medical School, 1919-1927, pp. 13, 144, Box 4, Folder 34, Minute on Dalhousie University: Public Health and Preventive Medicine, [1938], Box 5, Folder 43, Series 427, RG1.1, RFA.

22 Stacy May, Notes on Dalhousie Project, 3 May 1936, RG1.1, Series 427, Box 33, Folder 345, RFA; see also the other relevant material in this folder.

23 Carleton Stanley to Donald Mainland, DAL/MS/1/3, Institute of Public Affairs, Dalhousie University Archives [DUA]. See also the documentation in the related files, Institute of Public Affairs-Dalhousie Bureau of Industrial Relations, and Institute of Public Affairs-Municipal Consulting Bureau.

24 Minutes on Dalhousie University Morbidity Studies, 5 August 1937 and 30 June 1938, RG1.1, Series 427, Box 32, Folder 341, RFA.

Health Centre, was singled out for special praise. "With Foundation aid", read an internal report of the foundation in 1938, "the [Dalhousie Medical] School has been singularly successful in establishing itself and the Center as part of the community"; it was, the report continued, "the only medical school in the four Maritime provinces — Nova Scotia, Newfoundland, New Brunswick and Prince Edward Island".[25] The achievement recognized, therefore, was the provision of modern, professionalized medicine on a central basis to a region perceived as comprising the Maritime provinces and Newfoundland. Efforts to work individually with the provincial governments in the generation of public health programmes were regarded as less uniformly successful. In accordance with normal foundation policies, the intervention of the foundation was directed at launching programmes which would eventually be carried on by governments out of their own resources. Grants for the establishment of a new sanitary engineering organization within the Nova Scotia Department of Health in 1934, and for the setting up of a model public health district in Cape Breton in 1936, were favourably appraised in 1939; so successful was the first public health district that the province had subsequently decided to establish a second district centred on Yarmouth.[26]

Other efforts met greater difficulties, or were conceived on a lesser scale. The early success of the Massachusetts-Halifax Health Commission in using the Halifax-Dartmouth area to give a "demonstration of what the introduction of public health methods could do for a community " — a venture with which the Rockefeller foundation was closely connected in giving advice and recommending personnel, though it did not contribute funds — was not long sustained after the commission phased out its work during the mid-1920s. Hopes that the cities of Halifax and Dartmouth, and the province, would provide for its continuation were never entirely fulfilled, and many trained public health workers thereupon left for the United States.[27] In New Brunswick, a Rockefeller Foundation grant of $27,000 voted in 1922 "for the purpose of carrying out a rural health program" was hindered by lack of investment by the provincial government, although a further effort was made in 1928.[28] In 1929, after cor-

---

25 Minute on Dalhousie University: Public Health and Preventive Medicine, [1938], RG1.1, Series 427, Box 5, Folder 43, RFA.

26 Minute on Nova Scotia Bureau of Sanitary Engineering, 27 October 1934, Box 23, Folder 218, Minute on Nova Scotia Local Health District, 19 September 1936, Box 19, Folder 176, Report on Public Health Progress in Nova Scotia, Box 23, Folder 218, Series 427, RG1.1, RFA.

27 Minutes of Massachusetts-Halifax Health Commission, 23 March 1928, MG20, Vol. 197, Public Archives of Nova Scotia [PANS]; G.F. Pearson to V.G. Heiser, RG1.1, Series 427, Box 2, Folder 20, RFA; Kathryn M. McPherson, "Nurses and Nursing in Early Twentieth-Century Halifax", M.A. thesis, Dalhousie University, 1982, pp. 17, 98-101, 110-11.

28 See the correspondence of 1922 in RG5, IHB, Series 1, Sub. II, Series 427, Canada 1922, Folder 1865, RFA; W.F. Roberts to F.F. Russell, 11 September 1923, RG5.2, Series 427, Roberts 1923 and 1924, RFA; G.G. Melvin to C.N. Leach, 31 July 1928, RG1.1, Series 427, Box 24, Folder 227, RFA.

respondence with Sir Wilfred Grenfell as well as with the government of New-foundland, the foundation resolved to cooperate in a public health initiative with the Board of Health in St. John's, but this project apparently failed to get underway.[29] On Prince Edward Island, meanwhile, the foundation's first initiative was a small vote of $15,300 over a five-year period, 1939-43, for support of a public health laboratory.[30]

In giving support to Dalhousie University, and in efforts to promote public health schemes in the Atlantic region, the Rockefeller Foundation was following its customary practices. This is not to say that these interventions were unimportant, or that their success or failure did not influence prevailing standards of education and health. Yet they were transactions largely governed by a commitment to the professionalization of health care and were arranged in consultation with government and university officials or health professionals whose assumptions did not essentially vary from those of the officials of the foundation.[31]

In the case of the initiatives launched by the Carnegie Corporation, however, this was not necessarily true. Undoubtedly, the report published by Learned and Sills in 1922 was based upon an intelligent appraisal not only of the situation of education in the Maritime provinces but also of the political and societal characteristics of the region. The commissioners noted, for example, the sense of injustice that informed the Maritime rights movement:

> In all the provinces, a condition of actual prosperity is translated into a feeling of comparative poverty for the reason that all the other Canadian provinces have inherited great resources thru [sic] the vast extension of their original territory, while for the Maritime Provinces there is no opportunity for expansion. It is thus possible for Ontario to finance an elaborate educational program without resorting to general taxation, while good schools in the Maritime Provinces must be paid for largely out of the earnings of the people themselves. The adjustment of this inequality is now an issue in Canadian politics, or at least in that aspect of it that especially interests the Maritime Provinces.[32]

Learned and Sills also commented upon the importance of small-town and rural societies within the region, which they linked with the strength of organized religion:

> Undisturbed by foreign immigration and maintaining a conservative,

29 See the correspondence in RG2, Series 427, Box 26, Folder 212, RFA; and H.M. Mosdell to J.A. Ferrell, 28 April 1930, Box 43, Folder 356, RFA.

30 Minute on P.E.I. Public Health Laboratory, 1936, RG1.1, Series 427, Box 23, Folder 221, RFA.

31 On the earlier evolution of the medical profession in the Maritimes, see Colin D. Howell, "Reform and the Monopolistic Impulse: The Professionalization of Medicine in the Maritimes", *Acadiensis*, XI, 1 (Autumn 1981), pp. 3-22.

32 Learned and Sills, *Education in the Maritime Provinces*, p. 5.

chiefly small-town and rural life, the people are thoroughly denominationalized, only a small fraction of one per cent of the population giving no specific religious affiliation in the census. Furthermore, these various groups form the best understood and most actively motivated social organizations in a small town régime, and wield relatively much larger influence than in large cities. People, including the men, go to church.[33]

Yet the commissioners did not allow these characteristics to influence significantly their findings or recommendations. For them, the principal justification for the reforms they advocated was that the cause of educational efficiency would be advanced. A by-product would be "an illuminating experiment almost certain to succeed" which would "serve as a model appropriate to many existing American situations".[34] What Learned and Sills did not anticipate was the extent to which support for their plan would be influenced by the notion that economic justice and educational development were directly and inseparably linked, and the extent to which opposition would focus on whether centralization was an appropriate strategy for a rural and small-town population struggling to cope with economic dislocation. These two concerns would eventually have an important influence on later schemes supported by the Carnegie Corporation in the Maritimes and in Newfoundland.

The events that led to the ultimate failure of the Learned/Sills university federation scheme are well known and need no repetition here.[35] Whether what Learned privately described in 1925 as "the foolish but tenacious notion of the wicked exposure of tender youth to the wicked influences of a bad city" caused the lack of response by most Maritime colleges and universities to the Carnegie Corporation's expressed willingness to contribute $3 million to support the expenses of implementation, or even the unreasoned opposition of "the poorer and weaker rural brethren", there was no doubt that opposition to centralization was a crucial issue in the debate.[36] At its most rational level, the argument could be made that to force young people to travel long distances to one central institution was not a sound way of attempting to provide educational opportunities given the economic and social circumstances of the day. Yet when Learned called, as he did in writing to the chairman of the Dalhousie board of governors, G.F. Pearson, in July 1922, for "frequent and thorough-going discussions [of] the strictly educational features of the proposed union", he was asking for more

33 *Ibid.*, p. 14.

34 *Ibid.*, p. 50.

35 For one treatment, and bibliography, see John G. Reid, "Mount Allison College: The Reluctant University", *Acadiensis*, X, 1 (Autumn 1980), pp. 35-66.

36 Learned to Keppel, 2 March 1925, Maritime Provinces Educational Federation Files, CCA; Learned to G.F. Pearson, 14 July 1922, *ibid.*; see also Lester, *Review of Grants*, pp. 11-13. For discussion of the issue of centralization in the wider context of the overall activities of the Carnegie Foundation for the Advancement of Teaching, see Lagemann, *Private Power for the Public Good*, pp. 179-93.

than many of the scheme's most vigorous supporters were willing to give. Some advocates of the scheme, such as Presidents A. Stanley Mackenzie of Dalhousie University and T. Stannage Boyle of King's, were evidently influenced by academic, as well as possibly by institutional, motivations; although even Mackenzie was not averse on occasion to linking the federation scheme with Maritime rights, and citing the achievements of the large western universities in the fields of research and extension work.[37] For many of the most vigorous and publicly committed supporters, however, the economic argument was paramount.

For J.J. Tompkins, for example, who waged a constant battle to rally opinion behind the federation scheme even after he had been relieved of his duties at St. Francis Xavier University in late 1922 and sent as parish priest to the outlying port of Canso, the federation scheme represented a final opportunity for the Maritime provinces to regain their prosperity through self-help. His sense of urgency was well expressed in the summer of 1922 in a letter to his ally, the Halifax lawyer and newspaper editor Angus L. Macdonald:

> Get your coat off in good earnest. We have the best case in the world and no better cause ever was placed before the people of these provinces....We *ought* to win and it will be *our own fault* if we don't. Failure will spell disaster for us all. Success will bring a new and glorious era to these provinces and give our poor people a chance for life in these strenuous days.[38]

The popular aspects of the scheme, and their relation to socio-economic issues, were continually stressed by Tompkins. Whether corresponding with the Cape Breton labour leader J.B. McLachlan in an effort to organize a "Labor College" within the federation, building on the existing programmes of the Workers' Educational Club in Glace Bay, or dismissing with near-contempt the inclination of Mackenzie and Pearson to work through established political channels, Tompkins consistently regarded popular support as the key to the federation issue. "The Labor idea", he wrote in September 1922, "is growing like a snowball. It is going to get the *people* on the run . . .".[39]

In his predictions of success for the federation scheme, Tompkins was over-optimistic. Yet even in defeat, the scheme had important consequences. One result of the negotiations was the allocation of substantial grants to individual universities: although Dalhousie and King's, as participants in the only actual

---

37 See, for example, A.S. Mackenzie to G.J. Trueman, 26 April 1926, DAL/MS/1/3, Mount Allison University: University Federation, DUA.

38 Tompkins to Macdonald, 30 July 1922, Angus L. Macdonald Papers, MG2, Cabinet 5, Folder 1348, Public Archives of Nova Scotia, [PANS].

39 Tompkins to Learned, 5 October 1922, J.B. McLachlan to Tompkins, 4 October 1922, Tompkins to Learned, 21 February 1923, Maritime Provinces Educational Federation Files, CCA.

union to result from the federation scheme, enjoyed the major share of such grants, Acadia and Mount Allison also benefited.[40] Less obvious than endowment grants, but also of great significance, was the way in which the scheme had brought into continuing contact with the Carnegie Corporation a number of supporters of federation who put a high priority upon the economic significance of education. These supporters had favoured the proposal not because of a desire for centralization *per se*, but because of the opportunities which they had expected would be offered to small towns and rural communities, as well as to cities, by the existence of the federation. As well as Tompkins and Angus L. Macdonald, this group included Tompkins's colleague at St. Francis Xavier, M.M. Coady, and the Newfoundland deputy minister of education, Vincent P. Burke.[41]

As the 1920s went on, new proposals were generated in the Maritimes and Newfoundland, based on the assumed linkage between education and economy, and found support from the Carnegie Corporation. The creation of Memorial College in St. John's, influenced by Burke among others, was facilitated by a grant of $75,000 over a five-year period from the Carnegie Corporation, which was voted in 1924. From the beginning, the new institution recognized an obligation to extend study opportunities throughout Newfoundland, and specific grants were made during the early years to provide for a summer school and for extension of library service to "those living in small, isolated settlements". In writing to Keppel in 1928 to request renewal and increase of the corporation's funding of Memorial College, Burke cited the need of young people in Newfoundland "to prepare to take their regular places in the development of those great resources in the midst of which they have always lived but, owing to lack of the necessary educational advantages...very few of them indeed have had the training required".[42] The connection between educational and economic issues was even more explicit in the work of the Extension Department of St. Francis Xavier University, which during the formative years 1931-1937 received the major part of its revenues in the form of grants from the Carnegie Corporation, voted at the urging of Coady and Tompkins in support of the department's main purpose as enunciated by the university's board of governors: "the improvement of the economic, social and religious conditions of the people of Eastern Nova Scotia".[43]

40 See Table Two.

41 See M.M. Coady to A.L. Macdonald, 1 December 1922, Macdonald Papers, MG2, Cabinet 5, Folder 1348, PANS; also [A.L. Macdonald] to V.P. Burke, 9 January 1923, Folder 1348A, PANS.

42 V.P. Burke, Traveling Library, Second Announcement, September 1928, and Burke to Keppel, 17 May 1928, Memorial University of Newfoundland Files, CCA; see also Lester, *Review of Grants*, pp. 23-4.

43 F.P. Keppel, Notes of Interview with M.M. Coady, 12 April 1929, Keppel, Notes of Interview with Coady, 8 October 1931, J.J. Tompkins to R.M. Lester, 12 November 1931, and Proposal of Extension Department of St. Francis Xavier University, 11 December 1931, St. Francis Xavier

In the winning of Carnegie Corporation support for the Antigonish experiment, and for other extension, co-operative, and travelling library projects in the Maritimes and Newfoundland, the personal prestige of Tompkins was one important factor. Tompkins's tireless advocacy of the federation scheme, his fortitude when exiled to Canso, and his continuing zeal on behalf of the cause of education in the region were enough to prompt the normally matter-of-fact president of the corporation, F.P. Keppel, to declare in a letter of 1939 that "he [Tompkins] is, quite literally, a saint and he is at the same time one of the most ingenious and adroit practical men I have ever known".[44] There was more to the relationship, however, than personal influence. Although a severe critic of unrestrained capitalism, Tompkins had long advocated a non-Marxist solution to labour-capital conflicts and to general economic problems in the Maritime region. Study and self-reliance, he believed, promoted by such educational ventures as the "people's school" he inaugurated at St. Francis Xavier in early 1921, were the routes to progress for the labour movement and for all who sought individual or communal self-improvement.[45] This emphasis was continued in subsequent educational ventures supported or influenced by Tompkins, and it was one that had clear affinities with the underlying philosophical principles of the philanthropic foundations. The commitment of both the Carnegie Corporation and the Rockefeller Foundation to human progress by means other than class struggle, and their insistence that their own role should be essentially that of a catalyst, agreed well with the concept of self-help through study and cooperation. In view of Andrew Carnegie's well-known reluctance to assist denominational institutions, there was a certain irony in that the Carnegie Corporation's support should so readily be given to projects closely associated with a Roman Catholic university. Tompkins had remarked in a letter of 1927 that the time was past "when a good christian was supposed to make a choice between God and Carnegie". The secretary of the Carnegie Corporation, J.B. Bertram, expressed support in 1931 for the corporation's funding of the St. Francis Xavier extension programme in terms that showed that he too was untroubled by any such supposed antithesis: "if we can help people to help themselves instead of putting out a life line to the Red Cross or their fellow tax payers' pockets every time they get in a jam, we shall be carrying out the ideas of the Founder".[46]

University Extension Department File, CCA. On the revenues of the Extension Department, see *Mobilizing for Enlightenment: St. Francis Xavier University Goes to the People* (Antigonish, n.d.), Appendix B, copy in St. Francis Xavier University Extension Department File, CCA.

44 [F.P. Keppel] to R. Wilberforce, 11 April 1939, Newfoundland File, CCA.

45 See the article by Tompkins in *The Casket* (Antigonish), 29 July 1920, and the report of his speech to a regional conference of Rotary Clubs in *The Daily Times* (Moncton), 17 March 1922. On the "people's school" at Antigonish, see the documentation in J.J. Tompkins Papers, MG10-2, 5 (a), Beaton Institute, University College of Cape Breton.

46 J.J. Tompkins to H.J. Savage, 3 October 1927, *ibid.*, 6 (a); J.B. Bertram to F.P. Keppel, 31 December 1931, St. Francis Xavier University Extension Department Files, CCA. On Tompkins

For Bertram, however, the extension movement at St. Francis Xavier had an even wider significance. "This experiment in the Maritimes", he declared to Keppel, "is of more moment than merely to raise the people there out of their parlous condition; it may well be a demonstration of what is needed in many sections throughout the United States".[47] During the 1920s and early 1930s, the perception of the Maritimes and Newfoundland in the minds of officials of the Carnegie Corporation had undergone considerable change. Rather than being seen as remote areas that needed an infusion of modern progressive ideas in order to become fully North American, or even as convenient laboratories for carefully-controlled experiments, initiatives such as the Antigonish movement were now regarded as capable of generating their own methods and their own distinctive insights. During the 1930s, Prince Edward Island provided another example: with support from the Carnegie Corporation for public library development and for a chair of sociology and economics at Prince of Wales College, study clubs, cooperatives and credit unions proliferated.[48] To be sure, it would be easy to claim too much for the significance of such projects, either as part of the Carnegie Corporation's overall activities in the Atlantic region or in terms of long-term social and economic significance. The Carnegie Corporation's programmes were by no means entirely given over to projects that directly combined economic and educational impulses, as witness the large sums devoted to more conventional endowment grants to established institutions such as Dalhousie, King's, Acadia and Mount Allison. Furthermore, in retrospect it may seem that to place as much faith as did Tompkins and his associates in the economic value of education was naive, and substituted a simplistic remedy for the complexities of regional underdevelopment. Nevertheless, to a significant extent, the perception of the Maritimes and Newfoundland entertained by officials of the Carnegie Corporation had been reshaped through the influence of advisers within the provinces themselves.

For the Atlantic region, the inter-war period was a time of intractable socio-economic problems that defied easy solutions. The intervention of major philanthropic foundations in areas such as health and education provided one possible avenue to beneficial change. Initially, the definition of the kind of change that would be beneficial was determined in large part by the perceptions that prevailed within the foundations. Insofar as the foundations dealt with officials of existing universities and of governments, little modification of those

and his relationship with the Antigonish Movement, see Daniel W. MacInnes, "Clerics, Fishermen, Farmers, and Workers: The Antigonish Movement and Identity in Eastern Nova Scotia", Ph.D. thesis, McMaster University, 1978, pp. 158-70, 187, 216-21.

47 J.B. Bertram to F.P. Keppel, 31 December 1931, St. Francis Xavier University Extension Department Files, CCA.

48 See J.T. Croteau, *Cradled in the Waves: The Story of a People's Co-operative Achievement in Economic Betterment on Prince Edward Island, Canada* (Toronto, 1951); also J.A. Murphy to F.P. Keppel, 5 July 1937, St. Dunstan's College File, CCA.

perceptions was brought about, even though important changes were achieved in the health care and higher education systems. Yet through certain less orthodox ventures, officials of the Carnegie Corporation in particular saw their earlier perceptions refashioned by the influence of their local advisers. At a time when the regional economies were at a low ebb, the result of the dialogues with the Carnegie Corporation was to obtain support for movements that at the least gave evidence of social and intellectual vitality. For the officials who looked on from New York, the result was acceptance if not full understanding. "It seems to me", concluded Cartwright in 1936, "that the end justifies the means. The people there are receiving educational advantages, and far be it from me to en-quire into their motives".[49]

49 Cartwright to Keppel, 24 April 1936, *ibid.*

Table One

Grants Approved by Rockefeller Foundation for Maritime
Provinces and Newfoundland, 1918-1940

Recipient	Year(s)	Purpose	Amount
Dalhousie University	1920	Medical school development	$500,000
	1921	Medical school development	50,000
	1928	Teaching in Department of Hygiene	10,000
	1933-38	Teaching of public health	65,400
		LESS unspent balance in 1940	(5,258)
	1936	Institute of Public Affairs	61,200
		LESS unspent balance in 1940	(7,799)
	1937-38	Institute of Public Affairs, morbidity studies[1]	10,000
			683,543
New Brunswick, Government of	1923-24	Rural health programme	45,000
			45,000
Nova Scotia, Government of	1934	Department of Health, sanitary engineering	8,500
	1936	Department of health, local health district	33,400
		LESS unspent balance in 1940	(16,597)
	1937	Department of Health, division of vital statistics	8,160
		LESS unspent blance in 1940	(5,675)
			27,788
Prince Edward Island, Government of	1938	Public health laboratory	15,300
		LESS unspent balance in 1940	(15,300)
			—
			$756,331

Source: Rockefeller Foundation, *Annual Reports*, 1918-1940.

1 These grants were not separately listed in the *Annual Reports* of the Foundation, but were taken from a fund designated for "grants-in-aid, social sciences, social security". See Minutes, 5 August 1937 and 30 June 1938, RG 1.1, Series 427, Box 32, Folder 341, RFA.

Table Two
Grants Approved by Carnegie Corporation of New York
for Maritime Provinces and Newfoundland, 1918-1940

Recipient	Year(s)	Purpose	Amount
Acadia University	1920-29	Endowment	$275,000
	1927	Arts teaching material	5,000
	1928	Adult education	5,000
	1932	Emergency support	10,000
	1932	Purchase of books for library	15,000
	1933	Music study material	2,500
	1934	Development of fine arts	200
	1934-40	Fine arts work	11,000
	1940	Research in mathematics	5,000
			328,700
Central Advisory Committee on Education in the Atlantic Provinces	1924-40	Expenses of meetings[1]	19,771
			19,771
Dalhousie University	1918-19	Repairs following Halifax Explosion	20,626
	1920	Endowment in medicine	500,000
	1921	Hospital teaching facilities	50,000
	1924	Payment of deficits	190,000
	1926	Arts teaching material	5,000
	1929	Books for dental school library	2,000
	1929	Endowment	400,000
	1932	Books for library	9,000
	1933	Endowment in geology	125,000
	1934	Professorship of German	8,000
	1934	Department of pathology	4,000
	1934	Research on pleochroic haloes	1,500
	1937	Medical school library development	50,000
			1,365,126

Organization	Year	Purpose	Amount	Total
Halifax Ladies College	1936	Music study material	1,475	1,475
Jubilee Guilds of Newfoundland	1935	Administrative expenses	4,000	4,000
Memorial University College	1924	Establishment of junior college	75,000	
	1926	Library service for isolated areas	5,000	
	1927	Summer session	4,000	
	1928-37	Support	185,000	
	1930	Additional equipment	7,500	
	1930	Scholarship fund	7,500	
	1932	Arts teaching material	5,000	
	1932	Books for library	3,000	
	1938	Music study material	1,325	293,325
Mount Allison University	1932	Support	10,000	
	1932	Books for library	4,500	
	1933	Arts teaching material	5,000	
	1933	Endowment in chemistry	125,000	
	1936	Music study material	2,550	
	1937	Professorship of Germanic Studies	5,000	152,050
New Brunswick Museum	1934	Educational Programme	9,000	9,000
Newfoundland Adult Education Association	1931-34	Support	18,500	
	1937	Experiment in adult education	1,000	19,500

Institution	Year	Purpose	Amount	Total
Newfoundland Public Libraries Board	1940	Books for travelling library programme[2]	2,000	2,000
Nova Scotia Regional Libraries Commission	1940	Purchase of books[3]	10,000	10,000
Prince Edward Island, Government of	1933-35	Demonstrations of library services	95,000	95,000
Prince Edward Island Libraries	1939	Arts teaching material	2,000	2,000
Prince of Wales College	1932 1933	Books for library Endowment in economics and sociology	4,500 75,000	79,500
Public Archives of Nova Scotia	1934	Educational programme	1,500	1,500
St. Dunstan's University	1932	Books for library	1,800	1,800
St. Francis Xavier University	1919 1932 1932 1932-40	Endowment in French Support Books for library Extension activities[4]	50,000 10,000 4,500 65,000	129,500
St. Joseph's University	1933	Books for library	1,000	1,000

Study by Learned and Sills	1921-24	Expenses	5,575	5,575
University of King's College	1922	Current Expenses	40,000	
	1923	Institutional co-operation in Halifax	52,500	
	1923	Endowment	600,000	
	1925-27	Support	105,000	
	1932	Books for library	3,000	
				800,500
University of New Brunswick	1932	Books for library	4,500	4,500
		TOTAL		3,325,822

Sources: Robert M. Lester, *Review of Grants in the Maritime Provinces of Canada and in Newfoundland, 1911-1933* (New York, 1934), pp. 31-3; Stephen Stackpole, *Carnegie Corporation Commonwealth Program, 1911-1961* (New York, 1963), pp. 39-49.

Notes:

1   Payments on behalf of the Central Advisory Committee to 1940 are calculated from the figure for 1924-42 in Stackpole, *Commonwealth Program*, by subtracting amounts paid after 1940. See R.M. Lester to G.J. Trueman, 5 August 1941, 2 December 1941, Trueman to Lester, 23 December 1941, Lester to Trueman, 20 May 1942, Trueman Papers, 7837-134, 7837-147, Mount Allison University Archives.

2   Of this grant of $10,000 spread over five years, $2000 was payable in 1940. See W.M. Woods to F.P. Keppel, 5 April 1940, Newfoundland Public Libraries Board Files, CCA.

3   Of this grant of $50,000 spread over five years, $10,000 was payable in 1940. See [H.F. Munro] to F.P. Keppel, 23 January 1941, J.J. Tompkins Papers, MG10-2, 5 (c), Beaton Institute, University College of Cape Breton.

4   In addition to Stackpole, *Commonwealth Program*, see also [R.M. Lester] to R.B. Fosdick, 28 February 1938, St. Francis Xavier University Extension Department Files, CCA.

MARGARET CONRAD

Reprinted from Vol. IX, No. 2
(Spring 1980)

Apple Blossom Time in the Annapolis Valley 1880-1957

The Annapolis Valley apple industry has been the subject of considerable academic scrutiny. During the heyday of the apple era, Willard V. Longley wrote a doctoral thesis for the University of Minnesota focusing, appropriately, on production and marketing trends in the industry.[1] When the apple export market collapsed after the Second World War, N.H. Morse, in another doctoral thesis, chronicled the history of apple growing in the Valley.[2] Not surprisingly, since that ubiquitous student of staple industries, University of Toronto Professor Harold Innis, was Morse's supervisor, the Innisian influence is obvious in Morse's detailed study. More recently, historians and sociologists interested in class structures and social movements have looked to the Annapolis Valley apple industry in order to understand the weakness of cooperative structures and third party movements in Atlantic Canada.[3] While the wise student might conclude from this that the topic has been sufficiently analyzed, recent work by David Alexander suggests that there is one aspect that merits closer attention. Alexander argues that Canadian policy after the Second World War "lumbered overseas export industries with an impossible burden". Because federal authorities were mesmerized by the American market, their policies, Alexander maintains, resulted in foreign domination of east coast fisheries and indirectly forced a painful and futile relocation of the under-employed outport population.[4] At the risk of being accused of comparing apples and cod fish, this paper proposes to show that the Annapolis Valley apple industry had much in common with the Newfoundland salt fish trade in the first half of the twentieth century and that, however generous, federal policies were short-sighted, if not deliberately perverse, in the period immediately following

1 Willard V. Longley, "Some Economic Aspects of the Apple Industry in Nova Scotia" (PhD thesis, University of Minnesota, 1931). The thesis was published as Bulletin No. 113 of the Nova Scotia Department of Agriculture (Halifax, 1932).

2 N.H. Morse, "An Economic History of the Apple Industry of the Annapolis Valley in Nova Scotia" (PhD thesis, University of Toronto, 1952).

3 Ian MacPherson, "Appropriate Forms of Enterprise: The Prairie and Maritime Co-operative Movements, 1900-1955", Acadiensis, VIII (Autumn 1978), pp. 77-96; R. James Sacouman, "The Differing Origins, Organization and Impact of Maritime and Prairie Co-operative Movements to 1940", in Robert J. Brym and R. James Sacouman, eds., Underdevelopment and Social Movements in Atlantic Canada (Toronto, 1979), pp. 37-58; Robert J. Brym, "Political Conservatism in Atlantic Canada", in ibid., pp. 59-79.

4 Dav'' Alexander, The Decay of Trade: An Economic History of the Newfoundland Saltfish Trade, 1935-1965 (St. John's, 1977), pp. viii, 163.

the Second World War. Moreover, the "shabby dignity" which was the consolation prize awarded to charter members of Confederation in the form of federal agricultural policy in the 1950s had implications as potentially disruptive for Valley people as the great resettlement plan did for Newfoundland's outport population.[5]

The Annapolis Valley of Nova Scotia is one of the most productive agricultural areas in the Atlantic region. Highlands to the north and south, reaching elevations of seven and eight hundred feet respectively, shut out the maritime fogs and northwest winds, giving the Valley more hours of sunshine and a longer growing season than most localities in the Atlantic Provinces.[6] Because of the fertility of the soil, the temperate climate and the relative accessibility of the area by sea, the Annapolis Valley was one of the first areas in Canada to produce a surplus of agricultural products for export. Both the Acadians and the New England Planters who succeeded them were noted for their productive farms, where fruit, vegetables, cattle and grains grew in abundance.[7] Apples had been a product of the Valley since the early days of French settlement, but the perishable nature of the fruit made them a risky export in the era of the sailing ship.[8] Although "gentlemen" farmers experimented with new varieties and growing techniques, lack of near-by markets and efficient transportation prior to the mid-nineteenth century prohibited further development of the fruit industry. As R.W. Starr, one of the pioneers of the apple industry, remarked in 1886, the 'old days' were not conducive to developing a market for Valley apples: "Prices were low. The markets of Saint John and Halifax were easily glutted; the fruit, itself carelessly harvested, badly packed and then transported for long distances over wretched roads or else in the hold of a small schooner with potatoes and turnips for two or perhaps four weeks, was apt to arrive [at] market in a condition better imagined than described".[9]

The completion of a railway from Halifax to Windsor in 1858 and to Annapolis Royal by 1869 marked the beginning of a new era for the farmers of

5   David Alexander, "Economic Growth in the Atlantic Region, 1880-1940", *Acadiensis*, VIII (Autumn 1978), p. 76.

6   Andrew Hill Clark, *Acadia: The Geography of Early Nova Scotia to 1760* (Madison, 1968), ch. 2; J.W. Goldthwait, *Physiography of Nova Scotia* (Ottawa, 1924).

7   Clark, *Acadia*, pp. 230-61; John Robinson and Thomas Rispin, *Journey Through Nova Scotia*, reprinted in *Report of the Public Archives of Nova Scotia, 1944-45*, pp. 26-7; Joseph Howe, *Western and Eastern Rambles: Travel Sketches of Nova Scotia*, edited by M.G. Parks (Toronto, 1973), pp. 81-3.

8   For an outline of the early history of apple growing in the Annapolis Valley see Morse, "An Economic History of the Apple Industry", ch. 2; F.G.J. Comeau, "The Origins and History of the Apple Industry in Nova Scotia", *Collections of the Nova Scotia Historical Society* (1936), pp. 15-40; R.W. Starr, "A History of Fruit Growing in Kings County", Nova Scotia Fruit Growers Association, *Annual Report*, 1886, pp. 153-60.

9   Starr, "A History of Fruit Growing in Kings County", p. 155.

the Annapolis Valley. In the early 1860s Haligonians — anxious to wrest their hinterland from the clutches of Saint John — began showing an increased interest in Valley produce. In 1862 a committee sponsored by the provincial government and under the secretaryship of Robert Grant Haliburton (son of the famous author and one of Nova Scotia's most ambitious native sons) offered prizes for the best specimen of fruit and vegetables to represent Nova Scotia in the International Exhibition and Horticultural Society Show held in London. Although Nova Scotia produce made a good impression generally, its apples were especially well received. The *Times* enthusiastically reported that "the beauty of the apples beats anything we have ever seen".[10]

Success in the British market did not follow immediately. Shipments from Annapolis Royal and Halifax in the early 1860s proved financial failures, despite the efforts of one enterprising shipper to prevent the fruit from spoiling by using frozen lumber to reduce the temperature in the ship's hold. R.W. Starr attributed the initial difficulties of marketing Nova Scotia apples in the United Kingdom to the problem of "cargoes arriving in bad order from long passages and want of ventilation" and the "prohibitory" costs of steam freight.[11] There was also stiff competition in the British market from continental fruit which did not experience the transportation costs and quality deterioration imposed by the long North Atlantic voyage. However, by the 1880s improved steamship service and reduced freight rates from Halifax to Britain permitted regular shipments of apples to arrive in satisfactory condition. When the McKinley Tariff of 1890 virtually excluded Nova Scotia apples from the American market,[12] Britain was already absorbing an increasing volume of the Valley output. As Dr. Henry Chipman observed in a paper he delivered to the Fruit Growers Association in 1887, the British market had "solved the problem of profitable agriculture in the whole Valley".[13]

By 1914 the apple industry had transformed agriculture in the Annapolis Valley. Increased orchard acreage was brought into production, warehouses to protect the fruit from frost sprang up along the railroad, and "speculators" representing British brokers combed the area for commission-earning consign-

10 Duncan Campbell, *Nova Scotia in its Historical, Mercantile and Industrial Relations* (Montreal, 1873), pp. 418-21. According to Campbell, the apples were arranged in flat trays with partitions, packed in bran and arrived in excellent condition.

11 Starr, "A History of Fruit Growing in Kings County", p. 159.

12 A tariff of 63¢ a barrel imposed by the McKinley legislation resulted in a decline in exports of Nova Scotia apples to the United States from 44,000 barrels in 1890 to 1000 in 1891. Morse, "An Economic History of the Apple Industry", p. 15. Regarding this problem, see also J.W. Longley, "Fruit Growing in the Annapolis Valley", *Canadian Magazine* (1893), pp. 621-7. The American market never returned except when the American crop was small, as in 1919 and 1921. See Longley, *Some Economic Aspects of the Apple Industry in Nova Scotia*, pp. 125-6.

13 Cited in Morse, "An Economic History of the Apple Industry", p. 19.

ments.[14] Individual farmers experimented with grafting, spraying and fertilizating techniques and, at the urging of the Nova Scotia Fruit Growers Association (NSFGA), a provincially-funded horticultural school associated with Acadia University was established in Wolfville to bring scientific methods to bear on fruit growing. When the provincial government moved the school to Truro in 1905, the Fruit Growers Association successfully petitioned for a federally-funded Experimental Farm located in Kentville to assist them in improving the quantity and quality of their fruit.[15] The large volume of apple exports also enabled Valley farmers to secure favourable rates from rail and shipping cartels. By 1911-12, when the Valley produced a bumper crop of over one million barrels of apples, the transportation costs had been sufficiently reduced — from $1.00 a barrel in the 1880s to 60¢ in 1912 — to put the Valley product in a favourable competitive position with respect to its European and North American rivals in the British market.[16] Production costs also benefited from the relative ease with which Valley growers could find labour and supplies. The nearby subsistence farms and fishing villages, locked into their own seasonal rhythms, supplied labour at harvest time and quality barrels crafted during the winter months for the multi-million dollar industry.[17]

Orchards planted prior to the First World War came into peak production in the 1920s and 1930s, resulting in huge crops (see Table I). During the 1930s Nova Scotia produced over 40% of the Canadian apple output and was a major supplier of the British market, which in most years absorbed over three-quarters of Nova Scotia's total commercial crop and over 90% of the apples exported.[18]

14 *Ibid.*, pp. 19-30.

15 J. Fred Hockey, *Agricultural Research in the Annapolis Valley, 1909-1960* (Ottawa, 1967), pp. 1-3.

16 Morse, "An Economic History of the Apple Industry", pp. 157-61. According to Morse, rates from Halifax to Britain were as low as 60¢ a barrel in the 1912-13 season and although prohibitively high during the First World War, they were gradually reduced to 90¢ in 1924-25 where they stayed until the 1930s when they were as low as 54¢. Part of the reason why shipping cartels caved in to grower demands in the 1930s was the decision on the part of George Chase and others to ship directly from Port Williams, by-passing the Halifax lines, Furness Withy and White Star.

17 T.A. Meister, *The Apple Barrel Industry in Nova Scotia* (Halifax, n.d.). Harold Innis was particularly impressed by the extent to which the apple industry was an integral part of the Nova Scotia economy: "Fertilizer comes from the Cape Breton mines, cooperage from the lumber industry, labour from the fisheries. And in its turn the beauty of the Valley from blossom time to harvest has contributed to the profit of the tourist business". Cited in J. Holland Rose *et al.*, eds., *The Cambridge History of the British Empire*, vol. VI (New York, 1930), p. 669. Although no study has yet been done of the overall impact of the apple industry on the economy of the Annapolis Valley, one commentator, in 1930, estimated that Valley growers annually spent $1 million for containers and $3/4 million for labour. See United Fruit Companies, *Minutes and Proceedings of Annual Meetings* (Kentville, 1930), p. 6.

18 Morse, "An Economic History of the Apple Industry", pp. 175-6; Longley, *Some Economic Aspects of the Apple Industry in Nova Scotia*, p. 123.

Table I

Disposition of Nova Scotia Apple Production
1880-1938*

Year	Production '000 Bu.	Export '000 Bu.	% of Crop	Processed '000 Bu.	% of Crop	Fresh Sales Canada '000 Bu.	% of Crop
1938	6,572	5,316	80.9	753	11.4	503	7.7
1937	6,458	3,905	60.5	1,754	27.1	799	12.4
1936	4,967	2,468	49.7	1,715	34.5	784	15.8
1935	5,418	4,125	76.1	858	15.8	435	8.1
1934	6,425	4,000	62.3	1,356	21.1	1,069	16.6
1933	8,288	6,803	82.1	1,273	15.4	212	2.6
1932	3,647	2,661	73.0	787	21.5	199	5.5
1931	4,534	3,657	80.6	551	12.2	325	7.2
1930	3,517	2,979	84.7	254	7.2	284	8.1
1929**	5,959	4,219	70.8	1,195	20.1	545	9.1
1928	3,285	2,097	63.8	454	13.9	734	22.3
1927	2,811	1,816	64.6	428	15.2	567	20.2
1926	2,649	1,883	71.1	317	12.0	449	16.9
1925	3,742	2,326	62.1	1,073	28.7	343	9.2
1924	4,413	3,380	76.6	584	13.2	449	10.2
1923	5,389	4,364	81.0	339	6.3	686	12.7
1922	5,096	3,603	70.7	615	12.1	878	17.2
1921	5,508	3,691	67.0	769	14.0	1,048	19.0
1920	3,502	2,737	78.2	204	5.8	561	16.0
1919	4,899	1,953	40.7	1,290	26.9	1,556	32.4
1918	1,884	833	44.2	259	13.7	792	42.1
1917	2,234	41	1.8	496	22.2	1,697	76.0
1916	2,044	1,250	61.1	195	9.6	599	29.3
1915	1,842	1,250	67.9	60	3.2	532	28.9
1910-14 av.	2,810	2,238	79.7	n.a.	n.a.	572	20.3
1905-09 "	1,746	1,467	84.0	n.a.	n.a.	297	17.0
1900-04 "	1,185	928	78.3	n.a.	n.a.	257	21.7
1895-99 "	1,113	785	70.6	n.a.	n.a.	328	29.4
1890-94 "	534	336	62.9	n.a.	n.a.	198	37.1
1885-89 "	428	244	57.0	n.a.	n.a.	184	43.0
1880-84 "	284	31	32.0	n.a.	n.a.	193	68.0

*Three bushels = one barrel

**Figures for 1880-1929 do not include estimates of farm consumption.

Source: W.V. Longley, *Some Aspects of the Apple Industry in the Annapolis Valley in Nova Scotia* (Halifax, 1932), p. 115; N.H. Morse, "An Economic History of the Apple Industry of the Annapolis Valley in Nova Scotia" (PhD thesis, University of Toronto, 1952), p. 310.

Although apple growing became popular all over the province, most of the commercial crop originated in the Valley counties of Annapolis, Kings and Hants. While apples in the 1930s represented only about 10% of the gross value of Nova Scotia farm production, in Kings County the apple crop accounted for nearly one-half of the income derived from agriculture and helped to make the Valley farms the most valuable in the province.[19] It was a source of great pride to the inhabitants of Kings county that, within a 25-mile radius of the shire town of Kentville, 75% of all Nova Scotia apples grown for export were produced.[20] Even the Valley's political orientation was influenced by the apple industry. The strong imperial sentiment which characterized much of English-speaking Canada in the first half of the twentieth century, was given substance in the Valley by the close economic ties with the 'Mother Country'. In the 1911 federal election, for example, Kings County voters, who had long sought a renewal of reciprocity with the United States and had supported the Liberal Party since Confederation, were now so confident in their alternative markets that they elected Conservative candidates who campaigned on the slogan, "no truck or trade with the Yankees".[21]

The success of the British market imposed structural constraints on the Valley industry that were to last until the Second World War. Prior to 1939 the competitive position of Valley apples depended on their price, not their quality. Late-keeping, medium-quality, cooking apples — Ben Davis, Russets, Starks, Gano, Baldwins — suitable for the barrel trade were produced rather than the more expensive dessert apples — McIntosh, Delicious, Cortland — packed in boxes.[22] Such was the dominance of the United Kingdom outlet for apples that

19 *Seventh Census of Canada, 1931,* vol. VIII, pp. 86-7.

	Gross Value of farm products	Fruits and Maple Products	Average Value of Farms per acre
Annapolis	$2,294,788	$457,040	$30.29
Hants	2,522,884	225,112	24.94
Kings	5,152,308	2,312,385	60.25
Nova Scotia	32,582,206	3,399,377	24.61

20 Charles C. Colby, "An Economic Analysis of the Apple Industry of the Annapolis-Cornwallis Valley", *Economic Geography,* I (1925), pp. 174-5.

21 Between 1867 and 1911 Kings County returned only one Conservative to the Commons, D.B. Woodworth, who sat for one term, 1882-87. *Parliamentary Guide* (Ottawa, 1955), p. 302. In the only detailed study of the 1911 federal election in Nova Scotia, the author concludes that the expansion of trade with Britain and the prosperity that resulted was the major cause for the Conservative sweep of the Valley constituencies. A. Gordon Brown, "Nova Scotia and the Reciprocity Election of 1911" (MA thesis, Dalhousie University, 1971).

22 The common culinary varieties produced for the British trade included Ben Davis, Gano, Stark, Baldwin and Wagener. Golden Russet, Ribston, King, Blenheim, Spy, Cox Orange, Cortland and the much favoured early variety, Gravenstein, were suitable for both cooking and eating out of hand. McIntosh, primarily a dessert apple, also ranked among the top 10 varieties in number of trees by 1939. See Morse, "An Economic History of the Apple Industry", p. 71.

domestic markets, including that of Nova Scotia itself, were almost completely ignored. Although attempts had been made early in the century to break into the western and central Canadian markets, these were more easily filled by orchardists in British Columbia, Ontario and Quebec. Shipments of Nova Scotia apples also were sent to continental Europe and the United States in years when these areas experienced a shortfall in their crop. However, the almost unlimited demand of the largest apple consuming nation in the world and Nova Scotia's favourable geographical position to fill that demand made the vigorous pursuit of alternative markets unnecessary.[23]

The continuing expansion of the apple industry in the interwar years enabled the Annapolis Valley to avoid the worst effects of the 1930s Depression. In 1933, for example, Valley growers produced 2,762,700 barrels of apples (48% of the Canadian output), the bulk of which was sold in the United Kingdom for over $4 million. This was the largest crop and the biggest financial return yet recorded in the "orchard of the British Empire".[24] Only a year before, the federal government, bowing to pressures from Canadian growers, had secured a preference for Canadian apples in the increasingly protective British market. So powerful were the apple mandarins that J.L. Ilsley, federal Liberal member for the Valley riding of Kings-Hants, felt compelled to vote in favour of the 1932 British-Canadian trade treaty negotiated by the Conservative government of R.B. Bennett.[25] The local authorities were equally respectful of their Annapolis Valley constituents. Provincial Minister of Agriculture O.P. Goucher, with an eye to the upcoming election in August 1933, made a Spring announcement that the government planned a new dehydration plant for the Valley.[26] At a time when many Canadian communities were experiencing the trough of the Great Depression, Valley farmers and the many who depended on the apple industry for their livelihood, were in an expansive frame of mind. They celebrated their good fortunes by inaugurating the annual Apple Blossom Festival, a document to the influence of the apple on the economic well-being of the Annapolis Valley.[27]

By the 1930s the Valley apple industry had undergone major structural changes since the beginning of the century. In 1900 independent farmers had barrelled their crop, "tree run", and consigned it to British brokers for disposal at auction or by private sale, primarily in London, Liverpool, Glasgow and Manchester.[28] This arrangement proved less than satisfactory since the growers

23 Longley, *Some Economic Aspects of the Apple Industry in Nova Scotia*, pp. 114-26, 131.

24 Morse, "An Economic History of the Apple Industry", p. 175.

25 *Ibid.*, p. 198; H. Blair Neatby, *William Lyon Mackenzie King*, vol. III, *1932-39: The Prism of Unity* (Toronto, 1976), p. 26; Ian M. Drummond, *Imperial Economic Policy, 1919-39* (Toronto, 1974), chs. 5-6.

26 *Wolfville Acadian*, 11 May 1933.

27 *Ibid.*

28 Longley, *Some Economic Aspects of the Apple Industry in Nova Scotia*, pp. 8-9, 123.

felt that shippers and brokers reaped an inordinate proportion of the profits realized by the industry. In 1911, the United Fruit Companies was incorporated, the culmination of a decade of discussion on the merits of cooperative marketing. For several years prior to the First World War it seemed as if the whole industry would become dominated by the aggressive cooperative organizations whose main aim was to wrest control of the industry from the shippers and brokers. However, the cooperative thrust was blunted by the disruption of British markets during wartime and in the 1920s Valley cooperatives faced stiff competition from corporate shipping organizations, particularly the British Canadian Fruit Association, W.H. Chase and Herbert Oyler, financed by local and British capital. These corporate shippers, organized in the Nova Scotia Shippers Association in 1919, enhanced their position *vis à vis* the cooperatives by operating a 'truck system' as effective as any exercised by the St. John's merchants in the salt fish trade. W.V. Longley, in 1931, described how the system 'worked':

> All three of these organizations have found it necessary to finance many individual growers. They furnish them with supplies in the way of fertilizers and spray materials, also tend to furnish them with sufficient funds to enable them to carry through to the marketing season. They, however, bind the growers so financed so that their crop must be sold through their organizations. Thus it is, that a considerable number of growers have during the difficult years of the post-war period become involved and have found it necessary to be so financed. The result is, these organizations have a certain quantity of the crop assured ahead of picking season. Financially on such risks these organizations have been much better protected than the cooperatives.[29]

By taking on the bad risk farmers, the "big three" also "found it necessary to take over a certain number of farms".[30] Thus, the shippers, operating their own warehouses, their own supply outlets and sometimes even their own shipping operations also acquired the orchards of bankrupt farmers. In the 1930s the big three handled over 50% of the Valley apple crop.[31] As with the salt fish trade the structure of the apple industry favoured "highly individualistic buccaneers" at the export end with the losses forced on the producers.[32] Moreover, the shippers, with an eye to short run profits, were more concerned with volume than with the quality of the exported product, unless it was from their own orchards. They (as well as many of the growers) tended to oppose regulations which would improve

29 *Ibid.*, pp. 43-4.
30 *Ibid.*, p. 44.
31 Nova Scotia Fruit Growers Association, *Annual Report* (Kentville, 1951), pp. 82-3.
32 Alexander, *The Decay of Trade*, p. 21.

the quality and unit price of the fruit at the expense of quantity and they feared bureaucratic organizations that might favour the growers over the real or imagined interests of the shippers.[33]

Given the strength of the independent shippers, the United Fruit Companies (UFC) and other cooperative organizations in the interwar years became little more than vehicles by which small and medium scale growers could reduce the charges of middlemen in the export process and reap the economies of scale with suppliers of sprays, fertilizer and equipment necessary for the industry. The UFC, which by 1930 represented 51 of the 60 cooperatives in the Valley, usually handled less than 40% of the Valley apple crop prior to 1939 and had little control over its affiliates.[34] Members of the UFC were inclined to withdraw their support if independent action in any given year seemed more advantageous and they refused to submit to a pooled pack. This made any strategy to stabilize the marketing process difficult to implement. Although in 1931 the UFC established a finance company to help make its services more attractive to capital-starved farmers and also invested in processing plants designed to use the lower grades for vinegar, dried apples and concentrates, the cooperative organization was able only with difficulty to hold the line in competition with the independent shippers prior to 1939.[35] As long as overseas markets dominated the industry, and especially after George Chase single-handedly reduced shipping charges by exporting directly from Port Williams after 1928, the independent shippers were a force to be reckoned with in the Annapolis Valley.[36]

33 Morse, "An Economic History of the Apple Industry", pp. 205-20.

34 *Report of the Royal Commision Appointed to Investigate the Fruit Industry of Nova Scotia* (Halifax, 1930), pp. 33-4.

35 United Fruit Companies of Nova Scotia Limited, *Minutes and Proceedings of Annual Meeting* (Kentville, 1921-38).

36 W.H. Chase of Port Williams in 1926 sold his line warehouses to the British Canadian Fruit Association with G.A. Chase continuing the Port Williams operations. Facilities established by the Chases at Port Williams in 1928-29 resulted in shipments of 250,000 to 500,000 barrels a year from that port during the 1930s. The BCFA was backed by the British firm of J. and H. Goodwin and was operated by Valley managers with its headquarters at Kentville. When the BCFA was reorganized in the 1930s, R.W. DeWolfe Limited of Wolfville developed some of its properties and became an important shipper. The firm of H. Oyler was based in Kentville. In 1951 it was purchased by Minas Pulp and Power Company, the empire of R.A. Jodrey of Wolfville and Hantsport. Other large "independents" included E.S. Elliott, W.B. Burgess, E.D. Haliburton, F.S. Hewitt, Manning Ells, F.A. Parker and Sons, G.N. Reagh and Son, R. and D. Sutton, A.R. Stirling and other smaller concerns, numbering, according to Morse, up to 150 shippers. Morse, "An Economic History of the Apple Industry", p. 85. It is significant that the industry remained primarily in the control of Valley growers and shippers both before and after the war. Little biographical data is available on these "captains" of the apple industry although a recent biography of R.A. Jodrey is a useful case study of a Valley entrepreneur who got his start selling apples. See Harry Bruce, *R.A.: The Story of R.A. Jodrey, Entrepreneur* (Toronto, 1979). A 1939 survey showed that there were 2509 apple growers in Nova Scotia, 33 of whom had over 60 acres of orchards, while 85% owned less than 20 acres. Clearly, the majority of growers

It was within this context that the Annapolis Valley apple industry struggled to maintain its competitive position in the British market during the interwar years. Although improvements had been made in grading, packing and handling techniques by the 1920s, there was still room for improvement. Valley growers tended to export a large number of varieties, a wide range of quality and an unevenly graded product. As early as 1922, Professor W.S. Blair of the Kentville Experimental Farm had returned from a trip to the United Kingdom convinced that Valley growers would have to improve the quality of their product to compete with exports from Australia, the United States, British Columbia and Ontario, where increasing emphasis was being placed on red dessert varieties and the box pack. Moreover, British growers were organizing to capture their domestic market which was being swamped by the cheap North American product.[37] Such was the uncertainty in the industry during the 1920s that the provincial government established a Royal Commission in 1930 to report on problems facing Nova Scotia's apple growers.[38] The commission's findings were by no means flattering. Valley growers were criticized for refusing to upgrade their orchards, for selling a bad pack — "good top and bottom and poor in the 'middle" — and for intimidating officials whose job it was to grade and inspect the product for export.[39] The commission report also expressed alarm at the extent of indebtedness of the apple growers and argued that extensive changes were necessary if the Nova Scotia product was to remain competitive in the international market:

> Poor and ill-kept orchards must be eliminated; varieties of apples must be grown that the modern market requires; modern practices with regard to spraying and fertilization must be intensified; methods of packing and shipping must be done under conditions meeting modern requirements; the pack must be made dependable; the last word which science can give must be obtained and applied; but not least, the Valley, which by its very nature forms a single industrial unit, must consolidate its interests for marketing purposes.[40]

The cooperative principle and centralized marketing, panaceas of the era,[41] were seen as the salvation of an industry suffering from excessive individualism.

pursued mixed farming operations with fruit-growing as a side-line. This may help to explain the difficulty in arriving at a consensus on growing and shipping practices. *Ibid.*, pp. 73-4.

37 NSFGA, *Annual Report*, 1922, pp. 90-4.

38 *Report of the Royal Commission Appointed to Investigate the Fruit Industry of Nova Scotia* (Halifax, 1930).

39 *Ibid.*, p. 70.

40 *Ibid.*, p. 41.

41 For a similar assessment of the Newfoundland saltfish trade see Alexander, *The Decay of Trade*, pp. 25-6.

Unfortunately, the commission's recommendations served only to interject more venom in the already heated debate over marketing organization and quality control. The Nova Scotia Fruit Growers Association, an organization representing large and small growers as well as shippers, was unable to establish a consensus on the major recommendations of the royal commission and individual farmers were left to their own devices in improving their orchard practices.[42] However, events in Britain transpired to produce the desired effect. In 1931 the British government passed an Agricultural Marketing Act, a piece of legislation designed to regulate the chaotic domestic market for the benefit of local producers.[43] The act did not authorize control of imported products but it was an omen for the future. That omen was temporarily forgotten in 1932 when Bennett "blasted" his way into the British market by securing a preferential tariff for Canadian apples and other natural products at an imperial trade conference held in Ottawa. This gave Nova Scotia growers exactly what they wanted, since the tariff was sufficiently high to partially exclude apple imports from the United States which was the biggest competitor for the Valley product.[44]

Although various leading lights (including the ubiquitous Lord Beaverbrook)[45] had been proposing an empire preference since the turn of the century, British producers were less than enthusiastic about the Ottawa agreements. In 1933 the British government responded to their pressure by passing a second marketing act aimed at regulating imported natural products that competed with the domestic output.[46] This threw Nova Scotia growers into a tail spin for, under the new legislation, Britain threatened to put an embargo on Canadian shipments of early varieties and low grade fruit. The Nova Scotia government reacted immediately by sending their Minister of Agriculture, former NSFGA President, John A. McDonald, to Britain to investigate the situation. The British government agreed to call an Imperial Fruit Conference in June 1934 at which time an Empire Fruit Council was established to regulate voluntarily the volume of fruit exports to the United Kingdom.[47] Meanwhile, the Canadian Horticultural Council, of which Nova Scotia growers were members and which represented British Columbia and Ontario apple growers who also had a stake

42 NSFGA, *Annual Report*, 1931, pp. 11-12.

43 *Ibid.*, 1933, pp. 20-1.

44 Drummond, *Imperial Economic Policy, 1919-1939*, ch. 6. The Nova Scotia growers had reason to be grateful for the preference. Canadian apple exports to the United Kingdom increased 48% in the 1933-36 period over 1929-32 while in the same years U.S. and other foreign sources of apples for the British market dropped 45% and 50% respectively. NSFGA, *Annual Report*, 1937, p. 57.

45 Ian Drummond, *British Economic Policy and the Empire, 1919-1939* (London, 1972), pp. 31-5; A.J.P. Taylor, *Beaverbrook* (New York, 1972), chs. 11-13.

46 NSFGA, *Annual Report*, 1933, pp. 20-1.

47 *Ibid.*, 1934, pp. 9ff.

in the British market, pressed the Bennett government for marketing legislation that would impose order on what threatened to be a chaotic situation in the Canadian apple industry. Bennett complied with this and other similar requests by passing the Natural Products Marketing Act (NPMA) in 1934. Canadian apple growers were the first to apply for a control board under the provisions of this act and the Fruit Export Board (FEB) began operations in the Fall of 1934.[48]

Under the regulations of the FEB, anyone wishing to export apples from Canada had to apply for a license at one of the three FEB offices in Kentville, Ottawa and Kelowna. No early varieties and only limited quantities of "Domestic" or "C" grade apples were to be shipped to Britain. The Board also determined when shipments could most profitably be placed on the British market. Inspectors were stationed at Vancouver, Montreal and Halifax to ensure that only quality fruit was exported and other officials inspected the fruit upon its arrival in Britain.[49] From the point of view of quality control the system worked well. S.B. Marshall who inspected Nova Scotia apples at the British end of the export process was enormously enthusiastic about the results. In December 1935 he reported to the annual meeting of the NSFGA that "there is no pack on the markets of the United Kingdom superior to that now being sent over. . .and the very highest market prices are being realized both at auction and private treaty".[50] As proof of the new confidence in Nova Scotia apples, Marshall cited the fact that buyers at auctions no longer demanded that sample barrels be dumped out to ensure a consistent pack.

Despite the improved reputation of Nova Scotia fruit in Britain, all was not well with the FEB and the Nova Scotia committee established by the NSFGA to advise the parent board. Some of the shippers objected to the 1¢ a barrel levy imposed to pay for the new bureaucratic structure and they complained, with some justification, that FEB activities were more restrictive and costly than was required by the British regulations.[51] At the December 1935 meeting of the NSFGA, the long-standing tension between growers and shippers erupted in a free-wheeling debate over the FEB report which passed by a divided vote of 183-86.[52] The rift also poisoned attempts to create a local marketing board designed to control domestic shipments. H.E. Kendall, Chairman of the Nova Scotia Marketing Board (NSMB) which was finally created in 1935, described the nature of the cleavage:

> The shippers claimed that being the more experienced and having large vested interests at stake they should have the predominating voice. In

48 *Ibid.*
49 *Ibid.*, 1935, pp. 39-40.
50 *Ibid.*, p. 64.
51 *Ibid.*, pp. 41-2.
52 *Ibid.*, pp. 43-7.

other words, that if it was a Board of five — there should be three shippers and two growers. Your Organization on the other hand contended that as the Grower always "pays the shot" when things go wrong they should have the last word in decisions. This view prevailed with the Parent Board at Ottawa and our Board was set up as it exists with three elected by the Growers Association and two by the Shippers Association. That the position has not been a comfortable one is obvious.[53]

The shippers registered their protest against the NSMB by boycotting the domestic market in 1935 and by withdrawing from the NSFGA. Their position was vindicated and they were the first to stop paying tolls when the NPMA was declared *ultra vires* in 1936.[54] Thereafter, a Voluntary Export Advisory Council composed of four growers, four shippers and a chairman continued to regulate exports to meet British standards but it stuck to the letter of the law and could do little to influence the direction of the Nova Scotia apple industry.[55]

It is difficult to ascertain to what extent a rigidly controlled marketing system would have spared the Nova Scotia growers the crisis that descended upon them in the 1940s. It had become obvious well before the Second World War that British buyers were increasingly impatient with the unreliability of the Nova Scotia product and that British orchardists were beginning to protect their domestic market for culinary apples under the shelter of national marketing legislation. The President of the NSFGA warned his listeners in 1934 that they must look to the day when Great Britain would be "self-sufficient in cooking apples" and that "only our quality apples" would sell.[56] Many growers were taking such warnings to heart and upgrading their orchards. On the other hand, the generalized uncertainty generated by the Depression made many willing to cash in on short term profits in an effort to squeeze the last penny out of old orchards; and, given the depressed prices of the period, it seemed unwise to do more than reinforce past successes in marketing behaviour. Such activities, however, would not long go rewarded.

With the outbreak of the Second World War, the British market closed abruptly as capital and shipping capacity were diverted to the military effort. This blow to the Valley apple industry was softened temporarily by federal government action. At the request of both growers and shippers, Ottawa established regional marketing boards to dispose of surplus Canadian apples. What could not be sold on the domestic market was sent to processing plants and any overseas markets that might become available (see Table II). Since the volume of the Nova Scotia output was sufficient to disrupt Canadian markets and prices, the

53 *Ibid.*, p. 47.
54 *Ibid.*, p. 23; 1936, p. 9.
55 *Ibid.*, 1936, pp. 9, 13, 31ff.
56 *Ibid.*, 1934, p. 9.

Table II

Disposition of Nova Scotia Apple Production

1938-1970

Year	Production '000 Bu.	Export '000 Bu.	Export % of Crop	Processed '000 Bu.	Processed % of Crop	Fresh Sales Canada '000 Bu.	Fresh Sales Canada % of Crop
1970	2,800	136	4.8	1,858	66.4	806	28.8
1969	3,050	240	7.9	2,034	66.7	776	25.4
1968	2,790	197	7.1	2,047	73.4	546	19.5
1967	3,500	283	8.1	2,561	73.2	656	18.7
1966	2,962	257	8.7	2,095	70.7	610	20.6
1965	3,100	328	10.6	2,232	72.0	540	17.4
1964	2,430	259	10.6	1,669˙	68.7	502	20.7
1963	3,180	368	11.6	2,265	71.2	547	17.2
1962	2,461	390	15.9	1,667	67.7	404	16.4
1961	3,151	638	20.2	1,921	61.0	592	18.8
1960	2,243	335	14.9	1,326	59.1	582	26.0
1959	2,260	470	20.8	1,352	59.8	438	19.4
1958	1,455	171	11.8	873	60.0	411	28.2
1957	2,918	935	32.0	1,537	52.7	446	15.3
1956	2,206	220	10.0	1,506	68.3	480	21.7
1955	3,250	471	14.5	1,573	48.4	1,206	37.1
1954	2,157	80	3.7	1,505	69.8	572	26.5
1953	1,087	113	10.4	564	51.9	410	37.7
1952	1,626	157	9.7	704	43.3	765	47.0
1951	1,539	203	13.2	971	63.1	365	23.7
1950	2,250	87	3.9	1,429	63.5	734	32.6
1949	3,742	1,583	42.3	1,303	34.8	856	22.9
1948	2,291	—	—	1,417	61.9	874	38.1
1947	3,631	—	—	2,661	73.3	970	26.7
1946	6,020	1,920	31.9	3,059	50.8	1,041	17.3
1945	1,087	76	7.0	575	52.9	436	40.1
1944	5,262	500	9.5	3,985	75.7	777	14.8
1943	4,846	483	10.0	3,308	68.2	1,055	21.8
1942	3,918	—	—	3,124	79.7	788	20.1*
1941	3,444	304	8.8	2,124	61.7	912	26.5*
1940	3,453	—	—	1,726	50.0	729	21.0*
1939	5,953	108	18.1	3,672	61.7	517	8.7*
1938	6,572	5,316	80.9	753	11.4	503	7.7

*Volume reduction due to shrinkage, dumping or return to growers.

Source: Nova Scotia, Department of Agriculture and Marketing, *Agricultural Statistics, 1971* (Halifax, 1972), p. 59; N.H. Morse, "An Economic History of the Apple Industry of the Annapolis Valley in Nova Scotia" (PhD thesis, University of Toronto, 1952), pp. 394-5.

country was zoned and the sale of fresh apples from Nova Scotia was confined to the Maritimes and Newfoundland. Although zoning restrictions were relaxed somewhat in 1940, Nova Scotia fruit movements still were carefully regulated to prevent chaos in other regions of the country. Such harsh restrictions seemed justified in view of the expectation that the British market would re-open after the war and given that the federal government was willing to make deficiency payments to growers who were forced to sell their crops at a loss to processors.[57]

The Nova Scotia Apple Marketing Board (NSAMB), created in 1939 by the federal government under the War Measures Act, was placed under the general management of R.J. Leslie, a long-time proponent of centralized marketing.[58] As was the case with the FEB, the NSAMB, under Leslie's direction, interpreted its mandate as broadly as possible. In addition to disposing of the yearly crop and distributing various subsidies,[59] the NSAMB encouraged the building of processing plants and cold storage facilities; advocated the use of the box pack and stricter grading standards; and urged the upgrading of orchards through grafting and tree-pulling programs.[60] Although initial arrangements for deficiency payments did not enable growers to cover the costs of production, as the war reached its end, they were receiving higher overall returns than in the pre-war period (see Table III). The balance of power in the industry also changed. Since the shippers were temporarily eclipsed by events, the UFC, of which Leslie was president after 1944, witnessed a marked increase in popularity.[61] So pleased were Valley growers with the operation of the NSAMB that in 1944 they voted overwhelmingly to extend cooperative marketing into peacetime.[62]

By the end of the war, the Valley apple industry had been considerably revitalized. In 1946, one third of the unusually large Nova Scotia crop was shipped to British markets where it fetched a good return. It seemed only a matter of time

57 Morse, "An Economic History of the Apple Industry", pp. 290-308.

58 *Ibid.*, p. 293.

59 In the 12 years of its operation, the NSAMB distributed $19,000,000 in the form of price supports, subsidies to processors and tree-pulling programs. During the period in which the Valley was experiencing a reduction in output, British Columbia was increasing its apple production. In 1939 British Columbia produced fewer apples than did Nova Scotia. By 1950 the British Columbia output was three times that of Nova Scotia. British Columbia, with its larger Canadian market, was also able to weather the wartime restrictions in markets better than the British oriented Maritimers and required only $5 million in aid from Ottawa during the war. A.E. Britnel and V.C. Fowke, *Canadian Agriculture in War and Peace, 1935-50* (Stanford, 1962), pp. 326-7.

60 NSFGA, *Annual Report*, 1951, p. 13; Nova Scotia Apple Marketing Board, *Office Reports* (Kentville, 1940-51).

61 Morse, "An Economic History of the Apple Industry", pp. 364, 456. Nearly 50% of the apple crop was handled by the UFC in 1945, and over 60% by 1950.

62 NSAMB, *Office Reports*, 1944-5, p. 3; 81.3% of the 74% of the growers who voted were in favour of continuing centralized marketing.

Table III

Value of Nova Scotia Apple Production, 1931-1960

Year	Production '000 Bushels	Farm Price Current Values $ per bushel	Farm Price* Constant Values $ per bushel	Total Farm Values Current Values $ '000	Total Farm Values* Constant Values $ '000
1960	2,243	.82	.58	1,839	1,310
1959	2,260	.64	.46	1,446	1,046
1958	1,455	.63	.47	917	680
1957	2,918	.66	.50	1,926	1,456
1956	2,206	.76	.59	1,677	1,305
1955	3,250	.40	.32	1,294	1,045
1954	2,157	.98	.80	2,114	1,716
1953	1,087	1.37	1.14	1,489	1,238
1952	1,626	1.00	.84	1,626	1,357
1951	1,539	0.77	.68	1,185	1,039
1950	2,250	0.68	.66	1,530	1,484
1949	3,742	0.62	.62	2,316	2,316
1948	2,291	0.84	.87	1,926	2,004
1947	3,631	0.72	.85	2,629	3,086
1946	6,020	0.94	1.21	5,689	7,322
1945	1,087	1.08	1.42	1,178	1,548
1944	5,262	0.92	1.24	4,872	6,548
1943	4,846	0.89	1.23	4,314	5,975
1942	3,918	0.83	1.19	3,252	4,666
1941	3,444	0.77	1.15	2,652	3,976
1940	3,453	0.61	.98	2,106	3,408
1939	5,953	0.43	.73	2,560	4,332
1938	6,572	0.80	1.35	5,258	8,837
1937	6,458	0.53	.89	3,423	5,743
1936	4,967	0.57	.98	2,831	4,881
1935	5,418	0.79	1.41	4,280	7,616
1934	6,425	0.58	1.04	3,726	6,666
1933	8,288	0.50	.91	4,144	7,507
1932	3,647	0.59	1.05	2,152	3,822
1931	4,534	0.67	1.08	3,038	4,892

*Series deflated by Gross National Expenditure Index (1949 = 100)

Source: Nova Scotia, *Agricultural Statistics, 1967* (Halifax, 1968), p. 56; Nova Scotia, *Agricultural Statistics, 1971* (Halifax, 1972), p. 58.

before the 'good old days' were re-established, providing, of course, that Valley growers continued to upgrade the quality of their fruit and the reliability of their pack. Two developments intervened to destroy such delusions. The first spanner in the works was a mysterious breakdown in Valley apples which caused them to deteriorate at an alarming rate. Storage problems, soil culture, and chemical fertilizers and sprays were blamed for the difficulty, which only could be remedied, Leslie told the NSFGA in 1946, by careful management.[63] The second obstacle was more difficult to overcome. Europe's post-war recovery proved less rapid than had originally been hoped. In August 1947 Britain was forced to suspend sterling convertibility which had been made a condition of Allied post-war planning. For the foreseeable future Britain's purchases in dollar countries such as Canada would be severely restricted.[64]

As David Alexander has explained, historically, Canada earned large trade surpluses overseas in order to balance trade deficits in North America. In other words, overseas exports were a means of earning dollars to acquire goods and services produced in North America. The key to this "financial operation" was the convertibility of sterling. When sterling convertibility was suspended indefinitely in 1947, a new national strategy was necessary. Unfortunately it was not forthcoming, or rather, it developed by default with uneven repercussions on regions and industries in Canada.[65] Since the long-term restriction of American imports into Canada was unthinkable, it was obvious that alternative dollar-earning markets had to be found. Rather than seeking markets in the wider context of international trade, Ottawa focused on improving sales of Canadian primary products in the United States. While this may have been a suitable solution for some primary industries, nothing would be more difficult for Valley apple growers than an invasion of American apple markets — except perhaps the conquest of the Canadian market. Oriented since the turn of the century to the British trade, Valley apples were virtually excluded from the North American market not only by their quality, which was rapidly being improved, but also by the very way they were packaged. Although Ottawa officials had been reluctant to continue war-time assistance to Valley growers, the events of 1947 convinced them that extraordinary measures were necessary. The NSAMB, which from 1939-45 had operated under the War Measures Act

---

63 *Ibid.*, 1945-46, pp. 6-7.

64 On the exchange crisis see Donald Creighton, *The Forked Road: Canada 1939-57* (Toronto, 1976), pp. 122-7; A.F.W. Plumptre, *Three Decades of Decision* (Toronto, 1977), ch. 4; C.L. Barber, "Canada's Post-War Monetary Policy, 1945-54", *Canadian Journal of Economics and Political Science*, XXIII (1957), pp. 349-62; J.D. Gibson, "Post-war Economic Direction and Policy in Canada", *ibid.*, XX (1954), pp. 439-54; J.R. Petrie, "The Impact of the Sterling-Dollar Crisis on the Maritime Economy", *ibid.*, XIV (1951), pp. 347-52; Robert Cuff and J.L. Granatstein, "The Rise and Fall of Canadian-American Free Trade, 1947-8", *Canadian Historical Review*, LVIII (1977), pp. 459-82.

65 Alexander, *The Decay of Trade*, pp. 39-44.

and in 1946-47 under the National Emergency Transitional Powers Act, was allowed to continue under the Agricultural Prices Support Act of 1944.[66]

The December 1947 Annual Meeting of the Nova Scotia Fruit Growers Association was conducted in an atmosphere of crisis and confusion. NSFGA President E.D. Haliburton offered an urgent plea for the fruit growers in the "horse and buggy era" to "get on with" changing their varieties and marketing techniques to meet the North American consumer demand, but R.J. Leslie's report hinted at problems which a revitalized Nova Scotia apple industry would face. A brief to the Transport Commission requesting lower freight rates for Nova Scotia apples sent to Canadian markets had not been acted upon.[67] Even more alarming was the bureaucratic ineptitude exhibited in Ottawa. In 1947 federal officials had secured an agreement which would allow Canadians to sell their apples on the American market. However, while this diplomatic coup was well publicized, it was less well known that permission to sell did not necessarily mean that markets were guaranteed and were in fact non-existent. To make matters worse, barrels were unwelcome in the North American trade and the boxes required for the American market had to be imported, tariff and all, from the United States.[68]

The 1947 crisis prompted the NSFGA executive to sponsor a panel on "Orchard Reconstruction Policy". R.J. Leslie opened the discussion by pointing out that the British market was gone for the foreseeable future and that government aid was essential for an orchard rehabilitation program. For those interested in staying in the apple industry, he warned, both crop specialization and centralized marketing were necessary. While even E.D. Haliburton, champion of the independent operators, conceded that "we no longer have a choice", he was reluctant to go all the way with controls. Central selling might be necessary, he concluded; centralized packing perhaps was not. George Chase, representing the large shipping interests, was the only panelist to question the validity of the federal government agreement not to ship to sterling countries: "if exchange could be arranged", he maintained, the British "would welcome our total crop of Starks and Ben Davis, as well, of course, our dessert varieties".[69]

In 1948, R.D. Sutton, an apple grower whose brother was Liberal member of the provincial legislature for Kings County, headed what was becoming the perennial pilgrimage to Ottawa. Opposition to aid for Nova Scotia growers from Ontario and Quebec made a subsidy arrangement particularly difficult to negotiate. Only the intervention of the Nova Scotia premier, Angus L.

66 Morse, "An Economic History of the Apple Industry", pp. 447-8. In 1949 the federal government bowed to pressure from agricultural groups and passed the Agricultural Products Marketing Act, which had the effect of protecting the regional markets and therefore making Central and Western Canadian markets less accessible to Maritime produce.

67 NSFGA, *Annual Report*, 1947, pp. 81-4.

68 *Ibid.*, pp. 2, 81-4.

69 *Ibid.*, pp. 118-25.

Macdonald and his Minister of Agriculture, A.W. Mackenzie, produced a price support agreement satisfactory to Valley growers.[70] But the receipt of price support payments of $1,443,808 in 1948 was only a temporary solution to the absolute loss of overseas markets and the dim prospects of alternative ones. Nor was it sufficient to produce new varieties, improve grading standards and modify packing techniques to meet North American standards. It was also necessary to find buyers for fresh fruit in a North American apple market that was already over supplied and contracting under the assault of vigorous citrus fruit competition and the restricting sterling markets.[71] The processing route also had its limitations. Return from sales to processors rarely covered costs of production although for the less marketable varieties, it was a welcome alternative to letting the crop rot on the trees. Unfortunately, by 1948 Nova Scotia-produced apple sauce, pie filling and juice had already saturated their market potential, leaving the processors with unsold surpluses.[72] In the face of this bleak outlook, farmers all over the Valley, who had hung on until the expected return to normal conditions after the war, finally decided to uproot their orchards, some turning to the production of poultry, cattle or vegetables, others deserting the farm completely.[73]

The political scene in the Annapolis Valley reflected the economic chaos. In 1948 J.L. Ilsley, exhausted by his wartime role as Minister of Finance and frustrated by the endless litany of complaints from his constituents,[74] decided to resign his commons seat of 22 years for a more secure position on the bench.[75] The December 1948 by-election in Digby-Annapolis-Kings became a forum for the pent-up anger of Valley producers and, not surprisingly, the Progressive Conservative Party represented by UFC and NSAMB solicitor George Nowlan captured the Valley seat.[76] On the day following the by-election, President E.D. Haliburton announced to the NSFGA membership that since the Federal government was responsible for British policies which had ruined the overseas market, it should subsidize a tree pulling program to "buy us off their

---

70 *Ibid.*, 1948, p. 37.

71 *Ibid.*, 1957, pp. 51-3, 107. Between 1909 and 1956 per capita consumption of apples in North America dropped from 75 lbs. a year to 25 lbs. a year.

72 NSAMB, *Office Reports*, 1948-49, pp. 5-6. By 1949, 33% of Canadian apple sauce was produced in the Annapolis Valley, *ibid.*, 1949-50, p. 6.

73 See H.A. Blackmer, "Agricultural Transformation in a Regional System: the Annapolis Valley, Nova Scotia" (PhD thesis, Stanford University, 1976), for a detailed discussion of this process.

74 E.S. Elliott reported to the Nova Scotia Fruit Growers in 1947 that Mr. Ilsley remarked "more than once": "When shall this thing end?" Nova Scotia Fruit Growers Association, *Annual Report*, 1947, p. 121.

75 From 1926 to 1935 J.L Ilsley represented Kings-Hants. After 1935 Ilsley sat for the constituency of Digby-Annapolis-Kings.

76 Margaret Slauenwhite Conrad, "George Nowlan and the Conservative Party in the Annapolis Valley, Nova Scotia, 1925-1965" (PhD thesis, University of Toronto, 1979), pp. 207-24.

necks once and for all". General Manager of the Nova Scotia Apple Marketing Board, R.J. Leslie, enraged by the radio publicity given to Haliburton's remarks, warned farmers that they should be doing much more than destroying apple trees. He outlined a five-year plan oriented around centralized marketing to rehabilitate the industry.[77]

The federal Minister of Agriculture, James Gardiner, announced early in June 1949 that the Canadian government had worked out a plan with the British Food Ministry for the purchase of Canadian apples under the Marshall Plan. Nova Scotia's share of the quota would be approximately half a million barrels.[78] This sudden overture, described by R.J. Leslie as a "political" transaction, was a one-shot deal, not an indication of a new national marketing policy for Nova Scotia apples.[79] The agreement perhaps helped fruit grower Angus A. Elderkin to regain the Valley seat for the Liberal Party in the general election of June 1949, but Gardiner could not pressure Britain to continue allocating her limited dollars for apples, even if it meant losing a government member of the House. In a letter to the NSFGA in September 1949, he reminded Valley growers that in his meeting with them, he had "made it very plain that the time had arrived when the [Nova Scotia] growers should make a real attempt to sell their own apples without depending in any way upon the Federal Government either to merchandise them or to assist in financing".[80] Despite this communication, Gardiner belatedly authorized a grant of $500,000 to compensate growers for losses on their 1949 crop. This and previous grants, Gardiner explained, were the result of Nova Scotia's unique position "with its historical relationship to external markets, particularly that in the United Kingdom". But, he warned, no further assistance would be provided on that account.[81] This statement was read into the Commons debates by Gardiner's Parliamentary Assistant, Robert McCubbin, on 3 April 1950. It did little to impress Valley voters who proceeded to return a Progressive Conservative to fill the Valley seat left vacant when the 1949 election was successfully challenged in the courts.[82] Although $300,000 was

77 NSFGA, *Annual Report*, 1948, pp. 10-1, 112-3.

78 *Ibid.*, 1949, pp. 95-6.

79 NSAMB, *Office Report*, 1949-50, p. 3.

80 Printed in NSFGA, *Annual Report*, 1949, p. 98.

81 Gardiner's letter to the NSFGA of 31 March 1950, read in the House on 3 April 1950, is printed in *ibid.*, p. 71.

82 Conrad, "George Nowlan and the Conservative Party in the Annapolis Valley, Nova Scotia, 1925-65", ch. V. Had Valley growers commanded a solid block of seats in the House of Commons, a third party alternative may very well have appealed to voters. However, with only one seat sprawling over the whole apple growing area, the most effective way of punishing Ottawa was by supporting the governing party's major rival. It is this powerlessness rather than any indigenous conservatism which has made third party politics so weak not only in the Valley but in the Atlantic Region generally. In this I would support Robert J. Brym's argument as articulated in "Political Conservatism in Atlantic Canada", in Byrm and Sacouman, *Underdevelopment and Social Movements in Atlantic Canada*, pp. 59-79.

granted in deficiency payments for the 1950 crop, Angus L. Macdonald was sent a "most definite note of finality". This time Gardiner meant it. To make matters worse, Sir Andrew Jones of the British Food Mission let it be known in 1950 that Britain would not accept any Nova Scotia apples since the 1949 shipment had arrived in such a bad condition. The latter objection was overcome by a small shipment of fancy grade apples in 1950 but this did nothing to restore the former volume of trade with Great Britain.[83]

Given this impasse, the Apple Marketing Board, blamed by many growers for the difficulties experienced in the apple industry, was disbanded by a majority vote of its members in 1951. A.R. Stirling probably reflected the feeling of most of the growers when he argued that the NSAMB had been useful for negotiations with Ottawa and distributing federal subsidies but not for marketing.[84] Thus the NSAMB which was perfectly situated (if for no other reason than it had managed for the first time in Valley history to gather all growers under one jurisdiction) to ease the transition in Valley apple production was allowed, in fact encouraged, to pass into limbo. The debate over centralized marketing which accompanied its collapse was really a bogus one — a kind of familiar Greek chorus to the general tragic drama — since without markets it mattered little how the growers grouped themselves or, indeed, how rapidly they modernized their industry.[85]

Had lucrative markets been available, Valley growers would almost certainly have made the necessary adjustments to meet the demand. Indeed, by 1951, the changes wrought in the industry in the previous decade had given Nova Scotia the most modern cold storage facilities on the continent, a quality box pack and a promising proportion of dessert varieties.[86] Only the continued reliance on processing outlets in the 1950s halted the transformation begun under the auspices of the Nova Scotia Apple Marketing Board. For the Nova Scotia apple industry to have continued at its pre-war level, federal authorities needed either to arrange to sell a larger volume of Nova Scotia's new dessert varieties in other regions of North America or to find markets in emerging Third World countries. Neither of these alternatives seemed worth the political manoeuvering that would have been necessary to secure the desired result. The best prospects from the point of view of government officials and, indeed, of many of the growers themselves, was to send the surplus apple crop to processors while developing other areas of specialization in the Annapolis Valley. In the short run there was little else that could have been done. The real tragedy of the situation

83 NSFGA, *Annual Report*, 1950, pp. 91, 99-100; NSAMB, *Office Reports*, 1950-51, pp. 9-11.

84 NSFGA, *Annual Report*, 1950, pp. 99-100.

85 See Alexander, *The Decay of Trade*, pp. 136-9 for parallels with the salt fish marketing agency, the Newfoundland Associated Fish Exporters Limited (NAFEL).

86 NSAMB, *Office Reports*, 1948-9, pp. 10-1; *A Second Census of Apple Orchards in Nova Scotia* (Halifax, 1950) indicated that the number of trees had been reduced 30% in the decade between 1939 and 1949 and that dessert varieties had increased from 16.7% to 32.3% in the same period.

in the 1950s was less that the Nova Scotia apple industry experienced a crisis but that the crisis was used as a justification for crippling an industry with considerable long-term potential for the Atlantic Region — and for Canada which by the mid-1950s was importing nearly a half million bushels of apples annually from the United States.[87] Of course, the Annapolis Valley was not the only area where farmers experienced difficult times in the 1950s. Moreover, a number of the apple growers actually managed to make very successful transitions to other areas of agricultural production. Still it was heart-breaking for those who had invested heavily in orchards to watch their horizons contract while producers in Ontario, the United States and Commonwealth countries maintained and even increased their production. Although occasional shipments were made to the West Indies, the United States and Great Britain in the 1950s, these markets never absorbed the annual volume that was necessary to establish the industry on a profitable and stable basis. World apple markets in the post-war period were gradually being realigned and, as with other commodities in the regional economy, the Maritime product was being squeezed out of the highly structured market picture.[88]

Despite the unreceptive atmosphere, Nova Scotia growers did not give up their attempts to secure marketing assistance from Ottawa. Recognizing the

---

87 While it may be argued that "crippled" is too strong to describe the fate of the Nova Scotia apple industry, the growers themselves recognized that a small output made it impossible for the region to supply chain stores and other large-volume buyers who required a large and reliable source of fruit to fill their massive orders. See NSFGA, *Annual Report*, 1949, p. 27.

World Apple Production 1935-57*
('000 bushels)

	Average 1935-39	Average 1945-49	Average 1952-57
Canada	14.6	14.8	13.9
Mexico	1.2	2.0	2.7
United States	127.3	104.4	104.1
Europe	289.	250.	388.
South America	2.	9.	16.6
Asia, Africa, Oceana	28.	29.	48.

*   NSFGA, *Annual Report*, 1957, p.51.

Canadian Apple Production**

	Nova Scotia	Quebec	Ontario	B.C.
1933-38	43.4%	—	—	36.2%
1951-55	13.8%	19.4%	21.9%	42.5%
1956-60	14.6%	22.3%	25.2%	35.2%
1961-65	14.1%	25.9%	27.5%	30.8%

** Morse, "An Economic History of the Apple Industry", p. 175; B.H. Sonntag, *Maritime Agriculture: A Comparative Regional Analysis*, II, p. 330.

88 Alexander, *The Decay of Trade*, ch. 6.

real power in the cabinet, Nova Scotia growers in 1952 teamed up with their counterparts from British Columbia in an appeal to C.D. Howe. They suggested that interest payments on Canada's loan to Britain be forgiven in return for British purchases of agricultural products. The minister refused to budge.[89] After their own initiatives to find foreign outlets failed in 1953 and a disastrous hurricane destroyed much of the crop in 1954, the Nova Scotia growers made another appeal to Howe in 1955. Again he rejected their urgent plea for government assistance in marketing the unusually large Nova Scotia crop. Moreover, that concession to Nova Scotia content in the St. Laurent cabinet, the Minister of Public Works, Robert Winters, added insult to injury by offering to assist in financing a national advertising campaign to encourage Canadians to eat more apples![90]

By this time the attitude of the apple growers and their sympathizers toward the federal government had reached an all-time low. F. Waldo Walsh, Deputy Minister of Agriculture and Marketing for Nova Scotia, broke civil service silence by publicly denouncing the Liberal government for their callous dismissal of Valley growers in 1955. Walsh, resorting to a familiar Maritime reflex, accused the Liberals of a "mis-carriage of justice" in submitting to Ontario pressure to destroy the Nova Scotia apple industry. If Nova Scotians bought tariff protected automobiles for Ontario, Walsh reasoned, the least they could do was to tolerate competition from a revitalized Nova Scotia apple industry.[91] Resentment and confrontation between federal and provincial authorities are not unusual in the Canadian political process. However, the following encounter which occurred before the NSAMB was disbanded is particularly revealing, less for the form it took than the content of the exchange. Walsh, a member of the annual "apple delegations" to Ottawa described the 'diplomatic exchange' in his recently published memoirs. According to Walsh, Winters, unlike Ilsley, was a known protégé of Howe and, despite his Nova Scotia origins, was under suspicion for putting his own personal ambition ahead of the well-being of his province. Winters apparently tried to influence members of the provincial apple committee to re-orient themselves toward American markets, since British markets, he asserted, were "dead". Walsh explains his reaction to this pressure:

We had had a couple of drinks before supper one evening, and Winters once again dragged out his view about selling apples to the Americans. At this point Bob Leslie, who had long since grown tired of the argument, said that one of the best reasons for not tieing up with the Americans was that "he didn't think they were politically mature. . .".

The statement was too much for Winters. He couldn't turn on Leslie, who

89 NSFGA, *Annual Report*, 1952, p. 55.

90 *Ibid.*, 1955, pp. 25, 30.

91 F. Waldo Walsh, *We Fought For the Little Man* (Moncton, 1978), pp. 118-25.

was a respected Valley farmer and a voter, and certainly he couldn't afford to antagonize Rowland Sutton, who was a key Liberal in the Nova Scotia farm organization. But I was a little civil servant from Nova Scotia, and as a public employee I was fair game. So he turned on me.

"Walsh, as far as you are concerned," he said, "You are nothing but an imperialist fool!"

Without too much thought I replied:

"Yes, I guess that can be said about me, Bob, but at least no one can ever say that I kissed C.D. Howe's arse!"

At this, Winters threw a punch at me, and the fight was on. . . .[92]

Walsh was not alone in his criticism of Ottawa. The federal policy toward Nova Scotia apple growers in the 1950s and the general direction of the St. Laurent government in re-orienting Canadian trade to a continental market was widely perceived in Nova Scotia as a deliberate attempt to destroy the region's economy. This resentment would be tapped to good effect in 1957 by John Diefenbaker who represented another area of the country whose economy had been damaged by the post-war political and economic re-alignment.[93]

Despite the tireless and perhaps heroic efforts of the Nova Scotia growers and provincial government officials to secure federal assistance in finding export markets, little help was forthcoming. By 1957 the apple output had stabilized at about 2 million bushels and the number of apple trees in the Valley was less than half of that recorded in 1939.[94] Over 60% of the crop was now processed in nearby factories, while under 20% was dispatched to foreign markets.[95] Understandably, confidence in the industry was low and few new trees were planted. A provincial Royal Commission in 1957 suggested a reorganization of the cooperative structure of the United Fruit Companies Limited and government assistance for cold storage facilities but these measures, coupled with a relaxing of British restrictions in the late 1950s, did little to restore the apple industry to its former greatness.[96] Meanwhile, the forces of continentalism so obvious in other areas of Canada's economy marched into the Annapolis Valley to fill the vacuum left by the declining apple industry. By the 1970s the largest landholders in the Valley included the multi-national processing corporations, Hostess Foods, and Stokeley Van Camp, neither of which had held land in the area

92 *Ibid.*, pp. 117-8.

93 In the 1957 federal election the Progressive Conservative representative from Digby-Annapolis-Kings was joined by nine more Progressive Conservative members, enough to give Diefenbaker a seven seat plurality.

94 Sonntag, *Maritime Agriculture: A Comparative Regional Analysis*, II, pp. 329-30.

95 *Ibid.* By the 1950s apples represented less than 4% of Nova Scotia's agricultural output and was no longer a major source of import dollars as it had been in the interwar period.

96 *Report of the Royal Commission on the Administration and Operation of Public Cold Storage Plants in Relation to the Annapolis Valley Apple Industry* (Halifax, 1957).

prior to the Second World War.[97] These vertically integrated firms competed with the locally-owned cooperatives for the produce of the rapidly shrinking number of farms. Restricted markets internationally and regional agricultural self-sufficiency in Canada forced diversified agricultural production for a limited Atlantic Provinces' market. The appearance of multinational agribusiness conglomerates and nation-wide chain stores complicated selling structures and made it difficult for farmers to control even their local markets. In addition, sophisticated technological innovations and competition on a continental basis required large-scale production, huge amounts of capital and rigorous specialization, while mechanization rendered certain lands, including abandoned orchards, less suitable for cultivation. Finally, government regulation in the form of marketing boards, price supports and feed grain subsidies made individual initiative on the part of Valley farmers sadly impractical.[98]

The effects of these pressures can be seen in the changed nature of Valley agricultural production in the two decades after the Second World War. The number of farms and total area under cultivation decreased and the size of farms increased while overall output and capital value of farms soared in Kings County but declined in the agriculturally less well endowed Annapolis and Hants Counties. Increasingly owners of family farms either sold their holdings to incorporated farmers or to one of the large multinational corporations operating in the Valley. Farming, as in other areas of North America, was now an industry rather than a way of life, and subsistence farming had almost disappeared. The planning process meant that fresh produce appeared in the stores during all seasons of the year but it also forced Valley people to pay more for the produce of their own region than did people in more competitive market areas of North America.[99]

The apple industry, stimulated by the Atlantic Region's proximity to the British market, prolonged the export-led growth that had begun in the Valley before the end of the eighteenth century. The transition after the Second World War to highly mechanized agribusiness geared to a domestic market and processing was achieved, at least in terms of modern economic values, with remarkable efficiency. And, it must be conceded that, in many respects, dramatic changes in the mid-twentieth century were inevitable. On the other hand, the timing of the

---

97 Blackmer, "Agricultural Transformation in a Regional System"; Harry E. Bronson, "Continentalism and Canadian Agriculture", in Gary Teeple, ed., *Capitalism and the National Question in Canada* (Toronto, 1972), pp. 121-40.

98 Blackmer, "Agricultural Transformation in a Regional System", p. 74ff.

99 *Census of Canada*, 1941, vol. 8; 1951, vol. IV; 1961, vol. 5, part I; 1971, vol. IV, part II. The value in current dollars of farm products in Annapolis County in 1941 was $2 million compared to $3 million in 1961. Kings County increased from $4 million in 1941 to $10 million by 1961. By the latter date government services were the major source of income for Valley inhabitants — Greenwood Air Force and Cornwallis Naval bases contributing substantially to this development. In agricultural terms, egg production had eclipsed apples as the most lucrative sources of farm income.

transition, the traumas which accompanied it and the loss of local control which characterized it were not acts of God. They were deliberate policy decisions on the part of government, particularly the federal government, which was the only agency in Canada with the power to create alternatives for Maritime producers. After all, markets, in the era of the International Monetary Fund, the General Agreement on Tariffs and Trade, and the Agricultural Products Marketing Act are political phenomena, not the miraculous result of the law of supply and demand. Nobody embraced this truth more fully than did C.D. Howe who frequently intervened on behalf of Canadian secondary industry. Canadian manufacturers needed Howe's midas touch but so did the primary sector of the Canadian economy; and nowhere was the state economic planning more necessary than it was in the primary sector of the Maritime Provinces after the Second World War. By purposely confining Valley agriculture to a limited regional market and by refusing to assist in the search for external markets Ottawa sealed the fate of agriculture in the Atlantic Provinces, permitting it to follow the route of secondary industry into a dependent and underdeveloped state.[100]

100 David Alexander, "Development and Dependence in Newfoundland, 1880-1970", *Acadiensis*, IV (1974), pp. 3-21; T.W. Acheson, "The National Policy and the Industrialization of the Maritimes, 1880-1910", *ibid.*, I (1972), pp. 3-28.

ERNEST R. FORBES

Reprinted from Vol. XV, No. 2
(Spring 1986)

Consolidating Disparity:
The Maritimes
and the Industrialization of Canada
during the Second World War

THE POLITICIANS AND BUREAUCRATS who directed Canada's economic development emerged from the Second World War with a profound sense of accomplishment. The Department of Munitions and Supply arranged for the writing of its own history so that what C.D. Howe called the "magnitude of our achievement" would not be forgotten. The accounts not only stress the quantity of munitions produced but also boast of the government's contribution to a new industrial base for the nation.[1] These claims have not been challenged. Howe's biographers credit the minister and his advisors with having "shaped Canada's war programme, renewed Canada's industrial plant and reconstructed the Canadian economy".[2] But the scholar interested in the problem of Canadian regional disparity might well ask why, if Canada's industrial development during the war was so largely a product of government initiative, it did not include the Maritimes? Indeed, it can be argued that the policies of Howe and his associates were detrimental not only to Maritime industries but also to Canada's war effort.

The events of the war period help illuminate the process by which regional disparity is created. They are particularly pertinent to the debate between "orthodox" scholars who have attributed the growth of regional disparity to the forces of the marketplace and "liberal revisionist" and "neo-Marxian" scholars who give greater prominence to political and social factors in the region's decline.[3] The war highlighted the role of government in spectacular fashion and

The research for this paper was funded by the Social Sciences and Humanities Research Council of Canada. The author is particularly indebted for advice and research leads to Marc Milner, Roger Sarty, Danny Moore, Elizabeth McGahan, and David Zimmerman, and to research assistant Twila Buttimer for work in newspapers.

1   J. de N. Kennedy, *History of the Department of Munitions and Supply: Canada in the Second World War* (Ottawa, 1951), vol. I, p. v. See also Canada, Department of Reconstruction and Supply, "Canada's Industrial War Effort, 1939-1945", unpublished manuscript, 1947, vol. 264, B2-B8, Records of the Department of Munitions and Supply [RG28], Public Archives of Canada [PAC].

2   Robert Bothwell and William Kilbourn, *C.D. Howe: A Biography* (Toronto, 1979), p. 350.

3   Michael Clow, "Politics and Uneven Capitalist Development: The Maritime Challenge to the Study of Canadian Political Economy", *Studies in Political Economy*, 14 (Summer 1984), pp. 117-40 and "Situating a Classic: Saunders Revisited", *Acadiensis* XV, 1 (Autumn 1985), pp. 145-52. See also T.W. Acheson's "Introduction" to S.A. Saunders, *The Economic History of the Maritime Provinces* (Fredericton, 1984 [1939]) and the bibliography in J.B. Cannon, "Explain-

removed much of the illusion that events were controlled by the invisible natural laws of Adam Smith. Prime Minister William Lyon Mackenzie King and his colleagues suspended the law of supply and demand for the duration of the war. They appointed controllers over each major industry to develop and implement plans for industrial expansion. They aided private companies directly through government grants and indirectly through accelerated depreciation of plants and equipment. Firms could not substantially alter patterns of production without the permission of a controller. Those which failed to cooperate or became bogged down in labour problems could be, and sometimes were, expropriated, although cooperation between industry and government for mutual advantage was the more common practice. When private firms proved unable to meet particular war needs, the government created new crown corporations for the purposes required. Wages and prices were governed by the Wartime Prices and Trade Board. Subsidies were paid to compensate firms for the rising cost of imports, and cost of living bonuses were awarded to workers in lieu of wage increases. Commodity shortages were met with rationing and limits were set on the production of consumer products.[4]

The government's policies regarding coal, steel, shipbuilding, ship repair and general manufacturing industries in the Maritimes formed a consistent pattern. For more than a year into the war C.D. Howe and his controllers withheld government funds for the modernization and expansion of Maritime industries while labour was drawn to Ontario and Quebec or into the armed forces. With the realization of impending commodity shortages and the growing strategic importance of the region, they finally turned to Maritime industries only to encounter manpower shortages and a limited infrastructure. Their failure to resolve these problems, especially in the matter of ship repair, undermined the effectiveness of the Royal Canadian Navy at a critical point in the war. What government investment the Maritimes did receive tended to be in industries of a temporary nature. It is ironic that the region which received the least wartime investment would later be identified by the Department of Reconstruction as the one which would have the greatest difficulty in adjusting to a peacetime economy.[5]

The motives for bypassing the Maritimes were seldom articulated and not

ing Regional Development in Atlantic Canada: A Review Essay", *Journal of Canadian Studies*, XIX, 3 (Fall 1984), pp. 81-6.

4   C.R. Waddell, "The Wartime Prices and Trade Board: Price Control in Canada in World War II", Ph.D. thesis, York University, 1981. See also Robert Cuff and J.L. Granatstein, *War and Society in North America* (Toronto, 1971); C.P. Stacey, *Arms, Men and Governments* (Ottawa, 1970); J.L. Granatstein, *The Ottawa Men: The Civil Service Mandarins, 1935-57* (Toronto, 1982); James Eayrs, *In Defence of Canada: Peacemaking and Deterrence* (Toronto, 1972); Robert Bothwell, Ian Drummond, John English, *Canada Since 1945: Power, Politics, and Provincialism* (Toronto, 1981); and Donald Creighton, *The Forked Road: Canada 1939-1957* (Toronto, 1976).

5   Canada, Department of Reconstruction, Economic Research Branch, "Area Study Tables", 30 September 1945, Vol. 264, B2-B8, RG28, PAC.

always clear. At the beginning of the war Ontario lobbyists stressed the value of a central location for industry safe from German attack. After the war a Dominion Bureau of Statistics profile on the Maritimes offered "strategic reasons" as one explanation for the location "of much new industrial plant in the Central Provinces".[6] During the war, however, bureaucrats justified their masters' decisions largely in terms of efficiency. The Maritimes, they claimed, suffered from the fatal flaw of "distance". To what extent efficiency was the actual motive or merely a rationale is difficult to discern. The British Admiralty Technical Mission in Canada, which, after June 1940, depended upon the Department of Munitions and Supply to place their contracts, reported that "political issues weigh heavily" in the decisions taken. Moreover, they raised issues of efficiency which the Canadians seldom mentioned. Specifically, they pointed to the difficulties of building ships in yards which were cut off from the ocean for five months of the year and in a climate where the vessels under construction ‍ were often damaged by the deep frosts. They also questioned the practice of requiring vessels to make the long trip up the St. Lawrence River for servicing.[7] While the demands of Canada's allies were concerned with immediate efficiency in wartime, C.D. Howe and his controllers often appeared to be following an agenda for industrialization based on their perception of Canada's needs after the war. Their vision of a centralized manufacturing complex closely integrated with the United States apparently did not include the Maritimes in any significant role.

The perception of Maritime industries as peripheral to Canada's needs emerged early in the war. In the summer of 1940 the senior bureaucrats who composed the Economic Advisory Committee prepared a memorandum recommending against transportation subsidies for Maritime and Western coal. It would be better, they argued, to purchase the coal from the United States. The government would gain revenue from tariffs and the surplus miners would be absorbed into other sectors of the war effort. The recommendation was partially implemented by the government when the coal subsidies were reduced by more than one-third.[8] The Steel Control, in planning for shipbuilding and other steel requirements, approved a large new ships' plate mill for the Steel Company of Canada at Hamilton and a new rolling mill for the Algoma Steel Company at Sault Ste. Marie, and also assisted both of these and the smaller steel producers to modernize and increase capacity.[9] The Dominion Steel

6   Dominion Bureau of Statistics, *The Maritime Provinces in Their Relation to the National Economy of Canada* (Ottawa, 1948), p. 97.

7   "History of the British Admiralty Technical Mission in Canada", 30 April 1946, especially pp. 3, 57 and 72-73, Vol. 29, RG28, PAC.

8   "Report of the Economic Advisory Committee on Wartime Organization regarding policies relating to Canadian coal", July 1940, p. C246240, W.L. Mackenzie King Papers, PAC; F.G. Neat, "Report of the Activities of the Dominion Fuel Board", 11 October 1945, vol. 1, pp. 31-3, file 50-1-1, vol. 45, Records of the Dominion Coal Board [RG81], PAC; PC 3969, file 91-3-3, vol. 138, RG81, PAC.

9   "Report on the Activities of Steel Control from its establishment...June 24th, 1940, to October

and Coal Corporation, another of Canada's "big three" steel producers and the largest industrial employer in the Maritimes, was conspicuously less fortunate. Efforts to negotiate federal assistance for modernization encountered inexplicable delays. A memorandum from Dosco's assistant manager to company president Arthur Cross detailed a meeting in July 1940 of three senior Dosco executives, including Cross himself, with steel controller Hugh Scully. On the basis of this meeting written proposals were presented to Scully with copies addressed to Howe. Later, however, the Controller denied any recollection of the meeting or Dosco's proposals.[10] Prominent in Dosco's plan was a scheme to re-open its ships' plate mill in Sydney, a plant which was built in 1918 but closed after the war. On the advice of W.S. Drysdale, Director of Production, Dosco obtained an independent engineering study which proved favourable and was duly forwarded to Ottawa. Meanwhile, the controllers approved and Stelco proceeded with the construction of a new ships' plate mill at Hamilton, Ontario. This plant opened in April 1941.[11]

Dosco's manufacturing potential in the Maritimes was finally discovered in the fall of 1940 by an industrial task force which, under the auspices of the Department of Munitions and Supply, toured the country in search of unused manufacturing capacity to develop for British orders. The visitors later recalled that they found industry fully engaged in Ontario and Quebec but that considerable excess capacity remained in the Maritimes and the West.[12] Their recommendations for investment to allow the production of shells and gun-mountings from Dosco's plants at Trenton, Nova Scotia were accepted by the British government. "The main thing, however, on our entire trip and what impressed us most", one member reported, "was the fact that the large [ships' plate] mill at Sydney is lying idle".[13] They enthusiastically recommended "that immediate arrangements should be made to put this mill into production". It would require much less time and money than the construction of a new one and would be needed to meet "a definite shortage of plate in Canada" which they predicted "by March 1, 1941".[14] Their recommendation ran into trouble in the upper

1st, 1943", 1943, p. 48, file 176-2-15, vol. 205, RG28, PAC.

10 C.M. Anson, "Memorandum for Mr. A. Cross", 21 September 1940, F1157 #6, Angus L. Macdonald Papers, Public Archives of Nova Scotia [PANS].

11 The historical sketch of the first three years of Steel Control implied that work on the Hamilton plant had begun before the war. This was corrected in the survey of the next three years, as someone specifically recalled approving the project in 1940: "Report on the Activities of Steel Control from October 1st, 1943 until its termination November 1st 1945", 1946, p. 48, file 196-14-13, vol. 261, RG28, PAC. See also Canada, *Debates of the House of Commons, 1941*, pp. 6928-9.

12 Kennedy, *History of the Department of Munitions*, vol. I, p. 229.

13 F.M. Ross to A.L. Macdonald, 24 October 1940, F1157 #1, Macdonald Papers, PANS.

14 The task force consisted of W.F. Drysdale (Director of Production), F.M. Ross (Director of Naval Supply), Commander E. Watson, R.N. (British Admiralty Technical Mission) and James Crone (Advisor to the Department of Munitions and Supply): "Memorandum Covering the Visit of Representatives of the Department of Munitions and Supply....", 7 October 1940, F1157 #7, Macdonald Papers, PANS.

echelons of the Department of Munitions. Frank Ross, Director of Naval Supply and president of the Saint John Dry Dock and Shipbuilding Company, noted the difficulty and urged the Naval Minister, Angus L. Macdonald, "to discuss this matter" with his colleagues. The task force was overruled. The controllers planned to purchase the balance of their plate needs from the United States.

Dosco itself persevered with a formal offer to open the plate mill and to expand production to meet additional requirements for basic steel at a total cost of $3.5 million, about one million of which would be borne by the corporation.[15] Queried by Maritime politicians, C.D. Howe later explained his rejection of the offer to Parliament on the grounds that it would cost $4.5 million, that Dosco's primary steel was already under longterm contract to Great Britain and that government expenditure to increase basic steel production in the Maritimes could not be justified.[16] Howe's letter of refusal was particularly disquieting to Dosco president Arthur Cross, less perhaps because of the rejection of the specific project than because of the rationale offered. Howe's phrase, "having in mind our needs after the war", seemed to imply that the government was directing investment according to its own plan for post-war development and that steel production in the Maritimes would have a very limited role. Moreover, in the anticipation of future needs the government appeared to be heedless of the impact of its interference on the existing equilibrium among competing industries. Noting the approximately $4 million in federal funds that had gone to each of his competitors, Algoma and Stelco, Cross protested to Howe that this left Dosco "the only primary steel producer in this country which is receiving no government assistance". While Cross was "reluctant to believe that your advisers have deliberately formulated a policy which is bound to discriminate against the post-war future of this corporation and in favour of its central Canadian competitors", a continued failure to grant Dosco "some reasonable measure of assistance" would render such a conclusion "inevitable".[17]

Meanwhile, the government financed two new shipbuilding plants on the Great Lakes and reserved for major naval contracts ten out of the 15 existing Canadian shipyards capable of producing freighter class vessels.[18] Conspicu-

---

15 Arthur Cross to C.D. Howe, 29 January 1941, F1157 #4, Macdonald Papers, PANS.

16 *Commons Debates, 1941*, p. 2104. See also *Halifax Chronicle*, 19 May 1941. According to the figures given by Dosco representatives before the Carroll Commission, the Sydney plate mill when later opened cost just more than three million dollars: "Statement Showing Additions and Reductions, Property Account Covering Period January 1st., 1939 to December 31, 1942", loose sheet inserted in Dosco's brief to the Carroll Commission, Box 15 #11, Records of Royal Commissions and Reports [RG 44], PANS.

17 Arthur Cross to C.D. Howe, 12 March 1941, F1157 #5, Macdonald Papers, PANS.

18 "History of the British Admiralty Technical Mission in Canada", p. 6; "Naval Construction Programme, 1942, 1943, 1944", vol. 42, C.D. Howe Papers, PAC; "Branch History, Shipbuilding Branch, Department of Munitions and Supply", 31 October 1945, pp. 5-6, file 5 of 12, vol. 29, RG28, PAC; *Commons Debates, 1941*, p. 1629. The concentration of production in Ontario became particularly embarrassing for the Canadians when frigates were required for escort duty

ously absent were the Halifax Shipyards and the Saint John Dry Dock and Ship-building Company. Angus L. Macdonald later defended the government for failing to develop steel shipbuilding at these yards on the grounds that they were needed for repairs and service.[19] This interpretation would appear more plausible had the Department of Munitions effectively developed Maritime ports for repair purposes or directed to them the business required for year-round operation. It did neither.

Both Halifax Shipyards and the Saint John Dry Dock Company were busy with service and repairs in November 1940 when the government appointed D.B. Carswell, formerly manager and vice-president of Canada Vickers Ltd. and vice-president of Montreal Dry Dock Company, as controller of ship repair and salvage. When the ice moved out in the spring of 1941, Carswell, from his office in Montreal, authorized the lay-off of skilled workers at the Maritime ports and shifted the repair industry up the St. Lawrence River. Thereafter, the controller maintained the same alternate use of summer and winter facilities in the repair yards as had characterized the use of ports in Canada's export trade. Maritime ports would be employed to the extent that Montreal was inaccessible.[20]

Just how little support the Department of Munitions and Supply channelled into the Maritimes for industrial expansion is confirmed in the first report on capital assistance to Canadian industries prepared by the department for the period up to 30 April 1941. Of the $484,299,078 committed to that cause by British and Canadian governments, Prince Edward Island received exactly nothing, New Brunswick the same amount, and Nova Scotia $8,759,430. The region's share of this investment was 1.81 per cent. Even disregarding its 9.8 per cent of the population and the strategic importance of the region in an Atlantic war, and considering only its five per cent share of the nation's manufacturing, the discrepancy is still striking. Moreover, of the Maritime portion, about half went to develop the region's service capacity: a Montreal firm received $3 million to build a floating dry dock for Halifax, and another $1 million served to outfit an aircraft depot at Dartmouth. Most of the remainder went to Dosco's Eastern Car Company and Trenton Steelworks as the British government financed the retooling required for its orders of shells and gun mountings.[21] Even

which were too long to go through the locks of the St. Lawrence canals. The Quebec yards began the production of frigates in 1941 but the Ontario yards could not make the transition. See G.N. Tucker, *The Naval Service of Canada* (Ottawa, 1952), vol. II, p. 66.

19 *Commons Debates, 1941*, p. 1666. See also Tucker, *The Naval Service of Canada*, vol. II, p. 39. The Saint John Dry Dock and Shipbuilding Company did build three corvettes during the first three years of the war.

20 See the order-in-council appointing a separate controller for ship repairs, 17 November 1940, file 196-38-1, vol. 30, RG28, PAC, and D.B. Carswell's, "Reports on Ship Repairs and Salvage", especially 4 November 1941, file 196-13-3, vol. 256, RG28, PAC.

21 Department of Munitions and Supply, "Digest of Canadian and British Programme of Capital Assistance to Industry...corrected as of April 30th 1941", Vol. 42, Howe Papers, PAC.

this operation was delayed, Arthur Cross complained, as the priority rating initially assigned the two Dosco plants by the Department of Munitions did not allow effective competition with other Canadian firms in the purchase of machinery. In two years the Maritime share of Canada's investment in manufacturing declined from 5.1 to 4.6 per cent and the region's share of the labour force in manufacturing fell from 5.1 to 4.7 per cent.[22]

The initial bypassing of the Maritimes for industrial investment would ultimately prove critical for its wartime development. A majority of workers in all the new industries had to be trained, and retooling and expansion were much easier with the surplus labour supply left by the Depression. Maritime industries which failed to gain that initial headstart tried to catch up. Yet their skilled workers had been drawn away, essential commodities were in short supply, and they found themselves in competition with the military services for a dwindling pool of manpower.[23] The labour shortages became the standard excuse for the Department of Munitions' failure to develop industries in the Maritimes which were later recognized as important to Canada's war effort.

By the spring of 1941 the government's economic policies drew vigorous protests from the Maritime press, boards of trade and politicians. In October 1939 the New Brunswick Advisory Board for Economic and Industrial Development joined with the Saint John Board of Trade in lobbying British and Canadian purchasing agents and later maintained a permanent "representative" at Ottawa for that purpose. Meanwhile, New Brunswick's Liberal premier A.A. Dysart called upon the federal government for a policy of "decentralization" in industrial development.[24] The following year his successor and former colleague J.B. McNair approached the federal cabinet to help his nearly-bankrupt province to develop the necessary infrastructure, such as roads and electricity, to participate more effectively in Canada's industrial war effort. McNair's request for $4.5 million was rejected by the cabinet, but King, perhaps mindful of the political implications of McNair's appeal, prevailed upon his colleagues for a grant of $100,000 specifically tied to the upgrading of roads and bridges in Northern New Brunswick.[25] Thereafter, the lack of electricity became a factor in, or at least a rationale for, the Department of Munition's failure to invest any money in New Brunswick before the summer of 1941. Saint John Board of Trade President Colin McKay protested that the department's refusal to grant federal funds for hydro development was a method of discrimination in favour

22 Arthur Cross to C.D. Howe, 7 January 1942, F1222 #54, Macdonald Papers, PANS; *The Maritime Provinces in their Relation to the National Economy*, p. 98.

23 By 1943 Maritime industries were prominent among those trying to receive labour from Newfoundland. See Peter Neary, "Canada and the Newfoundland Labour Market, 1939-45", *Canadian Historical Review*, LXII, 4 (December 1981), pp. 470-95.

24 *Telegraph-Journal* (Saint John), 14, 17 October 1939 and "Report...of the New Brunswick Advisory Board for Economic and Industrial Development", September 1940, Box 14, RS 415, J.B. McNair Papers, Provincial Archives of New Brunswick.

25 Minutes of the Cabinet War Committee, 17 July 1940, Vol. 424, King Papers, PAC.

of the wealthier provinces. "Our shortage of power is definitely and directly due to our shortage of money", McKay declared. The government, he reported, had missed "a wonderful opportunity" to redress the problems arising from centralization and to redistribute industry more evenly throughout the country.[26]

In Nova Scotia, from early in the war, newspapers complained of the loss of skilled workers, in both metal and wood, to shipbuilders in Central Canada and blamed both levels of government for failing to develop an industry so natural to their region.[27] Through the later months of 1940, Premier A.S. MacMillan of Nova Scotia bombarded the federal cabinet with warnings of the damage which the public criticism was doing to the Liberal Party and called for the construction of steel shipbuilding plants in his province. He offered on behalf of the Nova Scotia government to deliver the electrical power required to any site in the province "as quickly as the plants can be produced". Finally, after a meeting with Howe in May 1941, MacMillan was able to report that the federal government would finance a plant in Nova Scotia provided that local entrepreneurs took the initiative.[28] The expanded programme for the construction of civilian shipping, announced in the summer of 1941, included a plant to build a small class of 4700-ton freighters at Pictou, Nova Scotia. The Pictou plant, although federally financed, was operated by a Halifax firm, Foundation Maritime, and constructed 24 freighters before the end of the war.

Angus L. Macdonald and the provincial minister of industry, Harold Connolly pressed the tiny shipyards of the outports to go after major contracts for the multitude of small wooden vessels needed in Canadian and Allied harbours. A few, such as Clare Shipbuilding of Meteghan, LeBlanc Shipbuilding of Weymouth and J.A. Urquhart of Parrsboro, were successful. In New Brunswick K.C. Irving at Buctouche and Ashley Colter at Gagetown turned out several million dollars' worth of barges and other wooden vessels.[29] Additional construction came to the Maritimes as an unexpected outgrowth of the problems of inland shipbuilding. The first ten corvettes completed for a British order narrowly escaped being trapped in the winter freeze-up and required substantial work in the Maritimes before they could risk an Atlantic crossing.[30] The Toronto Shipbuilding Company, the crown corporation which built the large Algerine class of minesweepers, established a subsidiary at Saint John to allow outfitting and sea trials in the winter months.[31] The additional demand ex-

26 President's Report, Minutes, Saint John Board of Trade, 20 January 1942, New Brunswick Museum, Saint John.

27 See for examples *Halifax Herald*, 19 February, 21, 22 March, 12 June 1941, *Post-Record* (Sydney), 29 April 1941.

28 See files on shipbuilding F1221 and F1222, especially A.S. MacMillan to A.L. Macdonald, 9 August 1940, 2 December 1940 and 16 May 1941, Macdonald Papers, PANS.

29 "Contracts for the Construction of Ships and Small Craft, Nova Scotia", file 5 of 12, vol. 29, RG28, PAC.

30 C.D. Howe to Admiral B.A. Fraser, 6 January 1941, file S9-25 (2), vol. 339, RG28, PAC.

31 Kennedy, *History of the Department of Munitions and Supply*, vol. I, p. 455.

hausted the electricity available from the limited hydro and coal plants and rationing was imposed in 1943.[32]

From an even weaker political base Prince Edward Island, under the leadership of Liberal Premier Thane Campbell, lobbied for a share of shipbuilding and munition plants. When this failed, he argued the need for federal funds to develop food processing plants to increase the Island's contribution to the war effort. From the fall of 1941 lobbying efforts concentrated on procuring a new car ferry, as the S.S. Charlottetown, the Island's largest and most modern ferry, sank on the Borden-Tormentine run.[33] J.L. Ralston waged a systematic campaign for the ferry and other Island causes but only after his resignation from the cabinet in 1944.[34]

Where were the federal Maritime politicians when decisions were taken which were so adverse to regional interests? It cannot be argued that the region lacked a voice at Ottawa. Indeed, the Maritimes had strong representation in the wartime cabinet. After the defeat of the Liberals in Nova Scotia in 1925, a little group of young lawyers or lawyer-academics conspired to remove their party's image as the mouthpiece for "big business" and the foe of progressive legislation.[35] While their electoral success was less than spectacular, their joint activities did establish lasting friendships. J.L. Ralston, a Halifax lawyer and war veteran originally from Amherst, might be considered the group's leader. He entered Mackenzie King's cabinet in 1926 seeking the implementation of the Duncan Commission Report and the protection of returned servicemen, with whom he strongly identified. After the government's defeat in 1930, Ralston continued as financial critic in the shadow cabinet. Another Amherst native, Norman MacLeod Rogers, whose military endeavours were followed by study in history and law at Oxford University, left a teaching appointment at Acadia to work as King's secretary and later returned to academic life at Queen's University.[36] Angus L. Macdonald, a Scottish Catholic from Inverness County who taught at the Dalhousie law school, became leader of the provincial party in 1930 and in 1933 premier of the province. J.L. Ilsley, a lawyer from Kentville, was one of the few Liberal candidates in Nova Scotia to overcome the Tory tides in the federal elections of 1926 and 1930. When the Liberals returned to power in Ottawa in 1935, Ilsley entered the cabinet in place of Ralston who stayed out,

32 *Annual Reports of the New Brunswick Electric Power Commission*, 1942, p. 4, 1943, p. 9, 1944, p. 8.

33 Scrapbook of reports of Prince Edward Island legislative debates, 14 April 1941, vol. 102, Records of the Department of Education [RG10], Public Archives of Prince Edward Island [PAPEI]. See also reports for 17 March 1942 and 11 and 13 March 1943.

34 See J.E. Michaud to J.L. Ralston, 8 February 1945, J.L. Ralston Papers, PAC and the *Summerside Journal*, 14 June 1945.

35 H.J. Logan to W.L.M. King, 16 February 1926, p. 113864, King Papers, PAC; E.R. Forbes, "The Rise and Fall of the Conservative Party in the Provincial Politics of Nova Scotia, 1925-1933", M.A. thesis, Dalhousie University, 1967, ch. 3.

36 J.R. Rowell, "An Intellectual in Politics: Norman Rogers as an Intellectual and Minister of Labour, 1929-1939", M.A. thesis, Queen's University, 1978.

rumour has it, to aid a financially-troubled law partner. Rogers, representing Kingston, became Minister of Labour.

With the outbreak of war Ralston became Minister of Finance. Rogers died in 1940, but with the expansion of the defence portfolio into three ministries, Ralston, now sitting for Prince County, Prince Edward Island, became Minister of National Defence. Ilsley took over Finance. Angus L. Macdonald was invited to become Minister of National Defence for Naval Services.[37] Macdonald's appointment had an additional logic as the strategic emphasis in Canadian naval planning had, near the outbreak of war, shifted from the west to the east coast.[38] Besides the three Nova Scotians, New Brunswick's J.E. Michaud held the fisheries portfolio from 1935.

Thus, the Maritimes had four representatives in the cabinet and three of them (later four when Michaud shifted to Transport in October 1942) on the powerful nine-member War Committee. This committee, as Macdonald put it, was regarded "more as a cabinet than a committee of the cabinet" in matters relating to the war.[39] The region appeared to enjoy the strongest representation in any cabinet since Confederation. There were some limiting factors, of course. Without previous experience at the federal level, Macdonald faced a formidable challenge in defending the interests of either navy or province. As Minister of Finance, Ilsley was hardly in a position for overt regional advocacy. Ralston had earlier remarked of that office, that its role of "barring the way to the money bags" left a new minister open to the "accusation...of having forgotten the rank and file alongside...whom he fought and having become a 'statesman'". Ilsley did indeed become a statesman — one who became increasingly alarmed at the unprecedented costs of modern warfare.[40] Nevertheless, one would expect that four senior cabinet ministers could have done more to protect the interests of the Maritimes during the preparations for war. That they failed to do so may be explained in part by the unusual delegation of responsibility within the wartime cabinet and by the extraordinary power of the Department of Munitions and Supply under the leadership of C.D. Howe.[41]

Howe's appointment as Minister of Transport in 1935 had initially pleased leaders of the Maritime Board of Trade. In their perpetual battle to defend the

---

37 J.W. Pickersgill, *The Mackenzie King Record* (Toronto, 1960), vol. I, p. 100-1.

38 R.F. Sarty, "Silent Sentry: A Military and Political History of Canadian Coast Defence, 1860-1945", Ph.D. thesis, University of Toronto, 1982, p. 455.

39 A.L. Macdonald, "Memorandum re Cabinet and War Committee of the Cabinet", 4 February 1943, F277 #2, Macdonald Papers, PANS.

40 J.L. Ralston to J.J. Cox, 22 February 1936, file 'C' Miscellaneous", vol. 18, J.L. Ralston Papers, PAC. See also H.M. Mackenzie, "Sinews of War: Aspects of Canadian Decisions to Finance British Requirements in Canada During the Second World War", paper presented to the Canadian Historical Association, June 1984.

41 Leslie Roberts, *C.D.: The Life and Times of Clarence Decatur Howe* (Toronto, 1957), chapters 5-10.

region's transportation interests, they had seen the 20 per cent regional freight rate reductions recommended by the Duncan Commission negated by a series of special competitive rates to which, the railways argued, the Maritime reductions could not apply.[42] Having lost all confidence in the minister previously responsible they hoped that Howe, who had once taught at Dalhousie University, would understand Maritime problems and appreciate the justice of their case. They were soon disillusioned.

Howe not only failed to sympathize with the Maritimes' representations on freight rates, but supported a series of initiatives which seemed to threaten the future of their ports. These included a bill to terminate the independence of the National Harbours commissions, to which the Maritime provinces had gained access only nine years before, and proposals to regulate freight rates between Atlantic and Great Lakes ports and to standardize wharf charges in Canadian harbours. Against the united representations of Maritime Liberals the latter proposals were not implemented, but the impression remained that Howe favoured the powerful Great Lakes ports lobby.[43] This was hardly a surprising position for someone who had built a business from constructing grain elevators on the Great Lakes and was Member of Parliament for Port Arthur.

Howe's regional orientation is further suggested by his close ties with Sir James Dunn, the piratical head of the Algoma Steel Corporation. In a recent account of that corporation, Duncan MacDowall notes Dunn's anti-Dosco lobby and his campaign to concentrate manufacturing on the Lakes. MacDowall implies that Howe's spectacular support of Dunn's empire, which received more than 80 per cent of the government's direct grants to the steel industry during the war, had less to do with lobbying and personal contact than with a shared perspective on continental development and the integration of the Great Lakes economy.[44]

There may have been an element of regional conflict in the occasional confrontations between Howe and the Maritimers. One of these involved the construction in wartime of the St. Lawrence Waterway, an international project for hydro development and the enlargement of the St. Lawrence canals for major ocean vessels. Howe's proposals, presented to the cabinet early in 1940, drew protests from J.L. Ralston that they would divert funds from the war effort. Ralston was overruled on the grounds that the project was important in retaining the goodwill of the United States. He objected again several months later at the projected $60 million price tag. According to King, Ralston could see no

42 E.R. Forbes, "Misguided Symmetry: the Destruction of Regional Transportation Policy for the Maritimes", in D.J. Bercuson, ed., *Canada and the Burden of Unity* (Toronto, 1977), pp. 75-6.

43 C.J. Burchell to J.L. Ralston, 12 March 1937, R.L. Matheson and F.M. Sclanders to J.L. Ilsley, 10 March 1937, file "'B' Miscellaneous", vol. 16, Ralston Papers, PAC; J.D. McKenna to T.A. Campbell, 29 July 1937, Rand Matheson to T.A. Campbell, 6 March 1938, T.A. Campbell Papers, Premier's Office Records, RG25, PAPEI.

44 Duncan McDowall, *Steel at the Sault: Francis H. Clergue, Sir James Dunn, and the Algoma Steel Corporation, 1901-1956* (Toronto, 1984), pp. 169-71 and ch. 8.

"corresponding advantage except what would accrue to Ontario for power". King concluded that Ralston "does not seem to regard Ontario as part of the Dominion". King was personally committed to the scheme which in 1941 he predicted would "prove one of the great achievements of the present administration".[45]

In other matters of industrial expansion Howe's views, backed by King, normally prevailed. The industrial controllers were his nominees and his responsibility. In the War Committee, Macdonald, Ralston or "Chubby" Power, Minister of National Defence for Air, might voice the needs of a service, but they had then to turn to Howe to learn whether the tanks, ships or aircraft could be built, where they would be built and when they might be delivered. When Angus L. Macdonald took office in July 1940, he could not hope to affect the decisions taken for the location of naval manufacture for which production lines had already been established. He could, however, propose classes of vessels not yet under construction for which Maritime yards were available. This may account for his enthusiasm for the building of destroyers in Canada. Howe was sympathetic to the idea, perhaps in part because the principal components other than the hull were to be manufactured by the John Inglis Company of Toronto, a firm whose close relations with the federal government had been the subject of the Bren Gun controversy.[46] In 1941 when Macdonald proposed to the War Committee the building of two Tribal class destroyers at Halifax, Howe endorsed the proposal as a supplement to repair work.[47]

On several other proposed naval projects Macdonald and Howe were far apart. The most serious confrontation involved ship repair. As the British analyzed their shipping and supply needs they became concerned with the lack of year-round repair facilities on the Atlantic coast. They regarded Halifax as the logical naval headquarters and terminus for their Canadian convoys and they begrudged the additional time and risk required in sending escorts to Montreal. Early in 1941 they specifically asked the Canadians to consider developing Halifax as a repair centre with multiple graving docks which could, if necessary, hold their largest vessels. Macdonald, supported by Ralston and acting on the advice of the Chiefs of Staff, proposed building a graving dock at Halifax. Citing the shortage of labour, Howe came out strongly against the proposal. He was backed by Mackenzie King who argued against "the dangerous concentration of nearly all naval facilities at Halifax".[48] King's strategic concern may have been political as well as military. Montreal would not surrender lightly the preeminent role which it had maintained in the repair industry and Saint

45 J.W. Pickersgill, *The Mackenzie King Record*, vol. I, pp. 61-2, 77, 165.

46 Roberts, *C.D.: The Life and Times of Clarence Decatur Howe*, pp. 52, 59-61.

47 Minutes of the Cabinet War Committee, 7 November 1940 and 21 May 1941, vol. 424, King Papers, PAC.

48 W.C. Hankinson to N.A. Robertson, 15 May 1941, file S-9-26, vol. 42, Howe Papers, PAC; Minutes of the Cabinet War Committee, 27 May 1941; "Appreciation...Canadian Military Effort as of May 28, 1941", file S 14, vol. 51, Howe Papers, PAC.

John was alarmed at a proposal which would so greatly strengthen its arch-rival. As though on cue, Opposition Leader R.B. Hanson, a New Brunswicker, wrote King expressing concern at the impact of the British plan on the postwar prospects of Saint John.[49]

Unable to create a major centre for ship repair in the Maritimes, Macdonald was reduced to a series of proposals for marine railways to be scattered about the region. When these were delayed by Howe, for whom the manpower barrier in the Maritimes seemed insurmountable, Macdonald successfully proposed a greater role by the three services in the determination of priorities within Howe's department. He also began to move the navy out from under Howe's empire through the recruitment and training of naval ratings for shipbuilding and repair.[50]

In December 1941 Howe objected to Macdonald's request for a second pair of Tribal destroyers on the grounds of a steel shortage. The problem was real enough. The military crisis in Europe had led to a greater urgency in shipbuilding construction. Shortages began to appear even before the United States' entry into the war limited exports of the ships' plate, steel and coal on which Howe's department had been relying. Certainly the Americans were not ungenerous. Their controllers often gave Canadian producers the same priority rating as their own. But in the general scramble for basic commodities, the Canadians could not expect to expand their supply from the south.[51] Howe withdrew his opposition to the destroyers for Halifax after the War Committee approved a $17 million government investment in a new blast furnace for Algoma at Sault Ste. Marie.[52]

The shortages signaled a new crisis stage in Canada's wartime economy as the controllers searched for ways of increasing production. The deficiencies surfaced first in ships' plate. In the summer of 1941 steel controller Fred Kilbourn gave the orders to Stelco to "shoot the works" by changing to a three-shift system and operating its new mill at maximum capacity. Since this operation now consumed all of the primary steel that Stelco could produce, the controller ordered Algoma and Dosco to supply Stelco's traditional customers in Ontario and Quebec. The government picked up the tab for transportation.[53] Howe proposed to meet long-term needs for primary steel with the new blast furnace for Algoma. About the same time the controller finally gave the green light to Dosco to "rehabilitate" its idle ships' plate mill at Sydney. Early in 1942 the cabinet granted Dosco $1.75 million to bring the shell of an old blast furnace

49 Minutes of the Cabinet War Committee, 27 July, 29 October and 12 November 1941.

50 Minutes of the Cabinet War Committee, 12 November, 17 December 1941; J.C. Mitchell, Memorandum to G.C.C., 26 May 1942, file NSS 830-2-9, vol. 5619, Department of National Defence Records [RG24], PAC.

51 See also R.D. Cuff and J.L. Granatstein, *American Dollars — Canadian Prosperity: Canadian-American Economic Relations, 1945-1950* (Toronto, 1978), p. 11.

52 Minutes of the Cabinet War Committee, 19 November, 17 December 1941, 28 January 1942.

53 M.A. Hoey to J.B. Carswell, 2 February 1943, file 196-14, vol. 3, vol. 257, RG28, PAC.

purchased in Ontario into production at Sydney. The plate mill began operations early in 1942 and in that year accounted for more than one-third of Canada's output of regular ships' plate.[54]

The shortages also led to a dramatic change in government coal policies. The industry which the mandarins were prepared to discourage at the beginning of the war was now seen as critical to steel production and domestic fuel needs. The coal industry did not thrive under the arbitrary control of the bureaucrats. Although the miners heeded the call of patriotism to enlist, many rejected the same call as a reason to accept lower wages than paid elsewhere in Canada. In 1941 the miners staged a five-month slowdown strike to protest the regional wage differential.[55] A year later the industry suffered a net loss of nearly 4,000 workers. Those who remained drew the ire of the controllers for persistent "absenteeism" as they closed the mines for traditional holidays, to protest specific grievances, and to attend the funerals of those killed in accidents.[56] But the key to the slump in coal production during the war was the loss of the "contract men", those workers at the coal face who actually mined the coal and were paid on the basis of output. It was this vital group of skilled miners which had responded most enthusiastically to the call for enlistment. Early in 1943 the cabinet declared coal production to be critical to the entire war effort, forbade further enlistment by skilled miners and ordered those who had done so to return to the mines. A disproportionate number of those returning appeared to be "datal men", and as production continued to decline, an investigator in 1944 reported that the "main trouble" was "a shortage of producers".[57]

Intensification of the war brought the predictable crisis in ship repair and harbour facilities in Maritime ports. Having failed in their efforts to interest the Canadian government in developing Halifax, the British turned to the United States for the North American refit of their larger vessels. The Americans too were surprised by Canadian nonchalance at the state of their repair facilities. In the spring of 1942 they completed their own survey of the port of Halifax and were strongly critical of facilities in general and the scarcity of repair berths in particular. The investigators recommended that the American government send tugboats to Halifax to rescue "vessels of all nationalities...detained for an unreasonable length of time in Canadian waters awaiting repairs".[58] C.D. Howe

54 See P.C. 6 and P.C. 85, 6 and 8 January 1942, file 196-14-1, vol. 258, RG28, PAC; "Report on the Activities of Steel Control 1940 to 1943", p. 50 and "Report on the Activities of Steel Control 1943 until 1945", p. 51.

55 Minutes of the Cabinet War Committee, 28 July 1941. See also Paul MacEwan, *Miners and Steelworkers* (Toronto, 1976), p. 265.

56 "Towards a Background for Solid Fuel Control", 29 March 1943, pp. 9-12, file 50-1-5A, vol. 45, RG81, PAC, and G.A. Vissac, "Emergency Coal Production Board Report on the Dominion Coal Co. Ltd.", September 1944, p. 114, file 196-37-6-1, vol. 328, RG28, PAC.

57 Minutes of the Cabinet War Committee, 5 May, 15 April 1943; G.A. Vissac to E.J. Brunning, 12 September 1944, file 196-37-6-1, vol. 328, RG28, PAC.

58 Captain N. Nicholson, A.J. Sullivan and C.G. Graham, "Report on Conditions in Halifax, Nova Scotia, and Saint John's, Newfoundland", 30 March 1942, file #111-45, Records of the

took umbrage at the Americans for undertaking the survey without his knowledge or permission. While the War Committee supported Howe in his indignation, its members also wanted assurance that the criticism was unfounded or that the deficiencies were being repaired. Howe advised them that the American survey was inaccurate and outlined new construction then in progress.[59]

In fact, despite Halifax's strategic location as convoy headquarters, Howe's department had continued to treat the port as secondary to Montreal. The Maritimes' shortage of repair berths and machinery was, at least in part, the result of priority decisions taken within the Department of Munitions and Supply. Confronted with shortages in the spring of 1941, Howe promised to "move heaven and earth to make sure that adequate repair facilities are available on the Atlantic coast before the St. Lawrence closes this year". But even specific commitments failed to materialize. In January 1942 Dosco president Arthur Cross reported to Howe that less than 13 per cent of the half-million dollars' worth of repair machinery, which the government had authorized for Halifax Shipyards, had been delivered by Citadel Company, the Montreal-based crown corporation responsible, and the harbour renovations announced the previous spring were incomplete or not even begun.[60] Moreover, the government's willingness to direct repair work to Montreal for half of the year made it difficult for Maritime firms to staff what facilities they had. After the layoffs in the Maritimes in the spring of 1941, D.B. Carswell reported great difficulty in recruiting skilled workers for the Maritime industry for the following winter.[61]

With repairs falling behind and the department seeking to train new workers, a worse crisis was avoided when naval authorities, short of both escorts and the facilities to service them, decided to forego their normally scheduled refits.[62] Yet in February 1942, at a meeting of the Advisory Committee on Ship Repair, Controller Carswell treated the approaching seasonal shift in repair work to Montreal as inevitable. In May he reported that volunteer workers recruited in Ontario and Quebec had been let go and expressed fear that the smaller plants would lose local workers in the slack period to follow.[63]

To Carswell's surprise the slack period did not materialize even after the St.

United States Maritime Commission and the War Shipping Administration, Washington National Records Center, Suitland, Maryland. This and other interoffice memoranda were made available to the author by the Freedom of Information Officer for the United States Maritime Administration.

59 Minutes of the Cabinet War Committee, 7 May 1942.

60 *Commons Debates 1941*, p. 1631; Arthur Cross to C.D. Howe, 6 January 1942, F1222 #54, Macdonald Papers, PANS.

61 See "Report on Ship Repairs and Salvage for the period ending, 31 October 1941" (Note that two different reports bear the same date. This reference is to the one near the end of the file). See also reports for 28 January and 28 February 1942, file 196-13-3, vol. 256, RG28, PAC.

62 G.L. Stephens to ACNS, 9 June 1943, file NSC 1057-1-35, vol. 1, vol. 3996, RG24, PAC.

63 "Minutes of the Advisory Committee on Ship Repairs", 23 February 1942, file 196-13 "General

Lawrence re-opened. There was a back-log from the winter, damage from U-boats continued high and still impending were the overdue naval refits. In the late summer another American investigator reported that, at Halifax, repair facilities were "taxed far beyond their capacity, causing great delays to vessels in need of drydockage and major repairs".[64] Severe additional pressure on all Canadian facilities came with the order in April 1942 to outfit the naval escorts with modern submarine detection equipment. The conversion involved reconstruction of the corvettes to receive the new equipment. Until this was completed the effectiveness of the Canadian navy for convoy protection — its principal responsibility in the war — was seriously impaired. Yet November of 1943 found the modifications completed on only 22 out of 74 corvettes. The navy was reduced to the desperate expedients of leaving some vessels frozen in St. Lawrence ports for the winter, routing others to British Columbia and sending still others on the dubious gamble of breaking into refit schedules at American ports.[65] Marc Milner's *North Atlantic Run: The Royal Canadian Navy and the Battle for the Convoys* shows the cost in naval efficiency of Canada's failure to develop an adequate repair service. The Canadian navy was forced to watch "from the sidelines" while the better-equipped British escorts brought victory to the allies in the Battle of the North Atlantic.[66]

Conditions were rendered even more chaotic at Maritime ports late in the summer of 1942 when the St. Lawrence suddenly closed three months early. British and Canadian naval authorities had noted the greater risks and strain on the escort system resulting from the dependence on Montreal. But the government failed to direct shipping or ship repair to the Maritimes until forced to do so by the activities of the German U-boats lurking within the narrow confines of the River and entrances to the Gulf. From the opening of the shipping season in 1942 U-boats sank 23 vessels. In August the Cabinet ordered the St. Lawrence closed to all but local traffic, for which convoys would be maintained.[67]

With the additional traffic and naval refit priorities, the repair facilities in Halifax and Saint John were in difficulty even before the freeze-up. Although the navy opened new repair facilities at Shelburne and Point Edward, it required time to "break in" the new operations. In the first six months they completed

Correspondence", vol. 1, vol. 256, RG28, PAC; "Report on Ship Repairs and Salvage for the period ending 31 May 1942".

64 "Memorandum", A.T. Cluff to C.G. Graham, 8 September 1942, file #111-45, Records of the U.S. Maritime Commission and the War Shipping Administration.

65 G.L. Stephens to CNS, 11 November 1943, F276 #37, Macdonald Papers, PANS; J.W. Keohane, memorandum to CNEC, 19 February 1944, file 35 vol. 2, vol. 3996,

66 Marc Milner, *North Atlantic Run: The Royal Canadian Navy and the Battle for the Convoys* (Toronto, 1985), ch. IX, and Marc Milner, "Royal Canadian Navy Participation in the Battle of the Atlantic Crisis of 1943", J.A. Boutilier, ed., *The RCN in Retrospect, 1910-1968* (Vancouver, 1982), pp. 158-74.

67 "Minutes of the Saint Lawrence Operations Conference", 22-24 February 1943, Appendix "G", file NSS 8280-166/16 vol. 3, vol. 6789, RG24, PAC. See also M.L. Hadley, *U-Boats Against Canada: German Submarines in Canadian Waters* (Toronto, 1985).

only four refits, although their combined capacity was projected to be 145 vessels a year. The naval authorities found that servicing in the little naval repair yards invariably seemed to require a further stop at Halifax for additional parts or expertise.[68] The construction of the tribal destroyers, which was intended to occupy workers in the summer months, became an embarrassment. Labour was diverted in order to rush completion of the hulls to free additional berths for repair purposes. The destroyers themselves would not be completed until after the war.

The shortage of facilities at Halifax and Saint John created a hopeless bottleneck for civilian shipping requiring maintenance or repair. By the spring of 1943 Carswell's desperation was reflected in instructions to port surveyors that dry docks limit repairs to problems which "seriously affect the sea-worthiness" of vessels. This order was sharply queried by the surveyors who informed him that a vessel is "either seaworthy or not seaworthy".[69] In his reports to Howe, Carswell was hard-pressed to find explanations for his problems which did not imply criticism of the department. He blamed the National Selective Service for failing to provide the skilled labour required, and in 1944 he attributed the shortage of berths in the repair yards to "Acts of God and perils of the sea". If the damaged vessels had only arrived "in reasonable numbers and at regular intervals", his yards might have coped, but they tended to come "in batches".[70]

In the spring of 1943, with Carswell, the navy and local port administrators all complaining of the labour shortage in Halifax, the government appointed a committee of interested parties to investigate. A survey of shipyard firms in the region reported a deficit of 4,872 workers. Discussions on how to meet the problem brought to light overcrowded conditions in the city which made temporary solutions difficult. As the navy expanded operations at Halifax, it tended to expropriate existing buildings. Overcrowding was aggravated by the congregation in the city of the dependents of service personnel who were stationed there or who had left from there to go overseas.[71] A local official complained of shortages in food and commodities which were still distributed on the basis of a census population of 65,000 at a time when 115,000 ration cards were issued exclusive of service personnel. He also protested the inability of the municipality

68 G.L. Stephens to A/CNS, 9 June 1943, file NSC 1057-1-35 vol. 1, vol. 3996, RG24, PAC.

69 D.B. Carswell to W. Bennett, 7 June 1943, A.R. Riddell to the Principal Surveyor, 21 June 1943, file 19-6-13 vol. 2, vol. 256, RG24, PAC.

70 "Report on Ship Repairs and Salvage for the period ending, 31 March 1944". Howe did not readily forgive anything which might be construed as criticism by subordinates. See *On the Bridge of Time: Memories of Hugh L. Keenleyside, Vol. 2* (Toronto, 1982), pp. 79-81.

71 "Minutes of the third meeting of naval and merchant ship maintenance committee on man power", 29 April 1943, file 196-13-8, vol. 257, RG28, PAC. See also Kay Piersdorf, "Anybody here from the West", *Nova Scotia Historical Review*, V, 1 (June 1985), pp. 5-14, Jay White, "'Sleepless and veiled am I': An East Coast Canadian Port Revisited", *ibid.*, pp. 15-29 and Jay White, "The Ajax Affair: Citizens and Sailors in Wartime Halifax, 1939-1945", M.A. thesis, Dalhousie University, 1984.

to provide the transportation, hospital and other services required by military activity and the increased population. His complaint was confirmed by Carswell, who reported "Good food...difficult to procure, sleeping space...not available...[and] transportation...inadequate...".[72] Their complaints resulted in a cabinet decision to place Halifax under the control of the harbour director who had the authority to restrict access and remove from it those deemed non-essential to the war effort. Nine months after the appointment of the committee, a naval memorandum complained that "Despite warnings and recommendations...no apparent action has been taken to move large bodies of skilled men...to...Nova Scotia where the demand has not only been urgent but has been long foreseen".[73]

The intensification of the war brought some industrial expansion, including plant renovation, to the Maritimes. These investments, however, tended to be limited in scope and featured types of industry which had very little chance of continuation after the war. None of the 28 crown corporations was located in the region. The Department of Munitions and Supply reported a total investment of $1.6 billion in the expansion of Canadian industry as of the end of December 1943, of which $823 million could be identified as located in particular provinces. The Maritimes' share of this, exclusive of housing, was a bit more than $27 million or 3.7 per cent. This was less than either British Columbia or the Prairies. Prince Edward Island received nothing, New Brunswick $6.5 million and Nova Scotia $20.8 million. New Brunswick obtained $1.5 million for aircraft repair, $1 million for naval construction and $2.7 million for ship repair. In Nova Scotia $5 million went to ship repair, $3.8 to the repair of aircraft, $3 million to steel and coal production, and $4.6 million to the manufacture of gun parts and ammunition. Shipbuilding totals also give an indication of the region's share of that industry: the Maritimes accounted for 6.2 per cent of the value of total contracts issued compared with 50 per cent for British Columbia, 28.6 per cent for Quebec and 15.1 per cent for Ontario. Within the region Nova Scotia's shipbuilding contracts totalled $62 million, New Brunswick's $9.8 and Prince Edward Island's $0.4 million.[74]

72 J.A. Hanway to Henry Borden, 22 June 1943, D.B. Carswell to C.D. Howe, 8 May 1943, file S-14 (2), vol. 51, Howe Papers, PAC. It is remarkable how casually the federal authorities appeared willing to discriminate against the Maritimes in the distribution of commodities. An oil shortage in 1941 resulted in a federal directive that ration coupons for gasoline would allow only two gallons in the Maritimes while continuing to yield five in the rest of the country: *Halifax Herald*, 19, 21, 23 May 1942 and interview with R.A. Tweedie of Fredericton, 26 February 1985.

73 Minutes of the Cabinet War Committee, 22 September 1943; K.F. Adams, "Inadequacy of Refitting Facilities on the East Coast of Canada", Memorandum to ACNS, 7 December 1943, file NSC 1057-1-35 vol. 2, vol. 3996, RG24, PAC.

74 Department of Munitions and Supply, Economics and Statistics Branch, "Report on the Government-Financed Expansion of the Industrial Capacity in Canada as at December 31, 1943", summary table 2, vol. 184, RG28, PAC; Shipbuilding summaries, file 5 of 12, vol. 29, RG28, PAC.

The regional inequities of the federal government's wartime industrial investments were amplified in a reconstruction policy of channelling more money into the same industries to enable them to make the transition to peacetime production. The depreciation formula ensured that only profitable companies which were in a position to make the conversion would receive assistance. By 1 July 1945, 48 per cent of the funds had gone to Ontario, 32 per cent to Quebec, 15 per cent to British Columbia and the other 5 per cent was divided among the remaining six provinces. The authors of a report to the Department of Reconstruction giving these figures observed that "the problems of the transition period" will be "most acute in the Maritimes...where wartime dislocations have been superimposed on the special problems of a depressed area".[75]

The transfer of shipping and ship repair to Maritime ports proved temporary and did not survive the crisis stage in the war. In justifying their return to the St. Lawrence, the controllers had ample evidence of the inability of Maritime ports to handle Canada's trade. The number of vessels travelling in the emergency convoys, supposedly for local needs on the St. Lawrence, tripled as exceptions were made in the ban on through traffic. By the winter of 1945 Howe reported an enormous quantity of stores backed up at Maritime ports and 13,000 Canadian railway cars stranded in the United States, a result of other attempts to bypass the Maritime bottleneck. The shipping directors called for the reopening of the St. Lawrence regardless of the U-boat threat or the strain on the escorts.[76] By early summer Carswell was able to report business as usual with the port of Montreal back in full service and two-thirds of the ship repair activity shifted to the St. Lawrence. At the end of July, he reported repairs to be proceeding "at full capacity" in Montreal and "fallen off substantially in the Maritimes". This was two months before the government officially lifted its controls on ship repair.[77]

The steel controller also began to emphasize the inefficiencies of the steel industry in the Maritimes. Dosco had suffered losses during the war as coal carriers were sunk in the St. Lawrence and ore carriers torpedoed on their way

75 Department of Reconstruction, Economic Research Branch, "Area Study Tables", 30 September, 11 July 1945, vols. 263, 264, B2-B8, RG28, PAC; "The transformation of the Canadian economy from a peacetime to a wartime basis and the machinery developed for that purpose", vol. 262, B2, RG28, PAC. For the role of the federal government in the problems of two primary industries adjusting to the postwar economy, see Margaret Conrad, "Apple Blossom Time in the Annapolis Valley, 1880-1957", *Acadiensis*, IX, 2 (Spring 1980), pp. 14-39 and David Alexander, *The Decay of Trade: An Economic History of the Newfoundland Saltfish Trade, 1935-65* (St. John's, 1977).

76 "Convoys In the Gulf of St. Lawrence", Memorandum from Deputy Secretary of the Naval Board to Commander-in-Chief, Canadian Northwest Atlantic, 28 August 1944, file NSS 8280-166 vol. 4, vol. 6789, RG24, PAC; Minutes of the Cabinet War Committee, 17 March 1945; E.S. Brand to W.G. Hynard, 2 February 1945, file NSS 8280-166 vol. 4, vol. 6789, RG24, PAC.

77 "Report on Ship Repairs and Salvage" for the periods ending 31 May, 31 July and 30 September 1945.

from Brazil. Like many firms it operated on a cost-plus basis, with the profits to be determined by a subsequent audit. In a firm as complex as Dosco, determining overall costs of operation was no mean feat and open to controversy. In 1944 the controller employed the costing of steel plate production derived from the audit — 68 cents for Dosco compared to 57 cents for Stelco — to record different prices in the books of the crown corporations buying it. As the demand for ships' plate declined, the difference in cost became the rationale for directing all domestic orders to Hamilton. With the decline in foreign orders, in February 1945 the Sydney plate mill closed down.[78]

The cost of producing steel, however, could not be separated from the pattern of previous government investment. Early in 1944 the steel controller sent T.F. Rahilly, a former general manager of Algoma, to report on the Sydney plant and its postwar prospects. Relentlessly, Rahilly compared the performance of each section with that of the new government-funded plants in other corporations. The Dosco coke ovens, for example, produced 100 tons of coke while the new ovens at Algoma could produce 160 tons. The blast furnaces were less efficient — one should be closed down immediately — and the iron ore was of a lower grade. But his conclusion was a surprising one and probably not welcome to Howe and his controllers. Rahilly argued that if the plant now had problems it was because "acts of the government have placed it in its present position". Dosco would "come out of the war period with less new plant than any of its competitors". Dosco was less efficient because of the government's intervention. In Rahilly's view the government had a clear responsibility to assist the company to reestablish itself in a peacetime economy.[79]

This view was not shared by Howe. Indeed Dosco's own efforts at survival proved embarrassing. Discouraged by the Maritimes' bleak postwar industrial prospects, the corporation turned to plants in Central Canada to provide captive markets for its primary products. Late in December 1943, having recently acquired the Canadian Tube and Steel Products Company of Montreal with its "extensive bolt and nut manufacturing plant", Dosco set out to close the bolt and nut department at Trenton and to lay off approximately 800 workers. A brief meeting of Arthur Cross with Howe sufficed to gain the minister's permission. To the surprise of both, this apparently routine shift in operations aroused extensive protest in the Maritimes. Maritimers were not strangers to the closure of their industries in periods of depression. But this closure, coming in wartime when business was booming, was recognized for what it was, a deliberate and conscious attempt to shift operations to a more promising location and, as the Dosco announcement proclaimed, to "consolidate operations now being conducted in the Montreal area".[80]

Pushed by a public outcry led by the trade unions, Premier A.S. MacMillan

78 F.H. Brown to C.L. Dewar, 22 September 1944, file 196-2D-2, vol. 195, RG28, PAC.

79 T.F. Rahilly to F.B. Kilbourn, 5 September 1944, file 196-2D-2, vol. 195, RG28, PAC.

80 "Proceedings of the Carroll Commission re. Trenton Steel Works Ltd.", vol. VI, pp. 406, 421-2, Box 15 #4, RG44, PANS.

appeared before the federal cabinet to urge that the government deny the corporation permission to close the Nova Scotia plant.[81] MacMillan did not accept the cabinet's rejection of his request but appointed a royal commission conducted by Judge W.F. Carroll to investigate. The hearings, which lasted from December 1943 to May 1944, kept the issue before the public. The unions accused the corporation of employing public funds to facilitate its shift from the region and its abandonment of its responsibilities to dependent communities. Clearly implied was a criticism of the government, and in particular the minister who originally gave permission for the plant's closure.[82] Nor was the criticism effectively rebutted by Howe's lame explanation that he "was not told" that the products of the Trenton plant were used for war purposes.[83]

Howe may not have forgiven either Dosco or the Nova Scotia government for this public embarrassment. In 1944, as Duncan McDowall records, Howe advised the steel controllers to use Dosco "to the minimum extent possible even if we have to buy the steel from the United States".[84] Howe's animus towards Dosco may have had even greater repercussions for the Maritime region. In 1943 the federal government invited the provinces to co-operate in appointing commissions to investigate each province's needs in adjusting to a postwar economy. The three Maritime provinces did so. Nova Scotia, as part of its study, retained the firm of Arthur McKee and Company of Cleveland, Ohio to investigate the Nova Scotia steel industry. Its report in the spring of 1944 proposed a sheet steel mill as a basic requirement for both Dosco and the manufacturing industries in the Maritimes. The McKee proposal included the results of a tentative market survey and diagram of the plant. In the same year Howe's department assisted Stelco to develop a mill for the production of sheet steel and invited other companies to submit proposals for a second mill to meet anticipated postwar needs. Dosco was not included in the invitation.[85]

The long-term impact of the government's wartime policies on the Maritimes was largely negative. While the government did generate economic activity, it created relatively little new industry in the region and even less of a permanent nature. It harmed existing industries which survived the war only to discover, as did Dosco, that their relative position in the country had been eroded by the expansion and modernization of their competitors. Even the service or repair industries did not escape damage from the increased capacity at the centre. The

81 Minutes of the Cabinet War Committee, 1 and 16 December, 1943.

82 "Submission of J.L. Cohen on behalf of United Steelworkers of America and District #26, United Mineworkers of America in the matter of...the curtailment of operations at DOSCO Trenton Steel Works...", 24 June 1944, Box 15 #12, RG44, PANS.

83 Province of Nova Scotia, *Report of the Commissioner on Trenton Steel Works* (Halifax, 1944), p. 26.

84 Quoted in McDowall, *Steel at the Sault*, p. 200.

85 A.G. McKee & Company, "Report on the Steel Industry" in *Report of the Royal Commission on Provincial Development and Rehabilitation* (Halifax, 1944), part XI, p. 19. This consulting firm had acted as consultants to Steel Control at the beginning of the war: M.A. Hoey to J.G. Godsoe, 10 May 1944, file 196-14-4, vol. 257, RG28, PAC.

Canadian National Railways' repair shops in Moncton, for example, found their position undermined by a big new machine shop in Montreal which, at Howe's suggestion, the railway built as a munitions plant and then converted at the war's end.[86] Maritime manufacturers who sought to develop lines of consumer products for the postwar era faced long odds in importing their sheet steel from Ontario while attempting to sell their products nation-wide. Companies which did so, such as Enterprise Stoves and the Enamel and Heating Products of Sackville, New Brunswick, found themselves doubly vulnerable to freight rate increases and a rate structure which increasingly favoured the central producers.[87]

By the pattern of its wartime investment, the federal government appeared to be telling businessmen that the Maritimes would have little part to play in Canada's new postwar industrial complex. Dosco responded to that message at first by vigorous protest and later by the transfer of secondary operations to Montreal. Meanwhile, with the taxable resources of the country now hived more than ever within the boundaries of Ontario and Quebec, provincial governments in the Maritimes were in no position to themselves finance the steps towards the re-industrialization of the region which their royal commission studies often suggested.[88]

While one can outline with precision the negative impact of the federal government's role, its motives remain open to controversy. There was, of course, no conspiracy to de-industrialize the Maritimes. Little more plausible is the suggestion that Howe and his controllers avoided the Maritimes in their investments from fear of German attack. It is true that Dosco was vulnerable to submarines in the acquisition of ores, and the corporation in 1942 went so far as to open emergency reserves of iron ore near Bathurst, New Brunswick, although these were never employed. Yet the strategic threat was not cited as a problem in the use of Maritime industry by the controllers at the time nor does it seem to have been a matter of discussion among their military advisors. The efficiency argument cannot so easily be dismissed, for it was the explanation most frequently offered by the bureaucrats in their industrial memoranda. But this rationale rings hollow when applied to the location of shipbuilding and ship repair industries or to the unnecessary delay in opening the Sydney plate mill.

86 See draft history of "National Railways Munitions Ltd.", file 3 of 12, vol. 29, RG28, PAC.

87 See their statements in "Submission of the Transportation Commission of the Maritime Board of Trade to the Royal Commission on Transportation", vol. 1, p. 119, Box 9, RG34, PAPEI. Appendix 46 in volume 2 suggests that competitive rates led to decreases of 10 to 35 per cent on basic steel to manufacturers in Central Canada, with the differential against the Maritime manufacturer increasing sharply after each rate increase.

88 Nova Scotia, *Report of the Royal Commission on Provincial Development and Rehabilitation;* New Brunswick, *Report of the New Brunswick Committee on Reconstruction* (Fredericton, 1944); Prince Edward Island, *The Interim Report of the Prince Edward Island Advisory Reconstruction Committee* (Charlottetown, 1945); J.R. Petrie, *The Regional Economy of New Brunswick: A Study Prepared for the Committee on Reconstruction* (Fredericton, 1944) and J.M. Beck, *The Government of Nova Scotia* (Toronto, 1957), p. 341.

The suggestion by officials of the British Admiralty Technical Mission, who were intimately involved in Canadian industry in an advisory capacity, that locational decisions were "heavily" political seems more plausible. Indeed the political hypothesis goes far in accounting for the entire pattern of economic development. The beginning of the war at the end of the Depression found Canadian industries starved for business and lobbying actively for the contracts anticipated from the war. Federal and provincial politicians were keenly interested. The earliest and biggest contracts went to the largest centres in the most influential provinces and with them went the federal assistance for industrial development.

The controllers' tacit respect for the political power of the Montreal metropolis also appeared obvious in their willingness to allow that city to dominate the lucrative ship repair industry. They persisted in this policy regardless of the inconvenience to convoys or the impediment to developing a stable industry, accessible during the winter months. Montreal's influence was also reflected in the discussions of the War Committee of the cabinet, which apparently found it easier to contemplate building destroyers at Halifax to provide off-season employment than to divert repair business from the St. Lawrence. Certainly the decision to locate one shipbuilding plant in Nova Scotia appeared to be largely a response to public protest. It should come as no surprise that politicians act from political motives.

One suspects, nevertheless, that there was more than the consideration of immediate political gain in the behaviour of C.D. Howe and his controllers. Howe's personal motives in decisions affecting the Maritimes cannot be shown conclusively at this stage of research. Letters and memoranda on controversial decisions involving the Maritimes are absent from his papers, and his public statements often appear as simplistic rationales. Howe's extraordinary support for Algoma and his apparent hostility towards Dosco, its most direct competitor, suggest that his friendship with Sir James Dunn might have been an influencing factor. His subsequent attempt to deny this relationship and his admission to destroying portions of their correspondence also point in that direction.[89] Yet his apparent preference for Algoma should not be exaggerated. Assistance to that corporation appeared outstanding largely because, unlike Stelco, its profit margin was too low to allow government investment to be hidden as depreciation.

Howe's general policies and occasional comments suggest that he was more than merely reacting to the hectic events of the period. Repeated references by Howe and his controllers to Canada's postwar needs, even during periods of crisis, suggest that they were working from a plan for the long-term industrial development of the country. Their blueprint included a continued industrial integration with the United States — a relationship which effectively undermined Dosco's claim to virtue as the only steel company not dependent on the

89 McDowall, *Steel at the Sault*, p. 205. See also S.R. Howe, "C.D. Howe and the Americans, 1940-1957", Ph.D. thesis, University of Maine, 1977, pp. 251-2.

Americans for primary materials. It also anticipated the St. Lawrence Waterway, an international project which promised to turn the cities of the Great Lakes into ocean ports. This scheme was abandoned by the Canadian government only after the Canadian-American treaty, signed in March 1941, failed to pass the United States Congress.[90]

From Howe's perspective, it may have appeared a more efficient use of Canada's resources to develop ports and concentrate industry on the Great Lakes and St. Lawrence rather than the coast. Moreover, such a plan had the practical advantage of meeting the long-term aspirations of the two politically powerful central provinces and their metropolises. Such an approach served the interests and regional prejudices of Howe, his controllers and influential friends. It even appeared to conform to the conventional wisdom of Canadian economists. If the weakness of Maritime industry in the 20th century was a natural outcome of the free interplay of the forces of the marketplace, as studies by S.A. Saunders and W.A. Mackintosh seemed to suggest, then it logically followed that government investment to develop industry there might be wasted in the long term. B.S. Keirstead probably reflected the thinking of many of his contemporaries when his studies in 1944 and 1948 set out the classic interpretation of the decline of manufacturing in the Maritimes as the inevitable result of economies of scale and agglomeration in Central Canada.[91]

One should not blame Howe, the politician, for responding to the political pressures of his day. He was not responsible for the structure of Confederation which some have aptly called an "unequal union". But neither the political pressures nor Howe's industrial blueprint served the interests of Canada's war effort in the Maritimes. Not only did Howe's department fail to develop the industrial potential of the region for the war, but hindsight also reveals the negative impact of spectacular errors in particular industries. The long delay in reopening the plate mill at Sydney contributed to severe shortages in ships' plate in Canada in 1941 and 1942. Howe and his controllers failed to develop in eastern Canada a major centre for the production of naval vessels. The construction of escorts on the Lakes led to battles against frost and freeze-up, a loss of flexibility in shifting to larger vessels and the lack of support capacity in refit

90 T.L. Hills, *The St. Lawrence Seaway* (London, 1959), pp. 66-7. The files of press clippings on this subject in Howe's papers suggest the enthusiasm of Great Lakes harbour communities at the prospects of becoming ocean ports.

91 Saunders, *The Economic History of the Maritime Provinces*, pp. 84-5 and W.A. Mackintosh, *The Economic Background to Dominion-Provincial Relations* (Ottawa, 1939), pp. 43-5. See also *Report of the Royal Commission on Dominion-Provincial Relations* (Ottawa, 1940), Book I, p. 119; B.S. Keirstead, *Theory of Economic Change* (Toronto, 1948), pp. 267-310 and *The Economic Effects of the War on the Maritime Provinces of Canada* (Halifax, 1944). W.Y. Smith pointed out, however, that although Howe and his adviser W.A. Mackintosh borrowed heavily from the work of British economist J.M. Keynes for their *White Paper on Employment and Income* (Ottawa, 1945), they conspicuously ignored his strictures on regional development: "Recognition of Regional Balance", *Policy Options*, 2 (5) (November/December 1981), pp. 41-4.

and ship repair. Their failure to heed the advice of major allies on developing a repair centre at Halifax and their persistence in maintaining that industry at Montreal seriously impaired the effectiveness of the Canadian navy.

Meanwhile, their policies, far from helping to overcome trends towards regional disparity of which some Canadians were conscious, served rather to accentuate and consolidate them. Howe may have sincerely believed, given his vision of Canada's future development, that the decline of industry in the Maritimes was inevitable. If so, with the mobilized resources of the Canadian state at his disposal, including billions of dollars in direct investment, his was a powerfully self-fulfilling prophecy.

_ ӠTER NEARY

Reprinted from Vol. XII, No. 2
(Spring 1983)

Newfoundland's Union with Canada, 1949: Conspiracy or Choice?

THE OPENING OF A MASS of papers at the British Public Record Office on the history of Newfoundland in the 1940s has rekindled the debate over the circumstances in which the province became part of Canada in 1949. The question at issue was, and is: did Newfoundlanders decide their own constitutional future after the war or was Confederation engineered by Great Britain and Canada? Conspiracy theories were popular in Newfoundland at the time and have never really died out. What are the facts? The events leading up to Confederation cannot be understood without reference to what happened to Newfoundland in the 1930s. As an export-oriented and debtor country, Newfoundland was economically savaged by the Great Depression and quickly pushed to the edge of bankruptcy. In 1933, with the agreement of the government formed in St. John's the previous year by Frederick Alderdice, a Royal Warrant was issued from London appointing a commission "to examine into the future of Newfoundland and in particular to report on the financial situation and prospects therein".[1] Chaired by Lord Amulree, a Scottish Labour peer, this royal commission advocated that Great Britain assume "general responsibility" for Newfoundland's finances; but it also recommended that Newfoundland give up democratic parliamentary government in favour of administration by a British-appointed commission.[2]

This scheme was accepted by the Newfoundland legislature and the new "Commission of Government" was inaugurated in St. John's in February 1934. The new administration was responsible to the parliament of the United Kingdom through the Secretary of State for the Dominions and combined a governor and six commissioners. Three of the latter were chosen from Great Britain and three from Newfoundland. The whole arrangement was not meant to be permanent but to last until Newfoundlanders could support themselves again, whereupon self-government would be restored at their request.[3] But no definition was given to self-supporting and no procedure was spelled out whereby responsible government might be resumed. These were critical omissions and left the British considerable scope for manoeuvre later on. Lord Amulree had investigated the possibility of Confederation as a solution to Newfoundland's problems but the idea had received a frosty reception in R.B. Bennett's Ottawa. The response of E.N. Rhodes, Bennett's Nova Scotian Minister of Finance, was especially chilling. "He was against Confederation", Rhodes told Amulree, "as

---

1 See S.J.R. Noel, *Politics in Newfoundland* (Toronto, 1971), p. 210.
2 *Newfoundland Royal Commission 1933 Report* (London, 1933), pp. 201-2.
3 Great Britain, *The Public General Acts, 1933-34*, p. 10.

the Newf[oundlande]rs would really in effect become another Ireland — not in the racial sense, but a nuisance and always grumbling and wanting something".⁴

During its first five years the Commission of Government effected many administrative changes and promoted various development schemes but Newfoundland remained economically downtrodden and was hit badly by the recession of 1937-38. Only an annual grant-in-aid from the United Kingdom permitted the Commission to balance its books in these years. In the summer of 1938 Governor Sir Humphrey Walwyn reported a more "bolshie" spirit among the St. John's hard-core unemployed and the following spring a *Daily Express* reporter concluded that the Commission was "overwhelmingly unpopular".⁵ It would take the outbreak of the Second World War to transform the Newfoundland economy. In an age of air and submarine warfare the Island was strategically located, and Canada and the United States had obvious military interests there. It was their defence spending on the Island and in Labrador that got Newfoundlanders out of the economic quicksand. Early in the war Canada took over the running of Gander airport, built by Great Britain and Newfoundland in the late 1930s and henceforth a crucial stopover point in the transatlantic ferrying of aircraft and supplies. Canada subsequently built air bases near St. John's and at Goose Bay, Labrador. St. John's was also a major centre of Canadian wartime naval operations and from 1941 the seat of a Canadian High Commission. In September 1940, Great Britain promised to secure for the United States "freely and without consideration" the grant for 99 years of base sites in Newfoundland.⁶ A lease was subsequently negotiated between Washington and St. John's and rapid development followed. During the summer of 1942, at the height of the base-building boom, approximately 20,000 Newfoundlanders were employed on defence construction.⁷ It was a measure of the turnabout in her fortunes that in 1941 Newfoundland made the first of a series of interest-free loans to the United Kingdom.⁸

Economic change of this magnitude clearly had political consequences and these, not surprisingly, invited Whitehall's attention. As one Dominions Office official wrote in June 1942, "a new and vigorous policy with regard to Newfoundland" had become imperative.⁹ In the heyday of the Atlantic Charter,

4 Amulree to Harding (draft), 21 May 1933, Amulree Papers, Bodleian Library. Quoted by permission of Lord Amulree.

5 Dominions Office [DO] series 35, file 725/N8/12, p. 23, Public Record Office; *Daily Express* (London), 27 March 1939, p. 10. All subsequent DO references are to material in the Public Record Office. Transcripts of Crown-copyright records in the Public Record Office appear by permission of the Controller of H.M. Stationery Office.

6 Great Britain, *Parliamentary Papers, Cmd. 6259* (London, 1941), p. 15.

7 Newfoundland Government, *Report of the Labour Relations Officer for the period June 1st, 1942, to February, 8th, 1944* (St. John's, 1944), p. 13.

8 DO 35/723/N2/73, p. 50; DO 35/749/N314/6, p. 77.

9 DO 35/723/N2/73, p. 5.

Newfoundland's existing form of government had become an anachronism, perhaps even an embarrassment; the war was being fought for democracy but, except in municipal elections in St. John's, Newfoundlanders did not vote. In the autumn of 1942, Clement Attlee, recently appointed to the Dominions Office, visited Newfoundland, observing that the Commission of Government had not prepared for the restoration of self-government and had no clear purpose. Political change, he believed, was both desirable and unavoidable, though the form it should take was by no means clear. "I sum up the attitude of most Newfoundlanders", Attlee wrote, "as being that of a man who having had a spell of drunkenness has taken the pledge . . . is tired of it and would like to be a moderate drinker but does not quite trust himself".[10] In 1943 another prominent British official wrote that what Newfoundlanders "universally" wanted was "to be on their own with a comfortable grant-in-aid, and little responsibility".[11] This was harsh but it was certainly true that Newfoundlanders, preoccupied with their sudden prosperity, never threatened the established political order during the war. The dissidents among them were divided in outlook and were easily deflected by Whitehall.

On Attlee's initiative a three man parliamentary "goodwill" mission was dispatched to Newfoundland in the summer of 1943. Then, in December of that year, it was announced in Parliament that "as soon as practicable" after the war in Europe had ended, Great Britain would provide Newfoundlanders with "machinery. . . to express their considered views as to the form of Government they desire, having regard to the financial and economic conditions prevailing at the time".[12] This promise meant business as usual for the Commission of Government in the interim and had two advantages: it would avoid any disruption of Newfoundland's war effort and would allow Newfoundlanders serving overseas to have a fair say in their country's future. Great Britain, the House of Commons was now also told, did not desire "to impose any particular solution" on Newfoundland but would be "guided by the freely expressed views of the people".[13]

The thinking behind Whitehall's first public policy step was that Confederation, while perhaps the best long-term solution for Newfoundland, was "wholly out of the question" and was, moreover, "a matter in which His Majesty's Government in the United Kingdom could not directly intervene".[14] The British further assumed that Newfoundland's existing prosperity was transitory and that the post-war period would be difficult. Though Newfoundlanders would be able to choose for themselves politically, in the British view they could not be

10 *Ibid.*, p. 63.
11 DO 35/1141/N402/11, p. 9.
12 DO 114/103, p. 24.
13 *Ibid.*
14 DO 35/1337/N402/1/11, pp. 208-09.

left to their own devices economically. If they were, Great Britain might soon be faced yet again with emergency requests for financial aid from St. John's. Above all, therefore, Great Britain wanted to avoid backing a Newfoundland government that would be free to borrow and spend as it pleased. In 1944 the Dominions Office attempted to refine the policy declaration of December 1943, to take account of all these factors. On the constitutional side, Lord Cranborne, Attlee's successor at the Dominions Office, opted for a procedure first suggested by Independent MP A.P. Herbert, one of the parliamentarians who had gone to Newfoundland on the goodwill mission.[15] The instrument through which Newfoundlanders would begin considering their constitutional future after the war would be a national convention elected, it was eventually decided, on a revised model of the pre-1934 local constituencies.

The Commission of Government resisted the national convention proposal, fearing that an elected body of Newfoundlanders would put it on trial, act as an alternative government, or do both.[16] But criticism from this quarter was brushed aside in London, and in any case the attitude of official St. John's changed when the Dominions Office made known the extent of the financial support it was willing to recommend for Newfoundland. In August 1944, Cranborne met in London with a three-man Commission of Government delegation which included two Newfoundlanders, L.E. Emerson and J.C. Puddester. Earlier he had asked the Commission to begin preparing a long-term reconstruction plan for Newfoundland. Now he revealed that he favoured a special parliamentary act to fund over about ten years the capital cost of development schemes in Newfoundland which he and the Chancellor of the Exchequer had previously approved.[17] Great Britain might also, he suggested, take over Newfoundland's sterling debt to offset the recurring costs of the development projects to be undertaken. This would be generous assistance indeed and the commissioners were quick to point out that its announcement before Newfoundlanders rendered an electoral verdict on their constitutional future would guarantee "an overwhelming vote in favour of a return to responsible government".[18] This being so, Great Britain would need some mechanism to safeguard her proposed investment.

Cranborne's answer here was a Joint Development Board. This would be established when the British Parliament voted funds for Newfoundland and while the Commission of Government was still in office, so as to avoid the coincidence of the restoration of self-governemnt and the imposition of new financial controls. As envisaged, the Board would be chaired by a judge of the Newfoundland Supreme Court and have six other members, three nominated by Great

15 *Ibid.*, p. 210; DO 114/103, p. 32.
16 DO 35/1338/N402/1/11, pp. 15-20.
17 DO 35/1142/N402/31, pp. 7-8.
18 *Ibid.*, p. 9.

Britain and three by Newfoundland.[19] Great Britain would also continue to appoint the Comptroller and Auditor-General of Newfoundland. The job of the Board would be to vet development schemes for funding, supervise the carrying out of work on approved projects, and report to both governments. Newfoundland would not be allowed to borrow externally without British agreement while the development scheme was in effect.[20] Eventually, the Commission of Government put forward a reconstruction program with an anticipated price tag of $100 million;[21] its plan was imaginative and presaged many of the developments which took place in Newfoundland in the 1950s. Assistance on this scale, the Dominions Office believed, would allow constitutional change to proceed without fear of the outcome, satisfy those parliamentarians who favoured generosity towards a gallant little ally, and bury once and for all the lingering suspicion that Great Britain had acted since 1933-34 as bailiff for Newfoundland's foreign bondholders.[22]

Cranborne was now ready to advance his brief, with its inextricably linked political and economic elements, within the British government. There he met immediate opposition from the Treasury: Great Britain simply could not pay for what was being proposed. The expenditures contemplated in Newfoundland would be mainly in Canadian dollars (Newfoundland's currency was tied to Canada's) and London was already borrowing massively from Ottawa. Great Britain's own financial situation in the post-war world would be perilous, and she would hardly look credible in negotiating loans for herself with the United States and Canada if she was simultaneously attempting to prop up Newfoundland. Great Britain had to look to her own concerns lest financial weakness endanger her position as a great power. "We have", one Treasury analysis concluded, "to face the fact that the expenditure now proposed and many other forms of expenditure may be in themselves politically and economically very desirable, but it is a melancholy fact that we cannot afford them".[23]

Cranborne resisted this approach, but the Treasury could not be moved and its view was unaffected by the coming to power of a Labour government in 1945. A new backer had to be found for Newfoundland, and Canada was the obvious candidate. What were the chances of success in Ottawa? Increasingly, the British believed they were good. Canada's stake in Newfoundland had been greatly increased by the war and the United States was now her direct competitor there. These new circumstances, the British believed, called for an active Canadian policy towards Newfoundland which would "gradually. . . build up an atmosphere of comradeship and practical co-operation in which the union of the two

19 DO 35/1342/N402/29, p. 165.
20 *Ibid.*, p. 186.
21 *Ibid.*, pp. 54-55.
22 *Ibid.*, pp. 172-86.
23 DO 35/1343/N402/32, p. 92.

countries could be seen to be in the common interest".[24] When the Canadians made informal soundings in 1945 about Great Britain's intentions in Newfoundland, Whitehall saw its opportunity. In September, P.A. Clutterbuck, a senior Dominions Office official who had served as secretary to the Amulree Commission and had remained close to Commission of Government affairs ever since, was sent to Ottawa to discuss the future of Newfoundland.[25] He did not find his Canadian hosts very forthcoming but he had a strong case. If Great Britian could not help a new administration in St. John's and Canada stood aside, American influence might well grow in Newfoundland. An understanding was soon reached. Canada would not back Newfoundland directly or indirectly through Great Britain, but she would welcome her into Confederation. Henceforth Great Britain and Canada would be as one in pursuit of this objective. Confederation, they agreed, was Newfoundland's "natural destiny".[26]

What could they do to forward their common cause? Clearly, they believed, the one thing they must not do was intervene directly in the constitutional debate among Newfoundlanders. Any hint of Anglo-Canadian cooperation to promote Confederation would be disastrous; the initiative for union had to come from Newfoundlanders themselves. It would, however, be possible for both parties to influence the development of Newfoundland opinion. Canada could do this best by welcoming any expression of interest in Confederation arising out of the national convention. If a signal came across the Gulf of St. Lawrence, Canada must be prepared to do "the handsome thing" by Newfoundlanders.[27] Great Britain could "assist" the latter "to turn their thoughts to Canada" by making clear to them that they could not rely on London for further financial help.[28] The British, of course, had another important lever in their ability to define the purposes for which the national convention would meet and the electoral procedure by which Newfoundlanders would subsequently make their constitutional choice.

The British had good cards and they played them skilfully. When the calling of a national convention was announced in Parliament on 11 December 1945, the Attlee government left itself great freedom for manoeuvre, while emphasizing to Newfoundlanders its inability to offer them much future help.[29] The convention would be an advisory body only, its job to recommend to the United Kingdom constitutional choices that might be put before the Newfoundland people in a referendum. Its views would clearly carry weight and be difficult to ignore; but it was not given final say on what would be on the referendum ballot.

24 *Ibid.*, p. 94.
25 For his report see DO 35/1347/N402/54, pp. 98-102.
26 *Ibid.*, p. 91
27 *Ibid.*, p. 101.
28 *Ibid.*, p. 102.
29 DO 114/103, pp. 54-63.

This prerogative the British kept carefully to themselves.

In the event, the national convention, which assembled in St. John's on 11 September 1946, following an election notable for its low voter turnout, decided to send delegations to Ottawa and London. The group that went to London was received politely but negatively. In offering thumbnail sketches of its members, K.C. Wheare, Fellow of All Souls and British-appointed constitutional advisor to the national convention, wrote, "I cannot believe that the resources of the Dominions Office will fail to cope easily and happily with these men".[30] They did not. British officialdom's special gift for saying no was on this occasion employed to full advantage. In effect the visit of the delegation served only to give the British another opportunity to demonstrate just how bare their cupboard really was. The delegation that went to Ottawa was accorded a very different reception. One of its members was Joey Smallwood, who had emerged among the convention delegates as the leading spokesman for Confederation. He and his colleagues were warmly received by Mackenzie King's government and returned to St. John's having worked out a possible scheme of union.

Before disbanding, the national convention recommended to Great Britain two possible forms of government for Newfoundlanders: "Responsible Government as it existed prior to 1934" and "Commission of Government".[31] When Smallwood had moved in the convention that the choice of Confederation also be recommended, his motion had been defeated 29-16. Undeterred, he had taken his case to the people, calling his opponents "twenty-nine dictators" and organizing a big petition in favour of what a majority of his national convention colleagues had spurned.[32] Much has been made of his success in this enterprise but he was really facilitating the inevitable. The British no doubt welcomed a pretext to add Confederation to the ballot but they really did not have to be persuaded to do so. Their final policy step, announced in Newfoundland on 11 March 1948, was masterful and was taken after close consultation with officials in St. John's and Ottawa, where P.A. Clutterbuck, freshly knighted, had gone as High Commissioner in 1946. The referendum would offer three choices — revised versions of the two recommended by the national convention, and Confederation. The form of words on the ballot was as follows: "1. COMMISSION OF GOVERNMENT for a period of five years"; "2. CONFEDERATION WITH CANADA", "3. RESPONSIBLE GOVERNMENT as it existed in 1933".[33] Interestingly, the formal justification advanced to the governor of Newfoundland for including Confederation did not mention the petition Smallwood had organized. Great Britain's initiative was justified because the issues involved in union with Canada had been "sufficiently clarified" to enable the people of

30 DO 35/3446/N2005/13, p. 27.

31 DO 114/103, p. 134.

32 Noel, *Politics in Newfoundland*, p. 254.

33 *Acts of the Honourable Commission of Government of Newfoundland, 1948* (St. John's, 1948), p. 49.

Newfoundland to pronounce on Confederation and because of the support this additional choice had commended in the national convention.[34] Three choices rather than two meant, of course, that a referendum might not produce an absolute majority for any one. Recognizing this and believing that majority support was crucial in so basic a decision, the British ruled that a second referendum on the two most favoured options would have to be held if the first failed to meet this requirement.

All elections hinge upon particular historical circumstances and there can be no doubt that the decisions made by Great Britain and Canada from 1945 onwards were important in establishing the framework of politics in which Newfoundlanders voted in 1948. But to influence is not to engineer. Once the form of the ballot and the procedure for voting were decided upon, Newfoundlanders were on their own and they had real choices. Rumours persist of electoral irregularities in Newfoundland in 1948, but not a shred of evidence has been produced to substantiate them. Great Britain and Canada had certainly worked together to put the choice of Confederation before Newfoundlanders but they could not and did not make that choice for them. The British were uncertain of the outcome in Newfoundland and had well-developed contingency plans to reintroduce responsible government should the vote go that way. If Smallwood's role in the national convention and in getting Confederation on the referendum ballot was perhaps less important than has heretofore been thought, there is no denying his achievement on the hustings. He did not win a "fixed" bout but a winner-take-all, bare-knuckle fight-to-the-finish. Indeed, on 3 June 1948, after the first round, he and his associates found themselves behind. On this occasion 69,400 votes were cast for responsible government, 64,066 for Confederation and 22,311 for continuing the Commission system.[35] But the result of the run-off, held on 22 July, was 78,323 for Confederation and 71,334 for responsible government.[36] These figures represented respectively 52.34 per cent and 47.66 per cent of the popular vote. Smallwood had triumphed and Great Britain and Canada had succeeded — but only just.

Is it surprising to find confirmed in the papers at the Public Record Office that Great Britain and Canada favoured a particular outcome in Newfoundland after the war? Not really. Given the substantial interests both countries had in Newfoundland, the real surprise would be to find that they did not have clearly-defined policy goals. Nor is it surprising to find that Great Britain and Canada had reached an understanding about the future of Newfoundland. Historians may not previously have known the details of Anglo-Canadian negotiations in the 1940s, but they have never doubted that Great Britain and Canada were players rather than spectators. Newfoundland's union with

34 DO 114/103, p. 143.

35 *Ibid.*, p. 191.

36 *Ibid.*, p. 192.

Canada was a complex diplomatic, constitutional and political event. It could not have been anything else and cannot otherwise be understood. Great Britain and Canada undoubtedly pursued their self-interest vis-à-vis Newfoundlanders but that too is neither surprising nor shocking. And it does not follow that because they did so they had necessarily to disregard the best interest of Newfoundland. Again, there were limits to what the British and Canadians could do to achieve their objectives. It is one thing to have the last word on what appears on a referendum ballot, as the British did in Newfoundland in 1948; it can be quite another thing to win the referendum, as René Lévesque discovered in 1980. Ultimately, in a fair and democratic electoral contest, Newfoundlanders had to decide their constitutional future themselves. If they had not wanted Confederation, they had other substantial choices before them. This was well understood at the time and should not now be obscured.

Perhaps the one real surprise at the Public Record Office is not that the British wanted Newfoundland to join Canada but that the Dominions Office for so long clung to the notion that Newfoundland could resume self-government with British financial support. Critics of Confederation and the means by which it was brought about in Newfoundland would do well to ponder the plan the Dominions Office had worked out for Newfoundland in 1944. If this had been implemented, Newfoundland might well have regained self-government but her freedom of action as an independent country would have been severely limited by the financial controls the British intended as the price for their continued support. As premiers of a Canadian province, Joey Smallwood and his Progressive Conservative successors have known no such constraints. Arguably, Newfoundland found greater independence within the loose structure of Canadian federalism than it could ever have achieved on its own. When Sir P.A. Clutterbuck made a nostalgic visit to Newfoundland in 1950, he was amazed at how fast Smallwood's government was moving economically and how far it intended to go. If the administration he had helped plan in 1944 had come into existence, things would have been very different. In effect the relationship St. John's achieved with Ottawa through Confederation was the very one that London was above all determined to avoid for itself. Newfoundland had found a backer but her backer could not necessarily control her financial course. There was no Dominions Office or Treasury in Ottawa to rein in Joey Smallwood, or Frank Moores or Brian Peckford.

All this, of course, means nothing if one believes as an article of faith that Newfoundland was the victim of an Anglo-Canadian plot. The fact that some files listed at Kew relating to Newfoundland affairs in the 1930s and 1940s remain either closed or, in one case at least, are "wanting" (in British archival parlance) will encourage such thinking. What has been held back, however, may well have more to do with personality than policy, though here there can be no certainty. On the other hand, the voluminous and comprehensive body of information that has been released lends cold comfort to those Newfoundlanders who now seem to hold a grudge against their own past and dream on of a glory that might have been but never was — before or after the upheaval of 1934. Conspiracy theories of history have a life of their own, for no amount of contrary evidence can ever conclusively refute them. After all, it is always possible to believe that the "real" evidence has been destroyed or hidden or the official record cunningly falsified, and that only when the secret archives are opened (or the long-lost diary found, and so forth) will the "true story" at last be told. Such notions are hardy perennials, especially in the case of historic events where the margin between success and failure, victory and defeat, was razor-thin, as it was in Newfoundland in 1948.

JIM OVERTON

Reprinted from Vol. XIV, No. 1
(Autumn 1984)

Coming Home:
Nostalgia and Tourism in Newfoundland

LIKE MOST OF ATLANTIC CANADA, Newfoundland has been since the 19th century an area of relative surplus population in a North American context. Since at least the 1860s a fairly constant stream of people have been forced by economic circumstances to seek temporary or permanent employment in Canada and the United States.[1] It is one thing, however, to describe the structures of uneven regional development and to chart the dynamics of the labour market which causes this process. It is another thing to appreciate the way in which such conditions are experienced by the people involved. The separation from friends, family, familiar landscapes and ways of working and living that leaving home usually involves has been a significant experience for many Newfoundlanders.

The word nostalgia comes from the Greek *nostos*, to return home, and *algia*, a painful condition. It describes a painful yearning to return home and was coined by a Swiss physician, Johannes Hofer, in the late 17th century.[2] Presumably homesickness or *maladie du pays* had existed before this time, but it was in the Enlightenment climate of the late 17th century that this emotion came to be characterized as a disease. In the 18th and 19th centuries nostalgia was increasingly recognized as a sickness of soldiers, sailors, emigrés and provincials. In the 19th century nostalgia also took on a romantic significance, especially in terms of recollections of a past, usually preindustrial, golden age of innocence and youth. Today nostalgia is no longer looked upon by the medical profession as a disease, and the symptoms are more likely to be discussed in terms of social maladjustment or depression. For Freudians, nostalgia is often considered a mild kind of neurosis stimulated by "a concern over, or denial of the future" rather than as a kind of "homing instinct".[3] The uncertainty and discomfort of

1 For background information and specific details on outmigration see, R.A. Mackay, *Newfoundland Economic, Diplomatic and Strategic Studies* (Toronto, 1946), David Alexander, "Development and Dependence in Newfoundland", *Acadiensis*, IV, 1 (Autumn 1975), pp. 3-31, David Alexander, "Newfoundland's Traditional Economy and Development to 1934", *Acadiensis*, V, 1 (Autumn 1976), pp. 56-78, Ralph Matthews, "The Pursuit of Progress: Newfoundland's Social and Economic Development in the Smallwood Era", in Neil B. Ridler, ed., *Issues in Regional/Urban Development of Atlantic Canada* (Saint John, 1978), pp. 27-49, Peter Neary, "Canada and the Newfoundland Labour Market", *Canadian Historical Review*, LXII, 4 (December 1981), pp. 470-495, Peter Neary, "Canadian Immigration Policy and the Newfoundlanders, 1912-1939", *Acadiensis*, XI, 2 (Spring 1982), pp. 69-83.

2 Jean Starobinski, "The Idea of Nostalgia", *Diogenes*, 53, 1966, pp. 81-103, George Rosen, "Nostalgia: A 'forgotten' psychological disorder", *Psychological Medicine*, 5, 1975, pp. 340-354, Fred Davis, *Yearning for Yesterday: A Sociology of Nostalgia* (New York, 1979).

3 M. Mike Nawas and J.J. Platt, "A Future Oriented Theory of Nostalgia", *Journal of Individual Psychology*, 21(1), 1965, pp. 55.

present life gives rise to a search for a more stable and secure world in the past. Various elements from the individual's past — places, events, people — become internalized as part of a fantasy-producing process.[4]

But this is not simply a fantasy, for it guides action and is a powerful creative force. Among Newfoundland emigrants, nostalgia has produced a variety of cultural expressions, not the least of which is the sentimental view which many expatriates have adopted towards the remembered way of life in Newfoundland. The idea of returning home is very often important for migrants. Going away to work is regarded as a necessary, but temporary, hardship to be endured.[5] As Teodor Shanin points out: "The dream of return, rich and successful, into one's own village, has been the grand utopia, around which strategies, norms and claims were structured by the migrants. Nor were these only dreams, for one can barely find a south Italian or Irish village without some 'Americans', i.e. returnees. Indeed, to sustain a dream one usually needs some consistent proofs of its realism, even if only limited in scope".[6] And migrants do return home in large numbers. Evidence cited by Shanin, for example, suggests that almost half of the European migrants to the United States went back home in the first 20 years of this century.

If returning home is the "grand utopia" for many migrants, the visit may be regarded as a little utopia. The visits of returning expatriates have, in fact, become a very significant form of tourism in Newfoundland. Surveys have shown that the VFR (Visiting Friends and Relatives) market accounts for a large part of the Newfoundland tourist trade.[7] The heritage of unemployment and poverty has thus offered the social and cultural basis for a developing tourist industry. Important ⚓

The process of adjusting to a new location may be a difficult one for migrants, depending particularly on the problems of finding employment and making friends. There is some evidence that migration is especially difficult for married women who do not work. Anne Martin's study of Newfoundland women in Hamilton suggests that this is the case. The words of one woman she interviewed show that dissatisfaction is the other side of the longing for home: "If I had my time over, I would have stayed in Newfoundland. I hate it up here. There's

---

4   Sigmund Freud, "Civilization and its Discontents", in J. Strachey, ed., *The Complete Psychological Works of Sigmund Freud* (London, 1930), pp. 64-145.

5   John Berger and Jean Mohr, *A Seventh Man* (Harmondsworth, 1975).

6   Teodor Shanin, "The peasants are coming: migrants who labour, peasants who travel and Marxists who write", *Race and Class*, 19(3), 1978, p. 285.

7   For example, the Government of Newfoundland and Labrador, *Non-Resident Auto Exit Survey* (June 20-Aug. 31, 1974) (Tourist Services Department, Department of Tourism), p. 4 showed that 37 per cent of the parties leaving Newfoundland for the mainland had come to visit friends and relatives. Similar figures emerged from two later surveys: Government of Newfoundland and Labrador, *Non-Resident Auto-Exit Survey (June 18-Aug. 30, 1977)* (Development Branch, Tourist Services Division, Department of Tourism) and Government of Newfoundland and Labrador, *Air Exit Survey Report* (Planning and Evaluation Division, Department of Tourism).

nothing here for me. People don't know how to be friendly. They don't have any respect for people here like in my home town. I will never stay in this God-forsaken bloody hole".[8] The insecurity and painfulness of adjusting to a new place are eased by association with people from similar backgrounds. Migrants from the same part of Newfoundland often tend to work and live together. Around such groupings of immigrants a whole cultural milieu tends to develop as people create some form of community, perhaps tied together, in part, by the common desire to eventually return home. Around the turn of the century the Cabot Club in Boston was a particularly important focus of attention for ex-Newfoundlanders. The heavy post-Second World War emigration also gave rise to associations in Canadian cities, such as the Terra Nova Club in Montreal and five or six clubs in Toronto.

People may maintain links with Newfoundland in a variety of ways, but music is especially important. The clubs in Toronto, of which the Caribou is the oldest, are a key element in the production and reproduction of exile culture, and a number of important musicians made their start in these clubs. Harry Hibbs went from Bell Island to Toronto in 1962 and worked in "the plants" until he was injured. As a result of his accident he became involved in the club run by Ray Kent, another former Bell Islander, playing the squeeze box. Similarly with Dick Nolan, Bert Cuff, Roy Payne and others. Eventually Hibbs started his own club — the Conception Bay Club and became a popular recording and T.V. star, producing record albums such as the recent *Memories of Newfoundland*.[9]

Much of this music is the epitome of emigré culture, containing recollections of "home" and expressing a longing for Newfoundland. Like the various artifacts and customs that people keep, music provides a symbolic link to the other life from which they have been exiled. A whole spate of "exile" songs date from the end of the 19th century, one of the periods of high outmigration from Newfoundland. These include the "Terra Novean Exile's Song" written by P. Dyer, an emigrant to the United States, "Newfoundland" written by Barrington Lodge, who "died in a foreign land some few years ago", and "The Exile's Christmas", written in Boston in 1892.[10] Another song from this period is "A Heart's Cry From the West", to be sung "*con expressione*".[11]

These romantic recollections of home are echoed in similar songs and verses from the post-1940s period, especially those from the singers associated with the Newfoundland clubs in Toronto. Consider the songs of Roy Payne, "Happy An-

---

8   Anne Martin, "The Case of the Migrant Wife: Looking at the World from the Underdog Perspective", *Occasional Papers of the McMaster University Sociology of Women Program*, 1, 1977, p. 185.

9   "The Newfoundland Herald Questions Harry Hibbs", *Newfoundland Herald*, 11 December 1979, pp. 18-20.

10 James Murphy, *Murphy's Songs and Ballads of Newfoundland* (n.p., 1902), pp. 36-8, 39-40, 54-6.

11 Gerald S. Doyle, *Old-Time Songs and Poetry of Newfoundland* (St. John's, 1966), p. 11.

niversary Newfoundland":

> Some like me, we waved goodbye, and went chasing after rainbows,
> Some left never to return again
> But I'm sure there's no Newfie alive
> Who doesn't wipe a tear from his eye
> When he recalls "God guard thee, Newfoundland",

and "There's No Price Tag on the Doors in Newfoundland":

> Surrounded by a mighty sea there's an island dear to me
> Described by some a place of rock and sand
> But so many a man has found when the world has turned you down
> There's no price tag on the doors of Newfoundland.[12]

The "Isle of Newfoundland" by Jason (Tex) Shaw is similar:

> Where the people make a living
> On the land and in the sea
> There are people on the island
> That mean the world to me
> I wish I had the power
> To change the course of time
> And live again in Newfoundland
> The home of childhood time.[13]

Many of the themes taken up in these songs are really no different from that whole genre of literature about Newfoundland which presents idyllic scenes from "old-fashioned" outport life. This literature flourished in the 1940s and 1950s in the pages of magazines such as the *Atlantic Guardian* and it is currently very popular in Newfoundland.

Ron Pollett's 1950 article in the *Atlantic Guardian*, "Summer Madness", can be seen as a classic account of the nostalgia of emigré Newfoundlanders. Nostalgia, writes Pollett, is "as much a disease as canker in potatoes": "There are an estimated 200,000 of us Newfoundlanders living on the mainland, mostly in cities. That's more than half as many as on the Island itself. Many were reared in seaside villages rimmed by woods and fields which, in summer setting etched pictures forever on our minds". It is the "summer madness", the "going home again" complaint, which is the permanent affliction of the exile and must

---

12 Bennett Brewing Co. Ltd., *The Ninth Edition of Newfoundland Songs* (St. John's, 1974), pp. 5, 27.

13 *Ibid.*, p. 16.

be cured sooner or later at least temporarily by a visit home. In the mind of the ex-resident of Newfoundland "in search of the Golden Fleece", images of home "dance like demons". The sweltering heat of summer in New York or Toronto helps create a longing for "home". Such homesickness in emigrants is made easier but is at the same time maintained by association with other emigrants:

> The biggest mistake the yearning exile in search of a cure could ever make is to marry one of his own kind. Yet that's what often happens since New-foundlanders, like other national groups, build their own nests in whatever foreign city they happen to settle in numbers. The folk-dance tempo of the get-togethers is far from waltz time, but it plays a gypsy tune for the homeside and the inevitable ensues.[14]

Together Newfoundlanders become "fully-fledged addicts" of nostalgia. With tales of outport life and adventure, they also "socialize" their children to an urge to "go home".

The literature of exile in general and Pollett's writing in particular contains an "out of time" vision of Newfoundland. One obvious clue to this is that it represents a vision of Newfoundland which is frozen at the time of the migrant's departure. As Pollett says:

> we envision tall-sparred schooners, white sails spread taughtly for spring airing, mirrored in the harbour calm. At least, that's the picture we are likely to recall. Most of us in the States came here before the high bars went up on the U.S. border in the early 30's. We can't picture the modern craft, which are mainly mechanized hulls sans canvas, sans romance. Anyway, who wants to dream about a steam trawler?[15]

But, more importantly, the golden age vision is a kind of utopia. It is less a description of Newfoundland than an expression of current alienation and a longing for a more satisfying life. Elements from people's pasts are incorporated into the vision, however, especially childhood memories, childhood being for many something of a golden age of innocence compared with adult life. Several writers have analysed this aspect of nostalgia; in particular, the way in which the images of past golden ages grow out of present dissatisfactions: "We are always dissatisfied enough to be ready for some form of flight into the past, a package tour to one of our preferred Arcadias".[16] In a way "golden ages" are imaginative constructions of a "fantasized past" which never existed, but which represent a

14 Ron Pollett, "Summer Madness", *Atlantic Guardian*, 7(8), 1950, pp. 18-25.

15 *Ibid.*, pp. 21-2.

16 Michael Wood, "Nostalgia or Never: You Can't Go Home Again", *New Society*, 30(631), 1974, p. 343.

"I want my Son to Know and Love Newfoundland, too"

This is Newfoundland's 450th anniversary year, and a fitting time for Newfoundland-born parents living abroad to return for a visit with their children. Plan your summer trip now to avoid disappointment and delays later.

The lad was born in the United States. Good schools, a high standard of living, fine opportunities in a great and rich country   these things were his by right of birth. But to his mother, who was born in Newfoundland, that was not enough. She wanted him to see and know her forbears and his, the folks back home who, knowing few of the amenities of modern life, had toiled through difficult times and developed sturdiness of character and resourcefulness. She wanted him to see the headlands and the bays of Newfoundland, to feel the thrill and the strength of the sea, to discover for himself that life for his ancestors had been a constant challenge . . . so the lad's mother took him "home" in the summer, and he learned to know and love Newfoundland as she did . . .

NEWFOUNDLAND TOURIST DEVELOPMENT BOARD

ST. JOHN'S and CORNER BROOK   -   NEWFOUNDLAND

Also: Newfoundland Government Information Bureau, 620 Fifth Ave., New York.

Figure One: The nostalgia theme in Newfoundland publicity, 1947 (Source: *Atlantic Guardian*, Vol. 3, No. 2 [1947])

future society which could and should exist.[17] This is the past as the "good life". This kind of valuing of rural society and community as a "locus of socially desirable characteristics" is of course a dominant feature of much 19th century thought, in particular in the romantic movement.[18] It is a current of thinking which informs literary and artistic production as well as the human sciences — forming one of the major paradigms in sociology and anthropology and human geography.[19] For small producers and rural dwellers forced by economic circumstances to leave and find work, the old way of life and the place they leave often continues to exist as a spiritual home, a world of friends, families, landscapes and communities which has been lost but which might in the future be recaptured. In the face of current difficulties and uncertainties, the old home exists as something to measure the present and future against, even if it is largely impossible to return except for visits.

A number of studies, especially those dealing with Scotland, have examined the economic and social roots of the kind of sentimental rural literature that is in a Scottish context called "kailyard" literature. Ian Carter points to the rise of tourism in those parts of Scotland which were the settings for many kailyard authors.[20] Tom Nairn links this literature with "cultural emigration" from Scotland, especially the areas which were the focus of "kailyard", and raises also the question of why such literature fell upon such fertile soil at that time.[21] A similar approach may be useful in explaining the outpouring of nostalgic sentimental culture in Newfoundland in the late 19th century and in the period after the Second World War. Both periods saw exceptional changes in rural Newfoundland, involving heavy outmigration. Some useful comments on this point are offered in the recent writings of Patrick O'Flaherty on Newfoundland, especially his comments on E.J. Pratt and the writers of the post-Second World War period. With regard to the latter period he argues that "the traditional, communal way of life" of the outports, "undermined in the hungry 1920s and 1930s, kept crumbling as more and more men left the fishery", first under the influence of the war and then of Confederation. Both opened up Newfoundland to the "vulgarity" of the North American way of life.[22] The development schemes of the 1950s and 1960s virtually completed the task.

17 Frank Hearn, "Remembrance and Critique: The Uses of the Past for Discrediting the Present and Anticipating the Future", *Politics and Society*, 5(2), 1975, pp. 201-27.

18 Malcolm Chapman, *The Gaelic Vision in Scottish Culture* (London, 1978), p. 201.

19 Robert A. Nisbet, *The Sociological Tradition* (New York, 1966), James Overton, "Promoting the 'Real' Newfoundland: Culture as Tourist Commodity", *Studies in Political Economy*, 4 (Autumn 1980), pp. 115-37.

20 Ian Carter, "'Kailyard': The Literature of Decline in Nineteenth Century Scotland", *The Scottish Journal of Sociology*, 1(1), 1976, pp. 1-13.

21 Tom Nairn, *The Break-up of Britain: Crisis and Neo-Nationalism* (London, 1977), p. 156.

22 Patrick O'Flaherty, *The Rock Observed: Studies in the Literature of Newfoundland* (Toronto, 1979), pp. 111-26, 144-83.

It was precisely in the post-war period that a group of what O'Flaherty calls "outraged patriots" started writing about Newfoundland.[23] Often distinctly nationalistic or chauvinist in their approach, these writers, including Harold Horwood and Herb Cranford, produced a number of small magazines. The most famous of these was the *Atlantic Guardian* produced by Art Scammell, Brian Cahill and Ron Pollett in Montreal, "three young Newfoundlanders who have left Newfoundland in body but not in spirit".[24] Advertised as "Every Issue a Souvenir", the *Atlantic Guardian* was a prime vehicle for the production and reproduction of the culture of exile. Often the tone of the publication was one which blended romantic and nostalgic scenes from outport life with short articles on current developments in Newfoundland. A populist literature, it was a celebration of the virtues of the vanished and vanishing way of life of the small producer in the fishery. For this group of exiled intellectuals with strong ties to rural Newfoundland, the outport way of life and stories about it had great symbolic value. For them it represented a supposedly happier past and a potentially happier future and a dissatisfaction with the present. It is also worth noting that this populist trend in culture corresponded with similar trends in politics. The period was that of Joey Smallwood's efforts to mobilize rural Newfoundland — especially the neglected small producer — to become a powerful political force and challenge the hegemony of the Water Street merchants in St. John's. These writers tended to articulate the values, concerns, hopes and anxieties of the small producer in rural Newfoundland in both cultural and political terms, demonstrating the essential link between these two spheres. In general, via various forms of literature and the media this group of people formed and shaped the Newfoundland of the mind for a large number of people both inside and outside the island in the years after the Second World War.

There are strong similarities between the meaning of the return visit for expatriates and pilgrimages. For many migrants, as for many members of particular religious groups, everyday life is lived in exile, in a profane space away from the sacred centre from which much of life's real meaning is drawn. Pilgrimages and the return visit are important, for as Erik Cohen points out, "The experience of life at the centre during his visit sustains the traveller in his daily life in 'exile', in the same sense in which the pilgrim derives new spiritual strength, is 're-created', by his pilgrimage".[25] Thus for many "existential tourists" the journey's goal is an almost indefinable one of travelling towards a spiritual centre, a sacred space in the migrant's memory. For many emigrants the Newfoundland of the mind is a metaphor: it represents tradition, the past,

23 *Ibid.*, p. 149.

24 *Atlantic Guardian*, 1(1), 1945, p. 12.

25 Erik Cohen, "A Phenomenology of Tourist Experiences", *Sociology*, 13(2), 1979, p. 190. Victor Turner's *Dramas, Fields, and Metaphors: Symbolic Action in Human Society* (Ithaca, 1974), pp. 166-230 is also useful here.

community, the sacred. In a temporary visit, one can celebrate the positive aspects of community, even though this may be a largely mythical community constructed in the memory of the exile. People may not be quite as friendly as expected, and the realities of life for the majority of people may be difficult to accept.[26] The small workless community is very different for a temporary visitor in summer than it is for the people who struggle to survive there year round. Yet returning migrants themselves have a profound effect on the local scene and local conceptions of their community. As studies of the Highlands and Islands of Scotland also suggest, returning exiles praise the special qualities of life in rural communities, and, while local residents may be sceptical of such praise, the emigrants do speak with authority — for after all they have been away and seen the world outside.[27]

Since the latter part of the 19th century efforts have been made to develop tourism in Newfoundland. Many of the earlier attempts were spearheaded by transportation interests, especially the railway company. Much early tourism was based on hunting and fishing, but sightseeing and science were also important. It is in this period around the turn of the century that an interest in tourism based on the return visits of expatriate Newfoundlanders first emerged. The high outmigration rate of the last 20 years of the 19th century was the basis for this tourism. In 1904, ex-Newfoundland residents throughout the United States, with the support of the Newfoundland government, organized an Old Home Week. This was to be a grand re-union in St. John's for exiles. Similar events were becoming popular in the United States, and the Cabot Club of Boston provided the initiative for arranging such an event in Newfoundland. The arrangements included cheap sea and rail excursions to the Island. James McAuliffe of Boston suggested that the Old Home Week would not only provide "a great source of revenue" for Newfoundland, but it would also promote a "spirit of patriotism" and be a means of "rolling back the clouds of misrepresentation and calumny indulged in by some of the representatives of the foreign press".[28] It would also, he argued, be a means of spreading tourist information about the country.

Old Home Week, 3-10 August 1904, attracted some 600 ex-Newfoundland residents from the United States.[29] Most came by rail and attended a public welcome in Bannerman Park in St. John's on August 1st. Several local "songsters" were published for the occasion, emphasizing the Newfoundland identity, often with a fine blend of patriotism and attempts to promote certain

26 There may be "no hello in the store", as a writer to the *Evening Telegram* (St. John's), 8 October 1979, pointed out.

27 Chapman, *The Gaelic Vision*, pp. 195-206.

28 James J. McAuliffe, "Old Home Week in Newfoundland", *Newfoundland Quarterly*, 3(4), 1904, p. 19.

29 H.M. Mosdell, *When Was That?* (St. John's, 1923), p. 93.

commercial products.[30] Many of these songs place great emphasis on New-foundland pride. The song "Avalon is Calling" was written especially for Old Home Week by Sir Cavendish Boyle:

> Avalon is calling you, calling o'er the main,
> Sons of Terra Nova, shall she call in vain?
> Dwellers in the new land gather to her shore,
> Gather in the Old Land, the Homeland loved of yore.[31]

Boyle was the Governor of Newfoundland from 1901 to 1904, between jobs as Colonial Secretary in British Guiana and Governor of Mauritius. He is well-known for his patriotic and sentimental verses, especially the "Ode to New-foundland". In fact, the folk music of Newfoundland increasingly became the symbol of national identity and pride in a fairly widespread growth of nationalist sentiment. At the same time the folklore representing local distinc-tiveness and ethnicity became important inputs into the tourist trade.

Nostalgia was fed on and fed by many entrepreneurs in the period. For exam-ple, in 1907 Dicks and Co. produced a "new album" of St. John's views printed in colour on toned cardboard. In their *Daily News* advertisement they stated: "Both album and art views will furnish pleasant memories of the Old Land, to Newfoundlanders abroad and to visitors, whilst in attractive terms they will tell to strangers the manner of the land in which we dwell".[32] Again, the nostalgia theme comes through in a discussion of picture post cards, the production of which was becoming an important activity for several enterprising firms. Reporting on those produced by Mr. Garrett Byrne, it was noted that he "deserves the thanks of all who love our Island Home for this offering...an op-portunity to remind their absent friends of the scenes of their youth".[33]

The development of tourism in Newfoundland continued, especially in the 1920s, but was interrupted by the depression of the 1930s and the Second World War. In the period after the war attempts were made to promote tourism again. One of the major themes that emerged in the promotional literature of this period was that of trying to encourage ex-residents to return home for a vaca-tion. An effort was made to excite and use nostalgic sentiments towards this end, by both government and non-government organizations. The *Atlantic Guardian* was from its inception committed to promoting Newfoundland as a tourist resort, aiming:

30 Paul Mercer and Mac Swackhammer, "The Singing of Old Newfoundland Ballads and a cold glass of good beer go hand in hand: Folklore and 'Tradition' in Newfoundland Advertizing", *Culture and Tradition*, 3, 1978, pp. 36-45.

31 Frank W. Graham, "*We Love thee Newfoundland*": *Biography of Sir Cavendish Boyle, K.C.M.G. Governor of Newfoundland 1901-1904* (St. John's, n.d.), pp. 183-4.

32 *Daily News* (St. John's), 1 July 1907.

33 *Daily News*, 13 July 1907.

To make Newfoundland better known at home and abroad: To promote trade and travel in the Island: To encourage development of the Island's natural resources: To foster good relations between Newfoundland and her neighbours.

Guardian Associates Ltd. also published guide books, postcards and a variety of other promotional literature. The editors of the *Guardian* recognized the potential for tourism in people like themselves. As a 1946 editorial claimed:

Scattered throughout Canada and the United States are thousands of Newfoundland born men and women, as many, it is said, as there are living in the Island...These colonies of Newfoundlanders in New York, Boston, Toronto, Montreal, Halifax, and other places represent a source of almost unlimited assistance to the homeland...At the present time, Newfoundlanders abroad make their greatest contribution to Newfoundland in the indirect form of money spent during vacation visits home.[34]

However, the *Guardian* recognized that to make such a trade viable much publicity would be needed. A later editorial urged Newfoundlanders to keep their relations homesick:

Now the whole point of this editorial on letters-to-the-editor is not to boast about the fact that we get scores of such letters every month (proud as we are of it), but to emphasize the importance of *keeping those Newfoundlanders abroad homesick.* Feed them with magazines, newspapers, clippings, pictures, letters — from home; give them by mail a steady diet of nostalgia, so that more of them will be stirred to say as James King of Windsor, Ont., says in this issue: "I am going home again".[35]

The prospect of economic depression and a surplus population problem, exacerbated by the phasing out of military bases, stimulated efforts to promote tourism in the post-Second World War period. The Newfoundland Tourist Development Board played a part in this and also exploited the nostalgia theme. In 1947, for example, "Newfoundlanders living abroad" were urged to "rediscover Newfoundland", and presumably their own past, to celebrate the 450th anniversary of John Cabot's discovery of the colony.[36] A second advertisement in 1947 portrayed the nostalgia theme in a slightly different way. Here we are presented with a young woman and her son looking over a peaceful outport

---

34 *Atlantic Guardian*, 2(7), 1946, p. 32.

35 Editorial, "Let's Keep Them Homesick!", *Atlantic Guardian*, 10(8), 1953, p. 3.

36 *Atlantic Guardian*, 3(1), 1947, end cover.

scene. The caption makes it clear that the advertisement is appealing to New-foundland war brides now resident in the United States.[37]

By the mid-1960s the provincial government was heavily involved in promoting this aspect of tourism. 1966 was designated Come Home Year, and organization was undertaken on a large scale to ensure its success. A newsletter was published, a committee formed, contacts with various Newfoundland clubs in Canada and the United States established, and efforts made to smarten up local communities and ensure sufficient accomodation for visitors. In fact, the year was also intended to be a celebration of the economic development and progress of the Smallwood era. An article by Dr. F.W. Rowe, chairman of the Come Home Year committee, made clear the celebratory nature of the event. In particular there was great emphasis on the infrastructure which has made the success of the Come Home Year possible:

> ...sleepy fishing and logging communities with primitive standards have been transformed into growing bustling municipalities with paved streets, water and sewer services, lovely homes and schools. Now both town and country can offer all the facilities and amenities essential to modern living. This process of modernization has been accelerated by a great program of electrification, which will soon encompass the entire province.[38]

The Trans-Canada Highway, the first paved road across the Island, was com-pleted only in 1966, the Gulf Ferry service was improved and, the Island was now ready for the influx of tourists. In addition, many small outports were now easily accessible for the first time by road and a network of provincial parks was completed to cater to the motorized tourist.[39] The government was, more generally, hoping to attract the new mass motorized tourist who had emerged in the affluence of the post war period of economic expansion. Ex-Newfoundland residents were invited back to witness the transformations which had taken place since they left: a "revolution" not only of physical things but of the "spirit" also.[40]

In a flurry of activity, bumper stickers, licence plates, maps and information booklets were produced for Come Home Year. Field workers visited various parts of the province organizing local committees to aid the celebrations. Crash courses for workers in the "hospitality field" were set up, and people were in-structed on their personal responsibility with regard to making the event a suc-cess and on the correct behaviour they should exhibit towards tourists. A

37 *Atlantic Guardian*, 3(2), 1947. See Figure One.

38 F.W. Rowe, "Come Home! Come Home!", *The Atlantic Advocate* (April 1966), p. 13.

39 Overton, "Promoting the 'Real' Newfoundland"; James Overton, *Restructuring Provincial Parks Policy in Newfoundland*. Working Papers on Contemporary Social Issues, Number 1 (Sociology Department, Acadia University, 1983).

40 Rowe, "Come Home!", p. 14.

number of promotional songs on the "Come Home" theme were penned, including one by Art Scammell which is included in his book of nostalgic scenes from outport life, *My Newfoundland*, which was especially published for the Come Home Year:

> Then come in your thousands our first Come Home Year(sic),
>   Give us your blessing and join in the cheer;
>   Though letters and phone calls we always enjoy,
>   You in the flesh is what we want, me boy![41]

If the appreciation of the new was one of the main themes of the Come Home Year - Canada Centennial celebrations of 1966-67, the other main theme was the attraction of the "old" qualities of Newfoundland. The new and the old together was the message: "But even with all the changes and progress, our people remain same as always; friendly, hospitable, proud and happy, the traits that have made us so well-known".[42] The Come Home Committee were responsible for the re-issue of Gerald S. Boyle's *Our Newfoundland Songs* — songs which, it was claimed, mirrored the "very soul of our Newfoundland people".[43] The express purpose of many of the songs was to excite nostalgia and pride in heritage: "To acquire the right interpretation to many of these songs one has to find not only the right singer, but also the right atmosphere which is quite often a fishing schooner's forecastle, an open motor boat, a lumber camp, or the banks of a fishing stream on a summer night, rather than a concert hall".[44] The book included a variety of old and new songs, including "The Emigrant's Return" by J.W. McGrath to the tune of Galway Bay.[45] Again, the song blends the old and the new:

> When the wind blows from the East, it brings sweet voices,
>   'Tis the Siren call, you hear as plain as day
> That says "Come Home" to every Newfoundlander
>   And when you hear it, you've got to obey.
>
> No more you'll hear the fishing skiffs at dawning,
>   But cars, and Trucks and Vans go all night long
> On that road that runs from Gambo down to Lumsden,
>   And now they want a Causeway to Greenspond.

---

41 A.R. Scammell, *My Newfoundland* (Montreal, 1966), rear cover.

42 "Come Home Year Ends", *Come Home Year Newsletter* (September 1966), p. 4.

43 F.W. Rowe, "Forword", in Doyle, *Old-Time Songs*, p. 5.

44 *Come Home Year Newsletter* (August 1966), p. 2.

45 Doyle, *Old-Time Songs*, pp. 13-14.

Now Joey says he's going to build a tunnel
Across Belle Isle, connecting Labrador
Through which we'll get Electric Power and Pulpwood,
And fish and Furs and many kinds of Ore.

But some things have not changed since when you left us,
The Sea Air, Ocean Rote and Northern Light
The Headlands, Rocks, and Ponds and Brooks and Marshes
Come feast on these unto your heart's delight.

It is clear that much contemporary "folk culture" has been shaped by and in turn has shaped the nostalgic and sentimental view of Newfoundland that is of key importance to the tourist trade for both ex-Newfoundland residents and other potential tourists.

Since the 19th century the nature of the Newfoundland economy has given rise to high rates of outmigration. Associated with this continuing exodus has been the destruction of many rural communities and the disruption of friendship and family ties. In the modern world people resist such changes in a variety of ways. Nostalgia, since the 17th century the disease of the exile, may be seen as one expression of dissatisfaction with the migrant's lot. Yet nostalgia is more than a "homing instinct", for it is also in many ways a yearning for a secure and stable existence in a more acceptable world. It is too pervasive a sentiment to be ignored, but it is highly unlikely that the promotion of tourism can satisfy the important needs, values and hopes expressed in nostalgia. As one element in the popular culture of Newfoundlanders, nostalgia contains the residuals of a powerful opposition to the contradictory changes which have resulted from capitalist development.

MAR 2 8 2009